Effective Human Relations
in Organizations

Effective Human Relations in Organizations

Seventh Edition

Barry L. Reece
Virginia Polytechnic Institute and State University

Rhonda Brandt
Springfield College

Houghton Mifflin Company   **Boston**   **New York**

Sponsoring Editor: *Kathleen L. Hunter*
Senior Associate Editor: *Susan M. Kahn*
Senior Project Editor: *Fred H. Burns*
Senior Production/Design Coordinator: *Jill Haber*
Manufacturing Manager: *Florence Cadran*
Marketing Manager: *Juli Bliss*

Cover design: Minko Dimov
Cover image: Minko Dimov

Printed in the U.S.A.

Library of Congress Catalog Card Number

ISBN: 0—395-90819-1

3 4 5 6 7 8 9 -CW- 03 02 01 00 99

*To Vera, Lynne, Mark, Monique,
Michelle, and Colleen*

BARRY L. REECE

To Matthew and Patrick

RHONDA BRANDT

About the Authors

The enduring strength of *Effective Human Relations in Organizations* reflects the diverse backgrounds of its authors, who bring together a wealth of experience to ensure the currency, accuracy, and effectiveness of this text.

BARRY L. REECE *Virginia Polytechnic Institute and State University*

Dr. Barry L. Reece is Professor at Virginia Polytechnic Institute and State University. He received his Ed.D. from the University of Nebraska. Dr. Reece has been actively involved in teaching, research, consulting, and designing training programs throughout the past three decades. He has conducted more than 600 workshops and seminars devoted to leadership, human relations, communications, sales, customer service and small business operations. Prior to joining the faculty at Virginia Tech he taught at Ellsworth Community College and The University of Northern Iowa. He has received the Excellence in Teaching Award for classroom teaching at Virginia Tech and the Trainer of the Year Award presented by the Valleys of Virginia Chapter of the American Society for Training and Development.

Dr. Reece has contributed to numerous journals and is author or co-author of twenty books including *Business, Human Relations—Principles and Practices, Supervision and Leadership in Action,* and *Selling Today—Building Quality Partnerships.* He has served as a consultant to Lowe's Companies, Inc., First Union, WLR Foods, Kinney Shoe Corporation and numerous other profit and not-for-profit organizations.

RHONDA BRANDT *Springfield College*

Rhonda Brandt received her M.Ed. from University of Missouri-Columbia. She is currently Chair of the Administrative Support Department of Springfield College in Springfield, Missouri. Prior to joining Springfield College, she served for ten years as the human relations instructor at the Hawkeye Institute of Technology in Waterloo, Iowa. Ms. Brandt has been active in the training and consulting industry for over twenty years, specializing in human relations and self-esteem programs for small businesses, large corporations, and educational institutions. She was a member of the National Council on Vocational Education's working committee for the Presidential White Paper *Building Positive Self-Esteem and a Strong Work Ethic.* Ms. Brandt is also the author of the Classroom Activities Manual that accompanies this text and co-author of *Human Relations—Principles and Practices.*

Brief Contents

Contents

9   Achieving Emotional Balance in a Chaotic World   225

10   Building Stronger Relationships with Positive Reinforcement   252

Preface

To be well prepared for employment in the year 2000 and beyond will require a greater understanding of human relations principles and practices. We have seen the evolution of a work environment that is characterized by greater cultural diversity, more work performed by teams, and greater awareness that quality relationships are just as important as quality products in our global economy. The ability to cope effectively with today's work/life issues and problems also requires extensive knowledge of human relations. The seventh edition of *Effective Human Relations in Organizations* has been updated to reflect these important trends and developments. As in earlier editions, the seventh edition includes a number of important components that have been praised by instructors and students for nearly two decades.

- The "total person" approach to human relations has been expanded and enriched in this edition. We continue to believe that human behavior at work and in our private lives is influenced by many interdependent traits such as emotional balance, self-awareness, integrity, self-esteem, physical fitness and healthy spirituality. This approach focuses on those human relations skills needed to be well-rounded and thoroughly prepared to handle a wide range of human relations problems and issues.
- This edition, like all previous editions, provides the reader with an in-depth presentation of the seven major themes of effective human relations: Communication, Self-Awareness, Self-Acceptance, Motivation, Trust, Self-Disclosure, and Conflict Resolution. These broad themes serve as the foundation for contemporary human relations courses and training programs.
- Self-development opportunities are provided throughout the entire text. One of the few certainties in today's rapidly changing work place is the realization that we must assume greater responsibility for developing and upgrading our skills and competencies. In many cases, self-development begins with self-awareness. The text provides multiple opportunities to complete self-assessment activities and then reflect on the results. Each chapter includes thinking/learning starters, application exercises, and case problems. Every effort has been made to encourage self-assessment, reflection, planning, and goal setting.
- A hallmark of this edition, and all previous editions, is the use of many real world examples of human relations issues and practices at respected organizations. These examples build the reader's interest and promote understanding of major topics and concepts. Many of the organizations cited in the seventh edition have been recognized by the authors of *The 100 Best Companies to Work for in America*, *100 Best Companies for Working Mothers*,

Hispanic Magazine's "100 Best Companies for Hispanics" and *Black Professional* magazine's "200 Great Places to Work." The seventh edition also includes many examples from successful smaller companies featured in *Inc.* magazine and from America's trading partners within the international community.

IMPROVEMENTS IN THE SEVENTH EDITION

The seventh edition of *Effective Human Relations in Organizations* reflects suggestions from the current adopters and reviewers, interviews with human resource development professionals, and a thorough review of the current literature. Up-to-date coverage of key topics is based on a careful review of over 3000 recent books, articles, and reports. It is a practical text that offers timely advice on how to effectively deal with the common human relations problems one will encounter in today's work place. It also offers valuable insights regarding ways that organizations can maintain the proper balance between concern for people and concern for productivity. The most significant changes include:

- A major effort was made to create a more concise, tightly focused textbook. Every sentence and every paragraph was carefully examined to be sure it is essential to coverage of the topic or concept. The finished product is very "reader friendly" because the text is focused on important information.
- Greater emphasis has been placed on "how to" information. In numerous areas of the text the reader is given specific guidelines to follow. For example, Chapter 4 now includes specific instructions on how to build an effective mentor relationship. Chapter 13 includes a new five-step approach to conflict resolution.
- The new edition includes expanded coverage of strategies that can be used to resolve work/life tensions. Throughout the past few years we have seen an explosion of books, articles, and reports on how to achieve work/life balance. We provide comprehensive coverage of this important area of human relations.
- The seventh edition keeps the reader in touch with what is happening in the real world with Internet application exercises. These exercises provide students with an opportunity to acquire additional information on important topics in each chapter. Also, the reader will develop a greater appreciation of the Internet as a source of additional information on human relations.
- This edition provides a three-dimensional approach to the study of ethical decision making. One dimension is a major segment of Chapter 5 that explains how to make the right ethical choices when faced with ethical and moral dilemmas. The second dimension is an exciting new instructional game entitled *Ethical Decision Making*. Participation in this game stimulates in-depth thinking about real-life ethical dilemmas. The third dimension is a new video entitled *Ethics* that includes five scenarios depicting typical ethical

dilemmas in an organizational setting. These materials can be used to enhance a teaching unit on character building and integrity.

- Many of the teaching/learning aids featured throughout the text have been updated. Most of the chapter opening vignettes are new to this edition. These real-world examples introduce chapter topics and build reader interest in the material. Over half of the case problems have been replaced or rewritten. Many of these focus on an employee issue or problem within the context of a specific organization. Several of the Thinking/Learning Starters within each chapter have been rewritten or replaced, and many new Total Person Insights appear throughout the text.

- The five chapters that make up Part II of the seventh edition are presented in a different sequence. We feel the new format provides a more logical presentation of material.

NEW LEARNING TOOLS THAT ENHANCE INSTRUCTION

The seventh edition of *Effective Human Relations in Organizations* includes several new learning tools that will aid both teaching and learning.

- **New video program.** The video package now includes five new segments that illustrate important concepts from the text. The videos focus on ethics, motivation, diversity, leadership, and organizational culture. These videos provide real-world examples from leading organizations and bring chapter content to life. The accompanying Video Guide provides a description of each video, suggested uses, and issues for discussion. Also included in the package is a segment about casual businesswear, which was well-received in the sixth edition.

- **New instructional games.** Two new instructional games entitled *Ethical Decision Making* and *Coping with Organizational Politics* have been developed for use with the text. The ethics game stimulates in-depth thinking about the ethical consequences of certain decisions and actions. Politics surface in every organization and the new instructional game prepares the student to cope effectively with common political situations. Each game simulates a realistic business environment where employees must make difficult decisions. Students play these games to learn without having to play for keeps.

- **New and revised application exercises.** Several new application exercises have been added to the text and the Instructor's Resource Manual. In addition, many of the existing exercises have been rewritten. The instructor can now choose from over 100 application exercises.

- **New transparency package.** Seventy-five two-color transparencies are available for use by adopters of the seventh edition of *Effective Human Relations in*

Organizations. The transparency program includes figures, graphs, and key concepts featured in the text, as well as pieces that are exclusive to the program.

CHAPTER ORGANIZATION

This book is divided into six parts. Part I, "Human Relations: The Key to Personal Growth and Career Success," provides a strong rationale for the study of human relations and reviews the historical development of this field. One important highlight of Chapter 1 is a detailed discussion of the major forces influencing behavior at work. This material helps students develop a new appreciation for the complex nature of human behavior in a work setting. The communication process, the basis for effective human relations, is explained from both an individual and organizational level in Chapter 2.

Part II, "Career Success Begins with Knowing Yourself," reflects the basic fact that our effectiveness in dealing with others depends in large measure on our self-awareness and self-acceptance. We believe that by building high self-esteem and by learning to explore inner attitudes, motivations, and values, the reader will learn to be more sensitive to the way others think, feel, and act. Complete chapters are devoted to such topics as communication styles, building high self-esteem, personal values, attitude formation, and motivation.

Part III, "Personal Strategies for Improving Human Relations," comprises chapters that feature a variety of practical strategies that can be used to develop and maintain good relationships with coworkers, supervisors, and managers. Chapters on constructive self-disclosure, learning to achieve emotional control, positive reinforcement, and developing a professional presence are featured in this part of the text.

In Part IV, "If We All Work Together . . . ," the concepts of team building and conflict resolution are given detailed coverage. Because employers are increasingly organizing employees into teams, the chapter on team-building leadership strategies (Chapter 12) takes on new importance. The chapter on conflict resolution (Chapter 13) describes several basic conflict resolution strategies and provides an introduction to the role of labor unions in today's work force.

Part V, "Special Challenges in Human Relations," is designed to help the reader deal with some unique problem areas—coping with personal and work-related stress, working effectively in a diverse work force, and understanding the changing roles of men and women. The reader is offered many suggestions on ways to deal effectively with these modern-day challenges.

Part VI, "You Can Plan for Success," features the final chapter which serves as a capstone for the entire text. This chapter offers suggestions on how to develop a life plan for effective human relations. Students will be introduced to a new definition of success and learn how to better cope with life's uncertainties and disappointments. This chapter also describes the non-financial resources that truly enrich a person's life.

INSTRUCTOR'S RESOURCE MANUAL WITH TEST BANK

The Instructor's Resource Manual is a complete teaching guide for the seventh edition of *Effective Human Relations in Organizations.* The opening material provides a review of the most important teaching and learning principles that facilitate human relations training, a review of several teaching methods, and a description of suggested term projects.

Part I provides a chapter preview, chapter purpose and perspective, a presentation outline, suggested responses to the Thinking/Learning Starters, review questions, and case problem questions for every chapter in the text. Answers, when applicable, are provided for the application exercises. Additional application exercises, suggested readings and video ordering information are included as well. Part II contains the test items and answers. True/False, multiple-choice, fill-in-the-blank, and short-answer questions are provided. Part III includes the instructional games entitled *Ethical Decision Making* and *Coping with Organizational Politics.* This section of the IRM includes complete instructions on how to administer these learning activities in the classroom. Part IV of this manual includes the answers to the cognitive study questions in the Classroom Activities Manual, as well as suggestions for effective implementation of each of the activities. Part V provides a list of videos that can be used in conjunction with the textbook, corresponding video vendors, and a list of suggested readings.

CLASSROOM ACTIVITIES MANUAL

This workbook serves as a student study guide/activities manual for independent work as well as in-class participation. Each chapter begins with twenty cognitive study guide questions and a list of the chapter objectives. Every workbook chapter includes a variety of questionnaires, self-assessment instruments, role-playing situations, and small group discussion exercises that will help students improve and internalize their human relations skills. Each chapter also includes an exercise that deals with valuing diversity, a critical skill that permeates all chapter topics. Each chapter concludes with a journal entry page.

THE SEARCH FOR WISDOM

The search for what is true, right, or lasting has become more difficult because we live in the midst of an information explosion. The Internet is an excellent source of mass information, but it is seldom the source of wisdom. Television usually reduces complicated ideas to a sound bite. Books continue to be one of the best sources of knowledge. Many new books, and several classics, were used as references for the seventh edition of *Effective Human Relations in Organizations*. A sample of the books we used to prepare this edition follow.

Anger, Rage, and Resentment by Kimes Gustin
Complete Business Etiquette Handbook by Barbara Pachter and Majorie Brody
Creative Visualization by Shakti Gawain
Data Smog—Surviving the Information Glut by David Shenk
Do What You Love . . . The Money Will Follow by Marsha Sinetar
Emotional Intelligence by Daniel Goleman
Empires of the Mind by Denis Waitley
Getting to Yes by Roger Fisher and William Ury
How to Win Friends and Influence People by Dale Carnegie
The Human Side of Enterprise by Douglas McGregor
I'm OK—You're OK by Thomas Harris
Minding the Body, Mending the Mind by Joan Borysenko
Multiculture Manners—New Rules of Etiquette For a Changing Society by Norine Dresser
The 100 Best Companies to Work for in America by Robert Levering and Milton Moskowitz
1001 Ways to Reward Employees by Bob Nelson
The Power of 5 by Harold H. Bloomfield and Robert K. Cooper
Psycho-Cybernetics by Maxwell Maltz
Re-Engineering the Corporation by Michael Hammer and James Champy
Reviving Ophelia by Mary Pipher
The Seven Habits of Highly Effective People by Stephen Covey
The Situational Leader by Paul Hersey
The Six Pillars of Self-Esteem by Nathaniel Branden
Spectacular Teamwork by Robert R. Blake, Jane Srygley Mouton, and Robert L. Allen
Stress for Success by James Loehr
The 10 Natural Laws of Successful Time and Life Management by Hyrum W. Smith
When Talking Makes Things Worse by David Stiebel
You Just Don't Understand: Women and Men in Conversation by Deborah Tannen

ACKNOWLEDGMENTS

Many people have made contributions to *Effective Human Relations in Organizations*. Throughout the years the text has been strengthened as a result of numerous helpful comments and recommendations. We extend special appreciation to the following reviewers and advisors who have provided valuable input for this and prior editions:

James Aldrich, *North Dakota State School of Science*
Garland Ashbacker, *Kirkwood Community College*
Sue Avila, *South Hills Business School*
Shirley Banks, *Marshall University*
Rhonda Barry, *American Institute of Commerce*
C. Winston Borgen, *Sacramento Community College*
Professor Charles Capps, *Sam Houston State University*
Lawrence Carter, *Jamestown Community College*
Cathy Chew, *Cedar Valley College*
John P. Cicero, *Shasta College*
Michael Dzik, *North Dakota State School of Science*
John Elias, *Consultant*
Mike Fernsted, *Bryant & Stratton Business Institute*
Dave Fewins, *Neosho County Community College*
Dean Flowers, *Waukesha County Technical College*
Jill P. Gann, *Anne Arundel Community College*
M. Camille Garrett, *Tarrant County Junior College*
Roberta Greene, *Central Piedmont Community College*
Ralph Hall, *Community College of Southern Nevada*
Sally Hanna-Jones, *Hocking Technical College*
Daryl Hansen, *Metropolitan Community College*
Carolyn K. Hayes, *Polk Community College*
John J. Heinsius, *Modesto Junior College*
Stephen Hiatt, *Catawba College*
Larry Hill, *San Jacinto College - Central*
Bill Hurd, *Lowe's Companies, Inc.*
Dorothy Jeanis, *Fresno City College*
Marlene Katz, *Canada College*
Robert Kegel, Jr., *Cypress College*
Vance A. Kennedy, *College of Mateo*
Deborah Lineweaver, *New River Community College*
Thomas W. Lloyd, *Westmoreland County Community College*
Jerry Loomis, *Fox Valley Technical College*
Roger Lynch, *Inver Hills Community College*
Russ Moorhead, *Des Moines Area Community College*
Marilyn Mueller, *Simpson College*
Erv J. Napier, *Kent State University*
Barbara Ollhoff, *Waukesha County Technical College*
Leonard L. Palumbo, *Northern Virginia Community College*
James Patton, *Mississippi State University*
C. Richard Paulson, *Mankato State University*
Naomi W. Peralta, *The Institute of Financial Education*

William Price, *Virginia Polytechnic Institute and State University*
Shirley Pritchett, *Northeast Texas Community College*
Linda Pulliam, *Pulliam Associates, Chapel Hill, N.C.*
Lynne Reece, *Four Oaks*
Jack C. Reed, *University of Northern Iowa*
Robert Schaden, *Schoolcraft College*
Mary R. Shannon, *Wenatchie Valley College*
J. Douglas Shatto, *Muskingum Area Technical College*
Marilee Smith, *Kirkwood Community College*
Cindy Stewart, *Des Moines Area Community College*
Rahmat O. Tavallali, *Wooster Business College*
V. S. Thakur, *Community College of Rhode Island*
Linda Truesdale, *Midlands Technical College*
Wendy Bletz Turner, *New River Community College*
Marc Wayner, *Hocking Technical College*
Tom West, *Des Moines Area Community College*
Steven Whipple, *St. Cloud Technical College*
Burl Worley, *Allan Hancock College*

We would also like to thank Dr. Denis Waitley and Mr. Charles Haefner for helping us develop a fuller understanding of human relations.

Over 200 business organizations, government agencies, and nonprofit institutions provided us with the real-world examples that appear throughout the text. We are grateful to organizations that allowed us to conduct interviews, observe workplace environments, and use special photographs and materials.

The partnership with Houghton Mifflin, which has spanned two decades, has been very rewarding. Several members of the Houghton Mifflin College Division staff have made important contributions to this project. Sincere appreciation is extended to Susan Kahn who has worked conscientiously on the text from the planning stage to completion of the book. We also offer a hearty thank you to other key contributors: Kathy Hunter, Fred Burns, and Juli Bliss.

BARRY L. REECE
RHONDA BRANDT

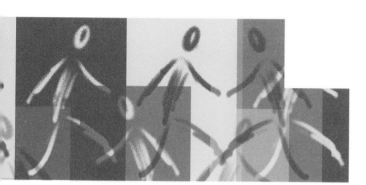

PART 1

Human Relations: The Key to Personal Growth and Career Success

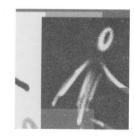

Chapter 1
Introduction to Human Relations

Chapter 2
Improving Personal and Organizational Communications

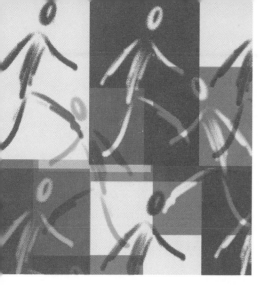

Chapter 1

Introduction to

Human Relations

Chapter Preview

After studying this chapter, you will be able to

1. Understand how the study of human relations will help you succeed in your chosen career.
2. Explain the nature, purpose, and importance of human relations in an organizational setting.
3. Identify major trends in the workplace that have given new importance to human relations.
4. Identify major forces influencing human behavior at work.
5. Review the historical development of the human relations movement.
6. Identify seven basic themes that serve as the foundation for effective human relations.

H OWARD SCHULTZ, CEO of Starbucks Coffee Company, grew up in a lower-middle-class family in federally subsidized housing in Brooklyn. His father was a blue-collar worker who held a variety of jobs. Schultz says, "He was not valued as a worker; the system he was part of beat him down and he became a bitter person who lost his self-esteem."[1] Motivated by memories of his father, Schultz is now working hard to make sure every employee feels valued and respected. At Starbucks the employee, not the customer, comes first. This policy is based on the belief that enthusiastic, happy employees will keep customers coming back. Starbucks offers workers an employee ownership plan, excellent training programs, full medical and dental benefits (available even to part-time employees), and career advancement opportunities.

During orientation new employees are introduced to guidelines for on-the-job interpersonal relations. The first guideline is to maintain and enhance self-esteem. Starbucks has discovered that when employees feel respected, they are less likely to leave the company. The annual employee turnover rate is less than 50 percent. The norm in this industry is more like 300 to 400 percent a year. Low employee turnover is important because the company is growing and needs experienced employees. From 11 Seattle stores and fewer than 100 employees, the company has grown to nearly 1,200 stores and several thousand employees.[2] ■

Starbucks' emphasis on relationships is not an isolated case. A growing number of U.S. organizations, from hospitals to hotels, are discovering and rediscovering the benefits of work environments that emphasize employee growth and development opportunities and the human side of enterprise. Most organizations that survive and prosper over a long period of time maintain a balance between concern for productivity and concern for people.

THE NATURE, PURPOSE, AND IMPORTANCE OF HUMAN RELATIONS

Many of America's best-managed organizations are not simply being "nice to people"; they are genuinely helping employees come alive through their work. We have learned that the goals of worker and workplace need not be in conflict. This chapter focuses on the nature of human relations, its development, and its importance to the achievement of individual and organizational goals.

Human Relations Defined

The term **human relations** in its broadest sense covers all types of interactions among people—their conflicts, cooperative efforts, and group relationships. It is the study of *why* our beliefs, attitudes, and behaviors sometimes cause relationship problems in our personal lives and in work-related situations. The study of human relations emphasizes the analysis of human behavior, prevention strategies, and resolution of behavioral problems.

Knowledge of human relations does not, of course, begin in the classroom. Although this may be your first formal course in the subject, your "education" in human relations actually began with your family, friends, and early employment experiences. You learned what was acceptable and what was not. You tested your behavior against that of others, formed close relationships, experienced conflict, developed perceptions of yourself, and discovered how to get most of your needs met. By the time you completed high school, you had probably formed a fairly complex network of relationships and had a pretty good idea of who you were.

The Importance of Human Relations

One of the most significant developments in recent years has been the increased importance of interpersonal skills in almost every type of work setting. In the minds of many employers, interpersonal skills represent an important category of "basic" or "transferable" skills a worker is expected to bring to the job. Technical ability is often not enough to achieve career success. Studies indicate that many of the people who have difficulty in obtaining or holding a job, or advancing to positions of greater responsibility, possess the needed technical competence but lack interpersonal competence.

Several important trends in the workplace have given new importance to human relations. Each of the following trends provides support for the development of competence in human relations:

• *The labor market has become a place of churning dislocation caused by the heavy volume of mergers, buyouts, and business closings.* These activities have been accompanied by nearly 3 million layoffs and the elimination of hundreds of product lines during the past decade. Even industries noted for job security have recently engaged in massive layoffs. A million U.S. defense workers have lost their jobs since the end of the Cold War. At International Business Machines Corp. (IBM), where a job once meant good pay and job security, 170,000 jobs have been cut worldwide in recent years. Even when the economy is strong, many companies continue to eliminate jobs.[3]

Downsizing has produced many negative consequences. The bond of employer-employee loyalty has all but been erased.[4] Large numbers of major U.S. companies are attempting to deal with serious problems of low morale and mistrust of management caused by years of upheaval and restructuring.[5]

• *Temporary work continues to grow.* Massive downsizing has created another phenomenon in the workplace—the large-scale use of temporary workers. Some companies that still have memories of painful layoffs are turning to temporary workers as a hedge against future layoffs. Strong demand for temps has

The Wall Street Journal.
*Permission, Cartoon Fea-
tures Syndicate.*

surfaced in such diverse fields as telecommunications, banking, heavy manufacturing, and computers. Manpower Inc., now the largest temp employer in the United States, is one of over 2,000 firms providing temporary workers. Today Manpower can provide temporary lawyers, accountants, engineers, and many other types of professional and technical workers.[6] Temporary work is growing in popularity among people who want more flexibility in their lifestyle. Others select this employment route because it can open the door to full-time employment.[7]

• *Organizations are increasingly oriented toward service to clients, patients, and customers.* We live in a service economy where relationships are often more important than products. Restaurants, hospitals, banks, public utilities, colleges, airlines, and retail stores all must now gain and retain the patronage of their clients and customers. In any service-type firm, there are thousands of "moments of truth," those critical incidents in which customers come into contact with the organization and form their impressions of its quality and service. Employees must not only be able to get along with customers; they must also project a favorable image of the organization they represent. Constant contact with the public requires a high degree of patience, versatility, and sensitivity to the needs of a diverse population. Critics of companies that engage in massive downsizing note that anxious survivors are more likely to focus inward on their own careers instead of outward on customer needs.[8]

• *A growing number of organizations are recognizing improved quality as the key to survival.* The notion of quality as a competitive tool has been around for many years, but today it is receiving much more attention. In a period of fierce global competition, a consumer does not have to tolerate poor-quality products or services. Stephen Shepard, editor-in-chief of *Business Week,* states that quality "may be the biggest competitive issue of the late 20th and early 21st centuries."[9] People are at the heart of every quality-improvement program. Committed, well-trained workers who are given authority and responsibility can do the most to improve quality.[10]

• *Many companies are organizing their workers into teams in which each employee plays a part.* Organizations eager to improve quality, improve job satisfaction, increase worker participation in decision making and problem solving, and improve customer service are turning to teams. Typical of the team approach is Motorola, Inc., which now has more than 5,000 specialized "customer satisfaction" teams that work on highly specific ways of improving efficiency or providing new and innovative services.[11] Along with increased use of teams at Motorola has come training to help employees improve their people skills.

Although some organizations have successfully harnessed the power of teams, others have encountered problems. One barrier to productivity is the employee who lacks the skills needed to be a team member. In making the transition to a team environment, team members need skills in group decision making, leadership, conflict resolution, and communications.[12] Another barrier is the poorly prepared team leader. Supervisory-management personnel who provide team leadership must assume the roles of teacher, mentor, and resource person. Leaders who can shift from manager-as-order-giver to manager-as-facilitator are more likely to bring out the best in the people they supervise. A leadership approach that emphasizes team building is introduced in Chapter 12.

• *Diversity has become a prominent characteristic of today's work force.* A number of trends have contributed to greater work force diversity. Throughout the past two decades, participation in the labor force by Asians, African Americans, and Hispanics has increased; labor force participation by adult women has risen to a record 60 percent—defying the widespread view that it had leveled off; the employment door for people with physical or mental impairments has opened wider; and larger numbers of young workers are working with members of the 50-plus age group. Within this heterogeneous work force we will find a multitude of values, expectations, and work habits. Today, the new buzzwords are "valuing differences" and "managing diversity." There is a need to develop increased tolerance for persons who differ in age, gender, race, physical traits, and sexual orientation. The major aspects of work force diversity are discussed in Chapter 15.

It is safe to say that no line of work, organization, or industry will enjoy immunity from these trends. Today's employee must be adaptable and flexible to achieve success within a climate of change and uncertainty. It is important for everyone to develop those interpersonal skills that are valued by all employers.

The Challenge of Human Relations

To develop and apply the wide range of interpersonal skills needed in today's workplace can be extremely challenging. You will be working with clients, customers, patients, and other workers who vary greatly in age, work background, communications style, values, cultural background, gender, and work ethic. When you make contact with these persons, you present yourself as a multifaceted being with a complex array of values, experiences, and perceptions. The authors of *Workforce America!* point out that "human beings are complex systems and [that] each dimension of diversity adds another element of complexity to the overall functioning of the system."[13] Because every person you come in contact with is unique, each encounter offers a new challenge.

Human relations is further complicated by the fact that we must manage three types of relationships. The first relationship is the one with ourselves. Many people carry around a set of ideas and feelings about themselves that are quite negative and in most cases quite inaccurate. In fact, many people reserve the very harshest criticism for themselves. People who have negative feelings about their abilities and accomplishments, and who engage in constant self-criticism, must struggle to maintain a good relationship with themselves. The importance of high self-esteem is addressed in Chapter 4.

The second type of relationship we must learn to manage is the one-to-one relationships we face in our personal and work lives. People in the health-care field, sales, food service, and a host of other occupations face this challenge many times each day. A nurse, for example, must build one-to-one relationships with patients. In some cases, racial, age, or gender bias serves as a barrier to good human relations. Communication style bias, a topic that is discussed in Chapter 3, is another common barrier to effective one-to-one relationships.

The third challenge we face is the management of relationships with members of a group. As already noted, many workers are assigned to a team on either a full-time or a part-time basis. At General Motors Corp.'s Saturn plant in Spring Hill, Tennessee, cars move along the line on wooden pallets, and teams of workers travel with them.[14] Lack of cooperation among team members can result in quality problems or a slowdown in production.

The Influence of the Behavioral Sciences

The field of human relations draws on the behavioral sciences—psychology, sociology, and anthropology. Basically, these sciences focus on the *why* of human behavior. Psychology attempts to find out why *individuals* act as they do, and sociology and anthropology concentrate primarily on *group* dynamics and social interaction. Human relations differs from the behavioral sciences in one important respect. Although also interested in the why of human behavior, human relations goes further and looks at what can be done to anticipate problems, resolve them, or even prevent them from happening. In other words, this field emphasizes knowledge that can be *applied* in practical ways to problems of interpersonal relations at work or in our personal life.

Human Relations and the "Total Person"

The material in this book focuses on human relations as the study of *how people satisfy both personal growth needs and organizational goals in their careers.* We believe, as do most authors in the field of human relations, that such human traits as physical fitness, emotional control, self-awareness, self-esteem, and values orientation are interdependent. Although some organizations may occasionally wish they could employ only a person's physical strength or creative powers, all that can be employed is the **total person.** A person's separate characteristics are part of a single system making up that whole person. Work life is not totally separate from home life, and emotional conditions are not separate from physical conditions. The quality of a person's work, for example, is often related to physical fitness and nutrition.

Many organizations are beginning to recognize that when the whole person is improved, significant benefits accrue to the firm. These organizations are establishing employee development programs that address the total person, not just the employee skills needed to perform the job. These programs include such topics as stress management, assertiveness training, physical fitness, balancing work and family life, and values clarification. A few examples follow:

Item: Employees at H. A. Montgomery—a chemical manufacturing firm in Detroit, Michigan—have the option of starting each workday with 20 minutes of Transcendental Meditation.[15]

Total Person Insight

"To me, there's no essential difference between the way we spend time in work and the way we spend the rest of our lives. Time is time; our working life adds up—in a few short decades—to be our life itself."

MARSHA SINETAR

Author, *Do What You Love . . . The Money Will Follow*

Item: Liz Claiborne, Inc. holds seminars on domestic violence issues for its employees.[16]

Item: Texas Instruments offers seminars for dads who need help juggling work and home.[17]

Item: Quaker Oats Company grants bonuses for employees who exercise and shun smoking.[18]

Some of the results of these programs may be difficult to assess in terms of profit and loss. For example, does a person in good physical health contribute more? If an employee is under considerable stress, does this mean he or she will have more accidents on the job? Specific answers vary, but most human resource management experts agree that total person development includes physical, mental, social, emotional, and spiritual development.

The Need for a Supportive Environment

John W. Humphrey, chief executive officer of the Forum Corporation, says, "These days, the only sustainable competitive advantage in any business is people, not product."[19] Unfortunately, not every CEO or manager attributes the same importance to people or people problems. Some managers do not believe that total person training, job enrichment, motivation techniques, or career development helps increase productivity or strengthen worker commitment to the job. It is true that when such practices are tried without full commitment or without full management support, there is a good chance they will fail. Such failures often have a demoralizing effect on employees and management alike. "Human relations" may take the blame, and management will be reluctant to try other human relations methods or approaches in the future.

A basic assumption of this book is that human relations, when applied in a positive and supportive environment, can help individuals achieve greater personal satisfaction from their careers and help increase an organization's productivity and efficiency.

Thinking / Learning Starters

1. How important will human relationship skills be in your future career(s)?

2. Do you believe the trends in the workplace described in this chapter will continue throughout the next decade? What new trends might develop?

THE FORCES INFLUENCING BEHAVIOR AT WORK

A major purpose of this text is to increase your knowledge of factors that influence human behavior in a variety of work settings. An understanding of human behavior at work begins with a review of the six major forces that affect every employee, regardless of the size of the organization. As Figure 1.1 indicates, these are organizational culture, supervisory-management influence, work group influence, job influence, personal characteristics of the worker, and family influence.

FIGURE 1.1

Major Forces Influencing Worker Behavior

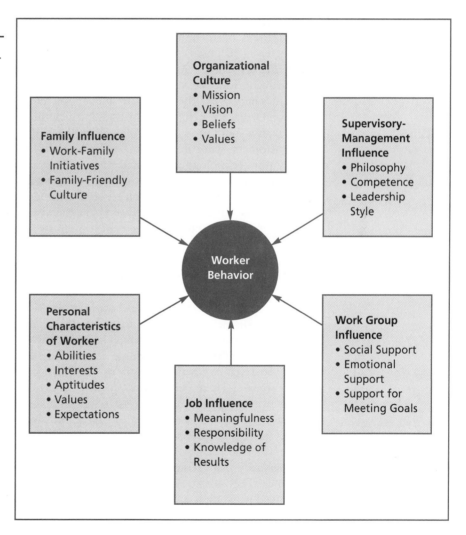

Organizational Culture

Every organization, whether a manufacturing plant, retail store, hospital, or government agency, is unique. Each has its own culture. **Organizational culture** is the collection of shared (stated or implied) beliefs, values, rituals, stories, myths, and specialized language that create a common identity and foster a feeling of community among organization members.[20] The culture at Lands' End, the Dodgeville, Wisconsin, mail order company, has been shaped by *Eight Principles of Doing Business* developed by its founder. One of those principles, "We believe that what is best for our customers is best for all of us," no doubt influenced the legendary friendliness of Lands' End telephone service representatives and the high quality of the products offered by the company.[21] By contrast, the U.S. Postal Service's authoritarian culture has resulted in poor labor-management relations, thousands of unresolved grievances, and customer service that is often mediocre.[22] The Postal Service hopes to achieve long-term culture change by emphasizing greater employee involvement and empowerment.

A growing number of organizations are creating vision statements that direct the energies of the company and inspire employees to achieve greater heights. Ortho Biotech, based in Raritan, New Jersey, begins its vision statement with a bold prediction: "We will be the best in our business by providing customers with innovative solutions to significant medical problems through biotechnology and related science."[23] Once a vision statement is created, leaders must help every employee see the connection between the employee's job and the organization's vision. Senior management must serve as "cheerleaders" to unify employees behind the vision. It takes a great deal of energy on the part of top management to keep a vision alive and vibrant.

Supervisory-Management Influence

Supervisory-management personnel are in a key position to influence employee behavior. It is no exaggeration to say that supervisors and managers are the spokespersons for the organization. Their philosophy, competence, and leadership style establish the organization's image in the eyes of employees. Each employee develops certain perceptions about the organization's concern for his or her welfare. These perceptions, in turn, influence such important factors as productivity, customer relations, safety consciousness, and loyalty to the firm. Effective leaders are aware of the organization's basic purposes, why it exists, and its general direction. They are able to communicate this information to workers in a clear and positive manner.

Supervisory-management personnel hold the key to both outlook and performance. They are in a unique position to unlock the internal forces of motivation and help employees channel their energies toward achieving the goals of the organization. Effective leadership is shaped by common sense, respect for each worker, good listening skills, and helping people to learn to work to-

---

Total Person Insight

"Jobs do a lot more than merely provide income. They provide the opportunity to learn and enhance skills, to have some control over one's fate and, perhaps most important, to gain a sense of self-worth, a sense of carrying one's own weight."

WILLIAM RASPBERRY

Syndicated Columnist

---

gether rather than just for themselves.[24] This leadership style is discussed in Chapter 12.

Work Group Influence

In recent years, behavioral scientists have devoted considerable research to determining the influence of group affiliation on the individual worker. They are particularly interested in group influence within the formal structure of the organization. This research has identified three functions of group membership.[25] First, it can satisfy *social needs*. Many people find the hours spent at work enjoyable because coworkers provide needed social support. Second, the work group can provide the *emotional support* needed to deal with pressures and problems on or off the job. Finally, the group provides *assistance in solving problems and meeting goals*. A cohesive work group lends support and provides the resources we need to be productive workers. The potential value of work group influence helps explain why so many organizations are using various types of teams to improve productivity.

Job Influence

Work in modern societies does more than fulfill economic needs. A job can provide a sense of meaning, a sense of community, and self-esteem.[26] As one organizational consultant noted, work has taken central stage in the lives of many people: "We spend most of our working hours doing our jobs, thinking about work, and getting to and from our workplaces. When we feel good about our work, we tend to feel good about our lives. When we find our work unsatisfying and unrewarding, we don't feel good."[27] Unfortunately, many people hold jobs that do not make them feel good. Many workers perceive their jobs to be meaningless and boring because there is little variety to the work. Some workers experience frustration because they are powerless to influence their working conditions.

Job satisfaction tends to increase when there is compatibility between the wants and needs of the employee and the characteristics of the job. To be completely satisfying, a job must provide three experiences for a worker: meaningfulness, responsibility, and knowledge of results.[28] To enhance both meaningfulness and responsibility, some organizations are redesigning jobs so they provide the employee with more challenge, variety, and personal growth. In Chapter 7 we discuss various design options.

Personal Characteristics of the Worker

Every worker brings to the job a combination of abilities, interests, aptitudes, values, and expectations. Worker behavior on the job is most frequently a reflection of how well the work environment accommodates the unique characteristics of each worker. For more than half a century, work researchers and theorists have attempted to define the ideal working conditions that would maximize worker productivity. These efforts have met with some success, but unanswered questions remain.

Patience and a caring attitude are two important personal characteristics needed by people who work in our expanding service economy. This elderly nursing home patient appreciates the warm, friendly approach used by this young staff member. (Therese Frare/The Picture Cube, Inc.)

Identifying the ideal work environment is difficult because today's work force is characterized by such great diversity. A single parent may greatly value a flexible work schedule and child care. The recipient of a new business administration degree may value challenging work and career advancement opportunities above other benefits. Other workers may desire more leisure time.

Coming into the workplace today is a new generation of workers with value systems and expectations about work that differ from those of the previous generation. Today's better-educated and better-informed workers value identity and achievement. They also have a heightened sense of their rights.

Family Influence

There is general agreement that people need to establish a balance between work life and family life. Balance implies an interconnection among many areas of work and the family.[29] We are just beginning to understand some of these strong linkages. For example, a study of blue-collar fathers in dual-earner households found a powerful tie between conditions at work and treatment of children. Fathers who experienced autonomy at work and worked for supportive bosses tended to have higher self-esteem and to treat their children with greater acceptance and warmth.[30] Researchers have also found fewer behavioral problems in children whose mothers have control over how, where, and when their work gets done.[31] These research studies indicate that children may be the unseen stakeholders in the workplace.

Many organizations have found that family problems are linked to employee problems such as tardiness, absenteeism, and turnover. The discovery has led many companies to develop work-family programs and policies that help employees juggle the demands of children, spouses, and elderly parents.[32] Marriott International, Inc., initiated a number of work-family initiatives after learning that family and personal problems fuel turnover as high as 300 percent at some of its hotels.[33] Johnson & Johnson, the New Jersey–based maker of health-care products, is considered to have one of the most family-friendly cultures in America. The company maintains four on-site child-care facilities, offers up to $3,000 help to workers who are adopting children, and supports a one-year parental leave program. The company credo includes this sentence: "We must be mindful of ways to help our employees fulfill their family responsibilities."[34]

THE DEVELOPMENT OF THE HUMAN RELATIONS MOVEMENT

The early attempts to improve productivity in manufacturing focused mainly on trying to improve such things as plant layout and mechanical processes. But over time, there was more interest in redefining the nature of work and perceiving workers as complex human beings. This change reflected a shift in values from a concern with *things* to a greater concern for *people*. In this section we examine a few major developments that influenced the human relations movement.

The Impact of the Industrial Revolution

The Industrial Revolution marked a shift from home-based, handcrafted processes to large-scale factory production. Prior to the Industrial Revolution, most work was performed by individual craftworkers or members of craft guilds. Generally, each worker saw a project through from start to finish. Skills such as tailoring, carpentry, and shoemaking took a long time to perfect and were often a source of pride to an individual or a community. Under this system, however, output was limited.

The Industrial Revolution had a profound effect on the nature of work and the role of the worker. Previously, an individual tailor could make only a few items of clothing in a week's time; factories could now make hundreds. Employers began to think of labor as another item in the manufacturing equation, along with raw materials and capital. Employers at that time did not realize how workers' needs affected production. As a result, few owners or managers gave any thought to working conditions, health and safety precautions, or worker attitudes and motivation. Hours were long, and pay was low.

Taylor's Scientific Management

Around the turn of the century, Frederick Taylor and other researchers interested in industrial problems introduced the concept of **scientific manage-**

Total Person Insight

"You can only get so much more productivity out of reorganization and automation. Where you really get productivity leaps is in the minds and hearts of people."

JAMES BAUGHMAN

Director of Management Development, General Electric Co.

ment. They believed that productivity could be improved by breaking a job into isolated, specialized tasks and assigning workers to each of those tasks. The development of scientific management coincided with the revolutionary concept of mass production. Needless to say, Taylor's theories became immensely popular among business owners and managers. Eventually, they helped pave the way for the assembly line.

Taylor's work was sharply criticized by those who believed it exploited, rather than helped, workers. The specialized tasks they performed required manual skills but little or no thinking.[35] More than ever, employees were treated as a commodity, as interchangeable as the parts they produced. Taylor originally thought that by increasing production, the company would end up with a larger financial pie for everyone to share: Management would earn higher bonuses; workers would take home more pay. He did not foresee that his theories would be applied in ways that dehumanized the workplace even further.

Mayo's Hawthorne Studies

Elton Mayo and his colleagues accidentally discovered part of the answer to variations in worker performance while conducting research in the mid-1920s at the Hawthorne Western Electric plant, located near Chicago. Their original goal was to study the effect of illumination, ventilation, and fatigue on production workers in the plant. Their research, known as the **Hawthorne studies,** became a sweeping investigation into the role of human relations in group and individual productivity.

For one part of their research, Mayo and his colleagues selected two groups of employees doing similar work under similar conditions and kept output records for each group. After a time, the researchers began to vary the intensity of light for one group while keeping it constant for the other. Each time they increased the light, productivity rose. To determine if better illumination was responsible for the higher outputs, they began to dim the light. *Productivity continued to rise.* In fact, one of the highest levels of output was recorded when the light was scarcely brighter than the full moon! The researchers realized some other influence was at work.

Mayo made two important discoveries. First, all the attention focused on the test group made these individuals feel more important. For the first time, they were getting feedback on their job performance. In addition, test conditions allowed them greater freedom from supervisory control. Under these circumstances, morale and motivation increased and productivity rose.

Second, Mayo found that the interaction of workers on the job created a network of relationships called an **informal organization.** This organization exerted considerable influence on workers' performance and could in some cases countermand orders handed down through the formal or managerial structure. For example, if management wanted to increase production, the workers could decide among themselves not to speed up the work. Thus, the informal organization could affect the rate of output substantially.[36]

Although some observers have criticized the Hawthorne studies for flawed research methodology,[37] this research can be credited with helping change the way management viewed workers.

From the Great Depression to the 1990s

During the Great Depression, interest in human relations research waned as other ways of humanizing the workplace gained momentum. During that period, unions increased their militant campaigns to organize workers and force employers to pay attention to such issues as working conditions, higher pay, shorter hours, and protection for child laborers. With the passage of the Wagner Act in 1935, businesses were required by law to negotiate contracts with union representatives. Other labor laws passed in the 1930s outlawed child labor, reduced the hours women worked, and instituted a minimum wage for many industries.

Completing a marathon in a wheelchair requires a great deal of motivation. The work of various psychologists and social scientists has added greatly to our understanding of what motivates people and how motivation works. (Gail Hilsenrath/The Picture Cube, Inc.)

During World War II and the years of postwar economic expansion, interest in the human relations field was revived. Countless papers and research studies on worker efficiency, group dynamics, organization, and motivational methods were published. Douglas McGregor, in his classic book *The Human Side of Enterprise,* argued that how well an organization performs is directly proportional to its ability to tap human potential.[38] He introduced his Theory X, a rather pessimistic, authoritarian view of human behavior, and Theory Y, a more positive, optimistic view. Abraham Maslow, a noted psychologist, devised a "hierarchy of needs," stating that people satisfied their needs in a particular order. Each theory had considerable influence on the study of motivation and is explored in detail in Chapter 7.

Since the 1950s, theories and concepts regarding human behavior have focused more and more on an understanding of human interaction. Eric Berne in the 1960s revolutionized the way people think about interpersonal communication when he introduced transactional analysis, with its "Parent-Adult-Child" model. At about the same time, Carl Rogers published his work on personality development, interpersonal communication, and group dynamics. In the early 1980s, William Ouchi introduced the Theory Z style of management, which is based on the belief that worker involvement is the key to increased productivity. Two books published by Jay Hall during the 1980s, *The Competence Process* and *The Competence Connection,* reminded management of the vast reserve of talent and the desire to perform embodied in most workers. Organizations must determine how to tap this reserve of competence.

There is no doubt that Management consultants Tom Peters and Robert Waterman also influenced management thinking regarding the importance of people in organizations. Their best-selling book *In Search of Excellence,* published in 1982, describes eight attributes of excellence found in America's best-run companies.[39] One of these attributes, "productivity through people," emphasizes that excellent companies treat the worker as the root source of quality and productivity.

In 1989 Stephen Covey authored a powerful book on leadership and human relations entitled *The Seven Habits of Highly Effective People.* He describes the principles of fairness, integrity, honesty, patience, and humility as essential ingredients in what he describes as the *character ethic.* Covey believes that character is the foundation for true success and happiness in life.

The most popular buzzword in the 1990s was *re-engineering,* a term coined by Michael Hammer and James Champy in their 1993 bestseller, *Re-engineering the Corporation.* Re-engineering is a radical approach to improving the performance of a company. Hammer and Champy suggest the starting point for re-engineering is a clean sheet of paper and answers to the question: If you could start the business today, how would you go about it now as opposed to how you have been doing it? Companies that took this challenge seriously often discovered that re-engineered work required fewer workers and far fewer managers.[40] Many workers who live through the re-engineering process say they feel overburdened by work and fear their own job loss.

Thinking / Learning Starters

1. What do you personally find to be the basic rewards of work?

2. The book *In Search of Excellence* cites "productivity through people" as an attribute of excellent companies. Do you agree or disagree with this view?

3. What degree of worker involvement have you experienced in places where you have worked or volunteered?

MAJOR THEMES IN HUMAN RELATIONS

Several broad themes emerge from the study of human relations. They are communication, self-awareness, self-acceptance, motivation, trust, self-disclosure, and conflict resolution. These themes reflect the current concern in human relations with the twin goals of personal growth development and the satisfaction of organizational objectives. To some degree, these themes are interrelated (see Figure 1.2) and most are discussed in more than one chapter of this book.

Communication

It is not an exaggeration to describe communication as the "heart and soul" of human relations. **Communication** is the means by which we come to an understanding of ourselves and others. To grow and develop as persons, we must develop the awareness and the skills necessary to communicate effectively. John Diekman, author of *Human Connections,* says that "if we are going to do anything constructive and helping with one another, it must be through our communication."[41] Communication is the *human* connection. That is why the subject is covered in more than one section of this book. In Chapter 2 we explore the fundamentals of both personal and organizational communication. It is these fundamentals that provide the foundation for all efforts to improve communication. Chapter 3 provides an introduction to communications styles and outlines several practical tips on how you can cope with communication style bias. Chapter 8 explains how constructive self-

FIGURE 1.2

Major Themes in
Human Relations

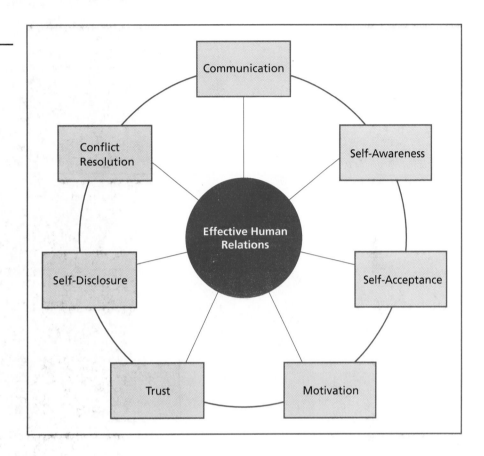

disclosure, an important form of personal communication, can be used to improve human relationships.

Self-Awareness

One of the most important ways to develop improved relationships with others
is to develop a better understanding of ourselves. With increased **self-awareness** comes a greater understanding of how our behavior influences others.
Stephen Covey says that self-awareness enables us to stand apart and examine
the way we "see" ourselves. He states that self-awareness "affects not only our
attitudes and behaviors, but also how we see other people."[42]
    The importance of self-awareness is being recognized by an increasing number
of authors, trainers, and educators. Daniel Goleman, author of the best-selling
book *Emotional Intelligence,* has given us new insights into the importance of
self-awareness. Goleman says IQ accounts for only about 20 percent of a

Communication plays a critical role in training programs that teach Samsung employees how to put on correctly a chip-plant bunny suit and mask. (Wyatt McSpadden)

person's success in life. The rest, he says, you can credit to "emotional intelligence." Of all the elements that make up emotional intelligence, Goleman asserts, self-awareness is the most important. He notes that a deficit in self-awareness can be damaging to one's personal relationships and career.[43] Self-awareness is discussed in greater detail in the chapters that are featured in Part II.

Self-Acceptance

The degree to which you like and accept yourself is the degree to which you can genuinely like and accept other people. **Self-acceptance** is the foundation of successful interaction with others. In a work setting, people with positive self-concepts tend to cope better with change, accept responsibility more readily, tolerate differences, and generally work well as team members. A negative self-concept, however, can create barriers to good interpersonal relations. Self-acceptance is crucial not only for building relationships with others but also for setting and achieving goals. The more you believe you can do, the more you are likely to accomplish. Chapter 4 explains why high self-esteem (complete self-acceptance) is essential for effective human relations. That chapter also helps you identify ways to achieve greater self-acceptance.

Motivation

Most people who engage in the study of **motivation** seek answers to two questions: "How do I motivate myself?" and "How do I motivate others?" If you are really committed to achieving peak performance, you must motivate yourself from within.[44] Inner drives for excellence can be very powerful. To motivate others, you need to understand time-proven research theories and well-established motivation strategies. Chapter 5 will help you identify the priorities and values that motivate you. Chapter 7 explores the complex nature of motivation, particularly of self and others, and examines various motivation strategies. In Chapter 10 you will learn how incentives and various types of positive reinforcement methods serve as external motivators.

Trust

H. Jackson Brown, Jr., author of *Live and Learn to Pass It On,* says that **trust** is the single most important factor in both personal and professional relationships.[45] Unfortunately, trust is often absent in organizations that are engaged in downsizing and implementing high-speed change. When a lack of trust exists in an organization, a decline in the flow of information almost always results. Employees communicate less information to their supervisors, express opinions reluctantly, and avoid discussions. Cooperation, so necessary in a modern work setting, deteriorates. When a climate of trust is present, frank discussion of problems and a free exchange of ideas and information are encouraged. The concept of trust is discussed in Chapters 8 and 12.

Self-Disclosure

Self-disclosure and trust are two halves of a whole. The more open you are with people, the more trust you build up. The more trust there is in a relationship, the safer you feel to disclose who you are. Self-disclosure is also part of good communication and helps eliminate unnecessary guessing games. Managers who let their subordinates know what is expected of them help those employees fulfill their responsibilities. Chapter 8 emphasizes the need of individuals to verbalize the thoughts and feelings they carry within them and provides many practical suggestions on how to use constructive self-disclosure.

Conflict Resolution

Conflict in one form or another surfaces almost daily in the lives of many workers. You may experience conflict during a commute to work when a careless driver cuts you off at a freeway exit ramp. If your job includes supervisory-management responsibilities, you will spend a great deal of time in **conflict resolution** attempting to resolve conflicts among members of your staff. As a team member, you may assume the role of mediator when other team members clash. Resolving conflict with coworkers can require a great deal of energy. Conflict also surfaces when working parents attempt to balance the demands of both work and family. Stressful conditions at home often interfere with work performance, and on-the-job pressures create or magnify problems at home.[46]

Conflict tends to obstruct cooperative action, create suspicion and distrust, and decrease productivity. The ability to anticipate or resolve conflict can be an invaluable skill. Although Chapter 13 deals specifically with the topic of conflict resolution, the chapters devoted to communication, achievement of emotional control, and team building provide many valuable suggestions on how conflict can be handled constructively.

Thinking / Learning Starter

Now that you have had an opportunity to read about the seven themes of human relations, what do you consider your strongest areas? In which areas do you feel you need improvement? Why?

HUMAN RELATIONS: BENEFITS TO YOU

As previously noted, the work force is currently characterized by downsizing, mergers, buyouts, and business closings. We are seeing more emphasis on quality products and quality services. In addition, diversity has become a more prominent characteristic of today's work force. These conditions will very likely continue into the twenty-first century. One of the best ways to cope with these changes is to develop and apply the interpersonal skills needed for success in today's working world.

A basic course in human relations cannot give you a foolproof set of techniques for solving every people-related problem that might arise. It can, however, give you a better understanding of human behavior in groups, help you become more sensitive to yourself and others, and enable you to act more wisely when problems occur. You may even be able to anticipate conflicts or prevent small problems from escalating into major ones.

Many leaders feel that courses in human relations are important because very few workers are responsible to themselves alone. These leaders point out that most jobs today are interdependent. If people in these jobs cannot work effectively as a team, the efficiency of the organization will suffer.

Summary

The study of human relations helps us understand how people fulfill both personal growth needs and organizational goals in their careers. Many organizations are beginning to realize that an employee's life outside the job can have a significant impact on work performance, and some are developing training and education programs in human relations that address the total person. Increasingly, organizations are discovering that many forces influence the behavior of people at work.

Human relations is not a set of foolproof techniques for solving people-related problems. Rather, it gives people an understanding of basic behavior concepts that may enable them to make wiser choices when problems arise, to anticipate or prevent conflicts, and to keep minor problems from escalating into major ones.

The development of the human relations movement involved a redefinition of the nature of work and the gradual perception of managers and workers as complex human beings. Two landmarks in the study of motivation and worker needs are Frederick Taylor's work in scientific management and Elton Mayo's Hawthorne studies. Many industry leaders predict an increased emphasis on human relations research and application. The reasons for this trend include greater awareness that human relations problems serve as a major barrier to the efficient operation of an organization, the employment of workers who expect more from their jobs, and worker organizations and government agencies pressing for attention to employee concerns.

Seven major themes emerge from a study of human relations: communication, self-awareness, self-acceptance, motivation, trust, self-disclosure, and conflict resolution. These themes reflect the current concern in human relations with personal growth and satisfaction of organizational objectives.

Career Corner

Q. The daily newspapers and television news shows are constantly reporting on mergers, business closings, and downsizing efforts. With so much uncertainty in the job market, how can I best prepare for a career?

A. You are already doing one thing that is very important—keeping an eye on labor market trends. During a period of rapid change and little job security, you must continuously study workplace trends and assess your career preparation. Louis S. Richman, in a *Fortune* magazine article entitled "How to Get Ahead in America," said, "Climbing in your career calls for being clear about your personal goals, learning how to add value, and developing skills you can take anywhere." After you clarify the type of work that would be rewarding for you, be sure you have the skills necessary to be competitive in that employment area. Keep in mind that today's employers demand more, so be prepared to add value to the company from day one. Search for your employer's toughest problems and make yourself part of the solutions.

The skills you can take anywhere are those transferable skills required by a wide range of employers. These are important because there are no jobs for life. Be prepared to work for several organizations.

Key Terms

human relations	communication
total person	self-awareness
organizational culture	self-acceptance
scientific management	motivation
Hawthorne studies	trust
informal organization	self-disclosure
	conflict resolution

Review Questions

1. Given the information provided in this chapter, define *human relations.*
2. List and briefly describe the major trends that have given new importance to human relations.
3. Describe the total person approach to human relations. Why is this approach becoming more popular?
4. List and describe the six major forces influencing human behavior at work.
5. In what ways can training in human relations benefit an organization?
6. How did Taylor's work help usher in the modern assembly line? What are some possible negative outcomes of the assembly-line approach?
7. Mayo's research indicated that workers could influence the rate of production in an organization. What discoveries did Mayo make that led to this conclusion?
8. Liz Claiborne provides seminars on domestic violence issues, and Quaker Oats Company grants bonuses for employees who exercise and shun smoking. Do these two programs represent a good use of company funds? Explain your answer.
9. What seven themes emerge from a study of human relations? Describe each one briefly.

10. Reread the Total Person Insight that quotes Marsha Sinetar and then indicate what you feel is the meaning of this quotation.

Application Exercises

1. Throughout this book you will be given many opportunities to engage in self-assessment activities. Self-assessment involves taking a careful look at the human relations skills you need to be well rounded and thoroughly prepared for success in your work life and fulfillment in your personal life. To assess your human relations skills, complete the Human Relations Abilities Assessment Form in the appendix of this text. This assessment form will provide you with increased awareness of your strengths and a better understanding of the abilities you may want to improve.

2. The seven broad themes that emerge from the study of human relations were discussed in this chapter. Although these themes are interrelated, there is value in examining each one separately before reading the rest of the book. Review the description of each theme and then answer these questions:

   a. When you take into consideration the human relations problems that you have observed or experienced at work, school, and home, which themes represent the most important areas of study? Explain your answer.

   b. In which of these areas do you feel the greatest need for improvement? Why?

Internet Exercise

 One of the most popular books among job seekers is *The 100 Best Companies to Work for in America* by Robert Levering and Milton Moskowitz. The goal of the authors is to identify and describe the best workplaces. Companies featured in this book are characterized by openness, fairness, camaraderie among employees, job security, opportunities for advancement, and sensitivity to work/family issues. These companies are concerned about the total person, not just the skills that help the company earn a profit. Here are some of the companies that have made the "best companies" list:

Company	Location	Type of Business
Southwest Airlines	Dallas, TX	Airline
SAS Institute	Carey, NC	Computer software
MBNA	Wilmington, DE	Issuer of credit cards
Corning	Corning, NY	Manufacturing
Weyerhaeuser	Federal Way, WA	Forest products

Develop a profile of two of these companies by visiting their Web sites and reviewing the available information. Also, visit Hoover's Online, a resource that provides access to profiles of about 2,800 companies. Additional information on each of these companies may be found in *Business Week, Forbes, Fortune, Working Mother,* and other business publications. For example, *Fortune* publishes an annual list of America's most-admired companies, and *Working Mother* publishes a list of the 100 best companies for working mothers.

Case 1.1   **In Search of Family-Friendly Firms**

A growing number of workers are searching for an employer that will help them manage the conflicting demands of home and work. Some are even willing to accept a somewhat smaller paycheck in return for such work-family benefits as child care, elder care, parental leave, and flexible scheduling.

Demographic trends indicate that conflict between family and work will likely increase in the years ahead. Sixty percent of all mothers are employed, and that figure is expected to increase steadily. By the year 2000, dual-earner couples will rise to a majority of all families—a dramatic departure from an earlier era when the husband provided most of the family income. And, as nearly half of marriages end in divorce, single parenting is increasing. Single parents sometimes face special problems balancing work and family responsibilities.

Each year *Working Mother* magazine publishes a list of the 100 best companies for working moms. Companies on the most recent list ranged from small Patagonia, Inc. (577 employees), to giant Eastman Kodak Company (47,014 employees). On-site child-care facilities and flexible work schedules helped Lucasfilm Ltd. (maker of the *Star Wars* trilogy) win a place on the list. The authors of *The 100 Best Companies to Work for in America* recognize many companies that have displayed sensitivity to work-family issues.

The success of family-friendly programs often depends on the attitudes of supervisory-management personnel. Even when employers offer leave for new parents and flexible scheduling, some managers exert subtle pressure to discourage employees from using them. And some companies with the best family-oriented benefits have the worst records for promoting women. Research conducted by Work/Family Directions, a Boston consulting group, found that many women feel that use of family-friendly programs will seriously hamper their career advancement. Deborah Donovan, a lawyer and new mother who works for E. I. du Pont de Nemours & Co., expressed the frustration felt by many other working mothers: "The pressures of middle management are such that flextime means you don't have to work Saturday afternoon. My pet peeve was the occasional Sunday morning meeting."

Questions

1. If you were searching for a new job, would you try to find work with a company that offers family-oriented benefits? Explain your answer.
2. Family-oriented programs such as flexible scheduling and parental leave are not used by some employees because they fear their manager will disapprove of their behavior. What can companies do to resolve this problem?
3. In some cases family-friendly policies breed resentment among employees who must step in when someone leaves work early to pick up a child at day care or takes leave time to care for an elderly parent. How would you respond to such a complaint?

Case 1.2   The Human Factor at Southwest Airlines

Many job applicants at Southwest Airlines Company are surprised to learn that a sense of humor is an important employment requirement. The company wants to hire people who work well in a collegial environment and feel that work should be an enjoyable experience. The result of this hiring practice is a group of employees who often go out of their way to amuse, surprise, and entertain the customer. Veteran Southwest fliers expect to have a few laughs on every flight. The customary no-smoking announcement on one flight was replaced by this effort: "Good morning, ladies and gentlemen. Those of you who wish to smoke will please file out to our lounge on the wing, where you can enjoy our feature film, *Gone with the Wind*." An attendant on another flight hid in the overhead luggage bin and then popped out when passengers started filing on board.

Herb Kelleher, Southwest's zany chief executive officer, says people are the most important company asset. He sees a strong connection between workplace satisfaction and company success. Kelleher's dedication to employees has earned his company recognition as a leader in good employee-management relations. Colleen Barrett, the number-two executive at Southwest, constantly reinforces the company's message that employees should be treated like customers, and she recognizes employees who go above and beyond the call of duty. Celebrations are an important part of the company culture, from spontaneous "fun sessions" to a lavish annual awards banquet where employee contributions are glorified.

Although Southwest has grown from 198 employees in 1971 to nearly 20,000 people today, the company has been able to maintain a close-knit family atmosphere. Herb Kelleher and Colleen Barrett have proven that a large company with a unionized work force can be a place where kindness, cooperation, and human spirit abound.

Can a company that emphasizes fun as a way of life operate efficiently and earn good profits? Apparently so. By almost every measure of efficiency in the airline industry, Southwest is at the top of the charts. Profitable every year since 1972, it has been recognized as the major airline with the fewest consumer complaints.

Questions

1. Southwest Airlines appears to be a very employee-oriented company. What aspects of the company's culture foster this loyalty?
2. Southwest is an airline serving the general public. Would the policies and procedures at this company work in an industry such as banking? Retailing? Auto manufacturing? Why or why not?

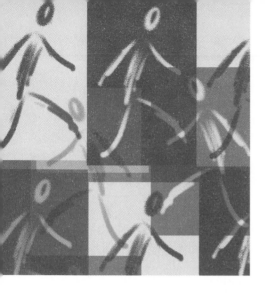

Chapter 2

Improving Personal and Organizational Communications

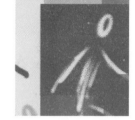

Chapter Preview

After studying this chapter, you will be able to

1. Differentiate impersonal from interpersonal communication.
2. Understand the communication process and the filters that affect communication.
3. Identify ways to improve personal communication, including developing listening skills.
4. Describe formal and informal channels of communication in an organization and recognize their strengths and weaknesses.
5. Identify ways to improve communications within an organization.
6. Understand how our global economy and advanced technology are changing the way we communicate.

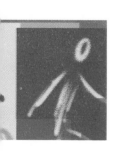

INTERNATIONAL HARVESTER CO. sold its failing Springfield, Missouri, plant to Jack Stack, the factory manager, and twelve other employees, who formed a new company, Springfield ReManufacturing Corp. (SRC). SRC buys worn-out engines and parts, fixes them to work like new, and sells them to companies such as Chrysler Corp., Mercedes-Benz AG, and General Motors Corp. Although SRC lost $60,000 in its first year, within a decade it showed profits of $1.3 million on sales of $65 million and employed over 650 people.

One reason for SRC's dramatic success is its open communication climate, which includes opening its financial records to employees. Strategic planning director Dave LaHay explains, "We don't keep any secrets. We get each person to understand the financial statement so they understand why we make the decisions we do."[1] *Inc.* magazine has documented how this "Open Book Revolution" is proving to be successful throughout the world as organizations teach employees how to read financial statements, share the statements with them, set goals to increase profits, and reward achievements toward those goals.[2]

All employees at SRC learn the meaning of such terms as *income statements, balance sheets, cash flow, equity,* and *retained earnings.* Then, on Wednesday afternoons, forty to fifty representatives from different parts of the company meet to play "The Great Game of Business." An exciting exchange of information takes place as some individuals shout out figures while everyone else busily writes them down. After the meeting, each representative reports the companywide results to coworkers in their department.

SRC employees explain their response to this open communication style: "They show us the sales and profits, what they ship; they go through every item. If you are not working up to standard, it's going to show up on that paper. With my prior company, . . . they would come down and say, 'You lost $200,000 this quarter.' [But we wouldn't] know where it was lost. Here you have a total view of everything that is going on." When SRC employees see where money is being lost, they take action to save it because they know that when the company reaches its profit targets at the end of the year, they will be rewarded with a cash bonus of up to 13 percent of their salary.[3] ■

Good communication, which is essential for the smooth functioning of any organization and for the personal development of each worker, depends on the orderly exchange of information. Managers need clear lines of communication to transmit orders and policies, build cooperation, and unify group behavior. Employees must be able to convey their complaints or suggestions and to feel that management has heard what they have to say. Clear communication among coworkers is vital to high productivity, teamwork, problem solving, and conflict management. In short, effective human relations is founded on good communication.

When people in organizations want to send messages, conduct meetings, or communicate person to person, they have many options. Some of these options are creating barriers to effective communication. The growing use of voice mail, electronic mail, fax machines, and pagers has created, for many workers, an information overload. A Gallup poll discovered that the average person working in a large organization sends and receives approximately 178 messages each day.[4] As the number of messages sent and received increases, workers often find themselves distracted and unable to concentrate because of the constant interruptions. This often leads to a breakdown in communications.

Although some communication breakdowns are inevitable, many can be avoided. Leaders like Jack Stack who are candid when sharing information avoid the communication problems so common in organizations. Employees who are treated with respect, are empowered to think for themselves, and feel a sense of responsibility are more likely to communicate openly with other workers and leaders throughout the organization.

THE COMMUNICATION PROCESS

Most people take communication for granted. When they speak or listen to others, they assume that the message given or received is being understood. In reality, most messages are distorted, incomplete, or lost on their way from one person to another. It is estimated that 80 percent of a message gets distorted or lost as it travels through an organization.[5] Therefore, it is important to understand something about the process of communication.

Impersonal Versus Interpersonal Communication

In a typical organization the types of communication used to exchange information can be placed on a continuum ranging from "impersonal" on one end to "interpersonal" on the other.[6] When we use such words as *transmit* or *transfer*, we are talking about a one-way information-giving process. This impersonal, one-way communication process can be used to give basic information such as company policies, instructions, or facts. Generally, organizations use memos, letters, electronic mail, computer printouts, voice mail, manuals, and/or bulletin boards as quick, easy ways to "get the word out." The major limitation of these forms of **impersonal communication** is that people receiving the information usually have no opportunity to ask the sender to clarify vague or confusing wording. Despite this limitation, some organizations are discovering creative ways to keep employees informed using impersonal communication methods. Cray Research, a company that makes supercomputers, uses a variety of communication methods. These include a print newsletter, a video magazine, a confidential question-and-answer program accessible on electronic mail, and frequent communication on business issues by means of E-mail.[7]

In many cases, the national and international geographical location of employees makes two-way communication almost impossible; then organizations often depend heavily on the one-way, impersonal methods such as fax machines, electronic mail, and the Internet. When Texaco Inc. was facing unfavorable publicity concerning a race-discrimination lawsuit, the CEO wasted little time in launching a campaign of damage control. Peter Bijur used the company's satellite broadcast network to address 27,000 employees. He carefully outlined steps that would be taken to redeem the company's reputation.[8]

Interpersonal communication is the verbal exchange of thoughts or information between two or more people. Such words as *share, discuss, argue,* and *interact* refer to this form of two-way communication. Interpersonal communication can take place in meetings, over the phone, in face-to-face interviews, or during classroom discussions between instructors and students. If interpersonal communication is to be effective, some type of **feedback,** or response, from the person receiving the information is necessary. When this verbal exchange happens, the person sending the information can determine whether or not the message has been understood in the way he or she intended. This form of communication is one of the most effective ways to build strong, trusting relationships among people throughout an organization.

Tom Chappell, owner of Tom's of Maine, which makes and sells natural toothpaste, shampoos, and deodorants, relies on face-to-face communication to cope with rumors, downturns in morale, and other communication problems. Several times each year Chappell gets together with his employees and talks about company performance and future plans. He says the best way to communicate with employees is to be honest, be informational, and tell it like it is.[9]

But interpersonal communication takes time, and because it does, many companies use the faster, impersonal means of conveying information. Indeed, the speed of information giving has increased dramatically through the use of computers and other technology. Yet many workers say they are out of touch.

Total Person Insight

"'Communication breakdown' has just about taken the place of original sin as an explanation for the ills of the world—and perhaps with good cause. As our world becomes more complex and we spend more time in organized activities, the need for interpersonal understanding has never been greater. And just as important, the cost of failure has never been higher."

PAUL R. TIMM

Educator; author, *The Way We Word*

A young narrator in a television commercial for Volkswagen expressed the feelings of many people:

> I've got gigabytes. I've got megabytes. I'm voice-mailed. I'm e-mailed. I surf the net. I'm on the Web. I am Cyber-Man. So how come I feel so out of touch?[10]

Computers and other forms of technology can be invaluable when it comes to impersonal information giving, but they cannot replace the two-way, interpersonal communication process when feedback and discussion are necessary.

Sender—Message—Receiver

Effective communication, in its most basic form, is composed of three elements: a sender, a receiver, and an understood message.[11] To illustrate, suppose your friend phones from your neighborhood convenience store and asks for directions to your home. You give your friend the appropriate street names, intersections, and compass directions so that he can drive to your door without getting lost. When your friend repeats his understanding of your directions, you clarify any misunderstandings, and he drives directly to your home. A simplified diagram of this communication process would look like Figure 2.1.

Now suppose you are late for an appointment, and the plumber you had requested three days ago calls you from her cellular phone and asks directions to your house. She explains that she has gotten lost in this neighborhood before, and it is obvious that English is her second language. The communication process becomes much more complicated, as shown in Figure 2.2. As your message travels from you to your plumber, it must pass through several "filters," each of which can alter the way your message is understood. Most

FIGURE 2.1

Diagram of Simple
Communication
Process

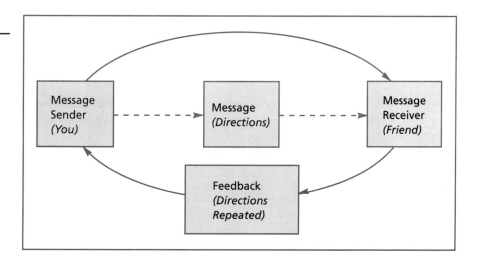

FIGURE 2.2

Diagram of
More Complex
Communication
Process

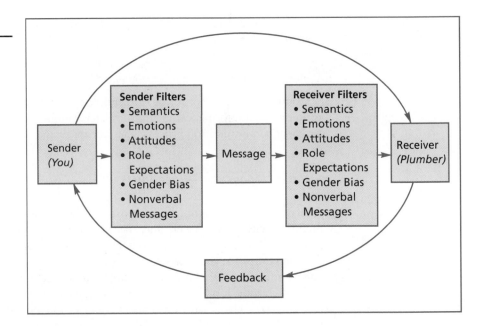

communication processes are of the complex type shown in Figure 2.2. Because these filters are so important, let's examine them in greater detail.

COMMUNICATION FILTERS

Messages are filtered through semantics, emotions, attitudes, role expectations, gender bias, and nonverbal messages. When the sender is influenced by any of these filters, the message relayed may be distorted. At the same time, the receiver's filters may further distort the message.

Semantics

We often assume that the words we use mean the same things to others, but this assumption can create problems. Words are not things; they are labels that stand for something. **Semantics** is the study of the relationship between a word and its meaning(s). We have agreed that particular words have associated meanings and usages. We can easily understand what words like *typewriter, computer,* or *envelope* mean. But more abstract terms, such as *job satisfaction, downsizing, internal customers,* or *word processing,* have less precise meanings and will be interpreted by different people in different ways. The more abstract the term, the less likely it is that people will agree on its meaning. Some professionals have been strongly criticized for using abstract words:

From May 1977 *Training* magazine. Used by permission.

" ... *PROMISE TO GET THE SHIPMENTS OUT ON TIME AND I'LL PROMISE YOU I WON'T TRY TO EXPLAIN THIS*...."

Item: Lawyers have been accused of using abstract words and "legalese" to confuse persons who turn to them for help. David Mellinkoff, a law school professor, says that lawyers' writing resembles a foreign language.[12]

Item: Corporate employees often use important-sounding jargon that is almost incomprehensible. Better Communications, a firm that teaches writing skills to employers, clipped this statement from a memo circulated at a Fortune 500 company: "Added value is the keystone to exponentially accelerating profit curves."[13]

People's attitudes, background, experiences, and culture also affect how they interpret the words and phrases they hear. For example, one Midwestern executive sent the following message to his manager, who was born and raised in Peru: "Send me factory and office headcount broken down by sex." The Peruvian manager replied, "249 in factory, 30 in office, 3 on sick leave, none broken down by sex—our problem is with alcohol."[14]

Emotions

Emotions can be a powerful communication filter. Strong emotions can either prevent people from hearing what a speaker has to say or make them too susceptible to the speaker's point of view. If they become angry or allow themselves to be carried away by the speaker's eloquence, they may "think" with their emotions and make decisions or take action they regret later. They have shifted their attention from the content of the message to their feelings about it.

You may have had the experience of your spouse or parent angrily demanding to know why you forgot to run an errand. If you allow someone else's anger to trigger your own, the conversation quickly deteriorates into an argument. The real issue—what happened and what is to be done about it—is lost in the shouting match. Detaching yourself from another's feelings and responding to the content of the message is often difficult. Yet many jobs require that employees remain calm and courteous regardless of a customer's emotional state. Emotional control is discussed in Chapter 9.

Attitudes

Attitudes are beliefs backed up by emotions. They can be a barrier to communication in much the same way emotions can—by altering the way people hear a message. The listener may not like the speaker's voice, accent, gestures, mannerisms, dress, or delivery. Perhaps the listener has preconceived ideas about the speaker's topic. For instance, a person who is strongly opposed to abortion will most likely find it difficult to listen with objectivity to a pro-choice speaker. Negative attitudes create resistance to the message and can lead to a breakdown in communication. Overly positive attitudes can also be a barrier to communication because the listener may hear only what he or she wants to hear. Biased in favor of the message, the listener may fail to evaluate it effectively. More is said about forming attitudes in Chapter 6.

Role Expectations

Role expectations influence how people expect themselves, and others, to act on the basis of the roles they play, such as boss, customer, or subordinate. These expectations can distort communication in two ways. First, if people identify others too closely with their roles, they may discount what the other person has to say: "It's just the boss again, saying the same old thing." A variation of this distortion occurs when we do not allow others to change their roles and take on new ones. This often happens to employees who are promoted from within the ranks of an organization to management positions. Others may still see the new manager as a secretary instead of a supervisor, as "old Chuck" from accounting rather than as the new department head. Coworkers may not take promoted employees seriously in their new roles or listen to what they have to say.

Second, role expectations can affect good communication when people use their roles to alter the way they relate to others. This is often referred to as "position power." For example, managers may expect employees to accept what they say simply because of the authority invested in the position. Employees are not allowed to question the manager's decisions or make suggestions of their own, and communication becomes one-way information giving.

Gender Bias

Men and women tend to color the messages they receive from people of the opposite gender strictly because of the other person's gender. This tendency is a form of **gender bias.**

Men no longer dominate the workplace because women are entering the workplace in greater numbers than ever before and are making major strides in achieving management positions within organizations. One consequence of these changing demographics has been a realization that men and women tend to speak in distinctly different "genderlects," just as people from various cultures speak different dialects.[15] Men are more likely to talk about money, sports, and business; women prefer talking about people, feelings, and relationships. Even when discussing the same topic, men and women may be on different wavelengths because their gender-specific focus is different. For example, if a man and woman are discussing a pending layoff in their organization, the man might approach it from a cost-cutting point of view, and the woman may focus on the feelings of the people involved. Neither view is wrong, but the resulting conversation can frustrate both parties. In her book *Genderflex: Men and Women Speaking Each Other's Language at Work,* Judith Tingle states:

> Men and women assume that the other gender is trying to accomplish the same goal as their own gender, but assume the other gender is going about it the wrong way. . . . Both men and women often become critical and angry at the other gender for not using the "correct" means to the desired end.[16]

This anger and frustration can create a major filter that interferes with effective communication between the genders. Chapter 16, "The Changing Roles of Men and Women," discusses specific techniques we can use to communicate more effectively with those whose gender differs from our own.

Nonverbal Messages

When we attempt to communicate with another person, we use both verbal and nonverbal communication. **Nonverbal messages** are "messages without words" or "silent messages." These are the messages (other than spoken or written words) we communicate through facial expressions, voice tone, gestures, appearance, posture, and other nonverbal means. Research indicates that our nonverbal messages have much more impact than verbal messages. Albert Mehrabian, author of *Silent Messages,* indicates that only 7 percent of the

Often our body language can help clarify the messages we are trying to send to others. (Spencer Grant/Stock, Boston, Inc.)

meaning attached to our messages is conveyed through our choice of words and 55 percent is conveyed by what is seen—facial expressions, posture, eye contact, and gestures. About 38 percent of the message meaning is conveyed by what others hear—tone of voice, vocal clarity, and verbal expressiveness.[17] This chapter limits its discussion to the form of nonverbal communication commonly referred to as "body language."

Many of us could communicate more clearly, more accurately, and more credibly if we became more conscious of our body language. We can learn to strengthen our communications by making sure our words and our body language are consistent. When our verbal and nonverbal messages match, we give the impression that we can be trusted and that what we are saying reflects what we truly believe. But when our body language contradicts our words, we are often unknowingly changing the message we are sending. If a manager says to an employee, "I am very interested in your problem," but then begins to look at his watch and fidget with objects on his desk, the employee will most likely believe the nonverbal rather than the verbal message.

Individuals can improve their communications by monitoring the nonverbal messages they send through the use of eye contact, facial expressions, gestures, and personal space.

Eye Contact   Eyes transmit more information than any other part of the body. Because eye contact is so revealing, people generally observe some unwritten rules about looking at others. People who hold direct eye contact for only a few seconds, or avoid eye contact altogether, risk communicating indifference. However, a direct, prolonged stare between strangers is usually considered impolite, even potentially aggressive or hostile. Generally speaking, when you are introduced to someone, maintain eye contact for 10 to 14 seconds.

Workers involved in customer service find that a certain amount of eye contact is necessary to build trust with a prospective customer. Research indicates that tips increase when food service personnel squat down beside the table. Apparently this informal posture promotes eye contact by placing the server on the same level as the customer. When customers perceive the server as friendly and attentive, they tend to give more generous tips.[18]

It is not always fair to base judgments about other people on their ability to make eye contact, however. One interviewer complained that a young man with excellent qualifications would not look him in the eye during the interview. A colleague discovered that the young man was Puerto Rican and explained that Puerto Rican youth are taught to look down as a mark of respect when speaking with adults.

As a general rule, when you are communicating in a business setting, your eyes should meet the other person's about 60 to 70 percent of the time. This timing is an effective alternative to continuous eye contact.

Facial Expressions If you want to identify the inner feelings of another person, watch facial expressions closely. A frown or a smile will communicate a great deal. We have all encountered a "look of surprise" or a "look that could kill." Most of our observations are very accurate. If we are able to assess the inner emotions of the other person, we can be sure that person is doing the same to us, drawing conclusions based on our facial expressions.

Gestures Did you know that you send a nonverbal message every time you place your hand over your mouth, clench your hands together, cross your legs, or grip your arms? These gestures send messages to people about how you are reacting to them and to the situation in which you find yourself.

The next time you are in a business meeting, watch the gestures of your colleagues. Some people will walk into the room with their shoulders slumped forward and head down. They will slouch into their chair, lean their chin on the palm of their hand, play with a pencil or paperclip on the table, or clutch their arms across their chest. Others will walk into the room with chin held high and shoulders back, sit straight in their chairs and lean slightly forward, and take notes with both arms "open" to whoever is speaking during the meeting. Experts agree that the words you say during a meeting with others, no matter how powerful, are often forgotten or disregarded unless your gestures command respect.[19]

In light of our expanding global marketplace, be aware that some gestures that may be common in the American culture may have dramatically different meanings to people from outside the United States (see Figure 2.3). Although nodding your head up and down means "yes" in most countries, it means "no" in Greece and Bulgaria.[20] To use your fingers to call someone forward in a crowd is insulting to most Middle and Far Easterners.[21] And that common American gesture of folding your arms in front of you shows disrespect in Fiji.[22]

Personal Space   Research conducted by Edward Hall provides evidence that people use the space around them to define relationships. It is possible to make others uncomfortable by standing too close to, or too far away from, them. A customer may feel uncomfortable if a salesperson stands too close. A job applicant may feel uncomfortable if the interviewer maintains a distance of several feet. Hall identified four "zones" of comfortable distances that help us understand this nonverbal effect on others:[23]

1. *Intimate distance* includes touching to approximately 18 inches from another person. Most people will respond with defensiveness when strangers intrude into this territory.
2. *Personal distance* ranges from 18 inches to 4 feet. This distance is usually reserved for people we feel close to such as spouses or close friends.
3. *Social distance* is 4 to 12 feet and is used for business meetings and impersonal social gatherings. Business can be conducted with a minimum of emotional involvement.
4. *Public distance,* which usually involves one-way communication from a speaker to an audience, is 12 to 15 feet.

It is important to keep in mind that these distances vary from one culture to another. For example, Asians are accustomed to close contact, but Americans want more space around them.

Thinking / Learning Starters

1. Are you aware of the messages you send through body language? Recall your nonverbal behavior in various situations, including a difficult meeting with a supervisor or a dinner party with friends. Was your behavior consistent with your words? Explain.

2. Acute sensitivity to nonverbal messages is an important skill for people to develop. In general, do you feel that nonverbal messages are more trustworthy than verbal ones? Describe specific nonverbal messages that you have learned to trust in your friends or coworkers.

Who Is Responsible for Effective Communication?

The sender and the receiver share equal responsibility for effective communication. The communication loop, as shown in Figure 2.2, is complete when the receiver understands, feels, or behaves according to the message of the sender. If this does not occur, the communication process has broken down.

FIGURE 2.3

The hand-ring finger gesture (hand displayed with the thumb and forefinger tips joined) is a sign of approval in North America. In Belgium, France, and Tunisia this gesture symbolizes the precise opposite—a "big zero." The thumb-up gesture means "OK" or "something good" in almost every part of the world. In Australia, however, it is considered an obscene gesture.

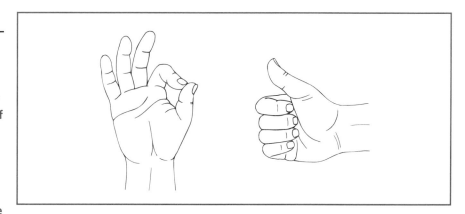

Sources: Hand-ring gesture taken from Desmond Morris, *Bodytalk: The Meaning of Human Gestures* (New York: Crown Trade Paperbacks, 1994), pp. 118–119 and pp. 129–130. Thumb-up gesture: Desmond Morris, *Bodytalk: The Meaning of Human Gestures,* and Rochelle Sharpe, "Work Week," *Wall Street Journal,* October 31, 1995, p. A-1.

Individuals can improve their human relations by basing all their communications on a simple premise: The message received *is* the message. If the message the receiver hears differs from the one the sender intended, the communication loop has not been completed. The message the receiver hears is, in effect, the only message that exists. If a serious discrepancy exists between what the sender intended to say and what the receiver heard, disagreements or even fights can occur. When emotions calm down, it does not help for the sender to say, "But that's not what I meant. You misunderstood!" By then, human relations between the sender and receiver have already been damaged.

When the sender accepts 100 percent of the responsibility for sending a clear, concise message, the communication process begins. But the receiver must also accept 100 percent of the responsibility for receiving the message as the sender intended. Receivers must provide senders with enough feedback to ensure that an accurate message has passed through all the filters that might alter it.

HOW TO IMPROVE PERSONAL COMMUNICATION

Now that you have been introduced to the communication process and the various filters messages must pass through, you can begin to take the necessary steps to improve your own personal communication skills.

Send Clear Messages

Become a responsible sender by always sending clear, concise messages with as little influence from filters as possible. As you formulate your messages, keep in mind how filters distort all messages from both the sender's and the receiver's vantage points. A general rule of thumb is to give clear instructions and ask clear questions so you won't be misunderstood. A new employee stood before the paper shredder in her new office. An administrative assistant noticed her confused look and asked if she needed some help. "Yes, thank you. How does this thing work?" "It's simple," said the assistant and took the thick report from the new employee and fed it through the shredder. "I see," she said, "but how many copies will it make?" This kind of miscommunication could easily have been avoided if both parties had followed a few simple rules.[24]

Use Words Carefully   As noted previously, abstract words, whether spoken or written, often become barriers to effective communication. Use words that are simple, clear, and concise. Avoid buzzwords or complex, official language. Tailoring the message to the receiver by using words the listener understands will help ensure that your message is understood.

Some companies are now sponsoring business writing courses for their employees. They focus on keeping messages short and simple. The opening and closing paragraphs should be limited to approximately three sentences. Condense the remaining information into three to four bulleted items. The skill of creating memos and letters that convey information clearly and concisely requires practice.[25]

Use Repetition   When possible, use parallel channels of communication. For example, by sending a memo and making a phone call, you not only gain the receiver's attention through dialogue but also make sure there is a written record in case specific details need to be recalled. Many studies show that repetition, or redundancy, is an important element in ensuring communication accuracy.

Use Appropriate Timing   Keep in mind that most employees, particularly at the managerial level, are flooded with messages every day. An important memo or letter may get no attention simply because it is competing with more pressing problems facing the receiver. Some organizations solve the problem by establishing standard times for particular messages to be sent and received. Important financial information, for example, may be sent on the second Thursday of every month. Timing the delivery of your message will help ensure that it is accepted and acted on.

Develop Listening Skills

In addition to sending clearer messages, we need to practice listening. Most of us are born with the ability to hear, but we have to learn how to listen. Tom Peters, in his book *Thriving on Chaos: Handbook for a Management Revolution,* entitles an entire chapter "Become Obsessed with Listening." Psychologist Carl Rogers has said, "Listening is such an incredible and magical thing." Peters, Rogers, and others agree: We need to accept listening as a skill that can be learned.

Many of the misunderstandings in life are due to poor listening. Most people never learn to listen. This helps explain why people listen at a 25 percent efficiency rate in typical situations. They miss about 75 percent of the messages spoken by other people.[26] All too frequently, most of us hear the message but do not take the time to really listen and blend the messages we hear with critical thinking and human understanding.

Active Listening **Active listening** means concentrating on what you are hearing, listening with your whole body, and feeding back to the speaker what you think the speaker meant.[27] By actively listening, you demonstrate sincere interest in what the other person is saying. This sets into motion a supportive chain in which the speaker feels more accepted and can be more open. When you truly want to create effective communications and enhance your relationships, there are several steps you can follow:

1. *Develop a listening attitude.* Regard the person as worthy of respect and attention. Empathize, or "feel with," the speaker, and really try to understand the other person's experience. Drop your expectations of what you are going to hear or what you would like to hear. Don't rush the speaker. Be patient, and refrain from formulating your response until the speaker has finished talking.
2. *Focus your full attention.* This is not easy because the delivery of the messages we hear is often much slower than our capacity to listen. So we have plenty of time to let our minds roam, to think ahead, and to plan what we are going to say next. Our senses are constantly feeding us new information while someone is trying to tell us something. Staying focused is often difficult and involves maintaining eye contact with the speaker and not letting distractions interfere.
3. *Take notes.* One way to focus your attention on what the speaker is saying and away from distractions is by taking notes. Although note taking is not absolutely essential in every verbal exchange, it will greatly improve communications in many situations. If your supervisor is giving you detailed instructions, taking notes will ensure greater accuracy and will build the supervisor's confidence in your ability to remember important details.

Total Person Insight

"Listening, really listening, is tough and grinding work, often humbling, sometimes distasteful. It's a fairly sure bet that you won't like the lion's share of what you hear."

GERRY MITCHELL

Chairman, Dana Corporation

4. *Ask questions.* This step ensures your own understanding of the speaker's thoughts and feelings and helps you secure additional relevant information. If you want the speaker to expand broadly on a particular point, ask open-ended questions, such as "How do you feel about that?" or "Can you tell us some ways to improve?"[28]

Critical Listening   The listening skills you use when you are trying to learn something new (giving your full attention, asking questions, repeating your understanding of the new idea) and those you use when you are in an argument with another person *should* be similar. However, emotions tend to distort your listening skills during an argument. **Critical listening** is the active, purposeful, organized cognitive process we use to carefully examine the thinking of others, in order to clarify and improve our understanding.[29]

When emotions are involved, it is important to critically examine what the speaker is saying. Ask yourself: Does the speaker's reasoning make sense? What evidence is being offered as part of each reason? Do I know each reason to be true from my own experience? Is each reason based on a source that can be trusted?[30] Attempt to see the topic of discussion from *the speaker's* point of view, and consider how the speaker's perception of the situation might be different from your own.

Critical listening is vitally important during interpersonal communication, but it is just as important during impersonal communication. When there is no opportunity for feedback, you must be careful to analyze the source of the information and determine its validity and credibility. Realize, for example, that viewing "tabloid" television news and network television news requires all of your critical listening skills.

Empathic Listening   Many workers today face serious personal problems and feel the need to talk about them with someone. They do not expect specific advice or guidance; they just want to spend some time with an empathic listener. Stephen Covey, the noted author and consultant, described **empathic listening** as listening with the intent to understand. This approach gives you an understanding of the other person's frame of reference and lets you understand how the person feels. Empathic listening, according to Covey, requires listening with your ears, your eyes, and your heart.[31] If you want to practice empathic listening, adopt the following practices:

1. *Avoid being judgmental.* Objectivity is the heart and soul of empathic listening. The person is communicating for emotional release and does not seek a specific response.
2. *Accept what is said.* You do not have to agree with what is being said, but you should let the person know you are able to understand his or her viewpoint.
3. *Be patient.* If you are unable or unwilling to take the time to hear what the person has to say, say so immediately. Signs of impatience send a negative message to the person needing to talk.[32]

As a coworker or supervisor, you will likely have many opportunities to engage in empathic listening. Effective empathic listening is one of the highest forms of interpersonal communications.

Thinking / Learning Starters

1. Think of some people you know who are active listeners. How can you tell? Describe an instance when their active listening improved their relations with you or another person.

2. Have you recently been approached by someone who wanted to talk to an empathic listener? Were you able to respond in the manner recommended?

COMMUNICATION CHANNELS IN ORGANIZATIONS

The healthy functioning of any organization, large or small, depends on teamwork. Good communication helps build teamwork by permitting a two-way exchange of information and by unifying group behavior. Poor communication can create an atmosphere of mistrust. Therefore, it is important that workers know the appropriate channels though which communication flows.

Organizations establish formal channels or structures through which communication travels. In most organizations, however, an informal channel, commonly referred to as the grapevine, offers a major communications link. For an organization to function smoothly, everyone needs to know how to use both formal and informal channels of communication.

Formal Channels

Communication in an organization generally moves along **formal channels:** Vertical channels carry messages between the top executive levels and the lowest level in the organization. Horizontal channels carry messages between departments, divisions, managers, or employees on the same organizational level.

Vertical Channels Communications moving through vertical channels from top management reach a great many people and carry considerable force. In general, if the level of trust between management and employees is fairly high, these messages will usually pass down through the organization effectively. Messages will be understood, believed, accepted, and acted on. If the level of trust is low, however, workers will tend to put more faith in rumors, even if such information conflicts with the formal message.

Communication traveling through vertical channels may be delivered face to face, by phone, or in written form. Many managers find that making brief phone calls to their staffs is much less expensive and more effective than sending memos or E-mail messages; phone calls also allow for immediate feedback. However, sensitive matters are best handled face to face. If someone is denied a promotion, has a personal problem that is affecting his or her work, or needs to be disciplined in some way, the manager can explain the situation in person rather than rely on a memo or letter. Written communications in such cases can be easily misunderstood. Talking things over not only allows for feedback but can also give the manager an opportunity to stress a worker's strengths once the negative information has been conveyed.

Communicating down vertical channels is fairly routine. Communicating back up can be more difficult. Top managers sometimes perceive themselves as the sender and their subordinates as the receivers of messages. Upward communication, however, is valuable in any organization because it gives employees the opportunity to contribute valuable ideas that may lead to substantial savings for the organization. When employees can participate in decisions that directly affect their work, they feel as if they are a part of the organizational community, not just individuals collecting a paycheck.

Horizontal Channels   People on the same level of authority communicate across horizontal channels. This communication may take place during structured meetings or informal conversations. Information dealing with a subject of interest to district managers is sent only to the personnel across that level in an organization. Managers may talk in an informal setting such as lunch and decide among themselves how directives that have come through the vertical channels are to be carried out. Even though the setting may be informal, the fact that only managers are present confirms that the communication is still proceeding through formal horizontal channels.

In some situations, horizontal channels may intersect with vertical authority lines. Project teams, for example, often bring together people from different departments and with different levels of authority. When Chrysler Corp. decided to build the Viper (a high-performance car developed to compete with General Motors Corp.'s Corvette), a project team was formed. The Viper project team included people from engineering, design, and manufacturing. With effective communication among team members, the project moved from the drawing board to production in a record thirty-six months, rather than the standard five years.[33]

Informal Channels

Top executives are often amazed at how quickly information passes along informal channels. A message, often referred to as gossip, may travel randomly throughout the formal channels of an organization from a vice president's administrative assistant to someone in the mailroom or from a janitor to a department supervisor.

Perhaps the best-known informal communications channel for gossip (the message) is the organization's **grapevine.** Grapevines exist in all organizations. This informal channel of communication can be positive or negative. The grapevine satisfies employees' social needs and provides a way to clarify orders that come through formal channels, particularly if upward communication is blocked or ineffective. Many officials have come to respect the grapevine's ability to convey even semisecret information quickly.

At times, however, messages that move through the grapevine may be distorted, abbreviated, exaggerated, or completely inaccurate. Many managers have found through personal experience how difficult it is to correct information that has been garbled by the grapevine. As the British politician James Gallagher once said, "A lie can be half-way around the world before the truth has its boots on."[34] When Chemical Bank initiated cuts in its work force and reorganized several divisions, rumors raced through the employee ranks, sapping productivity. Bruce Hasenyager, senior vice president at Chemical Bank, found a unique way to squelch gossip in the bank's Corporate Systems Division. He let employees post anonymous questions on an electronic bulletin board that was accessible to everyone connected to the office computer network. He then responded to the questions on-line. Hasenyager said, "It became a powerful tool for building trust."[35] One of the best ways for management to cope with an active grapevine is to be candid about information whenever possible. An organization with a reputation for honesty will find it easier to squelch the spread of inaccurate information than will an organization without such a reputation.

HOW TO IMPROVE ORGANIZATIONAL COMMUNICATION

SUPERVISOR: "We've really got to get closer to our employees, communicate with them better."

TRAINER: "Yes, we have a big problem there."

SUPERVISOR: "They don't understand the new changes, even though they have all the details."

TRAINER: "We just need to spend time with them."

SUPERVISOR: "Yes, you're right. We've got to educate them."

In this dialogue, notice the quick deterioration from "get closer" and "communicate" to "they don't understand' and "educate them." Note how quickly the concept of two-way communication was transformed into one-way instruction. This "talking down" style of communication is common in many organizations. Individuals can learn how to effectively communicate with each other, but until the organization itself develops an effective "listening environment," the benefits it reaps from that communication will be limited. Some of the possible benefits can be as tangible as increased productivity and higher profits.

Create a Climate That Encourages Upward Communication

One of the most effective ways to improve organizational communication is for leaders to create a nonthreatening environment where employees can communicate upward through the organization without endangering their career. In a typical organizational hierarchy, employees with limited power are naturally very cautious about discussing mistakes, complaints, and failings with a more powerful person. Management must demonstrate the desire to listen and the patience to persevere until ideas, suggestions, and complaints begin to flow upward. Employees at all levels must also be given a structured opportunity to participate in the communication process. Here are a few examples of leaders who have taken steps to improve upward communications:

Item: Rick Shaw, vice president of communications for Applied Industrial Technologies, Inc., believes in drawing knowledge from employees. To obtain information from workers at hundreds of operating locations, he created an on-line network for employees to share their best practices and ideas for improving operations. Contributors are rewarded with shares of stock.[36]

Item: When Pillsbury asked employees to identify problems, the silence was deafening. After all, during times of terrifying job loss, who wants to criticize their supervisor or manager? To overcome this problem, employees were given the option of calling a third party anonymously. Every word of each call is transcribed, and the transcript is sent to Pillsbury CEO Paul Walsh. This system exposes inefficiencies, douses brushfires, and builds employees' interest in the company because they know all transcripts get read and action is taken when problems exist.[37]

Item: Phyllis Apelbaum, founder of Arrow Messenger Service in Chicago, regularly rides with her couriers so she can hear "the kind of things you just don't hear in the office."[38]

These organizations actively pursue ways to remove barriers that prevent open communication. They recognize that improving communications will inevitably help build trust among all employees, regardless of their position in the organization. Given that there are natural obstacles to trust, such as internal politics, cultural differences, pride, and perceived lack of fairness, leaders must work hard to keep employees informed.

HIGH-TECH COMMUNICATION

The idea that we need to communicate more so that individuals and their organizations can be more successful is widely accepted. But technological advancements have so dramatically advanced the communications process beyond the traditional memo/letter/telephone that people are often overwhelmed with too much information. Top executives, in particular, are bombarded daily with useless data that they must wade through to find the information they are seeking. High-tech communications alternatives need to be carefully examined to determine their ability to provide useful information, not just masses of data.[39]

Modems, electronic mail, voice mail, faxes, cellular phones, laptop computers, hand-held pen-based electronic notepads, CD-ROM information storage, and the Internet are making it possible for people scattered all over the world to communicate without ever being in the same room. Many organizations now operate from **virtual offices,** which are companies that function like traditional businesses but are actually a network of workers connected with the latest technology.[40] Often a laptop computer, complete with an internal fax/modem, combines with a cellular phone to function effectively as "an office in a briefcase." **Telecommuting,** an arrangement that allows employees to work from their homes, enables people scattered all over the country to work as one office.

The telecommuting trend is increasing dramatically. The greatest boost to this trend has been the expansion of electronic mail, often referred to as E-mail. **E-mail** is a message you send or receive through a computer and its modem (the computer's connection to a telephone line). During recent years, most companies have added E-mail capabilities to their computer networks. In such companies, a salesperson calling on a customer can receive up-to-date information on the status of the customer's order by means of a quick E-mail message to the shipping department. An executive could convene an emergency meeting of all department managers by transmitting an E-mail message directly to their computer monitors. With the inception of the Internet, the service that links computers and databases of libraries, universities, and government agencies throughout the world, E-mail can now travel on a massive global communications "superhighway."

The advantages of using E-mail, both within an organization and globally, are obvious. Time efficiency is unsurpassed, for people can send detailed messages at any time, across all time zones, and the receivers can retrieve their messages as their schedule allows. The cost of an E-mail transmission is usually less than postage and dramatically less than a trans-Atlantic or trans-Pacific phone call. The potential for efficient customer service is enhanced because orders can be placed and changed, and shipping tracked, within seconds.

As E-mail use expands, subtle advantages are beginning to surface. E-mail is now referred to as the "great equalizer." Because the sender's gender and skin color are not immediately obvious, prejudiced attitudes are less likely to alter the message. Before E-mail, lower-level workers had little access to the president or CEO of their organizations. Now they can contact these individuals electronically without anyone in between misinterpreting, sabotaging, or blocking the message. In addition, electronic messages are a wonderful alternative for those individuals who are painfully shy and find it difficult to express themselves when communicating with others face to face.

Despite all these advantages, E-mail has some disadvantages you should be aware of if you are going to be using it. Because E-mail is used to speed up the communications process, many people compose and send hastily written messages, which can be confusing. If you have to send a second message to clarify your first message, E-mail does not save you any time.

Some people believe electronic mail is reviving the lost art of letter writing. If it has been a while since you had to write a letter to anyone, consider these guidelines before you create an E-mail message:

- Think before you write. Take time to compose your thoughts. Don't just "dash out an E-mail."
- Carefully edit your message on the screen before sending it. A typographical error, plural subject and singular verb, or "there" used instead of "their" in a sentence will reflect poorly on your professionalism and intelligence.
- Summarize your main points, indicate the action or response you are seeking, and be sure you provide all the details the receiver needs to take action.
- Be very careful about the tone of your messages. Remove any potentially offending words and phrasing from your documents. Since correspondents cannot see each other's body language, some mistakenly feel they must use stronger language to get their message across.[41]
- Since E-mail is transmitted instantaneously, be sure you have entered the correct E-mail address! There is no way to retrieve the message once you "send."

Another potential hazard in the use of E-mail is lack of privacy. As communication technology advances, individuals and organizations are devising safeguards that will maintain every individual's right to privacy.

COMMUNICATION IN A GLOBAL ECONOMY

Worldwide telecommunications and international business competition are creating additional communication problems and challenges for modern organizations. U.S. corporations employ more than 60 million overseas workers. More than 100,000 U.S. firms are engaged in global ventures valued at more than $1 trillion.[42] For example, since 1986 American Telephone & Telegraph Co. (AT&T) has grown from 50 people in 10 foreign countries to 52,000 overseas employees in 105 countries.[43] New York–based Colgate-Palmolive

Most progressive organizations understand the critical importance of cross-cultural communication in today's global economy. Marriott makes an effective marketing statement with this ad for their hotels located in twenty-seven countries. (Courtesy of the Marriott Corp.)

Co. currently operates in more than 170 countries and receives about 70 percent of its $7 billion revenues from overseas markets.[44] When we hear the word *transnational* (conducting business with several foreign countries at one time), we may think only of giant corporations like AT&T and Colgate-Palmolive. However, there has been a major increase in middle-size and even small businesses operating transnationally rather than restricting their activities to one or two countries.[45]

As more and more companies send their employees abroad on temporary or permanent assignments, effective communication becomes more critical. Recent studies indicate that more than 25 percent of U.S. corporate overseas assignments fail, at a cost of more than $2 billion a year.[46] Inadequate communication seems to be at the root of many of these failed assignments. For example, learning the language of the new country may be an obvious training need, but more organizations are beginning to realize they must prepare their expatriates—their foreign-based employees—in the language and culture of their host countries.[47] Each country has its own unique view of various aspects of doing business, such as how to spend time, share information, or handle relationships. American employees will function better if they know what to expect. Women should be prepared to cope with far more male chauvinism than they would encounter in the United States. Men and women alike must learn that aggressiveness may be counterproductive in some countries, and that physical contact beyond a handshake is strictly forbidden in many countries. Consider these subtle communication traps for the unwary:

Arab countries: Don't use your left hand to hold, offer, or receive materials because Arabs use their left hand to touch toilet paper. If you must use your left hand to write, apologize for doing so.

China: Don't refuse tea during a business discussion. Always drink it, even if you're offered a dozen cups a day. Never begin to eat or drink before your host does in China. Also, printed materials presented to Chinese business leaders should be in black and white, since colors have great significance for the Chinese.

France: Don't schedule a breakfast meeting. The French tend not to meet until after 10 A.M.

Germany: Don't address a business associate by his or her first name, even if you've known each other for years. Always wait for an invitation to do so. Also, breakfast meetings are unheard of here too.

Latin America: People here don't take the clock too seriously. Scheduling more than two appointments in one day can prove disastrous.

Japan: Don't bring up business on the golf course—always wait for your host to take the initiative. Don't cross your legs in Japan. Showing the bottom of the foot is insulting.

Mexico: Don't send a bouquet of red or yellow flowers as a gift. Mexicans associate those colors with evil spirits and death. Instead, send a box of premium chocolates.[48]

While many companies are sending employees abroad, others are employing more foreign-born workers than ever before. This trend means that supervisors and managers must have the communication skills to manage a multilingual, multicultural work force here at home. Many of these workers speak English only as a second language and may not be fully fluent in either speaking or receiving English messages.

Summary

Impersonal, one-way communication methods can be effectively used to share basic facts, policies, instructions, and other such information that requires no feedback from the receiver. Interpersonal communication involves a two-way exchange in which the receiver understands the message in the same way the sender intended it.

Communication is often filtered through semantics, emotions, attitudes, role expectations, gender bias, and nonverbal messages. Body language conveys information about a person's thoughts and feelings through eye contact, facial expressions, gestures, and use of personal space.

Individuals can make their messages clearer by choosing words carefully, using repetition, and timing the message so that the receiver can focus on what is being said. They can also learn active, critical, and empathic listening skills.

Communication in organizations unifies group behavior and helps build teamwork. Formal communication channels follow the structure of the organization and can be vertical or horizontal. Informal channels, such as the grapevine, often transmit information more rapidly than formal channels but can also have an extremely negative effect on the organization if the rumors are untrue. Organizations can improve their internal communications by creating a climate that encourages upward communication.

The communications superhighway that connects computers throughout the world has brought with it tremendous opportunities. This technology has also created a major concern about each individual's right to privacy.

The dramatic expansion of the global marketplace means that companies must train their employees to be able to communicate in spite of language and cultural differences.

Career Corner

Q. In our company, all of our individual computer terminals are networked through a mainframe computer. We can access documents and files from any terminal at any time. The human resources department has given us direct access to our individual personnel files and asked us to update our personal data, recording such changes as a new address or an increase or decrease in declared dependents.

Recently, I have received harassing phone calls on my unlisted home telephone. Although I cannot prove it, I believe someone at work has accessed my personnel file and discovered my private phone number. My company has no written policy regarding accessing information electronically. All information, including E-mail messages, can be read by anyone connected to the mainframe. What should I do?

A. Most computer programs that allow information input from multiple sources within a company also have a strong password management device to prevent anyone from accessing sensitive information. Request, in writing, that your organization initiate a password protection system. Different levels of information could be made available to various levels of personnel based on their "need to know" the information.

Currently, employers have the right to monitor employees at work. This includes recording phone conversations, video monitoring, and inspecting employees' personal property on company premises, which can include E-mail. However, because of the increase in the number of lawsuits based on intrusion of privacy and the increase in the use of electronic mail, your organization should establish clear and concise policies as to who can access what information. The policies should include guidelines on such issues as access, business versus personal messages, and offensive messages such as pornography or sexual harassment. If these policies are not firmly established, individual workers tend to lack trust in their coworkers. This atmosphere will eventually interfere with effective human relations throughout the organization.

Key Terms

impersonal communication
interpersonal communication
feedback
semantics
emotions
gender bias
nonverbal messages

active listening
critical listening
empathic listening
formal channels
grapevine
virtual office
telecommuting
E-mail

Review Questions

1. Describe the difference between impersonal and interpersonal communication. Explain the communication process in your own words.
2. Why is feedback essential to good communication?
3. What are the responsibilities of both sender and receiver in the communication process?
4. What are communication filters? How can they be stumbling blocks to effective communication?
5. What techniques can be used to send clear messages? How can you know if you have been successful?
6. What happens when a sender's nonverbal cues do not agree with the verbal message being sent?
7. Why do organizations have formal communication channels? When are they most effective?
8. Describe the strengths and weaknesses of informal communication channels in an organization.
9. List the advantages and disadvantages of using E-mail.
10. What types of communication problems exist in an organization that actively participates in the global economy? What steps should organizations take to help eliminate these problems?

Application Exercises

1. Susan Campbell, author and consultant in the area of interpersonal communication, says the starting point for effective communication is to make sure your intentions are clear. What do you want to accomplish with the next phone call, letter, E-mail message, or visit with a coworker? Sometimes we seek control over the receiver of our message. In some cases, our intention is spiteful or to avoid being blamed for something. If you are honest with yourself about the intention of your communication, you can improve the planning and delivery of your messages. If you are honest with yourself, you are more likely to get what you want. Reflect on your most recent written or spoken communications with another person. What were your intentions? Did you get what you wanted?

2. We can all improve our listening efficiency. First, we need to be aware of our listening habits. By completing this form, you can become more aware of poor listening habits that might reduce your listening efficiency. The results will give you an idea of some listening habits you might want to change.

   A—Almost never   *B*—Occasionally   *C*—Frequently   *D*—Most of the time

   _____ 1. Do you fail to pay attention? Some listeners allow themselves to be distracted or to think of something else.

   _____ 2. Do you give the appearance of listening when you are not? Some people who are thinking about something else deliberately try to look as though they are listening.

   _____ 3. Do you tune out the person who says something you don't agree with or don't want to hear? Some people are concentrating on what they are going to say next rather than truly listening to the other person's point of view.

   _____ 4. Do you listen only for facts? Some people listen only to facts or details and miss the real meaning of what is being said.

   _____ 5. Do you rehearse what you are going to say? Some people listen until they want to say something, at which point they stop listening and begin planning their response.

   _____ 6. Do you interrupt the speaker? Some people do not wait until the speaker has completely expressed his or her views.

   _____ 7. Do you fail to take notes at a meeting? Some people do not bother to take notes when necessary; consequently, they often forget important details.

Internet Exercise

As noted in this chapter, we spend more time listening than we spend speaking, reading, or writing. However, most of us are not good listeners. To learn more about listening and how to improve your listening skills, visit the Internet and determine what types of resources (such as books, articles, and training programs) are available. Using your search engine, type in "active listening" and "empathic listening," and then examine the information available on these topics. Will this information be useful as you attempt to improve your listening skills? Explain.

Case 2.1   ## General Electric's Chilling Tale

To compete effectively in the global marketplace, General Electric Co. (GE) built a $120 million futuristic factory in Columbia, Tennessee, to make refrigerators with a newly designed compressor—the rotary—using a technology that GE had invented but used only in air conditioners. Unfortunately, the rotary compressor ran too hot and soon failed in many of the GE refrigerators sold throughout the nation. The organization had to replace compressors in more than 1.1 million of these refrigerators at an estimated cost of $450 million. The replacement compressors were purchased from Italian producers.

The problems were traced back to poor corporate communication. Several of the technicians who did the actual preproduction testing had suspected that the compressor might be defective and had told their superiors. But senior executives six levels above heard only good news. Roger Schipke, the project division's former chief, admits, "It was your worst nightmare come true." Richard Burke, the appliance division's current chief of technology and manufacturing, says in retrospect, "I'd have gone and found the lowest damn level people we had . . . and just sat down in their little cubbyholes and asked them 'How are things today?'"

Key Events

- Peter Davey, retired chief design engineer for refrigerators, warned GE that rotaries ran too hot to be useful in refrigerators.
- Rotary compressors were removed from the larger air conditioners because they could not hold up in hot climates.
- The design team had no compressor-design experience and rejected help from Milton Kosfeld, the GE design engineer for the rotary air conditioners.
- Field tests were rushed, and 15 percent showed warning signs of excessive heat. Supervisors discounted the findings and did not pass them upward.

Questions

1. Many people might believe GE's huge loss was the result of technology. Why do you think Burke blames poor communication? Explain your reasoning.

2. GE has unveiled plans to build a 30-cubic-foot, side-by-side refrigerator that is being hailed as "the world's largest free-standing refrigerator." They gained the extra interior space by redesigning the gasket system and making the walls thinner. Not all retailers are convinced the larger refrigerator will sell well. If you were a GE employee who had been involved in the company's rotary compressor problem, what steps would you consider appropriate to prevent another disaster?

Case 2.2   **Mercedes Learns to Speak 'Bama**

The German Chamber of Commerce and Industry conducted a survey of 10,000 businesspeople and discovered that 30 percent of them are considering moving their production outside Germany. The reason: German workers earn wages and benefits that, on the average, are worth $25 an hour (the highest in the world), yet in terms of output per hour they are only two-thirds as productive as their American counterparts. In light of this crushing cost of doing business in Germany, Mercedes-Benz AG in Stuttgart formed a new globalization strategy that included building its new $300 million auto plant nearer to its customers. Mercedes was the top-selling import car in Japan, but the company did not choose that country for its new factory. It could have gone to Mexico and hired low-wage workers, but the company did not make that choice either. Instead, Mercedes chose Vance, Alabama (population 400), for the factory that builds its new sport-utility vehicles.

Not only did the Mercedes management team have to design a new car and a new factory, but they also had to prepare for the cultural upheaval of moving approximately forty German engineers, managers, and their families to Alabama. They conducted seminars at a retreat in the Black Forest to help their employees adjust to the strange habits of their new home and flew some native Alabamians to Stuttgart to help with these "cross-cultural encounter groups."

But Roland Folger, who moved from Germany to Alabama, explained, "We don't want a German enclave in Alabama. We want a real cultural mixing." The Alabamians have learned that Germans are very blunt, perfectionistic, formal, and sometimes humorless, but they love good wine. The German employees have learned that Americans call strangers by their first names, that they leave their office doors open, and that they rarely use public transportation. They have also learned the meaning of such strange expressions as "y'all" and "Howdy."

Despite all the cultural differences, the Vance factory has proven to be a success. Mercedes-Benz has clearly gained valuable experience in how to set up and operate a plant in a distant land and has recently established another new plant in São Paulo, Brazil. The company may well transfer an employee born in Alabama to its plant in Brazil!

Questions

1. Both the Americans and the Germans seem committed to making this multicultural factory operate effectively. What types of training exercises or activities would you use to help these two cultures understand each other better?

2. How might each of the communications filters identified in this chapter affect the messages sent between German-born and American-born workers?

3. What additional communications problems might have been encountered if Mercedes had chosen to build its plant in Japan instead of Alabama? What types of problems might they encounter with an Alabamian working in a German plant in Brazil? Are there any advantages to this situation?

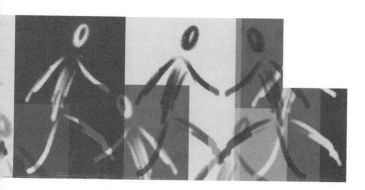

PART ll

Career Success Begins with Knowing Yourself

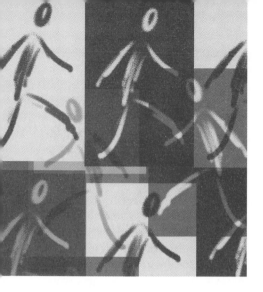

Chapter 3

Understanding

Your

Communication Style

Chapter Preview

After studying this chapter, you will be able to

1. Understand the concept of communication style bias and its effect on interpersonal relations.
2. Realize the personal benefits that can be derived from an understanding of communication styles.
3. Discuss the major elements of the communication style model.
4. Identify your preferred communication style.
5. Improve communications with others through style flexing.

I N TERMS OF CAREER SUCCESS, Oprah Winfrey and Lou Gerstner have a great deal in common. *The Oprah Winfrey Show* has won twenty-five Emmy Awards throughout the past eleven years, and Oprah is recognized as the reigning queen of talk TV. Lou Gerstner, IBM's chief executive officer, is credited with bringing the company back from the dead. A long period of depressed sales ended under his strong leadership. If these two respected people ever meet, communication problems are likely to surface. Oprah Winfrey is witty, laughs easily, and openly displays her emotions. People who watch her show say the experience is like spending time with a close friend.[1] By his own admission, Lou Gerstner is intense, blunt, and competitive and dislikes chitchat. He's not likely to disclose anything of a personal nature about himself.[2] Each of these successful people has a dominant communication style that influences the way each interacts with others. ■

COMMUNICATION STYLES: AN INTRODUCTION

Have you ever wondered why it seems so difficult to talk with some people and so easy to talk with others? Can you recall a situation where you met someone for the first time and immediately liked that person? Something about the individual made you feel comfortable. You may have had this experience when you started a new job or began classes at a new school. A major goal of this chapter is to help you understand the impact your communication style has on the impression others form of you. This chapter also provides you with the information you will need to cope effectively in today's workplace, which is characterized by greater diversity and teamwork.

Communication Style Defined

The impressions that others form about us are based on what they observe us saying and doing. They have no way of knowing our innermost thoughts and feelings, so they make decisions about us based on what they see and hear.[3] The patterns of behavior that others can observe can be called **communication style.**

Each person has a unique communication style. By getting to know your style, you can achieve greater self-awareness and learn how to develop more effective interpersonal relations with coworkers. Accurate self-knowledge is truly the starting point for effectiveness at work. It is also essential for managing the three key relationships described in Chapter 1: relationships with self, with another person, and with members of a group. If your career objective is to become a supervisor or manager, you will benefit by being more aware of your employees' communication styles. Job satisfaction and productivity increase when employees feel that their leaders understand their personal needs and take these into consideration.

It is sometimes difficult for us to realize that people can differ from us and yet not be inferior. Understanding other people's communication styles improves working relationships by increasing our acceptance of other people and their way of doing things. Knowledge of the various communication styles helps us communicate more effectively with people who differ from us.

In recent years, thousands of people have sought to improve their interpersonal relationship skills through the study of communication styles. They seek not only greater awareness of their own style but also greater sensitivity to and tolerance for other persons' styles. And they learn how to use the strengths of their styles in organizational settings.

Fundamental Concepts Supporting Communication Styles

This may be your first introduction to communication styles. Therefore, let's begin by reviewing a few basic concepts that support the study of this dimension of human personality.

1. *Individual differences exist and are important.* Length of eye contact, use of gestures, speech patterns, facial expressions, and the degree of assertiveness people project to others are some of the characteristics of a personal communication style. We can identify a person's unique communication style by carefully observing these patterns of behavior.[4]

2. *Individual style differences tend to be stable.* The basics of communication style theory were established by the famous Swiss psychiatrist Carl Jung. In his classic book *Psychological Types,* he states that every individual develops a primary communication style that remains quite stable throughout life. Each person has a relatively distinctive way of responding to people and events.[5] Many psychologists now believe that people are born with a predisposition to prefer some behaviors (actions) over others. Because these preferred behaviors are easily and naturally used, they are exercised and developed further over least-preferred preferences. For example, a gregarious child—one who enjoys the company of others—will seek ways to experience a wealth of relationships. This personality trait (often described as extroversion) will be nurtured and strengthened over the years.[6]

3. *There is a limited number of styles.* Jung observes that people tend to fall into one of several behavior patterns when relating to the world around them.

He describes four behavior styles: intuitor, thinker, feeler, and sensor.[7] Those in the same behavior category tend to display similar traits. The thinker, for example, places a high value on facts, figures, and reason. This person is not likely to leap to conclusions but likes to "sleep on it." He or she tends to follow an orderly approach to task completion. Very often the thinker is seen by others as cautious and structured.

4.   *To create the most productive working relationships, it is necessary to get in sync with the behavior patterns (communication style) of the people you work with.*[8] Differences between people can be a source of friction unless you develop the ability to recognize and respond to the other person's style. The ability to identify another person's communication style, and to know how and when to adapt your own preferred style to it, can give you an important advantage in dealing with people. Learning to adapt your style to fit the needs of another person is called "style flexing," a topic that is discussed later in this chapter.

Learning to Cope with Communication Style Bias

Several forms of bias exist in our society. People over 40 sometimes complain that they are victims of age discrimination. Gender bias problems have made headlines for several years. And people of color—blacks, Hispanics, Native Americans—say that racial and ethnic bias is still a serious problem today. Communication style bias represents another common form of prejudice.

Almost everyone experiences **communication style bias** from time to time. The bias is likely to surface when you meet someone who displays a style distinctly different from your own. For example, a quiet, reflective person may feel uncomfortable in the presence of someone like Oprah Winfrey who dis-

Total Person Insight

"By knowing our own communicating style, we get to know ourselves better. And we get along with others better as we develop the ability to recognize—and respond to—their styles."

PAUL MOK AND DUDLEY LYNCH

Human Resource Development Consultants

plays a dynamic, outgoing style. If, however, the person you encounter has the same communication style as yours, your message is less likely to be misunderstood. We could say, using the analogy of radio, that you are both on the same wavelength.

At this point, you may be saying to yourself, "But in the world of work, I don't have a choice—I have to get my message across to all kinds of people, no matter what their communication style is." You are right. Office receptionists must deal with a variety of people throughout each day. Bank loan officers cannot predict who will walk into their offices at any given time.

How can you learn to cope with communication style bias? First, you must develop awareness of your own unique style. Recall from Chapter 1 that self-awareness is one of the major themes of this text. Accurate self-knowledge is essential for developing strong interpersonal relationships. Knowledge of your communication style gives you a fresh perspective and sets the stage for improved relations with others. The second step in coping with communication style bias is learning to assess the communication style of those people with whom you have contact. The ability to identify another person's communication style, and to know how and when to adapt your own preferred style to it, can afford you a crucial advantage in dealing with people. The ability to "speak the other person's language" is an important relationship-management skill.[9]

THE COMMUNICATION STYLE MODEL

This section introduces a model that encompasses four basic communication styles. This simple model is based on research studies conducted over the past sixty years and features two important dimensions of human behavior: dominance and sociability. As you study the communication style model, keep in mind that it describes your *preferences*, not your *skills* or *abilities*.

The Dominance Continuum

In study after study, those "differences that make a difference" in interpersonal relationships point to dominance as an important dimension of style. **Dominance** can be defined as the tendency to display a "take-charge" attitude. Every person falls somewhere on the **dominance continuum,** illustrated in Figure 3.1. David W. Johnson in his book *Reaching Out—Interpersonal Effectiveness and Self-Actualization* states that people tend to fall into two dominance categories: low or high.[10]

FIGURE 3.1

Dominance Continuum

1. *Low dominance.* These individuals are characterized by a tendency to be co-operative and eager to assist others. They tend to be low in assertiveness and are more willing to be controlled by others.
2. *High dominance.* These people give advice freely and frequently initiate demands. They are more assertive and tend to seek control over others.

The first step in determining your most-preferred communication style is to identify where you fall on the dominance continuum. Do you tend to be low or high on this scale? To answer this question, complete the dominance indicator form in Figure 3.2. Rate yourself on each scale by placing a checkmark at a point along the continuum that represents how you perceive yourself. If most of your checkmarks fall to the right of center, you rank high in dominance. If most fall to the left of center, you are low in dominance.

Another way to assess the dominance dimension is to ask four or five people who know you well to complete the dominance indicator form for you. Their assessment may provide a more accurate indication of where you fall on the continuum. Self-assessment alone is sometimes inaccurate because it is difficult to observe yourself objectively.[11] Once you have received the forms completed by others, try to determine if a consistent pattern exists. (Note: It is best not to involve parents, spouses, or close relatives. Seek feedback from coworkers or classmates.)

Where Should You Be on the Dominance Continuum?

Is there any best place to be on the dominance continuum? Not really. Successful people can be found at all points along the continuum. Nevertheless, there are times when people need to act decisively to influence the adoption of their ideas and communicate their expectations clearly. This means that someone low in dominance may need to become more assertive temporarily to achieve an objective. New managers who are low in dominance must learn to influence others without being viewed as aggressive or insensitive. The American Management Associations offers a course entitled "Assertiveness Training for Managers," which is designed for managers who want to exercise a greater influence on others, get their proposals across more effectively, and resolve conflict situations decisively yet diplomatically.[12] Persons low in dominance may need to learn how to be responsive to others without giving up their own convictions.

FIGURE 3.2

Dominance Indicator
Form

I Perceive Myself as Somewhat

Cooperative			Competitive

Submissive			Authoritative

Accommodating			Domineering

Hesitant			Decisive

Reserved			Outgoing

Compromising			Insistent

Cautious			Risk Taking

Patient			Hurried

Passive			Influential

Quiet			Talkative

Shy			Bold

Supportive			Demanding

Relaxed			Intense

Restrained			Assertive

Persons who are high in dominance must sometimes curb their desire to express strong opinions and initiate demands. A person who is perceived as being extremely strong-willed and inflexible may fail to establish a cooperative relationship. In an organizational setting, it is important to learn how to get the job done without stepping on toes.

Thinking / Learning Starters

1. After you have determined your own place on the dominance scale, think about your closest coworkers and friends. Who is most dominant in your circle? Who is least dominant? Under what circumstances have they displayed high dominance? Under what circumstances have they displayed low dominance?

2. Complete the dominance indicator form shown in Figure 3.2 for one of the people you have just listed.

The Sociability Continuum

Have you ever met someone who was open and talkative and who seemed easy to get to know? An individual who is friendly and expresses feelings openly can be placed near the top of the **sociability continuum.**[13] The continuum is illustrated in Figure 3.3. **Sociability** can be defined as the tendency to seek and enjoy social relationships.

Sociability can also be thought of as a measure of whether you tend to control or express your feelings. Those high in sociability usually express their feelings freely, whereas people low on the continuum tend to control their feelings. The person who is classified as being high in sociability is open and talkative and likes personal associations. The person who is low in sociability is more reserved and formal in social relationships.

The second step in determining your most-preferred communication style is to identify where you fall on the sociability continuum. To answer this question, complete the sociability indicator form shown in Figure 3.4. Rate yourself on each scale by placing a checkmark at a point along the continuum that represents the degree to which you feel you exhibit each of the characteristics. If most of your checkmarks fall to the right of center, you are high in sociability. If most fall to the left of center, you are low in sociability.

The sociability indicator form is not meant to be a precise instrument, but it will provide you with a general indication of where you fall on each of the

FIGURE 3.3

Sociability Continuum

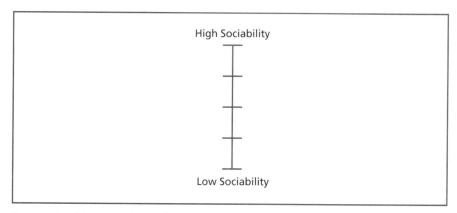

Source: Gerald L. Manning and Barry L. Reece, *Selling Today: Building Quality Partnerships,* Seventh Edition, Copyright ©1998. Adapted by permission of Prentice-Hall, Inc., Englewood Cliffs, N.J.

scales. You may also want to make copies of the form and distribute them to friends or coworkers for completion. (Remember, it is advisable not to involve parents, spouses, or close relatives in this feedback exercise.)

Where Should You Be on the Sociability Continuum?

Where are successful people on the sociability continuum? Everywhere. There is no best place to be. People at all points along the continuum can achieve success in an organizational setting. Nevertheless, there are some common-sense guidelines that persons who fall at either end of the continuum are wise to follow.

A person who is low in sociability is more likely to display a no-nonsense attitude when dealing with other people. This person may be seen as impersonal and businesslike. Behavior that is too guarded and too reserved can be a barrier to effective communication. Such persons may be perceived as unconcerned about the feelings of others and interested only in getting the job done. Perceptions are critical in the business world, especially among customers. Even a hint of indifference can create a customer relations problem.

Persons who are high in sociability openly express their feelings, emotions, and impressions. They are perceived as being concerned with relationships and therefore are easy to get to know. At times, emotionally expressive people need to curb their natural exuberance. Too much informality can be a problem in some work relationships. The importance of adapting your style to accommodate the needs of others is discussed later in this chapter.

FIGURE 3.4

Sociability Indicator
Form

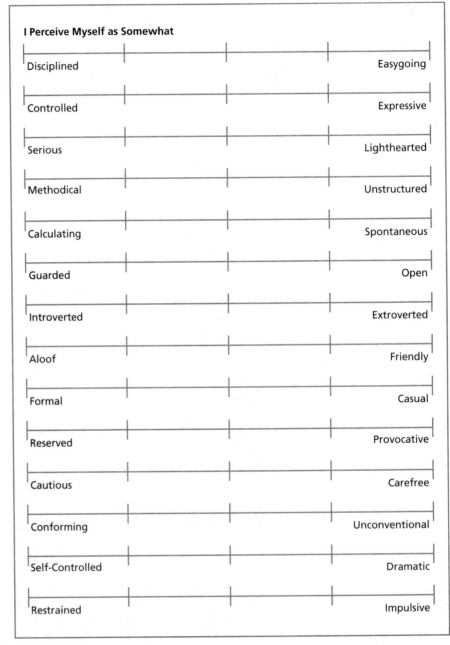

I Perceive Myself as Somewhat

Disciplined				Easygoing
Controlled				Expressive
Serious				Lighthearted
Methodical				Unstructured
Calculating				Spontaneous
Guarded				Open
Introverted				Extroverted
Aloof				Friendly
Formal				Casual
Reserved				Provocative
Cautious				Carefree
Conforming				Unconventional
Self-Controlled				Dramatic
Restrained				Impulsive

Source: Gerald L. Manning and Barry L. Reece, *Selling Today: Building Quality Partnerships,* Seventh Edition, Copyright ©1998. Adapted by permission of Prentice-Hall, Inc., Englewood Cliffs, N.J.

Thinking / Learning Starters

1. After you have determined your own place on the sociability scale, think about your closest coworkers and friends. Who is most sociable in your circle? Who is least sociable? Under what circumstances have they displayed high sociability? Under what circumstances have they displayed low sociability?

2. Complete the sociability indicator form shown in Figure 3.4 for one of the people you have just listed.

Four Basic Communication Styles

The dominance and sociability continua can be combined to form a rather simple model that will tell you more about your communication style (see Figure 3.5). The **communication style model** will help you identify your most-preferred style. Dominance is represented by the horizontal axis and sociability by the vertical axis. The model is divided into quadrants, each representing one of four communication styles: emotive, director, reflective, or supportive. As you review the descriptions of these styles, you will likely find one that is "most like you" and one or more that are "least like you."

Emotive Style The upper-right-hand quadrant combines high sociability and high dominance. This is characteristic of the **emotive style** of communication (Figure 3.6).

You can easily form a mental picture of the emotive type by thinking about the phrases used earlier to describe high dominance and high sociability. A good example of the emotive type of person is comedian Jay Leno. Rosie O'Donnell also projects an outspoken, enthusiastic, and stimulating style. Sandra Bullock, a popular actress, displays the emotive style. She is animated, frequently laughs at herself, and seems to like an informal atmosphere. Larry King, popular talk-show host, and President Bill Clinton also project the emotive communication style. Here is a list of verbal and nonverbal clues that identify the emotive person:

1. *Displays action-oriented behavior.* The emotive person seems to be constantly on the go. He or she is likely to talk rapidly and express views with vigorous hand gestures. David Letterman and Jim Carrey fit this description.
2. *Likes informality.* This person usually likes to operate on a first-name basis. Emotive-type people often share personal points of view soon after meeting you.

FIGURE 3.5

Where the dominance and sociability dimensions are combined, the framework for communication style classification is established.

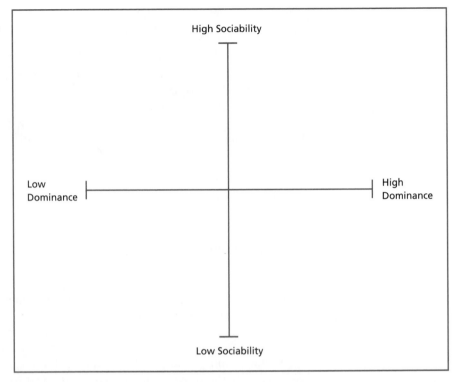

Source: Gerald L. Manning and Barry L. Reece, *Selling Today: Building Quality Partnerships,* Seventh Edition, Copyright ©1998. Adapted by permission of Prentice-Hall, Inc., Englewood Cliffs, N.J.

3. *Possesses a natural persuasiveness.* Combining high dominance and high sociability, this person finds it easy to express his or her point of view dramatically and forcefully.

Director Style The lower-right-hand quadrant represents a communication style that combines high dominance and low sociability—the **director style** (Figure 3.7). Television interviewer Barbara Walters and House Speaker Newt Gingrich project the director style. So is ABC reporter Sam Donaldson. Bob Dole, former presidential candidate, easily fits the description of this communication style.[14] All these people have been described as frank, assertive, and very determined. Some behaviors displayed by directors include the following:

1. *Projects a serious attitude.* Mike Wallace, one of the reporters on the popular television show *60 Minutes,* usually communicates a no-nonsense attitude. Directors often give the impression that they cannot have fun.

FIGURE 3.6

The emotive style combines high sociability and high dominance.

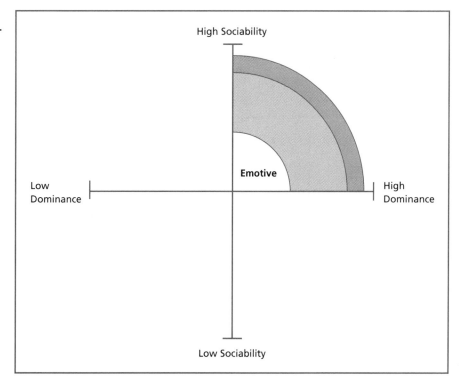

Source: Gerald L. Manning and Barry L. Reece, *Selling Today: Building Quality Partnerships,* Seventh Edition, Copyright ©1998. Adapted by permission of Prentice-Hall, Inc., Englewood Cliffs, N.J.

2. *Expresses strong opinions.* With firm gestures and a tone of voice that communicates determination, the director projects the image of someone who wants to take control. General Norman Schwarzkopf displays this behavior.
3. *May project indifference.* It is not easy for the director to communicate a warm, caring attitude. He or she does not find it easy to abandon the formal approach in dealing with people. Lou Gerstner, CEO of IBM, faces this challenge.

Reflective Style   The lower-left-hand quadrant of the communication style model features a combination of low dominance and low sociability. This is the **reflective style** of communication (Figure 3.8).

The reflective person is usually quiet, enjoys spending time alone, and does not make decisions quickly. The late physicist Albert Einstein fits this description. He once commented on how he liked to spend idle hours: "When I have

FIGURE 3.7

The director style combines high dominance and low sociability.

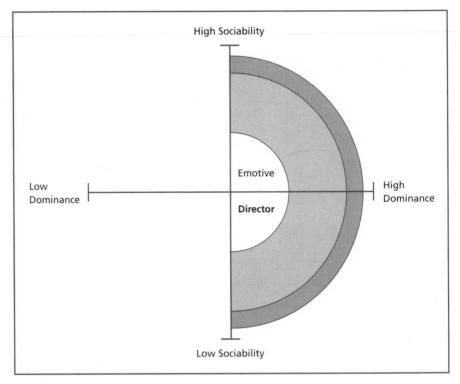

Source: Gerald L. Manning and Barry L. Reece, *Selling Today: Building Quality Partnerships,* Seventh Edition, Copyright ©1998. Adapted by permission of Prentice-Hall, Inc., Englewood Cliffs, N.J.

no special problem to occupy my mind, I love to reconstruct proofs of mathematical and physical theorems that have long been known to me. There is no goal in this, merely an opportunity to indulge in the pleasant occupation of thinking."[15] Alan Greenspan, chairman of the Federal Reserve, former president Jimmy Carter, former Dallas Cowboy coach Tom Landry, and Dr. Joyce Brothers also display the characteristics of the reflective communication style. Some of the behaviors characteristic of this style are as follows:

1. *Expresses opinions in a formal, deliberate manner.* The reflective person does not seem to be in a hurry. He or she expresses measured opinions. Emotional control is a common trait of this style.
2. *Seems to be preoccupied.* The reflective person is rather quiet and may often appear preoccupied with other matters. As a result, he or she may seem aloof and difficult to get to know.
3. *Prefers orderliness.* The reflective person prefers an orderly work environment. At a meeting, this person appreciates an agenda. A reflective person enjoys reviewing details and making decisions slowly.

Aaron Feuerstein (left), chief executive officer of Malden Mills, located in Lawrence, Massachusetts, displays the characteristics of the supportive communication style. He has been described by his workers as sensitive, patient, and a good listener. A person exhibiting characteristics of the director style, such as this police officer (right), projects the image of someone who takes a serious, no-nonsense approach to work. (Ed Quinn/SABA (left); Michael Newman/PhotoEdit (right))

Supportive Style   The upper-left-hand quadrant combines low dominance and high sociability—the **supportive style** of communication (Figure 3.9). People who possess this style tend to be cooperative, patient, and attentive.

The supportive person is reserved and usually avoids attention-seeking behavior. Additional behaviors that commonly characterize the supportive style include the following:

1. *Listens attentively.* Good listeners have a unique advantage in many occupational settings. This is especially true of loan officers, sales personnel, and supervisors. The talent comes more naturally to the supportive person.
2. *Avoids the use of power.* Supportive persons are more likely to rely on friendly persuasion than power when dealing with people. They like to display warmth in their speech and written correspondence. The late Charles Kuralt, CBS News journalist, and Neil Armstrong, Apollo 11 crew member, fit this description.
3. *Makes and expresses decisions in a thoughtful, deliberate manner.* Supportive persons appear low-key in a decision-making role. Meryl Streep, Paul Simon, Kevin Costner, the late Princess Di, and Harrison Ford all display characteristics of this style.

FIGURE 3.8

The reflective style combines low dominance and low sociability.

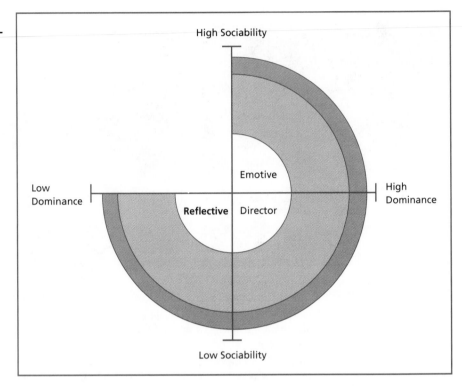

Source: Gerald L. Manning and Barry L. Reece, *Selling Today: Building Quality Partnerships,* Seventh Edition, Copyright ©1998. Adapted by permission of Prentice-Hall, Inc., Englewood Cliffs, N.J.

Did you find one particular communication style that is most like yours? If your first attempt to identify your most-preferred style was not successful, do not be discouraged. No one conforms completely to one style. You share some traits with other styles. Also, keep in mind that communication style is just one dimension of personality. Your personality is made up of a broad array of psychological tendencies that you reveal while you are interacting with the environment.[16] Communication style refers only to those behaviors that others can observe. Although we tend to repeat certain behaviors more than others, we all display a wide range of behaviors at various times. Nevertheless, others will react to us on the basis of our observable, repetitive patterns of behavior (communication style), rather than on the basis of our capacity for variation.[17]

Did you discover a communication style that is least like yours? In many cases, we feel a sense of tension or discomfort when we have contact with persons who speak or act in ways that are at odds with our communication style. For example, the person with a need for orderliness and structure in daily work

FIGURE 3.9

The supportive style combines low dominance and high sociability.

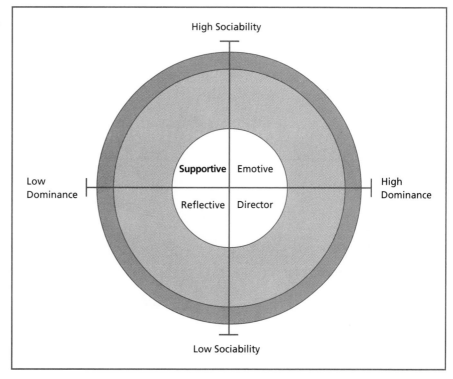

Source: Gerald L. Manning and Barry L. Reece, *Selling Today: Building Quality Partnerships,* Seventh Edition, Copyright ©1998. Adapted by permission of Prentice-Hall, Inc., Englewood Cliffs, N.J.

may feel tension when working closely with someone who is more spontaneous and unstructured.

Variation Within Your Communication Style

Communication styles also vary in intensity. For example, a person may be either moderately or strongly dominant. Note that the communication style model features zones that radiate outward from the center, as illustrated in Figure 3.10. These dimensions might be thought of as **intensity zones.**

Zone 1 People who fall within Zone 1 will display their unique behavioral characteristics with less intensity than people in Zone 2. This means that it may be more difficult to identify the preferred communication style of people in Zone 1. They will not be as obvious in their gestures, tone of voice, speech

FIGURE 3.10

Communication Style
Intensity Zones

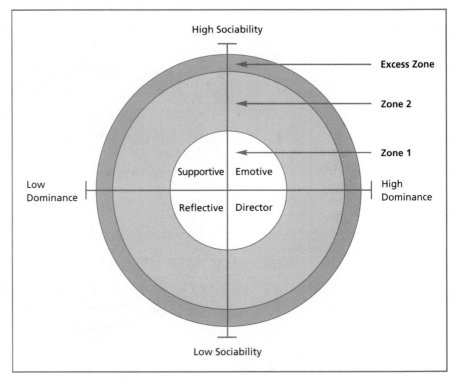

Source: Gerald L. Manning and Barry L. Reece, *Selling Today: Building Quality Partnerships,* Seventh Edition, Copyright ©1998. Adapted by permission of Prentice-Hall, Inc., Englewood Cliffs, N.J.

patterns, or emotional expressions. You may have trouble picking up the right clues to identify their communication style.

Zone 2   People who fall within Zone 2 will display their behavioral characteristics with greater intensity than those in Zone 1. For example, on the following dominance continuum, Sue, Mike, Harold, and Deborah each fall within a different zone.

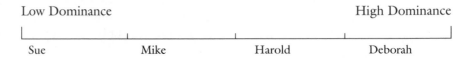

In terms of communication style identification, it is probably easier to distinguish between Sue and Deborah (who are in Zone 2) than between Mike and Harold (who are in Zone 1). Of course, the boundary line that separates Zone

1 from Zone 2 should not be viewed as a permanent barrier. Under certain conditions, people will abandon their preferred style temporarily, a process we call "style flexing."

You can sometimes see style flexing when a person is upset or angry. For example, Sue is a strong supporter of equal rights for women. At school she hears a male student say, "I think a woman's place is in the home." At that point, she may express her own views in the strongest possible terms. This forcefulness will require temporarily abandoning the comfort of her low dominance style to display assertive behavior.

Excess Zone The **excess zone** is characterized by a high degree of intensity and rigidity. It can also be labeled the "danger" zone. When people occupy this zone, they become inflexible and display a lack of versatility (see Table 3.1). Extreme intensity in any quadrant is bound to interfere with good human relations.

TABLE 3.1

Behaviors Displayed in the Excess Zone

Supportive Style	Attempts to win approval by agreeing with everyone
	Constantly seeks reassurance
	Refuses to take a strong stand
	Tends to apologize a great deal
Director Style	Is determined to come out on top
	Will not admit to being wrong
	Appears cold and unfeeling when dealing with others
	Tends to use dogmatic phrases such as "always," "never," or "You can't"
Emotive Style	Tends to express highly emotional opinions
	Is outspoken to the point of being offensive
	Seems unwilling to listen to the views of others
	Uses exaggerated gestures and facial expressions
Reflective Style	Tends to avoid making a decision
	Seems overly interested in detail
	Is very stiff and formal in dealing with others
	Seeks to achieve perfection

People often move into the excess zone when they are under stress or not feeling well. A person who feels threatened or insecure may also move into the excess zone. Even a temporary excursion into the excess zone should be avoided if at all possible. Inflexible and rigid communication styles are likely to lead to a breakdown in human relations.

Tips on Style Identification

To identify a person's communication style, focus your full attention on observable behavior. The best clues for identifying styles are nonverbal. Learn to be observant of people's gestures, posture, and facial expressions, and the rapidity and loudness of their speech.[18] Animated facial expressions and high-volume, rapid speech are characteristic of the emotive communication style. Infrequent use of gestures, speaking in a steady monotone, and few facial expressions are characteristic of the reflective style. Of course verbal messages will also be helpful. If a person tends to be blunt and to the point and makes strong statements, you are likely observing a director.

We have noted that communication style is determined by where a person falls on the sociability continuum and the dominance continuum. Once you have identified as many verbal and nonverbal clues as possible, use this information to place the person on each continuum. Let's assume that the clues indicate that the person is low in dominance. This means you can automatically eliminate the emotive and director styles because both are characterized by high dominance. The next step is to place the person on the sociability continuum. If the clues indicate that the person is low in sociability, you automatically eliminate the style. By the process of elimination, you conclude that this person is probably reflective. The authors of *People Styles at Work,* however, warn that your initial perception of another person's style should not be carved in stone. You should continue to collect new information and reassess your initial observations.[19]

VERSATILITY: THE THIRD DIMENSION

Earlier in this chapter we described two important dimensions of the communication style model: dominance and sociability. You will recall that these dimensions of human behavior are independent of each other. Now we are ready to discuss versatility, an important third dimension of human behavior.

Persons who can create and maintain interpersonal relations with others, regardless of their communication styles, are displaying versatility. **Versatility** can be defined as acting in ways that earn a social endorsement. Endorsement

---

Total Person Insight

"When we speak of interpersonal relationships (an interaction involving at least two people), we contend that no one can do much about what another person says or does, but each of us can do something about what we say and do. And because dealing with others is such a major aspect of our lives, if we can control what we say and do to make others more comfortable, we can realistically expect our relationships to be more positive, or effective, ones."

DAVID W. MERRILL AND ROGER H. REID

Authors, *Personal Styles and Effective Performance*

---

means simply other people's approval of our behavior. People give us their endorsement when they feel comfortable and nondefensive with us.[20]

The dimension of versatility is independent of style. This means that the emotive style is no more or less likely to be versatile than is the reflective style. Communication style remains relatively stable throughout life, whereas versatility is changeable.

Versatility is a trait we exhibit ourselves rather than elicit from others. Versatile people recognize that they can control their half of relationships and that it is easier to modify themselves than it is to modify others. The versatile person asks, "What can I do to make it easier for the other person to relate to me?"[21]

Achieving Versatility Through Style Flexing

Getting classified according to communication style doesn't mean you are "typecast" for life. You can always learn to strengthen areas of your most-preferred communication style in order to get along better with others.[22] One way to broaden your personality is to engage in style flexing. **Style flexing** can be described as a deliberate attempt to change or alter your style to meet the needs of another person. It is a temporary effort to act in harmony with the behavior of another person's communication style. Style flexing is communicating in a way more agreeable to persons of other styles. As noted earlier in this chapter, you can learn to adapt your style to accommodate others.

Style flexing has proven to be an important skill needed in many occupations. In personal selling, for example, research indicates that salespeople with high versatility scores were more likely to outperform salespeople with low versatility.[23]

To illustrate how style flexing can be used in an organizational setting, let's take a look at a communication problem faced by Jeff Walker, buyer of sporting goods for a small chain of sporting goods stores. Jeff has a strong emotive communication style and usually gets along well with other emotive communicators. His immediate supervisor is Rhonda Greenbaum, a reflective person who tends to approach her work in an orderly, systematic manner. Jeff finds it difficult to curb his stimulating, promotional style and therefore is sometimes viewed as "unstable" by Ms. Greenbaum.

What might Jeff do to improve communication with his supervisor? Jeff is naturally an open, impulsive communicator. During meetings with a reflective person, he should appear less spontaneous, slow his rate of speech, and avoid the use of dramatic gestures. He should try to appear more reserved.

The reflective person admires orderliness, so Jeff should be sure he is well prepared. Prior to each meeting, he should develop a mental agenda of items that he wants to cover. At the beginning of the meeting he might say, "Ms. Greenbaum, there are three things I want to discuss." He would then describe each item concisely and present information slowly and systematically. This businesslike approach will be appreciated by the reflective supervisor.

How could Jeff's boss use style flexing to foster better communication? She could avoid appearing too stiff and formal. During meetings, the reflective person should try to avoid being "all business." (The emotive person does not object to small talk during meetings.) The reflective communicator might also be more informal about starting and ending meetings exactly on time, might allow the emotive person to depart from the agenda now and then, or might bring up an item spontaneously. The reflective person should try to share feelings and concerns more openly in the presence of an emotive person.

Strategies for Adapting Your Style

Once you have identified the dominant style of the other person, begin thinking of ways to flex your style to gain a social endorsement. Remember, you can control your half of the relationship. What can be done to meet the interpersonal needs of the other person? Here are a few general style adaptation strategies:

Flexing to the Emotive Style

- Take time to build a social as well as a business relationship. Leave time for relating and socializing.
- Display interest in the person's ideas, interests, and experiences.
- Do not place too much emphasis on details. Emotive people like fast-moving, inspirational verbal exchanges.
- Maintain a pace that is fast and spontaneous.

Brad Anger, a marketing manager for a French-based company, is shown in a street in Ho Chi Minh City (formerly Saigon). Versatility is an important skill needed by this American working in Vietnam. (Gideon Mendel/ Network/SABA)

Flexing to the Director Style

- Be specific, brief, and to the point. Use time efficiently.
- Present the facts logically, and be prepared to provide answers to specific questions.
- Maintain a pace that is fast and decisive.
- Messages (written or oral) should be short and to the point.

Flexing to the Reflective Style

- Appeal to the person's orderly, systematic approach to life. Be well organized.
- Approach this person in a straightforward, direct manner. Get down to business quickly.
- Be as accurate and realistic as possible when presenting information.
- Messages (written or oral) should be detailed and precise. The pace of verbal messages should be slow and systematic.

Flexing to the Supportive Style

- Show a sincere interest in the person. Take time to identify areas of common interest.

- Patiently draw out personal views and goals. Listen and be responsive to the person's needs.
- Present your views in a quiet, nonthreatening manner. Do not be pushy.
- Put a priority on relationship building and communication.

In those situations where you are attempting to win the support or cooperation of another person, try to avoid saying or doing things that might cause tension to arise. Tony Alessandra and Michael O'Connor, authors of *People Smart,* state that if we don't think first of the other person, we run the risk of unintentionally creating a tension-filled relationship.[24]

Style Flexing: Pitfalls and Possibilities

Is style flexing just another way to manipulate others? The answer is yes if your approach is insincere and your only objective is to get something for yourself. The choice is yours. If your objective is to build an honest, constructive relationship, then style flexing can be a valuable and productive communication strategy.

In an organizational setting, it is usually best to flex your style when something important is at stake. Let's assume that you are head of a major department in a large hospital. Tomorrow you will meet with the hospital administrator and propose the purchase of new x-ray equipment that will cost a large amount of money. This is a good time to think about the administrator's communication style and make decisions regarding style-flexing strategies. You do not want communication style bias to become a factor during this important meeting.

Coping with Change

In an age of accelerating change, you are wise to develop a high degree of versatility. The adaptive, resourceful ways of the versatile person enable him or her to cope with changing conditions. Generally, the more versatile person has a competitive edge over the less versatile person. Just as a person can become technically obsolete in knowledge and skills, the less versatile person can become obsolete from the standpoint of interpersonal skills.[25]

A FINAL WORD OF CAUTION

A discussion of communication styles would not be complete without a few words of caution. It is tempting to put a label on someone and then assume the label tells you everything you need to know about that person. In *The Name of Your Game,* Stuart Atkins says we should be careful not to use labels that make people feel boxed in, typecast, or judged. He says we should not classify *people;* we should classify their *strengths* and *preferences* to act one way or another under certain circumstances.[26] As noted in Chapter 1, the "total person" is made up of such interdependent traits as emotional control, values orientation, self-esteem, and self-awareness. To get acquainted with the whole person takes time and effort. Atkins makes this observation: "It requires much more effort to look beyond the label, to experience the person as a dynamic process, to look at the fine print on the box and carefully study the ingredients inside the package. We have been conditioned to trust the label and look no further."[27]

You must also be careful not to let the label you place on yourself become the justification for your own inflexible behavior. If you discover that your most preferred communication style is reflective and take the position that "others will simply have to get used to my need for careful analysis of data before making a decision," then you are not displaying the characteristics of a versatile person. Try not to let the label justify or reinforce why you are unable to communicate effectively with others.[28]

Strength/Weakness Paradox

As noted previously in this chapter, there is no "best" communication style. Each style has its unique strong points. Supportive people are admired for their easygoing, responsive style. Directors are respected for the thoroughness and determination they display. The stimulating, personable style of emotive persons can be very refreshing. And the emotional control and industrious nature of reflective persons are almost universally admired.

Problems arise when people overextend or rely too much on the strengths of their style. The director who is too demanding may be viewed by others as "pushy." The supportive person may try too hard to please others and risk being viewed as "wishy-washy." An emotive person may be viewed as too excitable or not serious enough in a business setting. The reflective person who cannot seem to make a decision without mountains of information may be viewed as too cautious and inflexible. Some people rely too heavily on established strengths and fail to develop new skills that will increase their versatility.

Summary

Communication styles are the patterns of behaviors that are observable to others. Communication style tends to be stable throughout a person's lifetime. Each person has a distinctive way of responding to people and events.

Communication style bias is a common problem in organizations and should be viewed as a major barrier to good human relations.

The communication style model is formed by combining two important dimensions of human behavior: dominance and sociability. Combinations of these two aspects create four communication styles—emotive, director, reflective, and supportive. With practice you can learn to identify other people's communication styles. A third dimension of human behavior—versatility—is important in dealing with varying communication styles. You can adjust your own style to meet the needs of others—a process called style flexing.

Career Corner

Q. The company I work for discourages personal phone calls during working hours. I am a single parent with two young children. How can I convince my supervisor that some personal calls are very important?

A. Placing personal phone calls during working hours is an issue that often divides employers and employees. From the employer's point of view, an employee who spends time on nonwork calls is wasting time, a valuable resource. Also, many organizations want to keep telephone lines clear for business calls. From your point of view, you need to know about changes in child-care arrangements, serious health concerns of family members, and similar problems. In fact, you will probably perform better knowing that family members are secure. Explain to your supervisor that some personal calls will be inevitable. It is very important that you and your supervisor reach an agreement regarding this issue. When possible, make most of your personal calls during your lunch hour or during work breaks. Encourage friends to call you at home.

To improve communications with your supervisor, get acquainted with his or her communication style. Once you have identified this person's dominant style, use appropriate style flexing strategies to gain a social endorsement.

Key Terms

communication style
communication style bias
dominance
dominance continuum
sociability continuum
sociability
communication style model
emotive style

director style
reflective style
supportive style
intensity zones
excess zone
versatility
style flexing

Review Questions

1. How would you define *communication style bias?*
2. What are the four basic concepts that establish a foundation for understanding communication styles?
3. How will someone employed in an organization benefit from an understanding of communication styles?
4. Explain the difference between the dominance continuum and the sociability continuum.
5. What are the four communication styles? Provide a brief description of each.
6. What are some nonverbal clues that might help you identify a person's most-preferred communication style?
7. Explain why there is no "best" communication style. Feel free to use examples from your personal life to support your answer.
8. Explain the strength/weakness paradox.
9. Define the term *versatility*. Explain the meaning of *style flexing*.
10. The Total Person Insight by David Merrill and Roger Reid suggests that we should try to control what we say and do to make others more comfortable. Would it be easy or difficult for people to follow this advice? Explain your answer.

Application Exercises

1. Oprah Winfrey has become one of America's most popular talk-show hosts. Consider the behaviors she displays on her show, and then complete the following exercises:
   a. On the dominance continuum, place a mark where you feel she belongs.
   b. On the sociability continuum, place a mark where you feel she belongs.
   c. On the basis of these two continua, determine Oprah Winfrey's communication style.
   d. In your opinion, does Oprah Winfrey display style flexibility?
2. To get some practice in identifying communication styles, watch two or three television shows and attempt to identify the style of individuals portrayed on the screen. To fully develop your skills of listening and observing, try this three-step approach:
   a. Cover the screen with a towel or newspaper and try to identify the style of one or two persons, using voice only.
   b. Turn down the volume, uncover the screen, and attempt to identify the style of the same persons, using visual messages only.
   c. Turn up the volume and make another attempt to identify the communication style of the persons portrayed on the screen. This time the identification process should be easier because you will be using sight and sound.

   These practice sessions will help you learn how to interpret the nonverbal messages that are helpful in identifying another person's communication style. When you select TV shows, avoid situation comedies that often feature persons displaying exaggerated styles. You may want to watch a talk show or a news program like *Meet the Press.*

Internet Exercise

The primary purpose of this chapter is to provide you with an introduction to communication styles and prepare you to apply at work and in your personal life the concepts presented here. You now have the foundation you need to continue your study. A great deal of information related to communication styles can be found on the Internet. Using your search engine, type in the following keywords, and then review the resources available:

communication styles

personality types

personality dimensions

psychological types

Examine the resources (such as books, articles, and training programs), and then prepare a brief summary of your findings. Pay special attention to new information that was not covered in your textbook.

Case 3.1   **A Matter of Style**

Betty Westmoreland is a sales representative for the World Travel Agency, a firm that specializes in packaged tours to foreign countries. She has spent two months training for this position and is now working with customers. Betty is an expressive person who is very enthusiastic about her job. She possesses all the characteristics of the emotive communication style. She is outspoken, excitable, and very personable. Betty is always attractively dressed and well groomed.

Monday morning Betty has an appointment with Raymond L. Fitz III, executive director of an association made up of bank loan officers. Raymond wants to arrange a package tour to England for about fifty persons that will include transportation, hotel accommodations, meals, and tickets to special events. He is classified as reflective in terms of communication style. People who know him well view him as industrious, cautious, and well organized. He is all business when it comes to representing the bankers' association.

Questions

1. At the initial meeting, do you anticipate that communication style bias will surface? If so, why? If not, why?
2. What will be Raymond's primary communication needs?
3. How should Betty speak and act throughout the meeting to develop an effective business relationship with him?

Case 3.2 **Communication Style Training Builds Teamwork**

Many organizations interested in improving customer service, promoting greater teamwork among employees, and increasing quality have developed training programs that emphasize an understanding of communication styles. These programs help employees understand the four communication styles one is likely to encounter on the job.

When General Electric Co.'s Business Information Center (GEBIC) was instructed to reduce the layers of management and create a self-directed work force, the staff wasn't sure how to carry out the downsizing effort. They did realize that with fewer supervisory-management personnel, employees would have to contribute more to solving problems and making decisions. With the assistance of a consultant, a decision was made to help employees develop the interpersonal skills needed to become effective team members. The newly formed GEBIC team completed the LIFO workshop offered by Stuart Atkins Incorporated, a California-based training company.

LIFO training invites self-examination and promotes self-development in a comfortable, nonthreatening environment. Workshop participants complete the LIFO Survey, a self-scoring instrument that helps them identify their most-preferred communication style. During the workshop, GEBIC employees also spent time learning how to identify the most-preferred style of others. LIFO scores for all team members were posted and discussed at the workshop. This information contributed to an understanding of the team members' communication style preferences. Upon completion of the LIFO training, employees reported that they felt greater confidence in their ability to communicate effectively with other team members and with the customers served by GEBIC. One person described her experience this way:

> LIFO not only empowers me as an individual in terms of my interaction with other people, but enables me to empower the other people I am dealing with. When you understand their strong points and blind sides, you both interact more effectively. For example, if I know my boss likes a lot of detail and nitty gritty, I'm going to be prepared when I present a new idea to him.

How has LIFO training influenced productivity at GEBIC? The major responsibility of this division is to handle outside calls from industrial customers or prospects who need assistance. Thus, one way to measure productivity is to examine call volume (customers served per employee) and cost per customer served. During the first two years of the self-directed work-team approach, call volume rose 53 percent, and during the same period the cost per call dropped 34 percent. Team members take pride in the fact that they can usually identify the caller's communication style and then quickly adjust their own style to communicate effectively with the customer.

Questions

1. Each GEBIC team member was given the LIFO scores of other team members. What are the advantages of this practice? Are there any disadvantages? Explain.
2. GEBIC team members reported that LIFO training gave them the skills needed to identify the communication style of most callers. If your contact with another person is a telephone call, what factors (clues) would influence your decision regarding the caller's communication style?
3. Would you recommend LIFO training, or a similar program that focuses on communication style theory, to an organization that is attempting to increase the level of teamwork among its employees? Explain.

Chapter 4

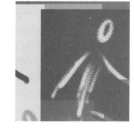

Building

High

Self-Esteem

Chapter Preview

After studying this chapter, you will be able to

1. Define self-esteem and discuss how it is developed.
2. Explain how self-esteem influences human relations and success at work.
3. Identify the characteristics of people with low and high self-esteem.
4. Explain the roles mentors can play in your professional life.
5. Identify ways to raise your self-esteem.
6. Understand the conditions organizations can create that will help workers raise their self-esteem.

C RYSTAL BURCH, A TEENAGER from a small town in Oregon, learned her early lessons about hard work from her grandmother, who raised four children on a paycheck from Dairy Queen after her husband lost a leg in a construction accident. Crystal's mother, one of 14 children, worked her way up to become supervisor at a packaging plant. Her father picked farm crops and moved irrigation pipe as a child, then rose through the blue-collar ranks to become production manager for a computer-furniture maker. These role models provided a powerful influence on Crystal's ever-changing adolescent view of her place in the world, but her annual visits to Nike Inc.'s Beaverton, Oregon, offices with her grandmother, Lauraine Burch, exposed her to people who wore suits and dresses to work, attended meetings, and solved marketing problems. Crystal noticed that people at Nike didn't have to lift 50-pound loads and were not in constant danger of physical injury. She thought, "I don't have to work like my mom. . . . I'd like to work my way up to be a manager, and maybe run my own business one day."[1]

But her image of her future became dim after entering a large middle school. She was bewildered by the crowds and was scorned by her fellow classmates when she eagerly asked questions in class. Soon she started missing homework deadlines, and her grades plummeted.

Once again a role model, this time Olympic athlete Jackie Joyner-Kersee, helped guide Crystal through her feelings of self-doubt. Grandmother Lauraine had worked with Ms. Joyner-Kersee on a Nike promotion and shared the materials with Crystal. The track star's humble childhood was very similar to Crystal's. She credited her solid hometown roots, close family ties, and the guidance of her role models for helping her achieve many of her goals. Her personal story of overcoming defeat at her first Olympic Games inspired Crystal to think differently.

Joyner-Kersee explained that she was physically ready to compete but lacked the proper mental conditioning: She did not *expect* to win. At the beginning of each event, she fed herself negative thoughts that drained her energy. Through proper mental training, however, Joyner-Kersee took control of her thoughts about her potential success, fed her mind positive self-talk, and came home with two gold medals from the Seoul Olympic Games.[2]

Crystal is once again back on track, and her grade-point average has skyrocketed. Many people, however, go through life never learning these lessons and are guided by negative role models and destructive self-talk that produce dramatically different results. The key seems to be how you feel about yourself and your future. ■

THE POWER OF SELF-ESTEEM

Nathaniel Branden, author of *The Six Pillars of Self-Esteem,* has spent the past three decades studying the psychology of self-esteem. In countless speeches, articles, and books, he has attempted to describe the connection between self-esteem and many of the human problems common to our society today. He notes that high self-esteem enhances our ability to build effective relationships with others:

> The healthier our self-esteem, the more inclined we are to treat others with respect, benevolence, goodwill, and fairness—since we do not tend to perceive them as a threat, and since self-respect is the foundation of respect for others.[3]

The belief that low self-esteem can cause serious problems throughout life prompted the California state assembly to establish the twenty-five-member Task Force to Promote Self-Esteem and Personal and Social Responsibility. This action followed testimony that people with low self-esteem are more likely to exhibit violent behavior, discriminate against others, and abuse drugs. The task force's final report defines **self-esteem** as appreciating your own worth and importance, having the character to be accountable for your own behaviors, and acting responsibly toward others.[4]

The importance of self-esteem as a guiding force in our lives cannot be overstated. Alfred Adler, a noted psychiatrist and author, observed, "Everything begins with self-esteem, your concept of yourself."[5]

Self-Esteem = Self-Efficacy + Self-Respect

Nathaniel Branden states that self-esteem has two interrelated components: self-efficacy and self-respect. **Self-efficacy** is the belief that you can achieve what you set out to do.[6] When your self-efficacy is high, you believe you have the ability to act appropriately. When your self-efficacy is low, you worry that you might not be able to do the task, that it is beyond your abilities. Your perception of your self-efficacy can influence which tasks you take on and which ones you avoid. Albert Bandura, a professor at Stanford University and one of the foremost self-efficacy researchers, views this component of self-esteem as a resilient belief in your own abilities. According to Bandura, a major source of self-efficacy is the experience of mastery, in which success in one area builds your confidence to succeed in other areas.[7] For example, an administrative assistant who masters a sophisticated computerized accounting system is more likely to master future complicated computer programs than is a person who feels computer illiterate and may not even try to figure out the new program, regardless of how well he or she *could* do it.

Self-respect, the second component of self-esteem, is what you think and feel about yourself. Self-respect is the deep-down-inside feeling of your own worth. The conviction of your own value is a primary factor in achieving career success. People who respect themselves tend to act in ways that confirm and reinforce this respect. People who lack self-respect may put up with verbal or physical abuse from others because they feel they are unworthy of praise and deserve the abuse.[8] One key to achieving a sense of self-worth is to set realistic standards. People with low self-esteem are often persons who set unrealistically high standards for themselves and then struggle to achieve them. The result is often a persistent need to prove themselves and an inability to enjoy what they have already accomplished.[9] When you respect yourself, you are less likely to feel a constant need to prove yourself to others. You are proud of your accomplishments and goals and are not dependent on the constant approval of others. One of the great tragedies in life is that people look for respect in every direction except within.

Self-esteem includes your feelings about your adequacy in the roles you play in life, such as that of friend, brother or sister, daughter or son, employee or employer, student or teacher, researcher, leader, and so on. Self-esteem also includes the personality traits you believe you have, such as honesty, creativity, assertiveness, flexibility, and many more. Often your self-esteem derives from your physical characteristics and your skills and abilities. Are you tall, slender, short, or heavy? Do you like what you see in the mirror? Are you good at writing, fixing appliances, researching topics, playing the piano, or engaging in some other skill?

Although high self-esteem is the basis for a healthy personality, it does not mean becoming egotistical—that is, thinking and acting with only your own interests in mind. Genuine self-esteem is not expressed by self-glorification at the expense of others or by the attempt to diminish others so as to elevate yourself. Arrogance, boastfulness, and the overestimation of your abilities reflect inadequate self-esteem rather than, as it might appear, too much self-esteem. Someone with an egotistical orientation to the world sees everything and everyone in terms of their usefulness to her or his own aims and goals. This attitude undermines good human relations.

How Self-Esteem Develops

A Sunday school teacher once asked her class of small children, "Who made you?" Instead of giving the expected reply, an insightful child responded, "I'm not finished yet!" You are not born knowing who and what you are. You acquire your image of yourself over time by realizing your natural abilities and by constantly receiving messages about yourself from the people closest to you and from your environment.

Childhood   Researchers have discovered that a child's potential is determined in the early years. The neurons of the brain—those long wiry cells that carry electrical messages through the nervous system and the brain—literally make their connections during the birth-to-preschool period. If these connections are not made, the child suffers later in life in a variety of ways. For example, emotional stability, which directly affects how individuals feel about themselves, is greatly affected by how the brain develops in the first two years of life.[10]

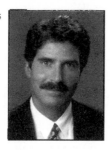

Beginning at about two months, the distress and contentment that newborns experience start to evolve into more complex feelings such as sadness and joy, envy and empathy, shame and pride. Sadly, children who do not play much or are rarely touched develop brains 20 to 30 percent smaller than normal for their age because of the lack of stimulation.[11] This underscores the importance of effective parenting—that is, finding time to cuddle a baby, talk with a toddler, and provide small children with stimulating experiences. Your potential adult vocabulary is determined by the words filtered through your brain before you were 3, and the foundations for math and logic were set before you were 4.[12] This early, powerful development, or lack thereof,

Total Person Insight

"Is it possible to have too much self-esteem? No, it is not; no more than it is possible to have too much physical health. Sometimes self-esteem is confused with boasting or bragging or arrogance. Such traits reflect, not too much self-esteem, but too little; they reflect a lack of self-esteem."

NATHANIEL BRANDEN
Author, *The Six Pillars of Self-Esteem*

serves as the basis for your success or failure at various endeavors throughout your life.

Do you remember that when you started school your childhood friends, siblings, teachers, and various authority figures began sending you messages such as these:

- Bad boy! Bad girl!
- You're so lazy!
- You'll never learn.
- What's wrong with you?
- Why can't you be more like . . . ?
- It's all your fault.

- You're great!
- You can do anything!
- You're a fast learner.
- Next time you'll do better.
- I like you just the way you are.
- I know you did your best.

In most cases, you probably did not stop and analyze these messages; you simply accepted them as true and recorded them in your memory. As a result, you gradually developed a picture of yourself, whether accurate or distorted, that you came to believe as real. The authors of *Staying OK* describe this subconscious level of activity:

> Everyone was once a child. Our experience today is filtered through the events and feelings of childhood, recorded in detail. We cannot have a feeling today that is "disconnected" from similar feelings recorded in the past, the most intense of which occurred to us in the first five years of life. This does not mean that today's feelings are not real, or that we are to discount them by claiming "they're just an old recording." We are today who we once were.[13]

Adolescence   The years from age 12 to age 18 are among the most crucial in developing and consolidating your feelings about yourself. During these years, you are moving away from the close bond between parent and child and are attempting to establish ideals of independence and achievement.[14] You fluctuate between determination to reach your goals and self-doubt about whether or not you are capable. You must also deal with physical changes, relationships with your peers, the loss of a carefree childhood, and the assumption of some adult responsibilities.

Society today, however, unlike previous generations when teens had to help out on the farm or in family business or care for siblings, does not "need" adolescents, and this lack of importance and direction can lead to feelings of insecurity and uncertainty. Teens often feel vulnerable as the media and real life expose them to more violence in the form of drive-by shootings, date rape, sexual harassment, and drug-induced behaviors than ever before. To compensate, they frequently adopt an attitude of not caring.[15] When you do not care about anything or anyone, you do not care about yourself, and the result is low self-esteem. Without some help, this insecurity and lack of direction can last far into adulthood.

A critical factor in self-esteem for large numbers of adolescents is physical appearance. Magazines such as *Glamour, Cosmopolitan,* and *GQ* portray the

thin body as the height of fashion. The common use of fad diets by young men and women, and eating disorders, can be traced to society's pressure to be thin.[16] It is easy to feel deficient or diminished in comparison to the images projected in movies, on television, or in our favorite magazines. It is also easy to form a negative self-image when making these comparisons.

Mary Pipher, author of the best-selling book *Reviving Ophelia,* says that girls, especially, face difficult challenges during adolescence. This is a time when everything is changing: body shape, hormones, skin, and hair.[17] Recent surveys have discovered that

- 40 to 50 percent of all females have negative body images.[18]
- 60 percent of elementary school girls report being "happy the way I am." But by the time they reach high school, only 29 percent say they are happy with themselves.
- Eighth- and tenth-grade girls were twice as likely as boys to report feeling sad and hopeless.
- 40 percent of the girls in Lancaster County, Nebraska (America's heartland), had considered suicide.[19]

Many people never move beyond the image they had of themselves while in high school. Adolescent problems should not be underestimated, for it is in the resolution of these problems that the self-esteem of the adult is born.

Adulthood When you reach adulthood, your mind has a time-reinforced picture of who you are, molded by people and events from all your past experiences. You have been bombarded over the years with positive and negative messages from your family, friends, teachers, strangers, and the media.

You may compare yourself to others, as was so common in adolescence, or you may focus on your own inner sense of self-worth. Emmett Miller, a noted authority on self-esteem, says that as adults we tend to define ourselves in terms of:[20]

1. *The things we possess.* Miller says this is the most primitive source of self-worth. If we define ourselves in terms of what we have, the result may be an effort to accumulate more and more material things to achieve a greater feeling of self-worth. People who define themselves in terms of what they have may have difficulty deciding "what is enough" and may spend their life in search of more material possessions.

2. *What we do for a living.* Miller points out that too often our self-worth and identity depend on something as arbitrary as a job title. Amy Saltzman, author of *Down-Shifting,* a book on ways to reinvent (or redefine) success, says, "We have allowed our professional identities to define us and control us."[21] She points out that we have looked to outside forces such as the corporation, the university, the media, counselors, or our parents to provide us with a script for leading a satisfying, worthwhile life. People pushed into a rigid career track that offers ample financial rewards but no fulfillment of personal needs may dread going to work in the morning even though others admire the job they hold.

3. *Our internal value system and emotional makeup.* Miller says this is the healthiest way for people to identify themselves:

> If you don't give yourself credit for excellence in other areas of life, besides your job and material possessions, you've got nothing to keep your identity afloat in emotionally troubled waters. People who are in touch with their real identity weather the storm better because they have a more varied and richer sense of themselves, owing to the importance they attach to their personal lives and activities.[22]

As an adult, you will be constantly adjusting the level of your self-esteem as you get in touch with your identity. Wally Amos is a prime example of a person who literally lost his identity. He started the gourmet-cookie craze with his Famous Amos Chocolate Chip Cookies, built an extremely successful company, then mismanaged it and lost everything, including two wives and the affections of his children. A court injunction denied him the use of his name and likeness in connection with any food-related venture. He was left without his family, his money, his company, or his name. In typical Wally fashion, however, he realized that there was only *one* name he could not use, and millions more names to choose from, and so the Uncle Noname Cookie Company was born.[23]

Learn to protect your self-esteem against those who try to diminish or limit your potential—by believing in yourself and going around, under, or through obstacles that get in your way. Listen to those who encourage and challenge you. This awareness of how other people are influencing you will help you dis-

> ## *Total Person Insight*
>
> *"If you keep on thinking what you've always thought, you'll keep on getting what you've always got."*
>
> WALLY AMOS
>
> Founder, Uncle Noname Cookie Company

tinguish between what is helpful and what is destructive, what is true and what is false. It will help you expand the range of what you believe you can be and do in the future.

> ## *Thinking / Learning Starters*
>
> 1. Can you recall two or three people from your childhood or adolescence who had a positive effect on your self-esteem? What did these people say or do? Were there any who had a negative effect on you? What did they say or do?
>
> 2. Identify at least two people who exhibit the characteristics of people with high self-esteem. What behaviors helped you identify them?

SELF-ESTEEM INFLUENCES YOUR BEHAVIOR

Your self-esteem has a powerful impact on your behavior at work and in your personal life. In general, people with low self-esteem tend to have more trouble with interpersonal relationships and to be less productive than people with high self-esteem.[24]

Characteristics of People with Low Self-Esteem

1. *They tend to maintain an* **external locus of control.** This means that they believe their behavior is controlled by someone or something in their environment. When you hear a person say, "It's not my fault. He made me do it," you can be assured that the speaker probably has low self-esteem. Rather than taking responsibility for their own choices, such people blame other people or events for controlling them. Even when they succeed, they tend to attribute their success to luck rather than to their own expertise and hard work. This often results in reliance on the approval of others. This seeking of others' approval often pressures us into behaving contrary to our deepest convictions. When we rely too heavily on validation from external sources, we can lose control over our lives.[25]

2. *They tend to participate in self-destructive behaviors.* If you do not like yourself, there is no apparent reason to take care of yourself. Therefore, people with low self-esteem tend to drink too much, smoke too much, and eat too much. Some may develop an eating disorder such as bulimia or anorexia, often with devastating results.

3. *They exhibit poor human relations skills.* Individuals with low self-esteem are more likely to feel hostile, show a lack of respect for others, and attempt to retaliate against others to save face in difficult situations. They tend to blame others for everything that goes wrong. In contrast, people with healthy self-esteem operate from a position of empathy, compassion, and cooperation.[26]

Workers with low self-esteem can reduce the efficiency and productivity of a group: They tend to exercise less initiative, hesitate to accept responsibility or make independent decisions, and refuse to ask for help, fearing that others might think them incompetent. Rather than admit an error and handle the consequences, they often lie in an attempt to cover their mistakes.

4. *They may experience the failure syndrome.* As noted previously in this chapter, you form a mental picture of yourself at a very early age. Your subconscious mind was, and continues to be, "programmed" by other people's negative and positive comments. If your subconscious mind has been saturated with thoughts of past failures, these thoughts will continue to undermine your efforts to achieve your goals. If you see yourself as a failure, you will usually find some way to fail. William Glasser, author of *Reality Therapy* and other books on human behavior, calls this the **failure syndrome.** Individuals with a failure syndrome think, "I always fail. . . . Why try?" They have a fear of taking action because they expect to fail . . . again.

Characteristics of People with High Self-Esteem

1. *People with high self-esteem are future oriented and not overly concerned with past mistakes or failures.* They learn from their errors but are not immobilized by them. They believe every experience has something to teach—if they are willing to learn. A mistake can show you what does not work, what not to do. One consultant, when asked whether he had obtained any results in trying to solve a difficult problem, replied, "Results? Why, I've had lots of results. I know a hundred things that won't work!" The same principle applies to your own progress. Falling down does not mean failure. Staying down does.

2. *People with high self-esteem are able to cope with life's problems and disappointments.* Successful people have come to realize that problems need not depress them or make them anxious. It is their attitude toward problems that makes all the difference. In his book *They All Laughed: From Lightbulbs to Lasers,* Ira Flatow examines the lives of successful, innovative people who had to overcome major obstacles to achieve their goals. He discovered that the common thread among these creative people was their ability to overcome disappointing events and press on toward their goals.

3. *People with high self-esteem are able to feel all dimensions of emotion without letting those emotions affect their behavior in a negative way.* This characteristic is one of the major reasons people with high self-esteem are able to establish and maintain effective human relations with the people around them. They realize emotions cannot be handled either by repressing them or by giving them free rein. Although you may not be able to stop feeling the emotions of anger, envy, and jealousy, you can control your thoughts and actions when you are under the influence of these strong emotions. Say to yourself, "I may not be able to control the way I feel right now, but I can control the way I behave." This may help you bring an emotionally charged situation under control.

4. *People with high self-esteem are able to help others and accept help.* They are not threatened by helping others to succeed, nor are they afraid to admit weaknesses. If you are not good at dealing with figures, you can bring in an accountant to manage the records. If you see someone whose abilities are not being used to their fullest, you can suggest ways that person might develop his or her talents. An old adage in business goes, "First-rate people hire first-rate people. Second-rate people hire third-rate people." Individuals with secure self-esteem realize that in helping others succeed, they benefit themselves as well.

5. *People with high self-esteem are able to accept other people as unique, talented individuals.* They learn to accept others for who they are and what they can do. Our multicultural work force makes this attitude especially important. Individuals who cannot tolerate other people who are "different" may find themselves out of a job. People with high self-esteem build mutual trust based on each individual's uniqueness. These trusting relationships do not limit or confine either person because of group attributes such as skin color, religion, gender, lifestyle, or sexual orientation. Accepting others is a good indication that you accept yourself.

6. *People with high self-esteem exhibit a variety of self-confident behaviors.* They accept compliments or gifts by saying, "Thank you," without making self-critical excuses and without feeling obligated to return the favor. They can laugh at their situation without self-ridicule. They let others be right or wrong without attempting to correct or ridicule them. They feel free to express opinions even if they differ from those of their peers or parents. They enjoy being by themselves without feeling lonely or isolated. They are able to talk about themselves to others without excessive bragging. But perhaps most important, they are able to maintain an **internal locus of control**—that is, they make decisions for their own reasons based on their standards of what is right and wrong, and they are not likely to comply with the inappropriate demands of others. This internal control helps raise self-esteem every time it is applied.

Thinking / Learning Starters

1. Have you ever felt envious of another person's possessions, relationships, or lifestyle? How did this feeling affect your relationship with that person? If you were able to raise your self-esteem, how might your behavior change? What effect would this behavioral change have on your relationship with that person?

2. When you make decisions in your personal life, do you operate from an internal or external locus of control? Give an example.

HOW TO BUILD SELF-ESTEEM

"The level of our self-esteem is not set once and for all in childhood," says Nathaniel Branden. It can grow throughout our lives or it can deteriorate.[27] Examining your present self-image is the first step in understanding who you are, what you can do, and where you are going.

The person you will be tomorrow has yet to be created. Most people continue to shape that future person in the image of the past, repeating the old limitations and negative patterns without realizing what they are doing. The development of a new level of self-esteem will not happen overnight, but it can happen. Such a change is the result of a slow evolution that begins with the desire to overcome low self-esteem.

Identify and Accept Your Limitations

The first step toward higher self-esteem is to accept yourself as you are now. Without acceptance, improving your self-esteem is not possible. Accept your limitations, and become realistic about who you are and what you can and cannot do. Demanding perfection of yourself is unrealistic—no one is perfect. The past cannot be changed, so stop dwelling on it. Your future, however, can be effectively shaped by how you think and act from this day forward.

Accepting ourselves begins with an honest look at who we are. We don't need to like everything we find. We can just say, for example, "Oh, yes, I can recognize that

Athletes and successful individuals from all walks of life understand the power of visualizing the successful completion of a difficult task. If you can see your goal, and sincerely believe you are capable, you can achieve it. (Michael McGovern/The Picture Cube, Inc.)

I sometimes feel impatient. This is a human feeling, and I don't need to deny it or dislike myself for feeling it."[28]

Acting as an observer and detaching yourself from negative thoughts and actions can help you break the habit of rating yourself according to some scale of perfection and can enable you to substitute more positive and helpful thoughts. A good first step is learning to hate a behavior you may indulge in, rather than condemning yourself. Hating yourself tends to make the behavior worse. If you condemn yourself for being weak, for example, how can you muster the strength to change? But if you become an "observer" and view the activity as separate from yourself, you leave your self-esteem intact, while you work on changing the behavior.

Take Responsibility for Your Decisions

Psychologists have found that children who were encouraged to make their own decisions early in their lives have higher self-esteem than those who were kept dependent on their parents for a longer period of time. Making decisions helps you develop confidence in your own judgment and enables you to explore options. Take every opportunity you can to make decisions both in setting your goals and in devising ways to achieve them. As you make your decisions, be willing to accept the consequences of your actions, positive or negative.

Total Person Insight

"To feel competent to live and worthy of happiness, I need to experience a sense of control over my existence. This requires that I be willing to take responsibility for my actions and the attainment of my goals. This means that I take responsibility for my life and well-being."

NATHANIEL BRANDEN

Author, *The Six Pillars of Self-Esteem*

When Jim Burke became head of a new products division at Johnson & Johnson, one of his first projects was the development of a children's chest rub. The product failed miserably, and Burke expected that he would be fired. When he was called in to see the Chairman of the Board, however, he met a surprising reception. "Are you the one who just cost us all that money?" asked Robert Wood Johnson. "Well, I just want to congratulate you. If you are making mistakes, that means you are taking risks, and we won't grow unless you take risks." Some years later, Burke became the chairman of J&J.[29]

The attitude that you must be right all the time is a barrier to personal growth. With this attitude you will avoid doing things that might result in mistakes. Much unhappiness comes from the widespread and regrettable belief that it is important to avoid making mistakes at all costs.[30] Taking risks that reach beyond what you already know how to do can often be fun and extremely rewarding.

Accepting full responsibility for your decisions and actions is an important key to building self-esteem. Most of the factors that generate self-esteem are under your control. Choose to participate in self-improvement activities that will enhance your career and your personal life. Choose to build harmonious relationships with your coworkers, supervisors, customers, and family members. Choose the values by which you want to live your life. Making your own decisions and taking responsibility for the consequences can become a habit that will be a powerful force in your life.

Develop Expertise in Some Area

Developing "expert power" not only builds your self-esteem but also increases the value of your contribution to an organization. Identify and cultivate a skill or talent you have, whether it is a knack for interviewing people, a facility with math, or good verbal skills. Alice Young, a resident partner in the law firm of Graham & James in New York, developed an expertise in her youth that she did not know would be a major asset in her career. "I speak Japanese, Chinese, French, and English," she says. "I have a knowledge of Asian cultures that I developed before trade with the East opened up." She has been able to capitalize on her expertise to help American and Asian companies do business with each other and to smooth over many cultural differences that would otherwise make negotiations difficult or impossible. She advises others to "use what you know to benefit yourself and your company."[31]

Developing expertise may involve continuing your studies after completing your formal education. Some institutions offer professional courses to enable people to advance in their careers. For example, the Institute of Financial Education conducts courses for persons employed by financial institutions, and the Certified Medical Representatives Institute offers a series of professional development courses for pharmaceutical representatives.

Seek the Support and Guidance of Mentors

Darryl Hartley-Leonard rose from being desk clerk at the Los Angeles Hyatt Hotel to become chief executive officer of the Hyatt Corporation. Ivan Seidenberg began his career at Nynex Corporation as a splicer's assistant earning $89.50 a week and went on to become the CEO. Both credit mentors for their rise from humble beginnings.[32]

Chip Bell, author of *Managers as Mentors: Building Partnerships for Learning,* defines a **mentor** as "someone who helps someone else learn something the learner would otherwise have learned less well, more slowly, or not at all." He also describes a mentor as a sensitive, trusted adviser.[33] Although mentoring is most often a one-on-one partnership, a mentor will sometimes guide a group of protégés through the process of developing their organizational savvy and their careers. In most organizations mentoring is carried out informally, but formal programs are common. Formal programs systematically match mentors and protégés.

Most people who have had a mentoring experience say it was an effective development tool. However, many surveys indicate that only a small percentage of employees say they have had a mentor. In today's fast-paced work environment, where most people have a heavy workload, you must be willing to take the initiative and build a mentor relationship. Here are some tips to keep in mind.

1. *Multiple mentors are recommended.* Some people feel the need for both internal and external mentors. Internal mentors, an experienced associate or supervisor, can provide guidance as you navigate the organizational bumps and potholes. An external mentor, someone who does not work for your company, can provide an objective, independent view of your skills and

talents.[34] Many people benefit from short-term "learning partners" who will coach them on specific skills. A busy person will be less threatened by a request for specific help with a marketing strategy or development of new computer skills.

2. *Search for a mentor who has the qualities of a good coach.* Mentors need to be accomplished in their own right, but success alone does not make someone a good mentor. Look for someone whom you would like to emulate, both in business savvy and in operating style. Be sure it is someone you trust enough to talk about touchy issues.[35] A good mentor is someone who will give you feedback in a straightforward manner.

3. *Market yourself to a prospective mentor.* The best mentor for you may be someone who is very busy. Sell the benefits of a mentoring partnership. For example, point out that you have something to give in return for assistance. You may offer a view from the front lines to a senior manager or some up-to-date technical expertise to an older coworker.[36] Describe specific steps you will take to avoid wasting the time of a busy person. You might suggest that meetings be held during lunch.

Although mentors are not mandatory for success, they certainly help. Indeed, there will always be days when you feel nothing you do is right. Your mentor can help repair damaged self-esteem and encourage you to go on. With the power of another person's positive expectations reinforcing your own native abilities, it is hard to fail.

Set Goals

Research points to a direct link between self-esteem and the achievement of personal and professional goals. People who consistently set goals are able to maintain high self-esteem. People who fail to set goals wander aimlessly through life with no purpose, and they are more likely to suffer from low self-esteem. The key is making your goals realistic. If they are too far out of sight, you might subconsciously say to yourself, "I can't really see myself doing that." If those are your thoughts, you will probably never succeed at accomplishing that goal. In most cases, you must be able to picture yourself accomplishing the goal.

Visualize Achievement of Your Goals

To **visualize** means to form a mental image of something. The power to visualize is in a very real sense the power to create. If you really want to succeed at something, picture yourself doing it successfully over and over again. Simulate every step in your brain before you ever attempt to make the goal a reality. Visualize yourself overcoming any obstacles that might interfere with your success.[37]

Shakti Gawain, author of *Creative Visualization,* states that when we create something, we always create it first in the form of a thought:

> Imagination is the ability to create an idea or mental picture in your mind. In creative visualization you use your imagination to create a clear image of something you wish to manifest. Then you continue to focus on the idea or picture regularly, giving it positive energy until it becomes objective reality . . . in other words, until you actually achieve what you have been visualizing.[38]

Many famous athletes choreograph their moves in their imagination before going into action. For example, champion skiers imagine themselves negotiating almost every inch of a slope, champion tennis players picture themselves executing successful shots, and gymnasts practice their moves as much in their imagination as in actual rehearsal.[39]

Mary Lou Retton, former Olympic gymnast, spent nine grueling years preparing herself physically and mentally for her performance on one event at the 1984 Olympics and won the gold medal by five one-hundredths of a point. She attributes much of her success to her ability to visualize her perfect performance. "Always prepare yourself for a perfect 10. When I visualized myself going through a beam routine, I didn't imagine myself falling. I visualized myself on the beam—perfect. Always picture it perfect. But also visualize what you can do if something does go wrong."[40]

Denis Waitley, former chair of psychology for the U.S. Olympic teams, believes it is possible to learn a new self-image through the same process—by vividly imagining yourself being the person you want to become.[41] This mental rehearsal can be a powerful step toward improving your self-image. Review the "Characteristics of People with High Self-Esteem" listed earlier in this chapter. If you would like to make them part of your behavior pattern, mentally rehearse these self-confident behaviors. See yourself walking with your chin up and your shoulders straight and speaking with a strong, confident voice. Picture yourself making appropriate eye contact with other people. As you gain confidence, practice these new skills by actually performing them when you are with your friends, family, and coworkers. You will begin to feel more comfortable with these behaviors every day, and soon they will become habits. If it works for the Olympic champions, it can work for you.

Monitor Your Self-Talk

To be sure you achieve the results you have visualized, you need to listen to your self-talk. **Self-talk** takes place silently in the privacy of your mind. It is the series of personal conversations you have with yourself almost continuously throughout the day. Just like statements from other people, your self-talk can dramatically affect your behavior and self-esteem.[42] Unfortunately, many people consistently tell themselves what they have done wrong or how incompetent they are. This negative self-talk often leads to a lack of self-confidence and unhappy relationships. Others talk to themselves with respect and encouragement that lead them toward successful behaviors even when faced with difficult situations. They focus on what they *can* do about the situation, rather than what they *cannot* do. Figure 4.1 indicates how self-talk is part of the cycle of self-esteem, whether that talk is negative or positive.

To constantly improve your self-esteem, you must monitor what you are saying to yourself. When negative thoughts attempt to take over, intentionally create self-talk statements that will replace the negative thoughts and counteract the damage those thoughts have had on your self-esteem in the past. Create self-talk statements for each of your goals by using the following guidelines:

1. Be *specific* about the behavior you want to change. What do you want to do to increase your effectiveness? You should firmly believe that what you want is truly possible.
2. Begin each self-talk statement with a first-person pronoun, such as *I* or *my*. Use a present-tense verb, such as *am, have, feel, create, approve, do,* or *choose*. Don't say "My ability to remember the names of other people *will* improve." Instead, focus on the present: "I *have* an excellent memory for the names of other people."
3. Describe the results you want to achieve. Be sure to phrase the statement as though you have already achieved what you want. Table 4.1 offers several general self-talk statements that might help you improve your self-esteem.[43]

FIGURE 4.1

Self-Esteem Cycles

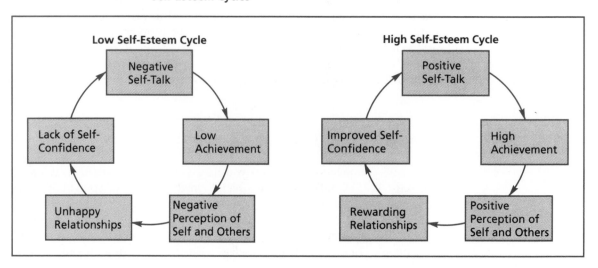

TABLE 4.1

Creating Semantically Correct Self-Talk

Wrong	Right
I can quit smoking.	I am in control of my habits.
I will lose twenty pounds.	I weigh a trim _____ pounds.
I won't worry anymore.	I am confident and optimistic.
Next time I won't be late.	I am prompt and efficient.
I will avoid negative self-talk.	I talk to myself, with all due respect.
I will not procrastinate.	I do it now.
I'm not going to let people walk all over me anymore.	I care enough to assert myself when necessary.

This last step is critical. Because your brain is merely a computer filled with various data from all your past experiences, you need to use literally the correct words. When you think of the words *spider, tornado,* or *blue,* your brain develops an automatic understanding of the word and a response or image based on years of conditioning and training. If you are attempting to quit smoking, don't mention the word *smoke* in your self-talk because your brain will react to the word. "I will not smoke after dinner" conjures an image in your subconscious mind, and your behavior follows accordingly. Say instead, "I am in control of my habits" or "My lungs are clean."

One warning: Every time your self-talk statements use the word *not* you are sending the wrong message to your brain. Consider the following statement: "I will not eat chocolate for dessert." Now remove the word *not* from the statement, and the remaining words represent the message being sent to your brain. Does the remaining statement represent your goal? Be careful to semantically design your self-talk statements so that they take you in the direction you want to go; otherwise, they will take you straight toward what you don't want.

Write positive self-talk statements for different facets of your personal and professional life. Put them on 3-by-5-inch index cards, and attach them to your bathroom mirror, refrigerator, car dashboard, desk blotter, and so on, and review them often. Barbara Grogan, a successful entrepreneur who founded Western Industrial Contractors, has a placard on the dashboard of her car that reads, "I am powerful, beautiful, creative, and I can handle it!"[44] This positive message helps her through the tough times.

Another technique for internalizing your thoughts is to record your affirming statements on a blank cassette tape while quiet, one-beat-per-second music (largo) is playing in the background.[45] Play the tape repeatedly, especially when you are in a relaxed state, such as just before you fall asleep at night. Your brain will accept the information without judgment. When these statements become part of your "memory bank," over time your behavior will follow accordingly. Your brain computer will put out exactly what you put in. If you put positive self-talk in, positive behavior will result.

ORGANIZATIONS CAN HELP

Even though each of us ultimately is responsible for raising or lowering our own self-esteem, we can make that task easier or more difficult for others. We can either support or damage the self-efficacy and self-respect of the people we work with, just as they have that option in their interactions with us. Organizations are beginning to include self-esteem modules in their employee- and management-training programs.

When employees do not feel good about themselves, the result will often be poor job performance. This view is shared by many human resource professionals and managers. Many organizations realize that low self-esteem affects their workers' ability to learn new skills, to be effective team members, and to be productive. Research has identified five factors that can enhance the self-esteem of employees in any organization[46] (see Figure 4.2).

- *Workers need to feel valuable.* A major source of worker satisfaction is the feeling that one is valued as a unique person. Self-esteem grows when an organization makes an effort to accommodate individual differences and to recognize individual accomplishments.
- *Workers need to feel competent.* Earlier in this chapter we noted that self-efficacy grows when people feel confident in their ability to perform job-related tasks. One of the best ways organizations can build employee confidence is to involve employees in well-designed training programs. Effective training programs give employees plenty of opportunities to practice newly acquired job skills.
- *Workers need to feel secure.* Employees are more likely to feel secure when they are well informed and know what is expected of them. Managers need to clarify their expectations and provide employees with frequent feedback regarding their performance.
- *Workers need to feel empowered.* Progressive organizations such as Corning Incorporated and Federal Express Corporation are demonstrating to employees that their opinions and views matter and that their ideas are being implemented in significant ways. These companies make sure that each person has a voice in helping the organization achieve its goals. This topic is discussed in more detail in Chapter 12, "Team Building: A Leadership Strategy."
- *Workers need to feel connected.* People are likely to achieve high self-esteem when they feel their coworkers accept, appreciate, and respect them. Many

FIGURE 4.2

Factors That Enhance the Self-Esteem of Employees

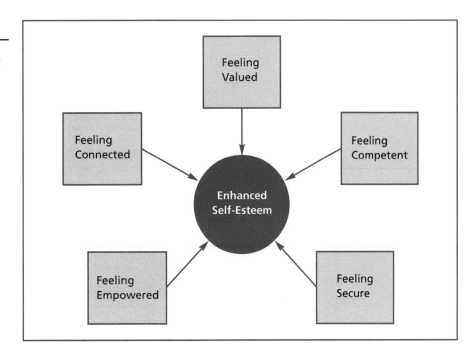

companies are fostering these feelings by placing greater emphasis on teamwork. Team-building efforts help promote acceptance and cooperation.

Summary

Self-esteem is a combination of self-respect and self-efficacy. If you have high self-esteem, you are more likely to feel competent and worthy. If you have low self-esteem, you are more likely to feel incompetent, unworthy, and insecure. Self-esteem reflects your feelings of adequacy about the roles you play, your personality traits, your physical appearance, your skills, and your abilities. High self-esteem is the foundation for a successful personal life and professional life.

A person starts acquiring and building self-esteem from birth. Parents, friends, associates, the media, and professional colleagues all influence the development of that person's self-esteem. As an adult, a person often defines herself or himself in terms of possessions, jobs, and/or internal values. People with high self-esteem tend to be future oriented, cope with problems creatively, handle their emotions, and give as well as receive help. They also accept others as unique, talented individuals and exhibit self-confident behaviors.

To build high self-esteem, individuals must accept the past and build for the future. They have to accept their limitations and develop expertise in some area. Making decisions and living with the consequences, positive or negative, can also help build self-esteem. Individuals need to set goals by visualizing the person they want to be and monitoring their self-talk.

Many organizations now realize that they need to help build employees' self-esteem and are doing so through training sessions, clear statements of expectations and feedback, giving greater respect to individuals in the workplace, and fostering teamwork.

Career Corner

Q. As a teenager, I was involved in a major car accident in which several bones in my face were broken. I was left with a large scar on my chin. Although I have had several operations to correct the visible damage, I still feel self-conscious whenever I meet new people. It is affecting my career opportunities. What can I do to gain more confidence?

A. In his book *Psycho-Cybernetics,* plastic surgeon Maxwell Maltz demonstrates that what your mind has been conditioned to believe about yourself can override or undermine what you actually see in the mirror. Throughout his twenty-five-year practice, Maltz operated on wounded soldiers, accident victims, and children with birth defects. Many of these individuals saw only their defects and doubted that they could ever be successful. Even after their corrective surgery, these patients' deformities continued to exist in their minds. Their inner self-images had not been changed.

You can learn to use the creative power of your subconscious mind. Even though your external image has been improved, you still need to change the inner self-image you carry within your mind. When you are successful in changing your mental image of yourself, your self-confidence will increase.

Key Terms

self-esteem
self-efficacy
self-respect
external locus of control
failure syndrome

internal locus of control
mentor
visualize
self-talk

Review Questions

1. What is self-esteem? Why is the development of high self-esteem important in a person's life?
2. What influences help shape a person's self-esteem?
3. What characteristics do people with high self-esteem exhibit?
4. Describe the behaviors of people with low self-esteem.

5. List the steps you can take to build high self-esteem. Which two do you feel are the most important? Why?
6. Define *internal* and *external locus of control,* and give an example of each.
7. What influence does self-talk have on a person's self-esteem? How can this influence be controlled?
8. In your own words, explain the two cycles portrayed in Figure 4.1.
9. List the three elements necessary for the construction of positive self-talk statements. Give three examples of such statements.
10. How can organizations help raise the self-esteem of workers?

Application Exercises

1. Describe a situation in which you achieved a goal you had set for yourself. Did any outside positive or negative forces influence your progress toward the goal? If there were negative forces, how did you overcome them? Did you visualize or mentally simulate the completed goal? If so, how did this simulation help?
2. Think about people you know at school, at work, or in your social environment who seem to exhibit low self-esteem. Describe the qualities that give you this impression. Now think about people you know who exhibit high self-esteem. List their qualities. Often these two lists will reflect direct opposites, such as "has a sloppy appearance/keeps a neat appearance," "slumps down the hall/walks tall," or "avoids eye contact during conversations with others/makes eye contact." What steps might the people you identified as having low self-esteem take to enhance their images? How might these steps improve their self-esteem? Could you take any similar steps to improve your own self-esteem? Explain.
3. Identify a quality that you would like to experience more frequently in your life. Examples might be the ability to develop rapport quickly with new acquaintances, the patience to enjoy leisure time, or the perseverance to maintain a daily exercise program. Once you select a specific quality, create in your mind a very detailed mental picture of this behavior. Now develop positive self-talk statements that will guide you toward the desired change in behavior. Use the guidelines on page 110 to ensure that you achieve your goal.

Internet Exercise

As noted in this chapter, self-esteem has two interrelated components: self-respect and self-efficacy. Self-efficacy can be thought of as the confidence you have in your ability to do specific things. Your confidence level can influence which tasks you take on and which ones you avoid. To learn more about self-efficacy and how it can influence your career, visit the Internet and determine what types of resources (such as books, articles, and training programs) are available on this topic. Using your search engine, type in "self efficacy" and "self esteem," and then study the available information. Pay special attention to information on how one achieves high self-efficacy. Prepare a written report of your findings.

Case 4.1   **Altering Your Body Image**

A growing number of people seem to be unhappy with how they look. Specifically, they are dissatisfied with the appearance of their body. *Psychology Today* uses the term "body image" to describe the perceptions people have of their physical appearance, attractiveness, and beauty. Body image is our mental representation of ourselves; it is what allows us to contemplate ourselves. The image we see in the mirror influences much of our behavior and self-esteem.

A negative body image can begin to take shape early in life. Teasing during childhood can have a crushing effect on body image. Memories of being teased haunt many people for years. Through adolescence the pressure to achieve an attractive body image is intense, especially among women. Body weight has a major influence on overall satisfaction with appearance. In many cases the ever-present media portray desirable women as thin.

Appearance is more important today than it was in the past, according to Mary Pipher, author of *Reviving Ophelia*. She notes that we have moved from communities of primary relationships in which people know each other to cities where secondary relationships are much more common:

> In a community of primary relationships, appearance is only one of many dimensions that define people. Everyone knows everyone else in different ways over time. In a city of strangers, appearance is the only dimension available for the rapid assessment of others. Thus it becomes incredibly important in defining value.[47]

Preoccupation with body image follows many people throughout adulthood. Large numbers of people wish to conform to the body-size ideals projected in the media. The motivation to be thinner helps support a $50-billion-a-year diet industry. People have learned to judge themselves, in many cases, by the standards of physical attractiveness that appear in fashion magazines and television commercials.

Some people have found ways to remake their self-image and move away from a preoccupation with body image. One approach is to develop criteria for self-esteem that go beyond appearance. To make appearance less significant in your life, you develop other benchmarks for self-evaluation. These might include succeeding at work, forming new friendships, or achieving a greater feeling of self-worth through volunteer work. Another approach is to engage in exercise that makes you feel good about yourself. Exercise for strength, fitness, and health, not just for weight loss. You can also identify and change habitual negative thoughts about your body. When you look in the mirror, try to say nice things about your body.

Questions

1. Professionals in the field of psychology say that people with low self-esteem rely too much on the views of others for a sense of self-worth. Is this a problem you currently face in your life? Explain.
2. Mary Pipher says that in large communities appearance is the only dimension available for rapid assessment of others. Do you find yourself placing a heavy emphasis on appearance when assessing the worth of others?
3. Joan Borysenko, director of the Mind/Body Clinic at Harvard Medical School, says you need to accept yourself as you are. Acceptance, she says, means actually honoring yourself as you are now. Is this good advice? Is it realistic advice? Explain.
4. If you currently have a negative body image, what other criteria could you use to help enhance your self-esteem?

Case 4.2   ## California Assembly Bill No. 3659

When the California legislature proposed a major study of the effects of self-esteem on the social ills of society, many critics across the country ridiculed the idea. Some California lawmakers were skeptical of anything dealing with self-esteem and agreed to the study only when the words "and Personal and Social Responsibility" were added to the original title, *The California Task Force to Promote Self-Esteem*. Garry Trudeau satirized the California study in his nationally syndicated comic strip "Doonesbury." Even when the final report was published, the media focused on the seven dissenting committee members, who refused to sign the final document, rather than on the commission's findings.

Behind the scenes, however, a different story emerged. Even though the work included no salary, more people applied to serve on the task force than on any other legislative body in the state's history. An unprecedented number of people asked to testify before the commission. Positive letters about the task force's work outweighed negative ones by a ratio of ten to one. Alfie Kohn, respected author and lecturer on education and human behavior, states that most research has indeed confirmed a positive association between self-esteem and achievement.

School districts that addressed self-esteem in light of the study's recommendations met with outstanding success. For example, student discipline problems dropped by 75 percent after self-esteem became part of the curriculum in one mostly Hispanic district that had one of the lowest per capita incomes in the state. In another high school, the number of teenage pregnancies dropped from 147 to 20 over a three-year period following implementation of self-esteem programs. Requests for more information poured in from experts from all fifty states and many foreign countries.

Although California's study focused on ways schools and families could improve self-esteem, one of the key principles listed in the final report was "When possible, we need to form our groups and organizations so that all members participate in establishing decisions, rules, and the consequences of breaking those rules." Since the report was published, companies across the country have begun to implement employee "empowerment" programs to help improve the self-esteem of their workers.

Questions

1. The entire three-year study cost California taxpayers $735,000, less than the cost of maintaining one prisoner facing a life sentence. Do you think the investment was cost-effective? Why?
2. Why do you think the task force received so much negative publicity even though the process and results were so dramatically positive?

Chapter 5

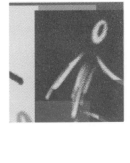

Personal Values

Influence

Ethical Choices

Chapter Preview

After studying this chapter, you will be able to

1. Explain the advantage of developing a strong sense of character.
2. Understand how personal values are formed.
3. Understand value conflicts and how to resolve them.
4. Identify ways to resolve value conflicts.
5. Learn how to make the right ethical decisions based on your personal value system.
6. Understand the danger of corporate crime and the steps being taken to eliminate it.

WHEN MICHAEL MILKEN MEETS with college students and members of the business community to talk about ethical issues, they pay attention. Most people know that in 1990 he pleaded guilty to six felony counts of securities law violations, paid more than $1 billion in fines and restitution, and served nearly two years in prison. He is still barred by the Securities and Exchange Commission from the investment brokerage industry. His employer, Drexel Burnham Lambert, one of the most powerful investment banks on Wall Street, pleaded guilty to a six-count felony indictment and was later forced into bankruptcy.[1] Dennis Levine, a leading merger specialist and partner at Drexel Burnham Lambert, also spent time in prison for illegal trading practices. In his book, *Inside Out,* we learn about the period of "easy morality" that existed on Wall Street. Reflecting on those fast-paced years at Drexel Burnham Lambert, Levine says, "The numbing effect of 60- to 100-hour work weeks helped erode my values and distort my judgment." He admits his ambition was so strong that it went beyond rationality and says, "I gradually lost sight of what constitutes ethical behavior."[2]

On leaving prison, Michael Milken was diagnosed with prostate cancer and immediately began a treatment program that yielded positive results. Today his cancer is in remission, and his image has been greatly enhanced. He started CaPCure, now the largest private provider of research funds for prostate cancer, and he gives large amounts of time and money to many education and medical causes. He is the featured speaker at many national conferences and serves as a consultant to prominent business leaders.[3] ■

CHARACTER AND INTEGRITY

"The candidate has the kind of work experience we are looking for, but can he pass the 'character' test?" "I always know exactly where she stands . . . she has character." "When I'm in a conflict with someone, I know I can defeat them if they lack character. If they don't stand for something, they'll fall for anything." Statements like these sprinkle daily conversations in every organization because character is such an important element of effective interpersonal relations. **Character** is composed of your personal standards of behavior, including your honesty, integrity, and moral fiber.[4] Your character is based on the judgments you make about what behaviors are right and what behaviors are wrong.

One dimension of character that is getting a great deal of attention today is integrity. Integrity is a basic ingredient of career success. Robert Ringer, author of *Million Dollar Habits,* defined **integrity** as adherence to your moral values, or practicing what you claim to believe in.[5] When your behavior is in tune with your professed standards and values—when you practice what you believe in—you have integrity.

From The *Wall Street Journal*—Permission, Cartoon Features Syndicate. Reprinted by permission.

I'm worried about Junior. He's put a picture of Michael Milken up on his wall."

In a world of uncertainty and rapid change, integrity has become a valuable character trait. People with integrity can be trusted to do what they say they will do. We know what they stand for and what they will fight for. On the other hand, it is difficult to trust people whose behavior contradicts their words. Stephen L. Carter, author of a book entitled *Integrity,* says that anyone who wants to act with integrity must first think hard about what is right and wrong.[6]

How can we achieve integrity? One approach, recommended by author Stephen Covey, is to keep your commitments. "As we make and keep commitments, even small commitments, we begin to establish an inner integrity that gives us the awareness of self-control and courage and strength to accept more of the responsibility for our own lives."[7] Covey says that when we make and keep promises to ourselves and others, we are developing an important habit. We cannot expect to maintain our integrity if we consistently fail to keep our commitments.

Your character and integrity strongly influence your relationships with others. But where can you learn these qualities? College catalogs rarely list a course like "Character Building 101." The Josephson Institute of Ethics acknowledged this lack of character training by forming the Character Counts Coalition. The coalition is an alliance of organizations such as the American Federation of Teachers, the American Association of State Boards of Education, and the American Association of Community Colleges. Their mission is to address the issue of character development through educational institutions and organizations throughout the country. Their efforts focus on a variety of grassroots training activities that encourage the development of the following six "pillars of character":

- **Trustworthiness** Be honest and sincere. Don't deceive or mislead and never betray a trust. Demonstrate your integrity by standing up for your beliefs. Never ask a friend or colleague to do something that is wrong.
- **Respect** Be courteous and polite by being appreciative and accepting of differences. Respect others' rights to make decisions about their own lives. Don't abuse, demean, mistreat, manipulate, exploit, or take advantage of others.
- **Responsibility** Be accountable for your actions. Think about the consequences of your behavior before you act. Don't make excuses or take credit for others' work.
- **Fairness** Treat all people fairly, be open-minded, and listen to opposing points of view. Don't take unfair advantage of others' mistakes.
- **Caring** Show you care about others through kindness, caring, sharing, compassion, and empathy. Be considerate and sensitive to others' feelings.
- **Citizenship** Play by the rules and obey the laws. Respect authority. Stay informed and vote.[8]

If you want to enhance your character, consider building these "pillars" into your lifestyle.

Total Person Insight

"People working together with integrity and authenticity and collective intelligence are profoundly more effective as a business than people living together based on politics, game playing, and narrow self-interest."

PETER SENGE

Author, *The Fifth Discipline*

HOW PERSONAL VALUES ARE FORMED

Hyrum Smith, founder of the Franklin Quest Company, says that certain natural laws govern personal productivity and fulfillment. One of these laws focuses on personal beliefs: Your behavior is a reflection of what you truly believe.[9] **Values** are your deep personal beliefs and preferences that influence your behavior. They are deep-seated in your personality and are more enduring than your attitudes. To discover what really motivates you, carefully examine what it is you value.

Table 5.1 details the values clarification process. These five steps can help you determine whether or not you truly value something. Many times you are not consciously aware of what is really driving your behavior because values exist at different levels of awareness.[10] Unless you clarify your values, life events are likely to unfold in a haphazard manner. Once you are aware of your value priorities and consistently behave accordingly, your character and integrity are enhanced, and life in general is much more satisfying and rewarding. Hyrum Smith says that everything starts with your **core values,** those general statements of principles and beliefs that guide the development of intermediate and long-range goals:

> If you set goals that aren't aligned with your values, you may accomplish a great deal, but you won't ever be satisfied, because you'll be neglecting the things that matter most to you.[11]

Our values may be influenced by our religious beliefs. Here students at Gujarat Vidyapith weave khadi, *a coarse fabric that has become a symbol of self-reliance for the people of India. Gandhi, religious leader and founder of the school, reasoned that if Indians could spin and wear their own cloth, they could get rid of their dependence on the British and their textile mills. (Steven McCurry/National Geographic Image Collection)*

TABLE 5.1

A Five-Part Valuing
Process to Clarify and
Develop Values

Thinking

We live in a confusing world where making choices about how to live our lives can be difficult. Of major importance is developing critical thinking skills that help distinguish fact from opinion and supported from unsupported arguments. Learn to think for yourself. Question what you are told. Engage in higher-level thinking that involves analysis, synthesis, and evaluation.

Feeling

This dimension of the valuing process involves being open to your "gut level" feelings. If it doesn't "feel right," it probably isn't. Examine your distressful feelings such as anger, fear, or emotional hurt. Discover what you prize and cherish in life.

Communicating

Values are clarified through an ongoing process of interaction with others. Be an active listener and hear what others are really saying. Be constantly alert to communication filters such as emotions, body language, and positive and negative attitudes. Learn to send clear messages regarding your own beliefs.

Choosing

Your values must be freely selected with no outside pressure. In some situations, telling right from wrong is difficult. Therefore, you need to be well informed about alternatives and the consequences of various courses of action. Each choice you make reflects some aspect of your values system.

Acting

Act repeatedly and consistently on your beliefs. One way to test whether or not something is of value to you is to ask yourself, "Do I find that this value is persistent throughout all aspects of my life?"

Source: Howard Kirschenbaum, *Advanced Values Clarification* (La Jolla, Calif.: University Associates, 1977).

Core values influence the actions of both individuals and organizations. Anne Mulcahy, an executive at Xerox Corporation and mother of two sons, says she and her husband make decisions at home and work based on their core values: "Our kids are absolutely the center of our lives—and we never mess with that."[12] Volvo, the Swedish automaker, has for years been guided by the core values of safety, quality, and environmental concern. Although some critics say the company makes solid, safe, but profoundly boring cars, its traditional core values will not be abandoned.[13]

As you engage in the values clarification process, it helps to reflect on those things that influence the development of your values. Let's look at some of the important factors that shape our values.

Environmental Influences

Aristotle said, "If you would understand virtue, observe the conduct of virtuous men." But where are these "virtuous men," the role models we should observe? As a nation, we have witnessed many examples of shabby values. When you look to Wall Street, you learn about the transgressions of Dennis Levine and Michael Milken. Turn to religion and you learn about the moral failures and financial excesses of leaders such as Jim Bakker and Jimmy Swaggart. Look at sports and you discover that some of our heroes are motivated by greed and lust. And our political leaders often seem to lack the moral courage to do the right thing.

Many events and individuals have influenced the formation of values in the United States in this century. Some of them are shown in Table 5.2. In general, the major environmental influences that shape our values are the family, religious groups, schools, the media, and people we admire.

Influence of the Family Katherine Paterson, author of books for children, says being a parent these days is like riding a bicycle on a bumpy road—learning to keep your balance while zooming full speed ahead, veering around as

TABLE 5.2

People and Events That Have Influenced the Formation of Values in the United States

Matures (born 1928–1945)	Baby Boomers (born 1946–1961)	Generation X (born 1962–1972)
Eisenhower	Television	AIDS
MacArthur	Beatniks	Wellness movement
A-bomb	Sputnik	Iran-Contra affair
Dr. Spock	Civil Rights Act	Operation Desert Storm
John Wayne	The pill	Glasnost
Mickey Mantle	Drug culture	Oklahoma City bombing
Doris Day	Women's movement	TV rating system
Frank Sinatra	Vietnam War	World Wide Web
The Waltons	Watergate	Health-care reform
Andy and Opie Taylor	JFK and MLK assassinations	Work/family-Balance concerns

many potholes as possible.[14] Parents must assume many roles, none more important than moral teacher. In many families in contemporary society, one parent must assume full responsibility for shaping children's values. Some single parents—those overwhelmed with responsibility for career, family, and rebuilding their own personal lives—may lack the stability necessary for the formation of the six pillars of character. And in two-parent families, both parents may work outside the home and at the end of the day may lack the time or energy to intentionally direct the development of their children's values. The same may be true for families experiencing financial pressures or the strains associated with caring for elderly parents. Author James Michener, who was an orphan and had no family, offered another perspective: "It is thoughtless beyond imagination for older people to say rigidly, 'The child must learn his or her values at home' when there is no home. Some substitution must be found."[15]

Influence of Religious Groups   Many people learn their value priorities through religious training. This may be achieved through the accepted teachings of a church, through religious literature such as the Koran and the Bible, or through individuals in churches or synagogues who are positive role models. William Wilson, founder of Pioneer/Eclipse Corporation of Sparta, North Carolina, when asked to comment on the impact of religious beliefs on his success, responded:

> I guess my religious beliefs did have one important impact on my approach to business—in terms of the ethics and principles I live by. I've always had the attitude that profits don't come first. They can never come first. People have to come first—customers and employees. The funny thing is, if you treat people right, the profits always follow.[16]

Religious groups that want to define, instill, and perpetuate values may find an eager audience. Stephen Covey and other social observers say that many people are determinedly seeking spiritual and moral anchors in their lives and in their work. People who live in uncertain times seem to attach more importance to spirituality.[17] Healthy spirituality is discussed in Chapter 17.

Influence of the Schools   Many parents, concerned that their children are not learning enough about moral values and ethical behavior, want character education added to the curriculum.[18] Some have been influenced by William J. Bennett's *The Book of Virtues*. Bennett sees moral education as a fundamental purpose of education. In support of this practice, Thomas Lickona, professor of education at the State University of New York, says children have very little sense of right and wrong, so schools must help out.[19]

In the 1970s, many schools included values clarification in their curriculum. As various factions of society objected, fearing that values would be "imposed" on children, schools eliminated these classes, and teachers learned to be "value neutral." Today, however, there is a nationwide resurgence of the movement to teach moral values and ethics in the classrooms. Sanford McDonnell, chairman of the Character Education Partnership, says the schools have the greatest potential for overcoming what he describes as "the national crisis of character." The Character Education Partnership defines "good character" as understanding, caring about, and acting on core ethical values. McDonnell says our nation will not be strong if we graduate young people who are brilliant but dishonest or have great intellectual knowledge but do not care about others.[20] In higher education, we are now seeing the addition of more courses on values and ethics. Over 500 business-ethics courses are currently taught on American campuses.[21] In some cases, entire departments or centers are devoted to this type of education.

Influence of the Media　Some social critics say that if you are searching for signs of civilization gone rotten, you can simply tune into the loud and often amoral voices of mass entertainment on television and radio. They point out that viewers too often see people abusing and degrading other people without any significant consequences. Mainstream television continues to feature a great deal of violence and antisocial behavior, and the programs are seen by a large number of young viewers. It is estimated that the average preschool child watches more than 27 hours of television per week and that the average teenager spends 21 hours watching TV.[22] Is it any wonder that, with this constant bombardment, our children have difficulty determining right from wrong?

Several organizations have taken steps to influence the content and presentation of mass entertainment. Children Now, a national children's advocacy group, has asked television programmers to show viewers the consequences of antisocial behavior. The National Political Congress of Black Women has initiated a campaign to get rid of recordings that contain messages that are demeaning to women. The Time Warner recording label has been a frequent target of this organization.[23] And in Richmond, Virginia, the owners of the Ukrop supermarket chain initiated an advertising boycott aimed at a radio station that began airing Howard Stern's controversial talk program. A letter from the Ukrop family described his program content as "racist, sexist, filth."[24]

Influence of People We Admire　In addition to being influenced by the media, your values are likely to be influenced by **modeling**—shaping your behavior to resemble that of people you admire and embracing the qualities those people demonstrate. The heroes and heroines you discover in childhood and adolescence help you form a "dominant value direction."[25] Opie and Andy Taylor were positive role models for most children growing up in the 1950s and 1960s. Today Bart Simpson's unique family relationships teach children a new way of interacting with authority figures. We would be better served to point children and adolescents in the direction of humanitarian and tennis champion Arthur Ashe, who led an exemplary family and professional life until his untimely death from AIDS contracted after heart bypass surgery, or Oprah Winfrey, whose open and honest style can have a positive effect on girls and women of all ages. If we truly want to develop a more moral society, we need to keep track of the men and women our children are modeling and encourage our children to look for positive qualities such as Ashe's integrity and

Winfrey's honesty. We would all be wise to focus on and emulate the positive qualities of those we admire.

Avoiding Values Drift

Core values represent the starting point for personal and organizational success. As individuals, we need to reflect on our core values when making decisions related to important work-life issues. All great institutions have answered the questions "What do we stand for?" and "Why do we exist?" Successful companies like Hewlett-Packard, Disney, and Boeing have one thing in common. They have successfully adapted over the decades to a changing environment without losing sight of their core values. They have not drifted away from their strong foundations.[26]

Debbie and Randy Fields, cofounders of Mrs. Fields' Cookies, hold strong opinions about what it takes to successfully operate a large chain of retail stores. They are constantly looking for "drift." Drift is the slow erosion of the company's standards and values. When the company was expanding, they opened a new store in Hawaii and staffed it with capable employees. Over a period of five months, the people made tiny, infinitesimal changes in the cookie recipes. When Debbie Fields visited the store, she discovered that her original chewy cookies had become spongy cakes.[27] Tiny changes in personal values can have a similar effect, steering a person slightly off course. That is why it is so important to constantly monitor your commitment to your values and make adjustments when necessary to get your life back on track. In his book *Conversations with God,* Neal Donald Walsch discusses the process of building a strong foundation for everything from your daily decisions to your long-range goals. He suggests: "Do not dismantle the house, but look at each brick, and replace those which appear broken, which no longer support the structure."[28] This careful examination of each of your values will help keep you on track toward your ideal future and help you avoid values drift.

Thinking / Learning Starters

1. Identify the events and individuals that have been influential in forming your value system. Are those of your childhood and adolescence still important to you?

2. Based on the media's influence and the concept of modeling, what do you predict the next generation's values will be? The children of today will be your coworkers in the future. Will their attitudes and values be a potential problem for you?

VALUES CONFLICTS

One of the major causes of conflict between people within an organization is a clash between each individual's personal values. There is no doubt about it, people are different. Everyone has been raised with different family backgrounds, religious experiences, education, role models, and media exposure. These differences can pop out anywhere and anytime people get together. Many observers suggest that organizations look for **values conflicts** when addressing such problems as declining quality, absenteeism, and poor customer service. The trouble may lie not so much in work schedules or production routines as in the mutual distrust and misunderstanding brought about by clashes in workers' and managers' value systems. Here are some examples of values conflicts:

Item: Manny Garcia, a very successful Burger King franchise owner, was upset when the company launched an advertising campaign that included the slogan "Sometimes you gotta break the rules." He felt the slogan sent the wrong message to his teenage customers. To protest the ad campaign, he flipped his Burger King signs upside down.[29]

Item: Workers struck the General Motors plant at Flint, Michigan, to protest excessive required overtime. They complained that workweeks that sometimes

People with shared values often unite against those whose values conflict with their group. Here a group opposed to David Duke confronts those in support of the political candidate and former Ku Klux Klan advocate. (Michael Dwyer/Stock, Boston, Inc.)

stretch to 66 hours disrupt their personal lives. Management says the overtime is necessary because the cost of health insurance and other benefits for new workers is so high the company cannot afford to hire more workers.[30]

Item: Herbert Lanese, former president of McDonnell Douglas Aerospace, was abruptly fired six months after he was hired because of a values clash with Chief Executive Harry Stonecipher. One problem became obvious during a 99-day machinists' strike at the St. Louis plant. Local newspapers quoted Lanese as saying that convenience store clerks with two weeks' training could do the machinists' jobs. Union members were elated when Lanese was removed.[31]

Internal Values Conflict

A person who is forced to choose between two or more strongly held values is experiencing an **internal values conflict.** As a manager, you may be torn between loyalty to your workers and loyalty to upper management. As an employee, you may find yourself in conflict between fulfilling family obligations and devoting the time and energy required to succeed at work. Trudy Desilets spent many years searching for a balance between her personal and professional life. Because travel demands left her exhausted, she gave up a fast-track sales job soon after the birth of her first child. When she asked to share her job with an equally qualified employee, her bosses turned her down. She loved her next job, but by the time her daughter was 3 she was facing burnout. The demands of being a good worker, a good mother, and a good wife were overwhelming.[32]

How you resolve internal values conflicts depends on how much time you are willing to invest in the values clarification process described in Table 5.1. Once you have completed the process and identified your core values, be sure to rank them in order of importance to you. This ranking process will help you make decisions when life gets complicated and you have to make difficult choices.[33] If one of your values is to be an outstanding parent and another is to maintain a healthy body, you should anticipate an internal values conflict when a busy schedule requires a choice between attending your daughter's soccer game and your weekly workout at the fitness center. However, when you rank which value is most important, the decision will be much easier.

Values Conflicts with Others

Some of the most common interpersonal values conflicts arise between workers of different generations, races, cultures, ethnic backgrounds, or religions; between men and women; and between supervisors and workers. Employees from diverse backgrounds may clash over different interpretations of the work ethic and the priorities of job and personal life. Unless such conflicts are handled skillfully, confrontation can make the situation worse, not better.

How will you handle a tense situation where it is obvious your values conflict with those of a colleague? You may discover your supervisor is a racist and you strongly support the civil rights of all people. Perhaps a coworker is a homosexual and your religious background does not accept this alternative lifestyle. These are highly emotional issues that can disrupt friendships, work teams, and the productivity of organizations. There are no easy answers. You *can* attempt, however, to develop respect for the other person, even though you disagree with his or her beliefs. Find a common ground concerning things you and the other person do agree on, and avoid discussions concerning your values conflict. Attempt to really listen to and understand where the other person is coming from, and share your thoughts and opinions in a calm manner. You will never be too old to learn something new and make adjustments to your beliefs based on new insights that may have never presented themselves during your formative years. If these techniques do not work and your values conflict continues to surface, you may need to determine whether or not the relationship is worth saving and make your decisions accordingly.

PERSONAL VALUES AND ETHICAL CHOICES

Ethics are the rules that direct your conduct and moral judgments.[34] They help translate your values into appropriate and effective behaviors in your day-to-day life. Personal ethics determine how you do business and with whom. Kickbacks and payoffs may be acceptable practices in some parts of the world yet may be viewed as unethical practices elsewhere. Where will you draw the line between right and wrong?

As competition in the global marketplace increases, moral and ethical issues can become cloudy. Although most organizations have adopted the point of view that "Good ethics is good business," exceptions do exist. Some organizations encourage, or at least condone, unethical behaviors. Surveys show many workers feel pressure to violate their ethical standards in order to meet business objectives.[35] Thus, you must develop your own personal code of ethics.

Every job you hold will present you with new ethical and moral dilemmas. These challenges can surface almost daily for people who direct and supervise the work of others. It may be tempting to tell employees to "do whatever is necessary" to get a job done on time, or to look the other way when employees engage in unethical or illegal acts. Simply taking credit for the accomplishments of others or displaying favoritism when establishing the work schedule represents a lapse in ethical conduct.

As a laborer, salesperson, or office worker, you too will be faced with ethical choices. Faced with the demands of overtime, balancing work and family, and layoffs due to downsizing, workers seem to feel more pressure to act unethically.[36] A survey by the International Association of Administrative Professionals found an alarming frequency of unethical behaviors including breaching confidentiality about hiring, firing, or layoffs, removing or destroying information, and falsifying documents.[37] Other studies indicate that underpaid employees who feel unappreciated are more prone to steal from their employers, with the price tag reaching over $120 billion a year—and climbing rapidly.[38]

How to Make the Right Ethical Choices

In today's turbulent, fast-paced, highly competitive workplace, ethical dilemmas surface frequently, and telling right from wrong has never been more difficult. Here are a few guidelines to help you make the right ethical choices.

Learn to distinguish between right and wrong.   Although selecting the right path can be difficult, a great deal of help is available today. Many current books and articles offer good advice. The book *The Measure of Our Success* by Marian Wright Edelman presents a collection of "lessons for life" that can offer guidance in making ethical choices. A few examples follow:

- There is no free lunch. Don't feel entitled to anything you don't sweat and struggle for.
- Never work just for money or for power. They won't save your soul or build a decent family or help you sleep at night.
- Be honest. Struggle to live what you say and preach. Act with integrity.
- Sell the shadow for the substance. Don't confuse style with substance; don't confuse political charm or rhetoric with decency or sound policy.[39]

Help in making the correct ethical choices may be as close as your employer's code of ethics, ethical guidelines published by your professional organization, or advice provided by an experienced and trusted colleague.

Make certain your values are in harmony with those of your employer. You may find it easier to make the right ethical choices if your values are compatible with those of your employer. Many organizations have adopted a set of beliefs, customs, values, and practices that attract a certain type of employee (see Figure 5.1). Harmony between personal and organizational values usually leads to success for the individual as well as the organization. These **shared values** provide a strong bond among all members of the work force.

Item: When selling their long-distance telephone service, employees of Working Assets assure their customers that 1 percent of every phone bill will be donated to liberal causes such as Greenpeace, the American Civil Liberties Union, gun control, abortion rights, and protection of redwoods. One marketing campaign read, "Be Socially Responsible: Talk on the Phone." Chief Executive Officer Laura Sure says that people are looking for other reasons to make a choice beyond the cost of services rendered.[40]

Item: In a Duke University survey of 650 M.B.A. graduates of eleven top schools, 70 percent indicated that they would not work for certain industries

FIGURE 5.1

Lotus Development Corporation's Operating Principles

OPERATING PRINCIPLES

These Operating Principles are intended to serve as guidelines for interaction between all employees. Their purpose is to foster and preserve the spirit of our enterprise and to promote the well-being of all concerned.

Commit to excellence

Insist on integrity

Treat people fairly; Value diversity

Communicate openly, honestly, and directly

Listen with an open mind; Learn from everything

Take responsibility; Lead by example

Respect, trust, and encourage others

Encourage risk-taking and innovation

Establish purpose before action

Work as a team

Have fun

Source: © Lotus Development Corporation. Used with permission.

Total Person Insight

"Nothing is more powerful for employees than seeing their managers behave according to their expressed values and standards; nothing is more devastating to the development of an ethical environment than a manager who violates the organization's ethical standards."

DAN RICE AND CRAIG DREILINGER

Management Consultants; Authors, "Rights and Wrongs of Ethics Training"

because of ethical or political concerns. About 82 percent said they would shun tobacco companies, 36 percent would avoid firms with environmental problems, 26 percent would refuse to work for liquor marketers, and 20 percent would not get involved with defense contractors. Dan Nagy, who conducted the survey for Duke's Fuqua School of Business, says, "Today's students have strong values and limit the compromises they're willing to make for money."[41]

Item: Lotus Development Corp. was awarded *Personnel Journal's* coveted Optimas Award, Quality of Life Category, for its continual re-evaluation of its values relative to its workers. One of Lotus's operating principles, treating people fairly and valuing diversity, led to the creation of an innovative benefits policy that offers medical, dental, vision, and hearing insurance benefits to gay and lesbian partners of employees. Russell Campanello, vice president of human resources for Lotus, stated this about the company's prior plan: "Our benefits program was out of synch with our stated values around not discriminating based on sexual orientation. It has to reflect the needs, interests and values [of the workers] because that's what makes [the relationship] mutual."[42]

Research conducted by the Families and Work Institute indicates that work/family decisions continue to be a battlefield for clashing values. Increasingly, employees want the opportunity to openly discuss family issues such as child care, requests for a flexible schedule, or care for an ailing parent. Johnson & Johnson is one of several companies that is training managers to sensitize them to values priorities that are different from their own.[43]

Don't let your life be driven by the desire for immediate gratification. Progress and prosperity have almost identical meanings to many people. They equate progress with the acquisition of material things. One explanation is that young business leaders entering the corporate world are under a great deal of pressure to show the trappings of success. This is the view expressed by John Delaney, who is a professor at the University of Iowa and has done extensive research on ethics. He says, "You're expected to have the requisite car and summer house to show you're a contributor to society, and many people do whatever it takes to get them."[44]

To achieve immediate gratification often means taking shortcuts. It involves pushing hard, cutting corners, and emphasizing short-term gains over the achievement of long-term goals. M. Scott Peck, author of the best-selling book *The Road Less Traveled,* discusses the benefits of delaying gratification: "Delaying gratification is a process of scheduling the pain and pleasure of life in such a way as to enhance the pleasure by meeting and experiencing the pain first and getting it over with. It is the only decent way to live."[45]

If delaying gratification is "the only decent way to live," why do so many people seek immediate gratification? The answer to this question is somewhat complex. Some people feel pressure from friends and family members to climb the ladder of success as quickly as possible and display the trappings of success such as a new car, boat, or house. They fail to realize that the road to peace of mind and happiness is not paved with Rolex watches, Brooks Brothers suits, and a Lexus. In Chapter 17 we describe a new definition of success and discuss the nonfinancial resources that make the biggest contribution to a happy and fulfilling life.

Thinking / Learning Starter

1. Think about the last time you felt guilty about something you did. Did you hurt someone's feelings? Did you take credit for something someone else accomplished? Which of your basic values did your actions violate?

2. When was the last time you broke off a friendship or relationship with another person in your personal or professional life? Does the reason for the breakup reflect back to a values conflict between the two of you? Explain.

CORPORATE VALUES AND ETHICAL CHOICES

This chapter began with a look at the dark side of Wall Street. In the securities industry, as in other industries, it is easy to focus on the individuals and organizations that have been motivated by greed and have failed to establish strict standards of business conduct. Nevertheless, some of the most successful companies play by the rules. At Legg Mason, one of the nation's top ten securities and investment management companies, employees are guided by strict standards of business conduct. Chip Mason, chief executive officer at Legg Mason,

Robert D. Haas, chairman and CEO of Levi Strauss & Company, believes that the corporation should be an ethical creature capable of both making profits and making the world a better place to live. He has established high standards regarding work environment, ethics, and social responsibility. He is pictured here in front of the Levi Strauss contribution to the AIDS quilt, a memorial to victims of the disease. (Andy Freeberg)

has told employees that honesty is the *number-one* business principle guiding the company. His leadership has been rewarded with steady revenue growth.[46] Similarly, Ben Edwards, chairman of A. G. Edwards and Sons, Inc., the seventh-largest securities firm in the nation, says that following the golden rule is still the best way to achieve success in business. This attitude has had a positive influence on the company's 7,400 employees. He encourages employees who are faced with an ethical conflict to ask the question "Is it right?"[47]

Corporate Crime

Many organizations have gotten into serious trouble by ignoring ethical principles. In recent years, the media have carried headlines concerning organizations involved in corporate crime.

Item: Eight former Honda Motor Co. executives pleaded guilty to bribery-related charges. The executives admitted that they accepted over $15 million in bribes from dealers in exchange for generous supplies of fast-selling Honda cars.[48]

Item: Prudential Insurance Company agreed to pay $410 million to customers who were misled by sales representatives. The agents involved were guilty of using a practice called "churning." Churning occurs when agents pressure customers to use built-up cash value in an old policy to buy a new, more expensive policy.[49]

Item: Stew Leonard, founder of the well-known Stew Leonard's Dairy Store, pleaded guilty to conspiring to defraud the federal government of taxes. He installed a computer software program that reduced sales data on an item-by-item basis and skimmed $17 million in cash.[50]

Those items represent only a small fraction of the corporate crime that goes on today. Many offenders are not caught or brought to trial. But, on the positive side, recent surveys indicate that a large majority of America's major corporations are actively trying to build ethics into their organizations.

Item: Minnesota Mutual Life Insurance Company has been able to steer clear of scandal for more than one hundred years by adopting a values-based management philosophy that rewards integrity and honesty. Success at the management level requires commitment to the company's core values. Managers must demonstrate their ability to infuse ethical values in their subordinates.[51]

Item: At Harley-Davidson the soul of the "Hog" can be traced to values that emphasize strong working relationships. The company's idea of a healthy working relationship is embedded in five formal values that constitute a code of behavior for everyone:[52]

- Tell the truth.
- Be fair.
- Keep your promises.
- Respect the individual.
- Encourage intellectual curiosity.

Many say they have difficulty determining the right course of action in difficult "gray-area" situations. And even when the right ethical course of action is clear, competitive pressures sometimes lead well-intentioned managers astray.[53] Tom Chappell, author of *The Soul of a Business* and founder of Tom's of Maine, explains why organizations often have difficulty doing what is morally right and socially responsible: "It's harder to manage for ethical pursuits than it is to simply manage for profits."[54]

How to Prevent Corporate Crime

Develop Ethics Codes Mark Twain once wrote, "To be good is noble. To tell people how to be good is even nobler, and much less trouble." Many corporate leaders have decided that it is time to put their views on ethics in writing. Most organizations today have written codes of ethics. A written code, highly publicized throughout the company and enforced without exception, can be a powerful force in preventing unethical behavior. A Tulane University study, however, discovered that the drive for a "comfortable life" and "pleasure" controlled the decisions of many managers even though their organizations had codes of ethics in place. Researchers say corporations need to do more to create an overall "ethical climate" that includes a reward system that recognizes acts of moral courage.[55] Also, organizations need to enforce their ethics codes with greater zeal.

Hire with Care   Thomas Melohn, president of North American Tool & Die Inc., located in San Leandro, California, says the key to operating a successful company is to first identify a guiding set of values and then "make sure you find people who have those values and can work together."[56] He says the hiring process should be given a very high priority. Melohn never hires any employee without checking references and conducting a lengthy job interview.

Jerry Pardue, vice president of loss and prevention for Super D Drugs, a southeastern drugstore chain, uses integrity tests (also called honesty tests) to screen out dishonest persons and drug users. He is one of a growing number of businesspeople who use some form of psychological testing. (Reid Psychological Systems developed the first honesty test more than forty years ago.) Company officials say that people who get involved in tangible theft (stealing cash or merchandise) are more likely to commit intangible thefts such as coming to work late or using the telephone for personal calls.[57]

As the popularity of integrity tests grows, so does the debate over their use. Many people are questioning the accuracy of the tests and the fairness of using them to hire or turn away applicants. Some states have made it illegal to deny someone a job on the basis of low test scores. Even the testing companies admit that the tests are not foolproof. But the American Psychological Association has studied the accuracy of integrity tests and has stated that some are in fact reliable.[58]

Provide Ethics Training   Many ethical issues are complex and cannot be considered in black-and-white moral terms. It is for this and other reasons that ethics training has become quite common in the business community. In some cases, the training involves little more than a careful study of the company ethics code and its implications for day-to-day decision making. Employees are notified where the code of ethics is displayed in the building and are asked to sign a document that verifies they have read, understand, and agree to abide by the code of ethics. In other cases, employees participate in in-depth discussions of ethical decisions. At Martin Marietta Corp., ethics training includes the use of a game called Gray Matters, in which a game leader presents mini-cases to teams of players. Each team also receives a list of potential responses to an ethical dilemma presented in the minicase. After discussing the responses, each team selects what it thinks is the best answer. The team leader then discloses the point value of each answer. Learning takes place as team members debate the pros and cons of each possible response.[59] Sears, Roebuck and Company provides its employees with a booklet entitled *Code of Business Conduct.* It outlines the company's position on a wide range of issues such as receiving gifts, employee discounts, care of company assets, and foreign business dealings. It also includes guidelines for making ethical decisions (see Table 5.3).

Is it possible to instill ethical values in employees through the use of training programs? Some critics say ethics training programs prepare employees to make the right decision only when actions are covered by specific rules. They see more merit in providing guidelines that employees can use to resolve many ethical issues. Almost everyone agrees that ethics training must start at the top of the organization. Business leaders must realize that unethical conduct is destructive and usually generates no more than short-term gains. The long-term consequences of ethical misconduct can be very costly.

Develop Support for Whistle-Blowing   When you discover your employer or a colleague is behaving illegally or unethically, you have three choices. You can keep quiet and keep working. You can decide you can't be party to the situation and leave. Or you can report the situation in the hope of putting a stop to it. When you reveal wrongdoing within an organization to the public or to those in positions of authority, you are a **whistle blower.**

Whistle blowers are sounding alarms in industries from tobacco companies to airlines. Jeffrey Wigand, a former chief researcher for Brown & Williamson Tobacco, testified that his company misled the public about the danger of nicotine. Sylvia Robins reported that she knew about a procedural flaw at Unisys, a National Aeronautics and Space Administration subcontractor that

TABLE 5.3

Sears's Guidelines for Ethical Decision Making

Guidelines for Making Ethical Decisions:
1. Is it legal?
2. Is it within Sears shared beliefs and policies?
3. Is it right/fair/appropriate?
4. Would I want everyone to know about this?
5. How will I feel about myself?

Source: *Code of Business Conduct,* Sears, Roebuck and Co., 3333 Beverly Road, Hoffman Estates, IL 60179. Courtesy of Sears, Roebuck and Co.

produces software programs for the space shuttle program, that resulted in invalid test results that endangered space shuttle crews. A Florida Power & Light engineer blew the whistle on safety concerns at a nuclear plant. Each of these individuals chose to come forward with information even though they knew they might be subject to harassment from their employers. And all were successful in their efforts. The tobacco industry is being forced to take legal and financial responsibility for years of tobacco-related health hazards. Engineers at Florida Power & Light and Unisys were severely punished for taking shortcuts that led to hazardous conditions, and both organizations were forced to pay huge penalties for their neglect.[60]

Many people were raised by parents who discouraged "tattling." Those who were raised during the baby-boom/Vietnam War era, however, learned to question authority and are now moving into the upper ranks of corporations and government agencies. Books such as *Blowing the Whistle: Organizational and Legal Implications* are finding an audience eager to learn how to effectively clean up unethical business practices without endangering their personal or professional futures. Cutting-edge management theories such as "total quality management" and "re-engineering" encourage workers to be a proactive part of the organization's team. If organizations focus on quality, then workers from the leadership ranks to the assembly lines must be able to report problems. Whistle-blowing is not an easy path to take. You may be right, win your case, and still lose friends and perhaps your job. However, taking steps to get rid of unethical practices is often your responsibility.

VALUES AND ETHICS IN INTERNATIONAL BUSINESS

If the situation is complex on the domestic scene, values and ethical issues become even more complicated at the international level. The subject is too broad to treat in detail in this chapter, but we can provide an overview of some conflicts that exist in international business. Here are some examples of situations in which a lack of shared values can create difficult situations:

Item: The values of Asian executives differ often from those of their American counterparts. To most Asians, the important values are hard work, respect of learning, and honesty. To most Americans, freedom of expression, personal freedom, and self-reliance are the important values, followed by individual rights, hard work, personal achievement, and thinking for oneself.[61] These contrasts offer special challenges in the global marketplace.

Item: In China, the highly regulated economy gives government officials many opportunities to seek payments for special favors. If you make the first payment, expect continued demands for money.[62] The United States Congress passed the Foreign Corrupt Practices Act, which bars American companies from the bribery of government officials common in many countries. In some cases, this law puts American businesspeople at a disadvantage because some representatives of other countries participate freely in bribery.

Item: As more Americans complete business transactions with the Japanese, value differences become clearer. **Naniwabushi** is the Japanese expression for establishing close personal terms with someone so that she or he will owe you a favor, a commonly accepted business practice in Japan. In this environment, potentially awkward obligations could arise for Americans if they accept gifts from Japanese business acquaintances.

Item: Value differences can also arise in business matters between French and American business representatives. The French tend to be prompt about considering a decision, but they like to examine all the details. This means that final decisions can be slow in coming. Once made, however, they are expressed candidly—whether the decision is in your favor or not.

Now that trade relations have been resumed with countries such as Vietnam, South Africa, and China, it is important for all parties to recognize value differences and to spend time and effort building mutual respect and understanding.

Summary

A strong sense of character grows out of your personal standards of behavior. When you consistently behave in accordance with your values, you maintain your integrity. Your values are the personal worth or importance you give to an object or idea. People's values serve as the foundation for their attitudes, preferences, opinions, and behaviors. Personal values are largely formed early in life and are influenced by family, religious upbringing, schools, the media, and role models.

Internal values conflicts arise when we must choose between strongly held personal values. Values conflicts with others, often based on age, racial, religious, gender, or ethnic differences, require skilled intervention before they can be resolved.

Once you have clarified your personal values, your ethical decisions will be easier. You must learn to distinguish right from wrong, choose an employer whose values you share, and avoid the pursuit of immediate gratification. Shared values unify employees in an organization by providing guidelines for behavior and decisions.

Corporate values and ethics on both the domestic and the international levels are receiving increasing attention because of the devastating effect and expense of corporate crime. Many organizations are developing ethics codes to help guide employees' behaviors, hiring only those individuals who share their corporate values, and offering ethics training opportunities to all employees. As multinational organizations increase in number, the individuals involved will need to consciously examine their values and ethical standards to deal effectively with differing value structures in each country.

Career Corner

Q. I will soon graduate from college and would like to begin my career with an organization that shares my values. I have carefully examined what is most important to me and believe I know the type of organizational culture in which I can thrive. But how do I discover the "real" values of an organization when my interviews are permeated with buzzwords such as "family-friendly" and "teamwork-oriented." How can I determine whether or not they truly mean what they seem to say?

A. Direct questions about an organization's values often result in well-rehearsed answers from the interviewer. Try using *critical incident* questions such as "How did you handle the recent downsizing of your middle managers" or "Tell me about the heroes in your organization." And don't depend solely on the interviewer's answers. Ask current and former employees as well as the organization's customers or clients. Listen carefully to the language used during your interviews. Do you hear a lot of talk about "love," "caring," and "intuition," or do you hear statements like "We had to send in the SWAT team," "They beat their brains out," and "We really nailed them!" If possible, sit in on a team meeting with your potential coworkers. A perfect match between your values and your potential employers' is hard to find, so be patient. You may need to compromise.

Key Terms

character
integrity
values
core values
modeling

values conflict
internal values conflict
ethics
shared values
whistle blower
Naniwabushi

Review Questions

1. How do values differ from attitudes, opinions, or behavior?
2. How are our values formed? How have the sources of our values changed in recent years?
3. Differentiate between internal values conflicts and values conflicts with others.
4. Explain the five dimensions of Kirschenbaum's valuing process (see Table 5.1).

5. Describe the advantages and disadvantages of employees sharing the same values as their organization.
6. Explain the negative effects of the pursuit of immediate gratification.
7. How do top management values affect the purpose and direction of an organization?
8. List some of the steps corporations are taking to eliminate crime in their organizations.
9. How might an ethics code help organizations be more productive?
10. How do seemingly accepted unethical business practices in foreign countries affect Americans' ability to compete for business contracts in those countries?

Application Exercises

1. Guilt and loss of self-respect can result when we say or do things that conflict with what we believe. One way to feel better about yourself is to "clean up" your integrity. Make a list of what you are doing that you think is wrong. Once the list is complete, look it over and determine if you can stop these behaviors. Consider making amends for things you have done in the past that you feel guilty about.[63]
2. In groups of four, discuss how you would react if your manager asked you to participate in some sort of corporate crime. For example, the manager could ask you to help launder money from the company, give a customer misleading information, or cover up a budget inaccuracy and keep this information from reaching upper management. You might want to role-play the situation with your group. Follow up with class discussion.
3. One of the great challenges in life is the clarification of our values. The five-part valuing process described in Table 5.1 can be very helpful as you attempt to identify your core values. Select one personal or professional value from the following list, and clarify this value by applying the five-step process.
   a. Respect the rights and privileges of people who may be in the minority due to race, gender, ethnicity, age, physical or mental abilities, or sexual orientation.
   b. Conserve the assets of my employer.
   c. Utilize leisure time in order to add balance to my life.
   d. Maintain a healthy lifestyle.
   e. Balance the demands of my work and personal life.

Internet Exercise

 As the Internet grows in popularity, we are seeing some unethical uses of this technology. Ethical issues related to privacy, security, and confidentiality are receiving increasing attention. Many sites on the World Wide Web focus on ethical issues pertaining to computers and technology. To learn about important ethical issues raised by the use of computers and the Internet, use your search engine to identify appropriate resources. Type in "computer ethics," and then examine the information available. Prepare a list of the most important ethical issues related to the use of computers, and place a checkmark next to each issue that currently affects you.

Case 5.1   ## Disney Versus the Southern Baptist Convention

If you look up *wholesome* in the dictionary, you might expect to discover the Walt Disney Company logo beside it because Disney has become *the* family-entertainment giant known for its theme parks and G-rated movies. The Walt Disney Company has been functioning on the family-oriented values passed on by its revered founder and is now the largest entertainment company in the world since purchasing the American Broadcasting Company. Recently, however, Disney's organizational culture has been changing to reflect new company initiatives and to value the diversity of its work force as well as its customers. Disney has extended health care benefits to all company employees with same-sex partners, allowed gays and lesbians to gather annually at Disney parks, and contracted with film producers that make R-rated movies.

In response, leaders of the 16-million-member Southern Baptist Convention voted to boycott Disney to protest what they see as its drift away from commitment to traditional family and Christian values. The Southern Baptists believe that same-sex relationships do not qualify as "family," that Disney should stop the annual gay/lesbian get-togethers, and that Disney should refuse to participate in the creation or marketing of R-rated movies. Their nonbinding resolution specifically requests members to cancel plans to visit Disney theme parks, refuse to pay to see Disney movies, and cut Disney product purchases by $100 each year. Sixteen million members times $100 can equal a devastating blow to any corporation's bottom line.

A Disney spokesperson called the boycott "misguided" because it targets the most family-friendly media company in the world.

Questions

1. Do you agree or disagree with the decision to launch a boycott? Explain.
2. If you were a Southern Baptist Convention member who did not vote at the convention and who had children who had saved money for their trip to Disney World, would you go on the trip? Explain.
3. If you were a Southern Baptist minister who did not vote at the convention and did not agree with the vote, how would you guide your church's membership?

4. What steps should Disney take to reduce the potentially destructive effect of the boycott? Would these actions violate the values of any other groups?

Case 5.2   **Tom's of Maine**

When Tom Chappell and his wife Kate founded Tom's of Maine in 1971, they had no idea that their earth-friendly detergents, toothpaste, and other cosmetics would meet with the success they have. Even though the company's products sell at a premium price, retailers and customers seem to appreciate the social responsibility that permeates the entire organization.

In 1986, Tom began to question his future and wonder what more he could do besides make money. He had gained tremendous financial success but he still felt empty. His next step was to enroll in the Harvard University Divinity School, where he earned a master's degree in theology. Rather than joining the ministry, however, he implemented his new insight in his own world of business and then wrote a book called *The Soul of a Business: Managing for Profit and the Common Good,* in which he outlined the relationship between solid values and business ethics.

Tom Chappell's message is simple: "Beliefs drive strategy. Your ethics can form the foundation of smart analysis and clear thinking." His strong spirituality has led him to select and cultivate employees who bring with them a strong respect for the beauty and goodness of nature and people. Ten percent of the company's pretax dollars goes to education, people in need, or efforts to save the environment. Employees are encouraged to spend 5 percent of their work time—two hours a week or one day a month—working for a cause of their choice. Employees report that they are proud to be part of Tom's of Maine and are happier with their own lives after helping the less fortunate in their community.

This humanitarian philosophy affects every aspect of the organization, including its marketing plan. Katie Shisler, vice president of marketing, points out that the company's advertising never claims its products are better than those of its competitors'. "We're not in the game of 'we're better.' We just recognize nature provides elegant solutions, and we share the same values you do." Tom's of Maine's market share has grown tenfold in recent years.

Questions

1. Identify the values that seem to be driving the management decisions at Tom's of Maine. Do you share any of these values?
2. What could other organizations learn from Tom Chappell's philosophy?

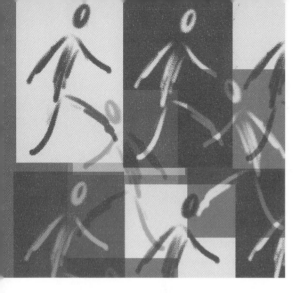

Chapter 6

Attitudes Can Shape
Your Life

Chapter Preview

After studying this chapter, you will be able to

1. Understand the impact of employee attitudes on the success of individuals as well as organizations.
2. List and explain the ways people acquire attitudes.
3. Describe attitudes that employers value.
4. Learn how to change your attitudes.
5. Learn how to help others change their attitudes.
6. Understand what adjustments organizations are making to develop positive employee attitudes.

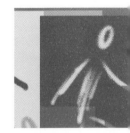

PRIOR TO THE OPENING of the Grand Hyatt Wailea Beach resort hotel on the island of Maui, the personnel department screened 6,000 applicants to fill 1,200 jobs. When Nordstrom opened its first department store on the East Coast, the company interviewed 3,000 people to fill 400 front-line jobs.[1] Both of these service-driven companies are searching for employees who display a positive attitude toward customer service.

When General Motors opened its Saturn plant, applicants were screened for "compatibility" from a huge pool of people. Hal Rosenbluth, CEO of Rosenbluth International, the nation's fourth-largest travel agency, interviews his potential executives by playing basketball with them. He explains, "I like to see who's passing the ball, who's hogging it, who's taking shots they shouldn't."[2] GM and Rosenbluth are searching for employees who exhibit attitudes that help them work effectively as team members.[3]

The National Center on the Educational Quality of the Work Force at the University of Pennsylvania asked 3,000 employers what matters most when hiring nonsupervisory workers. The applicant's attitude ranked number one among eleven characteristics.[4] A close look at this survey and at similar studies tells us that the qualities that make up "attitude" vary from one employment setting to another. Lynn Mercer, manager of a Lucent Technologies plant, says she is guided by the principle that you should hire attitude over aptitude. She searches for employees who display initiative, curiosity, and collegiality—characteristics that she views as hallmarks of a self-directed work force. Mercer is searching for self-starters and team players.[5] John Guffey, Coltec Industries Inc. CEO, is continuously searching for employees who do not have an attitude of entitlement. In other words, he wants to avoid hiring a person who is continually asking, "What's in it for me?"[6] ■

WHAT IS AN ATTITUDE?

An **attitude** is a relatively strong belief about or feeling toward a person, object, idea, or event. It is an "emotional readiness" to behave in a particular manner.[7] Values serve as a foundation for attitudes, and attitudes serve as a foundation for behavior (see Figure 6.1). Throughout life we form attitudes toward political movements, religions, national leaders, various occupations, government programs, laws, and other aspects of our daily lives. They become deeply ingrained in our personalities as we learn and grow. We tend to be very much in favor of those things toward which we have a positive attitude. And we are very much against those things toward which we have a negative attitude. Some of our attitudes are so strong that we encourage others to adopt

Habitat for Humanity International is a nonprofit ministry dedicated to providing housing for the homeless by making adequate, affordable shelter a matter of conscience and action. Volunteers and the selected homeowners invest hundreds of hours to reduce the monetary cost of the house, increase the personal stake of the family members in their house, and foster attitudes of partnership with other people in the community. (David Young-Wolff/PhotoEdit)

our views and copy our behaviors. When others hold strong contrasting attitudes, based on their values and past experiences, a potential human relations challenge exists.

Some attitudes, such as job satisfaction, are multidimensional. The feelings we have about our work, for example, are made up of attitudes toward the company's compensation plan, opportunities for promotion, coworkers, supervision, the work itself, and other factors.[8] Job satisfaction is usually of major concern to an employer because management knows there is a link between attitudes and behavior. Persons who are dissatisfied with their jobs are more likely to be late or absent from work, become unproductive, or quit. Therefore, improved job satisfaction can reduce tardiness, absenteeism, and employee turnover.[9]

FIGURE 6.1

The Relationship Between Values, Attitudes, and Behaviors

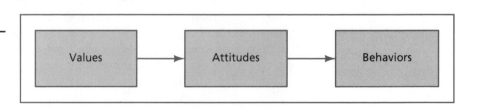

Total Person Insight

"Your attitudes can be the lock on, or the key to, your door of success."

DENIS WAITLEY

Author, *The Winning Generation*

The Powerful Influence of Attitudes

Charles Swindoll is credited with saying, "The longer I live, the more I realize the impact of attitude on life." He is convinced that attitude is more important than appearance, giftedness, or skill.[10] For example, people who go through life with a positive mental attitude see daily obstacles as opportunities rather than roadblocks and are therefore more likely to achieve their personal and professional goals. People who filter their daily experiences through a negative attitude tend to focus on what is going wrong and find it difficult to achieve contentment or satisfaction in any aspect of their lives. It makes no difference how attractive, intelligent, or skilled they are; their attitude holds them back.

Our attitudes can greatly influence our mental and physical health. Bernie Siegel, author of *Peace, Love and Healing* and *Love, Medicine and Miracles,* sees a strong connection between a patient's mental attitude and his or her ability to heal. Siegel, who is a surgeon, says that when a doctor can instill some measure of hope in the patient's mind, the healing process begins. As part of his treatment plan, Siegel attempts to give patients a sense of control over their destinies. He wants his patients to believe in the future and know that they can influence their own healing.[11]

Attitudes represent a powerful force in any organization. An attitude of trust, for example, can pave the way for improved communication and greater cooperation between an employee and a supervisor. A sincere effort by management to improve working conditions, when filtered through attitudes of suspicion and cynicism, may have a negative impact on employee-management relations. These same actions by management, filtered through attitudes of trust and hope, may result in improved worker morale. As another example, a caring attitude displayed by an employee can increase customer loyalty and set the stage for repeat business.

HOW ATTITUDES ARE FORMED

Throughout life you are constantly making decisions and judgments that help formulate your attitudes. These attitude decisions are often based on behaviors your childhood authority figures told you were right or wrong, childhood and adult behaviors for which you were rewarded or punished, role models you selected, and the various environmental and corporate cultures you chose to embrace.

Socialization

The process through which people are integrated into a society by exposure to the actions and opinions of others is called **socialization**.[12] As a child, you interacted with your parents, family, teachers, and friends. Children often feel that statements made by these authority figures are the "proper" things to believe. For example, if a parent declares, "People who live in big, expensive houses either are born rich or are crooked," the child may hold this attitude for many years.

Children learn a great deal by watching and listening to family members, teachers, and other authority figures. In some cases, the influence is quite subtle. Children who observe their parents recycling, using public transportation instead of a car to get to work, and turning off the lights to save electricity may develop a strong concern for protection of the environment.

Peer and Reference Groups

As children reach adolescence and begin to break away psychologically from their parents, the **peer group** (persons their own age) can have a powerful influence on attitude formation. In fact, peer-group influence can sometimes be stronger than the influence of parents, teachers, and other adult figures. With the passing of years, reference groups replace peer groups as sources of attitude formation in young adults. A **reference group** consists of several people who share a common interest and tend to influence one another's attitudes and behaviors. The reference group may act as a point of comparison and a source of information for the individual member. For example, a fraternity or sorority may serve as a reference group for a college student. In the business community a chapter of the American Society for Training and Development or of Sales and Marketing Executives International may provide a reference group for its members. As members of a reference group, we often observe other people in the group to establish our own norms. Reference groups often have a positive influence on the professional development of members.

Rewards and Punishment

Attitude formation is often related to rewards and punishment. People in authority generally encourage certain attitudes and discourage others. Naturally, individuals tend to develop attitudes that minimize punishments and maximize rewards. A child who is praised for sharing toys with playmates is likely to develop positive attitudes toward caring about other people's needs. Likewise, a child who receives a weekly allowance in exchange for performing basic housekeeping tasks learns an attitude of responsibility.

As an adult, you will discover that your employers will continue to attempt to shape your attitudes through rewards and punishment at work. Many organizations are rewarding employees who take steps to stay healthy. Dominion Resources, a Virginia-based utility, rewards healthy checkups for both employee and spouse. Some companies offer employees annual health checkups with precise targets for blood pressure, cholesterol levels, and other indicators of good health. Those who achieve the targets get a discount on their health premiums; those who fall short of the goal pay the standard rates.[13]

Role Model Identification

Most young people would like to have more influence, status, and popularity. These goals are often achieved through identification with an authority figure or a role model. A **role model** is that person you most admire or are likely to emulate. Preschoolers are most likely to identify their parents as their role models. At this early stage parents are seen as almost perfect, as real heroes. During early elementary school, children begin to realize that their parents have flaws, and they search for other heroes—perhaps a popular athlete, a rock star, or an actor. During later stages of development, new role models are adopted. As you might expect, role models can exert considerable influence—for better or for worse—on developing attitudes.

The media have a tremendous influence on people's selection of role models. By the time they graduate from high school, most young adults will be spending about four hours a day watching television.[14] Many of the programs they watch are dominated by crime, violence, and stereotyped or deviant characters and life situations. At the other extreme, other programs present positive superheroes with superhuman abilities. With this constant reinforcement from fictional negative and positive role models, young people sometimes have difficulty sorting out which behaviors and attitudes are acceptable in the real world.

Role models at work can have a major influence on employee attitude development. The new salesperson in the menswear department naturally wants help in adjusting to the job. So does the new dental hygienist and the recently hired auto mechanic. These people will pay special attention to the behavior of coworkers and managers. Therefore, if a worker leaves work early and no negative consequences follow, new employees may develop the attitude that staying until quitting time is not as important as they had thought. If a senior employee is rude to customers and suffers no negative consequences, new employees may imitate this attitude and behavior.

The late Princess Di successfully used her highly publicized life to share her humanitarian actions and attitudes with people around the world. (AP/Wide World Photos)

In most organizations, supervisory and management personnel have the greatest impact on employee attitudes. The supervisors' attitudes toward safety, cost control, accuracy, dress and grooming, customer relations, and the like become the model for subordinates. Employees pay more attention to what their supervisors *do* than to what they *say*.

Cultural Influences

Our attitudes are influenced by the culture that surrounds us. **Culture** is the sum total of knowledge, beliefs, values, objects, and customs that we use to adapt to our environment. It includes tangible items, such as foods, clothing, and furniture, as well as intangible concepts, such as education and laws.[15]

People strive to define themselves in every culture. The definition varies from culture to culture. If you ask an adult living in Japan, "Who are you?"

that person is likely to respond, "I'm an employee of Sony Corporation." In Japanese culture, people are more likely to define themselves by the organization that provides them with lifetime employment.[16] In the United States, a person's job and employer are somewhat less likely to be the major source of identity. For instance, a young woman who spends hours each week trying to improve the environment may define herself as an environmentalist. That she works as a department supervisor at a local supermarket may be incidental to how she defines herself.

As noted in Chapter 1, many organizations today are striving to define their own culture in order to influence the attitudes of their workers. Generally speaking, organizational culture represents the "social glue" that binds members of an organization together.

Item: Federal Express Corp., America's first nationwide overnight delivery service, recognizes that a successful service company must do everything possible to keep employees satisfied and highly motivated. After all, it is the employees who make the guaranteed overnight deliveries possible. The Federal Express culture incorporates four basic beliefs that many companies would consider revolutionary: (1) Be as concerned about investments in people as about investments in machines. (2) Use technology to support the efforts of men and women on the front line. (3) Make recruitment and training as crucial for salespeople and housekeepers as for managers. (4) Link compensation to performance for employees at the entry level, not just for those at the top.[17] Does all this attention to employees make a difference? The customers say yes. Ninety-five percent of Federal Express customers say they are completely satisfied with services provided.

Item: When Amy Miller started her first ice cream store, her market niche was safe from competition. However, it was not long before national companies such as Baskin-Robbins and Steve's were setting up shop nearby. Miller decided the best way to differentiate her store from the others was to provide some entertainment along with each purchase. When you visit an Amy's Ice Creams store, you may see an employee break-dance on the freezer top or juggle serving spades. Employees might be wearing pajamas (because it's Sleep-Over Night) or masks (because it's Star Wars Night). Employees are likely to do anything to create fun, including contests that involve the customers. Miller communicates her cultural message to prospective employees the day they show up looking for a job. Instead of a formal application form, they are given a white paper bag along with instructions to do anything they want with it and bring it back in a week. Applicants use the bag to create masks, cartoons, and works of art. Today Amy's Ice Creams is a seven-store chain of shops in Austin and Houston, Texas, with annual sales of $2.2 million.[18]

Item: The United States Marines have developed an eleven-week basic training program that has a dramatic impact on those who complete it. Recruits emerge as self-disciplined Marines who are physically fit, courteous to their elders, and drug-free. Many have had to overcome deep differences of class and race and have learned to live and work as a team. They live in an organizational culture where a hint of racism can end a career and the use of illegal drugs is minimized by a "zero tolerance" policy.[19]

Thinking / Learning Starters

1. Identify at least one matter you feel strongly about. Do you know how you acquired this attitude? Is it shared by any particular group of people? Do you spend time with these people?

2. Think of an attitude that a friend or coworker holds but that you strongly disagree with. What factors do you believe contributed to the formation of this person's attitude?

ATTITUDES VALUED BY EMPLOYERS

Chapter 1 noted that the current labor market is characterized by churning dislocation and uncertainty. The large number of mergers, buyouts, business closings, and downsizing efforts has resulted in the loss of many jobs. Layoffs have come in every segment of the work force. Even managers and professionals have experienced job losses. As these victims of job turnover seek new employment opportunities, they are discovering that employers are looking for candidates who display several important attitudes. The following discussion suggests several of these attitudes.

Be Self-Motivated

Dawn Overstreet, a lecturer associated with the Americana Leadership College, once said, "People need to be leaders of themselves." In her presentations she emphasizes the importance of self-sufficiency—the ability to handle life despite difficulties.[20] People who are self-motivated are inclined to set their own goals and monitor their own progress toward those goals. They do not need a supervisor hovering around them making sure they are on task and accomplishing what they are supposed to be doing. Many find ways to administer their own rewards after they achieve their goals. Employers who are participating in

Raised in a welfare family, Michael Bradford was homeless, battled drug and alcohol addiction, and spent time in jail for burglary. Today, Bradford has turned his life around by changing his out-look on life and graduating from a welfare-to-work program sponsored by Marriott Corporation. (David Peterson)

downsizing often retain those employees who are capable of making their own decisions and following through.

Become a Self-Directed Learner

Organizations from hospitals to retail outlets are being forced to train and re-train employees quickly and more frequently. Established industries are discovering the advantages of adopting new technology, and new industries are developing new processes that offer them a competitive edge in the market-place. Given this enormous demand for the work force to learn new things faster, people with curiosity and a desire to keep up-to-date will be in great demand.

But most organizations depend on each individual becoming a **self-directed learner.** Self-directed learners take responsibility for their own learning; they diagnose what it is they need to learn, develop objectives, discover learning experiences, find resources, and evaluate learning outcomes.[21] They seek out opportunities to enhance their skills and knowledge through on-the-job training as well as seminars and workshops offered outside the workplace. They read professional journals and monitor news media for research and technology advances that might affect their jobs in the future. Ideally, employees should prepare a self-directed learning plan that targets where they would like their professional life to lead them and indicates how they will get there.

Most people are eager to learn new jobs or new ways of doing their old jobs, but many do not know *how* to learn. Do you learn best by reading about a new process, by listening to someone describe it, by watching someone perform the new procedure, or by doing it yourself with an expert's guidance? Although there is no right or wrong learning style, it is important to understand the way you learn. Employees who know how to approach and master any new situation are more cost-effective to their employers because the time and other resources spent on their training can be reduced.[22] Employees who have the desire and ability to learn fast will have the cutting edge when it comes time to get their dream job or retain their position during downsizing.

Be a Team Player

In sports, the person who is a "team player" receives a great deal of praise and recognition. A team player is someone who is willing to step out of the spotlight, give up a little personal glory, and help the team achieve a victory. Team players are no less important in organizations. Employers are increasingly organizing employees into teams (health teams, sales teams, product development teams) that build products, solve problems, and make decisions. Saturn's automobile manufacturing plant is made up of a network of highly effective teams. Each team functions as a small-business unit responsible for its own product, budget, and accounting, and for doing business with the other teams within the organization. Management screens potential employees, but each team has the final say on whether a person will be hired. An employee who is not an effective team member can be thrown off the team.[23] Chapter 12 contains some tips on how to become a respected team member.

Be Concerned About Your Health and Wellness

The ever-growing cost of health care is one of the most serious problems facing companies today. Many organizations are promoting wellness programs for all employees as a way to keep costs in line. These programs include tips on healthy eating, physical-fitness exercises, stress management practices, and other forms of assistance that contribute to a healthy lifestyle. Employees who actively participate in these programs frequently take fewer sick days, file fewer medical claims, and bring a higher level of energy to work. Some companies even give cash awards to employees who lose weight, quit smoking, or lower their cholesterol levels. Employees who pay a great deal of attention to their health needs can be a real asset. In Chapters 14 and 17 we discuss health and wellness in greater detail.

Value Coworker Diversity

To value diversity in the work setting means to make full use of the ideas, talents, experiences, and perspectives of all employees at all levels within the organization. People who differ from each other often add richness to the organization. An old adage states: If we both think alike, one of us is not necessary.

Development and utilization of a talented, diverse work force can be the key to success in a period of fierce global competition. Women and people of color make up a large majority of the new multicultural, global work force. Many people, however, carry prejudiced attitudes against those who differ from them. They tend to "prejudge" others' value based on the color of their skin, gender, age, religious preference, lifestyle, political affiliation, or economic status. Although deeply held prejudices that have developed over a long time are difficult to change, employers are demanding these changes. Wisconsin Power and Light is typical of many organizations that have made a strong commitment to valuing diversity. One of the company's expectations concerning diversity says, "Employees at all organizational levels must be intolerant of

"I'm giving you a 'marginal' on your attitude toward constructive criticism." (*Kaser,* Phi Delta Kappan. *Reprinted by permission.*)

behaviors in the workplace that are inconsistent with the objectives of equal opportunity and the building of a diverse workforce.[24] Chapter 15 contains specific guidance on how to develop positive attitudes toward joining a diverse work force.

HOW TO CHANGE ATTITUDES

If you begin to notice that successful people will not associate with you, that you have been overlooked for a promotion you thought you should have had, or that you go home from work depressed and a little angry at the world, you can almost always be sure you need an attitude adjustment. Unfortunately, people do not easily adopt new attitudes or discard old ones. It is difficult to break the attachment to emotionally laden beliefs. Yet attitudes *can* be changed. There may be times when you absolutely hate a job, but you can still develop a positive attitude toward it as a steppingstone to another job you actually do want. There will be times as well when you will need to help colleagues change their attitudes so that you can work with them more effectively. And, of course, when events, such as a layoff, are beyond your control, you must strive to maintain a positive attitude. It is often said that life is 10 percent what happens to you and 90 percent how you react to it. Knowing how to change attitudes in yourself and others can be essential to effective human relations—and your success—in an organization.

Changing Your Own Attitude

You are constantly placed in new situations with people from different backgrounds and cultures. Each time you go to a new school, take a new job, get a promotion, or move to a different neighborhood, you may need to alter your attitudes to cope effectively with the change. In all these situations, the events are out of your control. But you can control your attitude toward these events. If you allow yourself to dwell on the negative aspects of change, you can expect to exhibit negative, self-destructive behaviors. When you make an effort to focus on the positive, you will find your world a much more pleasant place in which to live. If you are happy, other people enjoy working with you.

Being able to control your attitudes is a powerful human relations skill that usually involves certain basic changes:

1.   *Become an optimist.* Optimistic thoughts give rise to good moods that tend to serve as a foundation for developing positive attitudes and effective human relationships. When you are an optimist, your coworkers, managers, and—perhaps most important—your customers feel your energy and vitality and tend to mirror your behavior. An optimistic view of life events can make life far less stressful.

Total Person Insight

"You'll never entirely get rid of the negative voices inside you—but that doesn't mean you have to listen to them. Get into the habit of challenging negative ideas."

PAMELA R. JOHNSON AND CLAUDIA RAWLINS

Authors, "Daydreams and Dialogues: Key to Motivation"

In a work setting, it does not take long to identify people with an optimistic outlook. Optimists are more likely to bounce back after a demotion, layoff, or some other disappointment. According to Martin Seligman, professor of psychology at the University of Pennsylvania and author of *Learned Optimism,* optimists are more likely to view problems as merely temporary setbacks on their road to achieving their goals. They focus on their potential success rather than on their failures.[25]

Pessimists, in contrast, tend to believe bad events will last a long time, will undermine everything they do, and are their own fault. A pessimistic pattern of thinking can have unfortunate consequences. Pessimists give up more easily when faced with a challenge, are less likely to take personal control of their life, and are more likely to take personal blame for their misfortune.[26] Often pessimism leads to **cynicism,** which is a mistrusting attitude regarding the motives of people. When you are cynical, you are constantly on guard against the "misbehavior" of others.[27] If you begin to think that everyone is screwing up, acting inconsiderately, or otherwise behaving inappropriately, cynicism has taken control of your thought process, and it is time to change.

Fortunately, pessimism and optimism are both learned attitudes, so they can be changed. If you feel the need to become a more optimistic person, you can spend more time visualizing yourself succeeding, a process that is discussed in Chapter 4. Monitor your self-talk, and discover whether or not you are focusing on the negative aspects of the problems and disappointments in your life or are looking at them as learning experiences that will eventually lead you toward your personal and professional goals. Try to avoid having too much contact with pessimists, and refuse to be drawn into a group of negative thinkers who see only problems, not solutions. Surround yourself with other optimists because attitudes can be contagious.

2. *Think for yourself.* Determine whether the attitudes that seem to get you in trouble are your own or the result of socialization. If you have been socialized into holding negative attitudes, you need to re-examine them. Authority figures, family ties, and peer pressure are strong influences. But you are an intelligent adult now, and you can control your own thoughts and feelings about people, ideas, and events, rather than being controlled by others' attitudes.

Buckminster Fuller, the respected architect and inventor, stated that learning to think for himself was the turning point in his life. He discovered at age 32 that he needed to become a more independent thinker and stop relying on others to influence every aspect of his life. Once he made the decision to think for himself, he became highly motivated to discover what he described as the "operating principles" of his world.[28]

3. *Keep an open mind.* We often make decisions and then refuse to consider any other point of view that might lead us to question our beliefs. Many times our attitudes persist even in the presence of overwhelming evidence to the contrary. If you have been raised in a family or community that supports racist views, it may seem foreign to you when your colleagues at work openly accept and enjoy healthy relationships with people whose skin color is different from your own. Pay attention. Expose yourself to new information and experiences beyond what you have been socialized to believe. Maybe your coworkers have discovered qualities of these individuals that you have overlooked because you could not see beyond the color of their skin.

We live in a world where generalizations are commonplace: Men are too competitive. Women are too emotional. People on welfare are lazy. You cannot trust government officials. These generalizations need to be assessed with an open mind if you want to advance in your chosen career. James Allen, the famous Harvard psychologist, discovered that you can change many of the outer aspects of your life by changing the inner attitudes of your mind. When you face things you cannot change, take a few moments to reflect on the Serenity Prayer.

FIGURE 6.2

Serenity Prayer

SERENITY PRAYER

Grant me the serenity to
accept the things I cannot change,
the courage to change the things I can,
and the wisdom to know the difference.

Source: "Serenity Prayer" by Dr. Reinhold Niebuhr.

Helping Others Change Their Attitudes

It is true that you are really in control of only your own attitudes. Although you can bend and flex and alter these as often as you find it beneficial, sometimes you need to stand firm and maintain your position. At that point, you may want to help other people change their attitudes. Unfortunately, you cannot hand your colleagues "a ready-made box of attitudes." But often you can help produce an atmosphere in which they will want to change their thinking.

Some people attempt to beg, plead, intimidate, or even threaten others into adopting new attitudes. This process is similar to attempting to push a piece of yarn across the top of a table. When you *push* the yarn in the direction you want it to go, it gets all bent out of shape. When you gently *pull* the yarn with your fingertips, it follows you wherever you want it to go. Two powerful techniques can help you pull people in the direction you want them to go, often without their even realizing that you are attempting to change their attitudes:

1. Change the *conditions* that precede the behavior.
2. Change the *consequences* that follow the behavior.

Change the Conditions If you want people to change their attitudes, identify the behaviors that represent the poor attitudes and alter the conditions that precede the behavior. Consider the following situation.

A new employee in a retail store is having a problem adjusting to her job. From the first day, she has found the job frustrating. Because the store is understaffed and the manager needed her on the sales floor as soon as possible, he rushed through her job training procedures without taking time to answer her questions. Now she finds there are many customers' questions she cannot answer, and she has trouble operating the computerized cash register. The manager does not seem to care whether she succeeds or fails; he apparently just wanted the job filled. She wants to quit, and her negative attitudes are affecting her job performance and the way she handles her customers.

The manager could easily have prevented this employee's negative attitudes by changing the conditions surrounding her training. He could have been careful to answer all her questions *before* she was placed on the sales floor. Perhaps he could have asked an experienced salesperson to stay with her as she helped her first few customers. Above all, he could have displayed a caring attitude toward her and her success.

Change the Consequences Another way to help other people change their attitudes is to alter what happens *after* they exhibit the behavior and attitude you are attempting to change. A simple rule applies: When an experience is followed by positive consequences, the person is likely to repeat the behavior. When an experience is followed by negative consequences, the person will soon learn to stop the behavior. For example, if you are a supervisor, and several of your employees are consistently late for work, you might provide some form of negative consequence each time they are tardy, such as a verbal reprimand or reduced pay. Keep in mind, however, that we tend to focus attention on the people who exhibit disruptive attitudes and to ignore the employees exhibiting the attitudes we want to encourage. Saying: "Thank you for being here on time. I really appreciate your commitment" can be an extremely effective reward for those who arrive at work on time. Attitudes rewarded will be repeated.

One note of caution: It is important to view consequences through the eyes of the person you are trying to influence. What you see as a negative consequence—a one-week leave of absence without pay—might be a positive consequence to someone else—an extra week's vacation. Robert Mager, a nationally known authority in the field of training and development, says:

> It doesn't matter what I might seek out or avoid: It is what is positive or aversive to the person whose behavior I am trying to influence that counts. And this, incidentally, is one reason we don't succeed more often than we do in the area of human interaction. We try to influence others by providing consequences that are positive to us but not to them.[29]

Thinking / Learning Starters

---

1. Are you holding a grudge against someone? Describe the situation. What are the benefits of holding on to this attitude? What are the benefits of letting go of it and moving on to a more productive atmosphere?

2. Think of a situation that is upsetting to you at work or home. How can you alter the situation to help change the other person's opinions? If it is absolutely impossible to change the situation, what will result if you change your attitude? Which direction is the best solution to the problem?

ORGANIZATIONS' EFFORTS TOWARD IMPROVING EMPLOYEES' ATTITUDES

Many companies are realizing that an employee's attitude and performance cannot be separated. When employees have negative attitudes about their

Employers like Hewlett Packard are seeking employees who are willing to be part of self-managed teams that create solutions to problems within the organization. This team of HP workers created a better system of moving boxes while management vigorously refused to tell any of them what to do. (Andy Freeberg)

work, their job performance and productivity suffer. When they have positive attitudes, job performance and productivity are likely to improve. For generations, employers and labor unions focused on salaries and fringe benefits as the rewards that would keep workers producing at top efficiency. But gradually, both labor and management discovered that money was not always the primary ingredient of a satisfying job.

People who are asked what they most want from their job typically cite mutual respect among coworkers, interesting work, recognition for work well done, the chance to develop skills, and so forth. If employers want to maintain or improve the positive attitudes of their workers, and thereby maintain or improve productivity, they need to provide the benefits workers consider important. Of course, workers expect the pay to be competitive, but they want so much more. As author and management consultant Peter Drucker says, "To make a living is not enough. Work also has to make a life."[30] Organizations are finding creative ways to influence worker attitudes.

Item: Greyhound Lines Inc., the Chicago-based bus company, developed a training program that put new employees in the role of customers and required them to endure realistic simulations of actual customer service failures. Trainees waited in long lines, were treated rudely and indifferently, and were given rides in dirty, smelly buses. One month after "reality training" began, Greyhound realized a 50 percent decrease in customer complaints. Employees who completed this training exhibited a better attitude toward customers than did employees who had not received the training.[31]

Item: Starbucks Coffee Company has taken the position that the quality of its work force provides the only sustainable competitive advantage. The business is built on making every employee feel respected. Full- and part-time workers receive a generous and comprehensive employee benefits package. Starbucks's company culture has a positive influence on employees' attitudes toward customer service, product quality, and honesty. Orin Smith, chief financial officer at Starbucks, says, "The biggest defense against pilferage is a strong culture."[32]

Item: Intracorp, a Philadelphia-based managed care services firm, has found a way to reduce clients' worker compensation claims and aid workers' recovery after a work-related injury:

1. Explain workers' compensation policies before on-the-job mishaps occur.
2. Demonstrate genuine concern after an injury.
3. Refer the injured worker to doctors who treat quickly and aggressively.

When Intracorp's clients took these steps, workers recovered and returned to work more quickly. They discovered that workers who were satisfied with their treatment were less likely to see a lawyer.[33]

   What do these organizations have in common? Each has given thought to the attitudes that are important for a healthy work environment and has taken steps to shape these attitudes. Many organizations are attempting to improve employee attitudes and productivity by enhancing the quality of their employees' work life. This might involve developing training programs that employees want, joint review of monthly profit and loss statements, enhanced fringe benefit programs, and collaborative efforts to improve safety. It might also include building day-care centers, sponsoring drug treatment programs for employees, or paying for employee memberships at local health clubs.

A FINAL WORD

Viktor Frankl, a survivor of the Auschwitz concentration camp and author of *Man's Search for Meaning,* said, "The last of the freedoms is to choose one's attitude in any given set of circumstances." We have noted throughout this chapter that attitudes have a major impact on our day-to-day lives. Given the importance of attitudes, you should regularly re-examine yours and choose the ones that will take you where you want to go in life. Changing an attitude that is detrimental to your personal or professional life can be a challenge, but the process can also be a critical step toward your continued growth and success. The happiest people don't necessarily *have* the best of everything; they just *make* the best of everything. It's all in their attitude.

Summary

An attitude is any strong belief toward people and situations. It is a state of mind supported by feelings. People possess hundreds of attitudes about work, family life, friends, coworkers, and the like.

Attitudes represent a powerful force in every organization. If the persons employed by a service firm display a caring attitude toward customers, the business will likely enjoy a high degree of customer loyalty and repeat business. If the employees of a manufacturing firm display a serious attitude toward safety rules and regulations, fewer accidents will likely occur.

People acquire attitudes through early childhood socialization, peer and reference groups, rewards and punishment, role model identification, and cultural influences.

Employers hire and attempt to retain employees who are self-motivated, self-directed learners, willing to be a team player, concerned about health and wellness, and value coworker diversity.

You can choose to change your attitude by becoming an optimist; thinking for yourself without undue pressure from your peers, family, and others; and keeping an open mind. You can help others change their attitudes by altering the consequences and conditions that surround the situation. Positive consequences and conditions produce positive attitudes. Organizations are taking steps to improve employee attitudes by enhancing the quality of their work life.

Career Corner

Q. I am a 24-year-old recent college graduate. Six months ago I accepted a job as assistant to the office manager of a small manufacturing plant. She is in her late 50s and has been with the company since she graduated from high school. She has made it perfectly clear that she never had the opportunity to go to college. Her attitudes about how work is to be done in our office seem so old-fashioned. I have so many creative ideas to improve our efficiency, but she seems to believe I am too young to know anything. Every time she says, "That's the way it has always been done; don't change it," my skin crawls and I feel very bitter for the rest of the day. What can I do to change her attitude toward my potential?

A. Begin by changing your attitude toward her traditional way of performing routine tasks in the office. Remember, she has had to adjust to many changes over the years to keep her organization running smoothly. Respect her past successes, and assure her that you are there to help with the changing demands of the future.

Second, begin to alter the conditions in the office so that they are conducive to your creative ideas. Bring your professional journals to work, and invite her to read various articles discussing innovative ideas that have been successfully implemented in other offices. Invite her to attend a seminar with you or to enroll in a class on some new software package that makes tedious office tasks easier. If she accepts a new idea, praise her intelligence and openness. When she receives positive feedback from you and others in the organization, she will likely repeat the behavior and seek out additional ways to improve the efficiency of the office. Changing attitudes is not easy, so be patient.

Key Terms

attitude
socialization
peer group
reference group
role model

culture
self-directed learner
cynicism

Review Questions

1. It has been said that "attitudes represent a powerful force in any organization." What examples can you give to support this statement?
2. List five ways in which we form our attitudes.
3. Describe how rewards and punishment can shape the attitudes of employees in an organization. Give at least one example of each.
4. How can selecting a positive role model within an organization help an individual reach his or her goals?
5. Describe the attitudes employers are looking for in their employees.
6. Explain how consequences can influence the shaping of attitudes in an organization.
7. Robert Mager says that the conditions that surround a subject can play an important role in shaping attitudes. Provide at least one example to support Mager's statement.
8. Identify the difference between a person with an optimistic attitude and one with a pessimistic viewpoint. Which one are you? Explain.
9. What are organizations doing to help improve the attitudes of their workers? Why do they bother to keep their workers happy?

10. Explain in your own words the meaning of Waitley's Total Person Insight on page 149.

Application Exercises

1. Describe your attitudes concerning
   a. a teamwork environment
   b. health and wellness
   c. life and work
   d. learning new skills
   How do these attitudes affect you on a daily basis? Do you feel you have a positive attitude in most situations? Can you think of someone you have frequent contact with who displays negative attitudes toward these items? Do you find ways to avoid spending time with this person?
2. Identify an attitude held by a friend, coworker, or spouse that you would like to see changed. Do any conditions that precede this person's behavior fall under your control? If so, how could you change those conditions so the person might change his or her attitude? What positive consequences might you offer when the person behaves the way you want? What negative consequences might you impose when the person participates in the behavior you are attempting to stop?
3. For a period of one week, keep a diary or log of positive and negative events. Positive events might include the successful completion of a project, a compliment from a coworker, or just finding time for some leisure activities. Negative events might include forgetting an appointment, criticism from your boss, or simply looking in the mirror and seeing something you don't like. An unpleasant news story might also qualify as a negative event. At the end of one week, review your entries and determine what type of pattern exists. Also, reflect on the impact of these events. Did you quickly bounce back from the negative events, or did you dwell on them all week? Did the positive events enhance your optimism? Consider each negative event in relation to the Serenity Prayer (Figure 6.2). What did you discover?

Internet Exercise

The qualities that make up the "right attitude" vary somewhat from one employment setting to another. To learn more about what attitudes employers view as important, visit the Internet and discover what information is available on this important topic. Using your search engine, type in "attitude," and then examine the resources (such as books, articles, and training programs) available on this topic. Pay special attention to information on how attitudes are formed, attitudes valued by employers, and efforts organizations are making to improve attitudes. Prepare a brief written report that summarizes your findings.

Case 6.1   ## The Prize: A Flounder Fish Light

For the twenty-five years Mary spent with various door-to-door sales organizations, she felt unappreciated. At one company's annual conference, she watched another woman receive an alligator-skin purse for reaching a sales goal. Mary wanted that purse and vowed she would surpass her sales goal the following year and win the coveted prize. Which she did—but that year's prize was a flounder light for night fishing. Years later, Mary told *Savvy* magazine, "I made up my mind right then that if I ever ran a company, one thing I would never do was give someone a fish light."

Today Mary Kay Ash, founder of Mary Kay Cosmetics, works hard to provide within her company the conditions that help maintain her employees' positive attitudes toward their work. She also monitors carefully to make sure the rewards her sales consultants earn are meaningful to individual prize winners. She personally sends a birthday card to each employee, a silver bank shaped like a duck to new children of employees, a silver bowl to newlyweds, and, on the Monday before Thanksgiving, a turkey to everyone. Outside her private office at her Dallas headquarters is a sign that says "Department of Sunshine and Rainbows." She imagines that every person she meets during the day has a sign around his or her neck that says "Make me feel important," and she strives to do just that. Her positive attitude permeates the entire organization, as one employee explained: "It's catching. I was surprised that kind of attitude could be transferred through the whole company."

Many of Mary Kay's 220,000 independent beauty-and-sales consultants attend the three-day seminar held each summer at the Dallas Convention Center. The women are rewarded for their sales achievements and receive queen-for-a-day treatment. Top sellers are crowned with diamond tiaras and wrapped in mink coats or given a set of keys to the Mary Kay trademark—a pink Cadillac.

Questions

1. This chapter states that you can affect other people's attitudes by monitoring conditions in the workplace and influencing the consequences of workers' behavior. How has Mary Kay Ash implemented these principles? Would the conditions and consequences she provides help improve your attitude at work?

2. Employee surveys at Mary Kay show that only 60 percent of the work force feel they are paid fairly. Recently, secretaries at the company were earning $23,000 and production line assemblers $16,800. Christmas bonuses ranged from $25 to $500. Yet turnover among Mary Kay employees is less than 10 percent. Why do you think these employees are staying in jobs that do not meet their financial goals?

Case 6.2   **Office Politics**

Typically, a workplace operates under two sets of rules: a formal system, which includes the publicly acknowledged reporting structure, rules, and regulations; and a political system, which is the dynamic informal network of friends and influence. Most people have an attitude of resentment about having to play office politics in order to get ahead. They want to be judged by their performance, skills, and knowledge as they strive to succeed in their chosen careers. However, when you reach a certain level, everyone is smart, works hard, and is competent. Then the standard may be "who you know, not what you know."

Office politics is part of being an effective team player in most organizations. It is nothing more than getting to know people on an informal basis and learning their strengths and weaknesses. It involves getting to know who can get things done, whose opinion is respected, who gets ignored and why. The better you understand the values and attitudes underlying others' behaviors, the better you will be able to adjust your behavior accordingly. At the same time, the informal network allows you to share your talents and abilities that might not be discovered merely by looking at the work you produce. The goal of the team is not to work within your personal comfort zone but to get things done quickly while taking into account members' emotions and personalities so the team can produce quality decisions. This often requires you to play the political game. There are a few guidelines for playing this game effectively:

1. *Don't try to please everyone.* One aspiring young executive was bemoaning the fact that someone in the organization did not like her. A respected colleague commented, "Who do you think you are that *everyone* is going to like you!"
2. *Build a solid base of trusted allies throughout the organization.* These are people who will tell you what is going on and stand up for you.
3. *Maintain your visibility outside the company.* Speak at community events, volunteer your help to local charities, or write an article for your professional journal or local newspaper. You will be bringing credit to yourself and your company, and fellow workers will notice.

4. *Confront anyone who attempts to stab you in the back.* If you ignore one attempt, you will increase your vulnerability to other attempts. Intercept any false rumors by finding the person responsible for the grapevine messages and explaining your side of the story. If you are left out of important meetings or decisions, explain to those in charge how valuable your input might be to them.

5. *If you are not a "politician," consider working for a small business.* It will be easier for you to get to know individuals and gain their trust when there are only a few players.

Questions

1. What is your attitude toward playing office politics? Is this attitude based on past experience or stories you have heard from others? Explain.
2. What can you do to maintain a positive attitude toward office politics? What would be the consequences of your positive attitude?
3. Is there any way to assess a company's political environment before you go to work for the company? What kinds of mistakes might you avoid if you were aware of this information?

Chapter 7

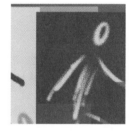

Motivating Yourself

and

Others

Chapter Preview

After studying this chapter, you will be able to

1. Differentiate between internal and external motivators in the workplace.
2. Identify the steps in the motivational cycle.
3. Explain the five characteristics of motives.
4. Describe Maslow's hierarchy of needs and Herzberg's motivation-maintenance theory.
5. Compare and contrast Theory X and Theory Y leadership styles.
6. Describe how expectations influence motivation.
7. List and describe contemporary motivation strategies.
8. Describe selected self-motivation strategies.

M ICHAEL QUINN JOINED WAL-MART as a part-time clerk and bathroom cleaner while attending high school. Later he switched to a full-time position and became an assistant manager at age 19 and a store manager at 23. "It amazes me that I'm in charge of a business that has sales of $22 million a year and more than 200 associates," says the young man whose serious manner and devotion to the company have won respect. As store manager, his workweek averages 60 hours, and the pressure to increase sales and profits is intense. When Quinn is working on specific goals, such as reducing inventory losses or preparing the store for a major sales event, 16-hour days become routine. If his store fails to achieve the profit margin established by the company, he faces the prospect of demotion. Two of his friends who were promoted to manager about the same time he was have already been demoted. "The bottom line is, if you don't keep performing, you don't last," Quinn says. But he is optimistic about his future. In the next two or three years he hopes to be managing a Wal-Mart supercenter and thinks he has a chance of becoming a district manager before the age of 30.[1]

Michael Quinn has chosen a career path that requires many sacrifices. He has very little time to spend with his wife, parents, and friends, and almost no time for leisure activities. What motivates him to thrive on the daily stress that comes with a front-line position in the fiercely competitive retail field? Is it the prestige that comes with the position, or is it the very attractive salary? Is it the opportunity to provide leadership to 200 associates, or is it his devotion to Wal-Mart Stores Incorporated—one of America's most successful companies? Questions about what motivates people are not easily answered because each individual differs so much in values, attitudes, and needs. ■

Learning what motivates you can be an essential part of knowing yourself. This process is possible once you understand your value priorities (Chapter 5) and have a clear understanding of how your attitudes affect your behavior (Chapter 6). The information on motivation presented in this chapter will help you gain some useful insights into your personal needs.

The material in this chapter also contributes to the development of your human relations skills. Knowing what motivates other people is basic to establishing and maintaining effective relationships with them.[2] This chapter also examines why management is so concerned with understanding the factors that motivate employees. Because productivity and profitability are crucial to the success of any organization, employees must be motivated to do their very best.

THE COMPLEX NATURE OF MOTIVATION

People are motivated by many different kinds of needs. They have basic needs for food, clothing, and shelter, but they also need acceptance, recognition, and self-esteem. Each individual experiences these needs in different ways and to

What motivates this stunt man to risk his life on top of Norway's Prekestolen Rock? We may never know the answer. Human motivation is very complex. (Gamma Liaison)

varying degrees. To complicate matters more, people are motivated by different needs at different times in their lives. Adults, like children and adolescents, continue to develop and change in significant ways throughout life. Patterns of adult development have been described in such important books as *Passages and Pathfinders,* by Gail Sheehy, and *Seasons of a Man's Life,* by Daniel Levinson. No one approach to motivation works for all people or for the same person all the time.

Motivation Defined

Motivation can be defined as the reason people do what they do.[3] It is an internal drive that encourages us to achieve a particular goal. In a work setting, this definition may suggest that all motivation is the result of the internal

Total Person Insight

"What motivates people? No question about human behavior is more frequently asked or more perplexing to answer. Yet knowing what motivates another person is basic to establishing and maintaining effective relations with others."

D. R. SPITZER

Consultant; Author, "30 Ways to Motivate Employees to Perform Better"

rewards a person receives while performing the job. But motivation at work can be triggered by rewards that occur apart from the job itself. These rewards are referred to as "external motivators." Motivation, then, is two-dimensional; it can be internal or external.

Internal motivation comes from the satisfaction that occurs when a duty or task is performed. If a nurse enjoys caring for a patient, the activity itself is rewarding and the nurse will be self-motivated. Psychologist Frederick Herzberg has said that motivation comes from an internal stimulus resulting from job content, not job environment. He has suggested that jobs be enriched to provide challenge, opportunity for achievement, and individual growth.[4] These intrinsic rewards motivate some people more than money, trophies for outstanding performance, or other similar external rewards.

External motivation is an action taken by another person. It usually involves the anticipation of a reward of some kind. Typical external rewards in a work setting include money, feedback regarding performance, and awards. Some organizations are using **incentives** to encourage workers to develop good work habits and to repeat behavior that is beneficial to themselves and the organization. An incentive can take the form of additional money, time off from work, or some other type of reward.

External rewards are rarely enough to motivate people on a continuing basis. Ideally, an organization will provide an appropriate number of external rewards while permitting employees to experience the ongoing, internal satisfaction that comes from a challenging job.

The Motivational Cycle

The **motivational cycle** describes how individuals go about satisfying a felt need. If your need is strong enough, such as acute hunger or thirst, you will be unable to concentrate on anything else until that need has been taken care of. Mahatma Gandhi reportedly said, "Not even God can talk to a hungry man."

There are five steps in the motivational cycle (see Figure 7.1). The presence of a sufficiently strong need (step one) creates tension (step two), which in turn makes a person take action to satisfy the need (step three.) Once the goal has been achieved (step four), there is a sense of satisfaction and reduction in tension (step five). For example, suppose you have a report due in two weeks, one that others are counting on to help them make a crucial decision. The tension builds, and your activities become focused on completing the report—your highest-felt need at the time. You may work evenings and weekends, turning down invitations to go out with friends. After several days of hard work, you achieve your goal: The report is finished. You experience an enormous sense of relief from the tension that has kept you at the job. Now you are free to relax and satisfy your other needs.

Characteristics of Motives

Motivators, commonly referred to as motives, prompt us to act in certain ways. Motives have been described as the "why" of human behavior. An

FIGURE 7.1

Steps in the Motivational Cycle

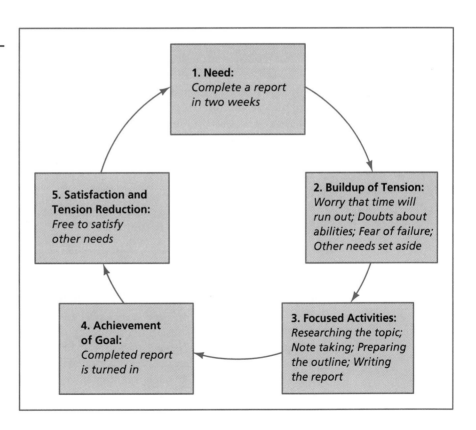

understanding of the following five characteristics of motives can be helpful as you seek to understand what motivates you, as well as what motivates others.[5]

Motives Are Individualistic   People have different needs. What satisfies one person's needs, therefore, may not satisfy anyone else's. This variation in individual motives often leads to a breakdown in human relationships unless individuals take the time to understand the motives of their colleagues.

Motives Change   As noted at the beginning of this chapter, motives change throughout our lives. What motivates us early in our careers may not motivate us later on. A moderate salary and opportunity for rapid advancement within the organization might motivate you to accept your first job. Many years later, however, you may experience the familiar midlife crisis and may be strongly motivated by cash bonuses that allow you to buy the things you never had while raising your family.

Motives May Be Unconscious   In most cases, we are not fully aware of the inner needs and drives that influence our behavior. The desire to win the "Employee of the Month" award may be triggered by unconscious feelings of inadequacy or the desire for increased recognition.

Motives Are Often Inferred   We can observe the behavior of another person, but we can only infer (draw conclusions about) what motives caused that behavior. The motives underlying our own behavior and the behavior of others are often difficult to understand.

Motives Are Hierarchical   Motives for behavior vary in levels of importance. When contradictory motives exist, the more important motive usually guides behavior. Workers often leave jobs that are secure to satisfy the need for work that is more challenging and rewarding.

INFLUENTIAL MOTIVATION THEORIES

The work of various psychologists and social scientists has added greatly to the knowledge of what motivates people and how motivation works. The basic problem, as many leaders admit, is knowing how to apply that knowledge in the workplace. Although many theories of motivation have emerged over the years, we will discuss only those that have become quite influential.

Thinking / Learning Starters

1. Look over Figure 7.1 and apply the motivational cycle to your own experience as you progressed toward accomplishing a goal. Choose an example from work or school, and fill in the steps.

    Need

    Buildup of tension

    Focused activities

    Achievement of goal

    Satisfaction and tension reduction

2. What needs have been competing for your attention lately? List them; then rank them in their order of importance, with number one representing your top priority. Is there anything you can do to ensure that your top priority needs are satisfied?

Maslow's Hierarchy of Needs

According to Abraham Maslow, a noted psychologist, people tend to satisfy their needs in a particular order—a theory he calls the "hierarchy of needs."[6] Maslow's theory rests on three assumptions: (1) People have a number of needs that require some measure of satisfaction. (2) Only unsatisfied needs motivate behavior. (3) The needs of people are arranged in a hierarchy of pre-potency, which means that as each lower-level need is satisfied, the need at the next level demands attention.[7] Basically, human beings are motivated to satisfy physiological needs first (food, clothing, shelter); then the need for safety and security; then social needs; then esteem needs; and, finally, self-actualization needs, or the need to realize their potential. Maslow's theory is illustrated in Figure 7.2. This theory can easily be applied to motivation on the job.

Physiological Needs The needs for food, clothing, sleep, and shelter, or **physiological needs,** were described by Maslow as survival or lower-order needs. When the economy is strong and most people have jobs, these basic needs rarely dominate because they are reasonably well satisfied. But, needless to say, people who cannot ensure their own and their family's survival, or are homeless, place this basic need at the top of their priority list.

Safety and Security Needs People's desire for order and predictability in life is reflected in **safety and security needs.** Safety needs usually focus on

FIGURE 7.2

Maslow's Hierarchy of
Needs

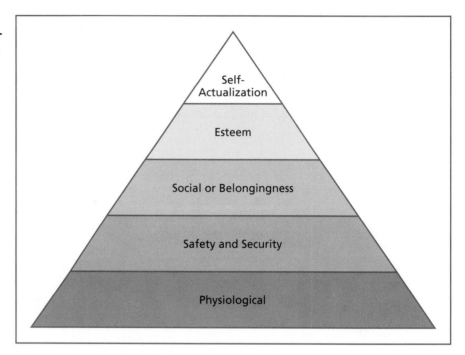

protection from physical harm. On the job, this means a guarantee of safe
working conditions. Unions or employee groups can make sure employers
maintain safety standards and reduce the risk of accidents or injuries resulting
from environmental hazards. Congress established the Occupational Safety and
Health Administration (OSHA) to help reduce deaths and injuries on the job.
Although this agency has had a positive impact on the problem, thousands of
workers die on the job or from work-related diseases each year, and several
million are injured.

But a person's need for safety and security is not limited to freedom from violence or injury. People have to know that they can provide for their families
and that they will have enough money and resources to take care of themselves
in sickness or old age. Mergers, buyouts, business closings, and downsizing efforts can create a feeling of insecurity among workers.

Social or Belongingness Needs   Whereas the first two types of needs deal
with aspects of physical survival, **social or belongingness needs** deal with
emotional and mental well-being. Research has shown that fulfillment of needs
for affection, for a sense of belonging, and for identification with a group are
as important to people's health as are food and safety. Although social needs
are felt throughout childhood, they may become more intense during adolescence, when the need to belong to a group becomes more important than
family ties or what parents think. In adults, the need for belonging may surface

Air-traffic controller and amateur pilot Scott Coleman receives personal satisfaction from volunteering his spare time, airplane operating costs, and fuel to fly seriously ill children to hospitals in the Boston area for vital medical tests and treatment. This type of activity could lead Scott toward achieving self-actualization, the ultimate motivational factor identified by Maslow (People Weekly © 1996 David Binder).

as a desire to join various organizations—professional associations, church groups, amateur sports teams, or social clubs. There are two major aspects of the need to belong: frequent, positive interactions with the same people and a framework of stable, long-term caring and concern.[8]

Esteem Needs   As discussed in Chapter 4, *self-esteem* is a term that describes how you feel about yourself. Self-esteem influences work behaviors and attitudes in two fundamental ways. First, employees bring to their work settings different levels of self-esteem, which in turn influence how they act, feel, and think while on the job. Second, individuals need to feel good about themselves; thus, much of what workers do and believe can serve to enhance, preserve, or restore their self-esteem. **Esteem needs** relate to a person's self-respect and to the recognition and respect he or she receives from others. Several esteem-building initiatives are discussed in this chapter.

Self-Actualization Needs   The four needs just described motivate people by their *absence*—that is, when people feel a lack of food and shelter, security, social relationships, or esteem. **Self-actualization needs,** however, represent the need for growth, and they motivate people by their *presence*. Self-actualization is people fulfilling their potential or realizing their fullest capacities as human beings.

Maslow used *self-actualization* in a very specialized sense to describe a rarely attained state of human achievement. Because of the uniqueness of each person, the form or content of self-actualization is an individual matter.[9] Most of us probably will not reach self-actualization in Maslow's sense of the term, but we do make steps toward it when we seek to expand ourselves by setting new goals and finding new means of expression. Table 7.1 summarizes some ways of satisfying self-actualization and other needs in the work situation.

Thinking / Learning Starters

1. Re-examine the "needs priority list" you created for the previous Thinking/Learning Starters. Consider Maslow's basic concept: People will satisfy their needs systematically, moving from physiological needs, to safety and security needs, to social needs, to esteem needs, and finally to self-actualization. How do the priorities on your list compare with this hierarchy?

2. What opportunities do you have to satisfy more than one of your needs at a time? Can you recall an occasion when you achieved self-actualization?

Maslow's Theory Reconsidered

Although Maslow's theory has helped us understand human behavior, his hierarchical arrangement of needs should not be accepted too literally. Human beings are motivated at any one time by a complex array of needs and may satisfy several of them through one activity. One familiar example is the business lunch. Not only are you conducting business with a client, but you are also satisfying your need to eat and drink, to engage in social activities, and perhaps to feel important in your own eyes and, you hope, the eyes of your client.

People will sacrifice lower-order needs to satisfy higher-order needs if the drive is strong enough. When individuals take up a dangerous sport such as skydiving or mountain climbing, they are placing self-actualization needs over security or safety needs. Or a young lawyer may decide to open a store-front office to serve the poor rather than enter the security of an established law firm. Despite these reservations, Maslow's contribution to the theory of motivation remains a landmark in the field.

TABLE 7.1

Ways of Satisfying
Individual Needs in
the Work Situation

Need	Organizational Conditions
Physiological	Pay Breakfast or lunch programs Company housing
Safety and security	Company benefits plans Pensions Seniority Pay
Social or belongingness	Coffee breaks Sports teams Company picnics and social events Work teams
Esteem	Recognition of work well done Responsibility Pay (as symbol of status) Prestigious office location and furnishings
Self-actualization	Challenge Autonomy

Source: Adapted from Judith Gordon, *A Diagnostic Approach to Organizational Behavior,* 3d ed. (Boston: Allyn and Bacon, 1991), p. 144.

Herzberg's Motivation-Maintenance Theory

Psychologist Frederick Herzberg proposes another motivation theory called the **motivation-maintenance theory.**[10]

Maintenance factors represent the basic things people consider essential to any job, such as salaries, fringe benefits, working conditions, social relationships, supervision, and organizational policies and administration. We often take such things for granted as part of the job. These basic maintenance factors do not act as motivators, according to Herzberg; but if any of them is absent, the organizational climate that results can hurt employee morale and lower worker productivity. Health insurance, for example, generally does not motivate employees to be more productive, but the loss of it can cause workers to look for employment in another organization that provides the desired coverage.

Motivational factors are benefits above and beyond the basic elements of a job. These benefits tend to increase employee satisfaction—employees like to feel they are getting something beyond a paycheck for their time and effort at work. Herzberg's list of motivational factors parallels, to some degree, Maslow's higher-order needs (see Table 7.2). It includes work itself, achievement, responsibility, recognition, and opportunities for advancement. When these factors are present, they tend to motivate employees to achieve higher production levels, to feel more committed to their jobs, and to find creative ways to accomplish both personal and organizational goals.

Herzberg theorizes that if employees' motivational factors are not met, they may begin to ask for more maintenance factors, such as increased salaries and fringe benefits, better working conditions, or more liberal company policies regarding sick leave or vacation time. Critics of Herzberg's theory have pointed

TABLE 7.2

Comparison of the
Maslow and Herzberg
Theories

	Maslow	Herzberg
Motivational factors	Self-actualization	Work itself Achievement Responsibility
	Esteem needs	Recognition Advancement Status
Maintenance factors	Social or belongingness needs	Social network Supervision
	Safety and security needs	Company policy and administration
	Physiological needs	Job security Working conditions Salary

out that he assumes that most, if not all, individuals are motivated only by higher-order needs such as recognition or increased responsibility, and that they seek jobs that are challenging and meaningful. His theory does not acknowledge that some people may prefer more routine, predictable work and may be motivated more by the security of a regular paycheck (a maintenance factor) than by the prospect of advancement.

McGregor's Theory X and Theory Y

In most organizations, day-to-day operations are significantly influenced by the relationship between workers and managers. Douglas McGregor, management consultant and author, accepted the concept of a needs hierarchy but felt that management had failed to do so.[11] In his influential book *The Human Side of Enterprise,* he outlines a set of assumptions that he says influence the thinking of most managers. He divides these assumptions into two categories: Theory X and Theory Y.

Theory X: A Pessimistic View **Theory X** represents a pessimistic view of human nature. According to this theory, people do not really want to work—they have to be pushed, closely supervised, and prodded into doing things, either with incentives such as pay or with punishments for not working.[12] Because they have little or no ambition, workers prefer to avoid responsibility and do only as much work as they have to. The general belief of management under this theory is that workers are paid to do a good job and management's function is to supervise the work and correct employees if they go off course.

Theory Y: An Optimistic View **Theory Y** reflects an optimistic view of human behavior. According to this theory, work is as natural to people as play or rest. People are capable of self-direction and can learn to both accept and seek responsibility if they are committed to the objectives of the organization. Another Theory Y assumption is that people will become committed to organizational objectives if they are rewarded for doing so.[13]

A healthy, mutually supportive relationship based on trust, openness, and respect can create a work climate in which employees want to give more of themselves. Goethe, German poet and philosopher, may have said it best: "Trust people as if they were what ought to be and you help them become what they are capable of being."

Theory X Versus Theory Y—The Debate Continues

Although Theory X and Theory Y were proposed years ago, the debate concerning which theory is valid continues. Thomas Stewart describes this debate as "The never-ending war for a manager's soul."[14] When an organization initiates a re-engineering effort (described in Chapter 1 as a radical approach to improving performance), you are likely to see a top-down, management-driven change process. Front-line employees are not likely to be involved in decision making, nor are they viewed as important company assets. On the other hand, many organizations have embraced Theory Y and have been rewarded with major performance gains. One example is Beth Israel–Deaconess Medical Center, a Boston-based employer of 8,000 people. Over the years it has created a high-trust environment by helping employees understand all aspects of the business, guaranteeing opportunities to participate in solving problems, and sharing gains when the organization succeeds.[15]

EXPECTATIONS INFLUENCE MOTIVATION

George Bernard Shaw, the noted British playwright, said, "Our lives are shaped not as much by our experience, as by our expectations." As we noted in Chapter 4, people tend to behave in ways that support their own ideas of how successful or unsuccessful they will be in certain endeavors. This somewhat mysterious power of expectations, often referred to as the **self-fulfilling prophecy,** is at the very heart of motivation. Self-fulfilling prophecies reflect a connection between your expectations for yourself and your resulting behavior. Let's assume that you want to lose a pound a week by following an exercise program and limiting your calorie intake. The success of this plan depends, in large part, on your belief that it will work. This belief might be influenced by your past experiences. However, encouragement of friends or a respected doctor who tells you, "If you follow this plan, I am sure you will lose weight," can help a great deal.

The Expectations of Others

Much research has confirmed that people tend to act in ways that are consistent with what others expect of them. The premise that there is a relationship between a person's level of motivation and the expectations of others has been extensively investigated by Robert Rosenthal and J. Sterling Livingston, professors at Harvard University. This theory has been applied in such diverse fields as education, sales, medicine, and manufacturing.

Item: In the classic study *Pygmalion in the Classroom,* Rosenthal described the effect of teachers' expectations of students' performance. The results of his research were astounding. When teachers had high expectations for certain students (those they had been led to believe had excellent intellectual ability and learning capacity), those students learned at a faster rate than other students in the same group—even though the teachers did not consciously treat the former students differently. These teachers unintentionally communicated their high expectations to the students they *thought* possessed strong intellectual abilities.[16]

Item: Research conducted by J. Sterling Livingston showed that sales managers' expectations can have a positive impact on sales productivity. When a group of "average producers" at Metropolitan Life Insurance Company were assigned to a district manager with high expectations, the salespeople accepted the challenge and outperformed another group of salespeople who had above-average performance records. In discussions with the group identified as "average salespeople," the district manager insisted that they had the ability to outperform the "supergroup." She did not permit them to think of themselves as "average" salespeople.[17]

This research, of course, has important implications for people who work in supervisory-management positions. Rosenthal said that forming expectations of the employees you supervise is unavoidable and that high expectations lead to high performance.[18]

CONTEMPORARY EMPLOYEE MOTIVATION STRATEGIES

The search for better ways to motivate employees has taken on a new level of importance. The rise of international competition, the growing demand for quality products and services, and the growing realization that technical solutions will not make a difference unless people are motivated to do their best have prompted organizations to seek more effective employee motivation strategies. After a decade of downsizing accompanied by massive layoffs, survivors have less reason to trust their employer. Employee loyalty has declined at many organizations. We will examine several motivation strategies that have merit even during times of great uncertainty.

Motivation Through Job Design

We have noted that today's workers place a high value on jobs that provide rewards such as a sense of achievement, challenge, variety, and personal growth. It is possible to redesign existing jobs so they will have characteristics or outcomes that are intrinsically satisfying to employees. There are at least three design options.[19]

Job Rotation **Job rotation** involves allowing employees to move through a variety of jobs, departments, or functions. Employees are encouraged to alternate tasks—two, three, or more—in a predefined way over a period of time. For example, a worker might attach a wheel assembly one week, inspect it the

At Compaq, "cell manufacturing" is used along with the traditional assembly line for producing many Compaq computers. This approach allows cell workers to build, test, and ship individual computers and make changes as they see necessary. Employees in these unique workstations have increased their output by 23 percent and product quality by 25 percent. (Chris Usher)

next, and organize the parts for assembly during the third week. Job rotation facilitates career advancement by cross-training workers, and it also allows management a hedge against absenteeism. In those cases where the job is highly repetitive, job rotation can reduce boredom.

Job Enlargement   **Job enlargement** means expanding an employee's duties or responsibilities. When a job becomes stale, motivation can often be increased by encouraging employees to learn new skills or take on new responsibilities. An administrative assistant may learn how to draft budgets, develop company manuals, or prepare spreadsheets; a manager may learn how to deliver training to employees in several departments. Lands' End, the mail order company, has developed a "job share" arrangement in which telephone sales representatives take one-day leaves to work in another area of the company. One person leaves the sales desk each Thursday to work in the returns department. Another employee works one day a week setting up product shots in the catalog photo shop. Employees enjoy the new challenges, and the company benefits by having employees who are trained in several facets of work. During busy periods these employees can fill strategic gaps.[20]

Job Enrichment   **Job enrichment** is an attempt to make jobs more desirable or satisfying, thereby triggering internal motivation. One approach assigns new and more difficult tasks to employees; another grants them additional author-

© 1993, Washington Post Writers Group. Reprinted with permission.

ity. The Ritz-Carlton Hotel Co. has used this job-enrichment strategy with great success. Its employees are authorized to handle customer complaints and solve problems without involving management.[21] Job-enrichment efforts recognize that many of today's workers value intrinsic rewards such as achievement, personal growth, and challenge.

Motivation Through Incentives

Incentives are often used to improve quality, reduce accidents, increase sales, improve attendance, and speed up production. Organizations frequently use some form of incentive to drive results. At Ohio-based Lincoln Electric Company, a piecework pay plan, coupled with a bonus, has been very successful. The company, which manufactures arc-welding products and industrial electrical motors, has not had a losing quarter since 1935 and has not laid off any workers at its U.S. operations in the 100 years of its existence.[22] Incentives and rewards are discussed in more detail in Chapter 10.

Many companies are experimenting with programs that reward the development of new ideas. These programs, known as **intrapreneurship,** encourage employees to pursue their ideas at work, with the company providing the money, equipment, and time to do so. For example, 3M Company permits employees to spend 15 percent of company time experimenting with their own ideas. This practice resulted in the development of Post-it Notes. Inventors at Texas Instruments who receive patents on their new product ideas can earn up to $175,000 in cash bonuses. Monsanto awards outstanding employees $50,000 for "significant life-time achievements." IBM annually awards approximately forty "Outstanding Innovation Awards" ranging from $2,500 to $25,000.[23]

Training and Education

Learning opportunities, both on and off the job, can be a strong motivational force. Employees realize that education and training are critical to individual growth and opportunity. Rosabeth Moss Kanter says, "The chance to learn new skills or apply them in new arenas is an important motivator in a turbulent environment because it's oriented toward securing the future."[24] Of course, employees will be more motivated to participate in training programs if they perceive that such participation will lead to salary increases, advancement, or more challenging work.

Organizations with 100 or more employees budget about $60 billion each year for formal training.[25] Many of these companies are using advanced communications technology to deliver instruction. Digital Equipment Corporation maintains its curriculum catalog on the World Wide Web. Employees located anywhere in the world have instant access to information on training opportunities. The Web enables Digital to offer self-paced courses that employees can access from their personal computer.[26]

Motivation Through Empowerment

Max DePree, retired CEO of Herman Miller, Inc., an office furniture company, and author of *Leadership Is an Art,* says the job of a manager is not to supervise or to motivate but to liberate and enable. He states that "most people come to work well prepared, well motivated, and wanting to reach their potential."[27] **Empowerment** means those efforts made to move authority and responsibility to the lowest ranks of the organization. The results of these efforts, according to the views of DePree and others, is to give workers a feeling of pride, self-expression, and ownership.

Empowerment as a motivation strategy is based on the premise that workers want challenge and personal meaning from their jobs. It also recognizes that lower-level employees often possess critical information about how to improve products and processes and better meet customer needs. Rowe Furniture Company, a Virginia-based manufacturer, saw productivity increase dramatically after

---

Total Person Insight

"You can get everything in life you want, if you help enough other people get what they want."

ZIG ZIGLAR

Author and Motivational Speaker

workers took over production scheduling and problem solving.[28] At a Xerox site in Dallas, 320 employees were allowed to arrange their own work schedule. Through group decisions, the flextime arrangements worked very well. Absenteeism dropped by 30 percent, and creativity increased.[29] Although empowerment efforts are growing in popularity, this motivational strategy should not be viewed as a quick fix. Empowerment calls for more than lip service by top management. It requires long-term commitment and resources. If often takes several years for employees to place full trust in managers who initiate an empowerment program.

Thinking / Learning Starters

1. In places where you have worked, would you say the managers believed in Theory X or Theory Y? Give specific examples to support your answer.

2. What types of incentives and rewards will motivate you? Money in the form of a year-end bonus? Recognition in front of your peers? A prize, such as a new car or a trip? Do you believe the factors that motivate you will change as you grow older? How?

SELF-MOTIVATION STRATEGIES

The material presented in this chapter helps make a strong case for the study of self-motivation strategies. Some supervisors and managers have a pessimistic view of human nature and are guided by a Theory X philosophy. Although some organizations understand how motivation power can be increased through job design, others seem unwilling or unable to implement creative job-design options. Many dull, routine jobs still exist. Long hours, stressful work, and too little leisure time can dampen the spirits of even the most dedicated worker who is performing interesting tasks. If you suddenly experience a layoff or demotion, you must be able to bounce back and move on with your life. The same is true for entrepreneurs, who are their own boss on a daily basis. They know that their livelihood depends on their ability to motivate themselves. The self-motivation strategies presented here can serve as valuable guidelines throughout your career.

Take control of your expectations. We have already noted the connection between your expectations for yourself and your resulting behavior. Dan Millman, in his book *The Laws of Spirit,* encourages us to frequently examine our beliefs and assumptions and replace self-defeating doubts with new beliefs based on clear intention. He reminds us that energy follows thought and that what we focus on will grow and develop. When we focus our attention on what is possible, our motivation power increases.[30]

Fight the urge to underachieve.   Many people do not achieve their full potential because they are afraid to venture outside their "comfort zone." These individuals often earn less than they deserve, exert little effort to win a promotion to a more challenging position, and refuse assignments that might enhance their career. Some people stay in their comfort zone because they fear success. This fear can stem from a variety of sources such as low self-esteem or family upbringing.[31]

How do you fight the urge to underachieve? A good starting point is to reflect on messages you received from family and friends while growing up. Did they resent people who experienced career success or were wealthy? Did they tell you to let other children win at games or various contests, because otherwise no one would like you? Do you see how a "fear of success" pattern might develop? Next, learn to showcase your abilities. This might involve volunteering to work on a new project that will allow you to demonstrate your skills. Finally, learn how to sell yourself to people who make decisions about your earnings and your advancement. Don't be afraid to toot your own horn.[32]

Learn to love the job you hate.   Most people start a new job with some degree of enthusiasm and dedication. Then, with the passing of time, job satisfaction decreases. The work may become routine, or the addition of new duties may result in greater stress. Janice Boucher, author of *How to Love the Job You Hate,* says it's possible to recapture your love for a job gone bad.[33] One approach is to redesign your job so that it offers more challenge, more variety, or less stress. Can you delegate to someone else some task that you do not like to do? Can you develop a special project that will give your job greater meaning? Can you do things that make you feel good about yourself and your job? For example, a supermarket cashier might begin to pay genuine attention to customers in order to improve service and learn more about their needs. A newspaper reporter who is being pressured to emphasize sensationalism when writing news stories might establish higher standards for truth in reporting. With some determination, you can make a job more personally meaningful.[34]

Build immunity to cynicism.   In Chapter 6 we described cynicism as a destructive thinking pattern. Ohio State University professor John Wanous states that employees grow cynical when employers make mistakes. These problems are magnified in the mind of the employee when employers are not open and honest. Unfortunately, a cynical attitude toward one aspect of company operations tends to color an employee's beliefs about all aspects of the company. To build immunity to cynicism, you must first maintain an open mind and avoid the temptation to blame management for every real or perceived problem. Take time to learn about the reasons for changes being made, and try to separate fact from fiction. Remember, the grapevine can be a source of accurate *and* inaccurate information. In most cases, bad news gets more attention than good news.

Strive for balance. Motivation often decreases when we no longer have a sense of balance in our life. Recent research has found that many employees are not being treated with respect or afforded dignity as "whole" people who have lives away from the job.[35] Conflicts between work and personal life surface when employees are ordered to work overtime on short notice, are required to change schedules abruptly, are required to travel away from home on business for long periods of time, or are denied requests for time off.[36]

To achieve balance, take time to reflect on what is most important in your life, and then try to make the necessary adjustments. Employees at Miller & Associates, a Dallas wholesaler of kitchen equipment, complete annual "life-purpose" statements. Each person records the ten most satisfying experiences in his or her life, making note of those that carry special meaning. This exercise is designed to promote self-awareness and guide the employee in setting annual goals. When David Rogers, a salesperson, finished his "life-purpose" statements, he realized that he wasn't taking time to do some of the things he most valued. He said, "I was so weighted toward work that it was getting in the way of work." Once he cut back on his hours, freeing up time for his social life, his sales actually increased.[37]

A FINAL COMMENT

Although there are many keys to success in your personal and professional life, self-motivation stands out as a major ingredient. Zig Ziglar, the noted author and speaker, says self-motivation is an ongoing process: "We need to continue to make choices about what level of self-motivation we want to maintain."[38]

Summary

Motivation is a major component of human relations training because it provides a framework for understanding why people do the things they do. In a work setting, it is what makes people want to work. Internal motivation occurs when the task or duty performed is in itself a reward. External motivation is initiated by another person and usually is based on rewards or other forms of reinforcement for a job well done. Most authorities on motivation recommend that organizations attempt to provide their employees with a mix of external rewards and internal satisfaction.

People are motivated by different needs. The motivational cycle describes the steps an individual goes through in satisfying a felt need. Motives are individualistic and can change over the years. Because there is no valid measure of a person's motives, motives can only be inferred. Motives vary in strength and importance and are therefore hierarchical. Maslow's hierarchy of needs theory states that physiological needs will come first, followed by safety and security, social, esteem, and then self-actualization needs. According to Maslow, although any need can be a motivator, only higher-order needs will motivate people over the long run. Herzberg's motivation-maintenance theory contends that when motivational factors such as responsibility, recognition, and opportunity for advancement are not present, employees will demand improvement in maintenance factors, such as higher salaries, more benefits, and better working conditions.

Managers must accomplish their goals through and with other people, and they are primarily responsible for motivating their subordinates. McGregor's Theory X and Theory Y reflect a pessimistic and an optimistic view of human behavior, respectively. Theory X managers believe that employees do not really want to work and can be motivated to do so only through close supervision and the threat of punishment. Theory Y managers attempt to understand what truly motivates employees and to give them due respect and consideration.

Personal expectations, as well as the expectations of others, have a powerful influence on a person's motivation. These expectations can become self-fulfilling prophecies. Managers can motivate employees by expressing belief in their abilities and talents.

Contemporary organizations attempt to motivate their employees through job-design modifications such as job rotation, job enlargement, and job enrichment. They are also discovering the effects of various incentives, intrapreneurship opportunities, additional training, and empowerment.

Often, however, people must make their own plan to keep themselves motivated. They need to control their expectations, strive to achieve regardless of past failures, learn to love the job they hate, avoid cynicism, and strive for a balance between their professional and personal lives.

Career Corner

Q. I am a member of a research team in a major pharmaceutical company. We are paid to create new and more effective drugs for our organization. Every time we have a "winner," the executives of the division receive large cash bonuses, the salespeople earn dramatically improved commissions, but we get just a pat on the back. I would like to quit my job, but I love it too much. What would you suggest?

A. To retain technical employees, many organizations are reviewing the way they reward and recognize them. One of the most effective strategies is the payment of royalties to the creators of successful new products. The Federal Technology Transfer Act of 1986 requires employee-inventors working on federally funded research projects to be rewarded with a royalty of at least 15 percent of any licensing income the project generates. Battelle Pacific Northwest Laboratory in Richland, Washington, uses both government and private research funds. Ten percent of the sales of "intellectual property" are set aside for key research personnel at Battelle to use as they see fit. Some technical employees are not motivated by cash and prefer to purchase updated equipment for their laboratories. Talk with your human resources division and suggest these ideas.

Key Terms

motivation
internal motivation
external motivation
incentives
motivational cycle
physiological needs
safety and security needs
social or belongingness needs
esteem needs
self-actualization needs
motivation-maintenance theory

maintenance factors
motivational factors
Theory X
Theory Y
self-fulfilling prophecy
job rotation
job enlargement
job enrichment
intrapreneurship
empowerment

Review Questions

1. Based on what you have read in this chapter, how would you define *motivation?*
2. Why is the motivational cycle activated only by a felt need? List the steps in the cycle.
3. Describe the difference between external and internal motivations and give examples.
4. Describe the needs present in Maslow's hierarchy. How do organizations attempt to meet these needs?
5. Who is the best judge of what is and what is not a motivating factor for employees? Explain.
6. Explain Herzberg's motivation-maintenance theory.
7. Describe McGregor's Theory X and Theory Y. What are the positives and negatives of each approach?
8. Identify the various ways a job can be redesigned to motivate an employee.
9. How might empowering employees with authority and responsibility affect their job performance? In what ways will this empowerment affect their human relations skills?
10. Identify five ways to motivate yourself.

Application Exercises

1. This chapter describes the following contemporary employee motivational strategies:
   a. job rotation
   b. job enlargement
   c. job enrichment
   d. intrapreneurial incentives
   e. training and education
   f. incentives
   g. intrapreneurship
   h. empowerment

To gain practice in identifying what motivates other people, select two people you think you know well, and write their names on a piece of paper. From the list above, choose three factors you believe would motivate each of these people at work. Then ask the same two people what really would motivate them to do their best. Did you accurately judge their motives? Explain. How might developing this skill of identifying others' motivating factors help you improve your human relations on the job?

2. What do you think it would be like to work for a company that embraces McGregor's Theory Y? Would this view of human behavior result in greater teamwork? Would it be easier to create a climate of trust? Would this view of human behavior help you be a more motivated person? Discuss your views with the rest of the class.

3. Self-motivation can begin with a review of the satisfying experiences in your life. List ten "life-purpose" statements on a piece of paper. Each statement should describe a satisfying experience in your life. An example might be, "I enjoy hiking trips with my friends." Once the list is complete, make note of the top three most satisfying experiences—those that have special meaning. Then answer two questions: Where can I find time to do the things that are most satisfying? How can I develop a self-motivation plan that focuses on the most important priorities in my life?

Internet Exercise

 Today's workers place a high value on jobs that provide rewards such as a sense of achievement, challenge, variety, and personal growth. Many organizations are attempting to design or redesign jobs so they will encompass features that provide employees with internal satisfaction. Visit the Internet, and study the information on motivation through job design. Using your search engine, type in "job design" and then review the resources (such as books, articles, and training programs) available. Examine the resources, and prepare a brief summary of your findings. Within your report, include job-design elements that would appeal to you.

Case 7.1   The Shift Toward Empowerment

The Federal Commission on the Future of Worker-Management Relations was assigned the task of exploring ways employee involvement could be increased in the workplace. The commission found that up to one-third of the workplaces now use employee participation in some form and that another 50 million workers would like to have more say about their jobs. Companies that have involved their employees in traditional management responsibilities show a clear pattern of high productivity and improved economic performance. Here are two examples.

Several years ago Chesapeake Packaging Corporation, a 145-employee corrugated-container manufacturer in Baltimore, was embroiled in a potential financial disaster. Management decided that one way to involve the employees in solving the problem was to open the books and ask for suggestions on how to improve profits. One suggestion was to carefully monitor who was hired, retained, and fired. Now every job applicant goes through a series of job-related tests, is interviewed by a four-employee panel, and is subject to a peer review every ninety days for the first year. Fellow workers determine whether new employees are taking their jobs seriously and contributing intellectually or are merely showing up for work and their paychecks. The panel makes the final decision on which new employees become part of the regular work force.

At Nucor, the minimill steel maker located in Charlotte, North Carolina, 80 percent of the employees are hourly wage earners organized into teams. Management believes in consistent employment, no matter what, and focuses on creative solutions when there is a downturn. For example, team members are encouraged to pretend they own their own franchise. They are totally in charge of completing their tasks as efficiently and effectively as possible. Nucor's bonus system allows employees to boost their pay to as much as three times the industry average, based on their team's productivity. Employees who are tardy lose their bonus for that day; those who are more than an hour late or who miss a day of work lose their bonus for the week. If one member of the team is not pulling his or her weight, team members work together to solve the problem quickly so that the team can get back on track.

Questions

1. How would you feel about the power of the peer-review panel if you were a new employee at Chesapeake Packaging? How would your opinion change if you were a member of the panel?
2. Does Nucor's bonus system enhance or inhibit teamwork? How?
3. Do you find the concept of empowerment frightening or exciting? Explain.

Case 7.2 **Different Strokes for Different Folks**

Former Labor Secretary Robert Reich believed that employees need to be regarded as potential profit centers, not as liabilities. He felt that organizations should establish goals that focus on developing the capacities of workers, enhancing their loyalty and commitment, and relying on them as a source of innovation and quality. But how can organizations motivate their diverse work force, from the lowest-level employees to the top executives, toward these goals? There is no simple answer to this question. Incentives work to a certain extent. A positive, motivational supervisor is always an asset. However, it has been discovered that if employees develop an *attitude* that prompts them to seek out opportunities to "go the extra mile," their *self-motivation* will result in success for both the individual and the organization.

Item: During the busy holiday season, a young stock boy at a specialty clothing store noticed customers with armfuls of clothes waiting in a long checkout line. He quickly pulled a rolling clothes rack parallel to the line and suggested that customers hang their items while they waited. He was not hampered by an "it's-not-my-job" or "it's not-my-department" attitude. No one told him what to do; he was self-motivated.

Item: Kathy Harless was asked to take on a special project to redesign GTE's Contact Center, the place where customers call to get phones installed or to make service changes. After months of meetings, gathering information, and observing all aspects of the customer contact process, Harless and her team designed a totally new approach to managing customer contact, but they knew it would involve an up-front investment of millions of dollars. Everyone agreed that telling GTE's chief executive officer that there were major problems and that the solution was going to cost millions was a career-suicide mission. But Harless stepped forward, risking her professional future, and presented her team's case. Months later, the GTE board of directors approved spending more than $1 billion to bring the plans to reality. As a result of her actions, Kathy Harless was promoted and became the first woman vice president in the history of GTE Telephone Operations.

Item: Bill Harris, chief financial officer of the Lurie Company, volunteers his professional expertise to help the Arlington Residences, a San Francisco shelter for recovering alcoholics. He states, "This is the most enjoyable work I do. I get a lot of personal satisfaction knowing that I am helping others who are not as lucky as I am, even if I don't know them or see them."

Questions

1. Each of these individuals was motivated by a different force. Can you identify the motivating factors? Explain your thoughts.
2. How can an organization instill self-motivation in its employees? What would be the advantages and disadvantages of accomplishing this goal?
3. What will motivate you to "go the extra mile" at work?

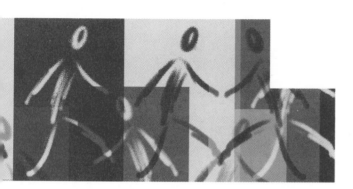

PART III

Personal Strategies for
Improving Human Relations

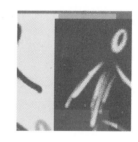

Chapter 8

Building Trust
with Constructive
Self-Disclosure

Chapter Preview

After studying this chapter, you will be able to

1. Explain how constructive self-disclosure contributes to improved interpersonal relationships and teamwork.
2. Understand the specific benefits you can gain from self-disclosure.
3. Identify and explain the major elements of the Johari Window model.
4. Explain the criteria for appropriate self-disclosure.
5. Understand the barriers to constructive self-disclosure.
6. Apply your knowledge and practice constructive self-disclosure.

O NE OF THE MORE CONTROVERSIAL employee development practices has been the introduction of an assessment approach known as 360-degree feedback. Organizations that have adopted this assessment strategy believe employees will benefit from feedback collected from several different sources. This means an employee may be evaluated not only by a supervisor but also by peers, subordinates, and sometimes even customers.[1]

Feedback often comes in the form of a completed questionnaire or inventory. This feedback—generally anonymous—usually provides some valuable insights regarding one's talents and shortcomings. An executive at Ameritech Corp. learned that his habit of making points by stabbing a person with his index finger, thumb upright, was threatening to some subordinates. A written anonymous comment from an employee said, "Don't make your hand into a gun and point at people. . . . It's very intimidating." The executive's reaction: "I wish someone had told me this thirty years ago."[2] ∎

A major goal of 360-degree feedback and other employee feedback programs is to increase self-awareness. Some people simply do not know themselves well enough. In companies that incorporate peer reviews into their 360-degree feedback effort, coworkers deliver performance reviews of one another. Peer appraisals have become quite common at companies that maintain a leaner, less hierarchical organization structure and rely more on teams. Although some employees pull punches to avoid hurting a coworker's feelings, others deliver criticism with candor. One goal of peer reviews is to give group members an opportunity to disclose feelings of frustration and to comment on others' behaviors that bother them. Another goal is to give group members a chance to boost one another's self-esteem by praising good performance.

SELF-DISCLOSURE: AN INTRODUCTION

Should the disclosure of constructive feedback be encouraged more in organizations? Although you may not fully support the use of some feedback practices, you will probably agree that much of the development and satisfaction you experience on the job is an outgrowth of open communication with coworkers and supervisors. You probably enjoy working in an environment where ideas, recommendations, and concerns can be exchanged freely. A spirit of openness often results in higher morale, greater teamwork, and increased productivity.

As a general rule, relationships grow stronger when people are willing to reveal more about themselves and their work experiences. It is a surprising but true fact of life that two people can work together for many years and never really get to know each other. In many organizations, people are encouraged to hide their true feelings. The result is often a weakening of the com-

Revealing one's thoughts, feelings, and needs to another person involves some risk, but the benefits of stronger, healthier relationships with others makes self-disclosure an important process on and off the job. (Michael A. Dwyer/Stock, Boston, Inc.)

munication process. Self-disclosure can lead to a more open and supportive environment in the workplace. This chapter focuses on constructive self-disclosure and the conditions that encourage appropriate self-disclosure in a work setting.

Self-Disclosure Defined

Self-disclosure is the process of letting another person know what you think, feel, or want. It is one of the important ways you let yourself be known by others. The primary goal of self-disclosure is to build strong and healthy interpersonal relationships.

It is important to note the difference between self-disclosure and self-description. **Self-description** involves disclosure of nonthreatening information, such as your age, your favorite food, or where you went to school. This is information that others could acquire in some way other than by your telling them. Self-disclosure, by contrast, usually involves some degree of risk. When you practice self-disclosure, you reveal private, personal information that cannot be acquired from another source. Examples include your feelings about being a member of a minority group, job security, and new policies and procedures.

The importance of self-disclosure, in contrast to self-description, is shown by the following situation. You work at a distribution center and are extremely conscious of safety. You take every precaution to avoid work-related accidents. But another employee has a much more casual attitude toward safety rules and often "forgets" to observe the proper procedures, endangering you and other workers. You can choose to disclose your feelings to this person or hide your reactions. If you stay silent, it is probably because you feel strongly about the situation and are afraid of showing those strong feelings or of failing to get your message across. In other words, either way there is risk.

Benefits Gained from Self-Disclosure

Before we discuss self-disclosure in more detail, let us examine four basic benefits you gain from openly sharing what you think, feel, or want.

1. *Increased accuracy in communication.* Self-disclosure often takes the guess-work out of the communication process. No one is a mind reader; if people conceal how they really feel, it is difficult for others to know how to respond to them appropriately. People who are frustrated by a heavy workload but mask their true feelings may never see the problem resolved. The person who is in a position to solve this problem needs to be made aware of it; he or she should not have to guess.

The accuracy of communication can often be improved if you report both facts and feelings. The other person then receives not only information but also an indication of how strongly you feel about the matter. For example, a department head might voice her concern about an increase in accidents this way: "Our accident rate is up 20 percent over last year, and to be honest, I am very concerned. Everyone must pay more attention to our safety procedures."

2. *Reduction of stress.* Sidney Jourard, a noted psychologist who wrote extensively about self-disclosure, states that too much emphasis on privacy and concealment of feelings creates stress within an individual.[3] To the extent that persons can share with others their inner thoughts and feelings, they experi-

Total Person Insight

"Almost any organization would operate more effectively with completely open and forthright employees, but absolute frankness is too much to hope for (and probably too much to bear)."

FERNANDO BARTOLOMÉ

Professor of Management, Bentley College

For Better or For Worse®   **by Lynn Johnston**

Lynn Johnston Productions, Inc. Distributed by United Feature Syndicate, Inc.

ence less stress. Constructive self-disclosure can be a very important dimension of a stress management program. Too many people keep their feelings bottled up inside, which can result in considerable inner tension.

3. *Increased self-awareness.* Chapter 1 stated that increased self-awareness should be one of the important outcomes of effective interpersonal relations. Self-awareness is the foundation on which self-development is built. To plan an effective change in yourself, you must be in touch with how you behave and how your behavior affects others. You make decisions regarding appropriate behavior based in large part on self-awareness. Once you are aware of how your behavior affects others, you can choose to change it. Self-awareness increases as you receive feedback from others.

One way to achieve increased self-awareness is to seek feedback from people who are familiar with your work habits and interpersonal skills. Jeannie Rice, manager of buildings and property information at Vanderbilt University, attended a workshop at the Center for Creative Leadership in Greensboro, North Carolina. Prior to the workshop her coworkers completed a leadership assessment questionnaire, and the results were given to Rice at the workshop. The anonymous comments from those who completed the questionnaire were quite critical of her leadership style. She was described as "demanding, blunt, critical, and opinionated." When she returned to her job, she made a special effort to meet with her staff and discuss these problem areas.[4] The use of some form of 360-degree feedback can help us understand how others view our performance at work.

The quality of feedback from others depends to a large degree on how much you practice self-disclosure. The sharing of thoughts and feelings with others often sets the stage for meaningful feedback (see Figure 8.1).

FIGURE 8.1

Self-Disclosure/Feed-
back/Self-Awareness
Cycle

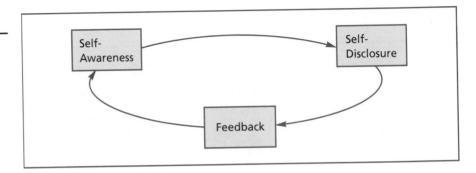

4. *Stronger relationships.* Another reward from self-disclosure is the strengthening of interpersonal relationships. When two people engage in an open, authentic dialogue, they often develop a high regard for each other's views. Often they discover they share common interests and concerns, and these serve as a foundation for a deeper relationship. John Powell, author of *Why Am I Afraid to Tell You Who I Am?* says this about the importance of openness: "Anyone who builds a relationship on less than openness and honesty is building on sand. Such a relationship will never stand the test of time, and neither party to the relationship will draw from it any noticeable benefits."[5] Of course, relationships can also be damaged by inappropriate self-disclosure. We discuss appropriate self-disclosure practices later in this chapter.

Thinking / Learning Starter

Mentally review your previous work or volunteer experience. Identify at least one occasion when you felt great frustration over some incident but avoided disclosing your feelings to the person who could have solved the problem. What factors motivated you not to self-disclose? In retrospect, do you now perceive any benefits you might have gained by choosing to self-disclose?

THE JOHARI WINDOW: A MODEL FOR SELF-UNDERSTANDING

A first step in understanding the process of self-disclosure is to look at the **Johari Window,** illustrated in Figure 8.2 (the word *Johari* is a combination of

FIGURE 8.2

Johari Window

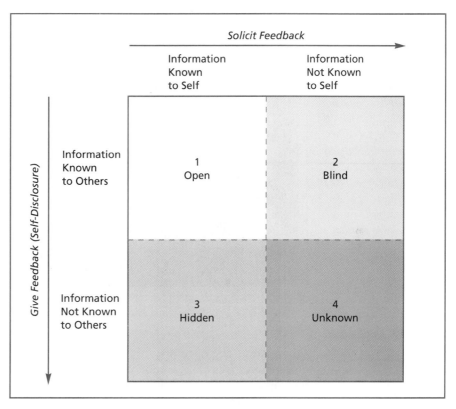

Source: Joseph Luft, *Group Processes: An Introduction to Group Dynamics.* Copyright © 1984 by Mayfield Publishing Company. Reprinted by permission of the publisher.

the first names of the model's originators: Joseph Luft and Harry Ingham). This communication model takes into consideration that there is some information you know about yourself and other information you are not yet aware of. In addition, there is some information that others know about you and some they are not aware of. Your willingness or unwillingness to engage in self-disclosure, as well as to listen to feedback from others, has a great deal to do with your understanding of yourself and with others' understanding of you.[6]

The Four Panes of the Johari Window

The Johari Window identifies four kinds of information about you that affect your communication with others. Think of the entire model as representing your total self as you relate to others. The Johari Window is divided into four panes, or areas, labeled (1) open, (2) blind, (3) hidden, and (4) unknown.[7]

One outcome of this mock job interview is greater self-awareness that comes as a result of feedback from the psychologist who is playing the role of an employer. Feedback from others can enlarge the open pane and reduce the size of the blind pane in our Johari Window. (Nicole Bengiveno/Matrix)

Open Area   The **open area** of the Johari Window represents your "public" or "awareness" area. This section contains information about you that both you and others know and includes information that you do not mind admitting about yourself. As your relationship with another person matures, the open pane gets bigger, reflecting your desire to be known.

The open pane is generally viewed as the part of the relationship that influences interpersonal productivity. Therefore, a productive interpersonal relationship is related to the amount of mutually held information. Building a relationship with another person involves working to enlarge the open area. As self-awareness and sharing of information and feelings increase, the open pane becomes larger.

Blind Area   The **blind area** consists of information about yourself that others know but you are not aware of. Others may see you as aloof and stuffy, whereas you view yourself as open and friendly. Or you may view your performance at work as mediocre, and others see it as above average. You may consider your dress and grooming practices appropriate for work, but others feel your appearance is not suitable for such a setting. Information in the blind area is acquired when you learn about people's perceptions of you.

Building a relationship and improving interpersonal effectiveness often involve working to enlarge the open pane and reduce the size of the blind pane. This can be achieved as you become more self-disclosing and thereby encourage others to disclose more of their thoughts and feelings to you (see Figure

8.1). People are more likely to give feedback to a person who is open and willing to share appropriate personal information with them.

Hidden Area The **hidden area** contains information about you that you know but others do not. This pane is made up of all those private feelings, needs, and past experiences that you prefer to keep to yourself. These could be incidents that occurred early in life or past work-related experiences you would rather not share.

You should not feel guilty about keeping some secrets. Everyone is entitled to conceal personal thoughts that are of no concern to others. Larry Bird, the former National Basketball Association superstar, once made a comment about those who wanted to probe deeply into his personal life: "You gotta be careful what you say around sportswriters because a lot of them want to find out what goes on inside you, the private you. . . . That's mine, you know."[8]

Unknown Area The **unknown area** of the Johari Window is made up of things unknown to you and others. Because you, and others, can never be known completely, this area never completely disappears. The unknown may represent such factors as unrecognized talents, unconscious motives, or early childhood memories that influence your behavior but are not fully understood. Many people have abilities that remain unexplored throughout their lives. A person capable of rising to the position of office manager may remain a receptionist throughout his or her career because the potential for advancement is unrecognized. You may possess the talent to become an artist or musician but never discover it. Elizabeth Layton did not discover her talent for drawing until she was 68. This artist, who spent most of her life as a homemaker in the small prairie town of Wellsville, Kansas, has exhibited her works of art in galleries and museums throughout the United States.[9]

Some of the unknown information that is below the surface of awareness can be made public with the aid of open communication. Input from others (teacher, mentor, or supervisor) can reduce the size of the unknown pane and increase the size of the open area.

The four panes of the Johari Window are interrelated. As you change the size of one pane, others are affected. At the beginning of a relationship, the open area is likely to be somewhat small. When you start a new job, for example, your relationship with your supervisor and other workers may involve a minimum of open communication. As time passes and you develop a more open relationship with coworkers, the open area should grow larger.

Self-Disclosure/Feedback Styles

Our relationship with others is influenced by two communication processes over which we have control. We can consciously make an effort to self-disclose our thoughts, ideas, and feelings when such action would improve the relationship. And we can also act to increase the amount of feedback from others. Figure 8.3a represents a self-disclosure/feedback style that reflects minimum use of self-disclosure and feedback processes. This style represents an impersonal approach to interpersonal relations, one that involves minimal sharing of information. Figure 8.3b represents a self-disclosure/feedback style that reflects considerable use of self-disclosure and feedback. Candor, openness, and mutual respect are characteristics of this style.

You can take positive steps to develop a larger open window (Figure 8.3b) by displaying a receptive attitude when others attempt to give you feedback. Openness to feedback from supervisors and coworkers, as opposed to defensiveness, is an important key to success in the workplace. If you become defensive, this behavior will likely cut off the flow of information you need to be more effective in your job. You can also actively solicit feedback from your supervisor and coworkers so that they will feel comfortable in giving it to you.

You can also develop a larger open window by constructively disclosing your perceptions, opinions, and feelings. In other words, let your supervisor or group members know where you stand. As you receive more feedback and engage in more self-disclosure, the open window will become larger, and you will benefit from improved interpersonal relationships.

Thinking / Learning Starter

To test your understanding of the Johari Window, write the term *open, blind, hidden,* or *unknown* in the appropriate space.

1. _____ Gary, a data entry clerk with a large insurance company, has the potential to become a proficient computer programmer. Neither he nor his coworkers are aware of this latent talent.

2. _____ Three years ago, Sara was fired from a job without any explanation from her employer. She has never shared this information with anyone.

3. _____ At a recent meeting with her sales manager, Jean expressed doubts about her ability to close sales. The sales manager indicated that he had experienced the same feelings early in his career.

4. _____ Jerry sees himself as humorous and entertaining. Coworkers view his type of humor as vulgar and offensive.

FIGURE 8.3

Johari Window at the Beginning of a Relationship (*left*) and After a Closer Relationship Has Developed (*right*)

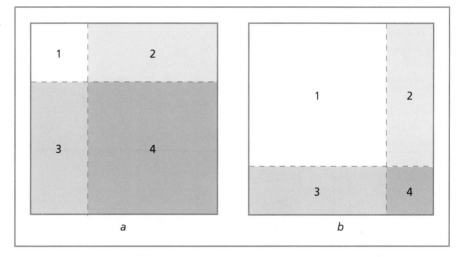

Source: Joseph Luft, *Group Processes: An Introduction to Group Dynamics.* Copyright © 1984 by Mayfield Publishing Company. Reprinted by permission of the publisher.

APPROPRIATE SELF-DISCLOSURE

At the beginning of this chapter, we stated that the primary goal of self-disclosure should be to build stronger relations. Self-disclosure is also a condition for emotional health, according to Sidney Jourard.[10] These goals (strong relationships and good emotional health) can be achieved if you learn how to disclose in constructive ways. Appropriate self-disclosure is a skill that anyone can learn.

In the search for criteria to determine the appropriateness of self-disclosure in a work setting, many factors must be considered. How much information should be disclosed? How intimate should the information be? Who is the most appropriate person with whom to share information? Under what conditions should the disclosures be made? In this section we examine several criteria that will help you develop your self-disclosure skills.

Use Self-Disclosure to Repair Damaged Relationships

Many relationships at work and in our personal life are unnecessarily strained. The strain often exists because people refuse to talk about real or imagined problems. Self-disclosure can be an excellent method of repairing a damaged relationship. The business manager for a large hospital and the physician in charge of the emergency room maintained a feud for three months because neither person was willing to sit down and openly discuss the problem. The problem began when a member of the physician's staff sent some incomplete medical records to the business office for processing. The business manager

Although it is most common to disclose ourselves through verbal communication, we often communicate what is important to us in the way we personalize our work environment. Shown here, in his office, is Alston Green, creative product designer at the ethnic business center of Hallmark Cards. (Don Ipock/ Gamma Liaison)

called the doctor and accused her staff of incompetence. As soon as he spoke the words, he was sorry. He had overreacted. The doctor in charge of the emergency room, anxious to defend her department, responded angrily with very strong language. She later regretted her lack of self-control. After several weeks, the business manager visited the emergency room and said, "Look, I'm sorry for what I said to you. You and your staff provide outstanding service to our patients, and I should not have reacted to the problem with such anger. Please accept my apology." The business manager and the doctor shook hands, and each returned to work feeling relieved that the problem was solved.

The Art of Apologizing   If your actions have caused hurt feelings, anger, or deep-seated ill will, an apology may be in order. A sincere apology can have a tremendous amount of healing power. In addition, it may set the stage for improved communications in the future. Many people avoid apologizing because they feel awkward about admitting they were wrong. If you decide to apologize to someone, the best approach is to meet with the injured party in private and own up to the wrongdoing. In a private setting, feelings can be exchanged with relative comfort. And do apologize completely. Don't say, "I'm sorry about what happened, but you shouldn't have. . . ." This is not an apology.[11]

The Art of Forgiveness   If someone you work with, a friend, or a family member apologizes, be quick to forgive. Forgiveness is almost never easy, especially when you feel you have been wronged. But forgiveness is the only way

---

Total Person Insight

"A genuine apology offered and accepted is one of the most profound interactions of civilized people. It has the power to restore damaged relationships, be they on a small scale, between two people, such as intimates, or on a grand scale, between groups of people, even nations. If done correctly, an apology can heal humiliation and generate forgiveness."

AARON LAZARE, M.D.

---

to break the bonds of blame and bitterness. To forgive means to give up resentment and anger. D. Patrick Miller, author of *A Little Book of Forgiveness,* says: "To carry an anger against anyone is to poison your own heart, administering more toxin every time you replay in your mind the injury done to you." He also says forgiveness provides healing and liberates your energy and your creativity.[12]

Present Constructive Criticism with Care

Constructive criticism is a form of self-disclosure that helps another person look at his or her own behavior without putting that individual on the defensive. Most people are very sensitive and are easily upset when they receive criticism. However, giving criticism effectively is a skill that can be mastered through learning and practice. Here are two effective methods for giving constructive criticism. First, avoid starting your message with "You," such as "You didn't complete your monthly inventory report" or "You never take our customer service policies seriously." For better results, replace "You-statements" with "I-statements." Say, "I am concerned that you have not completed your monthly inventory report." Another way to avoid defensiveness is to request a specific change in the future instead of pointing out something negative in the present. Instead of saying, "You did not have authorization to order office supplies," try saying, "In the future, please obtain authorization before ordering office supplies."[13]

Discuss Disturbing Situations As They Happen

You should share reactions to a work-related problem or issue as soon after the incident as possible. It is often difficult to recapture a feeling once it has passed, and you may distort the incident if you let too much time go by. Your memory is not infallible. The person who caused the hurt feelings is also likely to forget details about the situation.

If something really bothers you, express your feelings. Clear the air as soon as possible so you can enjoy greater peace of mind. Some people maintain the burden of hurt feelings and resentment for days, weeks, even years. The avoidance of self-disclosure usually has a negative effect on a person's mental and physical health as well as on job performance.

Accurately Describe Your Feelings and Emotions

It has been said that one of the most important outcomes of self-disclosure is the possibility for others to become acquainted with the "real" you. When you accurately describe your feelings and emotions, others get to know you better. This kind of honesty takes courage because of the risk involved. When you tell another person how you feel, you are putting a great amount of faith in that person. You are trusting the other person not to ridicule or embarrass you for the feelings you express.[14]

Too often, people view verbalizing feelings and emotions in a work setting as inappropriate. But emotions are an integral part of human behavior. People should not be expected to turn off their feelings the moment they arrive at work. Experiencing feelings and emotions is a part of being human.

What is the best way to report emotions and feelings? Some examples may be helpful. Let's suppose you expected to be chosen to supervise an important project, but the assignment was given to another worker. At a meeting with your boss, you might make the following statement: "For several weeks I've been looking forward to heading up this project. I guess I didn't realize that anyone else was being considered. Now I feel not only disappointed but also embarrassed."

Or suppose a coworker constantly borrows equipment and supplies but usually fails to return them. You might say: "Thanks for taking a few minutes to meet with me. I'm the type of person who likes to keep busy, but lately I've spent a lot of time retrieving tools and supplies you've borrowed. I've experienced a great deal of frustration and decided I should tell you how I feel."

As you report your feelings, be sure the other person realizes that your feelings are temporary and capable of change. You might say, "At this point I feel very disappointed, but I am sure we can solve the problem." Expressing anger can be especially difficult. This special challenge is discussed in Chapter 9.

Select the Right Time and Place

Remarks that otherwise might be offered and accepted in a positive way can be rendered ineffective not because of what we say but because of when and where we say it.[15] When possible, select a time when you feel the other person is not preoccupied and will be able to give you his or her full attention. Also, select a setting free of distractions. Telephone calls or unannounced visitors can ruin an opportunity for meaningful dialogue. If there is no suitable place at work to hold the discussion, consider meeting the person for lunch away from work or talking with the person after work at some appropriate location. If necessary, make an appointment with the person to ensure that time is reserved for your meeting.

Avoid Overwhelming Others with Your Self-Disclosure

Although you should be open, do not go too far too fast. Many strong relationships are built slowly. The abrupt disclosure of highly emotional or intimate information may actually distance you from the other person, who may find your behavior threatening. Unrestricted "truth" can create a great deal of anxiety, particularly in an organization where people must work closely together. Dr. Joyce Brothers says we must balance the inclination to be open and honest with the need to be protective of each other's feelings.[16] Disclosure of areas of privacy, in some cases, can create a barrier to building a close relationship.

Buddha gave some good advice about what to say and not say to others. The founder of Buddhism recommended that a person ask three vital questions before saying anything to another person: (1) Is the statement *true?* (2) Is the statement *necessary?* (3) Is the statement *kind?* If a statement falls short on any of these counts, Buddha advised that we say nothing.[17] His recommendations establish a high standard for anyone who engages in self-disclosure.

Thinking / Learning Starter

Review the criteria in the text for appropriate self-disclosure. On a sheet of paper, describe at least two situations in which another person violated one or more of these criteria while self-disclosing information to you. Describe your feelings at the time these experiences occurred. What impact did the person's behavior have on your relationship?

Be Aware of Your Nonverbal Cues

As you consider ways to disclose what you think, feel, or want in a constructive manner, remember that you reveal a great deal through nonverbal messages. If someone says, "How do you like my choice of office furniture?" a note of hesitation in your voice and an expression of doubt on your face may tell the other

person you are not very enthusiastic about it. A long pause, or complete silence, following the question will sometimes communicate that you do not
know how to phrase your reaction tactfully or that you dislike the office furniture and prefer to say nothing. The emotion in your voice, your eye contact,
your gestures, and your body posture will communicate a great deal about
your inner thoughts.

BARRIERS TO SELF-DISCLOSURE IN AN ORGANIZATIONAL SETTING

At this point you might be thinking, "If self-disclosure is such a positive force
in building stronger human relationships, why do people avoid it so often?
Why do so many people conceal their thoughts and feelings? Why are candor and openness so uncommon in most organizations?" To answer these
questions, let's examine some of the barriers that prevent people from self-
disclosing.

Lack of Trust

The word **trust** (derived from the German word *Trost,* meaning "comfort")
implies instinctive, unquestioning belief in another person or thing. In a two-
person relationship, trust exists when you fully believe in the integrity or character of the other person. When the trust level in an organization is high, we
see greater employee loyalty, better customer service, lower operating costs,
and other positive outcomes. Unfortunately, in a work environment characterized by rapid change and uncertainty caused by massive layoffs, trust has
greatly declined in many organizations. When the level of trust is low, people
are less likely to openly discuss problems and issues.[18]

Lack of trust is perhaps the most common—and the most serious—barrier
to self-disclosure. Without trust, people usually fear revealing their thoughts
and feelings because the perceived risks of self-disclosure are too high. When
trust is present, people no longer feel as vulnerable in the presence of another
person, and communication flows more freely. If the level of trust declines,
people tend to raise their defenses, and communication suffers. If you are not
trusted, people will not believe you even when you tell the truth.[19]

You have confidence in people you trust and tend to feel open, relaxed, and
comfortable in their presence. Jack Gibb, in his book *Trust: A New View of
Personal and Organizational Development,* points out that the trust level is the
thermometer of individual and group health. When trust is present, people
function naturally and openly. Without it, they devote their energies to mask-
ing their true feelings, hiding thoughts, and avoiding opportunities for personal growth.[20] Jess Lair, author of *I Ain't Much, Baby—But I'm All I've Got,*

Total Person Insight

"Trust has been called the 'ultimate intangible,' and though it can't be touched or held, it functions as a tangible force in powering our actions, enabling us to focus our efforts, and underpinning our cooperation in organizations. It is the cement that holds the organization together, the lubricant that enables it to function, and the currency that allows it to transact business with clients or customers."

GORDON F. SHEA

Author, *Building Trust for Personal and Organizational Success*

---

describes the effect of trust, or lack of it, in organizations: "The more you trust your associates, the more you believe in them, the better they are. The less you believe in them, the worse they are. And yet they are the same people. It's just a difference in what you expect of them."[21]

When *Fortune* magazine asked a group of management consultants, business school professors, and corporate chief executive officers to identify the keys to business leadership, their first choice was "Trust your subordinates."[22] It is also important that employees trust their leaders. Researchers have found a strong link between overall trust and responsive communication. The researchers also concluded that trust and communication are major factors in human relationships.[23]

Thinking / Learning Starters

1. Recall a situation in which a friend or coworker created the impression that he or she did not trust you. What did the person do or say to create this impression? How did you react to this behavior?

2. If you have a manager in your work setting, do you trust him or her? Why or why not?

One organization that realizes the importance of trust and self-disclosure in its working environment is The Forum Corporation, a leading provider of training programs. All employees, when hired, are given a framed copy of the "Forum Code" (see Figure 8.4) to hang on their office walls. Note that the

FIGURE 8.4

The Forum Corporation Code

FORUM CODE

Responsibility:
I will take responsibility for my own actions.

Esteem:
I will build esteem in myself, the company, and the client franchise.

Stay Healthy:
I will insist on maintaining and improving my own physical and mental health and will encourage others to do the same.

Planning and Executing:
I will develop, execute, and stick to a realistic plan.

Empathy:
I will anticipate the impact that decisions and actions have on others. I will put myself in the other person's shoes.

Confront:
I will confront differences honestly, quickly, and directly with the person involved.

Trust:
I will listen with respect. I will keep my commitments. I will be open and honest. I won't say what I don't mean.

Source: Used with permission from The Forum Corporation.

large capital letters, reading down, spell "respect." Note also the last two items, which deal specifically with self-disclosure and trust.

Jack Gibb states that the normal fears people bring to a new job are magnified when they encounter tight controls, veiled threats, and impersonal behavior. This climate sets the stage for what he describes as the "fear/distrust cycle" (see Figure 8.5).[24] The cycle begins with the management philosophy that people are basically lacking in motivation and cannot be trusted (discussed in Chapter 7 as Theory X). To bring about maximum production, management tries to maintain tight control over employees by initiating a series of strict rules and regulations. As management increases the controls, workers often become more defensive and resentful. The spirit of teamwork diminishes, and everyone in the organization begins talking in terms of "we" versus "they." When employees display a defensive attitude, management becomes more fearful and less trusting, responding with even tighter controls and more attempts to manipulate members of the work force. The fear/distrust cycle is now a reality, and the spirit of teamwork is lost completely.

Role Relationships Versus Interpersonal Relationships

Self-disclosure is more likely to take place within an organization when people feel comfortable stepping outside their assigned roles and displaying openness and tolerance for the feelings of others. In our society, role expectations are often clearly specified for people engaged in various occupations. For example, some people see the supervisor's role as an impersonal one. Supervisors are supposed to enforce rules and regulations, maintain high production, and avoid getting too close to the people they supervise. The advice given to some new supervisors is "Don't try to be a nice guy, or people will take advantage of you." Yet often the most effective supervisors are those who are approachable, display a sense of humor, and take time to listen to employee problems.

Some newly appointed supervisors may deliberately try to build barriers between themselves and subordinates. They draw a sharp distinction between

FIGURE 8.5

Fear/Distrust Cycle

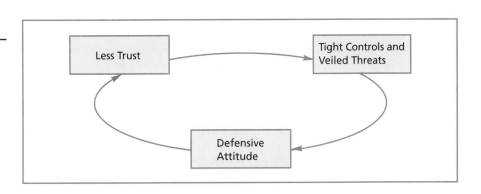

role relationships and **interpersonal relationships.** They are impersonal and aloof, thinking that this is appropriate "role" behavior. Employees usually respond to these actions by becoming defensive or less trusting.

Roles are inescapable, but they need not contribute to the depersonalization of relationships. Role expectations should be clearly stated within an organization, but role differentiation should not lead to a breakdown of interpersonal relations. Each role is played by a person. Others should be able to get to know that person regardless of the role the individual has been assigned. If you do not let others get to know you, they will probably never disclose their feelings, beliefs, and thoughts to you. To the extent that you remain a mystery, others may decide the risks of self-disclosure are too high.

PRACTICE SELF-DISCLOSURE

Many people carry around an assortment of hurt feelings, angry thoughts, and frustration that drains them of the energy they need to cope with life's daily struggles. Although self-disclosure provides a way to get rid of this burden, some people continue through life imprisoned by negative thoughts and feelings. If you avoid disclosing your thoughts and feelings, you also make it harder for others to know the real you. You will recall from the beginning of this chapter that self-disclosure involves revealing personal information that cannot be acquired from other sources. This type of information can often improve the quality of your relationships with others.

Could you benefit by telling others more about your thoughts, wants, feelings, and beliefs? To answer this question, complete Figure 8.6, which will give you an indication of your self-disclosure style. If you tend to agree with most of these items, consider making a conscientious effort to do more self-disclosing.

Becoming a more open person is not difficult if you are willing to practice. If you want to improve in this area, begin by taking small steps. You might want to start with a nonthreatening confrontation with a friend or neighbor. Pick someone with whom you have had a recent minor problem. Tell this person as honestly as possible how you feel about the issue or problem. Keep in mind that your objective is not simply to relate something that is bothering you but also to develop a stronger relationship with this person.

As you gain confidence, move to more challenging encounters. Maybe you feel your work is not appreciated by your employer. Why not tell this person how you feel? If you are a supervisor and one of the people you supervise seems to be taking advantage of you, why not talk to this person openly about your thoughts? With practice you will begin to feel comfortable with self-disclosure, and you will find it rewarding to get your feelings out in the open. As you become a more open person, the people you contact will be more likely

FIGURE 8.6

Self-Disclosure
Indicator

Instructions: *Read each statement and then place a checkmark (✓) in*
the appropriate space.

	YES	NO
1. In most cases I avoid sharing personal thoughts and feelings with others.	————	————
2. My relationships with others tend to be quite formal.	————	————
3. I would not be comfortable discussing personal problems at work.	————	————
4. I tend to avoid discussing my concerns even when feelings of frustration build inside me.	————	————
5. I tend to avoid giving praise or criticism to others.	————	————
6. I tend to believe that familiarity breeds contempt.	————	————

to open up and share more thoughts, ideas, and feelings with you. Everyone wins!

Summary

Open communication is an important key to personal growth and job satisfaction. Self-disclosure—the process of letting another person know what you think, feel, or want—promotes communication within an organization. It differs from self-description in that it usually involves some risk. Most people want and need accurate feedback from coworkers and the person who supervises their work.

Constructive self-disclosure can result in many rewards to people and organizations. It can pave the way for increased accuracy in communication, reduction of stress, increased self-awareness, and stronger interpersonal relationships.

The Johari Window helps conceptualize four kinds of information areas involved in communication: the open area, what you and others know about you; the blind area, what others know about you that you don't know about yourself; the hidden area, what you know but others do not; and the unknown area, what neither you nor others know. Most people gradually increase the open area as they learn to communicate with others.

Everyone can learn how to use self-disclosure in a constructive way. Your goal should always be to approach self-disclosure with the desire to improve your relationship with the other person. Describe your feelings and emotions accurately, and avoid making judgments about the other person. Disturbing situations should be discussed as they happen; it is difficult to recapture feelings once they have passed. Select the right time and place to share your thoughts, and avoid inappropriate disclosure of highly emotional or intimate information.

A climate of trust serves as a foundation for self-disclosure. In the absence of trust, people usually avoid revealing their thoughts and feelings to others. Self-disclosure is also more likely to take place within an organization when people feel comfortable stepping outside their assigned roles and displaying openness for the feelings of others than when they do not.

Lack of familiarity can be a barrier to constructive self-disclosure. To the extent that you remain a mystery, other people may decide the risks of self-disclosure are too high.

As with learning any new skill, you can improve your ability to disclose your thoughts and feelings by starting with less threatening disclosures and proceeding slowly to more challenging situations.

Career Corner

Q. The company I work for recently adopted the assessment approach known as 360-degree feedback. Every department head completed a three-day workshop on this feedback strategy. When my boss returned from the workshop, she held a staff meeting and said she wants to know what we think of her performance. We have been instructed to schedule a meeting with her and be prepared to "tell it like it is." I think she sincerely wants feedback regarding her strengths and areas needing improvement. Should I share with her the "good" and the "bad"?

A. Although your boss may be seeking assessment feedback, she could be turned off by your complaints or by criticism of the way she manages the department. Most managers respond poorly to direct criticism—even when they seek feedback. Criticism of her leadership may damage your career. Of course it would be a mistake to bottle up a major source of frustration inside you. If you are upset about a particular policy or practice, find the right time and place to disclose your feelings. Before the meeting, try to think of a good solution to the problem. Most bosses are turned off by employees who complain about something but fail to offer an alternative way of doing things.

Key Terms

self-disclosure
self-description
Johari Window
open area
blind area
hidden area

unknown area
constructive criticism
trust
role relationships
interpersonal relationships

Review Questions

1. What is the major difference between self-disclosure and self-description?
2. How can self-disclosure contribute to improved teamwork within an organization?
3. List four major rewards to be gained from self-disclosure.
4. Describe how self-disclosure can contribute to increased self-awareness.
5. What is the major difference between the blind area and the hidden area of the Johari Window?
6. What types of interpersonal relationship problems are overdisclosers and underdisclosers likely to encounter?
7. List the guidelines to follow when making appropriate self-disclosure.
8. In the absence of trust, what major problems can surface in an organization?
9. Describe the fear/distrust cycle.
10. List and explain two effective ways to give constructive criticism.

Application Exercises

1. To learn more about your approach to self-disclosure, complete each of the sentences below. Once you have completed them all, reflect on your written responses. Can you identify any changes in your approach to self-disclosure that would improve communications with others? Are there any self-disclosure skills that you need to practice?
   a. "For me, the major barrier to self-disclosure is . . ."
   b. "To establish a more mutually trusting relationship with others, I need to . . ."
   c. "In order to receive more feedback from others, I need to . . ."
   d. "In situations where I should apologize for something or voice forgiveness, I tend to . . ."

2. On Friday afternoon a coworker visits your office and requests a favor. She wants you to review a proposal she will give to her boss on Monday morning at 10:00 A.M. You agree to study the proposal sometime over the weekend and give her feedback on Monday before her meeting. You put a photocopy of the proposal in your briefcase and take it home. Over the weekend you get busy and forget to review the proposal. In fact, you are so busy that you never open your briefcase. On Monday morning you make a call on a customer before reporting to the office. While sitting in the customer's office, you open your briefcase and see the report. It is too late to study the report and give feedback to your coworker. Which of the following actions would you take?
   a. Try to forget the incident and avoid feeling guilty. After all, you did not intentionally avoid your obligation.
   b. Call the person's boss and explain the circumstances. Confess that you simply forgot to read the report.
   c. Meet with your coworker as soon as possible and offer a sincere apology for failing to read the report and provide the feedback.
   Provide a rationale for your choice.

3. Constructive self-disclosure is based on a foundation of trust. When the trust level is low, open and honest communication is unlikely to occur. We inspire trust by what we say and what we do. Some behaviors that inspire trust are listed below. Rate yourself with this scale: U = Usually; S = Sometimes; I = Infrequently. After you finish the self-assessment, reflect on your ability to inspire trust, and think about ways to improve yourself in this area.

	U	S	I
I disclose my thoughts and feelings when appropriate.	☐	☐	☐
I admit my mistakes.	☐	☐	☐
Others know that I keep confidences.	☐	☐	☐
I keep my promises and commitments.	☐	☐	☐
I avoid distortion of information when communicating with others.	☐	☐	☐

Internet Exercise

A careful study of the Johari Window communication model can provide helpful information about constructive self-disclosure. The Internet provides additional information about this model. Using your search engine, type in "Johari Window," and then review the available resources (such as books, articles, and training programs). Provide a brief summary of your findings. Pay special attention to new information that was not covered in your textbook.

Case 8.1   The Art of Giving Criticism

Large numbers of employees feel uncomfortable giving negative feedback to people they work with. Robert A. Baron, chair of the management department at Rensselaer Polytechnic Institute in Troy, New York, says, "Everybody is reluctant to give negative feedback, so all they do is bite their tongue until they can't stand it anymore." If someone is doing something that interferes with your work, causes you discomfort, or puts you in danger, do not remain silent. When you allow someone to do something you do not want, you become part of the problem. By remaining quiet, you allow the behavior to continue.

We live in a culture that encourages outspokenness, but the disclosure of thoughts and feelings must be handled with care. How something is said can be more important than what was said. Robert Genua, author of *Managing Your Mouth,* says that the most important thing is to pause before you speak and think about what you are going to say. If you are highly critical of someone's suggestion and express your views with strong sarcasm, the people who work with you may not remember that you happen to be right. However, they will remember your insensitive behavior. Genua says, "People who choose their words carefully come across as well-mannered, polished and refined."

Although some people are too direct in giving feedback and may actually be perceived as threatening, others make passive statements and fail to solve the problem. When giving negative feedback, you should look the person in the eye and be straightforward in expressing your thoughts and feelings. If someone is taking credit for your suggestions and ideas and has ignored your protests, you might say, "I want you to stop taking credit for my ideas. If you do not stop, I will ask our department head to schedule a meeting of the three of us so we can discuss the problem." To leave some things unchallenged can have negative results. Your reputation is formed not only by what you stand for but by what you won't stand for.

If you are a supervisor, the major reason you give negative feedback is to improve performance. Robert Baron has researched how bosses criticize employees and says some criticize too much and others criticize too little. Some give negative feedback for the wrong reasons, such as to reinforce their sense of power or to get revenge. To improve performance, you want to avoid comments that will make the other person angry or defensive. When it comes to giving criticism, do it with sensitivity.

Questions

1. Do you agree that speaking out at work is generally beneficial to you and your employer? Explain your answer.

2. Why are many people reluctant to give negative feedback to another person? What are some of the reasons some people are afraid to speak out?
3. If a coworker openly criticizes your work in a meeting and says things that are not true, what should be your immediate response? Should you make contact with this person after the meeting and try to resolve the problem? Explain your answer.

Case 8.2   ## A Manager's Perceptions of Self-Disclosure

In the process of collecting information for her book *The Androgynous Manager,* Alice Sargent conducted in-depth interviews with dozens of managers. (Sargent defines *androgyny* in the following way: "As a psychological term, androgyny suggests that it is possible for people to exhibit both masculine and feminine qualities and that such values, attitudes, and behaviors reside in varying degrees in each of us.") One of these managers, a man named Buford Macklin, shared some doubts about the merits of the androgynous style of management:

> If you're conciliatory and try to fit in, then you're homogenized and invisible. Your energy must go to convincing people you're competent. It's never a given, but instead, time and again, it's an uphill battle to prove competence. It's like you're incompetent until you prove otherwise. This means you must be focused and single-minded in your actions. The qualities of androgyny detract from this.

Macklin said that disclosing personal feelings did little to help him climb the management ladder. "It's construed as being soft, indecisive, and unclear. It just does not score the right kind of points to share personal data in the organization with my boss, subordinates, or even colleagues." According to Macklin, style is important. "Credibility requires you to have a strong rational style."

Questions

1. Do you agree or disagree with Macklin's point of view? Explain.
2. In what ways can openness, sensitivity, and concern for people aid Macklin? In what ways will these behaviors hinder his chances for promotion?

Chapter 9

Achieving

Emotional Balance

in a Chaotic World

Chapter Preview

After studying this chapter, you will be able to

1. Describe how emotions influence our thinking and behavior.
2. Understand the factors that contribute to emotional balance.
3. Explain the critical role of emotions in the workplace.
4. Describe the major factors that influence our emotional development.
5. Learn how to deal with your anger and the anger of others.
6. Understand the factors that contribute to workplace violence.
7. Identify and explain the most common emotional styles.
8. Describe strategies for achieving emotional control.

C AN A PILOT'S MIND-SET be a factor in airline crashes? The National Transportation Safety Board (NTSB), investigating the fatal crash of a Northwest Airlink commuter plane, thinks the answer is yes. The plane was landing at Hibbing, Minnesota, when it clipped a pine tree, lost a wing, and careened into a ridge. All eighteen people on board were killed. The plane was hundreds of feet lower than it should have been during the approach to the airport. The NTSB cited a "breakdown in crew coordination" and suggested that the pilot's history of "intimidation" kept his copilot from warning about the plane's continued descent. The board member in charge of the crash inquiry noted that the pilot had an angry argument with a gate agent over paperwork prior to takeoff. He also loudly criticized the copilot for not checking the landing light from outside the plane. Was anger a factor in this plane crash? John Nance, an aviation safety consultant, said, "We have people every day who end up in automobile accidents because they let their anger push the pedal to the floor. Nobody should think it's any different in an airplane."[1] ■

Anger is one of a vast array of emotions that can influence our behavior at work and in our personal world. To the extent that we can become more aware of our emotions and assess their influence on our daily lives, we have the opportunity to achieve a new level of self-understanding. That greater awareness can help us avoid inappropriate behavior.

EMOTIONS—AN INTRODUCTION

An **emotion** can be thought of as a feeling, such as jealousy, fear, love, joy, and grief, that influences our thinking and behavior. It is not an exaggeration to say that much of the human behavior we observe every day springs from feelings. An emotional experience often alters thought processes by directing attention toward some things and away from others.

Throughout each day our feelings are activated by a variety of events (see Figure 9.1). You might feel a sense of joy after learning that a coworker has just given birth to a new baby. You might feel overpowering grief after learning that your supervisor was killed in an auto accident. Angry feelings may surface when you discover that someone borrowed a tool without your permission. Once your feelings have been activated, your mind interprets the event. In some cases, the feelings trigger irrational thinking: "No one who works here can be trusted!" In other cases, you may engage in a rational thinking process: "Perhaps the person who borrowed the tool needed it to help a customer with an emergency repair." The important point to remember is that we can choose how we behave.

Feelings provide us with knowledge of our current emotional condition and the energy to act out our beliefs.[2] For example, after an argument with a coworker you may experience anger over your coworker's comments or regret about your own. Feelings serve as communication links with your emotions.

FIGURE 9.1

Behavior Is Influenced
by Activating Events

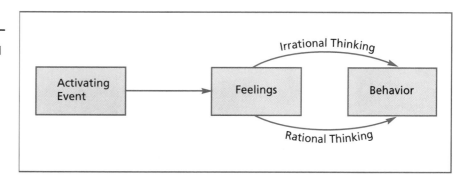

Emotional Intelligence

Daniel Goleman, author of the best-selling book *Emotional Intelligence,* challenges the traditional view of the relationship between IQ and success. He says there are widespread exceptions to the rule that IQ predicts success: "At best, IQ contributes about 20 percent to the factors that determine life success, which leaves 80 percent to other forces."[3] The focus of Goleman's book are the human characteristics that make up what he describes as *emotional intelligence.* He identifies five fundamentals of emotional intelligence:[4]

- *Self-awareness.* This is awareness of our own thoughts and feelings and of the meanings of these inner states. Self-awareness gives us the ability to monitor feelings and understand how they influence behavior.
- *Handling emotions.* The ability to keep distressing emotions in check is a major key to emotional intelligence. Distressing feelings that become too intense (raging anger, for example) undermine our stability.
- *Self-motivation.* To achieve a goal may require delaying gratification (studying for an examination rather than attending a movie) or stifling impulsiveness. The capacity to resist an impulse in order to achieve emotional self-control is a fundamental psychological skill.
- *Empathy.* This is the ability to sense how someone else feels. The key to understanding another person's feelings is the ability to read nonverbal cues such as tone of voice, gestures, and facial expressions. Empathy, according to Goleman, is the single human quality that leads us to override self-interest and act with compassion and kindness.
- *Social skills.* These are the skills that permit us to be effective in dealings with others. Social skills include the ability to build rapport quickly, mediate conflict, and help others soothe their feelings.

Research in the area of emotional intelligence continues. Toronto-based Multi-Health Systems Incorporated has developed the BarOn EQ-i, an assessment instrument designed to measure emotional intelligence. Although several companies are using this instrument, critics question whether a person's

We often see a variety of emotions expressied at sporting events. Here we see Michelle Kwan, Olympic ice skater, crying after completing her silver medal perfor-mance. (AP/Wide World Photos)

"emotional quotient," or EQ, can be measured with the precision of the IQ.[5] The connection between emotional intelligence and career success is also being debated. What we do know is that each of the five fundamentals of emotional intelligence can be learned and improved on.

Emotional Balance

We carry inside us a large array of emotions that have been with us since birth and will be with us until death. However, we sometimes suffer from a lack of emotional balance because we learn to inhibit the expression of certain emotions and to overemphasize the expression of others. Some families, for example, discourage the expression of love and affection. Some people are taught from an early age to avoid expressing anger. Others learn that a public display of grief (crying, for example) is a sign of weakness. If as a child you were strongly encouraged to avoid the expression of anger, fear, love, or some other emotion, you may repress or block these feelings as an adult.[6]

Emotional imbalance also develops if we become fixated on a single emotion. The high incidence of violent crime in America has motivated some people to become almost totally infused with the emotion of fear. One writer noted that people who are preoccupied with fear may be intensifying the problem: "We have a habit of keeping ourselves overwhelmed, through the news media, with bad and scary things that have happened all over the world each day; and then the chronic pattern of worrying about which of these bad things might happen to us in the future."[7] To focus on one emotion to the exclusion of others creates a serious imbalance within us. A person obsessed with hatred toward a specific minority group will find it difficult to display compassion toward persons who are members of that group. The emotion of hatred can overpower and extinguish the emotion of love.

The Myth of Negative Emotions

In our culture we have a tendency to label emotions as either "positive" or "negative." Love, bliss, joy, and compassion are described as positive emotions. Guilt, fear, anger, grief, and envy are labeled negative emotions. Furthermore, negative emotions are often viewed as bad. Joan Borysenko, author of *Minding the Body, Mending the Mind,* states that negative emotions are human and, most of the time, appropriate: "The only negative emotions are emotions that you will not allow yourself or someone else to experience. Negative emotions will not harm you if you express them appropriately and then let them go. . . . Bottling them up is far worse."[8]

The sudden loss of one's job, the breakup of a marriage, failure to win a promotion, or the death of a loved one requires us to cope with powerful feelings. Learning how to cope with negative emotions is an important step toward achieving emotional health.

The Emotional Factor at Work

Emotions play a critical role in the success of every organization, yet many people in key decision-making positions—leaders with outstanding technical skills—fail to understand the important role emotions play in a work setting. In part, the problem can be traced to leadership training that emphasizes that "doing business" is a purely rational or logical process. One consultant put the problem into proper perspective when he said, "We are still trying to do business as if it requires only a meeting of the minds instead of a meeting of the hearts."[9]

In some cases, emotional blindness can be very costly. Helen Barrett, a 57-year-old social work manager and former employee of Yale–New Haven Hospital, was awarded $105,000 by a jury that decided she was fired in a manner that caused emotional distress. Barrett was forced to leave her personal belongings in a plastic bag and was escorted out the door by security guards in full view of coworkers. A supervisor told her she would be arrested for trespassing if she returned. This threat was made even though there had been no indications of disloyalty or criminal wrongdoing.[10]

Total Person Insight

"All of our technology is underutilized and will remain so until we put the emotion of doing business onto parity with the logical and rational aspects of performance improvement."

JAMES C. GEORGES

Chief Executive Officer, The Par Group

Emotional undercurrents are present in almost every area of every organization. Most banks, hospitals, retail firms, hotels, and restaurants realize that they need a relationship strategy—a plan for establishing, building, and maintaining quality relationships with customers. This type of plan is essential for success in today's marketplace, which is characterized by vigorous competition, very similar products, and customer loyalty dependent on quality relationships and quality products.[11] Front-line employees, those persons responsible for delivering quality service and building relationships, engage in "emotional labor," and those who have frequent contact with the public often find the work very stressful.[12] *Emotional labor,* which taxes the mind, is often more difficult to handle than physical labor, which strains the body.

Relationships are no less important in the international arena. James Georges, a consultant with considerable international experience, believes our preoccupation with purely rational processes is a barrier to success in the global marketplace. "Our preoccupation with logic, knowledge, data, facts, rational systems and procedures gets in the way of developing the 'heart skills' we need in order to do business successfully in a highly competitive, global market."[13]

Thinking / Learning Starters

1. Recall a situation at work or at school where the leadership displayed emotional blindness. What are some of the reasons the important role of emotions was not taken into consideration?

2. Do you agree that emotional undercurrents are present in almost every area of the typical organization? Can you think of any exceptions?

FACTORS THAT INFLUENCE OUR EMOTIONS

The starting point in achieving greater emotional control is to determine the source of emotional difficulties. Why do we sometimes display indifference when the expression of compassion would be more appropriate? Why is it so easy to put down a friend or coworker and so hard to recognize that person's accomplishments? Why do we sometimes worry about events that will never happen? To answer these and other questions, it is necessary to study the factors that influence our emotional development.

Temperament

Temperament refers to a person's individual style and frequency of expressing needs and emotions; it is biological and genetically based. It reflects a contribution by nature to the beginning of an individual's personality.[14] Researchers have found that certain temperamental characteristics are apparent in children at birth and remain somewhat stable over time. For example, the traits associated with extroversion and introversion can be observed when a baby is born. Of course, many events take place between infancy and adulthood to alter or shape a person's temperament. Personality at every age reflects the interplay of temperament and of environmental influences, such as parenting.[15]

Subconscious Influences

The **subconscious mind** is a vast storehouse of forgotten memories, desires, ideas, and frustrations, according to William Menninger, founder of the famed Menninger Foundation.[16] He noted that the subconscious mind can have a great influence on behavior. It contains memories of past experiences as well as memories of feelings associated with past experiences. The subconscious is active, continuously influencing conscious decision-making processes.

Although people cannot remember many of the important events of the early years of their lives, these incidents do influence their behavior as adults. Joan Borysenko offers this example:

> Inside me there is a seven-year-old who is still hurting from her humiliation at summer camp. Her anguish is reawakened every time I find myself in the presence of an authority figure who acts in a controlling manner. At those moments, my intellect is prone to desert me, and I am liable to break down and cry with the same desolation and helplessness I felt when I was seven.[17]

This example reminds us that childhood wounds can cause us to experience emotions out of proportion to a current situation. Also, we often relive the experience in a context very different from the one we experienced as a child. A worker who is strongly reprimanded by an angry supervisor may experience the same feelings that surfaced when he was scolded by his mother for breaking an expensive vase.

A promising breakthrough in understanding the influence of the subconscious came many years ago with the development of the transactional analysis (TA) theory by Eric Berne. After years of study, Berne concluded that, from the day of birth, the brain acts like a two-track stereo tape recorder. One track records events, and the other records the feelings associated with those events.

To illustrate how feelings associated with early childhood experiences can surface later in life, picture in your mind's eye a 3-year-old walking around his mother's sewing room. He picks up a pair of sharp scissors and begins walking toward the staircase. The mother spots the child and cries, "Tommy, drop those scissors! Do you want to kill yourself?" Tommy's tape recorder records both the event (walking with scissors) and the emotions (fear and guilt). Ten years later, Tommy is taking an art class and his teacher says, "Tommy, bring me a pair of scissors." As he begins to walk across the room, his mind is flooded by the feelings of fear and guilt attached to that earlier childhood event.

The practical applications of transactional analysis were discussed in such books as *I'm OK—You're OK,* written by Thomas Harris; *Staying OK,* by Amy Bjork Harris and Thomas Harris; and *Born to Win,* by Muriel James and Dorothy Jongeward. TA concepts have been incorporated into many corporate training programs.

Cultural Conditioning

A professor at Dartmouth College said, "Culture is what we see and hear so often that we call it reality. Out of culture comes behavior."[18] A number of cultural influences are currently having a dramatic impact on the emotional health of American children and adults. According to the National School Boards Association, U.S. schools are being hit by an epidemic of violence. About one-quarter of all students say they have been victims of violence in or near their public schools.[19]

The rate of interpersonal violence in the United States is the highest among all industrialized countries. Americans of all ages are preoccupied with violence and encounter fictionalized violence in movies, TV programs, and video games. Research indicates that by the time most Americans reach the age of 18, they will have seen 40,000 made-for-TV murders and 200,000 acts of violence. The negative effects of televised violence appear to be increased aggression—both immediate and long term—in children and adults.[20] In addition to mass media violence, there is the real violence in sports as fights occur more frequently during games.

We are just beginning to understand the extent and seriousness of family violence in America. It appears to be far more common than most experts imagined. The authors of *No Safe Haven,* a major report on violence against

Azim Khamisa (second from left) and Ples Felix, with students at Birney Elementary School in San Diego, organized the first Violence Impact Forum—a program aimed at ending the culture of gang violence. After Khamisa's only son was killed by Felix's grandson, the two men put aside their differences and decided to join together to try to prevent further violence. (James Aronovsky)

women by an American Psychological Association task force, notes that as many as 4 million women experience a severe or life-threatening assault from a male partner in an average twelve-month period.[21] Domestic abuse is the leading cause of injury to women in this country. Many people—both men and women—are victims of verbal aggression, which may take the form of insults or swearing. Verbal aggression can affect people in ways similar to physical aggression, and it is also sometimes the first step toward physical aggression.[22]

Significant levels of violence, most commonly pushing, shoving, or slapping, occur in dating couples attending high school and college. These and other violent acts are committed by and against male and female students. The emotional reactions to these violent acts include confusion, anger, and sadness.[23]

Too much violence makes it difficult for us to achieve an emotional balance. People who have experienced violence, or the threat of violence, express high levels of distress. As life becomes a constant state of tension and anxiety, their ability to build and maintain good relationships with others decreases.

Thus far we have established two important points regarding the role of emotions in our life:

1. *It is important that we remain open to the full range of emotions that influence our thinking and behavior.* Shakti Gawain, a pioneer in the field of personal growth, says, "Our feelings are an important part of the life force that is constantly moving through us. If we don't allow ourselves to fully experience our emotions, we stop the natural flow of that life force.[24]

2. *Emotional undercurrents are present in every aspect of our work, and separating our mental and emotional energies at work is very difficult because they are so closely intertwined.*[25] We live in a society where many people are openly suspicious of emotions, so it is not surprising that in many work settings employees are encouraged to express their thoughts but not their feelings.

COPING WITH YOUR ANGER AND THE ANGER OF OTHERS

In the presence of disagreement or conflict we often experience primary feelings such as frustration, hurt, embarrassment, guilt, or insecurity. These feelings are often followed by the secondary feeling of anger. If someone strongly criticizes your work in front of coworkers, you may experience shame, alarm, or insecurity, which are primary feelings. Later, in the privacy of your office or home, you may begin to feel a strong sense of anger. You may say to yourself, "She didn't have to criticize my work in front of everybody!"

Anger may be defined as the thoughts, feelings, physical reactions, and actions that result from unacceptable behavior by others.[26] The negative emotion of anger often triggers hostility. Learning to deal effectively with anger is a key to a healthy relationship and to your physical and mental health. The authors of *Anger Kills* say that about 20 percent of the general population has levels of hostility high enough to be dangerous to health, another 20 percent has very low levels, and the rest of the population falls somewhere in between.[27] Learning to deal with your anger, and the anger of other people, is one of the most sophisticated and mature skills people are ever required to learn. Intense anger takes control of people and distorts their perceptions, which is why angry people often make poor decisions.[28]

Taking Control of Your Anger

When anger surfaces, we usually have several options. If another driver pulls out in front of your car and almost causes an accident, you will likely feel fear (a primary feeling) followed by anger (a secondary feeling). One option is to suppress the angry feelings. Another is to give way to irrational thinking and act out your angry feelings. You may be tempted to pull alongside the other driver and make a threatening gesture or shout obscenities. The consequences of this action may be quite negative. The other person may respond with further threats, and conflict may evolve to a point where violence takes place. Even if no such response takes place, you may experience feelings of guilt or embarrassment after acting out your anger in a destructive manner.

Appropriate expressions of anger can reduce your anxiety and help you get rid of unhealthy stress. An expression of anger may also improve communication because the other person learns exactly how you feel. In deciding whether to express your anger, consider these factors:

1. *Try to determine what impact your message will have on the self-esteem of the other person.* Is this person able to hear and understand your feelings without feeling threatened, inferior, or defensive?
2. *Consider the stability of the relationship between yourself and the other person.* Is the relationship strong enough to withstand the impact of your anger? Will your expression of anger evoke defensiveness, resentment, or violence?
3. *Reflect on your need to express anger.* Would it be unhealthy to suppress this anger? Are there less risky outlets for your anger? For example, your anger might dissipate after you discuss the problem with a close friend or colleague who is a good listener.[29]

It is often a good idea to engage in a quick self-examination before you express your anger. Try to pinpoint what triggered the anger. Are you relying on rational or irrational thinking? Anger is often the result of not having our needs met, so reflect on the source of the anger. Can it be traced to unfulfilled needs for belonging? For recognition? For security?

Effective Ways to Express Your Anger

Buddha said, "You will not be punished for your anger, you will be punished by your anger." Intense anger that is suppressed will linger and become a disruptive force in your life unless you can find a positive way to get rid of it. Expressing feelings of anger can be therapeutic, but many people are unsure about the best way to self-disclose this emotion. To express anger in ways that will improve the chances that the other person will receive and respond to your message, consider these suggestions:

1. *Avoid reacting in a manner that could be seen as emotionally unstable.* If others see you as reacting irrationally, you will lose your ability to influence them.[30] Failure to maintain your emotional control can damage your image.
2. *Do not make accusations or attempt to fix blame.* It would be acceptable to begin the conversation by saying, "I felt humiliated at the staff meeting this morning." It would not be appropriate to say, "Your comments at the morning staff meeting were mean spirited and made me feel humiliated." The latter statement invites a defensive response.[31]
3. *Express your feelings in a timely manner.* The intensity of anger can actually increase with time. Also, important information needed by you or the

Total Person Insight

"We all want to live sufficiently free from anger so that it isn't a problem, so that it doesn't prevent us from living successfully and harmoniously with other people and at peace within ourselves. This requires not just a philosophy, or a way of looking at things, it requires some skill-building."

KIMES GUSTIN

Author, *Anger, Rage, and Resentment*

person who provoked your anger may be forgotten or distorted with the passing of time.

4. *Be specific as you describe the factors that triggered your anger, and be clear about the resolution you are seeking.* The direct approach, in most cases, works best.

In some cases the person who triggers your anger may be someone you cannot confront without placing your job in jeopardy. For example, one of your best customers may constantly complain about the service he receives. You know he receives outstanding service, and you feel anger building inside you each time he complains. But any display of anger may result in loss of his business. In this situation you rely on your rational thinking power and say to yourself, "This part of my work is very distasteful, but I can stay calm each time he complains." Similarly, if the person who triggers your anger is your boss, and you cannot confront her without risking the loss of your job, you may have to defuse your anger in some other way. You might practice deep breathing, going for a long walk after work, or taking a few minutes out of your work to meditate.[32]

How to Handle Other People's Anger

Dealing with other people's anger may be the most difficult human relations challenge we face. Most of us are not well prepared to deal with our own anger or the anger of others. The following skills can be learned and applied to any situation where anger threatens to damage a relationship.

1. *Recognize and accept the other person's anger.* The simple recognition of the intense feelings of someone who is angry does a lot to defuse the situation.[33] In a calm voice you might say, "I can see that you are very angry," or "It's obvious that you are angry."

2. *Encourage the angry person to vent his or her feelings.* By asking questions and listening carefully to the response, you can encourage the person to discuss the cause of the anger openly. Try using an open-ended question to encourage self-disclosure: "What have I done to upset you?" or "Can you tell me why you are so angry?"

3. *Do not respond to an angry person with your own anger.* To express your own anger or become defensive will only create another barrier to emotional healing. When you respond to the angry person, keep your voice tone soft. Keep in mind the old biblical injunction, "A soft answer turns away wrath."[34]

4. *Give the angry person feedback.* After venting feelings and discussing specific details, the angry person will expect a response. Briefly paraphrase what seems to be the major concern of the angry person, and express a desire to find ways to solve the problem. If you are at fault, accept the blame for your actions and express a sincere apology.

VIOLENCE IN THE WORKPLACE

An angry Ford Motor Company employee who recently had been disciplined carried a 9mm handgun into the Ford plant in Plymouth Township, Michigan. He killed a supervisor and then himself. This was the sixth shooting at a Detroit-area auto plant in three years.[35] Although this type of violence in the workplace is not a frequent occurrence, homicides committed by disgruntled current and former employees are increasing. Such attacks are often triggered by loss of a job, conflict between the employee and management, or a personal tragedy, such as divorce or separation. Abusive behavior by supervisors and managers is widespread, according to Columbia University psychologist Harvey Hornstein. In his book *Brutal Bosses and Their Prey,* Hornstein says the abusive behavior takes the form of verbal and physical threats, lying, deviousness, and sexual harassment.[36] A rigid, autocratic, impersonal work environment also appears to foster violence. Over the past decade, thirty-six people have been killed and twenty wounded at U.S. post office facilities across America. Over 10,000 Postal Service employees called a toll-free hotline during a recent twelve-month period to report potentially violent coworkers.[37]

The person most likely to commit murder in the workplace is a middle-aged white male who is a loner without a family. He may have a fascination with weapons. Some are vengeful workers who have suffered other setbacks in their career, and being fired, passed over for a promotion, or abused in some way is the final insult. The perpetrator of workplace violence is often someone who finds his or her identity in the job, so its loss is a major blow to the person's self-esteem.[38]

Although homicides get the most attention, they do not represent the most common form of workplace violence. Workplace violence encompasses a wide range of behaviors including hostile remarks, intimidating another employee by stalking, physical assaults, and threatening phone calls. Nor is violence always directed toward a coworker or manager. As Martin Sprouse describes in *Sabotage in the American Workplace,* some disgruntled employees take out their rage and despair by damaging their employer's equipment, deliberately causing customer relations problems, or stealing office supplies.[39]

Preventing Workplace Violence

The National Safe Workplace Institute estimates that incidents of workplace violence cost employers and others several billion dollars each year. This figure does not, of course, reflect the human suffering caused by acts of violence. Can workplace violence be prevented? Although violence cannot be eliminated, some steps can help curb violent behavior in the workplace.

1. *Use hiring procedures that screen out unstable persons.* In-depth interviews, drug testing, and background checks can help identify signs of a troubled past.
2. *Develop a strategy for responding to incidents* before *they actually occur.* Adopt a zero-tolerance policy that makes it clear that violent incidents will not be tolerated.[40]
3. *If someone must be demoted, fired, or laid off, do it in a way that does not demoralize the employee.* Some rigid, authoritarian companies handle such personnel actions in a very dehumanizing manner.
4. *Provide out-placement services for laid-off or terminated employees.* These services may include development of job-search skills, retraining, or, in cases where the employee is displaying signs of aggression, counseling.
5. *Establish a systematic way to deal with disgruntled employees.* Federal Express Corp. developed the Guaranteed Fair Treatment program to provide a forum for employees who feel they have been treated unfairly. (Chapter 13 covers this and other conflict resolution programs in more detail.) Employee frustration builds in organizations where employees do not feel valued, respected, and heard.
6. *Provide supervisors and managers with training that will help them prevent workplace violence and deal effectively with violence if it does occur.* Workplace violence is a growing problem in America, but it is not a problem without solutions. As the workplace gets leaner, it need not become meaner.

EMOTIONAL STYLES

A good starting point for achieving emotional control is to examine your emotional style. How do you deal with emotions? Your style started taking shape before birth and evolved over a period of many years. As an adult, you are likely to display one of four different emotional styles when confronted with strong emotions.

Suppressing Your Emotions

Many people have learned to suppress their feelings as much as possible. Some have developed intellectual strategies that enable them to avoid dealing directly with emotional reactions to a situation. In response to the loss of a loved one, a person may avoid the experience of grief and mourning by taking on new responsibilities at work. This is not, of course, a healthy way to deal with grief. Some people become upset but keep their anger bottled up inside. Controlling your anger does not mean ignoring injustices by others. The inability to express emotions has been linked to a number of mental and physical health problems. Research indicates that migraine headaches and back pain can sometimes be traced to suppressed emotions.[41] Some heart attack patients are victims of their inhibited anger. They have blocked the feeling of anger and avoided the expression of this emotion toward the person or situation that provoked the feeling.[42]

Capitulating to Your Emotions

People who display this emotional style see themselves as the helpless victim of feelings over which they have no control.[43] By responding to emotion in this manner, one can assign responsibility for the "problem" to external causes, such as other people or unavoidable events. For example, Paula, a busy office manager, is frustrated because her brother-in-law and his wife frequently show up unannounced on weekends and expect a big meal. Paula has a tight schedule during the week, and she looks forward to quiet weekends with her family. She has never expressed her anger to anyone because the uninvited guests are, after all, "family." People who capitulate to their emotions often experience feelings of helplessness and simply suffer in silence.

Overexpressing Your Emotions

In a work setting, everyone needs to be seen as a responsible and predictable person. Angry outbursts can damage credibility. One of the quickest ways to lose the respect and confidence of the people you work with is to display a lack of emotional control. Foul and vulgar language in conjunction with an angry outburst can seriously damage a person's image.

One acceptable way to release anger is to sit down with pen and paper and write a letter to the person who triggered your anger. Don't worry about grammar, spelling, or punctuation—just put all your angry thoughts on paper.

Write until you have nothing more to say. Then destroy the letter. Once you let go of your angry feelings, you will be ready to deal constructively with whatever caused you to become upset.[44]

Accommodating Your Emotions

At the beginning of this chapter we said an emotion can be thought of as a feeling that influences our thinking and behavior. Accommodation means you are willing to recognize, accept, and experience emotions and to attempt to react in ways appropriate to the situation. This style achieves an integration of one's feelings and the thinking process. People who display the accommodation style have adopted the "think before you act" point of view. Let's assume that as you are presenting a new project proposal at a staff meeting, someone interrupts you and strongly criticizes your ideas. The criticism seems to be directed more at you than at your proposal. Anger starts building inside you, but before responding to the assailant, you pause and engage in some rational thinking. During the few seconds of silence, you quickly make a mental review of the merits of your proposal and consider the other person's motives for making a personal attack. You decide the person's comments do not warrant a response at this point. Then you continue with your presentation, without a hint of frustration in your voice. If your proposal has merit, the other members of the group will probably speak on your behalf.

Do we always rely on just one of these four emotional styles? Of course not. Your response to news that a coworker was killed in an auto accident may be very different from your response to a demeaning comment made by your boss. You may have found appropriate ways to deal with your grief but have not yet learned to avoid lashing out at persons who trigger your anger. Dealing with our emotions is a very complex process. Selecting the most appropriate response can be very challenging.

Thinking / Learning Starters

1. Think about the last time someone expressed his or her anger to you. Were you able to respond in an appropriate way? Was the relationship between you and the angry person damaged?

2. Try to recall a situation where you either suppressed your feelings or overexpressed your feelings. How did your behavior affect the other person?

Gender Differences in Emotional Style

Men often complain that women are too emotional. Women often complain that men are too rational and too insensitive to the emotions of others. Although these complaints are not valid in all cases, they can help us understand gender differences in emotional styles.[45] In many families, males are encouraged to hide their feelings, to appear strong and stable. Participation in team sports and work may reinforce this early conditioning. Many women say that when women talk about their emotions, men do not take their emotional needs seriously enough and do not respond with support and understanding. Joan Borysenko suggests that men take time to comfort a woman who wants to talk about an important problem and to validate her right to feel her emotions. An appropriate male response in this situation might be nothing more than a sincere acknowledgment of the problem: "Gee, Susan, I can see that you are really upset. Let's talk about the problem." Borysenko suggests that women keep in mind that many men find it difficult to talk about emotions and to display emotions. For example, many men still cling to the notion that crying is not a manly thing to do. Borysenko emphasizes that awareness of our own emotional style and that of the other person is very important. A good relationship does not require both people to have the same emotional style, but it does require each person to respect the other person's style.[46]

Male versus female aggression has been the subject of much discussion in recent years. Men are much more violent than women, but we are not sure why. Anne Campbell proposes one explanation in *Men, Women, and Aggression*. She believes that men's and women's experience in society teaches them to view aggression differently. Women, according to Campbell, feel aggression is the failure of self-control. Men see aggression as a way of imposing control over

Reprinted with special permission of King Features Syndicate.

others and are therefore more likely to regard it as a legitimate means of assuming authority over the disruptive and frightening forces they encounter in life.[47]

STRATEGIES FOR ACHIEVING EMOTIONAL CONTROL

We live our lives in two distinct worlds—one of fact and certainty and one of emotions and ambiguity. The world of certainty is that part of our lives that deals with objects and our rational side; the world of ambiguity deals with people and our feeling, or emotional, side—our human world. Too often we try to handle our human world in the same way that we handle our factual world.[48] Most of us are better prepared to deal with the rational side of our life because most of our previous education (formal and informal) emphasized this area. In this, the final part of the chapter, we share with you some practical suggestions for achieving greater control of the emotions that affect your life. Although emphasis is on the emotion of anger, the information pre-

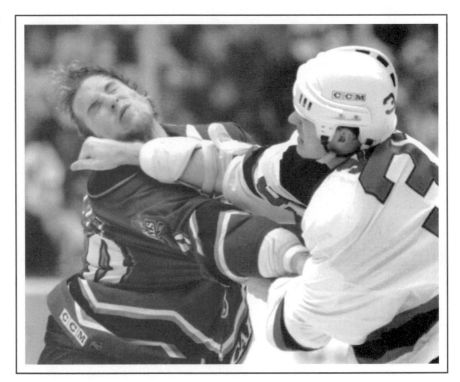

New Jersey hockey player Reid Simpson (right) lands a punch to the jaw of Washington's Brendan Witt. Each of us must learn to take control of our anger. (AP/Wide World Photos)

sented here will help you deal with other emotions, such as fear, jealousy, hurt, and grief.

Identifying Your Emotional Patterns

We could often predict or anticipate our response to anger if we would take the time to study our emotional patterns—to take a running inventory of circumstances that touch off our anger and our response to anger. An easy way to do this is to record your anger experiences in a diary or journal, noting such details as when, where, with whom, and to what degree you became angry. How did you respond to the anger? How long did the feelings of anger last? If you expressed your angry feelings to the person who upset you, how did you feel afterward? These journal entries can provide a path to greater self-awareness and help you determine changes you want to make in your emotional style.

Tamra Reed, a graphic designer employed by a large newspaper, felt anger and frustration every time a coworker delivered material late. New to her position, Tamra was hesitant to discuss her feelings with the offending person, but she did record them in a journal. She recorded not only her conscious feelings, such as anxiety, but also other feelings in her body—a knot in her stomach and muscle tension when material arrived late. Tamra soon began to identify some patterns. The late arrival of the material meant she had less time to work on the final design, so her completed work often fell short of the high-quality standards she set for herself.

The journal entries helped Tamra become aware of ways to cope with her problem. She discovered that she had lost touch with the power of her own resources. Each time she accepted late material, she gave her power to the offending person. This was followed by feelings of anger toward herself and toward the person who turned in the material late. She finally resolved to stop accepting late material and made her intentions known to those who were missing deadlines.

If you don't feel comfortable with journal writing, consider setting aside some quiet time to reflect on your emotional patterns. Try to answer some specific questions about the way you deal with anger. What makes you angry? Have others learned which "buttons" to push in order to make you angry? What is your typical response to strong feelings of anger? Do you feel guilty after expressing anger? Do you find it hard to let go of resentment? A period of quiet reflection will help you focus your thoughts and impressions. Becoming a skilled observer of your own emotions is one of the best ways to achieve greater emotional control.

In addition to journal writing and quiet reflection, there is one more way to discover emotional patterns. At the end of the day, construct a chart of your emotional landscape. Make a chart (see Table 9.1) of the range of emotions you experienced and expressed during the day.[49] Your first entry might be "I

TABLE 9.1

Charting Your
Emotional Landscape

Time	Circumstance	Emotion
6:00 A.M.	Alarm goes off. Mind is flooded by thoughts of all the things that must be done during the day.	Anxiety
7:10 A.M.	Depart for work. Heavy traffic interferes with plan to arrive at work early.	Anger and helplessness
8:00 A.M.	Thirty-minute staff meeting scheduled by the boss lasts fifty minutes. No agenda is provided. Entire meeting seems a waste of time.	Anger and frustration
9:35 A.M.	Finally start work on creative project.	Contentment
10:15 A.M.	Progress on project interrupted when coworker enters office, sits down, and starts sharing gossip about another coworker.	Anger and resentment
11:20 A.M.	Progress is made on creative project.	Contentment
1:45 P.M.	Creative project is complete and ready for review.	Joy and contentment
2:50 P.M.	Give project to boss for review. She says she will not be able to provide any feedback until morning. This delay will cause scheduling problems.	Frustration
4:00 P.M.	Attend health insurance update seminar sponsored by human resources department. No major changes are discussed.	Boredom
5:40 P.M.	Give up on a search for a missing document, turn off computer, and walk to parking lot.	Relief and fatigue

woke up at 6:00 A.M. and immediately felt _____." The final entry might be "I left the office at 5:30 P.M. with a feeling of _____." What emotions surfaced throughout your workday? Resentment? Creative joy? Anxiety? Boredom? Contentment? Anger? Satisfaction? Reflect on the completed chart and try to determine which patterns need to be changed. For example, you might discover that your behavior is too often influenced by irrational thinking. Repeat this process over a period of several days in order to identify your unique emotional patterns.

Fine-Tuning Your Emotional Style

Once you have completed the process of self-examination and have identified some emotional patterns you want to change, it is time to consider ways to

Total Person Insight

"It's unfortunate that we're never really taught how to show emotion in ways that help our relationships. Instead, we're usually told what we should not *do. However, too little emotion can make our lives seem empty and boring, while too much emotion, poorly expressed, fills our interpersonal lives with conflict and grief. Within reason, some kind of* balance *in the expression of emotion seems to be called for."*

GERARD EGAN

Author, *You and Me*

fine-tune your emotional style. Getting rid of emotional imbalances can help you to live a fuller, more satisfying life. Here are four things you can begin doing today.

- *Take responsibility for your emotions.* How you view your emotional difficulties will have a major influence on how you deal with them. If your anger is triggered by thoughts such as "I can never make my boss happy" or "Things always go wrong in my life," you may never find an effective way to deal with this emotion. By shifting the blame to other people and events, you cannot achieve emotional control.
- *Put your problems into proper perspective.* Why do some people seem to be at peace with themselves most of the time while others seem to be in a perpetual state of anxiety? People who suffer from an emotional imbalance often are unable or unwilling to look at problems realistically and practically, and they view each disappointment as a major catastrophe. Some things are not worth getting upset about. When faced with unpleasant events, pause and ask yourself, "Is this problem worth getting angry about?"
- *Take steps to move beyond anger and resentment.* Some people are upset about things that happened many years ago. Some even nurse grudges against people who have been dead for years. The sad thing is that the anger remains long after we can achieve any positive learning from it.[50] Studies of divorce, for example, indicate that anger and bitterness can linger a long time. Distress seems to peak one year after the divorce, and many people report that it takes at least two years to move past the anger.[51] When anger dominates one's life, whatever the reason, therapy or counseling may provide relief. Membership in a support group is often helpful.
- *Give your feelings some exercise.* Several prominent authors in the field of human relations have emphasized the importance of giving our feelings some exercise. Leo Buscaglia, author of *Loving Each Other*, says, "Exercise feelings. Feelings have meaning only as they are expressed in action."[52] Sam

Keen, author of *Fire in the Belly,* said, "Make a habit of identifying your feelings and expressing them in some appropriate way."[53] If you have offended someone, how about sending that person a letter of regret? If someone you work with has given extra effort, why not praise that person's work? If you have been nursing a grudge for some time, how about practicing forgiveness?

Every day of our personal and work life we face some difficult decisions. One option is to take only actions that feel good at the moment. In some cases, this means ignoring the feelings of customers, patients, coworkers, and supervisors. Another option is to behave in a manner that is acceptable to the people around you. If you choose this option, you will have to make some sacrifices. You may have to be warm and generous when the feelings inside you say, "Be cold and selfish." You may have to avoid an argument when your feelings are insisting, "I'm right and the other person is wrong!" To achieve emotional control often requires restructuring our ways of feeling, thinking, and behaving.

Summary

We carry inside us a vast array of emotions that help us cope with our environment. An emotion can be thought of as a feeling that influences our thinking and behavior. We sometimes experience emotional imbalance because we learn to inhibit the expression of certain emotions and overemphasize the expression of others. Emotions play a critical role in the success of every organization. Emotional undercurrents are present in almost every area of the organization, and they influence employee morale, customer loyalty, and productivity.

Our emotional development is influenced by temperament (the biological shaper of personality), our subconscious mind, and cultural conditioning. These influences contribute to the development of our emotional intelligence. Throughout the long process of emotional development we learn different ways to express our anger. Appropriate expressions of anger contribute to improved interpersonal relations, help us reduce anxiety, and give us an outlet for unhealthy stress. We must also learn how to handle other people's anger. It takes a great deal of effort to learn how to deal with our own anger and the anger of others.

In recent years we have seen an increase in workplace violence. Workplace violence encompasses a wide range of activities, including homicides, hostile remarks, physical assaults, and sabotage directed toward the employer. Although violence cannot be eliminated, steps can be taken to curb violent employee behavior.

To achieve emotional balance, we need to start with an examination of our current emotional style. When confronted by strong feelings, we are likely to display one of four different emotional styles: suppressing emotions, capitulating to them, overexpressing them, or accommodating them. Researchers suggest that there are gender differences in emotional style.

Emotional control is an important dimension of emotional style. The starting point in developing emotional control is to identify your current emotional patterns. One way to do this is to record your anger experiences in a diary or journal. Additional ways to identify emotional patterns include setting aside time for quiet reflection and developing a chart of your emotional landscape. Once you have completed the process of self-examination, you should consider appropriate ways to fine-tune your emotional style.

Career Corner

Q. When I started working for this company, I was never put in a situation where it was necessary to make presentations to others. After receiving a promotion to department head, I was expected to make monthly reports to my staff. I never feel comfortable in the role of group presenter. Hours before the monthly meeting I start feeling tense, and by the time the meeting begins I am gripped by fear. Two weeks ago, my boss asked me to make a presentation to senior management. Shortly before the meeting I started experiencing chest pain, sweating, and trembling. I told my boss I was sick and went home. Why am I so frightened of speaking to a group? Should I seek professional help?

A. It appears that you may have developed a social phobia. Social phobias are fears of situations in which the person can be watched by others. Phobias of various types are quite common—they currently afflict over 11 million Americans. Your problem could be serious, and you might consider seeking help from a qualified therapist. Psychotherapy can result in greater self-understanding and self-expression. Throughout the treatment you will learn new ways to cope with your problem. It is encouraging to note that about 80 percent of psychotherapy patients benefit from treatment.

Key Terms

emotion
temperament

subconscious mind
anger

Review Questions

1. What is the relationship between feelings and emotion? What role do feelings play in our life?
2. What is meant by the term *emotional balance?* What factors create an *emotional imbalance?*
3. List and briefly describe the three factors that influence our emotional development.
4. Emotions play a critical role in the success of every organization, yet many leaders seem unaware of this fact. Why?

5. Describe the human emotion we call anger, and explain why it is important to learn to control one's anger.
6. What four steps can improve the chances that another person will receive and respond to your feelings of anger?
7. List four skills that can be used to effectively handle anger in other people.
8. Discuss what it means to accommodate your feelings. What are the positive aspects of this emotional style?
9. List and briefly describe four ways to fine-tune your emotional style.
10. Explain your understanding of the Gerard Egan Total Person Insight.

Application Exercises

1. Recall the last time you were angry at another person or were a victim of a situation that made you angry. For example, perhaps a housemate or roommate refused to pay her share of the grocery bill, or your manager accused you of wrongdoing without knowing all the facts. Then answer the following questions:
   a. Did you express your anger verbally? Physically?
   b. Did you suppress any of your anger? Explain.
   c. What results did you experience from the way you handled this situation? Describe both positive and negative results.
   d. If you could relive the situation, would you do anything differently? Explain.
2. To learn more about the way you handle anger, record your anger responses in a journal for a period of five days. When anger surfaces, record as many details as possible. What triggered your anger? How intense was the anger? How long did your angry feelings last? Did you express them to anyone? At the end of the five days, study your entries and try to determine whether any patterns exist. If you find this activity helpful, consider keeping a journal for a longer period of time.
3. To learn more about how emotions influence your thinking and behavior, complete each of the following sentences. Once you have completed them all, reflect on your written responses. Can you identify any changes you would like to make in your emotional style?
   a. "When someone makes me angry, I usually . . ."
   b. "The most common worry in my life is . . ."
   c. "When I feel compassion for someone, my response is to . . ."
   d. "My response to feelings of grief is . . ."
   e. "When I am jealous of someone, my response is to . . ."

Internet Exercise

This chapter provides an introduction to important strategies for achieving emotional control. The Internet provides additional information about this important topic. Using your search engine, type in "emotional control," and determine what types of resources (such as books, articles, and training programs) are available. Pay special attention to information on how one can achieve greater emotional control. Prepare a written report on your findings, and note any strategies that you would consider adopting.

| Case 9.1 | **Love in the Workplace** |

S hould the emotion of love be allowed to flourish in a business setting? Wal-Mart Stores, Inc., says the answer is no if the romance involves coworkers who are married to other people. Two Wal-Mart employees were fired when a manager learned they were dating. One was separated from her husband but not divorced. At that time, Wal-Mart Stores had a policy that said married employees cannot date coworkers. This policy has since been modified to ban dating between supervisors and their subordinates. The Richards Group, a Dallas advertising agency, has a similar policy. New employees are told at the outset that dating someone from the agency—married or single—is not tolerated. Stan Richards, founder of the company, believes that office romances interfere with providing good service to clients. Those who support Richards's position say that workplace romances often result in lower productivity when the couple takes extra-long lunches or long breaks. If fellow staffers feel that the couple is not doing their share of the work, feelings of anger or jealousy may develop.

George Mitchell, chief executive officer of Mitchell Energy & Development Corporation, takes a very different view of romance in the office. He says, "People meet and get married, and you can't really stop that. It's the way the world goes." Bill Gates, CEO of Microsoft Corp., would no doubt agree. He married Melinda French, a Microsoft employee he met at work. A number of social and economic trends seem to be encouraging romance at work. There are more women in the workplace than ever before. People with similar talents, backgrounds, and aspirations often meet on the job. An increasing number of men and women work long hours and have less leisure time than they used to have.

Corporate America seems to be getting more comfortable with love in the workplace. A large number of companies now employ married couples. Steelcase Inc., the Grand Rapids, Michigan, office furniture manufacturer, has over 300 married couples on its payroll. And most executives seem unconcerned about office romances. Nearly three-quarters of the CEOs who participated in a *Fortune* magazine poll said romances between workers are "None of the company's business."

Questions

1. Can you think of a situation where employment of married couples would create problems for a firm? Explain your answer.

2. Should organizations establish policies that prevent dating a coworker? A supervisor? Explain your answer.
3. Is an office romance likely to affect the productivity of the two workers involved? Is it likely to affect the people who work around the persons involved in the romance?

Case 9.2   **Helping Employees Who Behave Badly**

O rganizations that want to survive in today's highly competitive global economy must learn how to deal with employees who behave badly. This includes the boss who frequently becomes angry and yells at employees. It also includes employees who treat customers with indifference and disrespect. Team members who cause friction and engage in infighting also need help. Many employees who behave badly are persons with valuable technical skills, so termination may not be an option. To salvage the career of an employee who possesses strong technical skills but lacks effective people skills is a challenge. Here is how some companies are meeting this challenge.

- At Chemical Bank, based in New York City, some candidates for management positions have been encouraged to complete the Dale Carnegie human relations course. A recent enrollee was a 32-year-old employee who had a degree in accounting. He had good technical skills, but Chemical wanted him to develop his people skills.
- David Prosser, chief executive officer of RTW Inc., a worker's compensation management firm in Minneapolis, received complaints about one of his managers. This person would become angry and yell at other employees. Most of the targets of his wrath were lower-level employees who wouldn't dare fight back. Other managers met with him to discuss his behavior, but he denied he had done anything wrong. Prosser viewed the manager as a valued employee, so he sent him to Executive to Leader Institute, a local coaching firm. After several months of personal coaching, the manager learned to control his anger.

More serious cases include employees who have substance addictions or serious personality disorders such as depression. A potentially violent employee can present the greatest challenge because discharging an employee with a mental disability may be viewed as illegal by the courts. Antibias laws such as the Americans with Disabilities Act can make it difficult for employers to fire mentally unstable workers. Legal pitfalls exist because it is often difficult to distinguish between conduct that is the result of a mental disability and conduct that is the result of generally unacceptable behavior. Companies must also determine the best way to deal with domestic violence that spills over to the job.

For example, many women who are victims of domestic abuse are threatened or abused while at work.

Questions

1. At Chemical Bank some employees are encouraged to complete the Dale Carnegie human relations course. What are the advantages and disadvantages of this approach?
2. A manager at RTW Inc. was given help in the form of personal coaching. What are the advantages and disadvantages of this approach?
3. What would be your response if a fellow worker suddenly became moody and caused friction in your department. Would you attempt to offer assistance, or would you wait for someone else to deal with the problem?

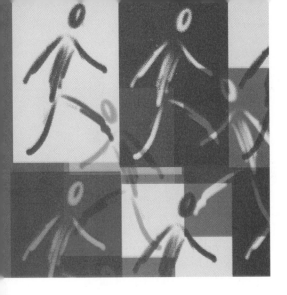

Chapter 10

Building Stronger Relationships with Positive Reinforcement

Chapter Preview

After studying this chapter, you will be able to

1. Create awareness of the strong need people have for positive reinforcement.
2. Understand how to use positive reinforcement to improve relationships and reward behavior.
3. Describe the major barriers to the use of positive reinforcement.
4. Explain how to reward individual and team performance.

T HROUGHOUT LIFE we are constantly buffeted by events that create within us either positive or negative energy. In many cases, seemingly minor events trigger this energy. Donald Peterson, former CEO of Ford Motor Company, recalls visiting a Ford plant and talking with a veteran production worker. The man said he had been with the company for twenty-five years and hated every minute of it until he was asked for his opinion. He said that question transformed his job.[1] David Overton, founder of the highly successful Cheesecake Factory restaurant chain, views positive energy as a major ingredient of his customer service program. At his eighteen locations the waiters and waitresses are urged to dole out "a little love" along with heaping plates of food.[2] Shake hands with Del Wallick, and you will see his prized wristwatch, given to him on his twenty-fifth anniversary with Timken Company. Wallick says, "I only take it off to shower and sleep."[3] ∎

This chapter discusses the impact of positive reinforcement on both individual and group behavior. We examine in detail the various types of positive reinforcement, and you will learn why many people have difficulty expressing positive thoughts and feelings. A special section is devoted to awards and incentive programs currently used by a variety of organizations.

PERSONAL AND ORGANIZATIONAL GROWTH THROUGH POSITIVE REINFORCEMENT

When a behavior is followed by a positive outcome, we are more likely to want to engage in that behavior again. In a work setting, **positive reinforcement** can be described as the practice of preparing written thank-you notes, providing an incentive or award, giving praise, or providing some other form of recognition that will increase the likelihood that the person will repeat the reinforced behavior. In this chapter we consider positive reinforcement in somewhat broader terms. We use the term to describe activities that not only increase productivity but also improve interpersonal relationships. Therefore, much of the information presented in this chapter will have application in your personal as well as your professional life.

Positive Versus Negative Energy

Throughout periods of great uncertainty and turbulence, negative energy can become a powerful force. Many people go to work everyday wondering if they will be the next victim of a merger, buyout, or business closing. Some

Employees at MBNA, a Wilmington, Delaware, financial services company, receive constant feedback concerning their performance. The company sets up electronic scoreboards in its offices to keep workers informed of how well they are doing in various areas of customer service. (Steve Rubin / The Image Works, Inc.)

wonder if they will be able to cope with rapid technological changes and a changing job market. Stressful working conditions caused by rising productivity demands and long hours can also be the source of negative energy. In a negative, stressful work climate, these pressures often result in physical fatigue, loss of energy, decreased optimism, and lower morale. A positive work climate is more likely to instill workers with positive energy, which results in greater strength of will, increased optimism, and higher employee morale.

Positive feedback can generate positive energy within us. It is positive energy that helps us cope with disappointments, uncertainty, and work that is physically and mentally demanding. In the presence of positive energy people feel uplifted, encouraged, and empowered. Positive energy helps us remain balanced in a work environment that is increasingly characterized by change and uncertainty.

Negative energy is created when good performance is ignored. Even the most confident, self-motivated employees eventually will feel taken for granted without occasional praise.[4] Employees who feel unappreciated do not perform to the best of their abilities. In the absence of positive feedback, the organization becomes a negative force because most of the information employees receive emphasizes what is wrong rather than what is right. In such a climate, employees feel their work is not appreciated, and they become progressively demoralized and defensive. Negative energy is also created when compensation is inadequate, when needed training is not provided, or when the employee's need for work/life balance is ignored.

The flow of negative energy within an organization creates barriers to the achievement of important goals. For example, negative energy will undermine efforts to provide good customer service. People who work in a negative climate will usually be less effective in developing positive relationships with customers. A partner with Arthur Andersen Consulting reminded employers that good service is more likely to be given by employees who gain satisfaction from their work: "You cannot expect your employees to delight your customers unless you as an employer delight your employees."[5]

Employee-Reward Preferences

Studies have pointed out that upper-level managers and supervisors frequently do not understand employee-reward preferences. Managers and supervisors often expect pay or monetary rewards and job security to rank highest as reward preferences among employees. But when employees are surveyed, a different picture emerges. Asked to rank morale-building factors according to what they feel their employees want from a job, supervisory-management personnel give high marks to such factors as good pay, job security, and good working conditions. When employees are asked to rank morale-building factors, they are more likely to give top place to full appreciation for work done, interesting work, and a feeling of being in on things.[6] If employee-

DUFFY © Joe Martin. Reprinted with permission of UNIVERSAL PRESS SYNDICATE. All rights reserved.

reward preferences are not in harmony with management's reward system, problems arise.

OUR NEED FOR POSITIVE REINFORCEMENT

How strong is an individual's need to receive positive reinforcement from others? Psychologist William James believed that the craving to be appreciated is a basic principle of human nature. Mark Twain, the noted author, answered the question by saying he could live for three weeks on a compliment. Twain was willing to admit openly what most people feel inside. Many have a deep desire for personal recognition but almost never verbalize these thoughts.

Few people have the strength of ego to maintain high self-esteem without positive feedback from others. We often are not certain we have performed well until some other person tells us. Kenneth Blanchard and Spencer Johnson, authors of *The One Minute Manager,* stress the importance of "catching people doing things right" and engaging in "one minute praisings."[7] Without this positive feedback, employees often suffer from a sense of incompleteness.

Support from Maslow

The hierarchy of needs developed by Abraham Maslow (discussed in Chapter 7) provides additional support for the use of positive reinforcement. In part, the need for security (a second-level need) is satisfied by positive feedback from an approving supervisor, manager, or coworker. You are likely to feel more secure when someone recognizes your accomplishments. A feeling of belonging (a third-level need) can be satisfied by actions that communicate, "You are part of the team." Maslow states that as each lower-level need is satisfied, the need at the next level demands attention. It would seem to be almost impossible to satisfy the esteem needs (fourth level) without positive reinforcement. A person's level of self-esteem may diminish in a work environment where accomplishments receive little or no recognition.

Support from Skinner

The research of B. F. Skinner at Harvard University has contributed to our understanding of reinforcement as a factor influencing the behavior of people in a work setting. Skinner maintained that any living organism will tend to repeat a particular behavior if that behavior is accompanied or followed by a reinforcer.[8] A **reinforcer** is any stimulus that follows a response and increases the probability that the response will occur again.[9] Skinner also demonstrated that the timing of reinforcement has an important effect on behavior change. He discovered that if the delay between a response (behavior) and its reinforcement is too great, a change in behavior is less likely to take place.

Support from Berne

In Chapter 9, you were given a brief introduction to transactional analysis (TA), a theory of communication developed by Eric Berne. TA is a simplified explanation of how people communicate. Berne's research also provided evidence that most people have a strong need for recognition, or "strokes."

The word *stroking* is used to describe the various forms of recognition one person gives another. Strokes help satisfy the need to be appreciated. A **physical stroke** may be a pat on the back or a smile that communicates approval. **Verbal strokes** include words of praise and expressions of gratitude.

Berne said that stroking is necessary for physical and mental health. He believed, as do others, that infants who are deprived of physical strokes (hugs, caresses, and kisses) begin to lose their will to live. As people grow into adulthood, they are willing to substitute verbal stroking for physical stroking. Adults still need and want physical stroking, but they will settle for words of praise, incentives, awards, and other forms of recognition.

A stroke can be positive or negative. Positive strokes, called "warm fuzzies" in TA language, include such behaviors as listening with genuine attention, smiling, or simply saying "Thank you" sincerely to a customer who has just made a purchase. Negative strokes, sometimes called "cold pricklies," produce "I'm not OK" feelings inside people. A negative stroke may take the form of being sarcastic, failing to remember the name of a regular customer, or making fun of another person's appearance.

Total Person Insight

"Reward for a job well done is often cited by experts as a way to increase employee satisfaction even when traditional sources of recognition, like raises or promotions, don't come through. Recognition gives people an opportunity to feel valued by both managers and peers, and it enhances interaction, communication, and team spirit."

ROGER L. HALE AND RITA F. MAEHLING

Authors, *Recognition Redefined*

Stroke Deficit: A Common Condition

Claude Steiner, author of *TA Made Simple,* says that most people live in a state of **stroke deficit.** They survive on a less-than-ideal diet of strokes, like people who never have enough to eat.[10] Some individuals are so hungry for positive recognition they will ask for strokes. The following statements made by an ad layout employee working for a large newspaper may reveal the need for positive feedback:

- "Did you see my appliance ad in today's edition?"
- "I've been thinking of entering some of my ads in the annual newspaper ad competition. Do you think my work is good enough?"

A person who is starved for recognition may say or do things that damage relationships with others. The individual who does not receive enough positive strokes may engage in exaggerated self-criticism. The newspaper employee just described might make these statements:

- "None of my ads look right. I think I'll quit this job."
- "The department manager must hate my work. He hasn't commented on any of my ads for weeks."

No one enjoys working around people who constantly fish for compliments or who spend a lot of time finding fault with themselves. Both these behaviors may indicate the need for more positive reinforcement.

Thinking / Learning Starter

Recall a situation when you accomplished something important but no one seemed to notice. Try to remember the feelings that surfaced inside you. Did you experience disappointment? Hurt? Anger? Feelings of inadequacy? Why do you now think your accomplishments were ignored?

FORMS OF POSITIVE REINFORCEMENT

You have no doubt heard of employees who worked thirty or forty years but did not receive any significant form of recognition until the traditional gold watch, or some other token of appreciation, was presented on the worker's final day. Times have changed. Most progressive organizations recognize that positive reinforcement should be provided as a reward for good performance.

Nathan Kane, a student at Massachusetts Institute of Technology, received the Lemelson-MIT prize of $30,000 for excellence in innovative thinking. Rewards of this type can serve as a powerful form of positive reinforcement. (Joanne Strohmeyer/ The Boston Globe)

Variety is an important element of a successful positive reinforcement program. The "one-size-fits-all" approach will not work, especially in organizations that have taken steps to enhance work force diversity. A comprehensive recognition program includes a blend of formal and informal types of recognition, as we shall see in this section.

Confirmation Behaviors

Evelyn Sieburg used the term **confirmation** to name a whole series of behaviors that have a positive, or "therapeutic," effect on the receiver.[11] In most cases, confirmation behaviors develop feelings of self-worth in the mind of the worker and may be reflected in increased productivity, less absenteeism, and greater interest in work. To understand the wide range of confirmation behaviors possible in a work setting, let's follow a new worker, Mary Harper, through her first year on the job.

Mary graduated from a local community college, where she had completed a legal assistant program, and then obtained a position with a large law firm.

Upon arriving at work, she was greeted warmly by the office manager, given a tour of the office complex, and introduced to the people with whom she would be working. A highlight of the tour was a stop at the president's office, where she met the founder of the firm. The president briefly reviewed the history of the firm and extended a warm welcome.

The orientation continued with a review of the firm's policies and procedures by the office manager as well as training that enabled Mary to use the firm's data retrieval system. As she demonstrated competence in using the equipment, the supervisor made comments such as "Well done . . . you're a quick learner," and "Good job . . . you're doing fine."

During the morning coffee break on her first day, she was surprised to see a notice on the bulletin board that said, "Please welcome Mary Harper to our office." This notice reminded other workers that a new person had joined the staff. The notice also made it easier for everyone to remember her name.

As the weeks passed, Mary was given positive reinforcement on several occasions. She received positive feedback from coworkers as well as her supervisor. When she had a problem, her supervisor proved to be a good listener. Every person Mary had contact with seemed to be instilled with positive energy. At the end of the first year, she received a letter from the president of the firm (see Figure 10.1).

Would you enjoy working in this organizational setting? Chances are your answer is yes. A host of confirming behaviors gave Mary encouragement and support during her first year on the job. Some of these confirmations follow.

Orientation and Training   The office manager realized that no orientation or poor orientation can reduce a new employee's effectiveness and contribute to dissatisfaction and turnover. She took time to give Mary Harper a thorough introduction to company policies and procedures and get her acquainted with other employees. A first-class orientation sends the message "You are important, and we want you to get off to a good start." The office manager also recognized the importance of effective training.

Praise   Giving praise is one of the easiest and most powerful ways to make an employee feel important and needed. The person who receives the praise knows that his or her work is not being taken for granted. When handled correctly, praise can be an effective reinforcement strategy that ensures repetition of desired behaviors.

Courtesy   The poet Alfred Tennyson once said, "The greater the man, the greater the courtesy." When Mary Harper reported to work, she was welcomed in a courteous manner and introduced to people throughout the office. Even the president of the firm was not too busy to greet her. Courtesy means being considerate of others in small ways, showing respect for what others revere, and treating everyone, regardless of position, with consideration.

FIGURE 10.1

Letter Providing
Positive Reinforcement

THOMAS, THOMAS, and ROYAL
Attorneys and Counselors at Law
Denver, Colorado

August 11, 19__

Ms. Mary Harper
Legal Assistant
Thomas, Thomas, and Royal
144 Walnut Street
Denver, CO 80204

Dear Mary:

You have now completed one year with our firm, and I want you to know we are very pleased with your work. Ms. Williams, your supervisor, has kept me posted: your performance to date is certainly praiseworthy.

I notice that you have not missed a single day of work in your first year. The enclosed gift certificate in the amount of $100 is an expression of our gratitude. We appreciate your dedication.

Best wishes for continued success with our firm.

Sincerely,

Stephanie Thomas

Stephanie Thomas
President

Active Listening As discussed in Chapter 2, everyone feels a sense of personal value when speaking with a good listener. Active listening can be a powerful reinforcer. **Active listening,** as noted in Chapter 2, is the process of sending back to the speaker what you as a listener think the speaker meant in terms of both content and feelings.

Positive Written Communication Most people respond positively to notes and letters that express appreciation. Unfortunately, this form of positive reinforcement is used all too infrequently. Mary Harper will probably keep the letter written to her by the president and may show it to friends and relatives. A letter of appreciation or a thank-you note can have considerable impact on employee morale and can improve interpersonal communication within the organization. To encourage workers to maintain the company's high quality standards and ensure that employees do not feel their good performance is taken for granted, Federal Express Corporation encourages the use of personal notes. During one recent year over 50,000 thank-you notes were sent to employees.[12]

Thinking / Learning Starter

Chances are you owe somebody a thank-you note. Think about the events of the past six months. Has someone given time and effort to assist you with a problem? Make a list of at least three people who deserve a thank-you note. Pick one, write that person a note of appreciation, and mail it today.

BARRIERS TO POSITIVE REINFORCEMENT

The material in this chapter is based on two indisputable facts about human nature. First, people want to know how well they are doing and if their efforts are satisfactory. Second, they appreciate recognition for their accomplishments. Performance feedback and positive reinforcement can satisfy these important human needs. People often say they prefer negative feedback to no feedback at all. "Don't leave me in the dark" is a common plea (spoken or unspoken) of most people.

As noted previously, positive recognition can generate positive energy within us. This energy can help sustain us during long hours of hard work and assignments that fail to challenge us. Positive energy can also help us overcome the challenges we face in our personal life. Most of us need this injection of positive energy, but many of those we spend time with on the job and off the job are unable or unwilling to provide it.

Barriers to positive reinforcement take many forms. When Jay Leno became host of *The Tonight Show*, his manager advised him not to say thank you to Johnny Carson, the person who had made the program an American institution. Leno later said that not thanking Carson was "the biggest mistake" he's ever made.[13] He had allowed someone else to talk him out of doing the right thing. Some additional reasons why we do not "do the right thing" are described in this section.

Preoccupation with Self

One of the major obstacles to providing positive reinforcement is preoccupation with self. The term **narcissism** is often used to describe this human condition. Narcissism is a Freudian term alluding to the mythical youth who wore himself out trying to kiss his own reflection in a pool of water.

Total Person Insight

"Feeling grateful is good for us. Gratitude is the opposite of the qualities of self-centeredness, indifference, and arrogance. Expressing gratitude affords each of us unique opportunities to reach out in love and share happiness. Saying thank you is a very positive thing to do."

MALCOLM BOYD

Episcopal Priest; Author, "Volunteering Thanks"

Deepak Chopra, author of *The Seven Spiritual Laws of Success,* encourages everyone to practice the "Law of Giving." This law states that you must give in order to receive. If you want attention and appreciation, you must learn to give attention and appreciation. If you want joy in your life, give joy to others. He says the easiest way to get what you want is to help others get what they want.[14] Put another way, when you do good for another person, you do good for yourself.

The publication of *Random Acts of Kindness* and many people's acceptance of its central theme may have signaled a movement away from self-preoccupation. Random acts of kindness are those little things that we do for others that have no payback. They involve giving freely, purely, for no reason.[15] Here are some examples from the book:

- Send a letter to a teacher you once had letting him or her know about the difference he or she made in your life.
- Write a card thanking a service person for his or her care and leave it with your tip.
- Organize your friends and workmates to gather their old clothes and give them to homeless people.

Misconceptions About Positive Reinforcement

Some people fail to use positive reinforcement because they have misconceptions about this human relations strategy. One misconception is that people will respond to positive feedback by demanding tangible evidence of appreciation. "Tell people they are doing a good job and they will ask for a raise" seems to be the attitude of some managers. Actually, just the opposite response will surface more often than not. In the absence of intangible rewards (such as praise), workers may demand greater tangible rewards.

A few managers seem to feel they will lose some of their power or control if they praise workers. Yet if managers rely on power alone to get the job done, any success they achieve will no doubt be short-lived. When employees are doing a good job, why not reinforce that behavior with a little praise or a thank-you or congratulatory letter, like the one in Figure 10.2?

Misconceptions about positive reinforcement are not limited to business and industrial settings. Students in our public schools complain that teachers too often focus on what is wrong (you missed 5 of the 20 test questions) rather than what is right (you answered 15 of the test questions correctly). Many teachers experience a life almost devoid of positive energy because students, parents, and administrators seldom say "thank you" for doing a good job. And many children say, "My parents are always commenting on the things I do wrong."

FIGURE 10.2

Congratulatory Letter Reinforcing Desirable Behavior

INFRA-DYNAMICS, INC.
BINGHAMTON   HOUSTON   PALO ALTO

May 19, 19__

Ms. Patty Morrison, Manager
Process Control Division
Plant Number Five
126 James Avenue
Binghamton, NY 13901

Dear Patty:

Once again it gives me great pleasure to recognize you and your staff for outstanding performance in the area of safety. You folks have maintained a perfect record throughout the past twelve months.

Congratulations to you and all your employees for your contributions to this important job responsibility. All of us here at the home office are proud of you. Keep up the good work!

Sincerely,

Ralph Plazio

Ralph Plazio
Vice President
Production and Quality Control

RP:br

The "Too Busy" Syndrome

Ken Blanchard, noted author and consultant, says, "We're often too busy or too stressed to remember that the recognition we crave, others crave as well."[16] When you are under a great deal of pressure to get your work done, and you are struggling to achieve some degree of work/life balance, it's easy to postpone sending a thank-you note or phoning someone simply for the purpose of saying, "Thank you." Bruce Baldwin, practicing psychologist and consultant, describes the problem this way:

> There is not enough positive feedback given these days. With intense life-styles and countless pressures on men and women at work and in the home, positive feedback may sometimes completely disappear. In many organizations and in just as many homes, an emotionally destructive pattern emerges. No one says a thing about what is positive or done well.[17]

The key to solving this problem is planning. A consciously planned PR program will ensure that recognition for work well done is not overlooked. One approach might be to set aside a few minutes each day to work on performance feedback and positive reinforcement activities. In *The One Minute Manager,* the authors point out that positive feedback need not take long. They suggest the simple plan outlined in Table 10.1.

TABLE 10.1

One-Minute Praisings

The one-minute praising works well, say authors Kenneth Blanchard and Spencer Johnson, when you

1. Tell people up front that you are going to let them know how they are doing.
2. Praise people immediately.
3. Tell them what they did right—be specific.
4. Tell them how good you feel about what they did right and how it helps the organization and others who work there.
5. Stop for a moment of silence to let them feel how good you feel.
6. Encourage them to do more of the same.
7. Shake hands or touch people in a way that makes it clear that you support their success in the organization.

Source: "One Minute Praisings" from *The One Minute Manager* by Kenneth Blanchard, Ph.D. and Spencer Johnson, M.D. Copyright © 1981, 1982 by the Blanchard Family Partnership and Candle Communications Corporation. By permission of William Morrow and Company Inc.

Failing to Identify Commendable Actions

There are numerous opportunities to recognize the people you work with. By exercising just a little creativity, you can discover many actions that deserve to be commended.

Assume you are the manager of a large auto dealership. One of the key people within your organization is the service manager. This person schedules work to be performed on customers' cars, handles customer complaints, supervises the mechanics, and performs a host of other duties. If you want to give your service manager performance feedback and positive recognition, what types of behavior can you praise? Table 10.2 lists some examples.

The approach to positive reinforcement should, of course, be tailored to the requirements of the job. Positive reinforcement strategies designed for the office staff may not work in the machine shop.

Not Knowing What to Say or Do

Bob Nelson, author of *1001 Ways to Reward Employees,* reminds us that we can provide praise, recognition, and rewards in a variety of ways. He encourages us

TABLE 10.2

Job-Performance
Behaviors to Be
Reinforced

1. *Performance Related to Interpersonal Relations*
   a. Demonstrates empathy for customer needs and problems
   b. Is able to handle customer complaints effectively
   c. Is able to keep all employees well informed
   d. Cooperates with supervisory personnel in other departments
   e. Recognizes the accomplishments of employees
   f. Exhibits effective supervision of employees
2. *Personal Characteristics*
   a. Is honest in dealings with people throughout the organization
   b. Is punctual
   c. Does not violate policies and procedures
   d. Maintains emotional stability
   e. Maintains a neat appearance
   f. Is alert to new ways to do the job better
3. *Management Skills*
   a. Avoids waste in the use of supplies and materials
   b. Maintains accurate records
   c. Spends time on short- and long-range planning
   d. Takes steps to prevent accidents
   e. Delegates authority and responsibility
   f. Maintains quality-control standards

to use thoughtful, personal kinds of recognition that signify true apprecia-tion.[18] Many words and phrases can communicate approval. Here are several examples (see also Table 10.3):

- "Good thinking!"
- "This is the best yet!"
- "Excellent idea."

- "Good answer."
- "Thank you."
- "Keep up the good work."

Of course, you can express appreciation without using verbal communica-tion. Nonverbal expressions of approval include:

- Making eye contact
- Nodding agreement
- Patting on the back

- Signaling okay with thumbs up
- Smiling
- Giving a firm handshake

And you can give recognition to others through some type of action. Here are some activities that show approval:

- Asking for advice
- Asking someone to demonstrate the correct performance or procedure for others
- Displaying another person's work, or discussing another person's ideas
- Recognizing someone's work at a staff meeting

Lack of Appropriate Role Models

We tend to look to our leaders for clues about what is acceptable behavior. These leaders provide a role model for us. If the store manager in your

TABLE 10.3

Six Phrases That Can Enrich Your Life

Six Phrases*

The following six phrases can be used every day to enrich your life and the lives of other people:

"I'm wrong."

"I'm sorry."

"I need you."

"Thank you."

"I'm proud of you."

"I love you."

*From a presentation by Rich DeVos, cofounder of Amway Corporation.

Source: "Rich DeVos Remarks—Delta Pi Epsilon Distinguished Lecturer," *Delta Pi Epsilon Journal* (Fall 1995), pp. 221–223.

Marylou Shockley (on the left) serves as mentor to Bree Bowman. Shockley is a senior executive at Pacific Bell and is in a good position to serve as a role model to Bowman. Positive reinforcement from a respected mentor can have considerable impact. (David Butow/SABA)

neighborhood supermarket is aloof, seems indifferent to the needs of employees and customers, and generally displays a negative attitude, the store's supervisors are likely to imitate this behavior. After all, if the boss behaves this way, it must be OK. Pretty soon the grocery clerks, baggers, and cashiers—who look to the supervisors for guidance—get the message: Customer relations is not important. Getting along with coworkers is not important. Providing positive reinforcement for one another is not important. The people at the top are always in the spotlight. Their actions are constantly being watched by the people they supervise, and their attitudes are contagious.

REWARDING INDIVIDUAL AND TEAM PERFORMANCE

In recent years we have seen major changes in the use of positive reinforcement strategies in the workplace. In the past we viewed positive reinforcement as the responsibility of supervisors and managers. This view was much too narrow. As shown in Figure 10.3, everyone in the organization has opportunities to recognize the accomplishments of others. Persons in supervisory and management positions can benefit from positive reinforcement initiated by subor-

FIGURE 10.3

Shared Responsiblity for Positive Reinforcement

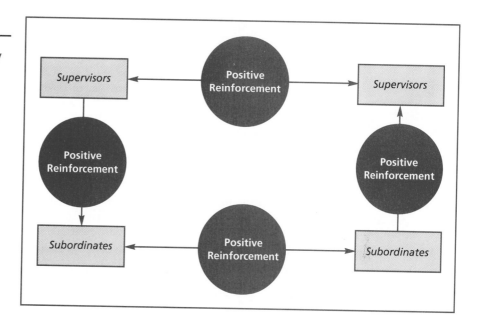

dinates. The authors of *How to Manage Your Boss* state that "subordinates too often wait until they have something negative to report before giving the boss feedback." Catching the boss doing something good and rewarding him or her is another appropriate use of positive reinforcement.[19]

Employees can also be encouraged to recognize the accomplishments of coworkers. In some cases, praise from a respected colleague is more important than praise from the boss. A survey conducted by Kuczmarski & Associates, a Chicago-based consulting firm, shed new light on the importance of peer recognition as a motivation factor. Members of new product development teams at seventy-seven Fortune 500 companies rated peer recognition second among factors that motivate them.[20]

The concept of teamwork, and the growing popularity of various types of teams, is changing the way companies structure their reward systems. If a work force is reorganized into self-directed work teams (discussed in Chapter 12), it makes sense to consider various types of team recognition plans. Such plans often emphasize the recognition of group performance rather than the recognition of individual performance.

Incentive Programs

Every year organizations spend billions of dollars for incentives and awards given to their employees. This money is spent on color TVs, vacation trips, rings, plaques, pins, certificates, merit pay, cash bonuses, and a host of other items. An **incentive program** is a planned activity designed to motivate employees to achieve an organizational objective.[21] The objective may be increasing quality, improving sales, ensuring safety, decreasing absenteeism, fostering teamwork, rewarding participation in wellness programs, or getting a job done quickly. Incentives represent a common form of positive reinforcement.

One of the most widespread developments in recent years has been the introduction of innovative incentive plans that reward increased productivity, improved quality, lower operating costs, or some combination of these factors. These plans include cash and noncash awards. The most common noncash awards include merchandise, travel opportunities, and recognition in the form of a plaque, trophy, pin, or letter of commendation. Noncash awards offer some advantages over cash awards, particularly "memory value." A weekend at a luxury hotel, valued at $250, will likely make a more lasting impression on the recipient than a $250 cash bonus. Noncash awards also have "trophy value." A high-quality gold pen or leather attaché case can be displayed and admired like a trophy.[22] Despite these advantages, many companies find that cash awards are needed to get employees to exert continuous effort. Some of the most common incentive programs involving cash payments are briefly described here.

Gain Sharing   In a **gain-sharing** plan, managers and employees develop methods of improving productivity, improving quality, and cutting costs. When a unit betters a predetermined performance objective, the resulting gains are divided according to a formula. One of the best examples of gain sharing is at the Rogan Corporation plant in Northbrook, Illinois. Rogan, a manufacturer of plastic knobs, uses gain sharing to reward employees for producing a premium-quality product and for reducing labor costs. After the program was started, employees contributed more than 300 ideas for making production more efficient. Efficiency improvements are reflected in worker bonuses.[23]

Profit Sharing   In a **profit-sharing** system, employees receive a share of the company's profits, which may be paid in cash or put into a retirement fund. Profit sharing is a successful motivator only when employees can influence profits. Critics of this plan say recipients often do not know exactly how they helped generate the profits, so they may not think or act differently because of the payment.[24]

Production Incentives   Under a **production-incentives** plan, employees receive payments based on how well they perform in relation to established standards. In a factory setting the rewards are often based on piecework. For each acceptable piece they produce, workers receive a specific payment. Safelite Glass Corporation of Columbus, Ohio, a nationwide installer of auto glass, moved from hourly to piece-rate pay. The payoff from piecework was significant. Average productivity per worker rose 20 percent, and the company experienced less absenteeism and lower employee turnover.[25]

Pay for Knowledge In a **pay-for-knowledge** system, workers are paid for the skills they master or the tasks they perform. This plan is often used by companies that want employees to be able to perform more than one job. When employees are organized into self-directed teams, it is common practice to encourage team members to learn all the jobs or tasks required of the entire team. Although training costs may be higher, workers who can perform several jobs become more valuable to the company.

Suggestion Programs Never underestimate the power of employee suggestions. When American Airlines, Inc., started offering noncash incentives to employees who came up with cost-saving ideas, the results exceeded expectations. The company saved over $50 million per year.[26] A formal **suggestion program** usually involves giving a monetary reward to employees who suggest ways to improve company operations. In most cases, the amount of the award is based on the estimated value of resulting increases in efficiency or cost cutting. Awards and incentives can also serve as the backbone of suggestion programs. To draw more ideas from employees, many companies are using merchandise awards in addition to, or in place of, the traditional cash award.

Criticisms of Incentive Programs

Although the vast majority of U.S. companies use some type of incentive program based on cash or noncash rewards, the practice is not without its critics. One of the foremost critics of incentive programs is Alfie Kohn, author of *No Contest: The Case Against Competition* and *Punished by Rewards: The Trouble with Gold Stars, Incentive Plans, A's, Praise, and Other Bribes.* Kohn states that reward systems often fail for these reasons:

1. *Pay is not an effective motivator.* Citing research by Frederick Herzberg and others, Kohn argues, "There is no firm basis for the assumption that paying people more will encourage them to do better work or even, in the long run, more work."[27]
2. *Rewards can punish.* Employees may view the reward as a form of manipulation: "Do this and you will get that." Kohn further notes that, in the mind of the employee, failing to receive a reward one has expected is indistinguishable from being punished.[28]
3. *Rewards can damage relationships.* A reward system that forces people to compete for awards or recognition may undermine cooperation and teamwork. In addition to damaged interpersonal relationships, the reward

plan may result in loss of self-esteem. Kohn says, "For each person who wins, there are many others who carry with them the feeling of having lost."[29]

4. *Rewards may mask real problems.* In some cases incentives treat the symptom, not the problem.[30] For example, a firm that gives merchandise awards or cash incentives may reduce absenteeism but fail to cure the real problem—which could be poor working conditions or poor supervision.

Although these criticisms have a great deal of merit, the fact remains that large numbers of organizations have achieved positive results with carefully developed incentive programs. It is possible to design programs that will have long-range benefits for both the organization and the individual employee. A well-designed program can help an organization achieve a variety of goals.

Planning the Incentive Program

The key to successful incentive programs is careful planning and implementation. The challenge is to develop a plan that motivates the right kinds of behavior. Any confusion about which behavior is to be rewarded can create serious problems. Programs must also be administered fairly, or some eligible employees may not participate or will participate with little enthusiasm. The following guidelines should be observed in the designing and implementing of an incentive program:

1. *Start with a well-defined purpose.* Companies with established incentive plans that are not related to specific goals almost always encounter problems.
2. *Consider individual employee needs.* If feasible, adapt rewards to the individual employee. The employee who is eager to build his or her personnel file might be given a letter of commendation instead of a wall plaque.[31] Theater tickets may be of little interest to an employee whose major interest is attending professional football games.
3. *Spell out requirements carefully before the program begins, and make rules easy to understand.* A written description of the incentive program should be given to every eligible employee. It is often a good idea to introduce new programs at meetings or conferences so that employees will have an opportunity to raise questions and discuss items that are not clear.
4. *Provide meaningful rewards.* If the rewards are not significant or if there are not enough of them, little interest in the program will develop. If achieving the award is too difficult, some employees may not even try. If rewards are too easily attained, participants will not be motivated to do their best.
5. *Administer the award program fairly.* Once the policies and procedures have been established, employees must be confident that the organization

will adhere to them. Incentives should be given only when results are achieved.

The Critical Importance of Environment

Positive reinforcement as a human relations strategy flourishes in a supportive environment. Within the organization, there should be respect for each person, regardless of job title, duties performed, or earnings. The prevailing climate within the organization should also be positive. People must feel good about the organization, its leadership, and other employees. Positive reinforcement comes naturally in a positive work environment. But positive reinforcement will almost never flourish in a negative work environment.

Summary

People usually feel good when their accomplishments are recognized and become upset when they are ignored. Positive reinforcement, when used correctly to reward accomplishments, is a powerful motivator. Everyone needs to receive personal recognition and to feel appreciated.

Although many studies indicate that recognition is an important employee reward preference, often ranked higher than monetary rewards and job security, many people seem unable or unwilling to reward a job well done. Confirmation behaviors must be used in organizational settings more often. Praise, simple courtesy, active listening, written thank-you notes, incentives, and awards represent some of the ways we can reinforce another's behavior.

Preoccupation with self is a major obstacle to providing reinforcement to others. Self-centered persons are likely to overlook the accomplishments of other people. Some people say a busy schedule does not allow time to give recognition to others. These and other barriers tend to minimize the use of positive reinforcement.

Common incentive programs were described, and suggestions for planning an incentive program were discussed. Some of the most common incentive programs involving cash payments are gain-sharing, profit-sharing, production-incentives, pay-for-knowledge and suggestion programs.

Career Corner

Q. Is "kissing up" to the boss an acceptable behavior today? I have heard that this practice can make a difference in today's competitive workplace.

A. Performance is what matters most, but it would be a mistake to disregard the impact of flattery on your boss. Complimenting your supervisor on how he or she conducted a business meeting or solved a major problem may enhance your career. Employees with good people skills—which include building rapport with the boss—are the ones most likely to advance. The primary rule to follow when praising your boss is *Don't fake it.* Don't give a compliment unless you genuinely believe it is deserved. To offer endless, insincere flattery will backfire. And don't forget to praise the accomplishments of your coworkers. The people you work with can often help or hinder your move up the ladder.

Key Terms

positive reinforcement
reinforcer
physical stroke
verbal strokes
stroke deficit
confirmation
active listening

narcissism
incentive program
gain-sharing plan
profit-sharing system
production-incentives plan
pay-for-knowledge system
suggestion program

Review Questions

1. What evidence supports the contention that positive reinforcement is a major employee reward preference?
2. What is the difference between a positive stroke and a negative stroke?
3. Why is positive energy so important in today's workplace?
4. How can a person's identity and self-worth be influenced by confirmation behaviors?
5. In a typical organizational setting, what confirmation behaviors might have a positive effect on employee performance?
6. What are some of the major criticisms of incentives and awards?
7. List and describe the most common incentive programs that involve the use of cash payments.
8. What are some common misconceptions about positive reinforcement?
9. What are some employee behaviors that might be recognized by a supervisor or manager? List at least five different performance-related behaviors.
10. Review the Total Person Insight by Malcolm Boyd. Do you agree? Explain your answer.

Application Exercises

1. Assume you are currently the owner of a small company with about one hundred employees. In recent years, rising premiums for employee health insurance have reduced profits. To encourage your employees to maintain a healthy lifestyle (which will reduce medical insurance claims), you are considering two options:

Option A: Add a $15 monthly surcharge to the health insurance premiums of employees who smoke. Establish healthy ranges for weight, cholesterol, and blood pressure, and assess small fines when employees fail to meet prescribed guidelines.

Option B: Provide a cash reward of $200 for any employee who quits smoking. Establish healthy ranges for weight, cholesterol, and blood pressure, and award small cash or merchandise incentives to employees who meet prescribed guidelines.

List the advantages and disadvantages of each proposal. Then select the proposal you feel will be most effective. Justify your choice.

2. Organizations are continually searching for ways to reward various employee behaviors. Pretend you are currently working at a retail shoe store and the manager asks you to help her design an incentive plan that would result in improved sales of shoes and accessories. She asks you to review and comment on the following options:

   a. Employee-of-the-month awards for highest sales. (A special plaque would be used to recognize each monthly winner.)

   b. Commission on sales. All employees would be given a 3 percent commission on all sales. Each salesperson would receive an hourly wage plus the commission.

   c. Time off. Employees who achieve sales goals established by management could earn up to four hours of time off each week.

   d. Prizes. Employees who achieve weekly sales goals established by management would be eligible for prizes such as sports or theater tickets, dinner at a nice restaurant, gift certificates, or merchandise sold by the store.

   Rank these four options by assigning "1" to your first choice, "2" to your second choice, "3" to your third choice, and "4" to your fourth choice. Provide a written rationale for your first choice.

3. The authors of *Random Acts of Kindness* tell us that the little things we do for others can have big payoffs. These acts give us an outward focus that helps us move away from self-preoccupation. Plan and initiate at least two acts of kindness during the next week, and then reflect on the experience. What impact did the act have on the other person? How did you feel about this experience?

Internet Exercise

Organizations spend millions of dollars on incentives and awards designed to motivate employees to achieve a specific objective. The Internet provides information on this topic. Using your search engine, type in the following keywords: "employee incentives," "production incentives," and "employee suggestion programs." Review the resources (such as books, articles, and training programs) that are available. Pay special attention to incentive programs that would appeal to you as a worker. Also,

describe resources you would recommend to someone who would like to develop an effective incentive program. Prepare a written summary of your findings.

Case 10.1   ## Do Incentives Encourage Healthier Lifestyles?

Throughout the 1980s and early 1990s many organizations invested heavily
in wellness programs in hopes that a healthier work force would result in
lower medical costs. Many discovered, however, that on-site gyms and classes
on nutrition did not deliver the expected savings. For example, Applied Materials Inc. started an exercise program with the goal of encouraging sedentary
workers to become more active. Most of the people who participated were already involved in some type of exercise program. Champion International
Corporation developed a wellness program that included weight-loss classes
and the installation of state-of-the-art fitness centers. Only a small number of
employees, as few as 10 percent, used the facilities.

As health insurance costs increase, organizations are searching for better
ways to help employees get healthy. Research conducted at the University of
Michigan indicates that big savings on insurance premiums can be achieved if
an employee exchanges bad habits for healthy ones. For example, a firm can
save over $1,000 if an employee quits smoking. Lowering cholesterol from
240 milligrams to 190 can reduce the annual bill for cardiac care by $1,200.
To develop a healthier work force, many organizations are turning to various
types of incentives. For example:

- L. L. Bean pays up to $200 to employees whose families take prenatal
  classes.
- Quaker Oats Company grants bonuses of as much as $500 for families who
  exercise, avoid smoking, and wear seat belts.
- Quad/Graphics printing company pays employees $30 to attend a seminar
  devoted to quitting smoking and gives $200 to anyone who quits for a year.

These examples seem to represent low-cost options for motivating employees
to avoid risks and develop a healthier lifestyle.

Questions

1. Is it appropriate for organizations to attempt to influence their employees'
   personal lifestyle decisions? Explain.
2. Is money the best incentive to use when you want to encourage an employee to adopt a healthy habit? What other types of incentives might be
   just as effective or more effective?

3. Would the incentives discussed in this case be effective in motivating you to make a healthy lifestyle change? Explain.

Case 10.2 Improving Quality with Suggestions

A growing number of companies are turning to their employees for suggestions for improving quality. Robin McDermott, coauthor of *Employee-Driven Quality*, says that throughout any organization there are thousands of opportunities for small improvements that employees can identify and in some cases implement. She suggests replacing traditional suggestion boxes with Employee-Driven Idea Systems. Her approach rewards all ideas submitted by employees equally, regardless of the idea's monetary value. Employees are encouraged to focus on making small improvements in their own jobs, and they receive recognition for quality improvements.

RLI Insurance in Peoria, Illinois, likes to encourage small ideas. The company found that large-money rewards tended to discourage the small suggestions that really make a difference. The team of workers that developed the RLI Insurance suggestion program found through research that employees value recognition more than cash prizes. Therefore, employee ideas receive a $2 bill—a token reward just big enough to show RLI's interest. When an employee's idea is used, that person enters a quarterly drawing for prizes that range from $50 to $100 in cash. Is the program working? Cindy Brassfield, coordinator of the recognition program, reports that 291 of the 340 employees eligible to participate submitted ideas—more than 1,300 of them—during a recent one-year period. RLI employees submit their ideas to Brassfield via E-mail.

Questions

1. Some companies have experimented with employee suggestion programs and have had great success. Other companies, however, say they receive very few ideas from employees. What factors might contribute to a successful employee suggestion program?

2. Do you agree or disagree with Robin McDermott's view that all employee ideas should be rewarded equally; regardless of their monetary value? Explain your answer.

3. Some companies are seeking suggestions from their customers. Do you support this practice? Explain your answer.

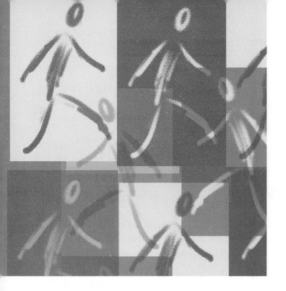

Chapter 11

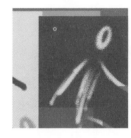

Developing

a Professional

Presence

Chapter Preview

After studying this chapter, you will be able to

1. Explain the importance of professional presence.
2. Discuss the factors that contribute to a favorable first impression
3. Distinguish between assumptions and facts.
4. Define *image* and describe the factors that form the image you project to others.
5. List and discuss factors that influence your choice of clothing for work.
6. Understand how manners contribute to improved interpersonal relations in the workplace.

HERTZ CORPORATION, the U.S. Air Force, Hyatt Hotels Corporation, the City of Dallas, and the Neiman-Marcus Group, Inc., have one thing in common: All have purchased the services of Feedback Plus, an agency that dispatches professional shoppers who pose as consumers. These "mystery" shoppers visit the client's business, purchase products or services, and report back to the client on the quality of service they receive. The City of Dallas hired Feedback Plus to see how car-pound employees treat citizens picking up their cars. The Air Force uses professional shoppers to assess customer service at on-base supply stores. Banks, hospitals, and public utilities are also hiring mystery shoppers. Vickie Henry, chief executive of Feedback Plus, notes that many similar firms compete for clients' business, and service really does differentiate one firm from another.[1] Sears, Roebuck & Company officials say Sears's mystery shopper program has helped the company achieve a new level of service and profitability. The amount that Sears and other companies spend on mystery shopper programs is estimated at $100 million a year.[2] ∎

As organizations experience increased competition for clients, patients, and customers, awareness of the importance of public contact increases. They are giving new attention to the old adage "First impressions are lasting impressions." Research indicates that initial impressions do indeed tend to linger. Therefore, a positive first impression can be thought of as the first step in building a long-term relationship.

Of course, it is not just *first* contacts with clients, patients, customers, and others that are important. Positive impressions should be the objective of *every* contact. A major goal of this chapter is to discuss the important factors that help us make positive impressions. Another important goal is to examine the factors that shape the image we project to others.

MAKING A GOOD IMPRESSION

There are many personal and professional benefits to be gained from a study of the concepts in this chapter. You will acquire new insights regarding ways to communicate positive impressions during job interviews, business contacts, and social contacts made away from work. You will also learn how to shape an image that will help you achieve your fullest potential in the career of your choice. Most important, the material in this chapter will very likely increase your self-awareness. As we noted in Chapter 1, self-awareness is an important first step toward building more effective relationships with others.

This is not a chapter about ways to make positive impressions with superficial behavior and quick-fix techniques. We do not discuss the "power look" or the "power lunch." The material in this chapter will not help you become a more entertaining conversationalist or win new customers by pretending to be interested in their hobbies or families. Stephen Covey, author of *The 7 Habits of Highly Effective People,* says that the ability to build effective, long-term relationships is based on character strength, not quick-fix techniques. He notes that outward attitude and behavior changes do very little good in the long run *unless* they are based on solid principles governing human effectiveness. These principles include service (making a contribution), integrity and honesty (which serve as a foundation of trust), human dignity (every person has worth), and fairness.[3]

Few people can fake a sincere greeting or a caring attitude. If you really do not care about the customer's problem, the customer will probably sense your indifference. Your true feelings will be difficult to hide. Ralph Waldo Emerson was right on target when he said, "What you are shouts so loudly in my ears I cannot hear what you say."

Professional Presence

We are indebted to Susan Bixler, president of Professional Image, Inc., and author of *Professional Presence,* for giving us a better understanding of what it means to possess professional presence. **Professional presence** is a dynamic blend of poise, self-confidence, control, and style that empowers us to be able to command respect in any situation.[4] Once acquired, it permits us to be perceived as self-assured and thoroughly competent. We project a confidence that others can quickly perceive the first time they meet us.

Bixler points out that, in most cases, the credentials we present during a job interview or when we are being considered for a promotion are not very different from those of other persons being considered. It is our professional presence that permits us to rise above the crowd. Debra Benton, a career consultant, says, "Any boss with a choice of two people with equal qualifications will choose the one with style as well as substance."[5] Learning to create a professional presence is one of the most valuable skills we can acquire.

The Primacy Effect

The development of professional presence begins with a full appreciation of the power of first impressions. The tendency to form impressions quickly at the time of an initial meeting illustrates what social psychologists call a **primacy effect** in the way people perceive one another. The general principle is that first impressions establish the mental framework within which a person is viewed, and information acquired later is often ignored or reinterpreted to coincide with this framework.[6]

During his first term as president, Bill Clinton often appeared in brief jogging shorts and garish print shirts; his suits were loose fitting and in need of tailoring; and his military salute was viewed as halfhearted by many observers.

Toby Fischer-Mirkin, fashion consultant and author of *Dress Code,* said the president did not communicate a very commanding image.[7] Early in his first term, Clinton appeared vulnerable to many people, and this image had a negative influence on his popularity. Later in his first term, he communicated a more "presidential" image and went on to be re-elected to a second term. He discovered, or perhaps rediscovered, the power of the primacy effect.

The First Few Seconds

When two people meet, their potential for building a relationship can be affected by many factors. Within a few moments, one person or the other may feel threatened, offended, or bored. Roger Ailes, communication adviser to three presidents and consultant to numerous Fortune 500 executives, says people begin forming an opinion of us in a matter of seconds. He believes that most people assess the other person very quickly and then settle on a general perception of that individual. Ailes says it is very difficult for us to reverse that first impression.[8] The following examples support his view of first impressions.

Dee Soder, a psychologist who helps unemployed senior executives find work, likes to give clients the fish test. If a person fails to comment on the wahoo, the large blue fish hanging on the wall outside her office, Soder sees a problem. When entering the office of a prospective boss, she says, you should pick out something unusual and comment on it. It creates a good first impression. (Nicole Bengiveno/Matrix)

Thinking / Learning Starter

To test the practical application of Roger Ailes's guideline in a real-life setting, examine it in the context of your past experiences. Review the following questions and then answer each with yes or no.

1. Have you ever entered a restaurant, hotel, or office and experienced an immediate feeling of being welcome after your first contact with an employee?

2. Have you ever met someone who immediately communicated to you the impression that he or she could be trusted and was interested in your welfare?

3. Have you ever placed a telephone call and known instinctively within seconds that the person did not welcome your call?

Item: Paula rushed into a restaurant for a quick lunch—she had to get back to her office for a 1:30 P.M. appointment. At the entrance of the main dining area was a sign reading "Please Wait to Be Seated." A few feet away, the hostess was discussing a popular movie with one of the waitresses. The hostess made eye contact with Paula but continued to visit with the waitress.

Item: When Sandy and Mike entered the showroom of a Mercedes-Benz dealer, they were approached by a salesperson wearing sport slacks (khaki color), a blue knit pullover shirt (short sleeve), and casual gum-soled shoes. The salesperson smiled and said, "Are you looking or buying?"

Total Person Insight

"If people aren't quickly attracted to you or don't like what they see and hear in those first two to four minutes, chances are they won't pay attention to all those words you believe are demonstrating your knowledge and authority. They will find your client guilty, seek another doctor, buy another product, vote for your opponent or hire someone else."

JANET G. ELSEA

President, Communication Skills, Inc.

In each of these examples, a negative first impression was created in a matter of seconds. The anxiety level of the restaurant customer increased because she was forced to wait while two employees talked about a personal matter. And the potential customers made judgments about the automobile salesperson based solely on his appearance. Unfortunately, these employees were probably not fully aware of the impression they communicated to customers.

Assumptions Versus Facts   The impression you form of another person during the initial contact is made up of both assumptions and facts. Most people tend to rely more heavily on **assumptions** during the initial meeting. If a job applicant sits slumped in the chair, head bowed and shoulders slack, you might assume the person is not interested in the position. If the postal clerk fails to make eye contact during the transaction and does not express appreciation for your purchase, you may assume this person treats everyone with indifference. Needless to say, the impression you form of another person during the initial contact can be misleading. The briefer the encounter with a new acquaintance, the greater the chance that misinformation will enter into your perception of the other person. The authors of a popular book on first impressions state that "Depending on assumptions is a one-way ticket to big surprises and perhaps disappointments."[9]

Cultural Influence

Cultural influences, often formed during the early years of our life, lead us to have impressions of some people even before we meet them. People often develop stereotypes of entire groups. Although differences between cultures are often subtle, they can lead to uncomfortable situations. We need to realize that the Korean shopkeeper is being polite, not hostile, when he puts change on the counter and not in your hand. Many Asian students do not speak up in class out of respect for the teacher, not boredom.[10]

Many American companies are attempting to create a new kind of workplace where cultural and ethnic differences are treated as assets, not annoyances. Yet some employees feel pressure to conform to dress and grooming standards that their employer considers "mainstream." When LaToya Rivers, a black college student, applied for a position at the Boston Harbor Hotel, she asked whether braids were allowed. She was told, "Yes, as long as they are neat and professional in appearance." Once hired, the policy seemed to change. A manager told her to restyle her braided hair or leave.[11]

Norine Dresser, author of *Multiculture Manners—New Rules of Etiquette for a Changing Society,* notes that it is becoming more difficult for organizations to develop policies that do not offend one ethnic group or another. She argues that it is the collective duty of the mainstream to learn the customs and practices of established minority groups as well as the ways of the latest arrivals from other countries.[12]

THE IMAGE YOU PROJECT

Image is a term used to describe how other people feel about you. In every business or social setting, your behaviors communicate a mental picture that others observe and remember. This picture determines how they react to you. Your image depends on more than exterior qualities such as dress and grooming. In the words of James Gray, author of *The Winning Image,* "Image is more than just a veneer."[13] He observes,

> Image is a tool for communicating and for revealing your inherent qualities, your competence, abilities and leadership. It is a reflection of qualities that others associate with you, a reflection that bears long-lasting influence in your bid for success. Image is not a tool for manipulation. Nor is it a false front. It cannot substitute for substance.[14]

In many respects, the image you project at work is very much like a picture puzzle, as illustrated in Figure 11.1. It is formed by a variety of factors, including manners, self-confidence, voice quality, versatility (see Chapter 3), integrity (see Chapter 5), entrance and carriage, facial expression, surface language,

FIGURE 11.1

Major Factors That Form Your Image

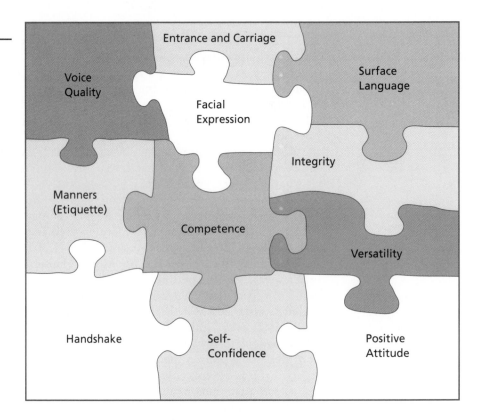

competence, positive attitude, and handshake. Each of these image-shaping components is under your control.

A growing number of organizations have discovered a direct link between profitability and the image projected by employees. Financial institutions, public utilities, airlines, retail stores, restaurants, hospitals, and manufacturers face the problem of not only gaining but also retaining the patronage of clients and customers. When the Oldsmobile division of General Motors Corp. decided to reshape the image projected by dealers, it developed a $25 million training program. Dealers and employees learned how to improve service to customers and to sell the Aurora, a more luxurious car than the models that Olds dealers were used to selling.[15]

Surface Language

As noted earlier, we base opinions about other people on both facts and assumptions. Unfortunately, assumptions often carry a great deal of weight. Many of the assumptions you develop regarding other people are based on **surface language,** a pattern of immediate impressions conveyed by appearance. The clothing you wear, your hairstyle, the fragrances you use, and the jewelry you display all combine to make a statement about you to others.

According to many writers familiar with image formation, clothing is particularly important. John Molloy, author of *Dress for Success* and *The Woman's Dress for Success Book,* was one of the first to acknowledge publicly the link between image and wardrobe. According to his research, what you wear influences your credibility and likability.[16]

Although a more relaxed dress code has evolved in recent years, people judge your appearance long before they judge your talents. It would be a mistake not to take your career wardrobe seriously. Bixler suggests that those making career wardrobe decisions should keep in mind that three things haven't changed:[17]

1. *If you want the job, you have to look the part.* Establish personal dress and grooming standards appropriate for the organization where you wish to work. Before you apply for a job, try to find out what the workers there are wearing. If in doubt, dress conservatively.

2. *If you want the promotion, you have to look promotable.* A good rule to follow is to dress for the job you want, not the job you have. If you are currently an office worker and want to become an office manager, identify the successful office managers and emulate their manner of dress.

3. *If you want respect, you have to dress as well as or better than your industry standards.* One would expect to find conservative dress standards in banking, insurance, accounting, and law, and more casual dress standards in advertising, sports entertainment, and agriculture. Spend time researching the dress and grooming standards in the industry in which you hope to find a job.

Thinking / Learning Starter

Do you recall a teacher, coworker, or supervisor whose surface language impressed you—either positively or negatively? What specific elements (such as dress or hairstyle) were evident in this person's surface language? What type of image do you think he or she was trying to project?

Selecting Your Career Apparel

Over 23 million American workers wear a uniform especially designed for a particular job. The judges on the U.S. Supreme Court and the technicians at the local Midas Muffler and Brake shop have one thing in common—both groups wear a special uniform to work. Today more and more people are donning uniforms to go to work. Companies that have initiated extensive career apparel programs rely on uniforms to project an image of consistent quality, good service, and uniqueness. Uniforms enhance company credibility, which in turn increases customer confidence in the firm.[18] Wearing a uniform can also have a positive effect on employees. Wearing the same uniform seems to create a sort of bond among coworkers. Thus, a uniform can make at least a small contribution to building company spirit at your local McDonald's restaurant or Holiday Inn hotel.

Wells Fargo Bank adopted a custom line of clothing for employees working at banking centers located in Safeway and other supermarkets. The goal was to create a professional look that would define the bank's identity and build customers' confidence in the financial services that Wells Fargo offered. The bank also wanted to make sure that people distinguished its employees from supermarket workers.[19]

The uniforms worn by United Parcel Service employees, United Airlines reservation clerks, and the employees at your local restaurant might be classified as special-design **career apparel.** In addition to special-design uniforms, there is another type of career apparel, somewhat less predictable, worn by large numbers of people in the labor force. Here are some examples:

- A female lawyer representing a prestigious firm would be appropriately dressed in a gray or blue skirted suit. A dress with a suit jacket would also be acceptable. She should avoid clothing in brash colors or casual styles that might reduce her credibility.
- A male bank loan officer would be appropriately dressed in a tailored gray or blue suit, white shirt, and tie. This same person dressed in a colorful blazer, sport shirt, and plaid slacks would be seen as too casual in most bank settings.

Millions of people wear a uniform at work. Many companies rely on uniforms to project an image of consistent quality, good service, and uniqueness. (Jeff Greenberg/The Picture Cube, Inc.)

- A female receptionist at a prominent accounting firm would be appropriately dressed in a skirt and blouse. This same person would be inappropriately dressed if she showed up for work wearing designer jeans, a sweater, and Birkenstock sandals.
- A technician employed by an auto dealership that sells new cars would be appropriately dressed in matching gray, tan, or blue shirt and pants. The technician would be inappropriately dressed in jeans and a T-shirt.

Many organizations seek advice about career apparel from image consultants. One source of image consultants is the Association of Image Consultants International.

Wardrobe Engineering

The term **wardrobe engineering** was first used by John Molloy to describe how clothing and accessories can be used to create a certain image. This concept was later refined by several other noted image consultants in hundreds of books and articles on dress and grooming. Although these authors are not in complete agreement on every aspect of dress, they do agree on a few basic points regarding wardrobe.

The quality of your wardrobe will influence the image you project.   A wardrobe should be regarded as an investment, with each item carefully selected to look and fit well. Purchase a few basic items each year and you will soon have everything you need.

The newest dress fad is often inappropriate in a business or professional setting.   In most cases, the world of work is more conservative than college, the arts, or the world of sports. If you are a fashion setter, you might be viewed as unstable or insincere. To be taken seriously, avoid clothing that is faddish or too flashy.

Women generally have more latitude than men in selecting appropriate attire, but they should still exercise some caution in choosing their wardrobe. In some cases, women are entering positions formerly dominated by men. They need to be taken seriously, and the wardrobe they select can contribute to this end.

Your wardrobe should be appropriate for your field and for you.   Although you should consider the dress and grooming standards of others in your field, don't give in to blind conformity or duplication. As one image consultant noted, "Effective packaging is an individual matter based on the person's circumstances, age, weight, height, coloring, and objectives."[20] In addition to these personal factors, you need to consider what's appropriate for your career. In general, four factors influence your choice of clothing for work:

1. *Products and services offered.* In some cases the organization's products and services more or less dictate a certain type of dress. For example, a receptionist employed by a well-established law firm would likely wear clothing that is conservative, modest, and in good taste. These same dress standards would apply to a pharmaceutical sales representative who calls on medical doctors.

2. *Type of person served.* Research indicates that first impressions created by dress and grooming are greatly influenced by unconscious expectations. Throughout life we become acquainted with real estate salespeople, nurses, police officers, and others employed in a wide range of occupations. We form mental images of the apparel common to each of these occupations. When we encounter someone whose appearance does not conform to our past experiences, we often feel uncomfortable.

3. *Desired image projected by the organization.* Some companies establish dress codes that help shape the image they project to the public. Walt Disney Company, for example, maintains a strict dress and grooming code for all its theme-park employees. They are considered "cast members" and must adhere to dress and grooming standards that complement the image projected by Disney theme parks.

4. *Geographic region.* Dress in the South and Southwest tends to be more casual than dress in the Northeast. Climate is another factor that influences

the clothing people wear at work. In Texas, for example, the warm climate calls for short sleeves and open collars in some work settings.

Thinking / Learning Starter

Assume you are planning to purchase (1) a life insurance policy, (2) a Rolex wristwatch, and (3) eyeglasses. What types of career apparel would you expect persons selling these products to wear? What grooming standards would you recommend?

The Business Casual Look

The terms *business casual* and *corporate casual* have recently been used to describe the movement toward dress standards that emphasize greater comfort and individuality. **Business casual** is clothing that allows you to feel comfortable at work but looks neat and professional. It usually means slacks, cotton shirts, and sports coats for men, and slacks, casual dresses, or skirts for women.[21] Business casual bridges the gap between the suits, white shirts, and silk blouses traditionally worn in business, and casual dress, such as jeans, shorts, and T-shirts. Some companies have established "casual Fridays" or "dress-down weeks," while others have shifted from a strict dress code to a relaxed dress code. The casual look in corporate America was triggered, in part, by efforts to improve teamwork and empower employees. Bottom-up initiatives often emphasize getting rid of symbols of top-down authority.[22] The casual

Reprinted with special permission of King Features Syndicate.

trend has also been fueled by the influx of Generation Xers who are entering the work force. These new workers are more relaxed and are looking for ways to express their individuality.

Growing acceptance of the casual look has created some problems for both employers and employees. Many companies are struggling to develop casual dress guidelines and offer assistance to employees who find dressing down for casual days a mind-boggling experience. What is business casual? What is "dressy" casual? The answer to these questions varies from one company to another. Some companies have developed written policies that describe what is and is not acceptable casual attire, but others say this approach is too intrusive. Chrysler Financial, a division of Chrysler Corporation, found that some employees did not follow the company's new casual-Fridays dress code. So the company hired a local department store to put on a fashion show involving professional models and Chrysler employees. The show gave employees many examples of casual clothing that is appropriate for work.[23]

Your Facial Expression

After your overall appearance, your face is the most visible part of you. Facial expressions are the cue most people rely on in initial interactions. They are the "TelePrompTer" by which others read your mood and personality.[24]

Studies conducted in nonverbal communication show that facial expressions strongly influence people's reactions to each other. The expression on your face can quickly trigger a positive or negative reaction from those you meet. How you rate in the "good-looks" department is not nearly as important as your ability to communicate positive impressions with a pleasant smile.

If you want to identify the inner feelings of another person, watch the individual's facial expressions closely. A frown may tell you "something is wrong." A smile generally communicates "things are OK." Everyone has encountered a "look of surprise" or a "look that could kill." These facial expressions usually reflect inner emotions more accurately than words.

In many work settings, a cheerful smile is an important key to creating a positive first impression. A deadpan stare (or frown) can communicate a negative first impression to others. If you find it hard to smile, take time to consider the reasons. Are you constantly thinking negative thoughts and simply find nothing to smile about? Are you afraid others may misinterpret your intentions?

Your Entrance and Carriage

The way you enter someone's office or a business meeting can influence the image you project, says Susan Bixler. She notes that "your entrance and the way you carry yourself will set the stage for everything that comes afterward."[25] A nervous or apologetic entrance may ruin your chances of getting a job, closing a sale, or getting the raise you have earned. If you feel apprehensive, try not to let it show in your body language. Hold your head up, avoid slumping forward, and try to project self-assurance. To get off to the right start and make a favorable impression, follow these words of advice from Bixler: "The person who has confidence in himself or herself indicates this by a strong stride, a friendly smile, good posture, and a genuine sense of energy. This is a very effective way to set the stage for a productive meeting. When you ask for respect visually, you get it."[26] Bixler says the key to making a successful entrance is simply believing—and projecting—that you have a reason to be there and have something important to present or discuss.

Your Voice

Several years ago, a Cleveland-based company, North American Systems, Inc., developed and marketed Mr. Coffee, an appliance that makes coffee quickly and conveniently. Some credited the quick acceptance of this product to an effective advertising campaign featuring baseball Hall of Famer Joe DiMaggio. He came across to the consumer as an honest, sincere person. When Joe DiMaggio said Mr. Coffee worked and made good coffee, people believed him.

The tone of your voice, the rate of speed at which you speak (tempo), and the volume of your speech contribute greatly to the meaning attached to your verbal messages. In the case of telephone calls, voice quality is critical because the other person cannot see your facial expressions, hand gestures, and other body movements. You cannot trade in your current voice for a new one, but with a little practice you can make your voice more pleasing to other people and project a positive tone.

Although there is no ideal voice for all business contacts, your voice should reflect at least these four qualities: confidence, enthusiasm, optimism, and sincerity. Above all, try to avoid a speech pattern that is dull and colorless. Joanne Lamm, founder of Professional Speech Associates, says the worst kind of voice has no projection, no color, and no feeling.[27]

African Americans, Hispanics, Asians, Native Americans, and recent immigrants to America often face special challenges in verbal communication. New arrivals may have a unique accent because the phonetic habits of the speaker's native language are carried over to his or her new language. Many people born and raised in America have a dialect that is unique. Should this uniqueness be viewed as a problem or an opportunity? Kim Radford, vice president of marketing at Wachovia Trust Company, had to answer this question soon after graduating from college. He took a position as a stockbroker in Charleston, West Virginia. Radford, a black, conducted most of his business on the telephone and seldom met clients face to face. Early on, someone said, "Kim, you need to get that black accent out of your voice if you're going to be successful in this business." Radford faced a real dilemma: He wanted to be successful, but he did not want to compromise his personal integrity. He talked to several people, black and white, and the advice he received boiled down to this guideline:

> Stay honest to yourself, but communicate and be understood. There's no need to clean up the fact that you sound black as long as you're articulate and your diction's good and people can understand you.[28]

Your Handshake

When two people first meet, a handshake is usually the only physical contact between them. A handshake is a friendly and professional way to greet someone, or take leave, regardless of gender. The handshake can communicate warmth, genuine concern for the other person, and strength. It can also communicate aloofness, indifference, and weakness. The message you send the other party through your handshake depends on a combination of the following factors:

1. *Degree of firmness.* Generally speaking, a firm (but not viselike) grip communicates a caring attitude, whereas a weak grip communicates indifference.

Secretary of State Madeleine Albright recognizes the powerful influence of a handshake. She is seen here visiting refugee children from Afghanistan. (Reuters/Muzammil Pasha/Archive Photos)

2. *Degree of dryness of hands.* A moist palm is unpleasant to feel and can communicate the impression that you are nervous. A clammy hand is likely to repel most people.

3. *Duration of grip.* There are no specific guidelines for the ideal duration of a grip. Nevertheless, by extending the handshake just a little, you can often communicate a greater degree of interest in and concern for the other person.

4. *Depth of interlock.* A full, deep grip is more likely to convey friendship and strength to the other person.

5. *Eye contact during handshake.* Visual communication can increase the positive impact of your handshake. Maintaining eye contact throughout the handshaking process is important when two people greet each other.[29]

Most individuals have shaken hands with hundreds of people but have little idea whether they are creating positive or negative impressions. It is a good idea to obtain this information from those coworkers or friends who are willing to provide you with candid feedback. Like all other human relations skills, the handshake can be improved with practice.

Your Manners

The study of manners (sometimes called etiquette) reveals a number of ways to enhance our professional presence. A knowledge of good manners permits us to perform our daily work with poise and confidence. Letitia Baldrige, author of *Letitia Baldrige's New Complete Guide to Executive Manners,* provides us with a basic definition of good manners: "It's consideration and kindness and thinking about somebody other than oneself."[30] Another writer says, "Manners are the grace woven into the knotty fabric of our lives. Without them, it's all knots and thorns."[31] Practical manners suitable for the workplace represent an important key to improved interpersonal relations.

Good manners is a universal passport to positive relationships and respect. One of the best ways to develop rapport with another person is to avoid behavior that might be offensive to that individual. Although it is not possible to do a complete review of this topic, some of the rules of etiquette that are particularly important in an organizational setting are covered here.

1. *When you establish new relationships, avoid calling people by their first names too soon.* Jacqueline Thompson, author of *Image Impact,* says assuming that all work-related associates prefer to be addressed informally by their first names is a serious breach of etiquette.[32] Use titles of respect—Ms., Miss, Mrs., Mr., or Dr.—until the relationship is well established. Too much familiarity can breed irritation. When the other party says, "Call me Susan," or "Call me Roy," it is all right to begin using the person's first name. Informality should develop by invitation, not by presumption.

2. *Avoid obscenities and offensive comments or stories.* In recent years, standards for acceptable and unacceptable language have changed considerably.

Total Person Insight

"In a society as ridden as ours with expensive status symbols, where every purchase is considered a social statement, there is no easier or cheaper way to distinguish oneself than by the practice of gentle manners."

JUDITH MARTIN
Author

Obscenity is more permissible in everyday conversation than it was in the past. But it is still considered inappropriate to use foul language in front of a customer, a client, or, in many cases, a coworker. According to Bob Greene, syndicated columnist, an obscenity communicates a negative message to most people:

> What it probably all comes down to is an implied lack of respect for the people who hear you talk. If you use profanity among friends, that is a choice you make. But if you broadcast it to people in general, you're telling them that you don't care what their feelings might be.[33]

Never assume that another person's value system is the same as your own. Foul language and off-color stories can do irreparable damage to interpersonal relations.

3. *Watch your table manners.* Business is frequently conducted at breakfast, lunch, or dinner these days, so be aware of your table manners. When you invite a customer to lunch, do not discuss business before the meal is ordered unless the client initiates the subject. Begin eating only when the people around you have their plates. If you have not been served, however, encourage others to go ahead. Assume responsibility for making sure the conversation moves from topic to topic and person to person. No one likes to be left out. Avoid ordering food that is not easily controlled, such as ribs, chicken with bones, or lobster. Thank the server when your meal is served.

4. *Express appreciation at appropriate times.* A simple thank-you can mean a lot. Failure to express appreciation can be a serious human relations blunder. The office worker who works hard to complete a rush job for the boss is likely to feel frustrated and angry if this extra effort is ignored. The customer who makes a purchase deserves a sincere thank-you. You want your customers to know that their business is appreciated.

5. *Be familiar with meeting etiquette.* Business meetings should start and end on time. When you attend a meeting, arrive on time and don't feel obligated to comment on each item on the agenda. Yes, sometimes silence is golden. In most cases, you should not bring up a topic unless it is related to an agenda item. If you are in charge of the meeting, end it by summarizing key points, reviewing the decisions made, and recapping the responsibilities assigned to individuals during the meeting. Always start and end the meeting on a positive note.[34]

6. *Be aware of personal habits that may offend others.* Sometimes an annoying habit can be a barrier to establishing a positive relationship with someone else. Chewing gum is a habit that bothers many people, particularly if you chew gum vigorously or "crack" it. Biting fingernails, cracking knuckles, scratching your head, and combing your hair in public are additional habits to be avoided. If you wear a fragrance (cologne or after-shave lotion), apply it in moderation when going to work. Do not risk causing a client or coworker discomfort with your fragrance.[35]

Letitia Baldrige says that in the field of manners, "Rules are based on kindness and efficiency." She also believes that good manners are those personal qualities that make life at work more livable.[36] Nancy Austin, co-author of *A Passion for Excellence,* says, "Real manners—a keen interest in and a regard for somebody else, a certain kindness and at-ease quality that add real value—can't be faked or finessed."[37] Real manners come from the heart.

Professional Presence at the Job Interview

The guideline that says "You seldom get a second chance to make a good first impression" has special meaning when you are preparing for a job interview. In most cases you are competing against several other applicants, so you can't afford to make a mistake. A common mistake among job applicants is failure to acquire background information on the employer. Without this information, it's difficult to prepare questions to ask during the interview, and decisions about what to wear will be more difficult. Let's assume you are planning to apply for a sales position at Abercrombie & Fitch, an upscale specialty chain that sells casual clothing for men and women. It would be helpful to know that the company maintains a very conservative dress code: Men are not permitted to wear necklaces or facial hair. Women cannot wear makeup or long nails. No piercing is allowed except for earrings (one for men, two for women.)[38]

One of the most important objectives of a job interview is to communicate the image that you are someone who is conscientious, so be prepared. If possible, visit the place of business before your interview. Observe the people already working there; then dress one step up in terms of professional appearance. When in doubt about what to wear, opt for a more formal look. What's most important is that you show that you care enough to make a good impression.

Summary

Professional presence permits us to be perceived as self-assured and competent. These qualities are quickly perceived the first time someone meets us. People tend to form impressions of others quickly at the time they first meet them, and these first impressions tend to be preserved. In an organizational setting, the time interval for projecting a positive or negative first impression is often reduced to seconds. Positive impressions are important because they contribute to repeat business and customer referrals.

The impression you form of another person during the initial contact is made up of assumptions and facts. When meeting someone for the first time, people tend to rely heavily on assumptions. Many of your assumptions can be traced to early cultural influences. Assumptions are also based on perceptions of surface language. Surface language is a pattern of immediate impressions conveyed by appearance. The clothing and jewelry you wear, your hairstyle, and the fragrances you use all combine to make a statement about you to others.

Image consultants contend that discrimination on the basis of appearance is still a fact of life. Clothing is an important part of the image you communicate to others. Four factors tend to influence your choice of clothing for work: (1) the products or services offered by the organization, (2) the type of person served, (3) the desired image projected by the organization, and (4) the region where you work.

In addition to clothing, research indicates that facial expressions strongly influence people's reactions to each other. The expression on your face can quickly trigger a positive or negative reaction. Similarly, your entrance and carriage, voice, handshake, and manners also contribute to the image you project when meeting others. All the factors that form your image should be given attention prior to a job interview or any other situation where a positive first impression is important.

Career Corner

Q. In the near future I will begin my job search, and I want to work for a company that will respect my individuality. Some companies are enforcing strict dress codes and other policies that, in my opinion, infringe on the rights of their employees. How far can an employer go in dictating my lifestyle?

A. This is a good question, but one for which there is no easy answer. For example, most people feel they have a right to wear the fragrance of their choice, but many fragrances contain allergy-producing ingredients. In some parts of California, you will find "nonfragrance" zones. Secondhand smoke is another major issue in the workplace because some research indicates that it can be harmful to the health of workers. Rules regarding weight, hair length, and the type of clothing and jewelry that can be worn to work have also caused controversy. There is no doubt that many companies are trying to find a balance between their interests and the rights of workers. Blockbuster Entertainment Corporation has placed restrictions on the length of an employee's hair and the amount of jewelry that can be worn during work hours. The company believes employee appearance is crucial to the success of the company. The best advice I can give you is to become familiar with the employer's expectations before you accept a job. The company has a responsibility to explain its personnel policies to prospective employees, but sometimes this information is not covered until after a person is hired.

Key Terms

professional presence
primacy effect
assumptions
cultural influences
image

surface language
career apparel
wardrobe engineering
business casual

Review Questions

1. Image has been described as "more than exterior qualities such as dress and grooming." What other factors shape the image we project?
2. Define the term *primacy effect.* How would knowledge of the primacy effect help someone who works in patient care or customer service?
3. Why do people tend to rely more heavily on assumptions than on facts during the initial meeting?
4. Why should career-minded people be concerned about the image they project? Do we have control over the factors that shape the image we project? Explain.
5. What are the four factors that influence your choice of clothing for work?
6. Susan Bixler suggests that when making wardrobe decisions, you should keep in mind that three things have not changed. List and discuss these three factors.
7. What is meant by the term *business casual?* Why have some organizations established a business casual policy?
8. Describe the type of speaking voice that increases a person's effectiveness in dealing with others.
9. Provide a basic definition of good manners. Why is the study of manners important?
10. Stephen Covey says that changing outward attitudes and behaviors does very little good in the long run unless we base such changes on solid principles that govern human effectiveness. Do you agree or disagree with his views? Explain your answer.

Application Exercises

1. Harvey Mackay, president of Mackay Envelope Corporation, has designed a sixty-six-question customer profile for his sales staff. Salespeople are encouraged to complete the form for each customer they call on. The profile includes such information as birth date, current position, marital status,

professional memberships, and special interests. Mackay takes the position that a salesperson cannot build long-term relationships with customers unless she or he takes a personal interest in them.

  a. Do you support the use of a customer profile to build relationships with customers or clients? Explain.

  b. What type of organization would benefit most from use of a detailed customer profile similar to the one used at Mackay Envelope Corporation?

2. The first step toward improving your voice is to hear yourself as others do. Listen to several recordings of your voice on a dictation machine, tape recorder, or VCR, and then complete the following rating form. Place a checkmark in the appropriate space for each quality.

Quality	Major Strength	Strength	Weakness	Major Weakness
Projects confidence	_____	_____	_____	_____
Projects enthusiasm	_____	_____	_____	_____
Speaking rate is not too fast or too slow	_____	_____	_____	_____
Projects optimism	_____	_____	_____	_____
Voice is not too loud or too soft	_____	_____	_____	_____
Projects sincerity	_____	_____	_____	_____

3. To survive in today's competitive climate, organizations must provide good service. Employees who have direct contact with the customer, client, or patient play a key role in the area of service. Effective front-line employees are able to express a warm, sincere greeting, display a caring attitude, and provide competent service. During the next seven days keep a record of all contacts you have with front-line people. After each contact, record your impressions of the experience. Was it positive? Negative? Briefly describe what the person said or did that caused you to view the contact as either positive or negative.

Internet Exercise

Throughout the past few years we have seen a movement toward casual dress in the workplace. Many companies have developed a casual dress code. Visit the Internet and determine what types of information are available on this topic. Using your search engine, type in the following keywords: "business casual dress" and "corporate casual dress." You may also want to visit the Web page of Levi Strauss & Company, a company that designs and sells clothes that can enhance a casual dress wardrobe. Review the available resources (such as books, articles, and training programs) related to this topic, and then prepare a written summary of your findings. Pay special attention to information that would help you develop a casual dress wardrobe.

Case 11.1   What You See Is Not Necessarily What You Get

The clothing we wear at work shapes other people's expectations of us. Feelings about people's competence, intelligence, attitudes, trustworthiness, and many other aspects of their personalities are conveyed by the colors, styles, and fit of their attire. Although some organizations such as Levi Strauss & Co. have adopted business casual dress codes, others encourage more conservative dress. Susan Bixler, well-known image consultant, says traditional business dress is generally classic and conservative and changes little from year to year. In a conservative business setting, men and women should avoid clothing that is more appropriate for leisure activities.

Some companies, such as the National Car Rental Company and the Century 21 Real Estate Corporation chain, encourage their employees to wear specially designed uniforms, called "career wear," to ensure that the employees will convey the "right" message and instill confidence in their customers.

Just how important is the "right look," and how does what people wear influence our expectations of them? Imagine that you have just checked into a hospital to be operated on the next day. When you get to your room, you are told that the following people will be coming to speak with you within the next several hours:

1. The surgeon who will do the operation
2. A nurse
3. The secretary for the department of surgery
4. A representative of the company that supplies televisions to the hospital rooms
5. A technician who does laboratory tests
6. A hospital business manager
7. The dietitian

You have never met any of these people before and do not know what to expect. The only thing you do know is that they are all women.

About half an hour after your arrival, a woman appears at your door dressed in a straight, red wool skirt, a pink-and-white striped polyester blouse with a bow at the neck, and red medium-high-heel shoes that match the skirt. She is wearing round gold earrings, a gold chain necklace, a gold wedding band, and a white hospital laboratory coat. She is carrying a clipboard.

Questions

1. Which of the seven people listed do you think is standing at your door? Why?
2. If the woman were not wearing a white hospital laboratory coat, how might your perceptions of her differ? Why?

3. If you find out that she is the surgeon who will be operating on you in the morning, but you initially thought she was someone different, how confident would you feel in her ability as a surgeon? Why?

Case 11.2   **Etiquette 101**

S hould I use call waiting in my home office? When introducing a female associate and a male client, whom do I introduce to whom? Do I need to thank the server when my food is served? What do I do when a customer tells a racist joke that offends me? Many people are seeking answers to such questions because knowing rules of etiquette can help us avoid embarrassing situations. The trend toward global partnerships, increased electronic communications, and the growth of the service economy pose new challenges on the etiquette front. Judith Martin, creator of the popular *Miss Manners* advice column, featured in over 200 daily newspapers, and author of several books on etiquette, notes that the irritations of modern life are so abrasive that people ignorant of the rules of etiquette may turn to the law to regulate everyday behavior. Today people who feel offended often take legal action.

Ann Marie Sabath, founder of At East Incorporated, an etiquette consulting company in Cincinnati, says details can make or break a business relationship. She teaches her clients to extend small courtesies such as writing personalized thank-you notes, personalizing voice mail boxes, and using a person's name when speaking to him or her. Those who cannot afford to hire a consultant or to attend a seminar on etiquette often turn to books such as *Complete Business Etiquette Handbook* by Barbara Pachter and Marjorie Brody or *Business Etiquette in Brief* by Ann Marie Sabath.

Colleges and universities are giving more attention to the role of good manners in achieving career success. Howard University has developed seminars for business students on such topics as telephone etiquette, table manners, and art appreciation. Texas Christian University has a seminar that includes a six-course dinner and instructions on how to order wine.

Questions

1. Some people say the study of etiquette is not necessary because good manners is nothing more than common sense. Do you agree or disagree? Explain your answer.
2. Should colleges and universities provide instruction on the rules of etiquette? Explain your answer.
3. Some organizations provide front-line employees with etiquette training. Do you support this practice? Explain your answer.

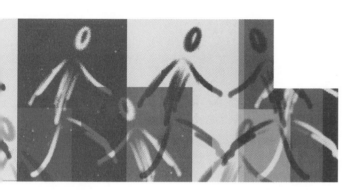

PART IV

If We All

Work Together . . .

Chapter 12

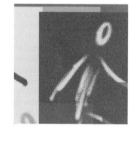

Team Building:

A Leadership

Strategy

Chapter Preview

After studying this chapter, you will be able to

1. Explain the importance of teamwork in an organizational setting.
2. Identify and explain common types of work teams.
3. List six characteristics of an effective work team.
4. Explain the behavioral science principles that support team building.
5. Describe the team-building skills that leaders need.
6. Describe the team-member skills that employees need.

STEINER/BRESSLER ADVERTISING received its first blow when Mary Faust, the major link to the agency's most important accounts, died in an airplane crash. The second blow came ten months later, when the firm's long-time president, Cy Steiner, committed suicide. Harry Bressler, the remaining partner, was preparing for retirement, so the job of running the company was given to John Zimmerman, the firm's creative director. He had no experience running an advertising agency, but he did know something about human behavior. Zimmerman asked himself, "What did I always want as an employee?" His answer? "Openness, honesty, and the ability to affect my future." With these thoughts in mind, he began the process of mobilizing his colleagues into a team and redefining the firm's culture.

Three months after Steiner's death, Zimmerman took all his employees to a retreat at a mountain-top lodge. After singing some inspiring songs, the staff formed small groups and focused on creating the ideal ad agency. After much discussion, they adopted a new way of doing business: "Serve however a client wishes." This meant that services would now be tailored to meet the specific needs of each client.

In the weeks following the retreat, Zimmerman distributed quarterly financial reports, and he placed a percentage of after-tax profits into a companywide bonus pool. In an effort to improve profits, everyone became more cost-conscious, and expenses dropped 25 percent. Weekly staff meetings are now held to keep everyone well informed. When Zimmerman became president, the agency was sliding toward financial ruin. Today Steiner/Bressler is a profitable agency with several new accounts. No one doubts that John Zimmerman's leadership style made the difference.[1] ∎

Teamwork is often cited as the key to cost reduction, large production increases, gains in quality, and improved customer service. One of the major values that has surfaced throughout the past decade is teamwork over individualism. Almost every organization today is trying to develop the spirit of teamwork, and many organizations have organized their workers into teams. When a person assumes the duties of team supervision, the individual's title is likely to be "team leader" or "team facilitator." The changing role of this new breed of leader is discussed in this chapter. In addition, we discuss ways in which you can become an effective team member.

TEAM BUILDING: AN INTRODUCTION

Can the element of teamwork make a difference between the successful and unsuccessful operation of an organization? Yes, there is evidence that a leadership style that emphasizes **team building** is positively associated with high productivity and profitability. Problems in interpersonal relations are also less common where teamwork is evident. Teamwork ensures not only that a job gets done but also that it gets done efficiently and harmoniously.

There is also evidence that team building can have a positive influence on the physical and psychological well-being of everyone involved. When employees are working together as a team, the leader and members often experience higher levels of job satisfaction and less stress.

Another positive outcome of teamwork is an increase in synergy. **Synergy** is the interaction of two or more parts to produce a greater result than the sum of the parts taken individually.[2] Mathematically speaking, synergy suggests that two plus two equals five. Teamwork synergy is encouraged at 3M Company, Quad/Graphics, Ford Motor Company, and other progressive companies.

Evolution of the Team Concept

Emergence of the team idea came with the now classic Hawthorne studies. Recall from Chapter 1 that this research was conducted by a group of Harvard professors at the suburban Chicago plant of Western Electric Company. Elton Mayo, one of the original researchers, noted that the Hawthorne experiment showed it was possible to take a random collection of employees and build them into a highly productive team. Mayo pointed out that certain factors were present that developed a spirit of teamwork. Teamwork was more likely to develop when the supervisor took a personal interest in each person's achievement, helped the group work together to set its own conditions of work, provided regular feedback on performance, and consulted the group before making changes.[3]

The concept of teamwork and the use of team-building activities to achieve teamwork have been around a long time. Some organizations work hard to get all employees to pull together as a team. Teamwork at a hospital, for example, may begin with acceptance of a common vision, such as providing outstanding health-care services. The only way to make this vision a reality is to obtain the commitment and cooperation of every employee. This will require meaningful employee participation in planning, solving problems, and developing ways to improve health care.

Thinking / Learning Starter

Review your work experience and try to recall situations in which a supervisor took a personal interest in you and your coworkers. What was the impact of this situation on members of the group? Did the supervisor fulfill Mayo's other three characteristics of a successful team manager?

The Transition to Team-Based Structures

One of the most popular workplace initiatives today is the development of organizations that are structured around teams. Over 40 percent of the organizations in America have adopted this approach.[4] Teams have become popular because they encourage **participative management,** the process of empowering employees to assume greater control of the workplace.[5] This section focuses on two of the most common types of teams: self-directed and cross-functional.

Self-Directed Teams　**Self-directed teams** assume responsibility for traditional management tasks as part of their regular work routine. Examples include decisions about production quotas, quality standards, and interviewing applicants for team positions. A typical self-directed (or self-managing) team usually has five to fifteen members who are responsible for producing a well-defined product (such as an automobile) or service (such as processing an insurance claim). Team members usually rotate among the various jobs and acquire the knowledge and skills to perform each job. Each member eventually can perform every job required to complete the entire team task. Employees formerly concerned only with their own jobs suddenly become accountable for the work of the total team.[6] One advantage of this approach is that it reduces the amount of time workers spend on dull and repetitive duties. Also, it taps the employees' full potential.

Published Image Inc., a small company that publishes shareholder newsletters for various mutual-fund companies, recently reorganized its employees into four largely autonomous teams. Each team has its own clients and its own staff of sales, editorial, and production workers. Team members can perform any task needed to meet daily deadlines. The use of self-directed teams at Published Image has resulted in lower employee turnover, improved morale, and better-quality newsletters.[7]

Cross-Functional Teams　**Cross-functional teams** are task groups staffed with a mix of specialists focused on a common objective.[8] These teams are usually temporary units with members from different departments and job levels. The teams are often involved in developing new work procedures or products, devising work reforms, or introducing new technology in an organization. Team members often provide a link among separate functions, such as production, distribution, finance, and customer service. If the workers are represented by a union, then union representatives are usually part of the team. Cross-functional teams often make major decisions that directly influence quality and productivity improvements. When the Cadillac Division of General Motors Corp. decided to build an all-new Seville, a cross-functional team made up of assembly workers, engineers, suppliers, and marketers designed the car. The result of this team effort was a sleekly styled, more agile auto designed to compete with Europe's best automobiles. The new Seville was an immediate sales success.[9]

Although we are seeing greater use of teams, this approach to employee participation is by no means a quick fix. In the case of self-directed teams, it can

Liberty Mutual has developed cross-functional teams made up of sales, underwriting, and loss-prevention experts. Here one of the teams helps customer Dale Shores (top) of the Roche Brothers grocery chain. (Steven Lewis)

sometimes take one or two years for members to learn all the tasks they will perform as they rotate from job to job. It also takes time for a team to mature to the point where it is comfortable making decisions in such areas as work scheduling, hiring, training, and ordering materials. Management must clearly state the purpose of the team and communicate clearly the interdependent nature of relationships among team members and other members of the organization.[10]

BASIC BELIEFS ABOUT TEAMWORK

Sam Walton, founder of Wal-Mart Stores, Inc., was at his best in the role of team builder. His coaching style was up close and personal, and he relied on face-to-face communication as a way of staying in touch with employees in Wal-Mart stores throughout America. Like all competent team leaders, Walton was a master of human nature and human relations, creating and nourishing team spirit throughout the company. Anyone who wants to develop the team-building style of leadership should study the basic beliefs and practices of people like Sam Walton.

McGregor's Influence

In the late 1950s, a book by Douglas McGregor entitled *The Human Side of Enterprise* presented convincing arguments that management had been ignoring certain important facts about people. He said that managers often failed to recognize the potential for growth and the desire for fulfillment characteristic of most workers. McGregor emphasized that "unity of purpose" is the main distinguishing characteristic of many productive work units. When a work group shares common goals and a common commitment, it accomplishes more than it would without them.

In *The Human Side of Enterprise,* McGregor discusses several characteristics of an effective work team.[11]

1. The atmosphere of the workplace tends to be informal, comfortable, relaxed. There are no obvious tensions. It is a working environment in which people are involved and interested.
2. There is a lot of discussion about work-related issues. Virtually everyone participates, but contributions remain pertinent to the task of the group. If the discussion gets off the subject, someone will bring it back in short order.
3. The tasks or objectives of the group are well understood and accepted by the members.
4. The members listen to one another. The discussion does not jump around. Every idea is given a full hearing.
5. There is disagreement. The group is comfortable with this and shows no signs of having to avoid conflict.
6. People freely express their feelings as well as their ideas, both on the problem and on the group's operation. There is little avoidance, and there are few "hidden agendas."

McGregor's views on the characteristics of effective work teams represent "classic" thinking. His thoughts continue to have merit today.

Total Person Insight

"We've felt that technical solutions would win the battle, but they never do. People win the battle of business. You could have the best technical solutions in the world, but if people don't join in and feel like part of the team, you just don't get anywhere."

FRAN TARKENTON

Author, *How to Motivate People* and "Tarkenton on Teambuilding"

The Leadership Grid®

In the early 1960s, Robert Blake and Jane Mouton authored a popular book entitled *The Managerial Grid*. As illustrated in Figure 12.1, the **Leadership Grid®** (formerly called the Managerial Grid®) is a model based on two important leadership-style dimensions: concern for people and concern for production.[12] Where work is physical, concern for production may take the form of number of units produced per hour or time needed to meet a certain production schedule. In an office setting, concern for production may take the form of document preparation volume and accuracy. Concern for people can be

FIGURE 12.1

The Leadership Grid®

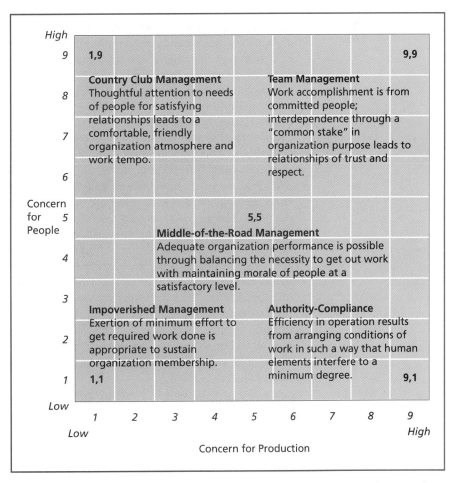

Source: From *Leadership Dilemmas-Grid Solutions* by Robert R. Blake and Anne Adams McCanse (formerly the Managerial Grid Figure by Robert R. Blake and Jane S. Mouton. Gulf Publishing Company, p. 29. Copyright © 1991 by Scientific Methods, Inc. Reprinted by permission of *Scientific Methods.*

reflected in the way a supervisor views work and safety conditions, compensation, recognition for a job well done, and awareness of employees' need to be treated with respect. The Grid helps clarify how these two dimensions are related and establishes a uniform language for communication about leadership styles and patterns. Although there are many possible leadership styles within the Grid, five encompass the most important differences among managers. Blake and Mouton developed descriptive names for each.[13]

- *Impoverished management* (1,1). People with the **impoverished management** orientation might be classified as "inactive" managers. They display little concern for people or production. These managers give very little of themselves and expect little from others.
- *Country club management* (1,9). Low concern for production and high concern for people characterize the **country club management** orientation. These managers take steps to prevent unhappiness and dissension. Country-club managers are eager to accommodate, to avoid being seen as aggressive or demanding. Managers who rely on this style want to keep unhappiness in the work group at a minimum.
- *Authority-compliance management* (9,1). The **authority-compliance management** style is task-oriented, placing much attention on getting the job done. Managers with this orientation display concern for production, not people. They see people as instruments of production. To these managers, achieving performance or production goals is essential, regardless of the human cost.
- *Middle-of-the-road management* (5,5). Managers with a **middle-of-the-road management** style display moderate concern for both people and production. They see a limited amount of participative management as practical. These persons are primarily concerned with maintaining existing conditions in the organization. Middle-of-the-road managers are likely to act in accordance with traditions and be satisfied with modest performance.
- *Team management (9,9).* The **team management** style is a proactive style of management. Persons with this orientation display a high concern for both people and production. They recognize that results are achieved through people. Team managers reward the contribution of ideas and recognize accomplishments, but they also clearly communicate their expectations, hold employees to high standards, and provide regular feedback on performance.

Blake and Mouton have devoted more than thirty years to the study of the team-building leadership style. They maintain that this style is the one most positively associated with productivity and profitability, career success and satisfaction, and physical and mental health. The term "one best style" is used by the authors to describe the 9,9 orientation. They feel this leadership style can be applied effectively in almost any type of organization. This style, they state, achieves production through a high degree of shared responsibility coupled with high participation, involvement, and commitment—all of which are hallmarks of teamwork.[14]

Hall's Contributions

Jay Hall, founder of Teleometrics International Inc., a Texas-based consulting firm, completed a large-scale research project that supports the work of Blake and Mouton.[15] He studied several thousand managers—their personalities and management styles and patterns. In his book *The Competence Process* he reports that high-achieving managers had a deep interest in both people and productivity and relied heavily on the participative approach. Low and moderate achievers, by contrast, avoided involving their subordinates in decision making.

Hall says the values that supervisors and managers hold dear flow from their basic convictions about the worth of the people who perform the work in an organization.[16] Participative management practices are more likely to be fostered in an organization where supervisory-management personnel project confidence in the potentialities of subordinates than in organizations where they do not.

Thinking / Learning Starter

Think about the supervisors and managers you have worked for or have observed. How much concern did each display toward people? Toward production? Assign each supervisor or manager one of the five leadership styles developed by Blake and Mouton.

Behavioral Science Principles Supporting Team Building

In almost every field of study there are a few universal principles (sometimes called fundamentals) that are supported by research evidence. Principles can be thought of as general guidelines that are true regardless of time, place, or situation. In the field of human relations there are several principles—based on the behavioral sciences—that support the team-building leadership style. Blake and Mouton have developed a list of these principles and have applied them to the art of leadership.[17]

1. *Shared participation in problem solving and decision making is basic to growth, development, and contribution.* When people are encouraged to participate in making decisions that affect them, they develop an identity and a sense of control over their destiny. Those employees who never get the opportunity to make such decisions may develop a feeling of powerlessness. They may become passive and avoid opportunities to make contributions to the organization.

The editors of American Political Hotline, *a daily faxed newsletter, must work as a team in order to maintain quality and meet deadlines. Here we see members of the staff making final decisions regarding newsletter format and content. (Gale Zucker/Stock, Boston, Inc.)*

2. *Mutual trust and respect undergird productive human relationships.* Trust is a catalyst. When trust exists within an organization, a spirit of teamwork is more likely to exist. As trust ebbs, people are less open with each other, less interdependent, and less willing to work as a team.
3. *Open communication supports mutual understanding.* Everyone has a need to communicate. People are naturally curious and interested in what is happening within the organization. The mutual sharing of thoughts through constructive self-disclosure promotes a deeper bond among people and a greater spirit of teamwork.
4. *Conflict resolution by direct problem-solving confrontation promotes personal health.* A primary goal of team building is to provide a natural forum for

Total Person Insight

"When I trust myself, trust you, and trust the process, my behavior becomes personal, regardless of other factors in the situation."

Jack Gibb

Author, *Trust—A New View of Personal and Organizational Development*

conflict resolution. Conflict can drain people of the energy they need to perform their regular duties. Conflict produces stress, and stress is a major contributor to physical exhaustion.

5. *Responsibility for one's own actions stimulates initiative.* As humans grow and mature, they become less dependent on others and seek more control over their own lives. Generally adults tend to develop a deep psychological need to be viewed by others as self-directing. When adults are not permitted to be self-directing, resentment and resistance build.

TEAM-BUILDING SKILLS FOR LEADERS

Although many organizations are making the transition to a team-based structure, and some of these teams need little or no supervision, demand for leaders who possess team-building leadership skills will continue to be strong.[18] This section discusses ways that supervisory-management personnel can become team builders. Later in this chapter, you will see how employees can contribute to the team-building process.

The wide range of types of supervisory-management positions may cause you to ask, Do people in these positions have much in common? Will team-building strategies work in most situations? The answer to both questions is yes. A great majority of successful supervisory-management personnel share certain behavior characteristics. Two of the most important dimensions of supervisory leadership—consideration and structure—have been identified in research studies conducted by Edwin Fleishman at Ohio State University[19] and validated by several additional studies.

Consideration

The dimension of **consideration** reflects the extent to which a supervisor's or manager's relationships with subordinates are characterized by mutual trust, respect for the subordinates' ideas, consideration of their feelings, and a certain warmth in interpersonal relationships. When consideration is present, the supervisor-subordinate relationship is characterized by a climate of good rapport and two-way communication.

Consideration is important because people holding supervisory positions must be able to establish a three-way relationship. They must be able to build rapport (1) with the person who supervises their work, (2) with those supervisors who hold similar positions at the same level (horizontal relationships), and (3) with their employees who look to the supervisor for guidance and direction. The quality of these relationships has a direct bearing on the supervisor's overall success. Consideration is the equivalent of "concern for people" on the Leadership Grid®.

Structure

The dimension of **structure** reflects the extent to which a supervisor is likely to define and direct his or her role and the roles of subordinates toward goal attainment. Managers who incorporate structure into their leadership style actively direct group activities by planning, setting goals, communicating information, scheduling, and evaluating performance. People who work under the direction of a highly structured supervisor know what is expected of them. Structure is the equivalent of "concern for production" on the Leadership Grid®.

It is interesting to note that the dimensions of consideration and structure are independent of each other. A supervisor may be well qualified in one area but lack competence in the other. The good news is that anyone can consciously work to develop competence in both areas.

Improving Consideration Skills

The effective use of consideration skills is needed to create a positive and productive work environment. To improve the dimension of consideration, the following practices can be adopted.

Recognize Accomplishments When individual achievements are overlooked, supervisors miss a valuable opportunity to improve job relationships with subordinates. As noted in Chapter 10, people need recognition for good work, regardless of the duties they perform or the positions they hold. Of course, recognition should be contingent on performance. When recognition is given for mediocre performance, the supervisor is reinforcing a behavior that is not desirable.

Provide for Early and Frequent Success According to an old saying, "Nothing succeeds like success." A supervisor should provide each employee with as many opportunities to succeed as possible. The foundation for accomplishment begins with a carefully planned orientation and training program. Supervisors and managers should review job duties and responsibilities, organizational policies and procedures, and any other pertinent information with their employees early in the relationship. No worker should have to rely on office gossip or the advice of a perennially dissatisfied employee for answers to important questions.

Take a Personal Interest in Each Employee Everyone likes to be treated as an individual. Taking a personal interest means learning the names of spouses and children, finding out what employees do during their leisure time, asking about their families, and acknowledging employee birthdays. Some supervisors keep a record of significant information about each of their workers (see Figure 12.2). This record is especially helpful for supervisors who are in charge of a large number of employees and find it difficult to remember important facts about each person.

Establish a Climate of Open Communication To establish a climate of open communication, the leader must be available and approachable. Employees should feel comfortable talking about their fears, frustrations, and aspirations. Communication is closely linked to employee morale—and morale is directly linked to productivity. Therefore, efforts to improve the communication process represent a good use of the supervisor's time and energy.

The supervisor who wants to foster a climate of open communication will schedule periodic meetings where employees can exchange ideas or discuss problems with one another and the supervisor. Periodic meetings represent a form of "team maintenance." Without such meetings, the work group may become less cohesive and less committed to common goals.

Discover Individual Employee Values Today's lean, flatter organizations offer employees fewer opportunities for promotion, smaller raises, and less job security. As a result, many workers no longer feel secure or identify with the company. Supervisors should encourage employees to explore their values and determine if there is a match between what matters most to them and the work they are doing. If a value conflict turns up, the supervisor may be able to redesign the job or give an employee a new assignment.[20] Supervisors should also attempt to find out whether there are any conflicts between the employee's job and personal life. A growing number of employees view their family and personal life as their primary source of satisfaction. The employee who feels pressured to work longer hours and assume greater responsibility may experience a major value conflict.[21] Supervisors who are able to meet the needs of

FIGURE 12.2

Employee Information Record

NAME: Sue Perez

DATE HIRED: 1/8/96

BIRTHDAY: 4/24/69

HOBBIES: Tennis and archery

FAVORITE MUSIC: Country-Western

SPECIAL INTERESTS: Active in the local recycling effort

COMMENTS: *Sue is interested in management*

employees who have work/life conflicts embrace an important leadership fundamental: Live by your values, and encourage others to live by theirs.[22]

Thinking / Learning Starter

Assume you are the manager of the record-keeping department at a small savings and loan association. Three of your employees are responsible for sorting and listing checks and keeping personal and commercial accounts up-to-date. A fourth employee handles all inquiries concerning overdrafts and other problems related to customer accounts. List five specific behaviors you could develop that would contribute to the supervisory-management quality described as *consideration*.

Improving Structure Skills

The supervisor who incorporates structure into his or her leadership style plays an active role in directing group activities. The team builder gives the group direction, establishes performance standards, and maintains individual and group accountablity. The following practices can be used to develop the dimension of structure.

Clearly Define Goals   Members of the group or team must possess a clear idea of what goals need to be accomplished. Supervisors and managers who are successful in motivating employees usually provide an environment in which appropriate goals are set and understood. Bob Hughes, a consultant in the area of team building, suggests establishing baseline performance data so progress can be assessed.[23] In an office that processes lease applications, where accuracy and speed are critically important, the baseline data might include the number of error-free lease applications the team processes in one day. In an ideal situation, team members will be involved in setting goals and will help determine how best to achieve the goals.

Encourage Individual and Team Goal Setting   Setting and achieving goals can provide individuals and teams with a sense of accomplishment. Specific goals are more likely to motivate us than general goals. The goal-setting process is described in Chapter 17.

Some supervisors and managers are using a formal approach to goal setting called **management by objectives (MBO).** Management by objectives is an approach to planning and evaluation in which specific targets are established for a specific period of time. Ideally, the personal goals of the individual employee mesh with the overall goals of the organization. At a date set in advance, the supervisor meets with each subordinate, and together they agree on targets of performance. Depending on the type of organization, the targets might relate to improved accuracy, reduced absenteeism, increased sales, fewer accidents, or decreased expenses. At the end of the established time period, a review of accomplishments is conducted. Hopefully, the involvement of the employee in setting performance goals results in a higher degree of commitment toward achieving the objectives.

Provide Specific Feedback Often   Feedback should be relevant to the task performed by the employee and should be given soon after performance. Feedback is especially critical when an employee is just learning a new job. The supervisor should point out improvements in performance, no matter how small, and always reinforce the behavior she or he wants repeated. The most relevant feedback in a self-directed work team usually comes from coworkers because team members are accountable to one another. Some self-directed work teams design their own performance appraisal system.

Deal with Poor Performance Immediately   As a supervisor, you must give feedback to the person who does not measure up to your standards of performance. When members of the group are not held accountable for doing their share of the work, group morale may suffer. Other members of the group will quickly observe the poor performance and wonder why you are not taking corrective action. To achieve the best results, focus feedback on the situation, issue, or behavior, not on the employee.[24] A person can make a mistake and still be a valuable employee. Correct the person in a way that does not create anger and resentment. Avoid demoralizing the person or impairing his or her self-confidence.

Structure Versus Control

Many times supervisors and managers confuse control with structure, states Mardell Grothe, training program design consultant to the National Tooling Machining Association. He says, "Structure is good. It means laying out very clearly what you want and when you want it done and letting the persons react. Control is trying to dictate how it should be done from moment to moment."[25] When structure is present, employees know what is to be done but realize that they have some latitude in how to complete the task. Today's better-educated and better-informed employees appreciate structure but usually react negatively to too much control.

SITUATIONAL LEADERSHIP

The **Situational Leadership Model,** developed by Paul Hersey and his colleagues at the Center for Leadership Studies, offers an alternative to the Leadership Grid®. **Situational leadership** is based on the theory that the most successful leadership occurs when the leader's style matches the situation. Situational leadership theory emphasizes the need for flexibility.[26]

Before we discuss the differences between the Leadership Grid® and the Situational Leadership Model, let's look at the similarities between the two. Both models are based on two nearly identical dimensions. Paul Hersey says that the primary behaviors displayed by effective managers in the Situational Leadership Model can be described as task behavior and relationship behavior. He offers the following definitions:

> Task behavior is defined as the extent to which the leader engages in spelling out the duties and responsibilities of an individual or group. The behaviors include telling people what to do, how to do it, when to do it, where to do it and who's to do it. Relationship behavior is defined as the extent to which the leader engages in two-way or multi-way communication if there is more than one person. The behaviors include listening, encouraging, facilitating, providing clarification, and giving socio-emotional support.[27]

Task behavior, concern for production, and structure really mean the same thing. And relationship behavior, concern for people, and consideration do not really differ. In essence, the situational leader and the person who uses the 9,9 team management style rely on the same two dimensions of leadership. Both use task behavior (concern for production) and relationship behavior (concern for people) to influence their subordinates.

What is the major difference between these two leadership models? Hersey says that, when attempting to influence others, you must (1) diagnose the readiness level of the follower for a specific task and (2) provide the appropriate leadership style for that situation.[28] In other words, given the specific situation, you must decide how much task behavior and how much relationship behavior to display. Consider the situation when a rescue squad arrives at an accident scene. In this crisis-oriented situation, the leader of the squad may rely on a very structured leadership style because there is no time to talk things over or to seek feedback from squad members.

Space does not permit an in-depth comparison of situational leadership with the 9,9 team manager style. But we can point out that it is not possible to become a situational leader without first developing task behavior (structure) and relationship behavior (consideration). Therefore, mastery of the skills needed to apply the 9,9 team management style is a prerequisite to becoming a situational leader.

TEAMWORK: THE EMPLOYEE'S ROLE

Each member should assume an active part in helping the work unit achieve its mission. This means that every member of the work group can and should be a team member and a team builder. These dual roles are achieved when employees assume greater responsibility for the success of the work unit. Today's most

When Mercedes-Benz began hiring workers for its new Alabama-based auto plant, more than 40,000 people applied for 650 well-paying jobs. Mercedes was searching for people who would be able to work effectively on teams. (Michael Schwarz)

Total Person Insight

"The idea of acting morally must extend to how a company treats its employees. Rather than focusing just on what they earn, you listen to what they need. You harness their energy and opinions. You empower them. The old authoritarian mode no longer works."

ANITA RODDICK

Founder, Body Shop International

---

valued employees are those who are willing to assume leadership responsibilities.

Employees As Leaders

In traditional organizations there were leaders and followers, and the followers were not expected to develop leadership skills. Today, some of the most effective leaders are helping their work team members develop leadership skills so that the team's success will not ride on one person. At a time when most organizations are attempting to compete in a complex, ever-changing global market, there is real merit in establishing a diversity of leadership within the work group. If we are willing to expand our definition of leadership, we can see leaders everywhere.[29]

- The passive "worker bee" frequently serves as a leader when the issue is how to get the work done.
- The "corporate counselor," who informally guides coworkers through stressful problems by merely listening, is an emotional leader.
- The rigid "rule follower" keeps our creativity from becoming irresponsible.

Will the "employees as leaders" approach catch on? J. Oliver Crom, CEO of Dale Carnegie & Associates, Inc., is optimistic. He says that leadership skills are needed at all levels of the organization and adds that "Every employee is a leader" might well be today's business slogan.[30]

Becoming a Valued Team Member

At the beginning of this chapter, we described two types of teams and noted that teams are becoming more common in organizational settings. Throughout your working life, your success will very likely depend on your ability to be

© 1997 by Wiley Miller. Distributed by The Washington Post Writers Group. Reprinted with permission.

an effective team member. Here are some tips on how to become a respected team member in any organization.[31]

1. *Avoid becoming part of a clique or subgroup within the team.* As a member of a clique you will very likely lose the trust and respect of other team members.

2. *Avoid any action that might sabotage the team.* By engaging in frequent criticism of other team members, gossip, or other unconstructive behaviors, you undermine team efforts.

3. *Keep in mind that effective team membership depends on honest, open communication among team members.* Use the fundamentals of constructive self-disclosure discussed in Chapter 8.

4. *As a team member, do not feel the need to submerge your own strong beliefs, creative solutions, and ideas.* If the team members are about to make a decision that in your opinion is not "right," do not hesitate to speak up and express your views.

Teamwork can be a very satisfying experience. It can generate positive energy and contribute to a sense of optimism about the future. As a team member you have the opportunity to assume a very important leadership role.

Managing the Relationship with Your Boss

The idea that you should manage the relationship with your boss may sound a little unusual at first. But it makes a lot of sense when you consider the advantages of assuming this responsibility. When the subordinate and the boss are both working to maintain a good relationship, conflict is less likely to surface. The boss-subordinate relationship is not like the one between parent and child—the burden for managing the relationship should not and cannot fall entirely on the one in authority.

When you take time to manage the relationship with your boss, he or she will become more effective in performing his or her job. In many cases, managers are no more effective than the combined competence of the people they supervise. Some employees do not realize how much their boss needs assistance and support from them.

How do you go about managing your boss? Here are some general considerations.

Assess Your Own Strengths   The boss represents only one-half of the relationship. The development of an effective working relationship also requires reflecting on your own strengths, weaknesses, work habits, communication style, and needs. What personal characteristics might impede or facilitate working with your boss? As one author puts it, the most important issue related to your adaptability to your boss's style is your own style. "The burden of assessment and adjustment falls more on you than on your boss."[32]

Develop an Understanding of Your Boss   Become familiar with this person's strengths, weaknesses, work habits, communication style, and needs. Spend time studying your boss. In some cases, the direct approach is best. Ask your boss, "How would you like me to work with you?" Try to determine his or her goals and expectations. What is the person trying to accomplish? Does your boss enjoy casual meetings to discuss business matters or formal meetings with written agendas?

Flex Your Communication Style   In terms of communication style, is your boss supportive, emotive, reflective, or director? Once you have answered this question, begin thinking of how to flex your style in ways that will build rapport and avoid unnecessary stress. Remember, style flexing is a temporary effort to act in harmony with another person's dominant communication style (see Chapter 3).

Be Frank and Candid   Suppose that to avoid conflict you almost never disagree with your boss—even when the boss is obviously wrong. Are you making a contribution to his or her growth and development? Obviously not. At times you must be your own person and say what is on your mind. The information you share with your boss may in fact contribute to his or her success. Chapter 8 provides some excellent tips on how to effectively self-disclose your thoughts and feelings.

As organizations become flatter, with fewer layers of management and more projects carried out by teams, collaboration will become more important. Effective team members are those who collaborate actively with their leader and other members of the team.[33]

Summary

Teamwork ensures not only that a job gets done but also that it gets efficiently. Therefore, successful teamwork can often make the difference between the profitable and the unprofitable operation of an organization. The team-building leadership style is effective because it is suited to the needs of most of today's employees.

Many companies are forming specific types of teams. Two of the most common are self-directed teams, and cross-functional teams.

An effective work team tends to be informal and relaxed, with no obvious tensions. People are involved, interested, and eager to participate in solving work-related problems. An effective work group also has clearly understood goals and objectives.

Two important dimensions of supervisory leadership contribute to team building. One of these dimensions, consideration, reflects the extent to which a supervisor maintains with employees relationships that are characterized by mutual trust, respect, and rapport. The other dimension, structure, reflects the extent to which a supervisor is likely to direct group activities through planning, goal setting, communication, scheduling, and evaluating. The Leadership Grid® helps clarify these two dimensions of leadership.

Members of an effective work group should assume effective leadership and membership roles. Each helps the group achieve its mission. Everyone assumes the role of team member and team builder.

Employees are in a unique position to give guidance and support to their supervisor or manager. Most bosses need this assistance and support to achieve success. To manage the relationship with your boss, it is first necessary to understand him or her. Next, you must assess your own strengths and try to identify personal characteristics that might impede or facilitate a working relationship. And finally, you must be frank and candid. Sometimes you need to disagree with your boss.

Career Corner

Q. I work for a company that frequently uses cross-functional teams to accomplish certain things. Whenever I serve on one of these teams, I feel frustrated. I want to get a promotion, but team assignments seem to hide my talents. How can I make the best of my next team assignment?

A. If your company is having success with these teams, the best way to get the attention of top management is to be an effective team member. When you get your next team assignment, make a quick study of how the group is working together and note any problems that could prevent the team from achieving its goals. Your visibility will increase if you find ways to enhance team performance. You might share important information with team members or offer to help team members develop some specific skills. In some cases it's possible to help your teammates grow while developing yourself.

Key Terms

team building
synergy
participative management
self-directed teams
cross-functional teams
Leadership Grid®
impoverished management
country club management
authority-compliance management

middle-of-the-road management
team management
consideration
structure
management by objectives (MBO)
Situational Leadership Model
situational leadership

Review Questions

1. In what ways did the Hawthorne studies contribute to the emergence of the team-building concept

2. In *The Human Side of Enterprise,* Douglas McGregor discusses several characteristics of an effective work team. What was his view on disagreement?

3. Describe the two management-style dimensions of the Leadership Grid® developed by Blake and Mouton.

4. List and describe the two types of teams that are currently used by organizations.

5. What are some of the behaviors displayed by supervisors who are strong in the area of consideration?

6. What are some of the behaviors displayed by supervisors who are strong in the area of structure?

7. Briefly describe the formal approach to goal setting called management by objectives. What targets of performance might be established jointly by the employee and supervisor?

8. Provide a brief description of situational leadership. What are the major similarities between the Situational Leadership Model and the Leadership Grid®?

9. Describe four major considerations that should guide you in any attempt to manage your boss.

10. Tarkenton discusses people versus technical solutions in the Total Person Insight. Do you agree or disagree with his point of view?

Application Exercises

1. Do women in managerial positions use a different approach than men? Judy Rosener, professor of management at the University of California and co-author of *Workforce America!,* says yes. She reports the following results of a survey sponsored by the International Women's Forum. First, women in this study were more likely to rely on personal characteristics such as charisma, interpersonal skills, and hard work as well as personal contacts (personal power) to achieve goals. They were less likely to use organizational position, title, and the ability to reward and punish (structural

power) to achieve goals. Second, women in this study used an "interactive" approach to leadership that encouraged participating, sharing power and information, and getting people excited about their work.[34]

    a. Do you feel the results of this study are accurate? Do you agree with the findings?

    b. Are there any risks involved in a leadership style that emphasizes personal power? Would this leadership style be appropriate for all types of organizations?

2. There is increasing pressure on organizations to allow employees' personal problems to be brought to the attention of the supervisor or manager. Personal problems that can disrupt people's lives include dealing with a teenager on drugs, coping with the needs of a frail parent, losing a babysitter, or getting a divorce. Schedule an interview with two persons who hold supervisory-management positions and ask these questions:

    a. Do you assume the role of mentor and counselor when an employee brings a personal problem to your attention?

    b. Should you give the person with a serious problem some special consideration, such as time off, less demanding work, or professional help that is paid for by the company?

3. The skills needed to be an effective leader can be developed by anyone who is willing to invest the time and energy. It is possible to practice important leadership skills before you assume the duties of a supervisor or manager. Review the various ways to improve consideration and structure skills discussed in this chapter, and then begin searching for opportunities to practice these skills. Here are some opportunities for practice:

    a. Volunteer assignments in your community

    b. Group assignments at work, at college, or at place of worship

    c. Involvement in political, professional, or social activities

Internet Exercise

Many organizations are forming specific types of teams in order to increase employee participation and productivity. The Internet is an important source of information concerning this topic. Using your search engine, type in the following keywords:

team building

self directed teams

cross functional teams

quality circles

Review the resources (such as books, articles, and training programs) that are available, and then prepare a written summary of your findings. Pay special attention to criteria for effective teams and information that would help you become a productive team member.

Case 12.1   Competition or Cooperation?

Is competitiveness vital to a successful career in business? Is it inevitable that we have winners and losers in the workplace? Is competition healthy or inherently destructive? Alfie Kohn, author of *No Contest—The Case Against Competition,* set out to answer these and other questions. As the title indicates, he is not in favor of competition. Here are some of his views:

1. Competition damages relationships among people and makes life more unpleasant than it needs to be.
2. Competition is not part of "human nature." Given a choice, most people will try to avoid unusually competitive activities and organizations. When people act competitively, it is because they are taught to do so.
3. Superior performance does not require competition.
4. Success often depends on the efficient sharing of resources, which is unlikely to happen if people are pitted against one another.
5. Competition makes people suspicious and hostile toward one another, thus damaging efforts to promote teamwork.
6. Bonuses and incentives should not be offered as prizes if only one person or group can win.

Stephen Covey, author of *The 7 Habits of Highly Effective People,* seems to agree with Kohn. He says that "people who are oriented toward competition tend to think defensively and protectively and in terms of scarcity."

What are the alternatives to competition? Kohn suggests placing more emphasis on cooperation. He suggests a move toward "positive interdependence," an approach where group members depend on each other and are accountable to each other.

Questions

1. Do you agree or disagree with Kohn's view that organizations should replace competition with cooperation?
2. Can an organization emphasize competition among workers and still maintain a spirit of teamwork?

Case 12.2   Wanted: A Few Good Women and Men

Throughout a long period of mergers, buyouts, downsizing efforts, and the organization of workers into teams, you would expect to see a major decrease in the number of supervisory-management positions. But, although we have seen some thinning of the ranks, the number of career opportunities in supervision and management is surprisingly high. Many skilled workers are promoted to first-line supervisory positions, and many first-line supervisors are promoted to middle-level managerial positions. You may have the opportunity to become a supervisor or manager sometime in the future, so now is the time to examine this career option. What qualities do you need to achieve success? What sacrifices might be needed if you accept a promotion to the position of supervisor or manager?

Today, supervisory-management personnel must be very adaptable and flexible, able to achieve success within a climate of change. The problems faced today are likely to be multidimensional and thus require a wide range of problem-solving skills and approaches. Here are some examples:

- Within today's work force you will find a multitude of values, expectations, and work habits. While maintaining high performance standards, leaders must display tolerance for persons who differ in age, gender, race, and physical traits. In some areas of the service industry, language barriers are common. Marriott International Inc. reports that members of its U.S. work force speak sixty-five different languages.
- The large-scale use of temporary workers is creating challenges for some supervisory-management personnel. We encourage supervisors to become well acquainted with each of their employees, but doing this is more difficult with temporary workers. More than 11 million workers telecommute from home, and many other employees work without a designated desk or office space—in an arrangement often described as "hoteling." These workers present another type of challenge.
- Employees who were born after 1964, described as Generation X or "post-boomers," may require a more flexible approach to supervision. Many of these people are not opposed to job hopping, take a dim view of written job descriptions and rules that crimp their freedom to be innovative, and seek work/life balance. These employees tend to be more individualistic than baby boomers.
- Organizations must continually make changes in order to adapt to a changing environment. Some of these changes will be descriptive. Supervisory-management personnel frequently introduce these changes and must win support for them.

Questions

1. Although supervisory-management positions are becoming more challenging, many people want these jobs. What motivates people to seek these positions?
2. Do you have the desire to become a supervisor or manager? If your answer is yes, discuss the reasons why you are interested. If your answer is no, explain the reasons why you are not interested.
3. Which of the challenges described above would be most difficult for you to deal with? Which of these challenges would you find most interesting?

Chapter 13

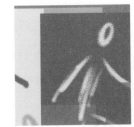

Effective

Conflict Resolution

Strategies

Chapter Preview

After studying this chapter, you will be able to

1. List and describe some of the major causes of conflict between people in the work setting.
2. Explain the three basic conflict resolution strategies.
3. Understand the role that assertiveness and cooperation play in personal conflict resolution.
4. Identify key elements of the conflict resolution process.
5. Understand the role labor unions play in conflict resolution.
6. Discuss contemporary challenges facing unions and management.

T ODAY WORKERS face subtle conflicts over issues that did not exist fifteen to twenty years ago. For example, most families now depend on two incomes for economic survival. As a result, working parents are demanding and getting new rights and benefits to help balance their personal and professional lives. Flextime, available at some companies, allows working parents to tailor their arrival and departure times at work to fit their child-care arrangements. Many family-friendly employers allow workers time off to attend special activities that involve their children. Some firms offer parental and maternity leave to both fathers and mothers of newborn babies. Conflicts can arise if workers who have not yet started their families or who have chosen to be child-free feel slighted when benefits and privileges are awarded to workers with children. Child-free workers in some organizations are expected to maintain regular working hours while their coworkers adjust to child-care challenges by arriving late for work or leaving early. Child-free workers may be denied personal leave time to care for a critically ill spouse while other workers have time off related to a pregnancy. And sometimes—when it comes time to work late into the evening or on weekends—child-free workers are asked or told to put forth extra effort by employers who fear they will be criticized for interfering with the "family time" of working parents. Of course, conflict can also arise if working parents feel employers are exhibiting favoritism when they choose a child-free worker for a special assignment that might eventually lead to a promotion. ■

What are employers to do? Should they change the rules and regulations to avoid conflict? This may not be economically feasible. Should they treat everyone the same? This would be a giant step backward in organizational management, since most employees now want to be treated as unique individuals. As organizations struggle to resolve nontraditional conflicts, traditional management-versus-labor disputes, as well as numerous other conflicts in the workplace, conflict resolution becomes a necessary human relations skill for workers and managers alike.

A NEW VIEW OF CONFLICT

Most standard dictionaries define **conflict** as a clash between incompatible people, ideas, or interests. These conflicts are almost always perceived as negative experiences in our society. But when we view conflict as a negative experience, we may be hurting our chances of dealing with it effectively. Many books and articles imply that we must do everything in our power to eliminate the conflicts in our professional and personal lives. In reality, conflicts can serve as opportunities for personal growth if we develop and use positive, constructive conflict resolution skills.[1]

Total Person Insight

"The rapid changes of the twentieth century have increased human conflict to the point that our sensibilities toward each other are becoming numb. The human capacity for adaptation may be working against our social relationships as we passively accept conditions that are not conducive to the effective resolution of interpersonal differences. Just as we adapt to bad air, tasteless food, polluted water, congested cities, and loud noise, we are also becoming callous and indifferent to the factors in our environment that are setting us at one another's throats."

GORDON LIPPITT

Consultant, Human Resource Development

Much of our growth and social progress comes from the opportunities we have to discover creative solutions to conflicts that surface in our lives. Dudley Weeks, professor of conflict resolution at American University, says conflict can be used to clarify a relationship, provide additional ways of thinking about the source of conflict, and open up possibilities for improving a relationship.[2]

Sometimes a difference of opinion is the first step in getting rid of outdated rules and regulations. When people work together to resolve conflicts, their solutions are often far more creative than they would be if only one person addressed the problem. Creatively managed conflict can shake people out of their mental ruts and give them new frameworks, new assumptions, and new points of view. The heart of effective human relations lies not in trying to eliminate conflict (an impossible task) but in making constructive use of the energy released by conflict.

Jerry Harvey, professor of management at George Washington University and author of *The Abilene Paradox and Other Meditations on Management,* says too much agreement is not always healthy in an organization. He points out that organizations, or departments within organizations, frequently take action that contradicts information they have for dealing with a problem or issue.[3] Members of a work team, for example, may be so anxious to be viewed as "team players" that they do not voice their concerns even when they have doubts about a decision being made. Experiments have shown that team members who have a strong need to be connected to the group often change their opinions to avoid being in conflict with the majority—even when they know they are right.[4] The result is that the team may decide on a course of action that some members know will fail.

The Cost of Conflict

The amount of time and money invested in conflict resolution is surprisingly high. It is estimated that management personnel spend about 20 percent of their time resolving disputes among staff members.[5] Most managers have learned that when they address the source of a conflict rather than suppress it, lines of communication open and people begin talking *to* each other rather than *about* each other. This open communication helps workers feel that their opinion is valued and that they are a part of the team.

In some cases, the revenue loss due to unresolved conflict can be extremely high. A strike by the International Brotherhood of Teamsters against United Parcel Service cost UPS more than $700 million in lost revenue.[6] A strike by the United Auto Workers against Chrysler cost the automaker an estimated $20 million a day in lost profits.[7] In addition to dealing with this loss of revenue, UPS and Chrysler had to find ways to rebuild employees' and customers' trust and loyalty after the conflicts were ended.

Causes of Conflict

Conflicts among workers are caused by a wide range of factors. Some are major and need to be addressed through the legal system or labor union negotiations. Others seem relatively minor but can still have a major impact on the productivity of an organization. Here we discuss several causes of conflict that may help you anticipate, and therefore solve, people problems in your organization.

Ineffective Communication A major source of personal conflict is the misunderstanding that results from ineffective communication. In Chapter 2 we discussed the various filters that messages must pass through before effective communication can occur. In the work setting, where many different people work closely together, communication breakdowns are inevitable.

Often it is necessary to determine if the conflict is due to a misunderstanding or a true disagreement. If the cause is a misunderstanding, you may need to explain your position again or provide more details or examples to help the other person understand. If a disagreement exists, one or both parties have to be persuaded to change their position on the issue. Those involved in the conflict can attempt to explain their position over and over again, but until someone changes, the root problem will persist.[8] This issue is discussed in greater detail later in this chapter.

Value Clashes In Chapter 5 you read that differences in values can cause conflicts between generations, among men and women, and among people with different value priorities. Consider the conflicts that might arise between "loyalists," who join their organization for life and make decisions for their own good as well as the good of the company, and "job-hoppers," who accept

Angry confrontations rarely result in effective conflict resolution. (Robert Brenner/ PhotoEdit)

a job in order to position themselves for the next opportunity that might further their personal career advancement. The opportunities for value clashes are almost limitless in today's diverse organizations.

Culture Clashes For generations, culture clashes have occurred between workers not only from other countries but also from different parts of the United States. Today's diverse work force reflects a kaleidoscope of cultures, each with its own unique qualities. The individual bearers of these different cultural traditions could easily come into conflict with one another. The issues may be as simple as one person's desire to dress in ethnic fashion and a supervisor's insistence on strict adherence to the company dress code, or as complex as work ethics.

Total Person Insight

"Everything that irritates us about others can lead us to an understanding of ourselves."

CARL JUNG, M.D.

Swiss Psychologist

Work Policies and Practices Interpersonal conflicts can develop when an organization has arbitrary or confusing rules, regulations, and performance standards. Workers will see little correlation between job performance and salary advancement if they discover that another worker doing the same job is making more money or is being promoted faster than they are. Conflicts often arise over rules about smoking. A fifteen-minute break might be reasonable for most workers but unreasonable for smokers who need fifteen minutes just to walk to and from a designated smoking area. But if smokers are allowed to be away from their work for a longer period of time, nonsmokers may be upset.

Adversarial Management Under adversarial management, supervisors may view their employees and even other managers with suspicion and distrust and treat them as "the enemy." Employees usually lack respect for adversarial managers, resenting their authoritarian style and resisting their suggestions for change. This atmosphere makes cooperation and teamwork difficult. Supervisors who display genuine concern for both people and production and are sensitive to employee needs have far fewer conflicts than do adversarial managers. Because of this, most organizations are encouraging a leadership style that encourages openness and mutual respect.

Noncompliance Conflict also surfaces when some workers refuse to comply with the rules and neglect their fair share of the workload. Coworkers get angry if they have to put forth extra effort to get the work done because others are taking two-hour lunch breaks, sleeping on the job, making personal phone calls during office hours, and wasting time. Now that so many organizations are organizing their work forces into teams, noncompliance has the potential for becoming a major source of conflict. The good news is that noncompliance is probably one of the easiest types of conflict to resolve. All employees—not just the supervisors—need to develop effective assertiveness skills so that they feel comfortable confronting the errant workers and asking for compliance. Some suggestions for appropriate assertive behaviors are offered later in this chapter.

Difficult People The focus of this book is to help you become a valued worker who is easy to get along with and productive regardless of your career path. However, you are likely to encounter coworkers who have not studied human relations. Some of them will be difficult to get along with, no matter what you do. In their book *Dealing with People You Can't Stand,* Rick Kirschner and Rick Brinkman identify ten types of difficult personalities (see Figure 13.1). They suggest four options you might consider when you work with difficult people:

1. Suffer in silence.
2. Change your attitude. You may not like the individual, but you can still work well together.
3. Change your behavior so that the difficult person has to learn new ways of dealing with you.
4. Look for a new job. Not all situations can be resolved.[9]

FIGURE 13.1

Dealing with People
You Can't Stand

Difficult People	Human Relations Strategies
The Tanks: Pushy and ruthless, loud and forceful, they assume that the end justifies the means.	When under attack, hold your position, make direct eye contact, focus on breathing slowly and deeply. When they finish, say, "When you're ready to speak to me with respect, I'll be ready to discuss this matter."
The Snipers: Identify your weaknesses and use them against you through sabotage behind your back or putdowns in front of the crowd.	Stop in midsentence and focus your full attention on them. Ask them to clarify their grievance. If it is valid, take action; if invalid, express your appreciation and calmly offer new information.
The Know-It-Alls: Will tell you what they know—for hours at a time—but won't take a second to listen to your "clearly inferior" ideas.	Acknowledge their expertise and be prepared with your facts. Use plural pronouns like *we* or *us*. Present your information as probing questions rather than statements so that you are less threatening and appear willing to learn from them.
The Think-They-Know-It-Alls: They don't know much, but they don't let that get in the way. They exaggerate, brag, mislead, and distract.	Acknowledge their input, but question their facts with "I" statements, such as, "From what I've read and experienced . . ."
The Grenades: When they blow their tops, they're unable to stop. When the smoke clears and the dust settles, the cycle begins again.	When the explosion begins, assertively repeat the individual's name to get his or her attention. Then calmly address the person's first few sentences, which usually identify the real problem. Suggest taking time out to cool down, then really listen to the problem.
The Yes Persons: They are quick to agree but slow to deliver, leaving a trail of unkept commitments and broken promises.	When they say yes, ask them to summarize their commitment and write it down. Arrange a weird deadline (9:11 A.M. on Thursday) and describe the negative consequences that will result if they do not follow through.

(continued)

FIGURE 13.1

(cont.)

Difficult People	Human Relations Strategies
The Maybe Persons: When faced with a crucial decision, they keep putting it off until it's too late and the decision makes itself.	List advantages and disadvantages of the decision or option. Help them feel comfortable and safe, and stay in touch until the decision is implemented.
The Nothing Persons: No verbal or nonverbal feedback. They tell you nothing and stare past you as if you're not there.	Use open-ended questions that begin with *who, what, where, when,* or *how;* use humor; describe negative results of not talking to you.
The No Persons: Doleful and discouraging, they say, "What goes up must come down." And what comes down must never be able to get back up again.	Ask them to critique your ideas. This shows you are approaching the problem realistically and with an open mind. Listen to their feedback, fix the problems, then present the plan.
The Whiners: They wallow in their woe, whine incessantly, and carry the weight of the world on their shoulders.	Listen and write down their main points. Interrupt and get specifics; identify and focus on possible solutions. If they remain in "it's hopeless" mode, walk away saying, "Let me know when you want to talk about solving the problem."

Source: From Rick Brinkman and Rick Kirschner, *Dealing with People You Can't Stand.* Copyright © 1994 by McGraw-Hill, Inc. Reprinted by permission of McGraw-Hill, Inc.

Thinking / Learning Starters

1. Have you ever experienced a conflict with a coworker? Explain. How did you handle the situation? Did you confront the other person? What were the results? Could you have handled the situation in a more productive manner? Explain.

2. Identify some of the causes of conflict in an organization in which you worked as an employee or volunteer. What types of conflict seemed to cause the most trouble among people?

DEALING WITH CONFLICT

In baseball, if two runners try to occupy the same base at the same time, there is conflict. It is an exciting situation, but if a positive solution is not found quickly, both they and their team will be losers. We must accept the fact that anytime two or more people are brought together, the stage is set for potential conflict. When conflict does occur, the results may be positive or negative, depending on how those involved choose to approach it.

When a difference of opinion has progressed to open conflict, various conflict resolution strategies may be needed to resolve the issue. When a conflict resolution strategy is applied, all opposing parties may or may not be satisfied with the outcome. Generally speaking, if any of the parties involved are dissatisfied, the conflict will probably arise again in the future.

Some of the most common approaches used to resolve conflict include withdrawing from an actual or potential dispute, smoothing it over, compromising, enforcing a solution, and confronting the situation directly. These and other approaches can be grouped into three basic conflict resolution strategies: win/lose, lose/lose, and win/win.

Win/Lose Strategy

When you rely on the **win/lose strategy,** you achieve your goals at the expense of others. Determining when to use this strategy depends on how severe the problem is and what results are desired from the solution. Although this approach may solve the conflict on a short-term basis, it usually does not address the underlying causes of the problem. When one person wins and the other loses, the loser is likely to resent the solution and may feel like a victim. In one sense, this approach simply sows the seeds for another conflict because the "loser" may seek revenge.

In a work setting, the strategy can be applied in either of two principal ways: The manager rules, or the majority rules. In the first way, the manager acts as an autocrat, deciding on the solution and stating that it is final; a mandate settles the matter. Indeed, the manager can threaten the security of the others if they refuse to accept the solution: "Either do as I say, or find a job somewhere else!" In the second way, a vote can be taken, and the majority wins. Unless the vote is unanimous, someone will be on the losing side.

When might the win/lose strategy be used? It can serve in situations where two factions simply cannot agree on any solution or may not even be able to talk to each other. A long-standing feud among workers may also be an instance where a solution may need to be imposed on all parties concerned. In such cases, the concern is not so much to maintain good human relations as it is to ensure that the work gets done.

Lose/Lose Strategy

All parties lose when the **lose/lose strategy** is used. Despite the negative over-tones associated with this term, the lose/lose strategy can be called on to elim-inate conflicts—again, depending on the results desired. Basically, this strategy can be applied in three ways.

First, both parties can be asked to compromise. Each person involved must "give in" to the other and must judge what degree of compromise is accept-able. When the sacrifices are too great, both parties may feel that too much has been given.

Second, an arbitrator, a neutral third party, can decide how the conflict should be resolved. This process often results in a solution being imposed on the disputing parties. The arbitration process may take from each side as much as it gives in the effort to reach a final settlement.

Third, going by the rules can also resolve a conflict, but it may not take into consideration the particulars of a case. If a worker requests more flexible work-ing hours because he or she must arrange child care, the manager may settle the issue by quoting the company rule that everyone starts at nine and leaves at five, no exceptions. This leaves the worker worrying about child-care concerns, while the manager may lose productivity from the employee.

The lose/lose strategy can be applied when there is little time to find a solu-tion through discussion and mutual problem solving or when the two sides cannot come to an agreement. Union-management disputes, for example, may be submitted to arbitration for a settlement.

In general, the lose/lose and win/lose strategies create a "we versus they" attitude among the people involved in the conflict rather than a "we versus the problem" approach. We versus they (or "my way versus your way") means that participants focus on whose solution is superior instead of working together to find a solution that is acceptable to all concerned. Each person tends to see the issue from his or her viewpoint only and does not define the problem in terms of mutual needs and goals.

Win/Win Strategy

The basic purpose of the **win/win strategy** is to fix the problem—not the blame! Those who use this strategy listen to all points of view, define the basic issues, and create an atmosphere of trust among all involved. Everyone must believe that the problem will be settled on the merits of the case rather than through political or personal influence. Those involved in the win/win process should be flexible, sensitive, patient, and calm. No one should feel threatened or humiliated. The result of the win/win strategy will be a solution to the problem that caused the conflict—one that meets individual needs, results in mutual benefits, and strengthens the relationship. Table 13.1 cites the assump-tions of the win/win strategy.

TABLE 13.1

Assumptions of the Win/Win Strategy

Given these assumptions and the opportunities to act on them, conflicts can be resolved to meet the needs of all involved, if sufficient information is available.

1. People want to work together.
2. People can work together to solve mutual problems.
3. People respect each other's right to participate in decisions that affect them.
4. People respect each other's integrity.
5. People respect each other's capabilities.
6. People working in the same organization share the common goals of the group.

Source: Excerpted with permission of the publisher from *Managing Conflict* by Donald H. Weiss. © 1981 AMACOM, a division of the American Management Association. All rights reserved.

Workers at this Georgia-Pacific sawmill have dropped recorded injuries to 70 percent of the industry average. They have learned that bypassing OSHA standards is literally hazardous to their health. They understand the same "macho" actions that used to make them heroes now get them in trouble with management. (Ann States/SABA)

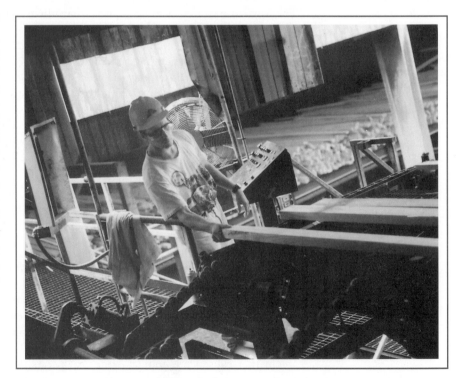

Fighting to win has become an extension of the skills we learn to succeed in a world characterized by competition. The winner becomes a powerful victor and the loser a resentful victim. Their interpersonal trust is diminished. When the parties in a conflict put aside their competitive urges and their pride, it is possible to open a sincere dialogue. Mutual trust is built by striving to protect the self-esteem and self-respect of the other person.

Assertiveness: A Personal Strategy for Resolving Conflict

Assertiveness is based on rights. **Assertive behavior** involves standing up for your rights and expressing your thoughts and feelings in a direct, appropriate way that does not violate the rights of others. It is a matter of getting the other person to understand your viewpoint.[10] People who exhibit assertive behavior skills are able to handle their conflicts with greater ease and assurance

On Manners by Jerry Marcus

"Let me finish! You always say 'You win' before I've won."

Total Person Insight

"Any method of negotiation may be fairly judged by three criteria: It should produce a wise agreement if agreement is possible. It should be efficient. And it should improve or at least not damage the relationship between the parties."

ROGER FISHER AND WILLIAM URY

Authors, *Getting to Yes*

---

while maintaining good interpersonal relations. Use assertive behaviors when you sense someone is taking advantage of you, ignoring your needs, or disregarding your point of view.

Some people do not understand the distinction between being aggressive and being assertive. **Aggressive behavior** involves expressing your thoughts and feelings and defending your rights in a way that violates the rights of others. Aggressive people may interrupt, talk fast, ignore others, and use sarcasm or other forms of verbal abuse to maintain control. They do not view conflict resolution as a strategy for improving relationships. Aggressive behavior, of course, may bring out the worst in those on the receiving end. The receivers are likely to behave defensively, which just escalates the conflict.

People who attempt to avoid conflict by simply ignoring things that bother them are exhibiting **nonassertive behavior.** Nonassertive people often give in to the demands of others, and their passive approach makes them less likely to make their needs known. If you fail to take a firm position when such action is appropriate, colleagues may take advantage of you, and management may question your ability to lead.[11] Table 13.2 may give you a clearer understanding of how assertive, aggressive, and nonassertive individuals respond when confronted with conflict situations.

How to Become More Assertive   If you are aggressive, nonassertive, or less assertive than you would like to be in certain situations, do not be discouraged. With practice, you can acquire the sense of well-being that comes with knowing that you can communicate your wants, dislikes, and feelings in a clear, direct manner without threatening or attacking others. Entire books are written describing assertiveness skills, so it is impossible to explain the various techniques within the context of this short chapter. Nevertheless, we can offer you practical guidelines that may help you develop assertiveness skills.

1. *In the beginning, take small steps.* Being assertive may be difficult at first, so start with something that is easy. You might decline the invitation to keep

TABLE 13.2

Behaviors Exhibited by Assertive, Aggressive, and Nonassertive Persons

	Assertive Person	Aggressive Person	Nonassertive Person
In conflict situations	Communicates directly	Dominates	Avoids the conflict
In decision-making situations	Chooses for self	Chooses for self and others	Allows others to choose
In situations expressing feelings	Open, direct, honest, while allowing others to express their feelings	Expresses feelings in a threatening manner; puts down, inhibits others	Holds true feelings inside
In group meeting situations	Direct, clear, "I" statements: "I believe that . . .	Clear but demeaning "you" statements: "You should have known better . . ."	Indirect, unclear statements: "Would you mind if . . ."

the minutes at the weekly staff meeting if you feel others should assume this duty from time to time. If you are tired of eating lunch at Joe's Diner (the choice of a coworker), suggest a restaurant that you would prefer. If someone insists on keeping the temperature at a cool 68 degrees and you are tired of being cold all the time, approach the person and voice your opinion. Keeping other people from getting what they want, while asking that your desires be considered, is not necessarily a bad thing.[12]

2. *Use communication skills that enhance assertiveness.* A confident tone of voice, eye contact, firm gestures, and good posture create nonverbal messages that say, "I'm serious about this request." Using "I" messages can be especially helpful in cases where you want to assert yourself in a nonthreatening manner. If you approach the person who wants the thermostat set at 68 degrees and say, "You need to be more considerate of others," the person will likely become defensive. However, if you say, "I feel

uncomfortable when the temperature is so cool," you will start the conversation on a more positive note.

3. *Be soft on people and hard on the problem.* The goal of conflict resolution is to solve the problem but avoid doing harm to the relationship. Of course, relationships tend to become entangled with the problem, so there is a tendency to treat the people and the problem as one. Your coworker Terry is turning in projects late every week, and you are feeling a great deal of frustration each time it happens. You must communicate to Terry that each missed deadline creates serious problems for you. Practice using tact, diplomacy, and patience as you keep the discussion focused on the problem, not on Terry's personality traits.

Conflict Resolution Styles

Depending on personality and past experiences in dealing with conflict in the workplace, individuals naturally develop their own conflict resolution styles. Through training in assertiveness and conflict resolution, individuals can learn to recognize their own style as well as the styles of others. They can learn how and when to adapt their behavioral style to deal effectively with conflict situations.

Robert Maddux has proposed a conflict resolution model that combines two factors: degree of assertiveness and degree of cooperation (see Figure 13.2). He suggests that there are five different styles resulting from various combinations of assertiveness and cooperation. Maddux takes the position that differing styles may be appropriate in different situations. He says, for example, if you must win at any cost, then the *win/lose style* may be your best option. If your goal is to maximize cooperation, even at the expense of personal goals, then the *accommodating style* would be your best choice.

Avoidance Style (Uncooperative/Nonassertive)   This style is appropriate when the conflict is too minor or too great to resolve. Any attempt to resolve the conflict might result in damaging a relationship or simply wasting time and energy. Avoidance might take the form of diplomatically sidestepping an issue or postponing your response until a more appropriate time.

Accommodating Style (Cooperative/Nonassertive)   This style is appropriate when resolving the conflict is not worth risking damage to the relationship or general disharmony. Individuals who use this approach relinquish their own concerns to satisfy the concerns of someone else. Accommodating might take the form of selfless generosity or blind obedience to another's point of view.

Win/Lose Style (Uncooperative/Aggressive)   This style may be appropriate when the conflict involves "survival of the fittest," when you must prove your superior position, or when your opinion is the most ethically or profes-

FIGURE 13.2

Conflict Resolution
Styles

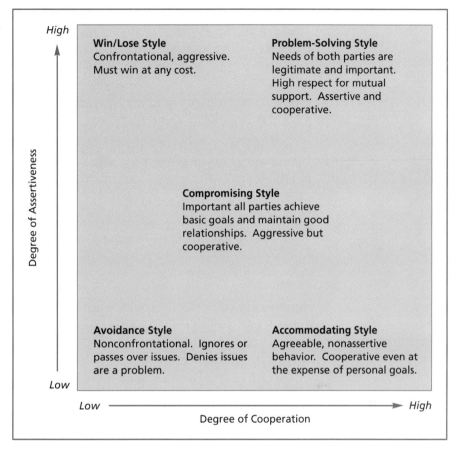

Source: Adapted from Robert B. Maddux, *Team Building: An Exercise in Leadership,* Crisp
Publications, Inc., Menlo, CA, 1986, p. 53. Reprinted by permission of the publisher.

sionally correct. This power-oriented position allows you to use whatever
means seem appropriate when it is time to stand up for your rights.

Compromising Style (Moderately Aggressive/Moderately Cooperative)
This style is appropriate when no one person or idea is perfect, when there is
more than one good way to do something, or when you must give to get what
you want. Compromise attempts to find mutually acceptable solutions to the
conflict that partially satisfy both sides. Never use this style when unethical activities are the cause of the conflict.

Problem-Solving Style (Assertive/Cooperative) This style is appropriate
when all parties openly discuss the issues and a mutually beneficial solution can
be found without anyone making a major concession. Problem solvers attempt

to uncover underlying issues that may be at the root of the problem and then focus the discussion toward achieving the most desirable outcome. They seek to replace conflict with collaboration.

Thinking / Learning Starters

1. Imagine and describe the human relations atmosphere in an organization where win/lose strategies are consistently applied.

2. Briefly describe the most recent conflict you had with another person. How assertive were you? How assertive was the other person? Who won? Who lost? How might you have changed your conflict resolution style to better handle the situation?

CONFLICT RESOLUTION PROCESS

In the past, the responsibility for conflict resolution was often given to supervisors, department heads, team leaders, shop stewards, mediators, and other individuals with established authority and responsibility. Today, the picture is changing as more companies are organizing workers into teams. The trend toward increased worker participation in decision making and problem solving (employee empowerment) is also having an impact on conflict resolution practices. Many progressive organizations want employees to resolve their own conflicts whenever possible. This means that every employee needs to possess conflict resolution skills. The **conflict resolution process** consists of five steps that can be used in both work and family situations.

Step One: Decide Whether You Have a Misunderstanding or a True Disagreement

David Stiebel, author of *When Talking Makes Things Worse!,* says a misunderstanding is a failure to accurately understand the other person's point. A disagreement, in contrast, is a failure to agree that would persist despite the most accurate understanding. In a true disagreement, people want more than your explanation and further details; they want to change your mind.[13] When we fail to realize the distinction between these two possibilities, a great deal of time and energy may be wasted. Consider the following conflict situation.

As Sarah entered the driveway of her home, she could hardly wait to share the news with her husband Paul. Late that afternoon she had met with her boss and learned she was the number-one candidate for a newly created supervisory position. Sarah entered the house and immediately told Paul about the promotion opportunity. In a matter of seconds, it became apparent that he was not happy about the promotion. He said, "We don't need the extra money, and you do not need the headaches that come with a supervisory position." Expecting a positive response, Sarah was very disappointed. In the heat of anger, Sarah and Paul both said things they would later regret.

If Sarah and Paul had asked each other a few questions, this conflict might have been avoided. Prior to arriving home, Sarah had already weighed the pros and cons of the new position and decided it was not a good career move; however, she wanted her husband's input before making the final decision. This conflict was not a true disagreement, in which one person tries to change the other person's mind; it was a misunderstanding that was the result of incomplete information. If Sarah and Paul had fully understood each other's position, it would have become clear that a true disagreement did not exist.

Step Two: Define the Problem and Collect the Facts

The saying "A problem well defined is a problem half solved" is not far from the truth. It is surprising how difficult this step can be. Everyone involved needs to focus on the real cause of the conflict, not on what has happened as a result of it. At this stage, it is helpful to have everyone write a one- or two-sentence definition of the problem. When everyone is allowed to define the problem, the real cause of the conflict will often surface.

As you begin collecting information about the conflict, it may be necessary to separate facts from opinions. Ask questions that focus on who is involved in the conflict, what happened, when, where, and why. What policies and procedures were involved? Collection of all the facts may be impossible in a particular case, but as long as the major points are identified, the process can keep moving.

Step Three: Clarify Perceptions

Your perception is your interpretation of the facts surrounding the situations you encounter. Perceptions can have a tremendous influence on your behavior. In a conflict situation, it is therefore very important that you clarify all parties' perceptions of the problem. You can do this by attempting to see the situation as others see it. Take the case of Laura, a sales representative who was repeatedly passed over for a promotion even though her sales numbers were among the best in the department.

Over a period of time Laura became convinced that she was the victim of gender discrimination. She filed charges with the Equal Employment Opportunity Commission (EEOC), and a hearing was scheduled. When Laura's boss was given a chance to explain his actions, he described Laura as someone who was very dedicated to her family. He said, "It's my view that she would be unhappy in a sales management position because she would have to work longer hours and travel more." He did not see his actions as being discriminatory. Laura explained that she valued the time she spent with her husband and children but achieving a management position was an important career goal. Laura and her boss's perceptions of the same situation were totally different.

Dudley Weeks says there are some important questions to be asked as you clarify perceptions of the conflict. What does each party think the conflict is about? Is the conflict over deeply held values or just preferences? Is the conflict over goals or methods? The answers to these questions can be important components of the conflict resolution process.[14]

Step Four: Generate Options for Mutual Gain

Once the basic problem has been defined, the facts surrounding it have been brought out, and everyone is operating with the same perceptions, everyone involved in the conflict should focus on generating options that will fix the problem. Some people, however, do not consider generating options to be part of the conflict resolution process. Rather than broadening the options for mutual gain, some individuals want to quickly build support for a single solution. The authors of the best-selling book *Getting to Yes* say, "In a dispute, people usually believe that they know the right answer—their view should prevail."[15] This is where brainstorming comes in. **Brainstorming** is a process that encourages all those involved in the conflict to generate a wide variety of ideas and possibilities that will lead to the desired results. No one should be allowed to evaluate, judge, or rule out any proposed solution. Each person is encouraged to tap his or her creative energies without fear of ridicule or criticism. Once all options are on the table, you will need to eliminate those that will not lead to the desired results and settle on the most appropriate ones.

Step Five: Implement Options with Integrity

The final step in the conflict resolution process involves finalizing an agreement that offers win/win benefits to those in conflict. Sometimes, as the conflict resolution process comes to a conclusion, one or more parties in the conflict may be tempted to win an advantage that weakens the relationship. This might involve hiding information or using pressure tactics that violate the win/win spirit and weaken the relationship. Even the best conflict solutions can fail unless all conflict partners serve as "caretakers" of the agreement and the relationship.[16]

Establish timetables for implementing the solutions, and provide a plan to evaluate their effectiveness. On a regular basis, make a point to discuss with others how things are going to be sure that old conflict patterns do not resurface. Conflict resolution agreements must be realistic and effective enough to survive as the challenges of the future confront them. Avoid the temptation to implement quick-fix solutions that may prove to be unsatisfactory in a few weeks.[17]

Beware of Defensive Behaviors

Progress toward conflict resolution is often slowed or sidetracked completely by defensive behaviors that surface when individuals are faced with unwarranted criticism, reminders of their shortcomings, or threats to their security. When one person in a conflict situation becomes defensive, others may mirror this behavior. In a short time, progress is slowed because people stop listening and begin thinking about how they can defend themselves against the other person's comments.

We often become defensive when we feel our needs are being ignored. Our needs form one of the essential foundations of our relationships, and when they are ignored or treated as unimportant, the relationship cannot realize its full potential.[18] For example, conflict can surface when the supervisor's need to meet a higher productivity quota collides with the workers' needs to have a life beyond the demands of the workplace. If the higher quota requires overtime, employees' need for leisure time or time with their families may be jeopardized. When the needs of both parties are jeopardized, defensive behaviors may result. In a conflict such as this, all parties involved should ask themselves: "What does the other person need so that he or she will feel positive about this relationship?" In this case, the conflict resolution process would then resolve around discovering ways to raise productivity within the current work schedule.

Another way to prevent defensive behavior from interfering with conflict resolution is to consciously maintain a positive image of the other people involved. Cleanse your mind of negative thinking, contempt, and regrets about things that may have caused the conflict.[19] Openly talk about your desire to keep the relationship strong, and praise their suggestions that contribute to resolving the conflict.

Alternative Dispute Resolution

At times, you and your coworkers or employer may not be able to reach a satisfactory resolution to your conflicts. You may believe you have been fired without cause, sexually harassed, discriminated against, overlooked for a promotion, or unfairly disciplined. Your only recourse may be to ignore the situation or take your employer to court. Ignoring the situation does not make it go away, and court battles can take years and can be extremely expensive. In some instances, you may have a legitimate complaint but not a legal claim. To help keep valued employees content and out of court, many organizations such as Levi Strauss, Alcoa, and TRW have created formal Alternative Dispute Resolution programs, or ADRs.

These programs usually involve any or all of the following: an open door policy that allows you to talk confidentially with upper management personnel, a toll-free hot line where employees can air grievances and get general advice, a peer review panel that investigates and attempts to resolve the problem, a third-party mediator who listens to arguments and attempts to forge a mutually acceptable solution, or an arbitrator who imposes a final and binding solution to the problem.[20] TRW's program offers an additional benefit. The ADR is mandatory for all employees with an unresolved grievance, but the arbitration option is *non*binding. If an employee is not pleased with the outcome, he or she is still able to take legal action. But if TRW is not pleased, the organization cannot appeal the arbitrator's decision but must abide by it.[21]

Federal Express Corp. has a similar procedure, which it calls the Guaranteed Fair Treatment process (GFT). Employees who believe they have been treated unfairly can appeal a manager's decision through the GFT. Each week the CEO and two top officers of the company personally hear appeals that have worked their way through the system. Cases that have merit are turned over to a panel of five employees, three of whom are picked by the appealing employee, for a final and binding decision.[22] Every effort is made to process a complaint within one or two weeks. Although Federal Express spends $2 million a year to administer the program, the company views it as a good investment that keeps the organization productive and out of court.

THE ROLE OF LABOR UNIONS IN CONFLICT RESOLUTION

Labor unions were given the legal right to organize and represent workers by the National Labor Relations Act of 1935 (the Wagner Act), and the Labor-Management Relations Act of 1947 (the Taft-Hartley Act). These two laws spell out the rights and obligations of both unions and management.

Before these laws came into effect, individual employees were virtually powerless against management. If a worker was injured, became ill and could not work, or had trouble keeping up with the production schedule, he or she could be fired and replaced with no recourse. Labor unions helped employees overcome this unfair treatment. By organizing their efforts, unionized employees were able to speak with one powerful voice when requesting resolution of their grievances to management. If their needs were not met, union members could fight back by walking out, slowing down productivity, or calling a strike against the company.

But the work force has changed dramatically during the past decade, and laws written in the 1930s and 1940s are not sufficient to meet today's environment. Traditional labor relations procedures have become outdated with the rapid growth of temporary and contract workers, dual-income families, and telecommuters. Only 16 percent of today's workers belong to a labor union. Subtract government workers and that figure falls to only 10 percent of private industry workers.[23] During the past few years, several employers have fired employees attempting to organize a union within their organizations, even though such punitive action is illegal.[24]

Because of this evolution, most union leaders are choosing to work more closely with management to achieve common goals rather than perpetuate the traditional adversarial relationship. Many employers working to build a partnership with unions have achieved economic gains greater than those of companies that use union-busting methods, such as firing striking workers and union organizers. A research team at Wayne State University studied both types of employers and concluded that cooperation provides the best payoff.[25] The old "us versus them" union is out, and the new cooperative, participative union emphasizing flexibility and innovation is in.

Item: Representatives of the International Association of Machinists contacted management at Alcoa's Denver plant asking if they could help create a high-performance work system. The company agreed to send three managers with IAM's Denver leaders to a weeklong union school in Maryland, where they learned how to set up a labor-management partnership and spur productivity—and in the process protect jobs. IAM then sent experts to the Denver location to help union leaders and managers from manufacturing to marketing create team systems and joint decision-making councils. Their focus was not on the traditional battle for improved wages and benefits; rather, it was on improving product delivery, customer satisfaction, and profitability.[26]

Item: Management at Inland Steel Co. agreed to place a union representative on the board, gave union members profit-sharing opportunities, and established strong job-security guarantees in return for simpler work rules and job reductions through attrition.[27]

Item: An agreement between the 6,200 members of the Amalgamated Clothing and Textile Workers Union and management at Xerox Corp. worked so well that Xerox brought 300 jobs from overseas to their plant in Utica, New York, where management expects higher quality and savings of $2 million a year. Xerox CEO Paul A. Allaire said, "I don't want to say we need unions if that means the old, adversarial kind, but if we have a cooperative model, the union movement will be sustained and the industries it's in will be more competitive."[28]

Most management–labor union disputes escalate when the employment contracts that establish the workers' wages, benefits, and working conditions expire and need to be renegotiated. The overwhelming majority of employment contracts are settled through **collective bargaining,** a process that defines the rights and privileges of both sides involved in the conflict and establishes the terms of employment and length of the contract (usually from three to five years). However, if labor and management cannot settle their differences, they may submit their disputes to one of the following:

- **Mediation**—A neutral third party listens to both sides and suggests solutions. It carries no binding authority. Both parties are free to reject or accept the mediator's decision.
- **Voluntary arbitration**—Both sides willingly submit their disagreements to a neutral party. The arbitrator's decision must be accepted by both sides.
- **Compulsory arbitration**—When the government decides that the labor-management dispute threatens national health and safety or will damage an entire industry, it can appoint an arbitrator who dictates a solution that is binding on both sides and can be enforced in a court of law.

When collective bargaining, mediation, and arbitration are not enough to settle disputes, union leaders may recommend and members may vote to go on strike against their employers. A strike generally results in a lose/lose situation in which workers lose paychecks, employers lose sales, customers lose products or services, and communities lose economic stability. Even if the workers receive a raise or increased benefits, it often takes a long time to overcome the negative economic impact and damaged relationships that often result from a strike.

Contemporary Issues Facing Labor Unions

A Purdue University labor relations expert stated that unions have declined in power and influence because of the rapid growth of advanced technology and their lack of planning for a changing society that includes working women, who are just as concerned about family issues as they are about their wages.[29]

Technology has changed the world's economy from a stable, manufacturing-dominated entity to a high-tech, service- and communications-oriented one. Technicians and engineers are less interested in being unionized. And telecommuters can create work environments to suit their own needs; they do not depend on a hierarchy to provide them with comfort and security. New laws and practices allow individuals to sue their employers, complain to regulators, or call the media's attention to a problem without the help of union leadership. If unions can identify unmet needs of these individuals, whatever they may be, and satisfy those needs, union membership will have an opportunity to grow.

For decades, labor unions were considered "brotherhoods." Men held the dominant leadership roles even though membership included millions of women. Although unions may say they are advocates for all members, in some cases their female members' needs have been ignored. In the famous Mitsubishi sexual harassment lawsuit, women reported at least twenty instances of widespread sexual harassment and sought help against their harassers from top officials at the United Auto Workers, but the union leadership refused to intervene.[30] With the help of the EEOC, the women pursued their case, and Mitsubishi agreed to pay an estimated $9.5 million to the women involved.

As the United States moves into a service economy (which is female dominated) from a manufacturing one (which was male dominated), unions are waking up to the fact that women's needs must become a top priority. Karen Nussbaum, former head of the Women's Bureau of the U.S. Department of Labor, is now director of the AFL-CIO's Working Women Department. Her task within the union is to "turn the labor movement into real advocates for women."[31] Nussbaum plans to increase bargaining on work-and-family issues, expand family leave, and improve child and elder care.[32]

As labor unions strive for survival, they may thrive in the next millennium if they increase their awareness and take action to address the needs of the current and future work force:

- Workers are vitally concerned about the inequities between executives' million-dollar salaries and climbing corporate profits while employees' compensation (in real dollars) declines.
- Health care continues to be a major concern for workers of all ages. It will be important to improve coverage of employees and try to find ways to provide coverage for all children. As the cost of Medicare goes up with the aging of the population, the probability of increased payroll taxes increases.[33]
- Workers are desperate for "good" jobs. The Los Angeles County Fire Department received 20,000 applications when it announced plans to hire 100 firefighters at an annual salary of $36,000. Michigan's state employment office was bombarded with 100,000 applications after the Big Three auto companies announced they would be hiring unionized jobs that paid $20 an hour after three years.[34]
- Economic conditions and labor laws make it far more feasible, and profitable, for organizations to hire temporary and part-time workers rather than highly trained, qualified, and experienced workers.

The Teamsters' successful settlement of the strike against United Parcel Service helped turn more part-time jobs into full-time opportunities and proved that unions still have a vital role to play in labor-management negotiations. But labor unions must look to the future needs of the work force rather than focusing on preserving union strongholds and traditions.

Summary

Conflicts among people in organizations happen every day and can arise because of poor communication, values and culture clashes, confusing work policies and practices, or adversarial management. Often, however, conflicts come from coworkers who refuse to carry their fair share of the workload or have a difficult personality. While unresolved conflicts can have a negative effect on an organization's productivity, a difference of opinion sometimes has a positive effect by forcing team members toward creative and innovative solutions to the problem.

There are several approaches for dealing with conflict: win/lose, lose/lose, and win/win. Using the win/win strategy not only can resolve a conflict but also can preserve relationships. Regardless of the strategy implemented, your level of assertiveness and desire for cooperation are key factors in the effective resolution of personal conflicts with others. When people cannot solve their conflicts in an informal manner, many organizations create solutions through a conflict resolution process. This process is dependent on win/win attitudes and a clear outline of the steps that need to be taken to resolve the conflict. Often an Alternative Dispute Resolution program (ADR) can resolve conflicts that might otherwise lead to legal action.

Labor unions were established to help balance the power between labor and management. But organizations today face complex problems that did not exist when many of the labor laws were established following the Great Depression. As unions' bargaining power and political clout diminish, labor leaders and business owners are finding new ways to cooperate with each other rather than negotiating with an "us versus them" attitude. They are finding that flexibility and innovation are far more productive than old adversarial styles. However, if labor and management cannot settle their differences, they may submit their disputes to mediation, voluntary arbitration, or compulsory arbitration.

Labor unions face a number of contemporary issues. Women expect unions to be more responsive to their needs. Many members want union leaders to be more aggressive in reducing the wage and salary inequities between executives and rank-and-file employees. Union leaders will also be under pressure to improve health-care coverage and create more well-paying jobs.

Career Corner

Q. I am in my mid-40s, have spent twenty-two years working my way up to be supervisor of my department in a major department store, and love my job. The new 31-year-old store manager has started to exclude me from memos and weekly management meetings, saying, "There's no reason for you to attend." Many of my coworkers are much younger than I, dress in jeans instead of professional suits, and seem to lack the traditional work ethic. Those of us over 40 are finding it difficult to keep our mouths shut. Any suggestions?

A. It is obvious your conflict stems from a values clash that sometimes develops between older and younger workers. There also seems to be a breakdown in communication. Your younger coworkers and the store manager may be consciously or unconsciously building an "us versus them" scenario in relation to the more experienced members of the team. You need to establish communication with your store manager. Openly discuss your concerns, and assertively seek an explanation for the changes that have taken place. When you allow others to ignore your needs and disregard your point of view, you display passive behaviors that will get you nowhere.

Key Terms

conflict
win/lose strategy
lose/lose strategy
win/win strategy
assertive behavior
aggressive behavior
nonassertive behavior

conflict management styles
conflict resolution process
brainstorming
collective bargaining
mediation
voluntary arbitration
compulsory arbitration

Review Questions

1. What are some of the major causes of conflict between people in organizations?
2. Discuss the positive aspects of conflict in an organization.
3. What results might you expect when you implement the win/lose strategy? The lose/lose strategy? The win/win strategy?
4. What options should you consider when working with difficult people?
5. Compare assertive behavior to nonassertive and aggressive behaviors.
6. What steps can you take to become more assertive?
7. Describe the steps in the conflict resolution process. Briefly describe the impact each step might have on the final outcome.
8. Explain the difference between arbitration and mediation.
9. Do you think the labor union movement is dead? Why or why not?
10. Explain your understanding of the Fisher and Ury Total Person Insight.

Application Exercises

1. Recall the last time you were angry at another person or were the victim of a situation that made you angry. For example, a housemate or roommate refuses to pay her share of the grocery bill, or your manager accuses you of wrongdoing without knowing all the facts. Then answer the following questions:
   a. Did you express your anger verbally, physically, or emotionally?
   b. Did you suppress any of your anger? Explain.
   c. What results did you experience from the way you handled this situation? Describe both positive and negative results.
   d. If you had the situation to do over again, would you do anything differently? Explain.
2. Describe a conflict that is disrupting human relations at school, home, or work. It might involve academic requirements at school, distribution of

responsibilities at home, or hurt feelings at work. Identify all the people involved in the conflict, and decide who should be involved in the conflict resolution process. Design a conflict resolution plan by following the steps given in this chapter. Implement your plan and report the results of this conflict resolution process to other class members.

3. To develop your assertiveness skills, find a partner who will join you for a practice session. The partner should assume the role of a friend, family member, or coworker who is doing something that causes you a great deal of frustration. (The problem can be real or imaginary.) Communicate your dislikes and feelings in a clear, direct manner without threatening or attacking. Then ask your partner to critique your assertiveness skills. Participate in several of these practice sessions until you feel confident that you have improved your assertiveness skills.

Internet Exercise

As noted at the beginning of this chapter, workers today are faced with subtle conflicts over issues that did not exist fifteen or twenty years ago. Effective conflict management strategies are needed in every type of work setting. Visit the Internet to discover what information is available on this topic. Using your search engine, type in the following keywords:

conflict resolution

conflict management

conflict resolution process

Review the available resources (such as books, articles, and training programs), and identify information that would be helpful as you attempt to resolve conflicts in your life. Prepare a written report of your findings.

Case 13.1   Will the UPS Strike Mark Unions' Resurgence?

When the employees of United Parcel Service responded to an internal employment-satisfaction survey, statistics showed they were happy and loyal to the company. However, when the International Brotherhood of Teamsters sent its questionnaire to its UPS unionized members, 90 percent of the respondents indicated their resentment that UPS was not offering enough full-time job opportunities for part-time workers. Union members threatened to strike UPS when the contract came up for renewal in 1997 unless changes were made. UPS officials didn't believe the threats, thinking that their employees were happy with the modest hourly-rate increase they were offering on the new contract.

Looking back, UPS executives agree they made a series of miscalculations that led the union and company to see the same situation in strikingly different ways. UPS grossly misjudged workers' allegiance to Teamster president Ron Carey, a veteran of twelve years as a UPS driver. UPS management did not believe drivers' willingness to actually go on strike. UPS vice chairman John Alden said, "We didn't expect a strike. Then we thought it would last only a day or two. And we thought the vast majority of our workers would cross picket lines."

The strike resulted in a public relations fiasco for UPS. Many Americans felt resentment toward corporate managers for holding down workers' wages at a time when profits and executives' salaries were soaring. The union's slogan, "Part-time America doesn't work," struck a chord with many of the everyday workers across the nation. A full-time UPS worker, a passive union member who turned activist during the strike, was quoted as saying, "With corporate America running all over us, there is never a time we've needed the unions more. Management only wants to chew them [part-time workers] up and spit them out. Who'll be their advocate?" The five-year contract that resulted from the strike converts 10,000 part-time jobs into full-time positions at double the hourly pay and provides raises over the life of the contract amounting to 15 percent for full-timers and up to 35 percent for part-timers.

UPS officials were shocked at the magnitude of the strike, which lasted fifteen days and cost the company over $600 million as well as an estimated 5 percent loss of long-term business. After the strike, a spokesperson for UPS said, "If we had known that it was going to go from negotiating for UPS to negotiating for part-time America, we would have approached it differently. The next time, we'll prepare for a multi-level grassroots political campaign, not a traditional labor-management dispute."

Questions

1. The union members received a great deal of sympathy during the strike from other workers across the country who struggle with two-tier wage systems and outsourcing jobs to part-time contractors. How do you feel the strike might influence the views of workers who face problems similar to those that Teamster members faced?

2. Many UPS customers were forced to lay off their own employees during the work stoppage, and some will never recover their losses. Bigger shippers have stated that they will never again rely on a single carrier for their ground-shipping needs. Federal Express paid $2.7 billion to acquire RPS to enhance FedEx's ground delivery service. After the strike, the U.S. Postal Service established cheaper rates and invested $270 million in advertising to spread the word about its overnight and parcel services. In your opinion, was the strike worthwhile? Explain your thinking.

Case 13.2   **Personal Assertiveness Pays Off**

J O Browning, a 5-foot-5-inch, 115-pound, soft-spoken daughter of an Air Force medic, never took up causes or ran for office in high school. In 1984 when she applied for a job building tires at Uniroyal-Goodrich, men in the plant took bets she wouldn't last and predicted, "That little skinny one ain't gonna be worth ———." But for twelve years, she proved her worth, married a coworker, gave birth to Whitney, then worked back-to-back shifts while her husband cared for their daughter. The couple had little time together, and Jo learned to live on three hours of sleep a day.

The global economy forced Uniroyal to cancel stable weekday and weekend work schedules and convert to rotating shifts in order to lower costs and improve quality control. The new scheduling plan involved the rotation of four factory crews among four cycles that combined eight- and twelve-hour shifts. The delicate balance Jo had established for her family was shattered. None of the 73 child-care providers she called was willing to give weekend care.

Jo turned her bitterness and anger into action. She researched child care at the library, contacted advocacy groups, contacted management personnel about the problem when no one else in the plant would, and keynoted a union-hall child-care meeting. She learned that Uniroyal had joined a nineteen-employer child-care alliance and was planning a joint study with the local nonprofit child care resource center. She badgered human resource managers to speed up the study and hand-carried the surveys to each worker. The results confirmed child-care problems among 86 percent of the parents. Child Care Systems of America saw the study and created a plan for an innovative seven-days-a-week child-care center. More hurdles put Jo in front of a city planning meeting, urging zoning approval for the center. The center, funded by parent fees, is now open in a sparkling three-bedroom house.

Jo Browning's coworkers recognized her efforts and elected her secretary of her local 1,325-member steelworkers' union. The first woman to hold officer status in her union, Jo is determined to make child care an issue at the bargaining table.

Questions

1. What role did assertiveness play in Jo Browning's approach to this conflict resolution?
2. Which steps of the conflict resolution process detailed in this chapter did she follow?
3. Was the result of this personal approach to conflict resolution a lose/lose, win/lose, or win/win solution? Explain.

PART V

Special Challenges

in Human Relations

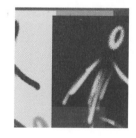

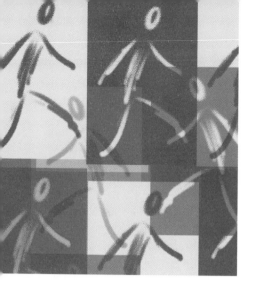

Chapter 14

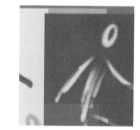

Responding to

Personal and

Work-Related Stress

Chapter Preview

After studying this chapter, you will be able to

1. Understand the stress factors in your life.
2. Identify the major personal and work-related causes of stress.
3. Learn how to assess the stress in your life.
4. Recognize the warning signs of too much stress.
5. Learn how to identify and implement effective stress management strategies.
6. Discover how to identify and prevent burnout.

WATCH OUT FOR THOSE FLYING MEMOS! On Frisbee Memo Day at Pacific Power and Electric in Portland, Oregon, all formal memos and other messages are delivered throughout the office attached to Frisbees. If you would like to hear a truly amateur band play, visit IBM's Inside Sales Center, a unit consisting of seventy-five telephone salespeople who sell computers. Each morning the musically inept salespeople playing tubas, accordions, drums, and other instruments perform a fifteen-minute concert. At Phelps County Bank in Rolla, Missouri, various departments discovered creative ways to let employees have a few laughs. The loan department staff decided to play charades to blow off a little steam. Now the game is a weekly thirty-minute event for employees while the managers cover the phones. One day, the bank tellers bunny-hopped through the lobby. Emma Lou Brent, CEO at Phelps, credits these initiatives with helping the bank improve employee morale and earnings.[1] ■

Organizations, large and small, are discovering that fun and laughter can counteract the negative effects of a stressful work environment. It is almost impossible to live in today's complex, fast-paced world without encountering some source of stress. The downsizing of organizations often results in a work force that is less secure and more competitive. Tensions build as we work longer hours and then try to cram too many activities into our dwindling leisure time. In this chapter we examine the most common sources of stress, help you assess your current stress load, and discover effective ways to respond to work- and personal-life stressors.

THE STRESS FACTOR IN YOUR LIFE

Stress can be defined as the behavioral adjustment to change that affects you psychologically and physically. It is a process by which your mind and body mobilize energy for coping with change and challenge.[2] Stress can come from our environment, from our bodies, or from our minds.[3] Environmental stress at work may be caused by noise, safety concerns, crowded work areas, pollution, windowless settings, or poorly designed workstations. Bodily stress can be caused by illnesses, injuries, or straining the body in some way. Some bodily stress can be attributed to chairs that lack lower-back support or keyboards that put too much stress on wrists, shoulders, and upper back.

The stress that comes from our minds is the most common type of stress. A great deal of the stress we encounter every day is caused by our negative thinking and faulty reasoning—creations of our own minds.[4] For example, someone with large house payments and a great deal of personal debt may begin to worry excessively about the possibility of a layoff; the individual who lacks self-confidence may develop a fear of every technology change that is introduced at

Stress factors are not limited to the workplace. Be aware of the stressors in every aspect of your life. Collectively they may have a negative effect on how you handle your day-to-day activities. (John Coletti/Stock, Boston, Inc.)

work; workers in organizations being merged may mentally anguish over who will be laid off next.

Of course, there are some positive aspects of stress. It can sharpen your resolve and stimulate you to do your best. Stress can build within you the energy and desire needed to perform effectively. As stress increases, so does your effectiveness—up to a point. Once you begin to feel distressed and anxious, the quality of your work will often suffer. At one point, stress can promote greater clear-mindedness, awareness, and focus. But with too much stress, you become tense and distracted.

Responding to Stress

The media are filled with stories of anxious, stressed-out workers, psychologists attempt to tell us how to eliminate stress from our lives, and organizations rush to adopt the most recent stess reduction approach on the market for their employees. As we consume all of this information, we struggle to control our environmental stressors, nourish and exercise our bodies for maximum performance, and allow only positive thoughts into our minds. But perhaps the most important aspect of stress is recognizing the difference between stress exposure and stress response. James Loehr, author of *Stress for Success,* says:

> Stress exposure is the most powerful stimulus for growth in life. People invariably grow the most in areas in which they've been pushed the most. Stress exposure expands stress capacity. The ultimate impact of stress in your life is determined not by the stress exposure itself but by your response to that exposure. The pressures of life in corporate America are not about to go away. If anything, they show every sign of increasing. High pressure is now a fact of life and a way of life. The only way to survive—and thrive—in today's workplace is not to get rid of stress but to deepen your capacity to handle stress.[5]

Loehr recommends that as we are exposed to new stressors, we need to develop new responses to stress and establish mental, physical, and emotional balance. He compares this process to weight training:

> To build strength, it is necessary to expose the muscles to increasing amounts of weight. Too much weight, though, can damage muscle tissue, and too little can break down muscle tissue and undermine strength. In other words, too much stress and you burn out; too little and you don't grow. . . . Grace under pressure is rarely inborn or God-given. The only way to meet the challenge of optimal performance is to train—mentally, physically, and emotionally.[6]

Unfortunately, most of us do not take the time to train our minds and bodies so that we build our capacity to handle the stress in our lives. Most of us merely attempt to handle stress as it comes along. Our natural response to stress is as old as life itself—adapted by almost all species as a means of coping with threats to survival.[7] When faced with an unexpected or possibly threatening situation, human beings—like animals—react with the **fight or flight syndrome:** Adrenaline pours into the bloodstream, heart rate and blood pressure increase, breathing accelerates, and muscles tighten. The body is poised to fight or run. Ironically, the same instincts that helped our ancestors survive are the ones causing us physical and mental health problems today.

The human response to stress is not easily explained. Repeated or prolonged stress can trigger complex physiological reactions that may involve several hundred chemical changes in the brain and body.[8] Everyone reacts differently to stress, so there is no single best way to manage it. Stress management methods must be tailored to individual needs.

As we discuss the major causes of stress, you will soon discover that it is virtually impossible to get rid of them and still function in today's society. Therefore, our approach is to help you train yourself to respond effectively to these stressors and thereby deepen your capacity to handle stress so that you will not only survive but thrive. The first step is to understand what might cause stress in your personal and professional life.

MAJOR CAUSES OF STRESS

Many years ago some scholars and consultants were making optimistic predictions about the nature of work in the year 2000. They talked about a new generation of technology that would make life easier for all of us. They promised us a paperless work environment, worker-friendly jobs, and more free time for leisure pursuits. Microsoft chairman Bill Gates predicted that business technology would soon allow people to do a full day's work in just four or five hours without reducing their productivity.[9] Something happened to change this positive view of life at work.

If you listen closely to workers today, you will hear them saying, "Nothing seems simple anymore," or "We are working twice as hard for the same results." Some say the pace at work is so dizzying it takes them hours to finally relax after the workday ends. A growing number of businesses, from hardware stores to hospitals, have become enormously complicated operations. Most of us can benefit from learning how to pinpoint the sources of stress in our life. If we can anticipate the stressors, we may be able to respond to them in a more effective manner.

Suppliers to the big three automakers were warned to implement tough new quality standards for their products. Jackie Parkhurst, the director of quality assurancy at Federal-Mogul, a maker of engine parts in Southfield, Michigan, calls the changeover a "brutal phenomenon" but agrees that employees can handle any change when they are adequately prepared to do so. (Will and Deni McIntyre)

Change

Changes in the workplace come in many forms, including the need to do a job faster, to master advanced technology, or to take on a new work assignment. Consider employees who have been accustomed to working alone and now must work with a team, or employees who have held jobs that required little contact with the public and now must spend a great deal of time with clients, patients, or customers. When companies restructure in an attempt to meet demands of the marketplace, they often do not take into consideration the life demands of the employees. Progressive companies such as Hewlett-Packard offer flexible work options, but many other companies do little or nothing to help employees balance jobs with personal and family life. In their efforts to lower costs and improve productivity, many organizations hand employees laptop computers, cellular phones, and a gasoline credit card, accompanied by orders to work from their cars, their homes, or their customers' offices. This high-tech approach to doing business is forcing hundreds of thousands of individuals to adjust their personal and professional lives.

Many people have witnessed drastic layoffs in their organizations. These survivors have something in common with their former colleagues: Both remember what it was like to work in a stable and secure work environment, and both know they might never experience the same job security again. The survivor has a job but may no longer have peace of mind and, in some cases, may even experience as much stress as the unemployed worker. During or after an employer's downsizing effort, the survivor is constantly thinking, "When will my turn come?" The survivor and the unemployed worker both struggle with the anxiety that surfaces when they realize the limited control they have over an important dimension of their lives.

Technostress

The computer revolution has created a form of stress that is causing mental and physical health problems among many workers. Craig Brod, a consultant specializing in stress reduction, was one of the first people to use the term *technostress* to describe this source of stress. **Technostress** is the inability to cope with computer and related technologies in a healthy manner. It may take several forms.[10]

Upgrade Anxiety As the processing speed of new computers increases, it is often necessary to acquire new equipment every one or two years in order to

Working parents often experience stress as they attempt to balance work and family responsibilities. Nancy Nicholl-Hasson is seen here reading to her 2-year-old daughter while her husband is hard at work at this home office. (Steve Rubin/The Image Works, Inc.)

keep up with the demands of customers, suppliers, and communications in general. With each upgrade, workers are forced to adapt to new technology just as they were adjusting to the previous system.

Addiction to Computers   Some psychiatrists submit that computers can be addicting. David Shenk, author of *Data Smog* and an authority in the area of technostress, makes this observation:

> Indeed, computers, the latest and most powerful engines driving the information glut, have provoked a certain compulsive behavior in a large number of people. The electrifying speed and strobe effect of the computer display monitor can be mildly hypnotic and addictive in the same way that television can, capturing people's attention for long, unhealthy periods of time.[11]

Many computer users develop deep feelings of dependency on their machines and thereby lose the capacity to feel or relate to other people. Some workers have adopted a machinelike mind-set that reflects the characteristics of the computer itself. Signs of the techno-centered state include a high degree of factual thinking, poor access to feelings, and low tolerance for the ambiguities of human behavior and communication.[12]

Information Overload   It is easy to experience sensory overload as you sort through the hundreds of messages that come to you daily by means of the Internet, E-mail, pagers, commercial advertising, and many other sources. Information overload is not just a workplace phenomenon. The lines between work and home have been blurring in recent years. With the aid of pagers and cellular phones, messages can reach you at the beach or during the backyard barbecue. *Data smog,* the term that David Shenk uses to describe the information-dense society we live in, is a problem because it crowds out quiet moments, obstructs much-needed contemplation, and often leaves us feeling confused.[13] In an age where information is viewed as a valuable commodity, we have too much of it!

The Computer Workstation   Many employees spend their entire workday confined to a computer terminal. Carpal tunnel syndrome, a repetitive-stress wrist injury, is often caused by constant computer keyboarding and is one of the fastest-growing occupational hazards. Computer-related vision problems are also very common. These computer-related ailments have focused more attention on **ergonomics,** the study of optimal work-area layout, lighting, furniture design, machine structure, and task limits. Today's computer workstation is often housed in a standard 8-foot-by-10-foot prefabricated cubicle. Such cubicles have become very popular because they reduce space needs and are easy to install and rearrange.[14] The merits of cubicles are still being debated. Some workers complain that cubicles are too open and noisy to permit concentration. Figure 14.1 presents some pointers that might help alleviate some of the effects of workstation-related technostress.

FIGURE 14.1

Suggestions for Alleviating Some of the Effects of Work-station-Related Technostress

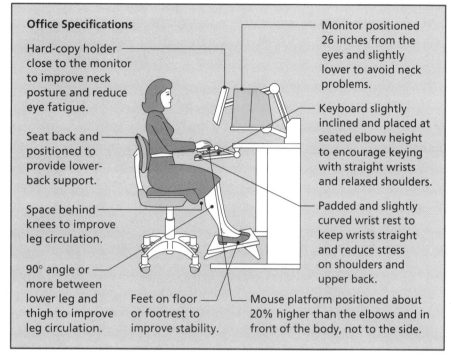

Office Specifications

Hard-copy holder close to the monitor to improve neck posture and reduce eye fatigue.

Seat back and positioned to provide lower-back support.

Space behind knees to improve leg circulation.

90° angle or more between lower leg and thigh to improve leg circulation.

Feet on floor or footrest to improve stability.

Monitor positioned 26 inches from the eyes and slightly lower to avoid neck problems.

Keyboard slightly inclined and placed at seated elbow height to encourage keying with straight wrists and relaxed shoulders.

Padded and slightly curved wrist rest to keep wrists straight and reduce stress on shoulders and upper back.

Mouse platform positioned about 20% higher than the elbows and in front of the body, not to the side.

Source: Gannett News Service. Used with permission.

Noise Pollution

The human auditory system influences the frontal lobe of the brain, which plays a primary role in personality and intellectual functions. Loud noise (above 80 decibels) can produce harmful physical and mental effects.[15] *Noise* can be defined as unwanted sound. The roar of traffic, the neighbor's loud stereo music, or the loud voice of the person who occupies the cubicle nearby can increase your stress without your conscious awareness. Researchers at Rutgers University's Noise Technical Assistance Center indicate that noise affects more people than any other pollutant[16] (see Figure 14.2).

The American Speech and Hearing Association estimates that about 40 million Americans live, work, or play everyday around noise that is dangerously loud. Many people experience hearing loss while working near loud machines, listening to loud music, or operating power equipment. About 36 million Americans have tinnitus in some form. Tinnitus is a persistent buzzing, ringing, or whistling sound that occurs in one or both ears. This very stressful hearing problem is usually worse when the tinnitus sufferer is around loud noises. Some companies are using carpeting, rugs, and extra wall insulation to help reduce noise levels. Many employers provide hearing protection devices.

FIGURE 14.2

Contribution to Work-
space Distractions
Overall

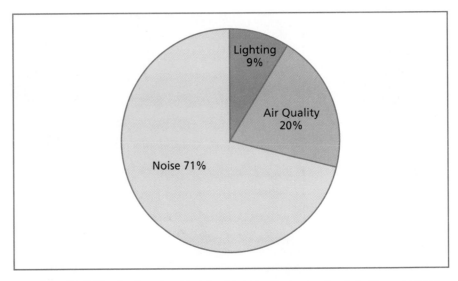

Copyright © 1996 by the American Society of Interior Designers. Reprinted by permission.

Irregular Schedules/Long Hours

As the nation moves steadily toward a 24-hour-a-day, 7-day-a-week economy, working from 9 to 5 is no longer the norm. Research conducted by Harriet Presser, professor of sociology at the University of Maryland, indicates that two-thirds of all workers in America work nontraditional hours.[17] Many service businesses open at 6 A.M. and close at midnight. Some are open 24 hours a day. Evening shifts, rotating shifts, 12-hour workdays, and weekend work may be good for business, but these schedules disrupt workers' lives. People who work evenings and nights are especially likely to experience fatigue, sleep disorders, and lack of opportunity to stay connected to friends and family members.

Total Person Insight

"We pride ourselves on speed—and forget that time goes by fast enough. The trick is to slow down long enough to listen, smell, touch, look, live."

ELLEN GOODMAN
Syndicated Columnist

Another source of worker fatigue is long hours coupled with an excessive workload. The traditional 40-hour workweek has almost disappeared in America. Understaffing due to a shortage of skilled workers often means that some workers must work overtime. Some companies avoid hiring new employees because they may have to lay them off later. Many organizations would rather maintain a smaller work force working time-and-a-half than pay a larger work force the full benefits package.[18] The result is a work force whose ability to handle stress is severely limited because workers are too tired to cope.

Incompetent Leaders

Organizations tend to promote individuals into supervisory positions when they exhibit extraordinary talents in a specific technical field. The most talented electrician becomes maintenance supervisor. The most efficient surgical nurse is promoted to nursing supervisor. The top salesperson is made sales manager. But technical superstars may be poor supervisors. And studies indicate that incompetent supervisors are a major source of stress in the workplace.[19] Incompetent leaders tend to ignore employee ideas and concerns, withhold information from employees, and fail to clarify roles and responsibilities. They may also set unrealistic deadlines and then blame employees for not meeting them.

Many supervisors are unable or unwilling to apply the leadership skills described in Chapter 12. Some of the reasons for incompetence include personality disorders, lack of training, and inability to learn from experience.

Work and Family Transitions

In our fast-moving world, most of us have learned that certain transitions are inevitable. A **transition** can be defined as the experience of being forced to give up something and face a change. Author Edith Weiner states, "People are now in a constant state of transitioning. It is difficult for anyone to say with any degree of certainty where he or she will be maritally, professionally, financially or geographically five years from now."[20]

When a single person marries or a married couple divorces, the transition can be extremely stressful and can affect job performance. A new baby and the challenge of child care can cause stress in working mothers and fathers. As double-income parents attempt to meet the needs of the family, they often feel guilty about the time spent away from their children. A Families and Work Institute survey found that children merely want their parents to come home from work less stressed.[21]

The twenty-something generation has produced a generation of concerned fathers, yet most organizations place little value on fathering as a workplace concern. A study conducted by Rosalind Burnett at Radcliffe College reinforced the results of many similar studies: Men are just as likely as women to worry about family problems while at work.[22] Yet many companies perpetuate the myth that men who want to be actively involved in the care and development of their children are not serious about their careers. The resulting stress can be detrimental to mothers, fathers, and the organizations they work for.

ASSESSING THE STRESS IN YOUR LIFE

Most of us would live longer and enjoy life more if we could answer two important questions: "How much stress do I have in my life?" and "What is stress doing to my physical and mental health?" Answering the first question is difficult because the sources of stress are so numerous in our personal and work lives. Also, stress can come from both positive and negative events in our life.

The Holmes-Rahe Social Readjustment Ratings Scale was developed to help people learn how much adjustment is needed to cope with various life events. The scale lists 42 life events with numerical values ranging from 100 (death of a spouse) to 11 (minor violation of the law). The more stressful the event, the higher the number is. Although we usually think of marriage and retirement as positive events, both require considerable adjustment, according to the authors of the scale. Divorce and dismissal from work, both negative events, also require considerable adjustment. Research indicates that your chance of suffering a serious medical problem in the coming year is related to the number of stressful events you are experiencing now.[23]

Try to develop an accurate picture of the sources of your stress. To learn more about possible sources of stress, complete the NWNL Workplace Stress Test provided in the appendix and in the *Classroom Activities Manual* that accompanies this textbook. It is typical of instruments designed to help employees become aware of stress sources on the job.

Warning Signals of Too Much Stress

In today's stress-filled world, it makes sense to become familiar with the most common warning signals of stress. Physical signs might take the form of lower-back pain, headaches, loss of appetite, hypertension, coronary problems, or fatigue. Psychological symptoms include anxiety, depression, irritability, paranoia, and reduced interest in personal relationships. Art Ulene, author of *Really Fit Really Fast,* says these unpleasant sensations may be your body's way of telling you that there is too much stress in your life.[24] The symptoms may be different for each person, but the message is the same: Listen to what your body is telling you.

Check the list of symptoms in Table 14.1 to see how many you are experiencing. If any of these symptoms is a stress-related problem for you, it may be

TABLE 14.1

Common Stress Signals

	How Often You Have It (Circle)			Occurs at Times of Stress (Circle)	
Anger	Never	Sometimes	Often	Yes	No
Backache	Never	Sometimes	Often	Yes	No
Blurry vision	Never	Sometimes	Often	Yes	No
Cough	Never	Sometimes	Often	Yes	No
Dermatitis	Never	Sometimes	Often	Yes	No
Diarrhea	Never	Sometimes	Often	Yes	No
Dizziness	Never	Sometimes	Often	Yes	No
Excessive sweating	Never	Sometimes	Often	Yes	No
Fatigue	Never	Sometimes	Often	Yes	No
Feeling rushed	Never	Sometimes	Often	Yes	No
Frequent urination	Never	Sometimes	Often	Yes	No
Headache	Never	Sometimes	Often	Yes	No
High blood pressure	Never	Sometimes	Often	Yes	No
Hyperventilation	Never	Sometimes	Often	Yes	No
Impotence	Never	Sometimes	Often	Yes	No
Insomnia	Never	Sometimes	Often	Yes	No
Itching	Never	Sometimes	Often	Yes	No
Gnashing teeth	Never	Sometimes	Often	Yes	No
Late menstruation	Never	Sometimes	Often	Yes	No
Muscle spasms	Never	Sometimes	Often	Yes	No
Nail biting	Never	Sometimes	Often	Yes	No
Palpitations	Never	Sometimes	Often	Yes	No
Rapid heart rate	Never	Sometimes	Often	Yes	No
Stomachache	Never	Sometimes	Often	Yes	No
Vaginal discharge	Never	Sometimes	Often	Yes	No

Source: "Common Stress Signals," Chart reprinted with permission from Feeling Fine Co. LLC.

time to begin using some type of stress management strategy. As you review these stress signals, see if you circled the words "often" and "yes" many times. This pattern may indicate that stress is responsible for the way you are feeling.

Thinking / Learning Starters

As you begin to "manage" your stress, consider these questions:

1. What forms of exercise do you do? Would you like to add some form of exercise to your schedule? Which one? When will you start?

2. To what extent do you monitor the foods you eat? Give examples.

STRESS MANAGEMENT STRATEGIES

It is not possible to eliminate stress from your life, but you can determine when you have passed your limits and then do something about it. Stress can be harmful when you neglect to take control of your life and your body. Some people hold up well under stress for extended periods; others do not. But everyone should make the effort to put stressful situations into proper perspective and deal with them accordingly. Once you become aware of what creates a stressful response in you (stress is very individualized), begin looking for stress management strategies that will help you cope with the stressful situations. Space does not permit an in-depth presentation of all stress management strategies, but we will describe those that are widely used today. You will be pleased to discover that many of these strategies require only a small investment of your time.

Sleep

Perhaps one of the most effective strategies for managing the negative aspects of stress is getting enough quality sleep. The amount of sleep your body requires is highly individualized, based on several factors including your age, fitness, amount of physical activity, diet, and chemical habits such as alcohol, nicotine, and caffeine consumption. Growth hormones and repair enzymes are released and various chemical restoration processes occur during sleep.[25] (This explains why children need considerably more sleep than adults.) In order to train your body so that you can deepen your capacity to handle stress, follow these guidelines to improve your sleep recovery periods:

- Develop a sleep ritual: Go to bed and get up at the same time as often as possible.
- Avoid strenuous exercise within two hours of bedtime.
- Avoid central nervous system stimulants near bedtime such as caffeine, chocolate, alcohol, or nicotine.
- Keep your bedroom cool, well ventilated, and dark.
- Get a half-hour of sunlight within thirty minutes of awakening. Light causes sleep hormones to be deactivated and replaced with hormones of arousal.[26]

Exercise

Every Saturday, from March through May, managers, bankers, and lawyers from Seattle to Atlanta shed their ties and put on their cleats to compete in one of the roughest games—rugby. The Harp USA Rugby Super League attracts mostly white-collar workers who say this sport helps them cope with the stress of office life. As one player explained, "After a hard day's work, rugby is a great release."[27] Terry Bradshaw, former NFL football player, says exercise tends to have a cleansing effect: "If I am stressed out, I go and run three miles, or play an hour and half of tennis. When I come back, I feel so good—I am ready to tackle the world."[28]

Exercise can act as a buffer against stress, so stressful events have less of a negative impact on your health. Regular aerobic exercise—walking, swimming, low-impact aerobics, tennis, or jogging, for example—can increase your stress capacity. Exercise does not have to be strenuous to be helpful. Even gentle exercise like yoga or tai chi will help you manage your daily stress load. Use these guidelines as you develop an exercise program that meets your needs:

- Before you begin a strenuous physical exercise program, check with your doctor to be sure it is appropriate for you.
- Engage in a warm-up activity before any aerobic exercise. You want to prepare the muscles and joints for the activity that follows.
- To avoid overuse injuries and boredom, consider alternating the types of exercise. For example, alternate swimming, which primarily works the upper body, with walking, which builds leg strength.
- Seek out exercise opportunities each day. Use stairs instead of the elevator. Ride your bicycle to school or work.
- Choose an exercise program you enjoy; otherwise, you will probably abandon it after a few weeks.

Nutrition

Health experts agree that the typical American diet—high in saturated fats, refined sugar, additives, caffeine, and even protein—is actually the wrong menu for coping with stress. The U.S. Senate Select Committee on Nutrition and Human Needs advises cutting down on fatty meats, dairy products, eggs, sweets, and salt. Fatty deposits can build up in the arteries, forming plaque. When stress increases the blood pressure, this plaque can tear away, damaging the arteries. Too much salt overstimulates the heart. Refined sugar acts first as a stimulant and then as a depressant to the central nervous system. The committee encourages greater consumption of fresh fruits, vegetables, whole grains, poultry, and fish. Eating the right foods in the proper amounts can replenish the vitamins and minerals the body loses when under stress and can also have a calming effect on your nervous system.

In recent years research into nutrition indicates that in many cases eating a carbohydrate-rich snack can actually help reduce feelings of impatience or distress. The best between-meal snacks are those that taste good to you but also are high in complex carbohydrates and fiber and low in fat.[29] Complex carbohydrates are found primarily in foods from plant sources such as fruits, vegetables, pasta, cereals, and breads. The exception is milk, which is an animal source. Some snacks to consider include raisins, a whole-grain cracker with a thin slice of low-fat cheese, a handful of almonds, a cup of bean or lentil soup, or a small serving of nonfat pasta salad. As you develop the nutrition phase of your stress management plan, consider these basics:

- Always start your day with a healthy breakfast to stabilize your blood sugar and start your metabolism.
- Eat often and light. Never eat large meals. Small meals every two hours throughout the day raise your metabolic rate, stabilize your moods and energy levels, and reduce cravings for food.
- Combine protein with carbohydrates to boost alertness.
- Reduce fat by baking, broiling, or grilling your foods instead of frying them.
- Drink eight glasses of water daily.
- Take a multivitamin, multimineral supplement daily.[30]

Meditation

Once the fight or flight syndrome was fully understood, researchers began searching for a way humans could respond to this condition. The stresses we face in today's world are likely to be psychological and interpersonal and not best handled by fighting or fleeing. A real breakthrough came with the discovery of the relaxation response by Herbert Benson at Harvard Medical School. The **relaxation response** is a simple meditation technique that can greatly reduce the damaging effects of stress. The technique slows your metabolism—including lowered pulse, respiration, brain-wave activity, and blood pressure. It is especially helpful in cases where people suffer from chronic stress such as being under constant deadline pressure or having serious difficulties with their spouse. Benson says that a majority of all physician visits in the United States stem from stress-related conditions that can be helped through the relaxation response and similar meditation techniques now widely accepted in medicine.

About 30 percent of the adult population in America uses some method to elicit the relaxation response.[31] Meditation, in one form or another, is probably the most common technique. Most meditation techniques involve these elements:[32]

1. Select a quiet place where you are not likely to be disturbed. Sit in a comfortable chair, or lie down on a couch or the floor.
2. Relax the muscles of your body from the top of your head to the tips of your toes. Let go of all the tension.
3. Focus on your breathing. Try to breathe naturally, letting the air come in through your nostrils and out of your mouth. Exhale slowly, letting all the air out of your lungs.
4. Every time you breathe out, repeat a word or phrase (mantra) that evokes the state you want to achieve. Your focus word might be "peace" or "relax."
5. Assume a passive attitude, and when other thoughts come to mind, simply say to yourself, "Oh well," and gently return to the repetition. With practice, you will find it easy to turn back intruding thoughts, and you will have fewer of them.

Practicing these five elements for ten to twenty minutes each day will help to perfect your ability to meditate as a general skill.

Why does this strategy work so well? As you inhale, you are bringing into your body fresh, clean air, and with it come sensations of peace, serenity, and regaining balance. With each exhalation, you are breathing out cynical thoughts and anxious feelings. With practice, the meditation technique will become more and more effortless.

In addition to meditation, there are other stress management activities that can be used during brief pauses in your day. Table 14.2 provides some examples.

Humor and Fun

The use of humor as a stress management strategy was introduced at the beginning of this chapter. Studies of the physiology of humor indicate that laughter is an invigorating tonic that heightens and brightens our mood and releases us from tensions. Laughter is a gentle exercise of the body, a

TABLE 14.2

5-Minute Stress
Busters

- Take 5 minutes to identify and challenge unreasonable or distorted ideas that precipitated your stress. Replace them with ideas that are more realistic and positive.
- Take a 5-minute stress-release walk outdoors: Contact with nature is especially beneficial.
- Relax your body and release tension with 5 minutes of deep breathing.
- Enjoy stress relief with a gentle 5-minute neck and shoulder massage.
- Spend 5 minutes visualizing yourself relaxing at your favorite vacation spot.
- Take a 5-minute nap after lunch.
- Spend 5 minutes listening to an audiotape featuring your favorite comedian.

form of "inner jogging."[33] A good laugh involves many physiological changes such as skin temperature, blood pressure, heart rate, brain-wave activity, and muscle tension.[34]

Constantly work on improving your sense of humor. This has nothing to do with your ability to tell a joke or make others laugh. It's all about accessing the chemistry of humor through everyday happenings. Humor can come from many sources—cartoons, humorous stories, jokes, or ridiculous events that

Laughter is often a major stress-reduction technique. Members of this laughing club begin their sessions with deep breathing exercises that involve reaching for the sky to reduce inhibitions, then force a "ho ho ha ha" until the laughter becomes contagious. (Steve McCurry/ National Geographic Image Collection)

Total Person Insight

"I try to find a reason to laugh under high stress. It's an important part of everything I do. When things get rough, I actually look for funny things, particularly in myself. The more stress I have, the more I use humor to break me up and then refocus."

CHARLES L. PEIFER

President and CEO, Prince Sports Group

---

occur in your life. The average number of laughs per day for adults is 25. The average for children is 400![35] Just because you are an adult does not mean you have to give up fun things. Is there time in your life for a little fun? If not, you may be missing a wonderful opportunity to recover from the stress in your life.

Some people have lost touch with what is fun for them. Ann McGee-Cooper, author of *You Don't Have to Go Home from Work Exhausted,* recommends making a list of things that are fun for you and then estimating the time they take.[36] This exercise may help you realize that there is plenty of time for fun things in your life. A walk in the park will require only twenty minutes, and reading the comics takes only five minutes out of your day.

Emotional Hardiness and Support

Employees who appear to be in great physical condition may be unable to cope with stress because their mental health is poor. This does not mean they are mentally ill; it means they feel they have lost control of their lives. This feeling adds to their stress.

It is impossible to be in control of every event in your life, but you can take the necessary actions to *feel* in control. Ronald Nathan, an M.D. and co-author of *The Doctors' Guide to Instant Stress Relief,* describes this quality as **emotional hardiness.** Those who possess it are in better control of their lives because they are committed to their goals, are challenged by change, and maintain their flexibility when their plans do not work as expected. Nathan says, "The key is to identify areas of your life where you do have control."[37] At Microsoft, such control results from scheduled evaluations in which personal calendars are critiqued in order to keep employees from overextending themselves. Technology overload is one area of concern. Some employees no longer carry a beeper but agree to check their voice mail regularly.[38]

In many cases, planning ahead is all that is needed. For example, if you have a deadline coming up, map out a plan that will prevent a crisis. You might schedule extra time between appointments to avoid feeling constantly under

---

Total Person Insight

"Today we are so thoroughly scattered by overcommitments to work, earning money, or commonplace socializing that a slower pace depresses us or seems humanly unattainable."

MARSHA SINETAR

Author, *Reel Power: Spiritual Growth Through Film*

---

pressure to stay on schedule. Or you might take the last hour of every Friday to straighten up your workstation so that you can start your workweek under control. Getting up fifteen minutes earlier in the morning will act as insurance that if anything does go wrong, you won't also have to deal with the stress of being late. Even little things like hanging a keyrack near your front door and forming the habit of always putting your keys there when you walk in can also help. This will prevent the frantic search for them if you are running late.

One of the major approaches to emotional hardiness is to examine your expectations. If you are trying to accomplish four or five major tasks in one afternoon but you know that pace is impossible, your expectations are out of line with reality. Of course you will feel out of control. Recognize your own limitations, and drop one activity at a time until the pressure is off.

Emotional Expression   Stress can trigger two of your strongest emotions, anger and fear. These emotions must be given a healthy outlet. Often you will feel better just by having someone listen to your concerns; everyone needs emotional support and a chance to vent feelings. The best listeners are usually those who have an understanding of the nature of your work but who are not directly associated with it. In some cases, you may want to consult a psychologist. Psychotherapy is no longer considered shameful, and it need not be time-consuming or expensive. As noted in Chapter 8, constructive self-disclosure often reduces stress when you discuss situations as they happen and attempt to describe your feelings and emotions accurately. When you select the right time, place, and listener, expressing your emotions can offset the detrimental physical effects of stress.

Counseling Programs   Sometimes stress manifests itself in behavioral changes that only one-on-one or group counseling can address. Many organizations therefore offer various counseling programs aimed at alcohol and drug abuse, emotional stress reduction, depression, career planning, and marital and financial matters. For example, several companies now use the National Depression Screening Project, which lets workers figure out over the phone if they are clinically depressed. Employees dial a toll-free number and then answer a ten-minute automated questionnaire. The employee, who remains anonymous, is told right away if treatment is recommended.[39]

Many companies have established employee assistance programs (EAPs). The typical EAP serves as a resource designed to prevent what may begin as a minor problem from becoming a career-ending disaster. Over half of the employees referred to EAPs have alcohol or other drug dependency problems. Some EAPs have libraries covering subjects such as elder care, stress reduction, or dispute resolution. Many EAPs offer counseling that is provided by licensed mental-health professionals.[40]

Twelve-Step Programs In addition to company-sponsored counseling programs, employees can join a twelve-step program. It has been estimated that every week, 3 million people attend one of the hundreds of different twelve-step programs for help with drug and alcohol abuse, eating disorders, or emotional disabilities.[41] Most of these programs rely on the fundamentals that have guided Alcoholics Anonymous (AA) for several decades. The format of all twelve-step programs is very similar and consists of two general aspects:

- *Working the steps.* This means admitting the problem, recognizing that life has become unmanageable, and turning life over to a higher power. Six of the steps included in the AA program mention a higher power.
- *Attending meetings.* Meetings of twelve-step programs are held in church basements, community centers, college campuses, and other locations where members describe their own problems and listen to others who have experienced similar problems. In most cases, strong bonding develops among group members.[42]

Do twelve-step programs such as Narcotics Anonymous, Overeaters Anonymous, Schizophrenics Anonymous, and Codependents Anonymous have a lasting impact? A few critics say these programs simply replace one form of addiction (drugs, alcohol, an unhealthy sense of shame, and so forth) with an addiction to group support. Instead, these critics advocate treatment programs that help people take control of their own lives and learn how to solve their own problems. Those who support twelve-step programs say that the emphasis on the connection to a higher power is the opposite of the isolated, unworthy feeling experienced by people who display addictive behaviors. Joan Borysenko, author of *Guilt Is the Teacher, Love Is the Lesson,* states that twelve-step programs are "psychologically sophisticated" and are "a potent force for healing shame and addiction."[43]

Seeking Solitude

Although some people feel uncomfortable when alone, many others feel "overconnected" due to the need to constantly respond to telephone calls,

E-mail messages, and pager signals. Those who are constantly in touch with others can benefit from the therapeutic effect of solitude. Solitude can be viewed as an emotional breather, a restorer of energy, and a form of rest similar to sleep. Ester Buchholz, author of *The Call of Solitude,* says alone-time is a great protector of the self and the human spirit. She also notes that solitude is often required for the unconscious to process and unravel problems.[44] To experience the benefits of solitude, consider getting up twenty minutes early in the morning, and use this time alone for reading or a short walk. If you usually eat lunch with a group, try eating alone from time to time.

BURNOUT

Burnout is feeling emotionally, intellectually, and physically drained day after day until you move beyond exhaustion and into a state of feeling numb. You feel as if your energy fuel tank is operating on empty. Burnout happens when you do not use the stress management strategies mentioned in this chapter. Just as the engine of a car literally stops running without fuel and oil, a complete mental or physical breakdown can result from burnout.

The most common symptoms of burnout include the following:

1. Increased detachment from coworkers: poor peer and group relationships, irritability with coworkers, decreased feelings of concern for coworkers
2. Increased detachment from clients: failure to initiate contact, labeling clients as objects, offering short or rude answers to clients' questions
3. Increased negative attitudes: constant complaining, cynicism, irritability, moodiness, a feeling of being under attack
4. Decreased energy: apathy, carelessness, clock watching, tardiness, and absenteeism
5. Questioning the validity of career goals and decisions
6. Increased disorientation: forgetfulness, low concentration, stumbling speech patterns
7. Increased physical problems: migraine headaches, backaches, ulcers, high blood pressure, sleep problems
8. Increased personal problems: eating disorders, drug or alcohol abuse, decreased social contacts, marital discord

Although all individuals experience one or two of these symptoms from time to time, a person experiencing burnout exhibits these characteristics with increasing frequency and severity. Burnout victims tend to accentuate the negatives and forget about the positives. The typical burned-out worker was a successful, motivated, committed, and valued worker. He or she often held a high-level position in which there was little feedback from others. Under such conditions, perspective is easily lost. A burnout victim often has a distorted view of reality and perceives everything through a cloud of depression.

The report *Employee Burnout: America's Newest Epidemic* reveals that stress-related disabilities have doubled over the last decade. What is even more distressing is that only 50 percent of these workers are being rehabilitated and returned to their jobs.[45] If you feel you are nearing burnout, take action immediately before it's too late. Follow these guidelines:

- Stop trying to do everything.
- When someone asks you to take on another task, always ask for its priority and a deadline. If necessary, explain how other projects will have to be delayed if you accept this one. Do this with family members as well as coworkers and supervisors.
- If you must refuse a task at home or at work, help devise an alternative solution so you do not alienate the people around you.
- Clarify your values priorities. If you had just one year to live, what tasks would you stop doing? What would you do instead?
- Fuel your body and mind: Get enough sleep, exercise, eat healthily, meditate, find humor in your life, develop emotional hardiness and support, and seek solitude.

Summary

When individuals cannot adequately respond or successfully adapt to a changing or unexpected set of circumstances, stress is usually the result. The stress that comes from attempting to balance work and family responsibilities cannot be eliminated, but individuals can learn how to manage it.

Many of the stressors we experience are generated at work. Technostress, the inability to cope with computer technology in a healthy manner, is a significant contemporary threat to individuals and organizations. The constant need to upgrade computer hardware and software, addiction to computers, the tremendous glut of information available through the Internet and E-mail, and poorly designed computer workstations are some of the elements that make technostress a negative force to be considered in the workplace. Noise pollution, irregular schedules, overtime mandates, and incompetent leaders add to the stress load of workers. In addition, transitions that occur in personal life, such as marriage, divorce, or relocation, may add more stressors that interfere with a person's effectiveness on the job.

Nevertheless, some stress in life is beneficial and helps keep a person motivated and excited. Therefore, the goal is not to eliminate stress but to learn how to assess the stressors in your life and increase your capacity to deal with them by participating in appropriate stress management strategies. You are more likely to handle the ever-increasing stress of today's demands when you sleep, eat, and exercise regularly. Integrating meditation and humor and fun into a daily routine will help offset the negative effects of stress. Discovering the power available through emotional hardiness and the support of others will also help.

Many organizations offer counseling services through employee assistance programs (EAPs). Some people turn to twelve-step programs for help in coping with the various addictions that often result from too much stress. When workers are unable to maintain an appropriate level of stress in their lives, they may be subjecting themselves to the effects of burnout. This debilitating condition requires effective self-help and help from others if it is to be overcome.

Career Corner

Q. I work for a large company and have a terrific job. Because of downsizing, all of us in the office are working sixty-hour weeks to get the work done. I take work home and do the work four people used to do. By the end of the week my mind is numb, my productivity is down, and I am exhausted. This not only is hard on my family but is bad for the company. It seems that if the work can't be handled during a normal workweek, then we need to hire more people to do the job. What do you suggest?

A. If you can get another job that is less stressful, then consider starting a job search. However, if you feel lucky to have your job, then let your boss know that you need help. Gather your colleagues together and present your case. Explain that mental activity becomes sharper when you are able to shift your focus by going home, being with your family, or socializing. Set limits at work and quit taking work home. Perhaps this will allow you to be more productive at work. Don't accept an unreasonable amount of work because you are afraid you will be laid off. A job that is causing you to burn out is not worth it.

Key Terms

stress   transition
fight or flight syndrome   relaxation response
technostress   emotional hardiness
ergonomics   burnout

Review Questions

1. Are there any positive aspects to stress? Explain.
2. Identify the various forms of technostress, and explain how they affect workers' productivity.
3. Discuss the major work-related stressors and their impact on employee productivity.
4. Identify four stress management strategies you will use to help improve your response to stress in your life.

5. List some of the warning signals of too much stress.
6. Explain emotional hardiness. How will you know when you have achieved it?
7. What benefits can organizations and individuals derive from participating in physical fitness programs?
8. Why should organizations try to eliminate or minimize worker stress?
9. What role does humor play in managing the negative effects of stress?
10. Describe burnout and the steps that can be taken to avoid it.

Application Exercises

1. Determine what set of circumstances is causing the most stress in your life. For example, are you trying to work too many hours while going to school? Are you experiencing parental or peer pressure? Then answer the following questions:
   a. What aspects of the situation are under your control?
   b. Are there any aspects of the situation that are out of your control? Explain.
   c. What steps can you take to help eliminate the stress?
   d. What individual stress management strategies could you use to counteract the effects of this stress?
2. Consider the following company-sponsored stress management programs. List them in order from most beneficial to you to least beneficial. Explain your reasoning.
   a. Access to on-site exercise facilities or company-sponsored health club membership
   b. A workshop on stress management sponsored by the company
   c. A cafeteria where healthy, nutritionally balanced foods are served
   d. Access to a soundproof audiovisual room for viewing relaxing videotapes and listening to soothing music
3. Stress often increases as we struggle with time management. How well do you manage your time? Take a few minutes and answer each question below. Then spend time developing a time management program that meets your individual needs.
   a. Do you develop a daily "to do" list that indicates the activities you hope to accomplish?
   b. Do you maintain a planning calendar—a single place to record daily appointments, deadlines, and tasks?
   c. Do you have a series of personal and professional goals that guide you in setting priorities for use of your time?
   d. Have you learned to say no to proliferating requests for your participation in team activities, projects, social activities, and so on, that may complicate your life?

Internet Exercise

Learning how to manage personal and work-related stress is a challenge that faces almost everyone today. Using your search engine, explore the Internet for information on this topic. Type in "stress management," and then examine the resources (such as books, articles, and training programs) available on this topic. Prepare a list of the stress management strategies discussed on the Internet that would help you manage the stress in your life.

Case 14.1

Programs for Healthy Lifestyles Start Small

Several years ago, Plaskolite, Inc., a medium-size producer of plastics, began a program to keep employees healthy. At first, the program was mainly a cash bonus plan: Bonuses were given to employees who participated actively in sports and to those who did not smoke. Now the program includes an in-plant weight room and periodic fitness tests as well as smoking cessation, weight loss, and stress management clinics.

The goal of the program is to reduce the company's medical costs over the long term by increasing employee fitness. Monetary benefits were not expected for perhaps ten years, when the effects of the program would show up in lower incidences of such "lifestyle diseases" as diabetes and heart attacks. Yet Plaskolite's insurance has already decreased, and the fitness tests show continual improvement. In addition, the firm has found that its program is of help in both recruiting and employee relations.

Cullinet Software, in Westwood, Massachusetts, has progressed from an initial small effort to a full commitment to improving their employees' health. The company employs many people who spend all day at computer terminals. When the building was designed, a fitness component was included to counteract the sedentary work style. Employees may now take a fitness break anytime during the day and then work until 7:00 P.M. When Maggie Weinstock, director of health and fitness for the company, talks about the program, she says, "It is a stress release and provides a social atmosphere at work. As a result, we see a definite positive impact on productivity and a lowering of absenteeism."[46]

Healthy lifestyle programs like these usually involve three stages:

1. An *informational* stage, in which the benefits of fitness are carefully explained to employees
2. A *motivational* stage, in which employees are encouraged to participate in the program
3. A *behavioral* stage, in which employees do participate and find that as a result they feel healthier and actually are in better physical shape

The cost of these programs depends on how extensive the programs are—and that obviously varies from organization to organization. But even the smallest firm can take steps toward employee health by spotlighting informational notices regarding health, offering small cash bonuses for participation (as Plaskolite did at first), and following through to ensure that employees' fitness goals are met.

Questions

1. Suppose you were asked to devise an inexpensive healthy lifestyle program for a real estate agency with about twenty-five employees. How would you determine which areas of fitness to work on first?
2. How would you implement the three stages of the program in the areas of (a) physical fitness and (b) smoking cessation?
3. How would you justify the cost of the program to the owner of the agency?

Case 14.2

I Ran My Life—Straight into the Ground

Sue Shellenbarger, a *Wall Street Journal* writer and radio talk-show host, is well known for helping her readers and listeners balance their work and family lives. She thought she was immune to burnout because she worked out of her home, loved her job, and spent time with her family. She learned, however, that burnout can sneak up on you. She outlines her three-month progression:

> *March:* Started work on a new project, manage son's T-ball team, drive daughter to soccer, volunteer at children's school. Phone rings nonstop, mail pours in, fax regurgitates all night. Enthused about everything, rise earlier and work later. *April:* Begin misfiring at work. Present a proposal editors call hairbrained. Spend days interviewing experts for a story, then realize information is useless. Excitedly call boss about a new idea and am informed I told her about it last week. *May:* To compensate for poorly managed time, I work longer and later, doze off during phone calls, and literally fall asleep sitting up while playing a game with the children. Irritability and impatience symptomatic of burnout set in. I haven't walked the dog in weeks. My son slams his bedroom door declaring I yell too much. He plants artificial flowers to create a substitute for the garden I haven't found time to plant. Cannot even imagine where there is time to plant it. My daughter is having problems at school, but I cannot see any solutions. Early June, after a month of minor illnesses, I see my doctor who asks: "Don't you write about balancing work and family?" He informs me I'm burning out!

As Sue shared her experiences through her columns, she received letters from readers. One man recounted a similar downward spiral as he extended his hectic professional life to a similar pace on weekends, cutting the lawn, cleaning, painting, and doing other odd jobs around the house. His weekends became a time of exhaustion, not relaxation. Another reader shared his resentment of Sue's telecommuter lifestyle, suggesting she didn't know what "real" stress was all about. He wrote:

> Try being the breadwinner in a one-paycheck family deep in office politics, other people snapping at your heels, trying to keep the world from the door. Don't feel like going on that business trip? That's OK; someone else from the office will go, and management will remember that at review time. Don't feel like working late? Someone else will. Can't work this weekend because of a family commitment? That's OK; your unmarried coworker will be in the office all day Saturday (and you can bet your next paycheck the boss will know all about it Monday).

As Sue looked back, she discovered she had probably burned out several times in the past but never acknowledged it. She continues to write her columns in hopes of helping others in stressful situations.

Questions

1. In Sue Shellenbarger's progression toward burnout, what guidelines for prevention of burnout should she have considered?
2. Do you think she was effective in helping her readers recognize behaviors that might lead to burnout? Explain.

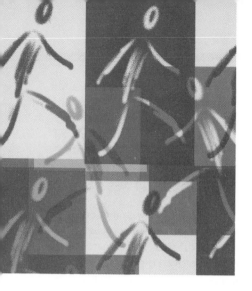

Chapter 15

Valuing

Work Force

Diversity

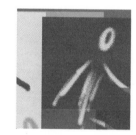

Chapter Preview

After studying this chapter, you will be able to

1. Define the primary and secondary dimensions of diversity.
2. Discuss how prejudiced attitudes are formed.
3. Develop an awareness of the various forms of discrimination in the workplace.
4. Understand why organizations are striving to develop organizational cultures that value diversity.
5. Identify ways in which individuals and organizations can enhance work force diversity.
6. Discuss the current status of affirmative action programs.

THE CITY OF MINNEAPOLIS conducted an affirmative action audit of BRW, a $38 million architecture and engineering firm with 350 employees. The results showed that BRW's rates of promotion and attrition for minorities and women were not good. A few simple adjustments such as advertising for new employees in minority publications would have satisfied the city, but CEO Don Hunt chose to take a much broader look at his organization and examine how it might become more competitive.

Hunt and his partners realized that 96 percent of BRW's managers were white males—a strong contrast to their client demographics. They realized that they would be less competitive if they remained a white-male-dominated firm. Therefore, they created a thirty-five-employee diversity committee that was challenged to examine BRW's personnel systems. The committee made these recommendations:

- Require all employees to attend "diversity training" sessions that help managers recognize how their preconceived ideas about race, sex, and national origin are affecting their hiring and retention practices.
- Advertise in minority and women's publications when positions open in the firm.
- Rewrite the company handbook to reflect a more aggressive commitment to work force diversity.
- Enhance the benefits package to include flextime and health benefits for all part-time workers in order to attract more women.
- Conduct annual "Respect Week" activities to help foster mutual respect among members of the firm's diverse work force.

After implementation of the recommendations, the number of employees rose to 400, work force diversity greatly increased, and the proportion of white male managers dropped to 81 percent.[1] ∎

A growing number of progressive organizations are realizing the impact a reputation for valuing diversity in the work force can have on a company's success . . . and they are doing something about it!

THE NATURE OF DIVERSITY

E Pluribus Unum—"Out of many, one." No other country on earth is as multiracial and multicultural as the United States of America. This diversity is a popular topic and common buzzword in newspaper and magazine articles focusing on the future of American organizations.

The strength of many other nations lies in their homogeneity. Japan is mostly made up of persons of Japanese descent, and their economy and business transactions reflect this heritage. The People's Republic of China is popu-

---

Total Person Insight

"Getting along with people from many backgrounds and interests is most important if you are going to be involved in society in any way. We are interdependent upon one another."

JACK PLUCKHAN

Vice President, Panasonic Corporation

---

lated mostly with persons of Chinese ancestry, and their values and culture are a major part of their global economic strength. But America has always been the "melting pot" of all the world's cultures. This diversity now represents the country's biggest crisis as well as its greatest opportunity.

The publication of *Workforce 2000,* a report prepared by the Hudson Institute for the U.S. Department of Labor, served as a powerful wake-up call for organizations throughout America. The report indicated that white males were already in the minority and would make up only 15 percent of the net additions to the labor force between 1985 and 2000. Authors of the report noted that the biggest gains would be made by women, minorities, and immigrants.[2] Progressive leaders immediately began to consider the implications of these demographic trends toward a more diverse work force. However, it took awhile for people to agree on a definition of the term *diversity.*

Ten years ago work force diversity was evident primarily in the increasing numbers of women, minorities, older workers, and immigrants. Today, diversity is about much more than visible, physical differences and demographic changes. At Pillsbury, for example, diversity is defined as "All those ways in which we differ."[3] We define **diversity** as valuing uniqueness while respecting differences and maximizing individual potentials.[4]

In the past, U.S. organizations attempted to assimilate everyone into one "American" way of doing things. The trend now, however, is to identify, respect, and value the individual differences in this new, diverse work force and to encourage every worker to make his or her full contribution. Organizations that foster the full participation of all workers will enjoy the sharpest competitive edge in the expanding global marketplace.

Dimensions of Diversity

There are primary and secondary dimensions of diversity. The **primary dimensions** are core characteristics of each individual that cannot be changed: age, race, gender, physical and mental abilities, and sexual orientation (see Figure

15.1). Together they form an individual's self-image and the filters through which each person views the rest of the world. These inborn elements are interdependent; no one dimension stands alone. Each exerts an important influence throughout life. Marilyn Loden and Judy Rosener describe individual primary dimensions in their book *Workforce America!* They say, "Like the interlocking segments of a sphere, they represent the core of our individual identities."[5]

The greater the number of primary differences between people, the more difficult it is to establish trust and mutual respect. When we add the secondary dimensions of diversity to the mix, effective human relations becomes even more difficult. The **secondary dimensions** of diversity are elements that can be changed or at least modified. They include a person's health habits, re-

FIGURE 15.1

Primary and Secondary Dimensions of Diversity

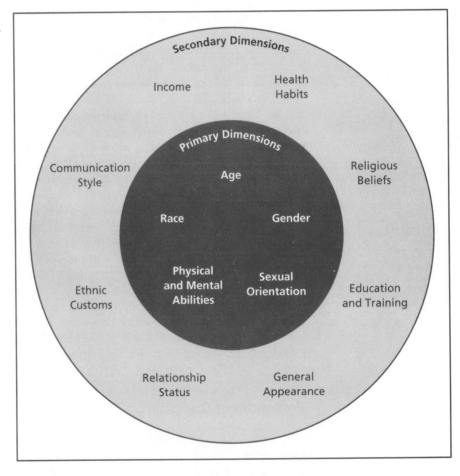

ligious beliefs, education and training, general appearance, relationship status, ethnic customs, communication style, and income (see Figure 15.1). These factors all add a layer of complexity to the way we see ourselves and others and in some instances can exert a powerful impact on our core identities. A single mother who loses her job may be severely affected by her loss of income, whereas a married woman with no children may not be as affected by a similar loss. A vocational-technical school graduate may have expectations far different from those of a four-year-college graduate. A member of the Baptist church may feel she has little in common with another woman who follows Islamic teachings.

Even though differences like these intensify the impact of particular secondary dimensions, they do not diminish the impact of primary dimensions.

Instead, they add depth to the individual. This interaction of primary and secondary dimensions shapes a person's values, priorities, and perceptions throughout life.[6]

Each of us enters the work force with a unique perspective shaped by these dimensions and our own past experiences. Building effective human relationships is possible only when we learn to accept and value the differences in others. Without this acceptance, both primary and secondary dimensions of diversity can become roadblocks to further cooperation and understanding.

PREJUDICED ATTITUDES

Prejudice can be defined as a premature judgment or an opinion that is formed without examination of the facts. Throughout life we often prejudge people in light of their primary and secondary dimensions. Attitudes in favor of or against people that are based solely on these traits are prejudices. Rather than treat others as unique individuals, prejudiced people tend to think in terms of **stereotypes**—generalizations made about all members of a particular group. They uncritically accept widely held beliefs about what various racial groups, socioeconomic classes, men, women, people living in a particular geographic region, and so forth are "really like." When we bring stereotypes to the workplace, we are likely to misinterpret or devalue some primary and secondary differences even after we have been exposed to them.

Stereotyping exists, in part, because it provides an easy and convenient way of dealing with people. Accepting a stereotype, you don't have to make the effort to understand who a person really is or might become.[7] Stereotypes bring some predictability to our lives and reduce the uncertainty of dealing with other people. Stereotypes are often based on one or several real experiences a

---

Total Person Insight

"So long as black and white Americans see each other as stereotypes and not as people with the same dreams, ambitions and values, this nation will be frozen in suspicion and hate."

VERNON E. JORDAN, JR.

Attorney and Civil Rights Leader

person has had in dealing with others, and they are resistant to change because people more readily believe information that confirms their previous experience than evidence that challenges it. For example, people without a tendency to gain weight sometimes view an overweight person as someone who lacks the self-discipline and motivation to lose weight.

Most of us object to being stereotyped but forget how often we stereotype others. Although the people most often hurt by stereotyping are women, minorities, older workers, and immigrants, white men are also victims. One dimension of the AT&T Corporation diversity program is a workshop entitled "What About White Males? Are They the Invisible Diversity Segment?" This workshop was created after many white male employees complained that conventional diversity courses perpetuated stereotypes about their supposed wealth, power, and insensitivity. More than 1,000 AT&T workers have participated in workshops aimed at dispelling myths about white men.[8]

How Prejudicial Attitudes Are Formed and Retained

Three major factors contribute to the development of prejudice: childhood experiences, ethnocentrism, and economic conditions.

Childhood Experiences   Today's views toward others are filtered through the experiences and feelings of childhood. Children learn attitudes and beliefs from family, friends, and other authority figures, and they learn how to view and treat different racial, ethnic, religious, and other groups. The *emotions* of prejudice are formed in childhood. Later in life you may want to change your prejudice, but it is much easier to change your intellectual beliefs than your deep feelings.[9]

Another way we develop prejudices is by allowing our experiences with one person to color our attitude toward that individual's entire group. For example, if a company brings in Asian laborers as replacements for striking employees, those employees may thereafter regard all Asians as potential "scabs" or strikebreakers. In the same manner, a manager who discovers that one young employee is negligent or careless may generalize these attitudes to include all young workers.

Ethnocentrism   The tendency to regard our own culture or nation as better or more "correct" than others is called **ethnocentrism.** The word is derived from *ethnic,* meaning a group united by similar customs, characteristics, race, or other common factors, and *center.* When ethnocentrism is present, the standards and values of our own culture are being used as a yardstick to measure the worth of other cultures.

Cultural conditioning tends to perpetuate ethnocentrism. As children, we are conditioned to respond to various situations as we see others in our culture respond to them. Some cultures value emotional control and avoid open conflicts and discussions of such personal topics as money or values. Other cultures encourage a bolder, more open expression of feelings and values and accept greater levels of verbal confrontation. Tension can result when people's cultural expectations clash in the workplace.

In their book *Valuing Diversity,* Lewis Brown Griggs and Lente-Louise Louw compare ethnocentrism in an organization to icebergs floating in an ocean. We can see the tips of icebergs above the water level, just as we can see our diverse coworkers' skin color, gender, mannerisms, and job-related talents and hear the words they use and their accents. These are basically "surface" aspects of a person that others can easily learn through observation. However, just as the enormous breadth of an iceberg's base lies beneath the water's surface, so does the childhood conditioning of people from different cultures. As icebergs increase in number and drift too close together, they are likely to clash at their base even though there is no visible contact at the water's surface.[10] As organizations increase the diversity of their work force, the potential for clashes resulting from deep-seated cultural conditioning and prejudiced attitudes also increases. These clashes will be emotional, and when they occur, effective human relations will become a challenge.

For example, a manager from one culture and his subordinate from another are talking together, and the manager begins to praise his employee for his insight and abilities. He adds that he has already told several people in the company how outstanding the employee is. This well-intentioned comment upsets the employee, who sees it as a breach of confidentiality. His deeply felt cultural conditioning has taught him to refrain from expressing any form of boastfulness in public.[11]

Economic Factors When the economy goes through a recession or depression, and housing, jobs, and other necessities become scarce, people's prejudices against other groups often increase. If enough prejudice is built up against a particular group, members of that group will be barred from competing for jobs. The recent backlash against immigrants can be traced, in part, to a fear that the new arrivals will take jobs that would otherwise be available to American workers. Some fear that new immigrant arrivals will work for rock-bottom wages and thus depress the earning power of low-income Americans. Prejudice based on economic factors has its roots in people's basic survival needs, and, as a result, it is very hard to eliminate.

Rising income inequality in America is viewed by many as a serious barrier to racial harmony. Ronald Walters, University of Maryland political scientist, says, "You can only have meaningful racial reconciliation when people of roughly equal socioeconomic status can reach across the divide of race."[12] Wide gaps between rich and poor exist, and the opportunities for upward mobility for many low-skilled, low-income workers have diminished in recent years. The gap between median weekly wages of black men and white men has widened since 1990.[13]

> ## *Thinking / Learning Starters*
>
> 1. Have you ever been the object of prejudice? What were the circumstances? How did this behavior affect your self-esteem?
>
> 2. Do you carry any prejudices that are obvious carryovers from your parents? Explain.
>
> 3. Are you doing anything to overcome these prejudices? What would the benefits be if you could overcome them?

DISCRIMINATION

Discrimination is behavior based on prejudiced attitudes. If, as an employer, you believe that overweight people tend to be lazy, that is an attitude. If you refuse to hire someone simply because that person is overweight, you are engaging in discriminatory behavior.

Individuals or groups that are discriminated against are denied equal treatment and opportunities afforded to the dominant group. They may be denied employment, promotion, training, or other job-related privileges on the basis of race, lifestyle, gender, or other characteristics that have little or nothing to do with their qualifications for a job.

Gender

Discrimination based on gender has been, and continues to be, the focus of much attention. The traditional roles women have held in society have undergone tremendous changes in the past few decades. More and more women are entering the work force not only to supplement family income but also to pursue careers in previously all-male professions. Men have also been examining the roles assigned them by society and are discovering new options for themselves. Most companies have recognized that discrimination based on gender is a reality and are taking steps to deal with the problem. Chapter 16 is devoted to an in-depth discussion of overcoming gender bias in organizations.

Age

Discrimination based on age can apply to the older worker—40 to 70—and the younger worker—18 to 25.

Youth can be a disadvantage when potential employers show a reluctance to hire young people because of their lack of practical experience in the work-place. Such employers fail to appreciate that everyone begins his or her career with no experience and needs an opportunity to prove himself or herself. Older workers between the ages of 40 and 70 are protected against discrimination by the Age Discrimination in Employment Act. The law states that if you are fired, demoted, denied a raise given to others, or otherwise mistreated primarily because of your age, you have legal recourse.

Even though organizations can no longer require mandatory retirement at a specific age, older employees are often victims of potent though subtle forms of discrimination. They may be laid off, have their workload cut back, lose their eligibility for promotion, or be given "make-work" projects that keep them out of the mainstream of the organization.

Americans tend to have a stereotypical notion that older workers are no longer capable of effective work performance. Many employers are reluctant to hire or retrain the older worker. They feel that those educated in the 1950s and 1960s will not understand the technology and methods of the new millennium. Studies indicate, however, that older workers tend to be more dependable, to stay on the job longer, and to learn new technologies in the same amount of time required by younger workers.[14]

The fact remains that the American work force is continuing to mature. By the year 2000, one in three Americans will be over 45 years old.[15] Although it would seem logical for employers to make a commitment to skill upgrading and retraining designed to facilitate acceptance of new techniques and procedures by older workers, many are unwilling to make this investment. In most cases you must take responsibility for your own career development. Keep up with what is going on at your company, and accept change. Take the initiative in learning and using new technologies. Keep fit—a regular fitness program can help you stay energized and competitive.[16]

Race

Racial discrimination is discrimination based on traits common to a person's ethnic origin or skin color. Because people cannot change their skin color or abandon their ethnic heritage, this is often the most difficult discrimination to overcome. As DeWayne Wickman, an African American and president of Vanita Enterprises, Inc., states it, "The melting pot does not melt blacks."[17]

Few areas are more sensitive and engender more passion than issues surrounding race. Throughout history we have seen attempts to place people in racial categories and judge them as racial symbols rather than as unique individuals. Until the early decades of the twentieth century, the Irish Catholic "race" was stereotyped as lazy and violent. In the 1930s Jews in the United States were considered a separate "race" by many Christian Americans. Italians were once considered "nonwhite."[18] The use of racial categories continues in America. The following nonwhite race categories appear on U.S. Census Bureau forms (*The American Heritage Dictionary* was consulted for the description of each category):[19]

Black	Persons who descended from peoples of African origin. Many blacks have a preference for the name African American or Afro-American. Blacks represent about 12 percent of the U.S. population.
Hispanic	This is the broadest term used to encompass Spanish-speaking peoples, such as Mexican Americans, Puerto Ricans, Cubans, and South Americans. The widely used term *Latino* is generally restricted to persons of Latin American descent. Hispanics make up about 10 percent of the U.S. population.
Asian	The term *Asian* is preferred over *Oriental* for persons of South and East Asian ancestry, such as Chinese, Koreans, Japanese, Indonesians, and Filipinos. Asians make up 3 or 4 percent of the U.S. population.
Native American	This term refers to peoples indigenous to America. The term *Indian* is used as a term of pride and respect by Native Americans.

Criticism of the racial categories used by the Census Bureau and other organizations is growing. Critics say the use of these categories only intensifies and reinforces the beliefs and actions of racists. They believe that one way to break down racial barriers and promote a race-free consciousness is to get rid of racial categories. A growing number of geneticists and social scientists reject the view that "racial" differences have an objective or scientific foundation.[20] Recently the 11,000-member American Anthropological Association (AAA) took the official position that "race" has no scientific justification in human biology. The AAA position is that "There is as much genetic variability between two people from the same 'racial group' as there is between two people from any two different 'racial' groups."[21] Put another way, individual differences are much greater than group differences, regardless of how the group is defined.[22] The AAA recommended that the Census Bureau drop the term *race* and replace it with *ethnic origins,* noting that many people confuse race, ethnicity, and ancestry.

Those who oppose getting rid of racial categories hold that in order to ensure that individuals of all races and national origins are treated fairly, we must categorize people according to these characteristics. They say the current system is needed to create minority voting districts and to administer an array of federal laws and programs designed to ensure that minorities get equal housing, education, health care, and employment opportunities.[23] Groups that are working to build race pride, such as the American Indian Movement, also oppose efforts to get rid of racial categories. There is no doubt that the pros and cons of classifying Americans by race will be hotly debated in the years ahead.

Many people still have an irrational suspicion of a particular ethnic or racial group. However, because of affirmative action programs and diversity training programs (discussed later in this chapter), and the threat of legal action, blatant racism has evolved into a new, more subtle form of discrimination that is difficult to recognize and hard to combat. Strategies to combat this subtle racism should be aimed at all levels within an organization, but they must start at the top.

Disability

Employees whose work assignments are limited by their mental or physical abilities have in the past been referred to as "handicapped" or "disabled." Today, a more acceptable term is *mentally challenged* for individuals who suffer from mental retardation or a serious emotional disturbance, and *physically challenged* for individuals who have hearing, speech, visual, orthopedic, or other health impairments, including long-term obesity.

Mentally or physically challenged people find it difficult to enter the job market even though their right to do so is protected by the Americans with Disabilities Act of 1991. That law bans discrimination against workers with disabilities and requires employers to make "reasonable accommodations" so they can work. It covers a wide range of disabilities, including mental impairments, AIDS, alcoholism, visual impairments, and physical impairments that require use of a wheelchair. The law sets forth requirements for businesses with fifteen or more employees.

Is the law working? Reports on employment of the disabled are mixed. The Census Bureau reports that the number of working disabled Americans ages 21 to 64 rose by more than 1.1 million between 1991 and 1994, including 800,000 severely disabled new workers who required special assistance.[24] But studies by Louis Harris and Associates indicate that about two-thirds of working-age people with disabilities are not working.[25] This means the talents of several million disabled people are not being utilized.

Discrimination against the mentally and physically challenged takes many forms, but the most common are

- Asking a job applicant about his or her impairment
- Requiring a candidate with a disability to have a medical exam
- Reducing health insurance for an employee with a particular infirmity
- Firing a staff member who develops a disability
- Refusing to serve a customer who has a disability[26]

Mentally or physically challenged people who try to get jobs often encounter such discrimination. Some companies are exceptions, however. Du Pont Cor-

For Better or For Worse®

by Lynn Johnston

© Lynn Johnston Productions, Inc. Distributed by United Features Syndicate, Inc.

poration, McDonald's, Marriott, Sears, Roebuck and Company, and IBM have specific recruiting, training, and retention programs that recognize the skills and abilities of this sector of the work force.

Sexual Orientation

Discrimination based on a person's sexual orientation is referred to as *homophobia,* an aversion to homosexuals. Not long ago, gays and lesbians went to great lengths to keep their sexuality a secret. But today many gay and lesbians are "coming out of the closet" to demand their rights as members of society. Indeed, many young people entering the work force who are used to the relative tolerance of college campuses refuse to hide their orientation once they are in the workplace. Activists want to make people aware that discrimination based on sexual orientation is as serious a problem as discrimination based on race, age, gender, or disability. And some, though not all, states have enacted laws that protect gays and lesbians from discrimination or illegal discharge from their jobs because of their sexual orientation.

An atmosphere in which gays and lesbians are comfortable about being themselves is often more productive than an atmosphere in which they waste their time and energy maintaining alternate, and false, personalities. Brian McNaught, a consultant who conducts a workshop called "Homophobia in the Workplace" at the largest factory in the AT&T Corporation system, states, "Homophobia takes a toll on the ability of 10 percent of the workforce to produce."[27] He points out that it is not productive to ask gays and lesbians to completely ignore their private lives when they come to work. Heterosexuals

Allan Gilmour, pictured here with his partner, was the first high-ranking auto executive to be publicly identified as gay. Throughout his long career at Ford Motor Company, he rose to become the company's second-highest officer and was twice considered for the CEO position. Like many other gays and lesbians who aspire to top corporate jobs, he kept his sexual orientation a secret during his career because he feared discrimination. (Louis Psihoyos/Matrix)

bring their personal lives to work all the time. Being unable to participate in casual conversations about weekend events or after-work activities leaves gays and lesbians feeling isolated. About 2,000 employees have attended Mc-Naught's workshops, all voluntarily. At the end of each session, employees are offered a magnetic pink triangle—the gay logo, so to speak—if they vow to make their office or work area a "safe space" for homosexuals. Thousands of these symbols can be seen throughout the plant.[28]

The authors of *Straight Talk About Gays in the Workplace* describe what Walt Disney Company, Polaroid, Lotus, Xerox, and other companies are doing to combat homophobia.[29] Some companies have established lesbian and gay employee associations that provide a point of contact for previously invisible employees. Many companies have added sexual orientation to their anti-discrimination policies, and nationwide about 140 major public and private employers have extended medical benefits to gay and lesbian partners.

Every organization must provide workers with an environment that is safe and free of threats and intimidation. Progressive companies are taking the additional step of discovering ways in which they can provide an open, productive work atmosphere. They do not want to lose their bright, intelligent, and highly motivated lesbian and gay employees to other companies that might provide a more open environment.

Subtle Forms of Discrimination

Discrimination based on gender, age, race, or disability is prohibited under Title VII of the 1964 Civil Rights Act. This prohibition applies to discrimination in all aspects of employment, including recruitment, hiring, promotion, discharge, classification, training, compensation, and other terms, privileges, and conditions of employment.[30] A person who feels she or he has been the victim of these types of discrimination can take legal action by filing a complaint with the state office of the Equal Employment Opportunity Commission.

But the laws do not specifically protect workers from more subtle discrimination. For example, although some state laws protect gay men and lesbians from discrimination or illegal discharge from their jobs, an atmosphere that allows cruel comments and jokes about their lifestyles can nevertheless occur, adversely affecting their job performance. This lower job performance can be used as a valid reason for dismissing the lesbian or gay person. This more subtle form of discrimination can, of course, be directed against any group and may be based on any of the secondary dimensions of diversity (religious beliefs, personal appearance, marital status). Those who are from another region of the country, speak with an accent, have too much education or too little, or possess some other personal characteristic that marks them as "different" may find themselves victims of subtle discrimination. Many people are inclined to equate a difference with a deficiency.

What Can You Do?

What can you do if you discover you are the target of discrimination? If you wish to stay in the organization, you will need to determine whether the "difference" is something you can change—your weight, the way you dress, your manner of speaking. If the difference is something you cannot or choose not to change, you may need to address the situation directly. Review the assertiveness skills you studied in Chapter 13. Assertiveness by you may help change other people's attitudes and in turn alter their discriminatory behaviors. Another powerful method of eliminating subtle discrimination is to compensate for it by excelling in your work. Become an expert on the job, and work to increase your skills and your value to the organization. As your colleagues gain respect for your talents, they will change their attitudes toward you. But if your future appears blocked, investigate other workplaces where management may be more open to diversity. The important point is that you should refuse to allow discrimination to limit your personal and professional success.

Thinking / Learning Starters

1. Describe your own primary and secondary dimensions of diversity.

2. Do you hold any prejudices that might create problems for you in your career? In your personal life?

THE ISSUE OF VALUING DIVERSITY

As we look back through the previous decades, we see a pattern of workers continually struggling to be treated alike:

- Labor unions were formed to ensure employees that everyone would be treated the same.
- The women's movement fought for equality in the workplace.
- Many organizations implemented strategies to duplicate the Japanese management style, which rewarded teamwork rather than individual accomplishments.

The 1990s, however, brought a strong shift away from treating everyone the same and toward **valuing diversity.** In a work setting, valuing diversity means that an organization intends to make full use of the ideas, talents, experiences, and perspectives of all employees at all levels of the organization.

Organizations have traditionally valued assimilation over diversity, placing emphasis on changing people to conform to traditional norms and performance expectations. Most American organizations have been shaped primarily by the values and experiences of western European, white, heterosexual, able-bodied men. Achieving high productivity has frequently been a matter of trying to fit all workers into the same mold and rewarding those who fit best. The dominant group set and controlled the agenda of the traditional organization and expected other groups to follow, conform, or disappear. As people moved up the career ladder, the range of acceptable behavior narrowed and reverted to the traditional mold of the male founders.

However, the changing demographics of the U.S. work force brings with it the realization that organizations must break away from this traditional management approach. To remain competitive, organizations are being forced to recognize and hire the best talent available in the labor pool, regardless of skin color, gender, and cultural background. Once on board, these talented individuals will choose to stay only in an atmosphere where they are appreciated and valued. If their organization does not acknowledge their unique contribution, these diverse employees are likely to move on to an employer that does.

The Economics of Valuing Diversity

Valuing diversity is not only a legal, social, and moral issue; it is also an economic issue because an organization's most valuable resource is its people. The price tag for *not* helping employees learn to respect and value each other is enormous in terms of lost time, wasted energy, delayed production, and increased conflict among employees.

- Highly skilled and talented employees will leave an organization that does not value diversity.
- Substantial dollars will be spent on recruiting and retraining because of high employee turnover.
- Discrimination complaints will result from mismanagement of diverse employees.
- A comment, gesture, or joke delivered without malice but received as an insult will create tension between coworkers.
- Deliberate acts of sabotage may be aimed at making coworkers who are different "look bad."

Total Person Insight

"More and more, organizations can remain competitive only if they can recognize and obtain the best talent; value the diverse perspectives that come with talent born of different cultures, races, and genders; nurture and train that talent; and create an atmosphere that values its workforce."

LEWIS BROWN GRIGGS AND LENTE-LOUISE LOUW

Authors, *Valuing Diversity: New Tools for a New Reality*

- Absenteeism associated with stress in the workplace will likely occur.
- Time will be wasted because of miscommunication and misunderstanding between diverse employees.[31]

Recognizing the value of diversity and managing it as an asset can help eliminate these negative effects and exert a positive influence on productivity and cooperation within the work force. Companies can succeed only when they have an environment that enables all employees, not just a few, to work to their full potential.

Mismanagement of employee diversity not only interferes with efficient production but also poses a significant threat to an organization's ability to provide outstanding service to its customers. In industries such as retailing, fast food, and banking, a complex set of employee transactions must take place to satisfy a customer's needs. If there is tension, infighting, disrespect, and a low level of trust among employees, there are likely to be human relations problems that stand in the way of high-quality customer service.

Thinking / Learning Starters

1. Describe how closely the student body of your school or your coworkers reflect the cultural makeup of your community.

2. Is there a disproportionate number of students of a certain race, sex, or age bracket in your college? What accounts for this situation? What effects does it have on the environment of your school?

ENHANCING DIVERSITY

By now you should be aware of the negative effects of prejudice and discrimination as well as the positive effects of valuing diversity. Many employers are no longer asking whether to diversify the work force but rather how best to manage diversity. After all, a person's differences don't create human relations problems. Other people's responses to those differences do.

What Individuals Can Do

People tend to hang on to their prejudices and stereotypes. If certain white people believe people of color are inferior, they are likely to notice any incident in which a person of color makes a mistake. But when a person of color exhibits competence and sound decision-making abilities, these same white people do not notice anything, or they attribute the positive results to other circumstances. You cannot totally eliminate prejudices that have been deeply held and developed over a long time. But you can learn to do the following:

1. *Monitor and analytically evaluate these prejudices in light of your increased personal involvement with others who are different from you.* As noted previously, it is not easy to free yourself from confining stereotypes. You need not only to change your intellectual beliefs but also to change the emotions of prejudice formed during childhood. If you feel you are prejudiced against a particular group, fine-tune your emotions by using the practices described in Chapter 9.

2. *Learn to look critically and honestly at the particular myths and preconceived ideas you were conditioned to believe about others.* Psychologists and sociologists have found that contact among people of different races, cultures, and lifestyles can break down prejudice when people join together for a common task. The more contact there is among culturally diverse individuals, the more likely it will be that stereotypes based on myths and inaccurate generalizations will not survive.

3. *Develop a sensitivity to differences.* Do not allow gender-based, racist, or antigay jokes or comments in your presence. If English is not a person's native language, be aware that this person might interpret your messages differently from what you intended. When in doubt as to the appropriate behavior, ask questions. "I would like to open the door for you because you are in a wheelchair, but I'm not sure whether that would offend you. What would you like me to do?"

4. *Use appropriate language.* In this way, you show diverse individuals your respect. For instance, the term *minority* is no longer acceptable in reference to people of color because "minority" gives the sense of less power, as in "majority versus minority." Table 15.1 offers some guidelines for appropriate terminology.

What Organizations Can Do

A well-planned and well-executed diversity program can promote understanding and defuse tensions between employees who differ in age, race, gender, religious beliefs, and other characteristics. Programs that are poorly developed and poorly executed often backfire, especially in organizations where bias and distrust have festered for years.[32] Most of the programs that fail are those that are not comprehensive and do not provide for ongoing cultural change. A

TABLE 15.1

Examples of Appropriate Language

When Referring To	Instead Of	Use
Women	Girls, ladies, gals, females	Women
Black people	Negroes, minorities	African Americans, Caribbean Americans, black people, people of color
Asian people	Orientals, minorities	Asian Americans, Japanese, Koreans, Pakistanis, etc. Differentiate between foreign-born and American-born people of color.
American Indians	Minorities	Native Americans; American Indians; name of tribe, e.g., Navajo, Iroquois; people of color
People of Hispano–Latin American origin	Minorities	Latinas/Latinos, Chicanas/Chicanos. Use country of national origin, e.g., Puerto Ricans, Chileans; people of color, Hispanics
Gay men and lesbians	Homosexuals	Gay men, lesbians
People with disabilities	Handicapped, crippled, disabled	People who are physically or mentally challenged, people with (the specific disability)
White people	Anglos, WASPS	European Americans. Use country of national origin, e.g., Irish American, Polish American. White people
Older or younger adults	Geriatrics, kids, yuppies	Older adults, elderly, younger people, young adults

Source: Adapted from *Workforce America!* by Marilyn Loden and Judy Rosener, Business One Irwin, 1991, p. 85. Reprinted by permission of the publisher.

comprehensive diversity program has three pillars:[33] organizational redesign, employment practices, and training and development (see Figure 15.2).

Organizational Redesign Do diversity programs make a difference? Companies that see diversity programs as an *event*—a one-day workshop that promotes the advantages of a diverse work force—will very likely answer no to this question. In fact, some of these quick-fix programs create greater, not less, di-

The Diversity Council at Levi Strauss & Company is seen here working on diversity and communication issues. The council is helping revamp policies, create new structures, and design a new human resource system. Like many other progressive organizations, Levi Strauss views diversity as a constructive force. (Mark Richards/ PhotoEdit)

visiveness among workers. Companies that see diversity programs as a *process*, are more likely to answer this question in the affirmative.

Denny's Inc., a large restaurant chain that had a reputation for racism, is an example of a company that has taken a comprehensive, long-term approach to making amends. After paying $54 million to settle two civil rights class actions, the company vowed to change its culture. It established long-term hiring and purchasing goals, developed nondiscriminatory training programs, created a program to increase the number of minority-owned franchises, and made it clear that evidence of bigotry toward customers or employees would result in immediate termination.[34]

Too often, diversity programs lack clear objectives and standards that will permit the organization to assess program outcomes. The diversity program developed by Allstate Insurance Company is an example of an initiative that is based on accountability standards. Diversity courses are carefully evaluated, and employees who complete the courses must pass tests with specified standards. Each quarter, employees complete a survey that probes how well their manager maintains a climate that emphasizes bias-free service to customers, respect for individuals, and sensitivity. Survey results are used to develop a "diversity index." Performance on this index determines 25 percent of a manager's merit bonus.[35]

FIGURE 15.2

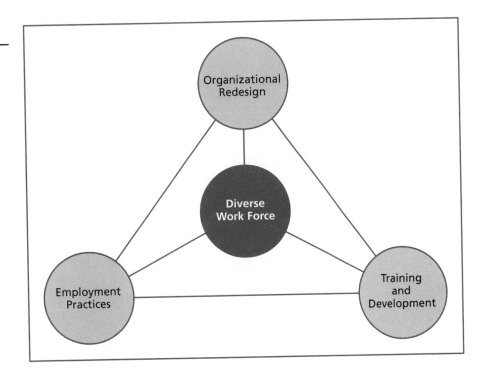

The Allstate program was implemented by a team of senior leaders. Any re-design effort must have the full support of senior management. Employees will take their cue from these leaders. If they see leaders promoting diversity at work yet joining segregated clubs, they will question how seriously top management is committed to equality. At Hoechst Celanese, the top twenty-six officers are required to join at least two organizations in which they are a minority. The company believes that managers can break out of their traditional white-male-dominated comfort zone by actually working beside people from diverse backgrounds.[36]

Employment Practices To achieve work force diversity, organizations need to seek out, employ, and develop people who have been victims of past discrimination. The starting point is active recruitment of people who are under-represented in the work force. One approach is to recruit in places where minorities attend school or work.

Some companies form partnerships with schools and colleges that have great diversity in the student body. Merrill Lynch & Co., Inc., for example, helps high schools in multiracial New Jersey prepare students for careers in the financial services area by teaching them to use personal computers and industry-specific software programs. Other companies sponsor professors' research, provide employees as guest lecturers, award scholarships, and hire students for

"GENTLEMEN, THERE'S BEEN SOME CRITICISM FROM SOME QUARTERS ABOUT THE SUPPOSED LACK OF DIVERSITY IN THE TOP RANKS OF THIS COMPANY."

summer jobs. These activities give company recruiters an opportunity to learn more about the specific details of the college's academic programs as well as the qualifications of individual graduates.[37]

Companies reviewing their standards for hiring and promoting also need to assess whether their assessment tools measure a candidate's actual abilities. Remember that many employment tests can be biased in favor of white, middle-class people. Organizations must also foster a climate for retention of women and minorities. To establish a culture of inclusiveness takes time. Some companies establish mentoring programs that pair each new employee with a senior employee of his or her choice. Mentors provide support and help steer the new employee toward promotability. Another approach is to develop career-planning sessions for all employees so they can clearly see their future within the company.

Training and Development To develop a culture that values and enhances diversity, organizations need training programs that give managers and employees the tools they need to work more effectively with one another regardless of their diverse backgrounds. These programs should also reduce an organization's liability for discrimination.[38]

Dallas-based Texas Instruments is often cited as a company that has distinguished itself through effective diversity training initiatives. It has been named to the honor roll of *Hispanic Magazine*'s "100 Best Companies for Hispanics"

FIGURE 15.3

Sears's Diversity
Guidelines

A Sears Manager's Guide to Diversity

❑ Give each individual—whether customer, associate or vendor—your uncompromising respect.

❑ Through selection, hiring and retention strive to maintain a balanced workforce that meets the needs of your customers and reflects the community in which you do business.

❑ Never treat any applicant or associate differently because of race, color, religion, gender, age, national origin, disability, citizenship status, sexual orientation or status as a veteran.

❑ Promote and continue Sears tradition of excellence in community involvement, cultural celebration and charitable contributions.

❑ Support vendors who understand and respect the importance of diversity.

❑ Recognize the diversity of your Sears community. Reflect it in the way your unit does business.

Source: *Courtesy of Sears, Roebuck and Company.*

and *Black Professional* magazine's "200 Great Places to Work." The starting point is a one-day seminar to learn to value diversity and uncover unconscious behavioral patterns that could impede the progress of women and minority employees. Senior managers attend a two-day session. Follow-up courses focus on ways to foster inclusiveness at Texas Instruments and respect for the individual.[39]

Many other companies have adopted the approach used at Texas Instruments. Done well, diversity training programs can promote harmony and reduce conflict. Training courses that are poorly designed and delivered by incompetent trainers, however, can end up alienating and offending employees. Training intended to dispel discriminatory attitudes may help perpetuate them. For example, an instructor who spends a great deal of time discussing characteristics of various cultures may actually reinforce stereotypical attitudes. Focusing on certain group differences also trivializes individuality. Each person has a unique individual identity created by a blend of primary and secondary characteristics such as communication style, ethnic heritage, religion, gender, education, and family structure. Sears, Roebuck and Company takes the position that diversity is an important source of competitive advantage. Management personnel at all levels are trained to follow the guidelines for enhancing diversity shown in Figure 15.3.

One goal of diversity training is to help employees avoid dwelling on their differences and begin to focus on what members of the organization have in common. Companies should emphasize that they have their own cultures to which every employee can belong and in which everyone abides by the same rules. Training programs need to clearly describe unacceptable conduct and explain that the organization will not condone it. The basic rules of civil behavior should be clearly spelled out. Most people want concrete examples of behavior that will not be tolerated. For example, employees would learn that humor that contains degrading racial or cultural content is unacceptable.[40] We cannot stop people from bringing prejudices to work, but we can explain that they must learn to act as though they have none.[41]

AFFIRMATIVE ACTION: YESTERDAY AND TODAY

Does affirmative action right the wrongs of the past or create new ones? This issue is being debated by some of America's best thinkers, and we are hearing strong arguments for and against this controversial program. **Affirmative action** can be defined as a program that encourages the hiring and promotion of members of groups that have been discriminated against in the past. Affirmative action, in all of its various forms, amounts to a major effort to make up for past wrongs.[42]

The Civil Rights Act of 1964, subsequent amendments, and related laws provide employment protection for women, minorities, and other categories of disadvantaged individuals. Affirmative action programs have attacked employment discrimination with four methods:[43]

1. Active recruitment of women and minorities
2. Elimination of prejudicial questions on employment application forms
3. Establishment of specific goals and timetables for minority hiring
4. Validation of employment testing procedures

Affirmative action was originally designed to level the playing field of employment by outlawing discrimination in hiring. Not so long ago "Whites only" was a common hiring standard, and you could find a "Help Wanted, Female" section in your daily newspaper.[44] There is no doubt that antidiscrimination legislation was needed. Affirmative action allowed a tremendous influx of diverse individuals through the front door of thousands of schools and organizations. Many were able to work their way into advanced, top-level positions. At the same time, however, affirmative action reinforced the historical view that the members of protected groups are not qualified for various positions and therefore need assistance just to get a job.

Many people say it is time to rethink affirmative action or even eliminate it. Recent political and legal interpretations of affirmative action have stimulated a nationwide debate over the merits of any program that grants preferential treatment to specific groups. Terry Eastland, author of *Ending Affirmative Action—The Case for Color Blind Justice,* has outlined some of the most common arguments voiced by those who want to end preferential policies:[45]

- *Preferences are discriminatory.* They tend to discriminate against those who are not members of the "right" race or gender.
- *Preferences do not counter discrimination.* Efforts by a company or a government to police presumed discrimination tend to move the focus away from real instances of discrimination that should be at the heart of law enforcement efforts.
- *Preferences do not make sense, given changing demographics.* The population eligible for affirmative action continues to grow several times faster than the nonpreferred population.

Colin Powell, a distinguished African American military leader, takes a more moderate position on affirmative action. He says, "If affirmative action means programs that provide equal opportunity, then I am all for it. If it leads to preferential treatment or helps those who no longer need help, I am opposed."[46] Barbara Bergmann, professor at American University and author of *In Defense of Affirmative Action,* presents the view that affirmative action is the only practical way to rectify discrimination in hiring. She states that many companies and government agencies will not embrace fairness in hiring and promotion as long as guidelines are voluntary.[47] Historian John Hope

Franklin, who was selected to lead President Clinton's advisory board on race, is one of several noted scholars who believe affirmative action policies are important to achieve full racial equality. He supports programs that open opportunities but do not lower standards.[48]

The debate about affirmative action will continue for many years. The concept and the means for implementing it are likely to be challenged in court repeatedly over the next decade. We can anticipate a move to focus preferences on class or socioeconomic status rather than race or gender. And we can anticipate that voluntary efforts to establish a diverse work force will likely continue because they can influence profits. As one author noted, "Appreciating diversity isn't just a nice idea, it's a business imperative."[49]

Summary

Work force diversity has become an important issue for organizations that want to remain competitive in a global economy. These organizations are beginning to move away from focusing on prejudice and discrimination and toward valuing diversity. Two dimensions, or sets of characteristics, are the basis of every individual's diversity. Primary dimensions include gender, age, race, physical and mental abilities, and sexual orientation. Secondary dimensions include health habits, religious beliefs, ethnic customs, communication style, relationship status, income, general appearance, and education and training.

Prejudice and discrimination are major barriers to effective human relations. Prejudice is an attitude based partly on observation of others' differences and partly on ignorance, fear, and cultural conditioning. Prejudiced people tend to see others as stereotypes rather than as unique individuals. Prejudicial attitudes are formed through the effects of childhood experiences, ethnocentrism, and economic factors. Discrimination is behavior based on prejudicial attitudes. Groups protected by law from discrimination in the workplace include women, people of color, older and younger workers, and those who have disabilities. More subtle forms of discrimination include discrimination arising from personal appearance, martial status, and so on. These subtle forms of discrimination are often difficult to prove but may be offset through assertiveness, a change in the behavior that causes the discrimination, or a move to a more tolerant organization.

The issue of valuing diversity is an economic one for most organizations. The changing demographics of American society mean that the work force will soon be made up of a minority of white men and a majority of women, people of color, and immigrants. Companies cannot afford to ignore this change in the pool of human resources.

Individuals can enhance diversity by letting go of their stereotypes and learning to critically and honestly evaluate their prejudiced attitudes as they work and socialize with people who are different. They will need to develop a sensitivity to differences and use language appropriately. Organizations must develop a culture that respects and enhances diversity. Their diversity training programs should become an internal process rather than an event. They need to seek out, employ, and develop people from diverse backgrounds.

Affirmative action guidelines have helped bring fairness in hiring and promotion to many organizations. Today, however, some people believe these guidelines are discriminatory because they allow preferential treatment for the people they were designed to protect. These preferences may no longer make sense, critics say, given the changing demographics of today's work force.

Career Corner

Q. I receive phone calls at work from customers located all over the world. Most of them speak English, but because of their accents, I often have difficulty understanding what they are trying to say to me. How can I handle these calls more effectively?

A. The fact that your customers can speak two languages indicates that they are probably educated and intelligent, so treat them with respect. Statements like "I can't understand you," or "What did you say?" are rude and should be avoided. Instead, take personal responsibility for improving the communications and gently say, "I am having a little difficulty understanding you, but if you will be patient with me I am sure I will be able to help." Ask them to slow down so that you can hear all the information correctly. Listen for key words and repeat them back to the caller. Identify coworkers who are fluent in a particular language, and ask them to help when calls come in from customers who share the same culture. Remember, people with foreign accents are not hard of hearing, so don't shout.

Key Terms

diversity
primary dimensions
secondary dimensions
prejudice
stereotypes

ethnocentrism
discrimination
valuing diversity
affirmative action

Review Questions

1. Distinguish between the primary and secondary dimensions of diversity, and give examples of each.
2. Why should organizations be concerned about valuing diversity?
3. How do the changing demographics of American culture affect the human resources pool of the future? Be specific.

4. Define *prejudice* and *discrimination*. How do these two terms differ in meaning?

5. What are some of the ways in which people acquire prejudices?

6. In what ways might valuing diversity impact an organization economically?

7. How can subtle forms of discrimination hurt the victim's chances to succeed in his or her career?

8. What role does affirmative action play in today's organizations? What are some of the positive and negative outcomes of affirmative action?

9. How can organizations enhance work force diversity?

10. What flaws in diversity training programs can cause a negative backlash among participants?

Application Exercises

1. Select a professional journal, the want ads from a local or national paper, or any magazine publication. Examine the ads, articles, and pictures for evidence that the publishers and advertisers are attempting to attract and respect readers from diverse races and cultures. For example, which racial or ethnic groups are pictured in expensive cars, offices, or homes? If your chosen career is traditionally dominated by one gender, do articles in your professional journals include references to both sexes?

2. For one week, keep a diary that records every instance in which you see actions or hear comments that reflect outmoded, negative stereotypes. For instance, watch a movie, and observe whether the villains are all of a particular race. As you read textbooks from other courses you are taking, notice whether the pictures and examples reflect any stereotypes. Listen to your friends' conversations, and notice any time they make unfair judgments about others based on stereotypes.

   Share your experiences with class members, and discuss what steps you can take to help rid the environment of negative stereotyping.

3. John Hope Franklin, professor of history at Duke University, was selected to lead President Clinton's advisory board on race. In an interview conducted shortly after he accepted the assignment, he noted that there are constant reminders of the deep racial divide that exists in America and that cannot easily be bridged unless people from different ethnic or racial groups begin to establish a dialogue.

   Meet with someone who is a member of a racial or ethnic group different from your own, and attempt to build a relationship by discussing the things that are important to each of you. As you get to know this person, become aware of his or her beliefs and attitudes. Try not to be diverted by accent, grammar, or personal appearance; rather, really listen to the person's thoughts and ideas. Search for things you and your new acquaintance have in common, and do not dwell on your differences.

Internet Exercise

Religious beliefs represent an important secondary dimension of diversity. Unfortunately, some people do not have very much tolerance for religious beliefs and practices that differ from their own. A 19-year-old woman living in Denver showed up for work at Domino's Pizza wearing a hijab, the traditional muslin head scarf. The manager told her to remove the scarf or leave. She had recently converted to Islam and was not sure if the manager was being rude or intolerant of her religion. Later, company officials discovered that the manager's order was a violation of Title VII of the Civil Rights Act of 1964. The employee was then told she could wear a scarf as long as it was red and blue, the company colors.[50] Visit the Web site of one or more religious advocacy groups and find out if it provides information on religious rights at work. Examples include the Anti-Defamation League and the Council on American-Islamic Relations. You may also type in "religious rights" and "religious freedom." Prepare a written summary of your findings.

Case 15.1

Denny's Racial Bias = $54 Million

Denny's, the $1.7 billion restaurant chain, has been fighting racial discrimination charges since the early 1990s. Court documents record a host of charges, including refusing to serve nonwhites, forcing African American customers to prepay for their meals, temporary closings of restaurants with mostly African American customers, unfair hiring and treatment of nonwhite employees, and blocking nonwhite employees from franchise opportunities and management positions.

One lawsuit was filed when six African American Secret Service officers, who had allegedly been snubbed by service personnel at a Denny's in Annapolis, Maryland, claimed Denny's "service lapse" had been "racially motivated." Another lawsuit filed in San Jose, California, alleged that thirty-two black customers were ordered to prepay for meals or pay a cover charge though white customers had no such requirement. Denny's parent company, Flagstar, agreed to pay $54.5 million to settle two class action suits. In addition, the landmark deal committed Flagstar to NAACP hiring and purchasing goals.

Since the settlement, Denny's has made major progress. Eight of the twelve all-white top executives have left the company; minority suppliers are awarded 12 percent ($50 million) of Denny's business each year; 27 of the chain's 600 franchised restaurants are black owned; and 5 percent of the managing partners are black. These statistics are not dramatic, but Denny's is pleased to be ahead of schedule as they attempt to reach the NAACP goals. The $1 billion diversity training program has created a new corporate culture that rewards managers for their sensitivity by tying 12.5 percent of managers' bonuses to their diversity hiring and promotion records. Flagstar CEO James B. Adamson sent a clear warning throughout the organization: "If you discriminate, you're history." He proved his commitment to the policy when a group of Asian American students filed a civil rights lawsuit against Denny's in Syracuse, New York. All management, staff, and security personnel were fired the day the report was received. In their response to the Asians' suit, Denny's management admitted that several of the employees involved in the incident had not received the nondiscrimination training required by the original decree. It is evident that simply having written policies in place is not enough to stop years of bigotry.

Questions

1. Beyond the $54.5 million fines, what other losses might Denny's experience as a result of the charges of discriminatory behaviors?
2. Do you believe that top management officials in the Denny's/Flagstar organization were responsible for creating a climate that encouraged restaurant managers to engage in racially biased activities? Why?
3. How would you respond if your manager asked you to blatantly discriminate against a minority?

Case 15.2   ## Piscataway Township Versus Taxman

Two business education teachers began teaching the same day in Piscataway, New Jersey: Sharon Taxman was white; Debra Williams was black. In 1989 the school board was forced to reduce the ten-person business education department by one person, and school protocol demanded "last one in, first one out." Both women, however, had been hired the same day.

To preserve an element of diversity, the school board fired Ms. Taxman and retained Ms. Williams, the only minority in the department. Ms. Taxman sued the school district, claiming violation of her rights guaranteed by the affirmative action guidelines of the 1964 Civil Rights Act, which prohibits discrimination based on race. The U.S. Court of Appeals for the Third Circuit decided that affirmative action could not be used for achieving diversity. The judges wrote that affirmative action could be justified only as a remedy for precisely identified past discrimination.

People trying to preserve affirmative action argue that Title VII of the 1964 Civil Rights Act permits the use of race- and gender-based preferences. Opponents argue that the attempt to maintain a diverse work force has nothing to do with remedying past discrimination and that firing decisions based on race represent blatant discrimination. The Supreme Court agreed to hear the case in January 1998.

However, two months before the Supreme Court docket date, Taxman and her attorneys accepted an out-of-court settlement for $431,000: $186,000 in back salary and interest, plus $245,000 to cover eight years of legal fees. Opponents of affirmative action expressed disappointment as their anticipated victory was taken away. Supporters of affirmative action not only were relieved that the case did not go to court but also were instrumental in raising approximately 70 percent of the cash settlement through the Black Leadership Forum, a coalition of major civil rights groups, including the Urban League and the NAACP Legal Defense and Educational Fund. Jesse Jackson, leader of the Rainbow Coalition, was one of the civil rights leaders who pushed for an out-of-court settlement and helped raise the money.

Although the U.S. Court of Appeals decided that affirmative action laws could not be used to justify the firing of Sharon Taxman, this decision does not set a precedent for other states. The rest of the nation must wait for the Supreme Court to resolve the issue.

Questions

1. If you were serving on the Supreme Court, would you have upheld the rights of the fired, white teacher, or would you have voted for the right of the school board to maintain faculty diversity? Explain.

2. Polls consistently show that a majority of Americans support efforts to help people who have been excluded from basic opportunities in areas such as education and employment. However, many people oppose race and gender "preferences." In place of preferences based on race and gender, some would substitute preferences for the economically disadvantaged. What is your position on preferences based on race and gender? On economic disadvantages? Explain your answer.

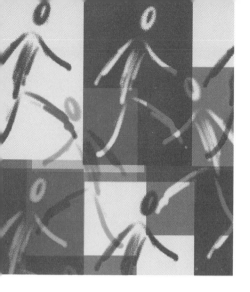

Chapter 16

The Changing Roles
of Men
and Women

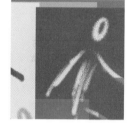

Chapter Preview

After studying this chapter, you will be able to

1. Describe how the traditional roles of men and women are changing.
2. Understand problems facing women and men as a result of gender bias in organizations.
3. Discuss ways to cope with gender-biased behaviors.
4. Identify ways to achieve work/life balance.
5. Explain the forms of sexual harassment and learn how to avoid being a victim or perpetrator of them.

WHEN DEBORAH KENT went to work at General Motors Corporation in the late 1970s, she told them the only thing she knew about cars was how to change a flat tire. In 1987 Ford Motor Company discovered this dynamic African American woman and hired her away from General Motors. Today she is manager of Ford's Avon Lake, Ohio, assembly plant and is responsible for building eighty-nine vehicles an hour, has over 3,500 workers, and a $300 million annual budget. The media suggested her steady stream of promotions was the result of "tokenism," but Kent and her boss, Dave Gorman, head of Ford's vehicle operations, agree it was her education and talent that helped her climb the corporate ladder.[1] She proved she was the best person—male or female—for the job.

Throughout his white-male-dominated corporate career, George Tunick never thought of women as possible candidates for top jobs or the boardroom. He had a smart and loyal female administrative assistant who took care of all his business needs and changed jobs every time he did. He realizes now that, had she been a man, she would have had twice the financial rewards for her twenty-five years of service to him. When he accepted the position as publisher of *Executive Female,* the professional journal of the National Association of Female Executives (an organization dominated by female employees and managers), Tunick admitted he went through "a real metamorphosis."[2] Because he is usually first to arrive at the office in the morning, he usually makes the coffee. He also makes his own appointments, is responsible for his own notes and record keeping, and answers his own phone. ■

Role reversals such as Kent's and Tunick's are happening in organizations all across America as men and women realize the limitations of their tradi-

---

Total Person Insight

"If a mandatory service period here at the [National Association of Female Executives] office could be arranged for all your male associates, it would enlighten them, as it did me. Since that isn't an option, and while men and women still are so different in their approaches and behavior, you still have to talk and talk to us until we all get it. Please give us a hand. It isn't that we don't want to understand. It's just that we have a few centuries of conditioning to overcome. As you do."

GEORGE TUNICK

Publisher, *Executive Female;* Author, "Re-educating Chauvinists"

tional, gender-based roles in society. Men and women alike are demanding equal rights with regard to nontraditional jobs, flexible work schedules, maternity/paternity leave, job sharing, child-care benefits, and so on.

TRADITIONAL ROLES ARE CHANGING

All cultures promote one set of behaviors for boys and a separate set for girls. Children generally learn their socially acceptable roles by the time they are 5 years old, but these roles are often continually reinforced throughout the life cycle by teachers, parents, authority figures, and the media. These traditional roles can be harmful to both men and women. For instance, the expectation that men should be aggressive and unemotional stifles their sensitivity and creativity. The assumption that women are emotional and weak hinders them in reaching leadership positions. Although men and women will always be different, their roles can and should be more nearly equal.

Gender bias (also known as **sexism**), or discrimination on the basis of gender, persists in America today. The women's movement that began in the 1960s with Betty Friedan's book *The Feminine Mystique* has helped women make tremendous strides toward equality with men in the workplace.[3] Only recently, however, have men begun to realize that they have been shortchanged when it comes to enjoying the options women have experienced for generations. Men have traditionally been the breadwinners while women had the option of staying home and caring for the children or choosing to work.

When employers base employment, promotion, and job-assignment decisions on a person's gender, human relations and productivity suffer. Gender bias is no longer a female-only issue, and many organizations are making the necessary adjustments.

Changes in the Role of Women

For generations, most women were encouraged to be passive, supportive of others, emotionally expressive, and physically attractive. These attitudes developed not only from what girls and boys were told but also from what they observed. Research indicates that boys and girls who see their mothers in traditional roles will tend to identify women as mothers, homemakers, and wives. Therefore, even though mothers encourage their daughters to adopt nontraditional roles and urge their sons to accept women in traditionally male roles, their own behavior will have far more influence than their words. If children see their fathers going to work each day while their mothers stay at home, they may expect to follow that pattern in their adult homes.[4]

Many women have found higher income potential in non-traditional jobs even though their new role may expose them to harassment from those who have not changed with the times.
(Eddie Adqams)

Schools are making some progress toward breaking these traditional expectations. Girls and boys are no longer tracked into homemaking and woodworking classes. Textbooks no longer portray men as doctors and women as nurses, or men as bosses and women as secretaries. However, teachers' conditioned attitudes often interfere with their classroom conduct. Some studies show teachers reward girls for being neat, pretty, compliant, and nice and reward boys for being smart. Teachers tend to interact with boys more frequently than with girls.

As a result of this cultural, social, and educational conditioning, some women are unaware of the range of opportunities open to them in today's world. They may continue to seek jobs with limited potential for advancement or economic gain. To combat this conditioning, women preparing for their role in the twenty-first century should select role models that will help them break away from traditional expectations. Such role models are women who have the ability to

1. Know what they want and plan for the future
2. Make decisions, live with the consequences, and learn from the process
3. Realize that with equal rights come equal responsibilities
4. Seek out opportunities that increase their abilities and personal fulfillment
5. Develop qualities of cooperation, dependability, self-control, and expertise in some area

In the past, many women shied away from behaviors such as these because they involve taking risks that might lead to failure. Many women today, however, embrace these risks as opportunities for success, recognition, and financial security. The "Crazy Dream" mentioned in Figure 16.1 may very likely become reality.

It has been more than thirty years since the National Organization for Women (NOW) was formed to fight discrimination against women; the changes in work force participation by women and in the opportunities available to women have been profound. Today working women make up 48 percent of the work force and may be the majority by the year 2000.[5] About 50 percent of the working women contribute more than half of their family's income.[6] In some segments of the work force, there is reason to be optimistic about the progress of women. Women have made significant gains in a wide range of traditionally male-dominated areas such as finance, marketing, law, medicine, accounting, and college teaching. More women than men are now enrolled in college.[7] But although women have made great progress, some problem areas persist. Studies indicate that just 1 in 10 of the most senior jobs at the 500 largest U.S. companies are held by women. Women now hold about 40 percent of the middle management jobs, but they almost always earn significantly less than their male counterparts.[8] Men continue to dominate craft, repair, and construction jobs. Women hold only 2 percent of the skilled trades jobs.[9] Later in this chapter we discuss how women can overcome gender bias and other work-related problems.

Regardless of all the changes in the role of women in today's society, they still have the primary and sometimes sole responsibility for child care. Therefore, the constantly expanding new role of women in the twenty-first century will include restructuring of home and work environments so that they are compatible with each other. Many women will seek out organizations that are not only women friendly in their hiring and promotion standards but are also family friendly in their employment practices.

Changes in the Role of Men

Many boys have been conditioned from their early years to be competitors and to win. They have been urged to be tough and aggressive, to learn

FIGURE 16.1

Thought-Provoking
Statement Published
by Nike

You keep having this dream, see, this

CRAZY DREAM.

This dream that someday
women will not be judged by their sex,
but for some wacky, zany reason,
by their performance alone.

This dream that someday
women will be allowed to do things
that are called "male things," only they
won't be called "male things" anymore
they'll be called "people things".

This dream that little girls will be
raised to believe they can do anything
and when they turn 13 or 18 or 21
or 30 or 65 it will still be true.

This dream that the word
"lady" isn't always preceded by the
word "old" and the word "weaker"
has nothing to do with sex.

We said it was a dream.

And dreams, occasionally,

DO COME TRUE.

Just do it.

Source: Reprinted with permission of NIKE.

teamwork, to select traditional male pastimes such as sports and cars, and to enter a masculine profession such as sales, automotive repair, management, engineering, or law. A boy was taught to withstand physical pain and to push his body to the limits. Above all, he was not to act like a girl, to take up interests that were considered feminine, or to show any tendencies that could be considered homosexual. A girl could be a tomboy, but a boy could not be a "sissy." Whereas a woman's worth was measured in terms of her physical attractiveness, a man's was measured by his ability to compete and achieve his goals and by his power to earn high salaries and material benefits. If women have been viewed as "sex objects," perhaps men have been seen as "success objects." A man is under constant pressure to prove himself and keep moving up the ladder. Even though men have learned the value of teamwork, they have also had to learn to look over their shoulders for whoever might be gaining on them.

Psychologists have become increasingly aware that we have neglected the stress associated with being male. Max Carey is someone who has experienced this stress in the extreme. Despite being the smallest football player in the league, he was an All-Ivy defensive halfback, setting five Columbia University records. He graduated number one in his U.S. Navy pilot flight school and came home from Vietnam a decorated war hero. When his business almost failed, he turned it around. Carey explains that he learned to deal with difficult emotional issues by stuffing them deeply into his subconscious. In combat, it was "keep up the bravado. Don't tell anyone you're scared or weak." In business, it was "God forbid anyone should know you're not perfect."[10] The cumulative stress of business and suppressed wartime memories eventually caused Max to have a breakdown. He was forced to do something he had never done before: admit weakness and ask for help.

Total Person Insight

"We are living at an important and fruitful moment now, for it is clear to men that the images of adult manhood given by the popular culture are worn out; a man can no longer depend on them. By the time a man is thirty-five he knows that the images of the right man, the tough man, the true man which he received in high school do not work in life."

ROBERT BLY

Author, *Iron John*

Jim Mains experiences mixed emotions as he treasures his private moments with his 10-month-old son and battles feelings of isolation as a stay-at-home father. (Kevin Horan Photography)

In her book *No Man's Land: Men's Changing Commitments to Family and Work,* Kathleen Gerson divides contemporary men—those struggling to identify their role in today's society—into three categories.[11] The first is the traditional breadwinner, in which the male identity revolves around being the sole provider of the family's income. Changes in the economy, however, make it almost impossible for a man to support his family by himself. As more women step in to share the burden, the male identity is eroded.[12]

The second category represents men who prefer to be autonomous and do not want the responsibilities connected with family role expectations. They therefore remain single; get a divorce and abandon their financial responsibilities to their family; or run away and escape their family commitment altogether.

The third group has moved in the opposite direction, toward greater involvement with child care and other family responsibilities. David Williams, tackle for the Houston Oilers, is a prime example of this new attitude toward a man's role. Williams paid a heavy fine for choosing to be with his wife during the birth of their son rather than playing in a professional football game. Fans across the country indicated their support for his decision by sending Williams money to help pay the fine. He donated it all to charity.[13]

Many men are tired of being in control, of not expressing their emotions freely, and of feeling they must constantly strive for achievement. They have discovered that the strong, unemotional, in-control image supported by previous generations is not realistic for men of today. They are learning to define the kind of life they want to lead rather than being restricted to traditional gender-role stereotypes.

Several individuals and groups have helped shape the men's movement. Robert Bly's book *Iron John* examined truths about masculinity that go beyond the stereotypes of our popular culture, and Warren Farrell's book *The Myth of Male Power* challenges the standard view of gender inequity. Family responsibility was a major theme of the Million Man March in Washington in 1995, and the revival-style meetings of the Promise Keepers encourage men to spend more time with their families. The National Center for Fathering promotes the value of greater balance between family involvement and work.[14]

As men re-examine their role in society, they are beginning to realize that the joys of parenting can be just as satisfying as the achievement of career goals. But such feelings are confusing for many men. Their wives often expect them to maintain their competitive nature at work while being attentive husbands and fathers at home. Men who were brought up in homes with single mothers or in homes where fathers were inaccessible because of the demands of their jobs have had few role models from which to learn the skills necessary to effectively balance career and family life. Is it any wonder many men feel frustrated as they strive to establish their role in society?

Total Person Insight

"We, as men, want to take back our full humanity. We no longer want to strain and compete to live up to an impossible oppressive masculine image — strong, silent, cool, handsome, unemotional, successful, master of women, leader of men, wealthy, brilliant, athletic, and heavy. We no longer want to feel the need to perform sexually, socially, or in any way to live up to an imposed male role, from a traditional American society or a counterculture."

BERKELEY MEN'S CENTER MANIFESTO

The men's movement is attempting to help men realize that their lives should be directed from within, not by external forces. In light of this evolution, men are beginning to speak up and demand the same rights the women's movement is seeking for women.

Thinking / Learning Starters

1. Do members of your immediate family hold traditional gender roles? If so, have any of these roles undergone changes during the past decade? In what way?

2. Before marriage, each partner should understand the other partner's expectations with regard to career, family responsibilities, and priorities. What are your expectations of your spouse (if you are married), or what do you imagine they would be (if you are not)?

PROBLEMS FACING WOMEN IN ORGANIZATIONS

When women pursue nontraditional jobs or are selected for management-level positions, they usually face two challenges: the wage gap and the glass ceiling. At the same time, many employers are gearing up for the predicted rise in the number of women available for work at the turn of the century by offering working women and mothers alternatives that allow them to reach their full potential. Although these alternatives offer tremendous opportunities, they also require tough choices.

The Wage Gap

The gap between women's and men's earnings has been shrinking in recent years, but wage inequality continues. The Bureau of Labor Statistics reports that women earn about 75 cents for every dollar men earn. This figure is somewhat misleading because the Bureau does not compare similar jobs held by men and women; it lumps together all jobs that women hold and all jobs that men hold. When surveys focus on specific fields such as engineering, banking, or accounting, women earn 85 to 95 percent of what men in similar jobs get.[15] Wage inequality is most apparent when you compare the earnings of men and women managers. For every dollar male managers earn, women earn about 60 cents.[16]

Many organizations are taking steps to deal with the problem of wage inequality. Some have adopted a comparable-worth policy, which requires that women and men be paid equally not only for the same jobs but also for jobs that require the same level of skill, effort, and responsibility, and the same working conditions. Employers who are searching for workers with specific skills have found that other characteristics such as gender or race no longer matter as much as they once did.[17] Employers who fail to adjust unequal pay scales can be sued under the Equal Pay Act of 1963.

The Glass Ceiling

There is a condition in the workplace that gives women a view of top management jobs but blocks their ascent. It is often referred to as the **glass ceiling.** The Glass Ceiling Commission, created by the U.S. Labor Department, has documented widespread limits on career advancement for women. Its research shows that about 95 percent of senior-level managers in the largest American companies are males.[18] Although we are seeing some positive change, especially among the middle-management ranks, women are still being held back by some widely held misconceptions. Top male executives say the major barrier for women is a lack of significant general management and line experience and less time in the "pipeline." Women in senior management positions say the *real* problems are (1) stereotyping and preconceptions of women held by men and (2) exclusion of women from informal networks of communication.[19]

Many companies are helping women break through the glass ceiling. Officials at Deloitte & Touche LLP, a large Wilton, Connecticut, accounting firm, were disappointed that too few women advanced to the level of partner and many talented women were leaving the company. Officials had mistakenly assumed that women were leaving only to start families. To help women move up in the company, they launched the "Advancement of Women" initiative. All of the organization's 4,700 managers and partners were sent to a two-day workshop where they could explore work-related gender differences. The company also set up a mentoring program, made sure women received career-advancing experience, and developed more family-friendly policies. The result after three years was a 30 percent increase in women partners and reduced turnover among women.[20] Allstate Insurance, J. C. Penney Company, and Dow Chemical Company are some other companies that have taken specific steps to make sure women move to the top.

Some employers mistakenly believe that women will not relocate or stick around long enough to be groomed for top-level positions. They argue that

---

Total Person Insight

"Ambitious women still face formidable resistance in many industries that have traditionally not welcomed them at any level. But they are chipping away at the so-called glass ceiling — the invisible barrier to female advancement to senior levels — in businesses where not so long ago there were no women at all."

ANN FISHER

Contributing Editor, *Fortune*

---

most women will get married and move as their husbands' job assignments dictate or will leave to devote themselves full-time to raising their families. These assumptions are incorrect! Studies indicate that a majority of women who quit working for large companies moved on to other companies that were more female friendly.

Women who find their advancement to the top blocked, or get tired of inflexible work schedules, often start their own business. Women today own one-third of all businesses and are starting businesses at twice the rate of men. We are seeing women start companies in industries such as manufacturing and construction, areas that were virtually closed to them in the past.[21]

Balancing Career and Family Choices

Women today know that they will probably be working for pay for part or all of their adult lives. This expectation is quite a departure from previous generations, when women were expected to maintain only the responsibilities of wife and mother. The challenge of performing multiple roles, however, can be stressful and tiring. A majority of the women in two-income families not only earn half of their family's income but also do most of their family's household chores. Lily Tomlin once said, "If I'd known what it was like to have it all, I would have settled for a lot less."[22] Many women in America no doubt share this thought.

When women began entering the work force in large numbers, they often did it on men's terms. Employers did not make an effort to meet the needs of women who wanted to balance career and family responsibilities. Although the demographics of work have changed dramatically over the past thirty years, some observers say the workplace has not changed very much. Elizabeth Perle

Linda Baran and Diana Lanza, New York-area senior account executives at UNUM, a large insurance company, share the same job. Each works three days a week, with one overlapping day for coordination. This arrangement allows both women to balance the demands of their work and family lives. (Len Rubenstein)

McKenna, in her book *When Work Doesn't Work Anymore,* says work often remains a place built for men who have full-time wives at home to take care of the rest of life.[23] When women mold themselves to fit the existing workplace and accept its values, they often pay a high price. In a world that requires long hours and "face time" to achieve recognition and advancement, women often find themselves neglecting the personal and family lives they hold so dear.[24] McKenna says that although earning money gives women economic power, more freedom, and an independent identify, these rewards may require some major sacrifices.

As we look for ways to help women balance career and family, we should not overlook the rewards that are experienced by women who work. Some studies have found that women who held both work and family roles reported better physical and mental health than was reported by women who stayed at home.[25] Joan Peters, in her book *When Mothers Work,* says work makes an important contribution to a woman's self-esteem and intellectual satisfaction.[26]

The "Mommy Track" Many women are delaying marriage or foregoing it altogether to pursue a meaningful and exciting career track. Similarly, many women marry but delay having children until they establish themselves in their field. Then, when they are ready to have children, many women choose the "mommy track," as opposed to a strict career track. The mommy track might temporarily slow a woman's career advancement, because some employers resist promoting these women until after their return to work. But it allows mothers to remain at home for a short time after the birth of their children and then return to their jobs. Recent studies indicate that the vast majority of women return to their jobs within six months after giving birth.[27]

The Family and Medical Leave Act of 1993 requires organizations with fifty or more employees to allow up to twelve weeks per year for health emergencies or the arrival of a child, including an employee's adopted or foster child. Employees forfeit their salaries while on leave, but they retain their benefits and the right to return to the same or a comparable job within the firm.[28] This security helps relieve the pressure many women feel when they take time off to start a family.

PROBLEMS FACING MEN IN ORGANIZATIONS

Many men are beginning to realize that they have been as rigidly stereotyped in their role as women have been in theirs. Men encounter resistance from their family, coworkers, and friends when they attempt to break out of their stereotypes. The changes a man makes to alter traditional masculine role characteristics can be threatening to others and can cause severe problems in his relationships. Yet it is common knowledge to individuals and organizations that the stress men are under today to conform to the expectations of society often leads to heart disease and other health problems. Many wonder if upholding the male image is worth the price.

Men Working with Women

Not long ago many men felt they had the corporate terrain all to themselves. Some felt discomfort, even resentment, when women became more visible and were promoted to management positions in corporations. But now, male attitudes toward female ambitions in the work world are greatly changing. One reason for this change is that men now in their 30s had a large number of female classmates in professional schools. These men learned during their training not only that they would be competing with such women but also that women are as smart and as ambitious as they are. Also, men who would like to see options available for their daughters are particularly helpful to women in business. An increasing number of men seem to be secure in their talents and abilities and welcome the opportunity to work beside equally self-assured women.

An example of lingering "male" attitudes toward women reaching the top can be as simple as semantics. A male CEO was sincerely proud to welcome a new member, who happened to be a woman, to the board of directors of his company. He started his introduction of her to his colleagues with "We will all have to clean up our jokes" and ended with "As you can all see from her appearance, she will add a lot to the looks of this board!" A subsequent training session taught this man that although it is correct to acknowledge the competence and past achievements that contributed to her promotion, it is not appropriate to discuss her physical appearance.

Men are learning that women can be excellent coworkers, team members, and leaders. Women are very comfortable with consensus building, an approach that can enhance teamwork. As leaders, women are more likely to use a collaborative, interactive management style and avoid the ineffective "command-and-control" style. Men admire women's abilities to be more perceptive and caring in business relationships.[29]

Balancing Career and Family Choices

Men, like women, now have more choices regarding marriage and family life. Men can choose to stay single to be free to relocate when their company asks them to. A man with traditional values may consciously decide to marry a woman who wants to be a nurturing mother and homemaker. By accepting full financial responsibility for his family, that man has made choices that will direct his lifestyle. Another man may choose to marry a woman with strong career goals. When a husband and a wife both pursue careers, responsibilities may have to be negotiated.

A growing number of men are learning to adjust to a marriage in which the wife brings home the family's biggest paycheck. Statistics compiled by the Department of Labor indicate that about 30 percent of the working wives make more than their husbands. Some men have difficulty coping with their wives' success.[30]

The "Daddy Track"   Many men, like many women, are choosing to place their relationship with their children on a par with, or even above, their career goals. They may join the "daddy track" and delay their career advancement while they spend time with their children. Magazine editor Robert Barker made this choice when he decided to cut his workweek and paycheck by two-fifths to share with his working wife child-care responsibilities for their infant daughter. After one year, the announcement of his wife's second pregnancy, and reorganization at work, Barker returned to his job full-time only to find his career goals and mind-set altered permanently. When offered a promotion, he turned it down, knowing he wanted to be able to spend time with his family.[31]

The Family and Medical Leave Act offers fathers paternity leave, just as it offers leave to mothers, but very few eligible men take advantage of this benefit. Many men still feel that taking parental leave will unofficially penalize them. They feel they may be passed over for promotions or for special assignments because of their family commitments. Men who do decide to take parental leave usually value the experience highly, says Deborah Lee, author of *Having It All, Having Enough.*[32]

Many men who have made conscious decisions to choose nontraditional lifestyles or careers emphasize the importance of not "going it alone." Men's support groups around the country have helped men examine traditional male roles, recognize and express their feelings, and support those who are making changes in their lives. Conferences for men, and books such as Sam Keen's *Fire in the Belly,* have helped men understand the available options and the extent to which women's struggle for equality is their fight as well. When women and men share equal status within the organization and the family, both are relieved of carrying the burden all by themselves.

Thinking / Learning Starters

1. Think of three men whom you know and admire. What roles do they play in their families? Have you observed any changes in these roles in recent years? Explain.

2. Men have traditionally expected to accept full financial responsibility for the family. How do you feel about this expectation in regard to your own future? Explain your options.

CHALLENGES AND OPPORTUNITIES FOR WORKING MEN AND WOMEN

As men and women struggle with their career and family choices, organizations are gearing up to meet the needs of their employees in the twenty-first century. They are recognizing the demands placed on working parents and are attempting to address the problems associated with quality child care. At the same time, they realize they must provide flexible work schedules that adjust to the changing roles of men and women.

The Challenge of Child Care

At the present time more than 50 percent of women with children under 6 years old are participating in the labor force. By the year 2001 about 70 percent of all families will be headed by single parents or dual-earner parents. The need for affordable, quality child care has never been greater.[33]

Mothers and fathers alike face forced overtime and unpredictable hours as their employers attempt to cut costs while improving service to customers. At the same time, many day-care providers shut their doors at 6 P.M. and on weekends. Workers who cannot balance the demands of work with available child care are often disciplined or fired. A mother of three was fired after she failed to report to a night-shift assignment with Federal Express when her child-care arrangements fell through. A single father and mechanic for a Minneapolis circuit-board maker was fired because he could not find child care for his shift.[34]

What is the best way to deal with this problem? Some companies provide on-site day-care centers and find this fringe benefit a strong factor in retaining valuable employees who are also parents. Some companies that cannot afford this option offer centralized information and referral services to off-site child-care centers. Some organizations offer "vouchers" to help subsidize the parents' costs; others deduct child-care costs from their employees' pretax earnings, similar to tax-deferred retirement withholding plans.

Keep in mind, however, the resentment that builds among the nearly two-thirds of the U.S. work force who see employees with children receiving special treatment.[35] These other workers are often expected to work overtime, the night shift, or weekends while their coworkers who are parents arrive late or leave early to manage child-care demands. During the workday, these workers frequently must absorb extra work to cover for parents called away for child-related emergencies. A secretary in Chicago states, "If you don't have kids, it's assumed you don't have a life outside the office."[36]

Some employers are beginning to get the message. Quaker Oats Company offers a benefits plan that gives child-free employees an annual credit of $300 because they generate lower medical insurance costs for the employer. They can use the credit to purchase extra vacation days, life insurance, or other benefits. Spiegel Inc. offers flexible hours to everyone. Corning Incorporated is training its managers to avoid dumping extra work on workers without children. A Corning work/life consultant states, "That has helped to reduce jealousy between employees."[37]

Flexible Work Schedule Opportunities

To recruit and retain the top talent in the labor market, many organizations offer a variety of flexible work schedules. Demand for greater flexibility has increased in recent years, and some predict that more than 80 percent of large companies will offer some form of flexible work schedules by the year 2000.[38]

Flextime   **Flextime** typically includes a core time when all employees work, often 10 A.M. to 3 P.M. Employees can choose their own schedule during the flexible time, which may mean arriving at 7 A.M. or leaving at 7 P.M.

Compressed Workweek   Typically, a **compressed workweek** consists of four ten-hour days—for example, Tuesday through Friday, or Thursday through Sunday. Employees may be given the opportunity to adjust their work schedules to fit their lifestyle. One of the newest compressed workweek schedules, often called the 9/80, is growing in popularity. Employees work one extra hour each day for nine days, a total of eighty hours, and receive a three-day weekend every other week.[39]

Job Sharing   With **job sharing,** two employees share the responsibilities of one job. For example, one employee might work the mornings and the other work the afternoons. At Schreiber Foods, Inc., in Green Bay, Wisconsin, job sharing has worked so well that the company has produced a video outlining the options. The firm encourages all of its 2,600 employees to work out the details with a coworker.[40]

Telecommuting   The availability of powerful home-office computer and communication technologies, large-scale use of temporary workers due to massive downsizing, and the demands of workers who want to blend work and family have fueled a major increase in **telecommuting**—employees working at home at a personal computer linked to their employer's computer. In the year 2000, the number of telecommuters is expected to reach 15 million, up from 2.4 million in 1990.[41] When done correctly, telecommuting can increase employee productivity 15 to 20 percent and increase employee retention and morale.[42]

Phased Retirement   Older workers may choose **phased retirement** to reduce the number of hours they work over a period of time prior to their retirement. This option gives workers an opportunity to adjust more easily into a new phase of their lives, and companies benefit when older workers train those who will replace them.

HOW TO COPE WITH GENDER-BIASED BEHAVIOR

Traditional attitudes, beliefs, and practices are not changed easily. If you are a man or woman breaking into a nontraditional role, you will encounter resistance. In addition, you may be confused about how to act or may be overly sensitive about the way others treat you. As a result, if you are choosing a new role for yourself, you will need to learn new skills to control your own behavior as well as to confront some of the very real obstacles you will encounter.

Eliminate Sexual Harassment

One of the most sensitive problems between men and women in organizations is **sexual harassment,** or unwelcome verbal or physical behavior that affects a person's job performance or work environment. Most people believe sexual harassment is a problem for women only, but each year a large number of sexual harassment cases are filed by men. Research indicates that 90 percent of Fortune 500 companies have dealt with sexual harassment complaints from their workers. It is estimated that the problem costs the average large corporation $6.7 million a year in increased absenteeism, staff turnover, low morale, and low productivity.[43]

Under the law, sexual harassment may take one of two forms. The first is **quid pro quo** (something for something), which occurs when a person in a powerful position threatens the job security or a potential promotion of a worker who refuses to submit to sexual advances. These kinds of threats are absolutely prohibited, and employers are liable for damages under the Fair Employment Practices section of the Civil Rights Act. These behaviors can take the form of comments of a personal or sexual nature, unwanted touching and feeling, or demands for sexual favors.

The second form of sexual harassment involves the existence of a **hostile work environment.** Supreme Court decisions have held that sexual harassment exists if a "reasonable person" believes that the behavior is sufficiently severe or pervasive to create an abusive working environment, even if the victim does not get fired or held back from a promotion. A hostile work environment exists when supervisors or coworkers use sexual innuendo, tell sexually oriented jokes, display sexually explicit photos in the work area, discuss sexual exploits, and so on. Unlike quid pro quo harassment, hostile work environment claims tend to fall in a gray area: What is offensive to one person may not be offensive to another. The bottom line is that most kinds of sexually explicit language, conduct, and behavior are inappropriate in the workplace, regardless of whether such conduct constitutes sexual harassment within the legal meaning of the term.

Some experts believe that sexual harassment may be more a power issue than a gender issue. Gender bias is based on the attitude that one gender is superior to the other. Neil E. Schermitzler, human resources director of the central region of Wang Laboratories Inc., comments, "I sometimes think we haven't touched the real issue. . . . [Sexual harassment] is an issue of power and exclusion."[44] It often results when a worker's livelihood and professional survival depend on the goodwill of a superior. The worker is made to feel vulnerable.

Women breaking into fields dominated by men are a common target of sexual harassment. Some of the most serious sexual harassment charges have been filed by women employed in the military, the brokerage industry, skilled trades, and manufacturing. Historically, these employment areas have employed mostly men.

Ever since Professor Anita Hill accused Supreme Court nominee Judge Clarence Thomas of lewd and overbearing conduct toward her, the country has been trying to determine the difference between innocent comments and sexual harassment. The key word is *unwelcome.* Victims of sexual harassment need to tell the harasser, in no uncertain terms, that his or her behavior is inappropriate. Meanwhile, victims should record the occurrence in a journal that includes the date and details of the incident. They should also talk with coworkers, who can provide emotional support and help verify instances of harassment. Chances are, if one person is being harassed, others are as well. If the harasser continues the behavior, the victim should go to a higher authority, such as the harasser's supervisor or the organization's human resources division. Under the law, companies are legally liable if they do not immediately investigate the situation and take action to eliminate the offensive behaviors. These actions can include reprimand, suspension, or dismissal of the harasser. If you are being harassed, put the company on notice that *it* has a problem. Then document everything: whom you talked with, when, what actions that person took, what he or she said, what you said in response, and what was agreed on. If you decide to file charges, you will have to substantiate your complaint. Before you file charges, however, be sure you have used all the remedies available to you through your employer. Such policies are established to allow employees to discuss their questions and resolve their concerns internally rather than through litigation. If you do not "go through the channels" set up by your employer, your case probably will be dismissed from court. For example, six former employees, all women, filed sexual harassment charges, seeking $60 million in damages from TGI Friday's Inc. and two of its managers. Friday's has a toll-free, twenty-four-hour hot line available for all employees to call and register any complaint about anything. The plaintiffs never used that number; they never complained. The case was dismissed.[45]

To prevent sexual harassment, every company should have a written policy saying that such behavior will not be tolerated under any circumstances. The policy should describe in clear, nonlegalistic terms what harassment is, and the company should explain how to file a complaint. Procedures for speedy, fair, and confidential investigations should be established. Offenders should be swiftly disciplined.[46] When legal action is taken by an employee and fines are issued, sexual harassment can be expensive, and the economic impact can be dramatic.

Item: Mitsubishi Motors Manufacturing of America was the target of the largest sexual harassment suit in EEOC history. In addition to paying millions of dollars in legal and consulting fees, the company agreed to make substantial cash payments to plaintiffs. The company was accused of condoning sexual harassment at its plant in Normal, Illinois.[47]

Item: Wal-Mart Stores Inc. was ordered to pay $50 million in punitive damages to a former employee after a jury found she and other women endured abusive remarks from male coworkers and supervisors. The award was later reduced to $5 million by the judge.[48]

Although the courtroom doors are open for individuals to protect themselves from unwanted behavior, pressing a sexual harassment charge is a lengthy, expensive, and psychologically draining experience. After Clarence Thomas's Supreme Court confirmation hearings, the entire nation became aware that resolving sexual harassment cases often comes down to one person's word against the other's.

Is there any recourse for being wrongfully accused of sexual harassment in the workplace? Two men filed charges against Polaroid Corporation, claiming they were wrongly accused. Similar charges were brought against the New York newspaper *Newsday*. The plaintiffs lost after Polaroid spent $100,000 and *Newsday* spent $200,000 in legal fees.[49] Most organizations are being extremely cautious and thorough in their investigations of all sexual harassment claims to avoid these time-consuming and expensive charges.

Learn to Understand and Respect Gender Differences

As mentioned in Chapter 2, gender bias often acts as a filter that interferes with effective communication between men and women. In recent years, popular books such as *You Just Don't Understand: Women and Men in Conversation* by Deborah Tannen and *Men Are from Mars, Women Are from Venus* by John Gray have heightened awareness of the differences between women's and men's communication styles. These differences, according to Tannen, are due to linguistic style. **Linguistic style** refers to a person's speaking pattern and includes such characteristics as directness or indirectness, pacing and pausing, word choice, and the use of such elements as jokes, figures of speech, stories, questions, and apologies. Linguistic style is a series of culturally learned signals that we use to communicate what we mean.[50] Communication experts and psychologists have made the following generalizations concerning gender-specific communication patterns:

- Women tend to use questions in a variety of ways—to seek information, to express an opinion, or to state an objection. Men tend to use questions only to request information, and they often miss opinions and objections when stated as questions.
- Men tend to speak in a steady flow, free of pauses, interrupting each other to take turns. Women tend to speak with frequent pauses, which are used for turn-taking.
- Male-style humor tends to focus on banter, the exchange of witty, often teasing remarks. A woman's style is often based on anecdotes in which the speaker is more likely to mock herself than she is to make fun of another person.
- Women are likely to downplay their certainty; men are likely to minimize their doubts.[51]

Does linguistic style really make a difference? Let's assume that two employees, Mary and John, are being considered for promotion to a management position. The person who must make the decision wants someone who displays a high degree of self-confidence. If John is regularly displaying the "male" communication patterns described above, he may be viewed as the more confident candidate. But if the person making the promotion decision is searching for someone who is sensitive, an attentive listener, and a consensus builder, Mary may win the promotion. We know that people in positions of power tend to reward linguistic styles similar to their own.[52]

Jayne Tear, a consultant who specializes in gender dynamics in organizations, says workplace tension based on gender differences need not be a major problem. Such tension can be avoided by teaching employees the linguistic styles that are most often used by each sex and encouraging the interchangeable use of these styles depending on the situation.[53]

Once you understand the concept that men and women communicate in different ways, you can begin to flex your style. Refer to Table 16.1 for

Reprinted with special permission of King Features Syndicate.

TABLE 16.1

Workplace Tips for Avoiding Gender-Specific Language Barriers

Men can . . .

- think about women as business beings rather than sexual beings.
- recognize that, within their gender group, women are as unique as men.
- communicate with women based on their individuality, rather than on the characteristics of a stereotyped group.
- use general humor, not sexual humor.
- remember that even when intentions are good, the impact of your communication may be bad.
- follow this rule: When in doubt, do not make the statement or act out the thought.

Women can . . .

- stay calm when expressing feelings if they don't want to be branded as overemotional.
- express feelings verbally rather than nonverbally. Men are not always good at reading behavior.
- avoid male bashing.
- use general humor, not self-effacing humor.
- say what needs to be said concisely, without excessive apologies or disclaimers.
- recognize that a man may not understand the impact of his sexually related comment. If you are offended, say something at the time.

Source: Anita Bruzzese, "Working Toward a Truce in the Battle of the Sexes," *Gannett News Service,* August 9, 1994, p. B1.

more specific suggestions on how to communicate better with the opposite gender.

It's true: Men and women are different, but they have so much to learn from each other. Harvard psychologist Carol Gilligan offers a musical metaphor: "One can think of the oboe and the clarinet as different, yet when they play together, there is a sound that's not either one of them, but it doesn't dissolve the identity of either instrument."[54]

Learn New Organization Etiquette

As women enter into upper levels of management and men begin to work in support positions, the ways in which men and women deal with each other

Total Person Insight

"The only realistic resolution to the enduring male-female communication problem will be adaptation, and ongoing adjustments, to the opposite sex. Proving who's right and who's wrong, or even waiting patiently for the other gender to 'get it' and change, are not likely solutions. If men and women are going to be more effective in understanding each other, influencing each other and working together, then each sex needs to become more skilled in changing its natural communication pattern and adapting to the other gender."

JUDITH TINGLEY

Author, *Genderflex: Men and Women Speaking Each Other's Language at Work*

change subtly. Does this change require new rules of etiquette? In some cases, yes. The following guidelines may help you understand how to act in these new situations:

1. When a woman visits a man's office, he should rise from his desk to greet her. When a man enters a woman's office, she should rise from her desk.
2. Whoever has a free hand (could be a small woman) should help anyone carrying too heavy a load (could be a large man).
3. Women resent being "go-fers." A man in charge of a meeting should not expect a woman to take notes, answer the phone, or type material. A woman should not leap to serve coffee when it is time for a break. Men and women should rotate such clerical duties as taking the minutes of a meeting.
4. Whoever arrives first at a door should open it, and whoever stands in the front row in the elevator should get off first.
5. Whoever extends an invitation to lunch or dinner should in most cases pay the tab.
6. Training materials, memos, and so on should be written in gender-free language. Clerical and secretarial personnel should not be referred to only as "she" or "her" and management personnel only as "he" or "him."

The new etiquette provides a means to overcome old stereotypes and traditional ways of setting men and women apart solely on the basis of gender. It is likely that both men and women will feel somewhat awkward at first relating to each other as equal colleagues. By practicing these points of etiquette and adopting a positive, helpful attitude toward each other, men and women can help ease the transition from traditional to nontraditional roles. Women and men both will be winners.

Summary

Gender bias is discrimination based on widely held beliefs about the abilities, characteristics, and behavior of men and women. The traditional roles assigned to both genders limit their opportunities to choose careers and lifestyles best suited to their abilities and true interests.

Many men and women are breaking out of these traditional roles. Over the past few decades, women have entered the job world in increasing numbers and in professions previously considered all-male. As a result, men and women have a wider range of choices regarding marriage and children than ever before. Organizations are beginning to offer their employees options such as job sharing, flextime, and home-based work so that they can better handle the demands of work and family.

Women are still subject to a wage gap, earning less than the wages men receive for similar work, but the gap is narrowing. Moreover, the Department of Labor has confirmed that the glass ceiling does exist and is holding women back from achieving high-level positions in organizations.

Men are also choosing new roles for themselves. They are working to dispel the myth that men must always be in control, emotionally unexpressive, logical, and achievement oriented. They realize that the rigid male role has had adverse effects on men's health and on their relationships with women and other men. Men are learning to make conscious choices about marriage, children, and career emphasis that better fit their values systems. Men are choosing more personally rewarding careers that allow time for family responsibilities, even if they must sacrifice some material gain to do so.

Sexual harassment may be a problem for some men as well as women. It may take one of two forms: quid pro quo, the threat of job security or promotion in exchange for sexual favors, or sexually explicit language, photos, or innuendo that creates a hostile work environment. Most organizations have developed guidelines to help employees avoid harassment or fight it when it occurs.

Methods of coping with gender-biased behavior include learning how to effectively communicate with the opposite gender and observing the new rules of etiquette in the workplace.

Career Corner

Q. I am a middle-aged man working in an organization that used to be dominated by men. Now almost half of my colleagues are women, most of whom I respect a great deal. But I have heard horror stories about sexual harassment charges, and I am scared to death that I will say or do something wrong around my female colleagues. Help!

A. You are not alone in your fears about potential sexual harassment charges. There are, however, a few rules that might be helpful for both men and women.

1. Use the "same-gender" standard: If you are not sure whether a comment is appropriate, determine whether you would make the comment if your colleague was of your gender.
2. Try the "candid-camera" test: Would you be embarrassed if someone videotaped your behavior or comment? If your answer is yes, don't do it or say it!
3. Compliment on merit, not appearance: Be sure to praise a person's job skills, not what the individual is wearing or how he or she looks. This puts the person's status as a coworker above that of gender or appearance.

Key Terms

gender bias (sexism)
glass ceiling
flextime
compressed workweek
job sharing
telecommuting

phased retirement
sexual harassment
quid pro quo
hostile work environment
linguistic style

Review Questions

1. List some of the qualities men and women traditionally have been encouraged to develop.
2. List some of the characteristics of traditional roles that men and women are changing as a result of the men's and women's movements.
3. Describe the flexible work schedules that many organizations now offer.
4. What are some of the nontraditional choices regarding marriage and children open to men and women today?
5. What are some of the problems women still face as a result of discrimination in organizations?
6. Describe some of the difficulties men encounter when they attempt to make changes in their traditional role.
7. Explain the benefits and drawbacks to careers that follow the "mommy track" or "daddy track."
8. Explain the two illegal forms of sexual discrimination in the workplace, and give an example of each.
9. What steps can individuals take to eliminate sexual harassment? What do organizations need to do to help reduce sexual harassment litigation?

10. List some reasons why men and women tend to have problems communicating. What adjustments can be made to remove these barriers to effective human relations?

Application Exercises

1. The following situations represent either quid pro quo or hostile environment forms of sexual harassment in the workplace. Identify the form represented by each situation, and explain your reasoning. Describe the actions you might take if you were the potential victim in each incident.
   a. Julie thinks David is very handsome. She often stares at him when she thinks he is not looking. David is aware of Julie's staring and is very uncomfortable but is too shy and embarrassed to say anything to her.
   b. While sitting at her desk, Karen receives the following electronic message from her boss on her computer screen: "Can we discuss your possible promotion over dinner this evening?"
   c. At a convention reception, one of Joan's most important clients invites her out for cocktails and dinner. She politely declines. He announces loudly, "She won't go out to dinner with me, and I'm her best customer!" Under his breath he says, "Honey, if you want my business, you'd better cooperate." Joan's boss insists she go to dinner with the client.
2. On a sheet of paper, list and explain the various choices you would make when attempting to balance your career and family responsibilities. For example, will marriage be a part of your future? Will you have children? When? How will you provide care for these children while you and your spouse are at work? Would you prefer home-based work? Which flextime options would you consider valuable? Do you want to work for someone else or own your own business?
3. Over a period of one week analyze your verbal and nonverbal communications with people who are of the opposite gender. Try to determine if any linguistic style differences are apparent during conversations. If you discover style differences, try to determine if they serve as a barrier to effective communication.

Internet Exercise

Discrimination on the basis of gender is still a common problem for persons who are seeking initial employment or for individuals who want to advance on the job. Persons with disabilities also face discrimination. Barriers that limit opportunities in the work force are often artificial and invisible. The Glass Ceiling Commission has created a Web site that features information concerning these forms of discrimination. The Equal Employment Opportunity Commission (EEOC) also offers information related to employment discrimination. Visit these and other appropriate Web sites to find out what is being done to help employers and employees deal with this problem. Pay special attention to the resources (such as books, articles, and training programs) described. Prepare a list of the resources you would recommend to business owners and managers.

Case 16.1   **Mitsubishi's Cement Ceiling**

Twenty-nine female employees at Mitsubishi Motor Manufacturing of America in Normal, Illinois, charged they were victims of blatant sexual harassment by their fellow workers. Their complaints included the following: Women had to agree to have sex to obtain jobs. Drawings of genitals, breasts, and various sexual acts were placed on car fenders during production, labeled with women workers' names, then sent through the assembly line for all to see. Pictures of sex parties were passed around in the workplace. The women received little support from United Auto Workers union leaders, who often catered to their white male majority constituency. Their attitude was evident during tailgate parties outside the union hall that occasionally featured a performing stripper. Their response to sexual harassment complaints: "Hey, McDonald's is always hiring." Three years after the charges were filed, twenty-seven of the twenty-nine women settled out of court for an estimated $9.5 million.

Mitsubishi hired former secretary of labor Lynn Martin to review its workplace policies and procedures. She criticized the company's labor-relations systems and made thirty-four recommendations. In an attempt to comply, the company sent all factory workers through an eight-hour course in sexual harassment awareness, created a unit to investigate harassment claims, and hired several female and minority executives. But Mitsubishi's problems persisted. In 1997 the EEOC filed a class-action suit for 330 women, and the result was a $34 million settlement.

Few employees, men or women, ever leave Mitsubishi, because their average pay of $19 an hour exceeds the pay offered by most other employers in the Normal, Illinois, area. But women complain bitterly that they are regularly subjected to ridicule, often in sexually explicit terms, from their managers; those who object are often excluded from overtime opportunities or are moved to undesirable work schedules.

In the 1980s, many foreign companies whose management personnel, like Mitsubishi's, were not familiar with the American culture searched for isolated, homogeneous communities for their U.S. manufacturing locations. During the past few years, however, such companies are being forced to examine their treatment of their increasingly diverse work force, which includes women, minorities, and men sensitive to behaviors that belittle others.

Questions

1. What would you do if you were a sexually harassed Mitsubishi employee? What would you do if you observed sexual harassment but were not actually the victim?
2. Assume you have been hired to study the sexual harassment problems at the Mitsubishi plant and recommend changes. What changes do you feel are needed to stop sexual harassment?
3. In light of current news stories about Mitsubishi and other organizations accused of having hostile work environments, what do you think the future holds for organizations that refuse to comply with the sexual harassment laws?

Case 16.2	## Is This Progress?

W omen police officers are poised to move from being token representatives to a significant presence in the nation's police cars. In Los Angeles, for example, the city council passed a resolution requiring its police department to boost the number of women in its ranks from 14 percent to 44 percent. But the council's bold move was not cheered by some male police officers who still believe that "women have no place in a patrol car and are stealing men's jobs."

Following the success of women in the military service in the Gulf War, armed service officials were told that they must let women fly aircraft into combat. Some observers predict, however, that women who break into all-male squadrons will face verbal and nonverbal abuse from their male coworkers. The Navy's Tailhook investigation revealed that women pilots were forced to experience a degrading "initiation" process.

Dee Dee Myers, the first woman to be a presidential press secretary, was constantly said to be "out of the loop, excluded from the white male tribal circle." Her office was smaller and her rank and pay were lower than those of her male predecessors.

Although women are experiencing some success as they attempt to break through the glass ceiling, some men still stand in the way of their progress. But there is hope: Some big companies, motivated by a desire to diversify upper management, are putting out the word that only women need apply for some of their top jobs. George Schmutz, president of Corporate Directions, a career counseling and search firm, said several companies have told him, "We will interview men, but we are only going to hire women." This may be great news for women, but companies that place gender limits on their executive recruiting expose themselves to attacks from qualified men, who may not be given a chance to compete for the top jobs.

Questions

1. How do you feel about women entering traditionally male jobs?
2. How do you feel about the men who object to women entering these jobs?
3. Do men have the right to object to "women only" executive job openings? How do you think a court would decide this issue? Explain your reasoning.

PART VI

You Can Plan

for Success

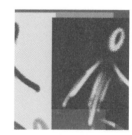

Chapter 17
A Life Plan for Effective Human Relations

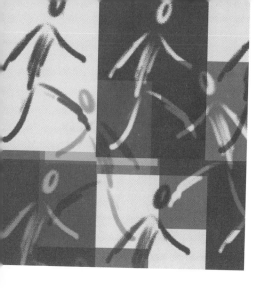

Chapter 17

A Life Plan

for Effective

Human Relations

Chapter Preview

After studying this chapter, you will be able to

1. Define success by standards that are compatible with your needs and values.
2. Learn how to better cope with life's uncertainties and disappointments.
3. Understand the forces that are influencing work/life balance.
4. Discuss the meaning of *right livelihood*.
5. Describe four nonfinancial resources that can enrich your life.
6. Provide guidelines for developing a healthy lifestyle.
7. Develop a plan for making needed changes in your life.

FOR YEARS CHARLES "ROCKY" RHODES worked seven-day weeks. As a cofounder and chief engineer of Silicon Graphics, he could pick among cutting-edge research and development projects at his company. He loved his work, but as the years passed, he felt the need for greater balance between work and family. One day Rhodes and his wife decided to take a hard look at their lives and develop some priorities. After much deliberation, they scribbled on a Post-it note the four priorities they agreed were most important: God, family, exercise, and work, in that order. They put the note on the refrigerator door, where it would be a daily reminder of what was really important in their lives. To reduce the tension between work and family, Rhodes gradually reduced his working hours. In the area of new product development, he assumed an advisory role that did not require full-time work. Today he works half-time and allocates the other hours to his family, volunteer work, and his church.[1] ■

No amount of training or education can fully prepare you for some of the experiences you will face in your career. There will usually be some unexpected rewards and a few major disappointments. Consider the experience of Lisa Latno, who found that a full-time job at Unum Life Insurance and a daily three-hour commute created major work/life tensions. She needed more time to raise her 2-year-old son and do the other things required of someone who blends work and family. Her request to work ten fewer hours a week was turned down by her supervisor, but another department manager invited Latno to take a thirty-hour-a-week job in her department.[2] Job flexibility helps many workers, men and women, achieve work/life balance.

The experiences of Rocky Rhodes and Lisa Latno remind us that our personal life and our work life are very much intertwined. The problems we experience at home (conflict with other family members, rebellion by a teenager, divorce) often have an influence on our performance at work. And a negative experience at work may influence how we feel and act away from the job. Working for a tyrannical boss may result in stress-filled days and sleepless nights.

In this chapter we help you construct a life plan that will enhance your relationships with people in your personal life and in your work life. This plan will also help you better manage the relationship you have with yourself. We discuss the meaning of success and suggest ways to cope with major disappointments such as losing your job or being passed over for a promotion. You will learn how to avoid being trapped by a lifestyle that offers financial rewards but little else. This chapter also helps you define your relationship with money and describes four nonfinancial resources that give meaning to life. Finally, you will learn how to develop the mental and physical fitness needed to keep up in today's frantic, fast-paced world.

TOWARD A NEW DEFINITION OF SUCCESS

Most of us have been conditioned to define success in narrow terms. Too frequently we judge our own success, and the success of others, by what is accomplished at work. Successful people are described as those who have a "good job" or have "reached the top" in their field. We sometimes describe the person who has held the same job for many years as successful. We do not stop to consider that such a person may find work boring and completely devoid of personal rewards.

From early childhood on we are taught to equate progress with pay increases and promotions. Amy Saltzman, author of *Downshifting*, notes that many people tend to set goals and measure success along a vertical career path that is often described as the "career ladder" or the "fast track." Saltzman says, "One is not successful, according to this school of thought, unless one is consistently moving up the ladder in some clearly quantifiable way."[3] Too often the person who is striving to achieve an immediate career goal (one more rung on the career ladder, for example) is forced to give up everything else that gives purpose and meaning to life. This may mean spending less time with family members and friends, spending less time keeping physically fit, abandoning vacation plans, and spending weekends at work. Achieving the next promotion may also require numerous relocations to places dictated by company officials.

Of course, the fast track is no longer an option for many employees. Today there are fewer rungs on the corporate ladder. One major goal of downsizing is to reduce the number of layers of management. The flattening of organizations will likely continue into the year 2000 and beyond.[4]

For those persons who have defined success in terms of larger paychecks earned by working overtime, the picture seems to be changing. Giving up time with friends and family, or giving up that part in the local community theater

---

Total Person Insight

"When it comes to defining a successful life in American Society, today's career professionals seem stuck between two ultimately dissatisfying extremes: dropping out completely and creating their own vision of a better world, or working within the system and speeding up their pace on the success treadmill."

AMY SALTZMAN

Author, *Downshifting: Reinventing Success on a Slower Track*

Here we see Tom Peters, noted author of best-selling business books, taking time to smell the flowers. Leisure time can provide us with the opportunity to relax and get rid of work-related stress. (Rafael Fuchs/Outline Press)

production, in return for more money seems to be less appealing to workers today. Juliet Schor, Harvard economist and author of *The Overworked American,* believes that during the next decade workers will give up income in exchange for more leisure time. She says, "People are very interested in issues like personal development, family, home and those kinds of things, so they are starting to want more from a job than just a paycheck; they're wanting flexibility, and that usually involves time."[5] She points out that many of the people who are continually required to work overtime feel trapped.

The Need for a New Model of Success

In recent years, a growing number of people are angry, disillusioned, and frustrated because they had to abruptly change their career plans. They gave their best efforts to an employer for ten, fifteen, or twenty years, and then the company eliminated their jobs. For years the firm said, "Take care of business and we'll take care of you," but then the situation changed. Under pressure from

new global competition, hostile takeovers, and the need to restructure, companies started getting rid of loyal workers. The unwritten and unspoken contract between the company and the employee was broken. Many of the people who lost their jobs during the past decade were once told that if they had ambition and worked tirelessly to achieve their career goals, success would be their reward. But the "reward" for many people has been loss of a job, loss of self-esteem, and increased anxiety about the future.

We should certainly feel sympathy for persons who have lost their jobs and watched their dreams dissolve. But there is another group of people who also merit our concern. These are the persons who put in long hours, climbed the ladder of success, and still have a job but have discovered that something is

---

Total Person Insight

"If I had only…
Forgotten future greatness
and looked at the green things and the buildings
and reached out to those around me
and smelled the air
and ignored the forms and the self-styled obligations
and heard the rain on the roof
and put my arms around my wife
… and it's not too late"

HUGH PRATHER

Poet; Author, *Notes to Myself: My Struggle to Become a Person*

---

missing from their lives. These people have a good job, a regular paycheck, and in some cases an impressive title, but they do not *feel* successful. How should we feel about the person who invested ten, fifteen, or twenty years in a job, gave up all or most of his or her leisure time, gave up quality time with friends and family, reached the top rung on the career ladder, and then discovered that life was empty and unfulfilling?

The traditional success model is slowly breaking down. This model defined success almost exclusively in terms of work life. The model emphasized working long hours, accomplishing work-related goals, and meeting standards often set by others. Lynn Lannon, president of the Lannon Group, a San Francisco–based consulting firm, says the old model results in "judging one's success by the standards of others, never feeling quite good enough and often feeling dissatisfied."[6]

The old model of success required us to be "one-dimensional" people for whom work is the single dimension. In the life of such a person, everything that has meaning seems to be connected to the job. When a person defines himself or herself by a job and then loses that job, what does that person have left? This is the question raised by Robert McCarthy, an outplacement counselor who works with people who have lost their jobs. He takes the position that people who are fired may be the fortunate ones if they come to the realization that they have meaning beyond their jobs. People who are able to broaden their perspectives, develop interests beyond their jobs, and put balance in their lives will usually not only achieve more self-fulfillment but also will be more valuable as employees.[7]

Loss of Leisure Time

Many Americans are beginning to understand that "all work and no play" is not good for their long-term mental and physical health. People who work too many hours often lose their ability to relate effectively to coworkers and family members. Some of America's best-managed companies are beginning to realize the negative consequences of long hours on the job and loss of leisure time. Perry Christensen, director of human resource strategy and planning for Merck and Company, says, "You can't build an effective company on a foundation of broken homes and strained personal relationships.[8]

In previous chapters we noted two trends that tend to erode leisure time: The number of hours people work per week has steadily increased over the years, and the use of pagers, fax machines, and cellular phones makes it increasingly difficult for people to escape the day-to-day demands of the workplace. The number of people who hold down more than one job has also increased.[9] U.S. workers work longer hours and spend less time on vacation than do workers in most other industrialized countries. A recent report by Hewitt Associates, an employee compensation firm, says a typical American worker with one year of service receives only ten days of paid vacation. By comparison, the same worker in Sweden, Denmark, Brazil, and Austria would receive thirty paid days off.[10] Germans, the very stereotype of industrious people, work 37.5 hours per week on average and receive several weeks of paid time off a year. In the United States many people work more than 55 hours a week.[11]

Developing Your Own Life Plan

The goal of this chapter is to help you develop a life plan for effective relationships with yourself and others. The information presented thus far has, we hope, stimulated your thinking about the need for a life plan. We have noted that personal life can seldom be separated from work life. The two are very much intertwined. We have also suggested that it is important for you to develop your own definition of success. Too frequently people allow others (parents, teachers, counselors, a spouse) to define success for them. Judging your success by the standards established by someone else may lead to a life of frustration.

Many people today are discovering that true success is a combination of achievements. Becoming too focused on one narrow goal may not provide the self-satisfaction you are seeking. One author makes this observation: "Everyone wants to be successful. But each person must have a personal definition of what success will feel like, and understand that true success rarely means having just one goal."[12] A narrow definition of success may actually prove to be counterproductive if it means giving up everything else that adds meaning to life.

Because work is such an important part of life, we now move to a discussion of items that will help you in your career planning. We discuss the concept of "right livelihood."

TOWARD RIGHT LIVELIHOOD

Visit Sena Plaza in downtown Santa Fe and you will see a public garden that is a wonderland of color and texture. The person responsible for this beautiful garden is Barbara Fix, a graduate of Stanford Law School who chose gardening over a high-powered law career. She says, "I've been offered many jobs in my life. I could have been on Wall Street making six figures, but the only job I ever hustled for was this one—six dollars an hour as the gardener at Sena Plaza."[13]

Barbara Fix is an example of someone who appears to have achieved "right livelihood." The original concept of right livelihood apparently came from the

The founders of Wild Rumpus Books, Collette Morgan and Tom Braun, have been able to compete successfully against the big megastores that are so common in Minneapolis. Many people who are in search of right livelihood are starting their own businesses. (David Graham)

teachings of Buddha. In recent years, the concept has been described by Michael Phillips in his book *The Seven Laws of Money* and by Marsha Sinetar in her book *Do What You Love . . . The Money Will Follow.* **Right livelihood** is work consciously chosen, done with full awareness and care, and leading to enlightenment. When Jason Wilson gave up a challenging business career to become a carpenter, he embraced the concept of right livelihood. He later started his own home construction business.[14] Ronald Sheade, once a vice president at a Fortune 1,000 company, now teaches eighth-grade science in a suburb of Chicago. He doesn't make big money anymore, but he loves teaching and now gets to spend more time with his family.[15] There are three characteristics to right livelihood.

Right Livelihood Is Based on Conscious Choice

Marsha Sinetar says, "When the powerful quality of conscious choice is present in our work, we can be enormously productive."[16] She points out that many people have learned to act on what others say, value, and expect and thus find conscious choice very difficult:

> It takes courage to act on what we value and to willingly accept the consequences of our choices. Being able to choose means not allowing fear to inhibit or control us, even though our choices may require us to act against our fears or against the wishes of those we love and admire.[17]

To make the best choices, you must first figure out what you like to do, as well as what you are good at doing. What you like doing most is often not obvious. It may take some real effort to discover what really motivates you. Students often get help from career counselors or explore a career option during a summer internship. If you are employed, consider joining a temporary project team. A team assignment may give you the opportunity to work closely with experts in such diverse areas as finance, marketing, or manufacturing.[18] If the team option is not available to you, seek a temporary assignment in some other department, or create a job that does not currently exist. The important thing is to try different things and discover what makes you happy.

Right Livelihood Places Money in a Secondary Position

People who embrace this concept accept that money and security are not the only rewards in life. Michael Phillips explains that "right livelihood has within itself its own rewards; it deepens the person who practices it."[19] In Chapter 7 we noted that internal motivation is often the result of doing work that is personally rewarding. For example, people who work in the social services usually do not earn large amounts of money, but many receive a great deal of personal satisfaction from their work. Barbara Fix does not make much money as a gardener, but the work provides enormous personal satisfaction. In her words, "Working in here is a privilege beyond measure. It's calming to the soul."[20]

Many people who once viewed success in terms of wealth, material possessions, and status are realizing that something is missing from their lives. They do not *feel* successful. They once felt pressured to "have it all" but now feel disappointed that their achievements have not brought them real happiness.

Right Livelihood Recognizes That Work Is a Vehicle for Self-Expression

Most of us spend from forty to sixty hours each week at work. Ideally, we should not have to squelch our real abilities, ignore our personal goals, and forget our need for stimulation and personal growth during the time we spend at work.[21] John Naisbitt and Patricia Aburdene, authors of *Re-Inventing the Corporation,* state that "in their hearts, people know that work should be fun and that it should be related to the other parts of their lives."[22] Most employees know intuitively that work should fulfill their need for self-expression, but this message has not been taken seriously by many leaders. Too few organizations truly empower workers and give them a sense of purpose. When employees feel that the company's success is their own success, they will be more enthusiastic about their work.

Marsha Sinetar says that although their jobs may differ, bicycle repair people, furniture makers, physicians, salespersons, and artists can use work as a means of self-expression and gain the satisfaction of growth and self-understanding.[23] In recent years, many people have abandoned secure, well-paying corporate jobs to start their own businesses. These entrepreneurs often report that their new businesses are a vehicle for self-expression.

For a growing number of people, right livelihood involves work/life balance. To achieve this balance, you will need the following skills:[24]

- *Clarify and act on your values.* This skill, discussed in Chapter 5, should be developed *before* you interview for a job. Mark Buzek, a recent graduate of Ohio State, decided not to take a job that would require frequent relocation and excessive travel. Although he is not married, he has strong ties with his parents, two sisters, and a brother in Ohio. Staying close to family members is an important value in his life. Sarah Schroeder, another recent graduate, says she cut off interviews with several employers who expect continuous sixty-hour-plus workweeks.[25]
- *Build trusting relationships at work.* What will be the reaction of coworkers if you take parental leave, leave work early to attend events that involve your children, refuse to work weekends? You are more likely to get support from those who know what is important in your life, value your friendship, and trust you to do the right thing.

- *Ask for what you need from bosses and family members.* Talk about your desire to maintain work/life balance. Be open and frank about what is important to you. Many people keep silent on work/life balance issues for fear of being seen as "uncommitted" to the job.
- *Learn to accept from yourself less than 100 percent some of the time.* Liz Landon, an employee of Andersen Consulting, recalls some advice she received from her boss: "Don't get crispy fried in the business. The insidious suction of achievement could leave you with no soul."[26] Do your best, but do not let the demands you place on yourself create major work/life tensions.

Thinking / Learning Starters

1. Do you agree that many people define success in terms that are too narrow? Reflect on your personal knowledge of friends and family members before answering this question.

2. In your opinion, does the concept of right livelihood seem realistic? Is right livelihood an option for everyone, or only a select few? Explain.

Defining Your Relationship with Money

Money is a compelling force in the lives of many people. It often influences selection of a career and the amount of time and energy invested in that career. Many people are pursuing money with the misguided belief that it is the key to happiness, and a significant number believe money is the only meaningful measure of success.[27] Melvyn Kinder, author of *Going Nowhere Fast,* says many people are on a money treadmill: "The money treadmill is built on a misconception about what money is, what it does, and what it means. We have been brainwashed into thinking money itself, once we amass it sufficiently, will bring us happiness and an end to insecurity."[28]

The money treadmill can be a trap, especially when you do not know what amount of money is enough. If you think that having *more* money is going to produce happiness or peace of mind, will you ever earn enough? Many people accept the "myth of scarcity." They have a mind-set or belief that "I don't have enough _____." Money becomes the lightning rod for the scarcity notion.[29] With this mind-set, any extra money earned is quickly spent on the things you think you do not have enough of. What might have been "wants" in the past (a big-screen TV set, a bigger home, a new car) now become "needs." Once you turn your wants into needs, then the need to work more overtime, hold down a second job, or continue a dual-earner arrangement intensifies. If you reject the myth of scarcity, you will have more time and energy to enjoy what you already have.[30]

Many Americans are locked into a work-and-spend cycle. As debts increase, people give up leisure time to make more money. As the treadmill continues to roll, some people become too tired to enjoy active leisure activities such as hiking, swimming, or playing a round of golf. The alternative is involvement in less satisfying activities such as sitting passively in front of the television set. The end result of the work-and-spend cycle is frequently a decline in the quality of life.

During the 1980s, the common view was that there would always be more money to pay off debts, so many people reduced or stopped saving and spent more. In the 1990s, we have seen growing income inequality and a decline in real compensation for many workers. Many economists predict that more workers will experience a decline in their standard of living during the years ahead.[31] These trends indicate that we must learn to manage our financial resources with as much efficiency as possible.

Competence in managing your personal finances is no less important than competence in managing your career. What matters most is not how much you earn but how much you keep. It is difficult to take career risks (leaving a job you dislike) unless you are able to build a financial cushion. Here are some tips on how to manage your personal finances:

- *Determine where your income is going.* With a simple record-keeping system, you can determine how much you spend each month on food, housing, clothing, transportation, and other things. Search for spending patterns you may want to change.
- *Spend less than you earn.* To do this, you may need to get rid of some credit cards, eat fewer meals at restaurants, use public transportation instead of driving your car, or make some other lifestyle change.
- *Maintain a cash cushion.* If you lost your job today, how long could you live on your current cash reserves? Financial consultants suggest that cash reserves should be equal to the amount you earn during a two-month period.
- *Develop a personal financial plan.* With a financial plan, you are more likely to achieve your financial goals. Without a plan, you will likely follow a haphazard approach to management of your finances.

Com-Corp Industries, a manufacturing plant based in Cleveland, Ohio, sees personal money management skills as one key to reducing conflict in the workplace. Employees who cannot live within their means are often under great stress and are more likely to experience interpersonal problems at work and at home. The company provides employees with classes on such subjects as developing a household budget and wise use of credit.[32]

Total Person Insight

"Keep in mind that there is no harder work than thinking—really thinking—about who you are and what you want out of life. Figuring out where your goals and your skills match up is a painful, time-consuming process."

JULIE CONNELLY

Contributing Editor, *Fortune*

Nonfinancial Resources

If you become totally focused on your financial resources, if you are caught up in the work-and-spend cycle, then chances are you have ignored your **nonfinancial resources.** And it is often the nonfinancial resources that make the biggest contribution to a happy and fulfilling life. A strong argument can be made that the real wealth in life comes in the form of good health, peace of mind, time spent with family and friends, learning (which develops the mind), and healthy spirituality. Paul Hwoschinsky, author of *True Wealth,* makes this observation about nonfinancial resources: "If you are clear about who you are, and clear about what you want to do, and bring your financial and non-financial resources together, it's extraordinary what can happen. I encourage people to really honor their total resources, and magical things happen. New options occur."[33] If you focus most or all of your attention on work, and you suffer a major work-related disappointment, then the result will likely be feelings of depression and despair. Thoughts such as "Now I have lost everything" can surface when you fail to get a promotion, find out that you were not selected to be a member of a special project team, or learn that your job has been eliminated. If you fully understand the power of your nonfinancial resources, then work-related disappointments are easier to cope with. The starting point is to realize that *most* of your resources are nonfinancial. During periods of great uncertainty, it is especially important that you think about your nonfinancial assets and consider ways to enhance them. We briefly discuss four nonfinancial resources that can enrich your life: physical and mental health, education and training (intellectual growth), leisure time (time for family, socializing, recreation), and healthy spirituality (see Figure 17.1).

Physical and Mental Health Is the statement "Health means wealth" just a worn-out cliché, or is this slogan a message of inspiration for people who want to get more out of life? If good health is such an important nonfinancial

FIGURE 17.1

Put Balance In Your Life

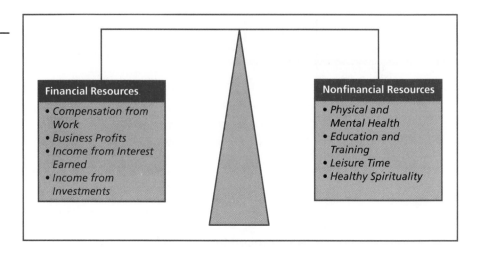

asset, then why are so many people flirting with self-destruction by eating the wrong foods, drinking too much, exercising too little, and generally choosing unhealthy lifestyles? The answer to the second question may be lack of awareness of the benefits of physical fitness. Susan Smith Jones, a fitness instructor at UCLA and author of *Choose to Be Healthy,* offers these benefits of good health:

- There is an interrelationship between health and outlook on life. For example, when the physical body is fit, toned, and strong, this condition has a positive effect on the mind. We are more likely to experience higher levels of self-esteem, feel a greater sense of self-confidence, and have a more positive outlook on life.
- Poor health tends to interfere with everything else in life: family harmony, work schedules, and relationships.
- Regular exercise and a healthy diet produce greater mental clarity, a higher energy level, and a more youthful appearance.[34]

Jones states that good health is something you must *choose* to have. She says, "Regardless of the lifestyle you've lived until now, you can, at any moment, choose differently."[35] If your breakfast is currently five cups of coffee and a danish, you can choose to change your diet. If you are spending thirty to forty hours a week sitting in front of a TV set, you can choose to spend that time in a different way. Your current level of health is the result of many choices you made in the past. Later in this chapter we discuss ways to form new habits that will help you achieve vibrant health.

Education and Training (Intellectual Growth)   It is sometimes easy to take for granted the time and energy required to earn a high school diploma, a certificate of completion in a technical field, a college degree, or some other form of recognition of achievement in education and training. We should view these achievements as important nonfinancial assets.

Throughout life we must continue to acquire this important resource. The time when you could achieve career success with just hard work and loyalty has passed. Today, employees are likely to be judged and rewarded on the basis of performance. Michael Hammer, co-author of *Re-Engineering the Corporation*, says, "You have to get results, and you have to continually update, train and develop yourself so that you're ready for tomorrow's jobs.[36] The expression "never stop learning" has never had more relevance than it does today. Here are some tips on how to acquire the skills and abilities you need:

- *Think of yourself as a unique product.* To maintain value in the marketplace, you must keep up-to-date. What skills and capabilities do you need to maintain or increase your value?[37]
- *Be selective in what you learn.* Learning often requires large amounts of time and energy, so consider carefully what unit of knowledge or skill will generate the most improvement.[38]
- *Take advantage of various learning pathways.* It helps to think of your job as a learning resource. Take full advantage of instructional programs offered by your employer. Volunteer for assignments that will provide new learning opportunities. And look outside the company at community college classes or programs offered by Toastmasters, Dale Carnegie, or other organizations.[39]

Leisure Time   Leisure time can provide an opportunity to relax, get rid of work-related stress, get some exercise, spend time with family and friends, or simply read a good book. Many people think they want more leisure time, but when it is available, they do not know what to do. Some people even feel guilty when they are not working. In her book *Downshifting,* Amy Saltzman talks about the problems Americans have with leisure time:

> The fact is, leisure today has something of a negative connotation. Having too much leisure implies we are wasting time and not working hard enough to get ahead. With so little time and so much of it devoted to professional pursuits, spending a Saturday afternoon on the front porch reading a book, talking to the neighbors or writing a letter to a friend is out of the question.[40]

If you are working for someone who is on the fast track, someone who may have given up all or most of his or her leisure time, you may be pressured to work at the same pace. If your boss is constantly trying to meet impossible deadlines and deal with last-minute rushes, you may feel the need to give up time for recreation or family. If this happens, try to identify the consequences of being overworked. Look at the situation from all points of view. If you refuse to work longer hours, what will be the consequences for your relationship with the boss, your relationship with other employees, your future with the organization?[41] You have choices, but they may be difficult ones. If it looks as though the pressure to work longer hours will never end, you may want to begin searching for another job.

Is it worth taking some risks to protect the leisure time you now have? Should you increase the amount of leisure time available in your life? Consider the following benefits of leisure time:

- Maintaining social connections with friends and family can be good for your health. A growing number of studies show that if you have strong and fulfilling relationships, you may live longer, decrease your chances of becoming sick, and cope more successfully when illness strikes.[42] Time spent with friends and family can be a powerful source of mental and physical renewal.
- One of the best ways to feel satisfied about your work is to get away from it when you begin to feel worn out. People who take time off from work often return with new ideas, a stronger focus, and increased energy. When you discover that end-of-the week exhaustion is still hanging around Monday morning, it's time to take some vacation or personal days.[43]
- An excellent way to increase your social connections and improve your own health is to become a volunteer. Research indicates that volunteers experience pleasurable physical sensations such as feelings of warmth, well-being, and calmness, and increased energy levels.[44] Polaroid Corporation will match time given to charitable groups with cash donations, and AT&T gives each employee a paid day for volunteer work.[45] A growing number of college students are getting involved in volunteer projects.

If you want more leisure time, then you must establish your priorities and set your goals. This may mean saying no to endless requests to work overtime or rejecting a promotion. Achieving success does not always require seven-day workweeks and time away from family and friends. Sometimes you must pull back from the endless demands of work and "get a life."

Healthy Spirituality   A discussion of nonfinancial resources would not be complete without an introduction to healthy spirituality. To become a "whole" or "total" person requires movement beyond the concrete, material aspects of life to the spiritual side of the human experience. Healthy spirituality can bring a higher degree of harmony and wholeness to our lives and move us beyond self-centeredness.

Spirituality can be defined as an inner attitude that emphasizes energy, creative choice, and a powerful force for living. It frees us to become positive, caring human beings.[46]

Spirituality encompasses faith, which can be described as what your heart tells you is true when your mind cannot prove it. For some people, faith exists within the framework of a formal religion; for others it rests on a series of personal beliefs such as "Give others the same consideration, regard, kindness, and gentleness that you would like them to accord you."[47]

An understanding of the many aspects of spirituality can give us an expanded vision of what it means to be human. Although spirituality is often associated with religion, it should be viewed in broader terms. Robert Coles, of Harvard Medical School, likes a definition of spirituality given to him by an 11-year-old girl:

> I think you're spiritual if you can escape from yourself a little and think of what's good for everyone, not just you, and if you can reach out and be a good person—I mean live like a good person. You're not spiritual if you just talk spiritual and there's no action. You're a fake if that's what you do.[48]

The words of this young girl remind us that one dimension of spirituality involves showing concern and compassion for others. It means turning away from rigid individualism and investing some time and energy in helping others. It means in some cases rolling up our sleeves and getting involved. We can enhance our spirituality through volunteer work, taking the time to listen to a coworker who is trying to resolve a serious personal problem, helping a stranded motorist, or simply writing a personal note of appreciation to someone at work who has given us assistance.

In many ways, large and small, work can be made more spiritual. Some of America's most successful business leaders have made this discovery. J. C. Penney, who built one of the nation's largest retail chains, adopted the golden rule as a key operating principle of his company. The philosophy of Worthington Industries is expressed in a single sentence: "We treat our customers, employees, investors and suppliers as we would like to be treated."[49] Hudson Food Inc. hired a chaplain to provide support and counseling to troubled employees.[50] Lotus Development Corporation formed a "soul" committee to examine the company's management practices and values. The company wants to find ways to make the work environment as humane as possible.[51] Edward Bednar teaches Zen Buddhist meditation techniques to employees working in the Wall Street area. He is attempting to help them live a more contemplative life.[52] At

Total Person Insight

"Not only is it possible to unite the worlds of business and spirituality, the resulting synergy creates benefits for both worlds."

FRED HUYGHUE

President, SSiM Group

the Hazelwood, Missouri, Ford Motor plant a nondenominational prayer group meets regularly.[53]

Spirituality is present in people who have a zest for life and are enthusiastic about experiencing its richness. Visiting an art gallery, listening to a concert, or walking near the ocean can stimulate healthy spirituality.

Healthy spirituality can often serve as a stabilizing force in our lives. As noted in Chapter 14, the various twelve-step programs (Alcoholics Anonymous is one example) emphasize the need for a spiritual connection. "Working the steps" means, among other things, turning life over to a higher power. This spiritual connection seems to give hope to persons who feel a sense of loneliness and isolation. Although the spiritual component of twelve-step programs has not been fully explained by the scientific community, it is viewed as an important part of the healing process.

For many people, a commitment to a specific religion is an important dimension of spirituality. Active membership in a religious group provides an opportunity to clarify spiritual values and achieve spiritual direction. If you do not attend the services of some religious group at a church, synagogue, temple, mosque, whatever—investigate a place of worship that seems compatible with your general orientation and attend a few times. If this experience tends to nurture your spiritual life, try to incorporate the core beliefs into your life.[54] For many people, membership in a religious community provides social connections—an extended family that they can depend on for social support.[55]

Healthy spirituality can be a positive, enlightening force in our lives. It can grow during quiet times when we reflect on the meaning of life, meditate, pray, or enjoy nature during a long walk in the woods. These activities draw our focus away from ourselves and the anxieties in our lives. We are more likely to experience healthy spirituality when we avoid self-pity and self-criticism and stay connected to others.

As more companies accept the whole person in the workplace, healthy spirituality will grow in importance. Hyler Bracey, consultant and author of *Managing from the Heart*, said, "We used to check our feelings, health, sexuality, spirituality and family problems at the door of the workplace. We've matured enough to get beyond that. The unspeakable is now acceptable."[56]

Total Person Insight

"Take time for nurturing your wellness. If you don't take time for wellness, you are going to have to make time for sickness."

Susan Smith Jones

Fitness Instructor; Author, "Choose to Be Healthy and Celebrate Life"

DEVELOPING A HEALTHY LIFESTYLE

Earlier in this chapter we noted that a healthy lifestyle can provide a higher energy level, a greater sense of self-confidence, and generally a more positive outlook on life. People who maintain good health usually have more endurance, spend less time feeling tired or ill, and miss less work than persons who are not physically fit. Good health is receiving greater attention today because many Americans are investing more time and energy in their work. They are being asked to work longer hours and do more in less time. Good health can help combat stress and tension at work and at home.

There is another important reason to adopt a healthy lifestyle. Throughout the past decade, the cost of health care has steadily increased, and several million Americans have lost their health insurance.[57] The old saying "I can't afford to get sick" is on the minds of many workers today.

The first step toward adopting a healthy lifestyle is to become well informed—to read, study, and learn what can be done to maintain your current level of health or improve your health. In this section we offer guidelines that form the framework for a good diet and a good exercise program. The second step is to determine what changes you need to make in your lifestyle and then make those changes. For many people, step one does not automatically lead to step two. Present-day Americans have access to more information about nutrition and exercise than any previous generation, but many refuse to give up poor eating habits and adopt an exercise program.

For a growing number of people, meditation is an important key to achieving a healthy lifestyle. Here we see a Hatha Yoga class at Yoga Works in Santa Monica, California, where people learn breathing techniques. (A. Ramey/ PhotoEdit)

Guidelines for a Healthy Diet

Eating the right foods can improve your health, boost your energy level, and in some cases extend your life. The link between health and diet is quite clear. Although we do not know enough about nutrition to identify the "ideal diet" for every person (food needs differ depending on age, body size, gender, physical activity, and other conditions), we can rely on dietary guidelines that are suitable for most Americans.[58]

Eat a Variety of Foods   Eating a variety of foods is important because you need more than forty different nutrients for good health: vitamins and minerals, amino acids (from proteins), essential fatty acids (from fats and oils), and sources of energy (calories from carbohydrates, fats, and proteins).[59] If you eat a variety of foods, you are more likely to maintain a well-balanced diet, because most foods contain more than one nutrient (see Figure 17.2).

FIGURE 17.2

Recommended Food
Groups and Amounts
Necessary for a
Healthy Diet

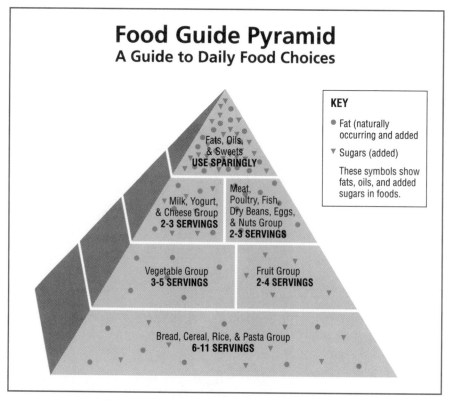

Source: U.S. Department of Agriculture/U.S. Department of Health and Human Services.

Cut Down on Fatty Foods The foods that are popular with many Americans are relatively high in fat, especially saturated fat, which contributes to high blood cholesterol levels. Many restaurant foods are high in fat because it gives menu items the flavor people often seek when eating out (see Table 17.1). Heart disease and certain kinds of cancer are byproducts of a high-fat diet.

Although diet is the most important factor in lowering cholesterol, exercise can help. About ninety minutes of aerobic exercise per week along with dietary changes has been found to lower total cholesterol.

Eat Foods with Adequate Starch and Fiber Foods high in starch, such as breads made with whole grains, dry beans and peas, and potatoes, contain many essential nutrients. Many starches also add dietary fiber to your diet. A growing number of scientists believe that high-fiber diets can help reduce the odds of getting cancer of the colon. Some cereals and most fruits and vegetables are good sources of fiber.

Avoid Too Much Sodium A common byproduct of excess sodium is high blood pressure. In the United States, where sodium-rich diets are very common, about one in four adults has elevated blood pressure. In populations with low sodium intakes, high blood pressure is very uncommon.[60] The recommended daily intake of sodium is 1,100 to 2,400 milligrams.

If You Drink Alcohol, Do So in Moderation Alcoholic beverages are high in calories and low in nutrients and cause serious health risks when used in

TABLE 17.1

Food Choices That Are High in Fat and Sodium

	Fat (grams)	Sodium (milligrams)	Calories
Sara Lee Bran Muffin (large)	22	470	440
Taco Bell's Taco Salad	61	910	905
Hot Pockets Ham 'n' Cheese	15	840	340
Long John Silver's Caesar with Chicken Wrap	73	3,710	1,450
Burger King's Double Whopper with Cheese	61	1,245	935

Source: *University of California at Berkeley Wellness Letter*, January 1998, p. 3; *University of California at Berkeley Wellness Letter*, July 1997, p. 3; *Tufts University Diet & Nutrition Letter*; Denise Webb, "Nutrition Now—Eat Right at a Fast-Food Restaurant," *Redbook Magazine*, July 1991.

excess. When alcohol is consumed in excess of one or two drinks per day, there tends to be a strong relationship between alcohol intake and high blood pressure. Excessive alcohol consumption has been linked to liver damage and certain types of cancer.[61]

With the help of these healthy diet guidelines, you can develop your own plan for achieving a healthful diet. Keep in mind that good nutrition is a balancing act. You want to select foods with enough vitamins, minerals, protein, and fiber but avoid too much fat and sodium. You want to consume enough calories to maintain the energy level required in your life but avoid weight gain. Get in the habit of checking the "Nutritional Facts" labels, which reveal the fat and sodium content of foods. Prior to developing your own diet plan, consider getting advice from a medical doctor or someone with expertise in nutrition.

Improving Your Physical Fitness

With regard to exercise, people often choose one of two extreme positions. Some adopt the point of view that only high-intensity activities (marathon running, high-impact aerobics) increase physical fitness. These people believe in the "no-pain, no-gain" fitness approach. The other extreme position is to become a "couch potato" and avoid all forms of exercise. Both positions should be avoided.

Physical fitness can be defined as the ability to perform daily tasks vigorously and have enough energy left over to enjoy leisure activities. It is the ability to endure difficult and stressful experiences and still carry on. Physical fitness, which involves the performance of the lungs, heart, and muscles, can also have a positive influence on mental alertness and emotional stability.[62] Research indicates that we can achieve and maintain physical fitness with a moderate exercise program. For most people, a program that involves regular physical activity at least three times a week and includes sustained physical exertion for twenty to thirty minutes is adequate.[63] This modest investment of time and energy will give you a longer and healthier life.

You do not need to become an obsessive fitness fanatic to achieve lifesaving benefits from exercise. Start slowly with an aerobic fitness activity you feel you will enjoy. Walking, swimming, running, low-impact aerobics, and jogging are aerobic exercise. When we engage in aerobic exercise, the body is required to improve its ability to handle oxygen.[64] These exercises strengthen the heart, burn up calories, increase stamina, and help release tension. Other examples of aerobic exercise are cross-country skiing, rope skipping, skating, rowing, and bicycling. Some people find it easier to stay with an exercise program that includes a variety of fitness activities, such as swimming, walking, and weight training. This approach helps exercise the whole body and avoid the boredom that sometimes comes with just one type of exercise.[65]

If you are younger than 35 and in good health, you probably do not need to see a doctor before beginning an exercise program. If you are older than 35 and have been inactive for several years, consult your doctor before engaging in vigorous exercise.[66]

PLANNING FOR CHANGES IN YOUR LIFE

Throughout this book we have emphasized the concept that you can control your own behavior. In fact, during these turbulent times changes in your behavior may be one of the few things under your control. If making changes in your life seems to be a logical course of action at this point, then it is time to do some planning. The starting point is to clearly identify the personal growth goals that can make a difference in your life. What are some behaviors you can adopt (or alter) that will make an important positive change in your life? Once you have identified these behaviors, you can set goals and do what is necessary to achieve them. At the end of Chapter 1 you were encouraged to complete the Human Relations Abilities Assessment (HRAA) Form that is in the appendix of this book (see Application Exercise 1 in Chapter 1). If you completed this instrument, then you no doubt gained awareness of your strengths and a better understanding of the abilities you want to improve. Now would be a good time to complete the instrument a second time and determine if your *X*s have moved to the right on the various scales. Completion of the HRAA Form will help you identify the behaviors you want to change.

The Power of Habits

Before we discuss specific goal-setting methods, let us take a look at the powerful influence of habits. Some habits, like taking a long walk three or four times a week, can have a positive influence on our well-being. Simply saying "Thank you" when someone does a favor or pays a compliment can be a habit. Other habits, such as smoking, never saying no to requests for your time, feeling jealousy, or constantly engaging in self-criticism, are negative forces in our lives. Stephen Covey, author of *The 7 Habits of Highly Effective People,* makes this observation: "Habits are powerful factors in our lives. Because they are consistent, often unconscious patterns, they constantly, daily, express our character and produce our effectiveness . . . or ineffectiveness."[67]

Breaking deeply embedded habits, such as impatience, procrastination, or criticism of others, can take a tremendous amount of effort. The influences supporting the habit, the actual root causes, are often repressed in the subconscious mind and forgotten.[68] How do you break a negative habit or form a positive habit? The process involves five steps.

Motivation Once you are aware of the need to change, you must develop the willingness or desire to change. After making a major commitment to change, you must find ways to maintain your motivation. The key to staying motivated is to create a sense of urgency that is so intense you feel compelled to act on your desire to change. You must continuously remind yourself why you want to change a bad habit or form a new habit.[69] If you are trying to break the habit of overeating, for example, try to visualize all of the benefits that will come from a change in your eating habits.

Knowledge   Once you clearly understand the benefits of breaking a habit or forming a new one, you must acquire the knowledge you need to change. Seek information, ask for advice, or learn from the experiences of others. This may involve finding a mentor, joining a group, or gathering sufficient material and teaching yourself. For example, suppose you decide you need to lose weight. Your first step might be to visit a bookstore and buy one or two books on weight reduction practices. Let's assume the books help but you discover that reading is not enough. Your next step might be to talk with others who share the same goal. You might consider joining a support group or talking to a counselor or an expert in nutrition. In the process of acquiring information, you are actually gaining a better understanding of the habit you want to learn or unlearn.

Practice   Information is only as useful as you make it. This means that to change your behavior you must *practice* what you have learned. If you are a shy person, does this mean you need to volunteer to make a speech in front of several hundred people? The answer is no. Although there is always the rare individual who makes a major change seemingly overnight, most people find that the best and surest way to develop a new behavior is to do so gradually. This is particularly true if you feel a lot of anxiety about changing. Take your time. Allow yourself to ease into your new behavior until you feel comfortable with it.

Feedback   Whenever you can, ask for feedback as you attempt to change a habit. Your progress will be much faster than it would be if you used only the trial-and-error method. Everyone has blind spots, particularly when trying something new. You will often need to rely on the feedback of others to tell you when you are off course or when you have really changed—sometimes you are too close to the process to tell.

Reinforcement   When you see yourself exhibiting the type of behavior you have been working to develop—or when someone mentions that you have changed—reward yourself! The rewards can be simple, inexpensive ones—treating yourself to a movie, a bouquet of flowers, a favorite meal, or a special event. This type of reinforcement is vital when you are trying to improve old behaviors or develop new ones. Do not postpone rewarding yourself until the goal is reached. Intermediate success is just as important as the final result.

The Goal-Setting Process

Many years ago J. C. Penney, founder of the large retail chain, made a strong statement regarding the value of having goals: "Give me a stock clerk with a goal, and I will give you a man who will make history. Give me a man without a goal, and I will give you a stock clerk."[70] Penney recognized that goals give direction to our lives. Setting and achieving personal goals contributes to emotional well-being. It gives us a sense of personal control and a greater feeling of confidence in ourselves.[71] With the awareness of self-control comes the strength to accept more responsibility for our own life.

Goals should be an integral part of your plan to break old habits or form new ones. You will need an assortment of goals that address the different needs of your life. After a period of serious reflection, you may be facing unlimited goal-setting possibilities. Where do you begin? We hope that reading the previous chapters in this book, completing the HRAA Form, and reviewing the material in this chapter will help you narrow the possibilities.

The goal-setting process requires that you be clear about what you want to accomplish. If your goal is too general or vague, progress toward achieving that goal will be difficult to observe. Goals such as "I want to be a success" or "I desire good health" are much too general. The more specific the goal, the easier it will be for you to achieve.[72]

A very important step in the goal-setting process is to put the goal in writing. Kazuo Wada, chair of the retail giant Yaohan International Group, strongly recommends written goals. He says, "If you write down a goal, it becomes part of your consciousness."[73] His approach is to put his goals in writing again and again until he achieves them. Although the power of written goals is widely recognized, many people do not put their goals in writing. A written goal, reviewed daily, is much more likely to be achieved. Achieving your goals will usually require hard work and effort over a period of time. The process of achieving your goals, however, can be very rewarding.

THE CHOICE IS YOURS

Are you ready to develop a life plan for effective human relations? We hope the answer is yes. One of the positive aspects of personal planning is that you are making your own choices. You decide what kind of person you want to be and then set your own standards and goals. The results can mean not only career advancement and financial benefits but also the development of strong, satisfying relationships with others. These relationships may be the key to future opportunities, and you in turn may be able to help others achieve their goals.

In the opening chapter of this text, we talked about the total person approach to human relations. By now, we hope you realize that you are someone special! You have a unique combination of talents, attitudes, values, goals, needs, and motivation—all in a state of development. You can decide to tap your potential to become a successful, productive human being, however *you* understand those terms. We hope this book helps you develop your human relations skills and to become what you want to be. You can turn the theories, concepts, and guidelines presented here into a plan of action for your own life and career. We wish you the best!

Summary

The traditional definitions of success that most of us know are too confining. They view success almost entirely in terms of measurable job achievements. These definitions leave out the intangible successes to be had in private and in professional life.

Many people today are discovering that true success is a combination of achievements. Achieving right livelihood is one important dimension of success. Right livelihood is work consciously chosen, done with full awareness and care, and leading to enlightenment. Right livelihood is based on conscious choice. Although right livelihood recognizes that work is a vehicle for self-expression, it is a concept that places money in a secondary position. People who choose right livelihood are more likely to have high self-esteem, are self-disciplined, and have established meaningful goals.

A person's nonfinancial resources make one of the biggest contributions to a happy and fulfilling life. Each of us has four nonfinancial resources that can enrich our lives: physical and mental health, education and training (intellectual growth), leisure time (time for family, socializing, recreation), and healthy spirituality. These nonfinancial resources can be acquired throughout our lives.

Many Americans are working to achieve healthy lifestyles. Healthy lifestyles can give us a higher energy level, a greater sense of self-confidence, and generally a more positive outlook. People who maintain good health usually have more endurance, spend less time feeling tired or ill, and miss less work than persons who are not physically fit.

Planning for changes in your life often requires breaking negative habits or forming positive habits. The process of breaking habits and forming new ones involves five steps: motivation, knowledge, practice, feedback, and reinforcement. Goal setting is also an integral part of a successful plan to make changes. Unspecified or vague goals, goals that are not put in writing, are harder to reach and contribute less than they could to a productive, enriching life.

Key Terms

right livelihood
nonfinancial resources

spirituality
physical fitness

**Review
Questions**

1. What have been the traditional criteria used to measure success? What are some of the reasons we need a new model for success in our society?
2. Explain the reasons many Americans have experienced a decline in leisure time.
3. What does the term *right livelihood* mean? What are the common characteristics of right livelihood?
4. What is the work-and-spend cycle?
5. List and describe four nonfinancial resources.
6. Julie Connelly in the Total Person Insight says there is no harder work than thinking about who you are and what you want out of life. Do you agree or disagree with her point of view? Explain.
7. What are the major reasons we should adopt a healthy lifestyle?
8. List and describe the guidelines for a healthy diet.
9. Provide a brief description of physical fitness. Why is physical fitness so important in the life of a typical worker?
10. What are the five steps involved in breaking a negative habit or forming a positive habit?

**Application
Exercises**

1. In recent years, it has become popular for organizations to develop a mission statement that reflects their philosophy and objectives. The Lotus Operating Principles prepared by Lotus Development Corp. (see Chapter 5) and the Forum Code (Chapter 8) prepared by the Forum Corporation provide examples of mission statements. Prepare a personal mission statement that reflects your goals and aspirations for a successful life. Your mission statement should cover the roles of financial and nonfinancial resources in your life.
2. Throughout this chapter you were encouraged to take control of your life and establish your own definition of success. This chapter has a strong "all development is self-development" theme. Can we really control our own destinies? Can we always make our own choices? Mike Hernacki, author of the book *The Ultimate Secret of Getting Absolutely Everything You Want,* says yes:

   > To get what you want, you must recognize something that at first may be difficult, even painful to look at. You must recognize that *you alone* are the source of all the conditions and situations in your life. You must recognize that whatever your world looks like right now, you alone have caused it to look that way. The state of your health, your finances, your personal relationships, your professional life—all of it is *your* doing, yours and no one else's.[74]

   Do you agree with this viewpoint? Take a position in favor of or in opposition to Hernacki's statement. Prepare a short one- or two-paragraph statement that expresses your views.

3. There are many ways to deepen and extend your spirituality. One way is to begin placing a higher value on silence, tranquillity, and reflection. If your life is extremely busy, you may not be taking time for thought or reflection. If you are accustomed to living in the presence of noise throughout the day, quiet times may make you feel uncomfortable at first. Over a period of one week, set aside a few minutes each day for your own choice of meditation, prayer, contemplation, or reflection. Try to find a quiet place for this activity. At the end of the week, assess the benefits of this activity, and consider the merits of making it part of your daily routine.[75]

Internet Exercise

Dale Carnegie Training offers human relations training programs to people in seventy different countries. Access the company's Web site, and review the information provided. Examine information about the company, and then review the books and courses available. Read the course description for *The Dale Carnegie Course.* Does it appear that this company offers courses and materials that would be of interest to you at some future date? Prepare a one-page summary of your views.

Appendix

HUMAN RELATIONS ABILITIES ASSESSMENT FORM

The purpose of this instrument is to help you assess those attitudes and skills that contribute to effective human relations. An honest response to each item will help you determine your areas of strength and those areas that need improvement. Completion of this self-assessment form will provide you with information needed to develop a plan for improved human relations.

Directions: Circle the number from 1 to 5 that best represents your response to each statement. Review the following information before you complete the form: (1) Strongly disagree (*never do this*); (2) Disagree (*rarely do this*); (3) Moderately agree (*sometimes do this*); (4) Agree (*frequently do this*); (5) Strongly agree (*almost always do this*).

1. I am an effective communicator who sends clear, concise verbal messages.   1 2 3 4 5

2. When people talk, I listen attentively and frequently use active listening skills.   1 2 3 4 5

3. I am conscious of how I express nonverbal messages (facial expression, tone of voice, body language, etc.) when communicating with others.   1 2 3 4 5

4. When forming attitudes about important matters I maintain an open mind, listen to the views of others, but think for myself.   1 2 3 4 5

5. I make every effort to maintain a positive mental attitude toward other people and the events in my life.   1 2 3 4 5

6. I seek feedback and clarification on the influence of my attitudes and behaviors on others.   1 2 3 4 5

7. I am willing to change my attitudes and behaviors in response to constructive feedback from others.   1 2 3 4 5

8. I constantly monitor my self-talk in order to maintain high self-esteem.   1 2 3 4 5

9. I tend to be future oriented and not overly concerned with past mistakes or failures.   1 2 3 4 5

10. I have developed and maintained high expectations for myself.   1   2   3   4   5

11. I accept myself as a changing, growing person capable of improvement.   1   2   3   4   5

12. My goals are clearly defined, attainable, and supported by positive self-talk.   1   2   3   4   5

13. I accept the fact that each communication style has its unique strong points and that there is no "best" communication style.   1   2   3   4   5

14. I make a deliberate attempt to change or alter my communication style (style flexing) in order to meet the needs of other persons.   1   2   3   4   5

15. I have identified my internal motivations and continue to seek opportunities to fulfill these motivations.   1   2   3   4   5

16. I base my personal and professional decisions on clearly defined personal values.   1   2   3   4   5

17. I accept the fact that others' values may differ from mine, and I respect their right to maintain a value system different from my own.   1   2   3   4   5

18. I have a clear sense of what is right and wrong, and my character reflects the fundamental strengths of honesty, fairness, service, humility, and modesty.   1   2   3   4   5

19. I maintain my integrity by practicing what I believe in and keeping my commitments.   1   2   3   4   5

20. I am able to share information about myself in appropriate ways, avoiding the extremes of complete concealment and complete openness.   1   2   3   4   5

21. I engage in appropriate self-disclosure in order to achieve improved communication and increased self-awareness and to build stronger relationships.   1   2   3   4   5

22. I am able to solve problems and make decisions in a logical manner without allowing my emotions to interfere.   1   2   3   4   5

23. My relationships with people at home, school, and work do not suffer because of my expressions of anger or impatience.   1   2   3   4   5

24. I have developed effective ways to cope with my own anger and the anger of others.   1   2   3   4   5

25. I am familiar with and can apply several strategies for achieving emotional control.   1 2 3 4 5

26. I make every effort to recognize the accomplishments of others and celebrate my own successes.   1 2 3 4 5

27. I understand and can apply several forms of positive reinforcement.   1 2 3 4 5

28. I project to others an image that matches my talents and aspirations.   1 2 3 4 5

29. The factors that form my image (career apparel, manners, facial expression, etc.) are appropriate and do not detract from the image I project to others.   1 2 3 4 5

30. In the role of team member, I listen carefully to the views of others and speak frankly about the issues that are uppermost in my mind.   1 2 3 4 5

31. I make every effort to screen out negative thoughts and accentuate positive thinking.   1 2 3 4 5

32. As a team member, I help create an atmosphere of mutual trust and respect.   1 2 3 4 5

33. When people disagree with me, I listen closely to what they have to say and do not try to respond immediately.   1 2 3 4 5

34. I do not hang on to grudges or resentments because these behaviors limit my personal growth and my effectiveness in the area of human relations.   1 2 3 4 5

35. When I experience conflict with others, I strive to be cooperative yet assertive.   1 2 3 4 5

36. In my attempts to resolve conflict I strive for a solution that all parties can accept.   1 2 3 4 5

37. I have developed good habits of diet, sleep, and exercise in order to cope more effectively with the negative stressors in my life.   1 2 3 4 5

38. I accept change as an ongoing process in my life and realize the need to establish new goals.   1 2 3 4 5

39. I manage stress and tension so I am not overwhelmed by the negative stressors in my life.   1 2 3 4 5

40. I refuse to perpetuate negative stereotypes and accept each person as a unique individual worthy of my respect.   1 2 3 4 5

41. I make every effort to identify my own prejudiced attitudes and avoid stereotypical attitudes
toward people of color, older people, persons
with disabilities, and others who are different
from me.   1   2   3   4   5

42. I work hard to combat prejudice because it has
a negative impact on my self-esteem and the
self-esteem of the victim.   1   2   3   4   5

43. I stay connected with family and friends and net-
work with professional and business associates.   1   2   3   4   5

44. I try to maintain balance in my life by avoiding
addiction to work and by engaging in leisure-
time activities.   1   2   3   4   5

45. I envision my existence in a larger context and
view healthy spirituality as a positive, enlighten-
ing force in my life.   1   2   3   4   5

46. I avoid rigid individualism (self-centered behavior) by investing time and energy in helping
others.   1   2   3   4   5

47. I seek advice and counsel from friends, coworkers,
and professionals in order to cope with life's
problems.   1   2   3   4   5

48. I constantly strive to improve my knowledge,
skills, and sense of purpose in my life's work.   1   2   3   4   5

49. I have established well-thought-out, realistic
goals for my life, and these goals are tied to my
values.   1   2   3   4   5

50. I take responsibility for my actions and do not rely
on others to plan my future.   1   2   3   4   5

THE NWNL WORKPLACE STRESS TEST

The issue of increased stress, especially in the workplace, is a growing concern today. The following material is part of a package prepared by Northwestern National Life Insurance Company. It is intended for both employees and employers to assess the levels of stress in their work environment. Read the sample letter to employees and complete the questionnaire that follows, keeping in mind a current or previous work environment.

Sample letter to employees

Date

Dear Employee:

Stress has become a serious problem in the workplace. Four in 10 American workers say they feel their job is very or extremely stressful, according to a study by Northwestern National Life. Employees who feel their job is highly stressful are twice as likely to burn out on the job.

Job stress can cause employee turnover, absenteeism and health problems, as well as lower productivity and job satisfaction. We at _____ are concerned about the effect of job stress on our work force. We would like to find out how serious stress is at our company and identify ways we can reduce job stress and burnout.

To help us evaluate job stress levels, we would like you to fill out the enclosed questionnaire by _____. It will take 10 minutes or less to complete.

Return it to _____ in the attached envelope. Confidentiality is guaranteed. Do not sign your name to the questionnaire.

Thank you for your cooperation. We value your opinion and will share the results of this survey with you.

Sincerely,

CEO or Human Resources Manager

The NWNL Workplace Stress Test

Instructions
Thinking about your work site, how strongly do you agree or disagree with the following statements? For each statement, fill in the circle with a pencil under the response that best describes your work site.

	Response				
	Disagree Strongly	Disagree Somewhat	Neutral or Don't Know	Agree Somewhat	Agree Strongly
SECTION A					
1. Management is supportive of employee's efforts.	O	O	O	O	O
2. Management encourages work and personal support groups.	O	O	O	O	O
3. Management and employees talk openly.	O	O	O	O	O
4. Employees receive training when assigned new tasks.	O	O	O	O	O
5. Employees are recognized and rewarded for their contributions.	O	O	O	O	O
6. Work rules are published and are the same for everyone.	O	O	O	O	O
7. Employees have current and understandable job descriptions.	O	O	O	O	O
8. Management appreciates humor in the workplace.	O	O	O	O	O
9. Employees and management are trained in how to resolve conflicts.	O	O	O	O	O
10. Employees are free to talk with one another.	O	O	O	O	O

	Response				
	Disagree Strongly	Disagree Somewhat	Neutral or Don't Know	Agree Somewhat	Agree Strongly
SECTION B					
11. Workloads vary greatly for individuals or between individuals.	O	O	O	O	O
12. Employees have work spaces that are not crowded.	O	O	O	O	O
13. Employees have access to technology they need.	O	O	O	O	O
14. Few opportunities for advancement are available.	O	O	O	O	O
15. Employees are given little control in how they do their work.	O	O	O	O	O
16. Employees generally are physically isolated.	O	O	O	O	O
17. Mandatory overtime is frequently required.	O	O	O	O	O
18. Employees have little or no privacy.	O	O	O	O	O
19. Performance of work units generally is below average.	O	O	O	O	O
20. Personal conflicts on the job are common.	O	O	O	O	O
21. Consequences of making a mistake on the job are severe.	O	O	O	O	O

Response

	Disagree Strongly	Disagree Somewhat	Neutral or Don't Know	Agree Somewhat	Agree Strongly

SECTION C

| 22. Employees expect the organization will be sold or relocated. | ○ | ○ | ○ | ○ | ○ |
| 23. There has been a major reorganization in the past 12 months. | ○ | ○ | ○ | ○ | ○ |

Response

	Disagree Strongly	Disagree Somewhat	Neutral or Don't Know	Agree Somewhat	Agree Strongly

SECTION D

24. Meal breaks are unpredictable.	○	○	○	○	○
25. Medical and mental health benefits are provided by the employer.	○	○	○	○	○
26. Employees are given information regularly on how to cope with stress.	○	○	○	○	○
27. Sickness and vacation benefits are below that of similar organizations.	○	○	○	○	○
28. Employee benefits were significantly cut in the past 12 months.	○	○	○	○	○
29. An employee assistance program (EAP) is offered.	○	○	○	○	○
30. Pay is below the going rate.	○	○	○	○	○
31. Employees can work flexible hours.	○	○	○	○	○
32. Employees have a place and time to relax during the workday.	○	○	○	○	○
33 Employer has a formal employee communications program.	○	○	○	○	○

Response

	Disagree Strongly	Disagree Somewhat	Neutral or Don't Know	Agree Somewhat	Agree Strongly

SECTION E

34. Child-care programs or referral services are available.	○	○	○	○	○
35. Referral programs or day care for elderly relatives are offered.	○	○	○	○	○
36. Special privileges are granted fairly based on an employee's level.	○	○	○	○	○
37. New machines or ways of working were introduced in the past year.	○	○	○	○	○
38. Employer offers exercise or other stress-reduction programs.	○	○	○	○	○

Response

	Disagree Strongly	Disagree Somewhat	Neutral or Don't Know	Agree Somewhat	Agree Strongly

SECTION F

37. Work is primarily sedentary or physically exhausting.   ○ ○ ○ ○ ○

40. Most work is machine-paced or fast-paced.   ○ ○ ○ ○ ○

41. Staffing or expense budgets are inadequate.   ○ ○ ○ ○ ○

42. Noise or vibration is high, or temperatures are extreme or   ○ ○ ○ ○ ○

    fluctuating.

43. Employees deal with a lot of red tape to get things done.   ○ ○ ○ ○ ○

44. Downsizing or layoffs have occurred in the past 12 months.   ○ ○ ○ ○ ○

45. Employees can put up personal items in their work area.   ○ ○ ○ ○ ○

46. Employees must react quickly and accurately to rapidly   ○ ○ ○ ○ ○

    changing conditions.

Please check that you have filled in one response for each statement. Thank you for completing the questionnaire.

Reprinted with permission from Northwestern National Life Insurance Company, "Employee Burnout: Causes and Cures," 1992.

For a copy of the stress test and scoring information please contact NWNL at (612) 342-7137.

Notes

Chapter 1

1. Mary Scott, "Interview with Howard Schultz," *Business Ethics,* November/December 1995, p. 28.
2. Kate Berry, "Starbucks Opens First Stores in Miami, Hoping to Woo Lovers of Cuban Coffee," *Wall Street Journal,* March 31, 1997, p. A9; Jennifer Reese, "Starbucks—Inside the Coffee Cult," *Fortune,* December 9, 1996, pp. 190–198.
3. John A. Byrne, "The Pain of Downsizing," *Business Week,* May 9, 1994, pp. 60–69.
4. "The Secret Purpose of Downsizing," *Business Ethics,* November/December 1996, p. 13.
5. Gene Koretz, "The Downside of Downsizing," *Business Week,* April 28, 1997, p. 26.
6. "Now Renting: Attorneys and Rocket Scientists," *Training,* February 1997, p. 10.
7. Hal Lancaster, "Managing Your Career," *Wall Street Journal,* February 18, 1997, p. B1.
8. Frederick F. Reichheld, "Solving the Productivity Puzzle," *Wall Street Journal,* March 4, 1996, p. 14.
9. Stephen B. Shepard, "Defining the Q-Word," *Business Week* (Quality Edition), 1991, p. 4.
10. "Questing for the Best," *Business Week* (Quality Edition), 1991, p. 8.
11. Bernard Avishai, "Companies Can't Make Up for Failing Schools," *Wall Street Journal,* July 28, 1996, p. A12.
12. Jeff Pettit, "Team Communication: It's in the Cards," *Training & Development,* January 1997, p. 12.
13. Marilyn Loden and Judy B. Rosener, *Workforce America!* (Homewood, Ill.: Business One Irwin, 1991), p. 23.
14. "Miles Traveled, More to Go," *Business Week* (Quality Edition), 1991, p. 71.
15. Haidee Allerton, "Working Life," *Training & Development,* August 1995, p. 72.
16. Joseph Pereira, "Employers Confront Domestic Abuse," *Wall Street Journal,* March 2, 1995, p. B1.
17. Maggie Jackson, "Dads Speak Up About Work-Family," *Roanoke Times,* June 15, 1997, p. B1.
18. Shawn Tully, "America's Healthiest Companies," *Fortune,* June 12, 1995, p. 276.
19. "Who Wins and Why," *Inc.,* April 1987, p. 103.
20. Robert Kreitner, *Management,* 7th ed. (Boston: Houghton Mifflin, 1998), p. 263.
21. David Stamps, "Relaxed Fit," *Training,* October 1996, pp. 90–100.
22. David Stamps, "Going Nowhere: Culture Change at the Postal Service Fizzles," *Training,* July 1996, pp. 26–34.
23. Chris Lee, "The Vision Thing," *Training,* February 1993, p. 27.
24. William W. Arnold and Jeanne M. Plas, *The Human Touch* (New York: Wiley, 1993), pp. 1 and 2.
25. D. R. Hampton, C. E. Summer, and R. A. Webber, *Organizational Behavior and the Practice of Management* (Glenview, Ill.: Scott, Foresman, 1973), p. 215.
26. J. David McCracken and Ana E. Falcon-Emmanuelli, "A Theoretical Basis for Work Values Research in Vocational Education," *Journal of Vocational and Technical Education,* Spring 1994, p. 7.
27. Betsy Jacobson and Beverly Kaye, "Balancing Act," *Training & Development,* February 1993, p. 26.
28. Roy W. Walters, "Improving Man/Machine Interface for Greater Productivity," *BNAC Communicator,* Summer 1982, p. 13.
29. Jacobson and Kaye, "Balancing Act," pp. 24–26.
30. Sue Shellenbarger, "Dad Takes Home a Tough Day at Work," *Wall Street Journal,* June 29, 1994, p. B3.
31. Sue Shellenbarger, "It's the Type of Job You Have That Affects the Kids, Studies Say," *Wall Street Journal,* July 31, 1996.
32. Rochelle Sharpe, "Labor Letter," *Wall Street Journal,* September 13, 1994, p. 1.
33. Sue Shellenbarger, "Keeping Workers by Reaching Out to Them," *Wall Street Journal,* June 1, 1994, p. B1.
34. Robert Levering and Milton Moskowitz, *The 100 Best Companies to Work for in America* (New York: Currency-Doubleday, 1993), p. 211.
35. George F. Will, "A Faster Mousetrap," *New York Times Book Review,* June 15, 1997, p. 8.
36. Bradley J. Rieger, "Lessons in Productivity and People," *Training & Development,* October 1995, pp. 56–58.
37. For a detailed examination of the Hawthorne criticisms and the legacy of the Hawthorne research, see David A. Whitsett and Lyle Yorks, *From Management Theory to Business Sense* (New York: American Management Association, 1983).
38. Jim Collins, "The Classics," *Inc.,* December 1996, p. 55.
39. Thomas J. Peters and Robert H. Waterman, Jr., *In Search of Excellence: Lessons from America's*

Best-Run Companies (New York: Harper & Row, 1982), p. 14.

40. John R. Diekman, *Human Connections* (Englewood Cliffs, N.J.: Prentice-Hall, 1982), p. xii.

41. Hal Lancaster, "Re-Engineering Authors Reconsider Re-Engineering," *Wall Street Journal,* January 17, 1995, p. B1.

42. Stephen R. Covey, *The 7 Habits of Highly Effective People* (New York: Simon & Schuster, 1989), pp. 66–67.

43. Richard Koonce, "Emotional IQ, a New Secret of Success," *Training & Development,* February 1996, p. 19.

44. Denis Waitley, *Empires of the Mind* (New York: Morrow, 1995), p. 133.

45. H. Jackson Brown, Jr., *Live and Learn to Pass It On* (Nashville, 1992), poster.

46. Harold H. Bloomfield and Robert K. Cooper, *The Power of 5* (Emmaus, Pa.: Rodale Press, 1995), p. 61.

Chapter 2

1. Robert Levering and Milton Moskowitz, *The 100 Best Companies to Work for in America* (New York: Currency-Doubleday, 1993), p. 419.

2. "The Open Book Revolution," *Inc.,* June 1995, cover story.

3. Levering and Moskowitz, *The 100 Best Companies to Work for in America,* p. 421.

4. Alex Markels, "Memo 4/8/97, FYI: Messages Inundate Offices," *Wall Street Journal,* April 7, 1997, p. B1.

5. "Effective Listening Skills," *Women in Business,* March–April 1994, p. 28.

6. John Stewart and Gary D'Angelo, *Together—Communicating Interpersonally* (New York: Random House, 1988), p. 5.

7. Patricia A. Galagan, "On Being a Beginner," *Training & Development,* November 1992, p. 36.

8. Mike France and Tim Smart, "The Ugly Talk on the Texaco Tape," *Business Week,* November 18, 1996, p. 58.

9. "Tom Chappell—Minister of Commerce," *Business Ethics,* January–February, 1994, p. 18.

10. David Shenk, *Data Smog—Surviving the Information Glut* (San Francisco: Harper Edge, 1997), p. 54.

11. Sy Lazarus, *Loud and Clear* (New York: AMACOM, 1974), p. 3.

12. Brian Hickey, "Throwing the Book at Legalese," *TWA Ambassador,* June 1990, p. 86.

13. "Memos from Hell," *Fortune,* February 3, 1997, p. 120.

14. Roger E. Axtell, ed., *Do's and Taboos Around the World,* compiled by Parker Pen Company, 3d ed. (New York: Wiley, 1993), p. 155.

15. Deborah Tannen, *You Just Don't Understand* (New York: Ballantine Books, 1991), p. 42.

16. Judith C. Tingley, *Genderflex: Men and Women Speaking Each Other's Language at Work* (New York: AMACOM, 1994), p. 33.

17. Ginger Trumfio, "More Than Words," *Sales & Marketing Management,* April 1994, p. 55.

18. "Server Posture Affects How We Tip," *The Menninger Letter,* November 1993, p. 5.

19. Phyllis Mindell, "The Body Language of Power," *Executive Female,* May/June 1996, p. 48.

20. Axtell, *Do's and Taboos Around the World,* p. 46.

21. Ibid., p. 47.

22. Ibid., p. 49.

23. William B. Gudykunst, Stella Ting-Toomey, Sandra Sudweeks, and Lea Stewart, *Building Bridges: Interpersonal Skills for a Changing World* (Boston: Houghton Mifflin, 1995), pp. 315–316.

24. Cheryl Hamilton, *Communicating for Results* (Belmont, Calif.: Wadsworth, 1990), p. 48.

25. Camille Wright Miller, "Working It Out," *Roanoke Times & World-News,* May 8, 1994, p. F4.

26. C. Glenn Pearce, "How Effective Are We As Listeners?" *Training & Development,* April 1993, pp. 79–80.

27. Gary Blake, "How to Become an 'Active Listener,' " *Fluid Power Journal,* January 1995, p. 6.

28. Donna Deepose, "Listen Your Way to Better Management," *Supervisory Management,* May 1993, pp. 7–8.

29. John Chaffee, *Thinking Critically,* 5th ed. (Boston: Houghton Mifflin, 1996), pp. 40, 72.

30. Ibid., p. 462.

31. Stephen R. Covey, *The Seven Habits of Highly Effective People* (New York: Simon & Schuster, 1989), pp. 240–241.

32. C. Glenn Pearce, "Learning How to Listen Emphatically," *Supervisory Management,* September 1991, p. 11.

33. Jean Lindamood, "The Very First Viper T/10 Drive," *Automobile Magazine,* 1991, pp. 64–73.

34. Alan Zaremba, "Communication: Working with the Organizational Grapevine," *Personnel Journal,* July 1988, p. 40.

35. John R. Wilke, "Computer Links Erode Hierarchical Nature of Workplace Culture," *Wall Street Journal,* December 9, 1993, p. 1.

36. Thomas Petzinger, Jr., "The Best Companies Get Their Looks from Their Employees," *Wall Street Journal,* December 20, 1996, p. B1.

37. Thomas Petzinger, Jr., "Two Executives Cook Up Way to Make Pillsbury Listen," *Wall Street Journal,* September 27, 1996.

38. "Assets Who Leave at 5 (or Work till 10)," *Inc.,* March 1994, p. 51.

39. Kenneth Labaich, "Rethinking Almost Everything," *Fortune,* May 13, 1996, p. 179.

40. "Business Being Built Without Bricks, Mortar," *Springfield News-Leader,* April 28, 1994, p. 1B.

41. Ginger Trumfio, "Liberty, Equality, E-Mail!" *Sales & Marketing Management,* March 1994, p. 38.

42. Charlene Marmer Solomon, "Global Operations Demand That HR Rethink Diversity," *Personnel Journal,* July 1994, p. 44.

43. Ibid.

44. Ibid., p. 40.

45. "Growing Your Business by Going Global," *Inc.,* January 1994, p. 65.

46. "Don't Be An Ugly-American Manager," *Fortune,* October 16, 1995, p. 225.

47. Lennie Copeland, "Training Americans to Do Business Overseas," *Training,* July 1983, p. 12.

48. Andy Cohen, "Small World, Big Challenge," *Sales & Marketing Management,* June 1996, p. 72.

Chapter 3

1. Betsy Morris, "He's Smart. He's Not Nice. He's Saving Big Blue," *Fortune,* April 14, 1997, pp. 68–81.

2. J. Randy Taraborrelli, "The Change That Has Made Oprah So Happy," *Redbook,* May 1997, pp. 95–96.

3. Robert Bolton and Dorothy Grover Bolton, *People Styles at Work* (New York: AMACOM, 1996), p. 10.

4. Tony Alessandra, *Behavioral Profiles: Participant Workbook* (San Diego: Pfeiffer & Company, 1994), p. 12.

5. Bolton and Bolton, *People Styles at Work,* pp. ix–x.

6. Karen Waner and Lonnie Echternacht, "Using the Myers-Briggs Type Indicator to Compare Personality Types of Business Teachers Who Teach Office Occupations with Personality Types of Office Professionals," *The Delta Pi Epsilon Journal,* Spring 1993, pp. 56, 58.

7. Bolton and Bolton, *People Styles at Work,* p. x.

8. Ibid.

9. Robert M. Hecht, *Office Systems,* February 1990, p. 26.

10. David W. Johnson, *Reaching Out—Interpersonal Effectiveness and Self-Actualization* (Englewood Cliffs, N.J.: Prentice-Hall, 1981), pp. 43–44. The dominance factor was described in an early book by William M. Marston, *The Emotions of Normal People* (New York: Harcourt, 1928). Research conducted by Rolfe La Forge and Robert F. Suczek resulted in the development of the Interpersonal Check List (ICL), which features a dominant-submissive scale. A person who receives a high score on the ICL tends to lead, persuade, and control others. The Interpersonal Identity

Profile, developed by David W. Merrill and James W. Taylor, features a factor called "assertiveness." Persons classified as high in assertiveness tend to have strong opinions, make quick decisions, and be directive when dealing with people. Persons classified as low in assertiveness tend to voice moderate opinions, make thoughtful decisions, and be supportive when dealing with others.

11. Hugh J. Ingrasci, "How to Reach Buyers in Their Psychological 'Comfort Zones,' " *Industrial Marketing,* July 1981, p. 60.

12. American Management Association, *Catalog of Seminars* (New York: American Management Association, 1995), p. 42.

13. The research conducted by La Forge and Suczek resulted in identification of the hostile/loving continuum, which is similar to the sociability continuum. Their Interpersonal Check List Features this scale. L. L. Thurstone and T. G. Thurstone developed the Thurstone Temperament Schedule, which provides an assessment of a "sociable" factor. Persons with high scores in this area enjoy the company of others and make friends easily. The Interpersonal Identity Profile developed by Merrill and Taylor contains an objectivity continuum. A person with low objectivity is seen as attention seeking, involved with the feelings of others, informal, and casual in social relationships. A person who is high in objectivity tends to be indifferent toward the feelings of others. This person is formal in social relationships.

14. Liz Stevens, "How to Deal with That Pain in the Office," *San Jose Mercury News,* September 4, 1996, p. 6G.

15. "On the Human Side," *Time,* February 19, 1979, p. 75.

16. Sandra Scarr and James Vander Zanden, *Understanding Psychology,* 5th ed. (New York: Random House, 1987), p. 564.

17. David W. Merrill and Roger H. Reid, *Personal Styles and Effective Performance* (Radnor, Pa.: Chilton, 1981), pp. 54–55.

18. Bolton and Bolton, *People Styles at Work,* p. 87.

19. Ibid.

20. Merrill and Reid, *Personal Styles and Effective Performance,* p. 88.

21. Wilson Learning Corporation, *Growth Through Versatility* (Eden Prairie, Minn.: Wilson Learning Corporation), p. 4.

22. Bob Reeves, "It Takes All Types," *Lincoln Star,* May 24, 1994, p. 11.

23. "People Skills Still a Sales Basic," *Training & Development,* December 1994, pp. 7–8.

24. Tony Alessandra and Michael J. O'Connor, *People Smart* (La Jolla, Calif.: Keynote Publishing, 1990), p. 10.

25. Wilson Learning Corporation, *Growth Through Versatility*, p. 6.

26. Stuart Atkins, *The Name of Your Game* (Beverly Hills, Calif.: Ellis & Stewart, 1981), pp. 49–50.

27. Ibid., p. 51.

28. Chris Lee, "What's Your Style?" *Training*, May 1991, p. 28.

Chapter 4

1. Sue Shellenbarger, "What Does Your Job Tell a Crystal Burch About Fulfillment?" *Wall Street Journal*, April 24, 1996, p. B1.

2. L. B. Gschwandtner, "Creating a Champion," *Personal Selling Power*, March 1992, pp. 57–60.

3. Nathaniel Branden, *The Six Pillars of Self-Esteem* (New York: Bantam, 1994), p. 7.

4. California State Department of Education, *Toward a State of Esteem* (Sacramento: Department of Education, January 1990), p. 19.

5. Quoted in A. H. Maslow, "A Theory of Human Motivation," in *Psychological Foundations of Organizational Behavior*, ed. Barry M. Stow (Santa Monica, Calif.: Goodyear Publishing, 1977), pp. 7–8.

6. David E. Shapiro, "Pumping Up Your Attitude," *Psychology Today*, May/June 1997, p. 14.

7. Richard Laliberte, "Self-Esteem Workshop," *Self*, May 1994, p. 201.

8. Branden, *The Six Pillars of Self-Esteem*, p. 39.

9. Laliberte, "Self-Esteem Workshop," p. 201.

10. Tim Simmons and Ruth Sheehan, "Even in Earliest Years, Brain Is 'Wiring' for Life," *News & Observer*, February 16, 1997, p. 1A.

11. Madeleine J. Nash, "Fertile Minds," *Time*, February 3, 1997, pp. 51–52.

12. Simmons and Sheehan, "Even in Earliest Years, Brain Is 'Wiring' for Life," p. 1A.

13. Amy Bjork Harris and Thomas A. Harris, *Staying OK* (New York: Harper & Row, 1985), p. 24.

14. Margaret Henning and Ann Jardim, *The Managerial Woman* (New York: Anchor Books, 1977), pp. 106–107.

15. Ellen Graham, "Leah: Life Is All Sweetness and Insecurity," *Wall Street Journal*, February 9, 1995, p. B16.

16. "The New American Body," *University of California at Berkeley Wellness Letter*, December 1993, p. 1.

17. Mary Pipher, *Reviving Ophelia* (New York: Ballantine Books, 1994), p. 23.

18. Stephanie Mehta, "Photo Chain Ventures Beyond Big Hair," *Wall Street Journal*, May 13, 1996, p. B1.

19. Ellen Uzelac, "In a Daughter's Voice," *Common Boundary*, September/October 1995, p. 49.

20. Emmett E. Miller, *The Healing Power of Happiness* (Emmaus, Pa.: Rodale Press, 1989), pp. 12–13.

21. Amy Saltzman, *Down-Shifting* (New York: HarperCollins, 1990), pp. 15–16.

22. Miller, *The Healing Power of Happiness*, pp. 12–13.

23. Belleruth Naparstek, "About Face," *Common Boundary*, July/August 1996, p. 64.

24. Richard Ringer, David Balkin, and R. Wayne Boss, "Matching the Feedback to the Person," *Executive Female*, November–December 1993, p. 11.

25. Hyrum W. Smith, *The 10 Natural Laws of Successful Time and Life Management* (New York: Warner Books, 1994), p. 178.

26. Branden, *The Six Pillars of Self-Esteem*, p. 48.

27. Ibid., p. 33.

28. California State Department of Education, *Toward a State of Esteem*, pp. 23–24.

29. Robert J. Kriegel, with Louis Platier, *If It Ain't Broke . . . Break It!*" audiocassette produced by Barr Audio, Irwindale, Calif., 1992.

30. Arnold A. Lazarus and Clifford N. Lazarus, *The 60-Second Shrink* (San Luis Obispo, Calif.: Impact Publishers, 1997), p. 40.

31. Cheri Burns, "The Extra Edge," *Savvy*, December 1982, p. 42.

32. Hal Lancaster, "It's Harder, but You Still Can Rise Up from the Mail Room," *Wall Street Journal*, June 18, 1996, p. B1.

33. Chip R. Bell, "Making Mentoring a Way of Life," *Training*, October 1996, p. 138; Lin Standke, review of *Managers as Mentors: Building Partnerships for Learning*, by Chip Bell, *Training*, April 1997, pp. 64–65.

34. Hal Lancaster, "You Might Need a Guide to Lead You Around Career Pitfalls," *Wall Street Journal*, July 30, 1996, p. B1.

35. Ibid.

36. Hal Lancaster, "How Women Can Find Mentors in a World with Few Role Models," *Wall Street Journal*, April 1, 1997, p. B1.

37. Lazarus and Lazarus, *The 60-Second Shrink*, pp. 3, 4.

38. Shakti Gawain, *Creative Visualization* (San Rafael, Calif.: Whatever Publishing, 1978), p. 14.

39. Lazarus and Lazarus, *The 60-Second Shrink*, p. 3.

40. L. B. Gschwandtner, "Mary Lou Retton," *Personal Selling Power*, 15th Anniversary Issue, 1995, p. 99.

41. Denis Waitley, "The Winning Generation Video Series," Advanced Learning, Inc., Cedar Falls, Iowa.

42. Lazarus and Lazarus, *The 60-Second Shrink*, pp. 1, 2.

43. Herb Kindler, "Working to Change Old Habits," *Working Smart*, May 1992, p. 8.

44. Julia Flynn Siler, "The Corporate Woman: Is She Really Different?" *Business Week*, June 25, 1990, p. 14.

45. Sheila Ostrander and Lynn Schroeder, *Superlearning* (New York: Dell Publishing, 1979), pp. 87–109.

46. Roy J. Blitzer, Colleen Petersen, and Linda Rogers, "How to Build Self-Esteem," *Training & Development,* February 1993, pp. 58–60.

47. Pipher, *Reviving Ophelia,* p. 183.

Chapter 5

1. O. C. Ferrell and John Fraedrich, *Business Ethics* (Boston: Houghton Mifflin, 1997), pp. 267–274.

2. Dennis Levine, "The Inside Story of an Inside Trader," *Fortune,* May 21, 1990, p. 82.

3. Kathleen Morris and Lisa Sanders, "Professor Milken's Lesson Plan," *Business Week,* August 4, 1997.

4. "The Strength of Character," *Royal Bank Letter* (Royal Bank of Canada) May–June 1988, p. 1.

5. "Practicing What You Preach," *The Pryor Report,* vol. 10, no. 1a.

6. Richard Brookhiser, "Why Virtue Is in Short Supply," *New York Times Book Review,* March 3, 1996, p. 12.

7. Stephen R. Covey, *The Seven Habits of Highly Effective People* (New York: Simon & Schuster, 1989), p. 92.

8. Joseph Josephson and Ednah Josephson, *Character Counts Wallet Card* (Marina del Ray, Calif.: Josephson Institute of Ethics, 1994).

9. Hyrum W. Smith, *The 10 Natural Laws of Successful Time and Life Management* (New York: Warner Books, 1994), pp. 14–15.

10. J. David McCracken and Ana E. Falcon-Emmanuelli, "A Theoretical Basis for Work Values Research in Vocational Education," *Journal of Vocational and Technical Education,* Spring 1994, p. 4.

11. Smith, *The 10 Natural Laws of Successful Time and Life Management,* pp. 66–67.

12. Sue Shellenbarger, "Some Top Executives Are Finding a Balance Between Job and Home," *Wall Street Journal,* April 23, 1997, p. B1.

13. Kevin A. Wilson, "Halo Car," *Autoweek,* April 7, 1997.

14. Katherine Paterson, "Family Values," *New York Times Book Review,* October 15, 1995, p. 32.

15. Tom Pickens, "Ethics: Easy as A-B-C?" *Creative Living,* vol. 22, no. 4, p. 8.

16. "Put First Things First," *Inc.,* December 1987, p. 168.

17. Chris Lee and Ron Zemke, "The Search for Spirit in the Workplace," *Training,* June 1993, p. 21.

18. Stanley M. Elam, Lowell C. Rose, and Alec M. Gallup, "The 26th Annual Phi Delta Kappa/Gallup Poll of the Public's Attitudes Toward the Public Schools," *Phi Delta Kappan,* September 1994, p. 49.

19. Sonia L. Nazario, "Schoolteachers Say It's Wrongheaded to Try to Teach Students What's Right," *Wall Street Journal,* April 6, 1990, p. B1.

20. Sanford N. McDonnell, "A Virtuous Agenda for Education Reform," *Wall Street Journal,* February 18, 1997, p. A22.

21. Andrew Stark, "What's the Matter with Business Ethics," *Harvard Business Review,* May–June 1993, p. 38.

22. William J. Bennett, *The Index of Leading Cultural Indicators: Facts and Figures on the State of American Society* (New York: Simon & Schuster, 1994), p. 103.

23. Richard S. Dunham and Michael O'Neal, "Gunning for the Gangstas," *Business Week,* June 19, 1995, p. 41.

24. Roy Furchgott, "Howard Stern's Battle of Richmond," *Business Week,* June 17, 1996, p. 6.

25. Morris Massey, *The People Puzzle* (Reston, Va.: Reston Publishing, 1979).

26. James C. Collins, "Change Is Good but First, Know What Should Never Change," *Fortune,* May 29, 1995, p. 141.

27. Jeffrey L. Seglin, "Playing by the Rules," *Inc.,* November 1996, p. 39.

28. Neal Donald Walsch, *Conversations with God, Book 1 Guidebook* (Charlottesville, Va.: Hampton Roads, 1997), p. 71.

29. "Newsbreakers," *Inc.,* October 1990, p. 25.

30. Joan E. Rigdon, "Some Workers Gripe Bosses Are Ordering Too Much Overtime," *Wall Street Journal,* September 29, 1994, pp. A1, A6.

31. "McDonnell Douglas Executive Ousted," Associated Press, *Springfield NewsLeader,* October 27, 1996, p. A1.

32. Sue Shellenbarger, "In Real Life, Hard Choices Upset Any Balancing Act," *Wall Street Journal,* April 19, 1995.

33. Smith, *The 10 Natural Laws of Successful Time and Life Management,* pp. 68–69.

34. Vivian Arnold, B. June Schmidt, and Randall L. Wells, "Ethics Instruction in the Classrooms of Business Educators," *Delta Pi Epsilon Journal,* vol. 38, no. 4, Fall 1996, p. 185.

35. "Workers Cut Ethical Corners, Survey Finds," *Wall Street Journal,* March 10, 1995, p. A2.

36. "Nearly Half of Workers Take Unethical Actions—Survey," *Des Moines Register,* April 7, 1997, p. 18B.

37. Paula Ancona, "How to Handle Unethical Situations in the Office," *San Jose Mercury News,* July 9, 1995, p. 1PC.

38. Sherwood Ross, "The Thief on the Payroll," *San Jose Mercury News,* April 14, 1996, p. 1PC.

39. Marian Wright Edelman, *The Measure of Our Success* (Boston: Allyn and Bacon, 1992), pp. 502–503.

40. "Long-Distance Services Target Customers' Values," *Springfield NewsLeader,* June 25, 1996, p. C1.

41. Eric D. Randall, "Money No Longer Tops for MBAs," *USA Today,* May 25, 1994, p. 5B.

42. Dawn Anfuso, "Soul-Searching Sustains Values at Lotus Development," *Personnel Journal*, June 1994, pp. 54–61.

43. Sue Shellenbarger, "Some Workers Find Bosses Don't Share Their Family Values," *Wall Street Journal*, July 12, 1995, p. B1.

44. Betsy Weisendanger, "Doing the Right Thing," *Sales & Marketing Management*, March 1991, p. 82.

45. M. Scott Peck, *The Road Less Traveled* (New York: Simon & Schuster, 1978), p. 19.

46. Michael H. Mescon and Timothy S. Mescon, "And Then Some . . . ," *Sky*, August 1989, p. 92.

47. George Kegley, "Broker with a Difference: A. G. Edwards, Chairman," *Roanoke Times & World-News*, April 13, 1990, p. B6.

48. Krystal Miller, "Former Honda Executives Plead Guilty to Charges Tied to Bribes from Dealers," *Wall Street Journal*, March 15, 1994, p. A4; Holman W. Jenkins, Jr., " 'Tis the Season of Sin at Honda," *Wall Street Journal*, December 17, 1996, p. A23.

49. Leslie Scism, "Prudential's New Chief Is Finding It Difficult to Avoid the Rock," *Wall Street Journal*, January 24, 1997, p. A1.

50. Richard Behar, "Skimming the Cream," *Time*, August 2, 1993, p. 49.

51. Mary Ellen Egan, "Old Enough to Know Better," *Business Ethics*, January/February 1995, p. 19.

52. Bob Filipczak, "The Soul of the Hog," *Training*, February 1996, pp. 38–42.

53. Andrew Stark, "What's the Matter with Business Ethics?" *Harvard Business Review*, May–June 1993, p. 38.

54. "Tom Chappell—Minister of Commerce," *Business Ethics*, January/February 1994, p. 17.

55. "Ethical Programs and Personal Values Are Still Not Enough," *Business Ethics*, May/June 1996, p. 12.

56. Joshua Hyatt, "How to Hire Employees," *Inc.*, March 1990, p. 2.

57. Claudia H. Deutsch, "You Want This Job? Pass the Integrity Test," *San Jose Mercury News*, February 25, 1990, p. 2.

58. "Honesty Tests: The Defense Rests," *Training*, May 1991, p. 12.

59. Phillip Barnhart, "The Ethics Game," *Training*, June 1993, pp. 65, 66.

60. Ellen Neuborne, "Whistle-Blowers Pipe Up More Frequently," *USA Today*, July 22, 1996, p. 2B.

61. Paul M. Sherer, "North American and Asian Executives Have Contrasting Values, Study Finds," *Wall Street Journal*, March 8, 1996, p. B12.

62. John Bussey and James McGregor, "What, Why, and How," *Wall Street Journal*, December 19, 1993, p. R19.

63. Chris Hill and Toby Hanlon, "26 Simple Ways to Change How You Feel," *Prevention*, August 1993, p. 126.

Chapter 6

1. Ron Zemke, "Custom Service As a Performing Art," *Training*, March 1993, p. 40.

2. Robert Levering and Milton Moskowitz, *The 100 Best Companies to Work for in America* (New York: Currency-Doubleday, 1993), p. 398.

3. Alex Taylor III, "Bla Car, Bad Book," *Fortune*, November 29, 1993, p. 17.

4. "What Matters Most to Employers?" *Inc.*, June 1995, p. 90.

5. Thomas Pelzinger, Jr., "How Lynn Mercer Manages a Factory That Manages Itself," *Wall Street Journal*, March 7, 1997, p. B1.

6. Ken Gepfert, "As Wage Edge Shrinks, Workers' Attitude Shines," *Wall Street Journal*, May 28, 1997, p. S2.

7. "A Matter of Attitude," *Royal Bank Letter*, May–June 1994, p. 2.

8. Wayne F. Cascio, *Costing Human Resources* (Boston: PWS-Kent Publishing, 1991), p. 130.

9. Ibid., p. 131.

10. Tom Lopp, "Attitude Makes the Difference," *Vocational Education Journal*, January 1996, p. 8.

11. Bernie S. Siegel, *Love, Medicine and Miracles* (New York: Harper & Row, 1986), p. 26.

12. Jerome Kagan, *Psychology: An Introduction* (New York: Harcourt Brace Jovanovich, 1984), p. 548.

13. "Tailored Health Plans Take Off," *Fortune*, June 27, 1994, p. 12.

14. Henry Labalme, "Breaking the Chains of Addiction to Television," *Roanoke Times*, April 23, 1996, p. A5.

15. William F. Schoell and Joseph P. Guiltinan, *Marketing*, 5th ed. (Boston: Allyn and Bacon, 1992), pp. 166–167; William M. Pride and O. C. Ferrell, *Marketing*, 10th ed. (Boston: Houghton Mifflin, 1997), p. 146.

16. Eamonn Fingleton, "Jobs for Life—Why Japan Won't Give Them Up," *Fortune*, March 29, 1995, pp. 119–125.

17. Michael R. Quinlan, "How Does Service Drive the Service Company?" *Harvard Business Review*, November–December 1991, p. 156.

18. John Case, "Corporate Culture," *Inc.*, November 1996, pp. 42–53.

19. Thomas E. Ricks, "New Marines Illustrate Growing Gap Between Military and Society," *Wall Street Journal*, July 27, 1995, p. A1.

20. Shawn Cavence, "Spiritual Doctor Sets Up Shop," *Collegiate Times*, February 20, 1990, p. A6.

21. Timothy G. Hatcher, "The Ins and Outs of Self-Directed Learning," *Training & Development*, February 1997, p. 35–39.

22. Anthony P. Carnevale, Leila J. Gainer, and Ann S. Meltzer, *Workplace Basics Training Manual* (San Francisco: Jossey-Bass, 1990), p. 3.

23. David Holzman, "When Workers Run the Show," *Working Woman*, August 1993, p. 74.

24. Nancy L. Mueller, "Wisconsin Power and Light's Model Diversity Program," *Training & Development*, March 1996, p. 57.

25. Patricia Sellers, "Now Bounce Back!" *Fortune*, May 1, 1995, pp. 49–62.

26. Martin Seligman, *Learned Optimism* (New York: Knopf, 1991), p. 4.

27. Redford Williams and Virginia Williams, *Anger Kills* (New York: Harper Perennial, 1993), p. 12.

28. Phil Catalfo, "Buckminster Fuller—the 50-Year Experiment," audiotape (San Francisco: New Dimensions Foundation, 1988).

29. Robert F. Mager, *Developing Attitudes Toward Learning* (Belmont, Calif.: Fearon-Pitman, 1968), p. 47.

30. Quoted in Nancy W. Collins, Susan K. Gilbert, and Susan Nycum, *Women Leading: Making Tough Choices on the Fast Track* (Lexington, Mass.: Stephen Greene Press, 1988), p. 1.

31. "Walking in Your Customers' Shoes," *Training*, February 1995, p. 16.

32. Matt Rothman, "Into the Black," *Inc.*, January 1993, pp. 59–65.

33. "Work Week," *Wall Street Journal*, January 7, 1997, p. A1.

Chapter 7

1. Kevin Helliker, "Retailing Chains Offer a Lot of Opportunity, Young Managers Find," *Wall Street Journal*, August 15, 1995, pp. 1, 4.

2. D. R. Spitzer, "30 Ways to Motivate Employees to Perform Better," *Training/HRD*, March 1980, p. 51.

3. Michael J. O'Connor and Sandra J. Merwin, *The Mysteries of Motivation* (Minneapolis: Performax Systems International, 1988), p. 1.

4. Robert Kreitner, *Management*, 7th ed. (Boston: Houghton Mifflin, 1998), pp. 388–389.

5. Cynthia Berryman-Fink, *The Managers' Desk Reference* (New York: AMACOM, 1989), pp. 156–157.

6. Abraham H. Maslow, *Motivation and Personality* (New York: Harper & Row, 1954).

7. H. C. Kazanas, *Effective Work Competencies for Vocational Education* (Columbus, Ohio: National Center for Research in Vocational Education, 1978), p. 12.

8. "Belonging Satisfies Basic Human Need," *The Menninger Letter*, August 1995, p. 6.

9. "Maslow's Term and Themes," *Training*, March 1977, p. 48.

10. Frederick Herzberg, Bernard Mausner, and Barbara Black Snyderman, *The Motivation to Work* (New York: Wiley, 1959).

11. David J. Rachman and Michael H. Mescon, *Business Today*, 4th ed. (New York: Random House, 1985), p. 235.

12. "Management Theory? Management Madness," *Psychology Today*, March/April 1997, p. 59.

13. Kreitner, *Management*, p. 49.

14. Thomas A. Stewart, "Which Side Are You On? The Never Ending War for a Manager's Soul," *Fortune*, May 15, 1995, pp. 123–124.

15. Chris Lee, "Trust Me," *Training*, January 1997, p. 34.

16. Berryman-Fink, *The Managers' Desk Reference*, pp. 156–157.

17. Judith Gordon, *A Diagnostic Approach to Organizational Behavior*, 3d ed. (Boston: Allyn and Bacon, 1991), p. 626.

18. Alison Furnham, "Expect Good Work and You'll Get It," *Executive Female*, September/October 1996, p. 13.

19. Berryman-Fink, *The Managers' Desk Reference*, pp. 156–157.

20. David Stamps, "Relaxed Fit," *Training*, October 1996, p. 96.

21. Gerhard Gschwandtner, "Quality: Selling Lessons from Baldridge Award Winners," *Personal Selling Power*, April 1993, p. 8.

22. Raju Narisetti, "Manufacturers Decry a Shortage of Workers While Rejecting Many," *Wall Street Journal*, September 8, 1995, p. A1.

23. Shari Caudron, "Motivating Creative Employees Calls for New Strategies," *Personnel Journal*, May 1994, p. 105.

24. Rosabeth Moss Kanter, "The New Managerial Work," *Harvard Business Review*, November–December 1989, p. 91.

25. "Industry Report 1996," *Training*, October 1996, p. 38.

26. Leslie Overmyer-Day and George Benson, "Training Success Stories," *Training & Development*, June 1996, p. 27.

27. "Today's Leaders Look to Tomorrow," *Fortune*, March 26, 1990, p. 36.

28. Thomas Petzinger, "Self-Organization Will Free Employees to Act like Bosses," *Wall Street Journal*, January 3, 1997, p. B1.

29. "Creativity, Productivity Rise When Workers Have More Say," *San Jose Mercury News*, March 12, 1997, p. 6G.

30. Dan Millman, *The Laws of Spirit* (Tiburon, Calif.: H. J. Kramer, 1995), pp. 60–64.

31. Sherri Eng, "Are You Scared of Success?" *San Jose Mercury News,* January 17, 1996, pp. 6G, 7G; Douglas A. Bernstein, Edward J. Roy, Thomas K. Srull, and Christopher D. Wickens, *Psychology,* 4th ed. (Boston: Houghton Mifflin, 1997), pp. 357–359.

32. Eng, "Are You Scared of Success?" p. 7G.

33. Margaret Kaeter, "Falling in Love Again," *Business Ethics,* November/December 1994, p. 44.

34. Mihaly Csikszentmihalyi, "Finding Flow," *Psychology Today,* July/August 1997, pp. 47–48.

35. Sherwood Ross, "How Companies Hurt Themselves," *San Jose Mercury News,* January 1, 1995, p. PC1.

36. Sue Shellenbarger, "Work-Family Issues Go Way Beyond Missed Ball Games," *Wall Street Journal,* May 28, 1997, p. B1.

37. G. Pascal Zachary, "The New Search for Meaning in Meaningless Work," *Wall Street Journal,* January 9, 1997, p. B1.

38. Gerhard Gschwandtner, "Zig Ziglar," *Personal Selling Power,* 15th Anniversary Issue, 1995, p. 105.

Chapter 8

1. Warren Shaver, Jr., *How to Build and Use a 360-Degree Feedback System* (Alexandria, Va.: American Society for Training and Development, 1995), pp. 1–16.

2. Srikumar S. Rao, "The Painful Remaking of Ameritech," *Training,* July 1994, p. 48.

3. James G. Carr, "Dare to Share," *Pace,* June 1988, p. 22.

4. Brian O'Reilly, "360 Feedback Can Change Your Life," *Fortune,* October 17, 1994, pp. 93–100.

5. John Powell, *Why Am I Afraid to Tell You Who I Am?* (Chicago: Argus Communications, 1969), p. 77.

6. Roy M. Berko, Andrew D. Wolvin, and Darlyn R. Wolvin, *Communicating* (Boston: Houghton Mifflin, 1995), p. 46.

7. *Communication Concepts—The Johari Window* (New York: J. C. Penney Company, Consumer Affairs Department, 1979).

8. Carrie Rickey, "A Rhinoceros Among the Gazelles," *New York Times Book Review,* December 11, 1988, p. 13.

9. Michael Ryan, "A Hidden Talent," *Parade Magazine,* May 28, 1989, p. 30.

10. Carr, "Dare to Share," p. 22.

11. Gary Blake, "Don't Use That Tone with Me!" *Wall Street Journal,* November 25, 1996, p. A18.

12. Sharon Nelton, "The Power of Forgiveness," *Nation's Business,* July 1995, p. 41.

13. Arnold A. Lazarus and Clifford N. Lazarus, *The 60-Second Shrink* (San Luis Obispo, Calif.: Impact Publishers, 1997), pp. 76–79.

14. John R. Diekman, *Human Connections* (Englewood Cliffs, N.J.: Prentice-Hall, 1985), p. 63.

15. Hendrie Weisinger and Norman Lobsenz, *Nobody's Perfect—How to Give Criticism and Get Results* (Los Angeles: Stratford Press, 1981), p. 39.

16. Joyce Brothers, "The Most Important People We Know . . . Our Friends," *Parade Magazine,* February 16, 1997, pp. 4–6.

17. Mark Matousek, "The Cat Is on the Roof," *Common Boundary,* January/February 1997, p. 64.

18. Shari Caudron, "Rebuilding Employee Trust," *Training & Development,* August 1996, pp. 18–21; Chris Lee, "Trust," *Training,* January 1997, pp. 28–37.

19. Aubrey C. Daniels, *Bringing Out the Best in People* (New York: McGraw-Hill, 1994), p. 41.

20. Jack R. Gibb, *Trust: A New View of Personal and Organizational Development* (Los Angeles: Guild of Tutors Press, 1978), p. 29.

21. Jess Lair, *I Ain't Much, Baby—But I'm All I've Got* (New York: Doubleday, 1969), p. 104.

22. Kenneth Labich, "The Seven Keys to Business Leadership," *Fortune,* October 24, 1988, pp. 58–66.

23. "Trust in Supervisors Fueled by Communication," *Menninger Letter,* July 1994, p. 1.

24. Gibb, *Trust: A New View of Personal and Organizational Development,* p. 192.

Chapter 9

1. Daniel Pearl, "One Air Crash Suggests How a Pilot's Mind-Set Can Pose a Safety Risk," *Wall Street Journal,* May 25, 1994, pp. A1, A10.

2. Willard Gaylin, *Feelings* (New York: Ballantine Books, 1979), p. 1.

3. Daniel Goleman, *Emotional Intelligence* (New York: Bantam Books, 1995), p. 34.

4. Daniel Goleman, "The Educated Heart," *Common Boundary,* November/December 1995, p. 27.

5. Jay Stuller, "EQ—Edging Toward Respectability," *Training,* June 1997, p. 45.

6. John Selby, *Conscious Healing* (New York: Bantam Books, 1989), p. 32.

7. Ibid.

8. Joan Borysenko, *Minding the Body, Mending the Mind* (New York: Bantam Books, 1987), p. 163.

9. James Georges, "The Not-So-Stupid Americans," *Training,* July 1994, p. 90.

10. Margaret A. Jacobs, "Brutal Firings Can Backfire, Ending in Court," *Wall Street Journal,* October 24, 1994, p. B1.

11. Gerald L. Manning and Barry L. Reece, *Selling Today—Building Quality Partnerships,* 7th ed. (Englewood Cliffs, N.J.: Prentice-Hall Business Publishing, 1998), p. 13.

12. Ron Zemke, "Contact! Training Employees to Meet the Public," *Service Solutions* (Minneapolis: Lakewood Books, 1990), pp. 20–23.

13. Georges, "The Not-So-Stupid Americans," p. 90.

14. Douglas A. Bernstein, Edward J. Roy, Alison Clark-Stewart, and Christopher D. Wickens, *Psychology,* 4th ed. (Boston: Houghton Mifflin, 1997), p. 403.

15. Ibid.

16. William C. Menninger and Harry Levinson, *Human Understanding in Industry* (Chicago: Science Research Associates, 1956), p. 29.

17. Joan Borysenko, *Guilt Is the Teacher, Love Is the Lesson* (New York: Warner Books, 1990), p. 70.

18. Donella H. Meadows, "We Are, to Our Harm, What We Watch," *Roanoke Times & World-News,* October 16, 1994, p. G3.

19. "Schools Hit by Epidemic of Violence," *Roanoke Times & World-News,* January 6, 1994, p. A1.

20. "Reducing TV Violence May Curb Antisocial Behavior," *Menninger Letter,* October 1995, p. 4.

21. Tori DeAngelis, "Women's Safety Illusory When Males Turn Violent," *APA Monitor,* September 1994, p. 1.

22. Jan E. Stets and Debra A. Henderson, "Contextual Factors Surrounding Conflict Resolution While Dating: Results from a National Study," *Family Relations,* January 1991, pp. 29–36.

23. Bonnie E. Carlson, "Dating Violence: A Research Review and Comparison with Spouse Abuse," *Social Casework: Journal of Contemporary Social Work,* 1987, pp. 16–23.

24. Shakti Gawain, *The Path of Transformation* (Mill Valley, Calif.: Nataraj Publishing, 1993), p. 96.

25. Ibid.

26. Harold H. Bloomfield and Robert K. Cooper, *The Power of 5* (Emmaus, Pa.: Rodale Press, 1995), p. 334.

27. Redford Williams and Virginia Williams, *Anger Kills* (New York: HarperCollins, 1993), p. 3.

28. Kimes Gustin, *Anger, Rage, and Resentment* (West Caldwell, N.J.: St. Ives' Press, 1994), p. 1.

29. Helen Hall Clinard, *Winning Ways to Succeed with People* (Houston: Gulf Publishing, 1985), p. 82.

30. Susan Bixler, *Professional Presence* (New York: G. P. Putnam's Sons, 1991), pp. 190–191.

31. Rolland S. Parker, *Emotional Common Sense* (New York: Barnes & Noble Books, 1973), pp. 80–81.

32. Jane Brody, "Turning Anger into Useful Force," *Roanoke Times & World-News,* November 30, 1993, p. E1.

33. Gustin, *Anger, Rage, and Resentment,* p. 37.

34. Les Giblin, *How to Have Confidence and Power in Dealing with People* (Englewood Cliffs, N.J.: Prentice-Hall 1956), p. 37.

35. Angelo B. Henderson and Oscar Suris, "Latest Shooting at Ford Assembly Plant Rekindles Calls for Safer Workplaces," *Wall Street Journal,* November 15, 1996, p. A6.

36. Kenneth Labich, "Psycho Bosses from Hell," *Fortune,* March 18, 1996, p. 123.

37. "Murder at the Post Office: Until Culture Change Is a Reality, It's a 'Ticking Bomb,'" *Training & Development,* January 1994, p. 29.

38. Helen Frank Bensimon, "Violence in the Workplace," *Training & Development,* January 30, 1994, p. 30.

39. Bob Filipczak, "The Rest of the Story," *Training,* July 1993, p. 40.

40. "Preventing On-the-Job Violence," *Inc.,* June 1996, p. 116.

41. Borysenko, *Minding the Body, Mending the Mind,* p. 160.

42. Selby, *Conscious Healing,* p. 32.

43. Walton C. Boshear and Karl G. Albrecht, *Understanding People: Models and Concepts* (San Diego: University Associates, 1977), pp. 41–46.

44. Chris Hill and Toby Hanlon, "Twenty-Six Simple Ways to Change How You Feel," *Prevention,* August 1993, p. 63.

45. Borysenko, *Minding the Body, Mending the Mind,* pp. 164–165.

46. Ibid.

47. Beryl Lieff Benderly, "The Perps Are Almost Always Male," *New York Times Book Review,* June 6, 1993, p. 26.

48. William J. Crockett, "Our Two Worlds," *Training & Development,* May 1982, p. 60.

49. Sam Keen, *Fire in the Belly—On Being a Man* (New York: Bantam Books, 1991), p. 242.

50. Borysenko *Minding the Body, Mending the Mind,* p. 169.

51. Ellen Safier, "Our Experts Answer Your Questions," *Menninger Letter,* May 1993, p. 8.

52. Leo F. Buscaglia, *Loving Each Other* (Thorofare, N.J.: Slack, 1984), p. 160.

53. Keen, *Fire in the Belly,* p. 242.

Chapter 10

1. Bob Nelson, *1001 Ways to Reward Employees* (New York: Workman, 1994), p. 106.

2. Ann Marsh, "Slice of Life," *Forbes,* April 21, 1997, pp. 64–66.

3. Alex Markels and Joann S. Lublin, "Longevity—Reward Programs Get Short Shrift," *Wall Street Journal,* April 27, 1995, p. B1.

4. Roger L. Hale and Rita F. Maehling, *Recognition Redefined* (Exeter, N.H.: Monochrome Press, 1993), p. 8.

5. Ronald Henkoff, "The Best Service Workers," *Fortune,* October 3, 1994, p. 116.

6. "Crossed Wires on Employee Motivation," *Training & Development,* July 1995, p. 59.

7. Kenneth Blanchard and Spencer Johnson, *The One Minute Manager* (New York: Morrow, 1982), p. 43.

8. Harry L. Miller, *Teaching and Learning in Adult Education* (London: Macmillan, 1964), pp. 34–36.

9. Sandra Scarr and James Vander Zanden, *Understanding Psychology,* 5th ed. (New York: Random House, 1987), p. 565.

10. Claude Steiner, *TA Made Simple* (San Francisco: Transactional Pubs, 1973), p. 6.

11. Evelyn Sieburg, "Confirming and Disconfirming Organizational Communication," in *Communication in Organizations,* ed. James L. Owen, Paul A. Page, and Gordon I. Zimmerman (St. Paul, Minn.: West, 1976), p. 130.

12. Jaclyn Fierman, "When Will You Get a Raise?" *Fortune,* July 12, 1993, p. 34.

13. "Leno Regrets Not Thanking Johnny," *San Francisco Examiner,* September 8, 1995, p. C17.

14. Deepak Chopra, *The Seven Spiritual Laws of Success* (San Rafael, Calif.: Amber-Allen, 1994), pp. 30–31.

15. *Random Acts of Kindness* (Berkeley, Calif.: Conari Press, 1993), pp. 1, 54, 68, 91.

16. Nelson, *1001 Ways to Reward Employees,* p. ix.

17. Bruce A. Baldwin, "Complimentary Guidelines," *Pace,* August, 1988, p. 19.

18. Nelson, *1001 Ways to Reward Employees,* p. xv.

19. Christopher Hegarty, with Philip Goldberg, *How to Manage Your Boss* (New York: Rawson, Wade, 1980), p. 125.

20. John E. Rigdon, "Bosses Everywhere Will Hold Them Up As Models," *Wall Street Journal,* August 8, 1993, p. B1.

21. "How to Run an Incentive Program," *Incentive,* July 1990, p. 2.

22. Susan Sonnesyn Brooks, "Noncash Ways to Compensate Employees," *HR Magazine,* April 1994, p. 39.

23. Tom Ehrenfeld, "The Productivity-Boosting Gain-Sharing Report," *Inc.,* August 1993, p. 87.

24. Jack Stack, "The Problem with Profit Sharing," *Inc.,* November 1996, pp. 67–68.

25. Gene Koretz, "Truly Tying Pay to Performance," *Business Week,* February 17, 1997, p. 25.

26. Brooks, "Noncash Ways to Compensate Employees," p. 40.

27. Alfie Kohn, "Why Incentive Plans Cannot Work," *Harvard Business Review,* September–October 1993, p. 58.

28. Ibid.

29. Ibid., pp. 58–59.

30. Ibid., pp. 61–62.

31. Bob Nelson, Lael Good, and Tom Hill, "You Want To-MAYtoes, I Want ToMAHtoes," *Training,* 1997, p. 57.

Chapter 11

1. Kevin Helliker, "Smile: That Cranky Shopper May Be a Store Spy," *Wall Street Journal,* November 30, 1994, p. B1.

2. Hal Kahn, "Secrets of a Mystery Shopper," *San Jose Mercury News,* September 22, 1996, pp. 1E, 2E.

3. Stephen R. Covey, *The 7 Habits of Highly Effective People* (New York: Simon & Schuster, 1989), pp. 22, 34.

4. Susan Bixler, *Professional Presence* (New York: G. P. Putnam's Sons, 1991), p. 16.

5. "Author: Success Pivots on First Impressions," *San Jose Mercury News,* November 8, 1992, p. 2 PC.

6. Douglas A. Bernstein, Alison Clarke-Stewart, Edward J. Roy, and Christopher D. Wickens, *Psychology,* 4th ed. (Boston: Houghton Mifflin, 1997), p. 241.

7. "Dress Codes for Presidential Candidates," *Parade Magazine,* November 5, 1995, p. 17.

8. Malcolm Fleschner, with Gerhard Gschwandtner, "Power Talk," *Personal Selling Power,* July/August 1995, p. 14.

9. Leonard Zunin and Natalie Zunin, *Contact—The First Four Minutes* (New York: Ballantine Books, 1972), p. 17.

10. Clyde Haberman, "No Offense," *New York Times Book Review,* February 18, 1996, p. 11.

11. Diane E. Lewis, "Some Firms in a Twist over Braids," *San Jose Mercury News,* May 25, 1997, p. 1 PC.

12. Haberman, "No Offense," p. 11.

13. James Gray, Jr., *The Winning Image* (New York: American Management Association, 1982), pp. 3–5.

14. Ibid., p. 6.

15. Robert L. Simison, "GM Is Spending $25 Million to Teach Good Olds Guys to Be Even Friendlier," *Wall Street Journal,* May 11, 1994, p. B5.

16. John T. Molloy, *Dress for Success* (New York: Peter H. Wyden, 1975); and John T. Molloy, *The Woman's Dress for Success Book* (New York: Warner Books, 1977).

17. Bixler, *Professional Presence,* p. 141.

18. Michael Solmon, "Standard Issue," *Psychology Today,* December 1987, pp. 30–31.

19. Haidee E. Allerton, "Dress Code Backlash," *Training & Development,* August 1997, p. 8.

20. Dave Knesel, "Image Consulting—A Well-Dressed Step Up the Corporate Ladder," *Pace,* July–August 1981, p. 74.

21. Haidee Allerton, "Working Life," *Training & Development,* April 1993, p. 96.

22. Bill Saporito, "Unsuit Yourself—Management Goes Informal," *Fortune,* September 20, 1993, p. 118.

23. "HR Shows Its Fall Collection." *Training,* August 1996, p. 14.

24. Janet G. Elsea, *The Four-Minute Sell* (New York: Simon & Schuster, 1984), p. 34.

25. Susan Bixler, *The Professional Image* (New York: Perigee Books, 1984), p. 217.

26. Ibid., p. 219.

27. Martha Sherrill Dailey, "The Way We Sound," *Roanoke Times & World-News,* May 8, 1988, p. 1.

28. Marc Hequet, "Giving Good Feedback," *Training,* September 1994, p. 74.

28. Adapted from Zunin and Zunin, *Contact,* pp. 102–108; "Handshake 101," *Training & Development,* November 1995, p. 71.

30. Amy Gamerman, "Lunch with Letitia: Our Reporter Minds Her Manners," *Wall Street Journal,* March 3, 1994, p. A14.

31. Barbara Lazear Ascher, "Mind and Manners," *Self,* May 1994, p. 129.

32. Jacqueline Thompson, *Image Impact* (New York: Ace Books, 1981), p. 8.

33. Bob Greene, "Why Must We Say Things Like . . . and . . . ?" *Roanoke Times & World-News,* April 27, 1980, p. 7.

34. Ann Marie Sabath, "Meeting Etiquette: Agendas and More," *DECA Dimensions,* January–February 1994, p. 8.

35. Susan Bixler, "Your Professional Presence," *Training Dimensions,* vol. 9, no. 1, 1994, p. 1.

36. Letitia Baldrige, *Letitia Baldrige's Complete Guide to Executive Manners* (New York: Rawson Associates, 1985), p. 13.

37. Nancy K. Austin, "What Do America Online and Dennis Rodman Have in Common?" *Inc.,* July 1997, p. 54.

38. Laura Bird, "No Detail Escapes the Attention of Abercrombie & Fitch's Chief," *Wall Street Journal,* October 7, 1997, p. B1.

Chapter 12

1. Patricia Sellers, "When Tragedy Forces Change," *Fortune,* January 10, 1994, p. 115.

2. "Synergy: Or, We're All in This Together," *Training,* September 1985, pp. 64, 65.

3. William G. Dyer, *Team Building: Issues and Alternatives* (Reading, Mass.: Addison-Wesley, 1977), p. 9.

4. "Industry Report—1997," *Training,* October 1997, p. 62.

5. Robert Kreitner, *Management,* 7th ed. (Boston: Houghton Mifflin, 1998), p. 402.

6. Rollin Glaser, *Helping Your Organization Gear Up for Self-Managing Teams,* (King of Prussia Pa.: Organization Design and Development, Inc., 1991), pp. 2–3.

7. Michael Selz, "Testing Self-Managed Teams, Entrepreneur Hopes to Lose Job," *Wall Street Journal,* January 11, 1994, p. B1.

8. D. Keith Denton, "Multi-Skilled Teams Replace Old Work Systems," *H.R. Magazine,* September 1992, pp. 48–56.

9. "Caddy Roars onto the Right Track," *Business Week,* December 23, 1991, p. 104.

10. J. Thomas Buck, "The Rocky Road to Team-Based Management," *Training & Development,* April 1995, pp. 35–38.

11. Adapted from a list in Douglas McGregor, *The Human Side of Enterprise* (New York: McGraw-Hill, 1960), pp. 232–235.

12. The Leadership Grid® appears in *Leadership Dilemmas—Grid Solutions* by Robert R. Blake and Anne Adams McCanse. Copyright ©1991 by Scientific Methods, Inc.

13. From *The New Managerial Grid,* by Robert R. Blake and Jane Srygley Mouton. Houston: Gulf Publishing Company. Copyright ©1978, p. 11. Reproduced by permission.

14. Robert R. Blake and Jane Srygley Mouton, "How to Choose a Leadership Style," *Training & Development,* February 1982, pp. 41–42.

15. Reported in Ron Zemke, "What Are High-Achieving Managers Really Like?" *Training/HRD,* February 1979, p. 35–36.

16. Jay Hall, *The Competence Connection* (The Woodlands, Tex.: Woodstead Press, 1988), p. 77.

17. Adapted with permission from the April 1998 issue of *Training* magazine. Copyright 1998. Lakewood Publications, Minneapolis, MN. All rights reserved. Not for resale.

18. "An Interview with Warren Bennis," *Training,* August 1997, p. 33.

19. These two dimensions can be measured by the *Leadership Opinion Questionnaire* developed by Edwin A. Fleishman and available from Science Research Associates, Inc., Chicago, Illinois.

20. "Making a Nickel Do a Dime's Work," *Training,* April 1994, p. 12.

21. "Managers Focusing More on Families," *Menninger Letter,* March 1993, p. 2.

22. Sue Shellenbarger, "Enter the New Hero: A Boss Who Knows You Have a Life," *Wall Street Journal,* May 8, 1996, p. B1.

23. "Tips for Teams," *Training,* February 1994, p. 14.

24. "The HRD Hall of Fame," *Training,* January 1994, p. 38.

25. "The Trouble with Kids," *Inc.,* January 1983, p. 63.

26. Kreitner, *Management*, p. 457.
27. Paul Hersey, *The Situational Leader* (Escondido, Calif.: Center for Leadership Studies, 1984), pp. 29, 30.
28. Ibid., p. 57.
29. Margaret Kaeter, "The Leaders Among Us," *Business Ethics*, July–August 1994, p. 46.
30. J. Oliver Crom, "Every Employee a Leader: Part One," *The Leader*, April 1997, p. 6.
31. Peter Koestenbaum, *Leadership—The Inner Side of Greatness* (San Francisco: Jossey-Bass, 1991), pp. 179–183.
32. Donald Sanzotta and Lois Drapin, "Getting Along with the Boss," *Supervisory Management*, July 1984, p. 16.
33. "The Art of Followership," *Personal Report*, June 15, 1988, p. 1.
34. Judy B. Rosener, "Ways Women Lead," *Harvard Business Review*, November–December 1990, pp. 119–125.

Chapter 13

1. Dudley Weeks, *The Eight Essential Steps to Conflict Resolution* (New York: G. P. Putnam's Sons, 1992), p. 7.
2. Ibid., pp. 7–8.
3. Jerry B. Harvey, *The Abilene Paradox and Other Meditations on Management* (Lexington, Mass.: Lexington Books, 1980), pp. 14–25.
4. "A Matter of Attitude," *Royal Bank Letter*, May–June 1994.
5. Annie Fisher, "Which One Should I Fire? . . . Is My Voice Mail Monitored? . . . and Other Queries," *Fortune*, November 25, 1996, p. 173.
6. Douglas A. Blackman and Glenn Burkins, "UPS's Early Missteps in Assessing the Teamsters Help Explain How Union Won Gains in Fight," *Wall Street Journal*, August 21, 1997, p. A16.
7. Bill Vlasic, "Trench Warfare in Detroit," *Business Week*, May 5, 1997, p. 130.
8. David Stiebel, "The Myth of Hidden Harmony," *Training*, March 1997, p. 114.
9. "Surviving the Office Jerk Takes Patience," *Springfield News-Leader*, November 6, 1994, p. 2E.
10. "Assertiveness: More Than a Forceful Attitude," *Supervisory Management*, February 1994, p. 3.
11. Stephen Ash, "How to Make Assertiveness Work for You," *Supervisory Management*, p. 8.
12. Albert Ellis, *Effective Self-Assertion*, Psychology Today audiotape, 1985.
13. David Stiebel, *When Talking Makes Things Worse!* (Dallas: Whitehall & Nolton, 1997), p. 17.
14. Weeks, *The Eight Essential Steps to Conflict Resolution*, pp. 90–101.
15. Roger Fisher and William Ury, *Getting to Yes* (New York: Penguin Books, 1981), p. 59.
16. Weeks, *The Eight Essential Steps to Conflict Resolution*, p. 228.
17. Ibid., p. 223.
18. Ibid., p. 127–129.
19. Harold H. Bloomfield and Robert K. Cooper, *The Power of 5*, (Emmaus, Pa.: Rodale Press, 1995), pp. 374–375.
20. Toddi Gutner, "When It's Time to Do Battle with Your Company," *Business Week*, February 10, 1997, pp. 130–131.
21. Ibid., p. 131.
22. Robert Levering and Milton Moskowitz, *The 100 Best Companies to Work for in America* (New York: Currency-Doubleday, 1993), pp. 123–124.
23. "Labor's Surprising Reemergence," *Business Week*, February 17, 1997, p. 110.
24. "Why America Needs Unions but Not the Kind It Has Now," *Business Week*, May 23, 1994, p. 78.
25. Aaron Bernstein, "Busting Unions Can Backfire on the Bottom Line," *Business Week*, March 18, 1991, p. 108.
26. Aaron Bernstein, "Look Who's Pushing Productivity," *Business Week*, April 7, 1997, pp. 72–76.
27. "Labor Deals That Offer a Break from 'Us vs. Them,'" *Business Week*, August 2, 1993, p. 30.
28. "Why America Needs Unions," p. 71.
29. "Unions Realizing Change Is Essential," *Denver Post*, June 21, 1995, p. 9G.
30. Kirstin Downey Grimsley and Frank Swoboda, "UAW Refused to Act on Complaints of Harassment, Former Official Says," *Denver Post*, June 8, 1996, p. P3.
31. Carol Kleiman, "More Than Just a 'Brotherhood,'" *San Jose Mercury News*, May 11, 1997, p. 1 PC.
32. Sue Shellenbarger, "Karen Nussbaum Plans to Focus Unions on Family Issues," *Wall Street Journal*, February 19, 1997, p. B1.
33. "Labor's Modest Quid Pro Quo," *Business Week*, November 11, 1996, p. 38.
34. Aaron Bernstein, "Sharing Prosperity," *Business Week*, September 1, 1997, pp. 64–69.

Chapter 14

1. Bob Filipczak, "Are We Having Fun Yet," *Training*, April 1995, pp. 48–56; Hal Lancaster, "Your Career May Be a Laugh Track Away from the Fast Track," *Wall Street Journal*, March 26, 1996, p. B1; Haidee Allerton, "Deposits? Try the Conga Line," *Training & Development*, May 1995, p. 103.
2. Arnold A. Lazarus and Clifford N. Lazarus, *The 60-Second Shrink* (San Luis Obispo, Calif.: Impact Publishers, 1997), p. 86; Howard I. Glazer, *Getting in Touch with Stress Management* (American Telephone and Telegraph, 1988), p. 2.

3. Lazarus and Lazarus, *The 60-Second Shrink,* pp. 86–87.

4. Ibid., p. 86.

5. James E. Loehr, *Stress for Success* (New York: Times Books, 1997), pp. 4, 17.

6. Ibid., pp. 18, 22.

7. Glazer, *Getting in Touch with Stress Management,* p. 2.

8. Harold H. Bloomfield and Robert K. Cooper, *The Power of 5* (Emmaus, Pa.: Rodale Press, 1995), p. 18.

9. Robert Carey, "A Balancing Act," *Performance Strategies,* June 1996, p. 14.

10. Craig Brod, *Technostress: The Human Cost of the Computer Revolution* (Reading, Mass.: Addison-Wesley, 1984), p. 16.

11. David Shenk, *Data Smog—Surviving the Information Glut* (San Francisco: Harper Edge, 1997), p. 43.

12. Brod, *Technostress,* p. 17.

13. Shenk, *Data Smog,* p. 31.

14. Kathleen Kerwin and Catherine Arnst, "A Cubicle with a View," *Business Week,* June 2, 1997, p. 8.

15. Bloomfield and Cooper, *The Power of 5,* p. 299.

16. John Grossman, "The Quest for Quiet," *Health,* February 1990, p. 59.

17. Jaclyn Fierman, "It's 2 A.M., Let's Go to Work," *Fortune,* August 21, 1995, pp. 82–88.

18. Mary Scott, "Interview with Jeremy Rifkin," *Business Ethics,* September/October 1996, p. 33.

19. Kenneth Labich, "Psycho Bosses from Hell," *Fortune,* March 18, 1996, p. 123; Vanessa Ho, "Companies Get the Message That Happy Workers Help Bottom Line," *Roanoke Times & World-News,* November 13, 1995, p. E6.

20. Edith Weiner, "The Fast Approaching Future," *Retail Issues Letter,* July 1994, p. 3.

21. Sue Shellenbarger, "Work and Family," *Wall Street Journal,* October 26, 1994, p. B1.

22. Sue Shellenbarger, "Work and Family," *Wall Street Journal,* November 2, 1994, p.B1.

23. Art Ulene, *Really Fit Really Fast* (Encino, Calif.: HealthPoints, 1996), p. 59.

24. Ibid., pp. 56–58.

25. Loehr, *Stress for Success,* p. 179.

26. Ibid., p. 183.

27. "Smart Managing," *Fortune,* May 26, 1997, p. 149.

28. "Overcoming Obstacles," *Personal Selling Power,* 15th Anniversary Issue, 1995, p. 101.

29. Bloomfield and Cooper, *The Power of 5,* pp. 25–26.

30. Loehr, *Stress for Success,* pp. 185–186.

31. Beth Baker, "The Faith Factor," *Common Boundary,* July/August 1997, pp. 20–26.

32. Adapted from Herbert Benson, *The Relaxation Response* (New York: Morrow, 1975), p. 19; Redford Williams and Virginia Williams, *Anger Kills* (New York: Harper Perennial, 1993), pp. 86–89; Bloomfield and Cooper, *The Power of 5,* pp. 34–35.

33. Robert Ornstein and David Sobel, *Healthy Pleasures* (New York: Addison-Wesley, 1989), pp. 215–217.

34. Norman Cousins, *Anatomy of an Illness: Reflections on Healing and Regeneration* (New York: Bantam Books, 1981).

35. Loehr, *Stress for Success,* p. 191.

36. Ann McGee-Cooper, *You Don't Have to Go Home from Work Exhausted* (New York: Bantam Books, 1992), pp. 52–53.

37. "Stress," *Men's Health,* November 1993, pp. 61–63.

38. Robert Carey, "A Balancing Act," *Performance Strategies,* June 1996, p. 18.

39. "Work Week," *Wall Street Journal,* July 25, 1995, p. A1.

40. Joan Hamilton, "Can Company Counselors Help You Cope," *Business Week,* November 14, 1994, pp. 140–141.

41. Juliet Bruce, "12-Step Research: Trying to Measure the Immeasurable," *Common Boundary,* September/October 1991, p. 33.

42. Ibid., p. 34.

43. Joan Borysenko, "Ridden with Guilt," *Health,* March 1990, p. 78.

44. Ester Buchholz, "The Call of Solitude," *Psychology Today,* January/February 1998, pp. 50–54.

45. *Employee Burnout: America's Newest Epidemic* (Minneapolis: Northwestern National Life Insurance Co., 1991), p. 17.

46. Leonard Abramson, "Boost to the Bottom Line," *Personnel Administrator,* July 1988, p. 38.

Chapter 15

1. Donna Fenn, "More Than Just Affirmative Action," *Inc.,* July 1995, p. 93.

2. Sharon Nelton, "Nurturing Diversity," *Nation's Business,* June 1995, p. 25.

3. "Diversity—Making the Business Case," *Business Week,* December 9, 1995, n.p.

4. Adapted from a definition developed by 3M Company published in Michael L. Wheeler, *Diversity: Business Rationale and Strategies* (New York: Conference Board, 1995), p. 9.

5. Marilyn Loden and Judy B. Rosener, *Workforce America!* (Homewood, Ill.: Business One Irwin, 1991), p. 18.

6. Ibid., p. 21.

7. Dudley Weeks, *The 8 Essential Steps to Conflict Resolution* (New York: G. P. Putnam's Sons, 1992), pp. 114–115.

8. Joann S. Lublin, "Companies Rethink Diversity Training," *Wall Street Journal,* June 16, 1995, p. B5A.

9. Daniel Goleman, *Emotional Intelligence* (New York: Bantam Books, 1995), pp. 156–157.

10. Lewis Brown Griggs and Lente-Louise Louw, *Valuing Diversity* (New York: McGraw-Hill, 1995), pp. 3–4, 150–151.

11. Ibid., p. 151.

12. Susan Garland, "Going Beyond Rhetoric on Race Relations," *Business Week,* June 23, 1997, p. 40.

13. Aaron Bernstein, "Is America Becoming More of a Class Society?" *Business Week,* February 26, 1996, pp. 86–91.

14. "Fifty-Something," *Training & Development,* May 1994, p. 143.

15. Griggs and Louw, *Valuing Diversity,* p. 17.

16. Haidee Allerton, "Not Older, Just Better," *Training & Development,* August 1995, p. 72.

17. Sam Fulwood III, "Black Still Isn't the Color of Money," *Venture,* March 1988, p. 32.

18. James Q. Wilson, "A Long Way from the Back of the Bus," *New York Times Book Review,* November 16, 1997, p. 10; Orlando Patterson, "Why Conduct a Racial Census?" *News & Observer,* July 13, 1997, p. 29A.

19. *American Heritage Dictionary,* 3d ed. (Boston: Houghton Mifflin, 1992), pp. 108, 195, 856, 918.

20. Robert S. Boynton, "Color Us Invisible," *New York Times Book Review,* August 17, 1997, p. 13.

21. Stephen Magagini, "A Race Free Consciousness," *News & Observer,* November 23, 1997, pp. 25a–26a.

22. Wilson, "A Long Way from the Back of the Bus," p. 10.

23. Lawrence Lindsey, "This Is a Political Matter," *Wall Street Journal,* December 26, 1996, p. 16A.

24. Gene Koretz, "A Law That Put People to Work," *Business Week,* February 10, 1997, p. 28.

25. "More of the Disabled Are Unemployed," *San Jose Mercury News,* August 18, 1996, p. 2 PC.

26. Deborah L. Jacobs, "The Americans with Disabilities Act," *Your Company* (Milwaukee, Wis.: Northwestern Mutual Life Insurance Co., Summer 1994), p. 10.

27. Thomas A. Stewart, "Gay in Corporate America," *Fortune,* December 16, 1991, p. 44.

28. Thomas Petzinger, Jr., "AT&T Class Teaches an Open Workplace Is Profitably Correct," *Wall Street Journal,* November 10, 1995, p. B1.

29. "Gays in the Workplace," *Inc.,* January 1996, p. 86.

30. U.S. Commission on Civil Rights, *Promise and Perceptions: Federal Efforts to Eliminate Employment Discrimination Through Affirmative Action* (Washington, D.C.: U.S. Government Printing Office, October 1981), p. 17.

31. Loden and Rosener, *Workforce America!,* p. 12.

32. Alex Markels, "A Diversity Program Can Prove Divisive," *Wall Street Journal,* January 30, 1997, p. B1.

33. Leone E. Wynter, "Do Diversity Programs Make a Difference?" *Wall Street Journal,* December 4, 1996, p. B1.

34. Nicole Harris, "A New Denny's—Diner by Diner," *Business Week,* March 25, 1996, pp. 166–168.

35. Lisa Lucadamo and Scott Cheney, "Learning from the Best," *Training & Development,* July 1997, pp. 25–26.

36. Faye Rice, "How to Make Diversity Pay," *Fortune,* August 8, 1994, p. 82.

37. Ibid., p. 84.

38. Stan Crock and Michele Galen, "A Thunderous Impact on Equal Opportunity," *Business Week,* June 26, 1995, p. 37.

39. Stephen M. Paskoff, "Ending the Workplace Diversity Wars," *Training,* August 1996, p. 44.

40. Cathleen Watson, "Making Diversity Work," *Executive Female,* September/October 1996, p. 42.

41. Paskoff, "Ending the Workplace Diversity Wars," pp. 46–47.

42. Joanne L. Symons, "Is Affirmative Action in America's Interest?" *Executive Female,* May/June 1995, p. 52.

43. Robert Kreitner, *Management,* 7th ed. (Boston: Houghton Mifflin, 1998), pp. 325–326.

44. Symons, "Is Affirmative Action in America's Interest?" p. 52.

45. Terry Eastland, "Endgame for Affirmative Action," *Wall Street Journal,* March 28, 1996, p. A15.

46. Michael K. Frisby, "Powell Reshapes Debate on Affirmative Action, Deepening Divisions Among Black Republicans," *Wall Street Journal,* August 13, 1996, p. A14.

47. Paul Berman, "Redefining Fairness," *New York Times Book Review,* April 14, 1996, p. 16.

48. Beth Baker, "Forcing America to Keep Faith," *AARP Bulletin,* vol. 38, no. 8, 1997, p. 8.

49. Geoffrey Brewer, "Why We Can't All Get Along," *Sales & Marketing Management,* December 1995, p. 32.

50. Katherine Roth, "God on the Job," *Working Woman,* February 1998, pp. 65–66.

Chapter 16

1. Earle Eldridge, "A Pioneer at Ford," *USA Today,* September 16, 1994, p. 2B.

2. George Tunick, "Re-educating Chauvinists,." *Executive Female,* January–February 1995, p. 82.

3. Wendy Kaminer, "Sexual Politics, Continued," *New York Times Book Review,* March 23, 1997, p. 12.

4. Elizabeth Holland, "Role Models," *Roanoke Times & World-News,* October 4, 1979.

5. Gene Koretz, "Women Swell the Workforce," *Business Week,* November 4, 1996, p. 32.

6. Naomi Freundlich, "Maybe Working Women Can't Have It All," *Business Week,* September 15, 1997, pp. 19–22; Keith H. Hammonds, "She Works Hard for the Money," *Business Week,* May 22, 1995, p. 54.

7. Gene Koretz, "Women's Work Is Still Waning," *Business Week,* November 3, 1997, p. 30.

8. Linda Himelstein, "Shatterproof Glass Ceiling," *Business Week,* October 28, 1996, p. 55; Leon E. Wynter, "Study Measures Status of Female Managers," *Wall Street Journal,* December 3, 1997, p. B1.

9. "No Easy Path for Women in Non-Traditional Careers," *Techniques,* April 1997, p. 17.

10. William R. "Max" Carey, Jr., "The Superman Complex," *Inc.,* October 1988, p. 84.

11. "Why Can't a Man Be More like . . . What?" *Business Week,* September 13, 1993, pp. 13–15.

12. Kim Clark, "Women, Men & Money," *Fortune,* August 5, 1996, p. 60.

13. "Work and Family," *Training & Development,* March 1994, p. 79.

14. Jerry Adler, "Building a Better Dad," *Newsweek,* June 17, 1996, pp. 58–64.

15. Tim Belknap, "Is the Grumble Gap Shrinking?" *Business Week,* October 28, 1996, p. 8; "Work Week," *Wall Street Journal,* January 16, 1996, p. A1.

16. Leon E. Wynter, "Study Measures Status of Female Managers," *Wall Street Journal,* December 3, 1997, p. B1; "Take No Comfort in Denial," *Executive Female,* July/August 1997, p. 70.

17. Gene Koretz, "Good News on Wage Inequality," *Business Week,* December 15, 1997, p. 30.

18. Keith H. Hammonds, "An Unbreakable Glass Ceiling?" *Business Week,* March 20, 1995, p. 42.

19. Gale Duff-Bloom, "Women in Retailing—Is There a Glass Ceiling?" *Retailing Issues Letter,* Center for Retailing Studies, Texas A & M University, May 1996, pp. 1–4.

20. "How to Crack the Glass Ceiling," *Training,* February 1995, pp. 19–21.

21. Kathleen R. Allen, "What Do Women Want?" *Inc.,* September 1996, p. 27; Thomas Petzinger, "Diane Dawson Keeps Focus on Business, Not on the Odds," *Wall Street Journal,* October 13, 1995, p. B1.

22. "Women Taking Care of Business," *Roanoke Times & World-News,* May 13, 1995, p. 16A.

23. Freundlich, "Maybe Working Women Can't Have It All," p. 19; Sue Shellenbarger, "Women Indicate Satisfaction with Role of Big Breadwinner," *Wall Street Journal,* May 11, 1995, p. B1.

24. Freundlich, "Maybe Working Women Can't Have It All," p. 19.

25. Rosalind C. Barnett and Caryl Rivers, "The Myth of the Miserable Working Woman," *Working Woman,* February 1992, pp. 62–67.

26. Freundlich, "Maybe Working Women Can't Have It All," p. 22.

27. "The Postpartum News: Moms Go Back to Work," *Training,* June 1994, p. 64.

28. "Family and Medical Leave Act: Does It Apply to You?" *Your Company,* Summer 1993, p. 10.

29. Chris Lee, "The Feminization of Management," *Training,* November 1994, pp. 25–31; "A Woman's Place? In Charge," *Business Week,* February 27, 1995, p. 8.

30. Kim Clark, "Women, Men & Money," *Fortune,* August 5, 1996, pp. 60–61.

31. Robert Barker, "One Man and a Little Lady," *Business Week,* April 15, 1991, p. 91.

32. Sherwood Ross, "More Fathers Taking Advantage of Parental Leave Time," *San Jose Mercury News,* April 13, 1997, p. 2 PC.

33. Seth Godin, ed., *The 1995 Information Please Business Almanac and Sourcebook* (Boston: Houghton Mifflin, 1994), p. 201; Sue Shellenbarger, "Deciding How Soon to Prepare Your Child to Stay Home Alone," *Wall Street Journal,* March 20, 1996, p. B1; Keith H. Hammonds, "Clinton's Child-Care Conference: Just Chatter?" *Business Week,* November 3, 1997, p. 46.

34. "Child-Care Crunch Puts Parents Between the Kids and the Boss," *Wall Street Journal,* October 12, 1994, p. B1.

35. Laurie M. Grossman, "What About Us?" *Wall Street Journal,* June 21, 1993, p. R8.

36. Ibid.

37. Ibid.

38. Wendy Lee Gramm, "The Economy, a Women's Issue," *Wall Street Journal,* March 22, 1994, p. B3.

39. Kathy Bergen, "Compressed Workweek Pays Off—on 10th Day," *Roanoke Times,* March 30, 1997, p. B2.

40. "There's Enough Work to Go Around Here," *Business Week,* March–April 1994, p. 31.

41. Sarah Priestman, "Hearth and Home Office," *Common Boundary,* July/August 1996, p. 55.

42. Marc Hequet, "How Telecommuting Transforms Work," *Training,* November 1994, p. 57.

43. Anne B. Fischer, "Sexual Harassment: What to Do," *Fortune,* August 23, 1993, p. 85.

44. Brian S. Moskal, "Sexual Harassment: An Update," *Industry Week,* November 18, 1991, p. 38.

45. Ron Ruggles, "California Jury Dismisses Friday's Harassment Suit," *Nation's Restaurant News,* November 21, 1994, p. 7.

46. "No Easy Path for Women in Non-Traditional Careers," *Techniques,* April 1997, p. 21.

47. De'Ann Weimer and Emily Thornton, "Slow Healing at Mitsubishi," *Business Week,* September 22, 1997, pp. 74–75.

48. "No Easy Path for Women in Non-Traditional Careers," p. 17.

49. "Men Start to Fight Back As Accusations Increase," *Wall Street Journal,* October 18, 1991, p. 3B.

50. Deborah Tannen, "The Power of Talk: Who Gets Heard and Why," *Harvard Business Review,* September–October 1995, pp. 129–140.
51. Jayne Tear, "They Just Don't Understand Gender Dynamics," *Wall Street Journal,* November 20, 1995, p. A14; Dianna Booker, "The Gender Gap in Communication," *Training Dimensions* (West Des Moines: American Media Incorporated, Fall 1994), p. 1; Jennifer J. Laabs, "Kinney Narrows the Gender Gap," *Personnel Journal,* August 1994, pp. 83–85.
52. Tannen, "The Power of Talk," p. 146.
53. Tear, "They Just Don't Understand Gender Dynamics," p. A14.
54. Anastasia Toufexis, "Coming from a Different Place," *Time,* Fall 1990, p. 66.

Chapter 17

1. Sue Shellenbarger, "Software Ace Turns His Life Upside Down, and Is Happier for It," *Wall Street Journal,* January 31, 1996, p. B1.
2. Keith H. Hammonds, "Balancing Work and Family," *Business Week,* September 16, 1996, p. 80.
3. Amy Saltzman, *Downshifting* (New York: HarperCollins, 1991), p. 16.
4. Marc Heguet, "Flat and Happy?" *Training,* April 1995, pp. 29–34.
5. Robert Kuttner, "No Time to Smell the Roses Anymore," *New York Times Book Review,* February 2, 1992, pp. 1, 21.
6. Lynn Lannon, "Giving Back: The Secret of Creating Success," *Training & Development,* April 1990, p. 58.
7. Robert McGarvey, "Softening the Blow," *U.S. Air,* September 1991, p. 18.
8. Sue Shellenbarger, "Keeping Your Career a Manageable Part of Your Life," *Wall Street Journal,* April 12, 1995, p. B1.
9. Kuttner, "No Time to Smell the Roses Anymore," p. 21; Gene Koretz, "Those Educated Moonlighters," *Business Week,* August 4, 1997, p. 22.
10. "U.S. Workers Suffer from a Time-Off Gap," *Business Week,* August 12, 1991, p. 16.
11. Edward Dolnick, "Trade Money for Time," *Health,* October 1994, p. 53; Stuart R. Levine, "The Case for Balance," *The Leader,* January 1996, p. 6.
12. "When Success Fails to Make You Happy," *Working Smart,* September 1991, p. 1.
13. Marsha McEuen, "A Natural Art," *Santa Fean,* August 1997, pp. 104–107.
14. Interview conducted on February 8, 1992.
15. Ronald Henkoff, "So You Want to Change Your Job," *Fortune,* January 15, 1996, p. 52.
16. Marsha Sinetar, *Do What You Love . . . The Money Will Follow* (New York: Dell, 1987), p. 11.
17. Ibid., pp. 11–12.
18. Anne Fisher, "Six Ways to Supercharge Your Career," *Fortune,* January 13, 1997, pp. 46–48; John Epperheimer, "If It Feels Good, Do It and Change Your Career," *San Jose Mercury News,* July 17, 1996, p. 7G.
19. Michael Phillips, *The Seven Laws of Money* (Menlo Park, Calif.: Word Wheel and Random House, 1997), p. 9.
20. McEuen, "A Natural Art," p. 105.
21. Sinetar, *Do What You Love,* pp. 14–15.
22. John Naisbitt and Patricia Aburdene, *Re-Inventing the Corporation* (New York: Warner Books, 1985), p. 5.
23. Sinetar, *Do What You Love,* p. 15.
24. Shellenbarger, "Keeping Your Career a Manageable Part of Your Life," p. B1.
25. Sue Shellenbarger, "New Job Hunters Ask Recruiters, Is There a Life After Work? *Wall Street Journal,* January 29, 1997, p. B1.
26. Patricia Sellers, "Don't Call Me Slacker!" *Fortune,* December 12, 1994, p. 196.
27. Howard Gleckman, "Generation $ Is More like It," *Business Week,* November 3, 1997, p. 44.
28. Melvyn Kinder, *Going Nowhere Fast* (Englewood Cliffs, N.J.: Prentice-Hall, 1990), p. 76.
29. Michael Toms, "The Soul of Money—A Conversation with Lynne Twist," *New Dimensions,* January–February 1997, pp. 7–8.
30. Ibid., p. 8.
31. Rudi Dornbusch, "Why Is the Middle Class Really Bogging Down?" *Business Week,* February 13, 1995, p. 25; Robert Kuttner, "Owning Up to the Costs of Free Trade," *Business Week,* April 28, 1997, p. 22.
32. Teri Lammers Prior, "If I Were President . . .," *Inc.,* April 1995, pp. 56–60.
33. Michael Toms, "Money: The Third Side of the Coin" (interview with Joe Dominguez and Vicki Robin), *New Dimensions,* May–June 1991, p. 7.
34. Susan Smith Jones, "Choose to Be Healthy and Celebrate Life," *New Realities,* September–October 1988, pp. 17–19.
35. Ibid., p. 18.
36. Hal Lancaster, "Re-Engineering Authors Reconsider Re-Engineering," *Wall Street Journal,* January 17, 1995, p. B1.
37. Derwin Fox, "Career Insurance for Today's World," *Training & Development,* March 1996, pp. 63–64.
38. Ibid., p. 63.
39. Ibid., p. 64.
40. Saltzman, *Downshifting,* p. 23.

41. Jay T. Knippen, Thad B. Green, and Kurt Sutton, "Asking Not to Be Overworked," *Supervisory Management,* February 1992, p. 6.

42. Art Ulene, *Really Fit Really Fast* (Encino, Calif.: HealthPoints, 1996), pp. 198–199.

43. Marilyn Chase, "Weighing the Benefits of Mental-Health Days Against Guilt Feelings," *Wall Street Journal,* September 9, 1996, p. B1.

44. Ulene, *Really Fit Really Fast,* p. 199.

45. Pam Sebastian, "Making Friends for Life," *Wall Street Journal,* December 11, 1996, p. A22.

46. Leo Booth, "When God Becomes a Drug," *Common Boundary,* September/October 1991, p. 30.

47. Harold H. Bloomfield and Robert K. Cooper, *The Power of 5* (Emmaus, Pa.: Rodale Press 1995), p. 484.

48. "Making the Spiritual Connection," *Lears,* December 1989, p. 72.

49. Robert Bolton and Dorothy Grover Bolton, *People Styles at Work* (New York: AMACOM, 1996), pp. 110–111.

50. Barnaby J. Feder, "Clergymen on the Job to Help Workers Deal with Problems," *Roanoke Times,* October 13, 1996. p. A-6.

51. G. Paul Zachary, "The New Search for Meaning in Meaningless Work," *Wall Street Journal,* January 9, 1997, p. B1.

52. Judith Valente, "Some Employ Faith to Get the Job Done," *USA Today,* June 16, 1995, p. B1.

53. Ibid., p. B2.

54. Redford Williams and Virginia Williams, *Anger Kills* (New York: HarperCollins, 1993), p. 181.

55. Ibid., p. 182.

56. Chris Lee and Ron Zemke, "The Search for Spirit in the Workplace," *Training,* June 1993, p. 25.

57. "Wellness Facts," *University of California at Berkeley Wellness Letter,* November 1995, p. 1.

58. *Dietary Guidelines for Americans* (Washington, D.C.: U.S. Department of Health and Human Services, December 1995), pp. 3–21.

59. Ibid., p. 5.

60. Ibid., p. 36.

61. Ibid., p. 40–41.

62. Ulene, *Really Fit Really Fast,* pp. 20–21.

63. "One Small Step . . . ," *University of California at Berkeley Wellness Letter,* January 1991, p. 1; Kenneth Blanchard, D. W. Edington, and Marjorie Blanchard, *The One Minute Manager Gets Fit* (New York: Morrow, 1986), p. 36.

64. Robert A. Gleser, *The Healthmark Program for Life* (New York: McGraw-Hill, 1988), p. 147.

65. Ibid., p. 143.

66. *Fitness Fundamentals* (Washington, D.C.: Department of Health and Human Services, 1988), p. 2.

67. Stephen R. Covey, *The 7 Habits of Highly Effective People* (New York: Simon & Schuster, 1989), p. 46.

68. James Fadiman, *Be All That You Are* (Seattle: Westlake Press, 1986), p. 25.

69. David L. Mortellaro, Response to question and answer interview, the *Roanoke Times,* July 29, 1995, p. A10.

70. Robert McGarvey, "Getting Your Goals," *U.S. Air,* July 1989, p. 28.

71. Bruce A. Baldwin, "Barriers to Success," *U.S. Air,* June 1992, p. 18.

72. Fadiman, *Be All That You Are,* p. 45.

73. Pete Engardio and Peter Finch, "Kazuo Wada's Answered Prayers," *Business Week,* August 26, 1991, p. 66.

74. Mike Hernacki, *The Ultimate Secret of Getting Absolutely Everything You Want* (New York: Berkley Books, 1988), p. 35.

75. Adapted from Bloomfield and Cooper, *The Power of 5,* pp. 492–493.

Credits

Case Credits

Case 1.1: Rochelle Sharpe, "Being Family Friendly Doesn't Mean Promoting Women," *Wall Street Journal,* March 29, 1994, p. B1; Sue Shellenbarger, "Work and Family," *Wall Street Journal,* June 1, 1994, p. B1; Milton Moskowitz, "Best Companies for Working Mothers," *Working Mother,* October 1996, pp. 10–45; Sue Shellenbarger, "Two-Income Couples Are Making Changes at Work and at Home," *Wall Street Journal,* February 14, 1996, p. B1.

Case 1.2: Kenneth Labich, "Is Herb Kelleher America's Best CEO?" *Fortune,* May 2, 1994, p. 50; Robert Levering and Milton Moskowitz, *The 100 Best Companies to Work for in America* (New York: Currency-Doubleday, 1993), p. 414; Scott McCartney, "Airline Industry's Top-Ranked Woman Keeps Southwest's Small-Fry Spirit Alive," *Wall Street Journal,* November 30, 1995, p. B1.

Case 2.1: Thomas O'Boyle, "GE Refrigerator Woes Illustrate the Hazards in Changing a Product," *Wall Street Journal,* May 7, 1990, pp. A1, A5; "GE's Betting on a Bigger Fridge—the World's Biggest," *Springfield News-Leader,* July 29, 1994, pp. 1B, 6B.

Case 2.2: Rick Atkinson, "Mercedes Workers Polish Their Y'Alls and Howdies," *Denver Post,* February 27, 1994, p. 3H; Jack Yamaguchi, "Eagles Are Landing in Japan," *Road & Track,* July 1994, p. 24; "White House Watch," *The New Republic,* October 25, 1993, p. 48; Justin Martin, "Mercedes: Made in Alabama," *Fortune,* July 7, 1997, p. 158.

Case 3.2: "The New Corporate World Is Flat," *LIFO Training News,* vol. 7, no. 1. (Beverly Hills, Calif.: Stuart Atkins, Inc.).

Case 4.1: David M. Garner, "The 1997 Body Image Survey," *Psychology Today,* January/February 1997, pp. 30–48; "Altering Your Image: Strategies from the Trenches," *Psychology Today,* January/February 1997, p. 80; Mary Pipher, *Reviving Ophelia* (New York: Ballantine Books, 1994), pp. 183–184.

Case 4.2: California Assembly Bill No. 3659; California State Department of Education, *Toward a State of Esteem* (Sacramento: Department of Education, January 1990), p. 37; Gloria Steinem, *Revolution from Within: A Book of Self-Esteem* (Boston: Little, Brown, 1992), pp. 26–31; Alfie Kohn, "The Truth About Self-Esteem," *Phi Delta Kappan,* December 1994, p. 275.

Case 5.1: Jennifer J. Laabs, "Beef About Employee Benefits Causes Religious Group to Boycott Disney," *Personnel Journal,* August 1996, p. 11; "Southern Baptists Take on Disney," *U.S. News & World Report,* June 24, 1996, p. 18; Kate Clinton, "The Lull Before the Lull," *Progressive,* August 1996, p. 46.

Case 5.2: "Paying Employees to Work Elsewhere," *Inc.,* February 1993, p. 29; "Interview with Tom Chappell," *Business Ethics,* January/February 1994, pp. 16–18; Milton Moskowitz, "Business Prophets," *Common Boundary,* March–April 1994, pp. 55–58; "Profiles in Marketing: Katie Shisler," *Sales & Marketing Management,* March 1993, p. 12.

Case 6.1: Robert Levering and Milton Moskowitz, *The 100 Best Companies to Work for in America* (New York: Currency-Doubleday, 1993), pp. 270–272.

Case 6.2: Hal Lancaster, "Office Politics: It's Almost Impossible to Get Ahead Without It," *San Jose Mercury News,* April 16, 1997, p. 6G; Cheryl Shavers, "Moving the Rock Called Organizational Politics," *San Jose Mercury News,* March 30, 1997, p. 3E; Cheryl Shavers, "Corporate Politics Part of Being Effective Player," *San Jose Mercury News,* June 15, 1997, p. 2D.

Case 7.1: "The Feds Study Employee Involvement," *Training,* August 1994, p. 12; Gillian Flynn, "Nonsales Staffs Respond to Incentives," *Personnel Journal,* July 1994, pp. 34–38; Chris Lee, "Open-Book Management," *Training,* July 1994, pp. 23–25; Keith H. Hammonds, "The Issue Is Employment, Not Employability," *Business Week,* June 10, 1996, p. 64.

Case 7.2: "An Interview with Labor Secretary Robert Reich," *Training,* August 1996, p. 41; Joseph McCafferty, "A Higher Reward," "Bureaucracy's Bright Side," *CFO,* August 1997, p. 28; "I'll Have to Check with the Manager," *Training,* March 1996, p. 18; "Turning Point: Frank Talk from Top Executives About the Moments That Changed Their Careers Forever," *Executive Female,* July/August 1997, p. 50; G. Pascal, "The New Search for Meaning in 'Meaningless' Work," *Wall Street Journal,* January 1, 1997, p. B1.

Case 8.1: Derek Reveron, "Employee Criticism: Do It with Sensitivity," *San Jose Mercury News,* July 12, 1992, p. 1 PC; "How to Sidestep Verbal Pitfalls," *San Jose Mercury News,* January 31, 1993, p. 2 PC; "Speaking Out Counts at Work," *San Jose Mercury News,* December 20, 1992, p. 1 PC.

Case 8.2: Alice G. Sargent, *The Androgynous Manager* (New York: AMACOM, 1981), p. 2.

Case 9.1: Anne B. Fisher, "Getting Comfortable with Couples in the Workplace," *Fortune,* October 3, 1994, pp. 138–144; Dianna Kunde, "Office Protocol Can't Always Squelch Romance," *San Jose Mercury News,* May 15, 1994, p. 1 PC; "Romance in the Office: One Court's View," *Supervisory Management,* July 1994, p. 4. "New York Court Backs Ban on Wal-Mart Staff Dating," *Wall Street Journal,* January 6, 1995, p. B6; Marc Hequet, "Office Romance," *Training,* February 1996, pp. 44–50.

Case 9.2: Perri Capell, "Salvaging the Careers of Talented Managers Who Behave Badly," *Wall Street Journal,* December 24, 1996, p. B1; Thomas A. Stewart, "Looking Out for Number 1," *Fortune,* January 15, 1996, p. 36; Edward Felsenthal, "Potentially Violent Employees Present Bosses with a Catch-22," *Wall Street Journal,* April 5, 1995, p. B1.

Case 10.1: Nancy Ann Jeffrey, "Wellness Plans Try to Target the Not-So-Well," *Wall Street Journal,* June 20, 1996, p. B1: Shawn Tully, "America's Healthiest Companies," *Fortune,* June 12, 1995, pp. 98–106; Bob Nelson, *1001 Ways to Reward Employees* (New York: Workman, 1994).

Case 10.2: "Small Ideas Are Big Hits," *Inc.,* August 1993, p. 28; "Capitalize on Kaizen Mine," *Training & Development,* February 1994, p. 14.

Case 11.1: "Don't Ignore Dressing for Success," *Supervisory Management,* September 1994, p. 5; Susan Bixler, "Your Professional Presence," *Training Dimensions,* vol. 9, no. 1, 1994, p. 1.

Case 11.2: "Brush Up Your Business Etiquette," *Training,* July 1997, p. 10; Susan Goodman, "Interview with Judith Martin," *Modern Maturity,* March–April 1996, pp. 56–64; Stephanie Shapiro, "Civility Movement Hopes to Put White Gloves on Clenched Fists," *News & Observer,* February 23, 1997, p. 3E.

Case 12.1: Alfie Kohn, *No Contest—The Case Against Competition* (Boston: Houghton Mifflin, 1986), pp. 96–131; Stephen Covey, "Transforming a Swamp," *Training & Development,* May 1993, p. 46.

Case 12.2: Ann Sample, "Don't Call Me Slacker!" *Fortune,* December 12, 1994, pp. 180–196; Catherine Yang, Ann Therese Palmer, Seanna Browder, and Alice Cuneo, "Low-Wage Lessons," *Business Week,* November 11, 1996, pp.

108–116; Camille Wright Miller, "Fair Treatment Avoids Bias Complaints," *Roanoke Times & World-News,* December 29, 1996, p. B2.

Case 13.1: Douglas Blackmon and Glenn Burkins, "UPS's Early Missteps in Assessing the Teamsters Help Explain How Union Won Gains in Fight," *Wall Street Journal,* August 21, 1997, p. A16; Linda Grant, "How UPS Blew It," *Fortune,* September 29, 1997, p. 29; Paul Magnusson, "A Wake-Up Call for Business," *Business Week,* September 1, 1997, pp. 28–29; Joseph Pereira, "UPS Strike Turns a Tepid Teamster Militant," *Wall Street Journal,* August 19, 1997, p. B1; Aaron Bernstein, "At UPS, Part-Time Work Is a Full-Time Issue," *Business Week,* June 16, 1997, pp. 88–90; Nicole Harris, "UPS Puts Its Back into It," *Business Week,* October 27, 1997, p. 50.

Case 13.2: Sue Shellenbarger, "Jo Browning Built a Child-Care Agenda into a Factory's Plan," *Wall Street Journal,* August 6, 1997, p. B1.

Case 14.1: Judith A. Webster and Vicki A. Moss, "To Your Health," *Nation's Business,* March 1986, p. 65; Donna Fenn, "Keeping Fit," *Inc.,* February 1986, pp. 101–102; Leonard Abramson, "Boost to the Bottom Line," *Personnel Administrator,* July 1988, pp. 36–39.

Case 14.2: Sue Shellenbarger, "No, You're Not Too Tough to Suffer a Bout of Burnout," *Wall Street Journal,* June 25, 1997, p. B1; and "Some Readers Saw the Burnout Coming, and Many Empathized," *Wall Street Journal,* July 7, 1997. p. B1.

Case 15.1: David Zuckerman, "Serving Up Apologics," *Sales & Marketing Management,* October 1993, pp. 133–135; Benjamin A. Holden, "Denny's Chain Settles Suits by Minorities," *Wall Street Journal,* May 24, 1994, p. A3; Stephen Labaton, "Civil Rights Milestone," *Denver Post,* May 25, 1994, p. 2A; "The Stiff Price of Bias: $35,000 a Customer," *U.S. News & World Report,* June 6, 1994, p. 14; "Denny's: The Stain That Isn't Coming Out," *Business Week,* June 28, 1993, pp. 98–99; "What to Do When Race Charges Fly," *Fortune,* July 12, 1993, p. 95; Nicole Harris, "A New Denny's—Diner by Diner," *Business Week,* March 25, 1996, pp. 166–168; "Flagstar's Denny's Unit Faces Suit Involving Discriminatory Action," *Wall Street Journal,* August 25, 1997, p. B5.

Case 15.2: Edward Felsenthal, "Supreme Court Agenda Touches Everyday Life," *Wall Street Journal,* September 29, 1997, p. B1; Elsa C. Arnett, *News & Observer,* November 22, 1997, n.p.; Linda Greenhouse, "Key Case on Racial Diversity Settled," *News & Observer,* November 22, 1997, p. 1A; "Affirmative Action Case Helps Define Boundaries," *USA Today,* November 24, 1997, p. 14A; Tony Mauro and Gary Fields, "Settlement Prolongs Affirmative Action Fight," *USA*

Today, November 24, 1997, p. 4A; Steven A. Holmes, "Tough Times for Affirmative Action," *News & Observer,* November 23, 1997, p. 18A.

Case 16.1: Mitsubishi Gets Its Report Card," *Business Week,* February 24, 1997, p. 46; De'Ann Weimer and Emily Thornton, "Slow Healing at Mitsubishi," *Business Week,* September 22, 1997, pp. 74–75; Edith Hill Updike and William J. Hostein, "Mitsubishi and 'The Cement Ceiling,'" *Business Week,* May 13, 1996, p. 62; Peter Elstrom and Edith Hill Updike, "Fear and Loathing at Mitsubishi," *Business Week,* May 6, 1996, p. 35; Rochelle Sharpe, "Women at Mitsubishi Say Union Fell Short on Sexual Harassment," *Wall Street Journal,* July 10, 1996, pp. A1, A12.

Case 16.2: Sonia Nazario, "Female Cops Not Tokens, Make Significant Presence," *Roanoke Times & World-News,* October 10, 1993, p. D5; "America's Fighting Women Take Off," *Roanoke Times & World-News,* May 1, 1993, p. A9; Anna Quindlen, "Smart Women Hang on for Dear Life—Even in the White House," *Springfield News-Leader,* September 25, 1994, p. B1. Joann S. Lublin, "Firms Designate Some Openings for Women Only," *Wall Street Journal,* February 7, 1994, p. B1.

Career Corner Credits

Chapter 1: Louis S. Richman, "How to Get Ahead in America," *Fortune,* May 16, 1994, pp. 46–54; Ronald Henkoff, "Winning the New Career Game," *Fortune,* July 12, 1993, pp. 46–49.

Chapter 2: Jennifer Laabs, "Personnel File Data Base: Universal Access?" *Personnel Journal,* July 1994, p. 85; Shannon Peters, "Standard Policy Clears Confusion Over E-Mail," *Personnel Journal,* June 1994, p. 123.

Chapter 3: Barry L. Reece and Gerald L. Manning, *Supervision and Leadership in Action* (New York: Glencoe, 1990); Camille Wright Miller, "Working It Out," *Roanoke Times & World-News,* July 17, 1994, p. F-3.

Chapter 4: Maxwell Maltz, *Psycho-Cybernetics* (New York: Pocket Books, 1972), pp. 6–7.

Chapter 5: Hal Lancaster, "You Have Your Values; How Do You Identify Your Employer's?" *Wall Street Journal,* April 8, 1997, p. B1.

Chapter 7: Shari Caudron, "Motivating Creative Employees Calls for New Strategies," *Personnel Journal,* May 1994, pp. 103–106; adapted from "The New Search for Meaning in 'Meaningless' Work" by G. Pascal Zachary, *The Wall Street Journal,* January 1, 1997, p. B-1.

Chapter 8: Joan E. Rigdon, "Even When They Ask, Bosses Don't Want Your Complaints," *Wall Street Journal,* August 10, 1994, p. B1.

Chapter 9: Glen O. Gabbard, "Are All Psychotherapies Equally Effective?" *Menninger Letter,* January 1995, pp. 1–2; "Fact About: Anxiety Disorders," published by Carrier Foundation, Belle Mead, N.J.

Chapter 10: Mitchell Schnurman, "Kissing Up: It Works. . . . But Only If You Mean It," *Roanoke Times & World-News,* September 28, 1993, p. E1.

Chapter 11: "How Much Can Employer Dictate Your Lifestyle?" *San Jose Mercury News,* May 2, 1993, pp. 1 PC and 2 PC; Susan Barciela, "Looks and Dress Still Count, Though the Lawyers Might Argue," *Roanoke Times & World-News,* June 19, 1993, p. D2; Susan Bixler, "Your Professional Presence," *Training Dimensions,* Vol. 9, No. 1, 1994, p. 1.

Chapter 12: Timothy D. Schellhardt, "To Be a Star Among Equals, Be a Team Player," *Wall Street Journal,* April 20, 1994, p. B1.

Chapter 13: Sue Shellenbarger and Carol Hymowitz, "As Population Ages, Older Workers Clash with Younger Bosses," *Wall Street Journal,* June 3, 1994, pp. A1 and A5.

Chapter 14: Based on Ann Landers, "Maybe It's Time to Change Jobs," *Roanoke Times & World-News,* September 1994. Camille Wright Miller, "'Prime' is performance, attitude issue," *The Roanoke Times,* September 22, 1996, p. B2.

Chapter 15: "Good Customer Phone Form," *Training & Development,* December 1992, p. 9.

Chapter 16: Based on Dianne Hales and Robert Hales, "Can Men and Women Work Together? Yes, If . . .", *Parade Magazine,* March 20, 1994, pp. 10–11.

Total Person Insight Credits
Chapter 1

p. 13: William Raspberry, "Topmost Priority: Jobs," *Washington Post,* (n.d.) 1977; **p. 9:** Marsha Sinetar, *Do What You Love . . . The Money Will Follow* (New York: Dell, 1989); **p. 16:** James Baughman quote from Frank Rose, "A New Age for Business?", *Fortune,* October 8, 1990, p. 162.

Chapter 2

p. 34: Paul R. Timm, "The Way We Word," in *Effective Communication on the Job,* ed. William K. Fallon (New York: AMACOM, 1981), p. 74; **p. 45:** Gerry Mitchell quote from "Listen, Listen, Listen," *Business Week,* September 14, 1987, p. 108.

Chapter 3

p. 66: Paul Mok and Dudley Lynch, "Easy New Way to Get Your Way," *Readers Digest*, November 1982, p. 73; **p. 83:** David W. Merrill and Roger H. Reid, *Personal Styles and Effective Performance* (Radnor, Penn.: Chilton Book Company, 1980), p. 2.

Chapter 4

p. 97: Nathaniel Branden, *The Six Pillars of Self-Esteem* (New York: Bantam, 1994), p. 19; **p. 101:** Belleruth Naparstek, "About Face," *Common Boundary*, July/August 1996, p.64; **p. 106:** Nathaniel Branden, *The Six Pillars of Self-Esteem* (New York: Bantam, 1994), p. 105.

Chapter 5

p. 122: Peter Senge quote from Brian Dumaine, "Mr. Learning Organization," *Fortune*, October 17, 1994, p. 147; **p. 134:** Dan Rice and Craig Dreilinger, "Rights and Wrongs of Ethics Training," *Training & Development*, May 1990, p. 105.

Chapter 6

p. 149: Denis Waitley, *The Winning Generation: The Self-Esteem Training Program for Youth* (Cedar Falls, Iowa: Advanced Learning, Inc., 1987), p. 18; **p. 159:** Pamela R. Johnson and Claudia Rawlins, "Daydreams and Dialogues: Key to Motivation," *Supervisory Management*, January 1991, p. 2.

Chapter 7

p. 174: D. R. Spritzer, "30 Ways to Motivate Employees to Perform Better," *Training/HRD*, March 1980, p. 51; **p. 188:** Zig Ziglar quote from Gerhard Gschwandtner, "Zig Ziglar," *Personal Selling Power*, 15th Anniversary Issue, 1995, p. 103.

Chapter 8

p. 202: Fernando Bartolomé quote from "Nobody Trusts the Boss Completely—Now What?" *Harvard Business Review*, March–April 1989, p. 135; **p. 211:** Aaron Lazare, "Go Ahead—Say You're Sorry," *Psychology Today*, January/February 1995, p. 40; **p. 215:** Gordon F. Shea, *Building Trust for Personal and Organizational Success: A Self-Paced, Skill-Building Training Manual for Individuals and Groups* (New York: Wiley, 1987), p. 1.

Chapter 9

p. 230: James Georges, "The Not-So-Stupid Americans," *Training*, July 1994, p. 90; **p. 236:** Kimes Gustin, *Anger, Rage, and Resentment* (West Caldwell, N.J.: St. Ives' Press, 1994), p. 13; **p. 245:** Gerard Egan, *You and Me* (Monterey, Calif.: Brooks/Cole, 1977), p. 73.

Chapter 10

p. 257: Roger L. Hale and Rita F. Maehling, *Recognition Defined* (Exeter, N.H.: Monochrome Press, 1993), p. 25; **p. 263:** Malcolm Boyd, "Volunteering Thanks," *Modern Maturity*, May–June 1997, p. 72.

Chapter 11

p. 282: Janet G. Elsea, *The Four-Minute Sell* (New York: Simon & Schuster, 1984), p. 34; **p. 294:** Judith Martin, "Low Income Is Not Low-Class," *Roanoke Times & World-News*, March 13, 1988, p. E 10.

Chapter 12

p. 308: Fran Tarkenton, "Tarkenton on Teambuilding," *Management Solutions*, October 6, 1986, p. 30; **p. 312:** Jack R. Gibb, *Trust—A New View of Personal and Organizational Development* (Los Angeles: Guild of Tutors Press, 1978), p. 45; **p. 320:** Anita Roddick quote from "What I Want Business to Do in '92," *Fortune*, December 30, 1991.

Chapter 13

p. 330: Gordon Lippitt quote from "Managing Conflict in Today's Organizations," *Training & Development*, July 1982, p. 3; **p. 332:** Harold H. Bloomfield and Robert K. Cooper, *The Power of 5*, Emmaus, Pa.: Rodale Press, 1995, p. 374; **p. 340:** Roger Fisher and William Ury, *Getting to Yes* (New York: Penguin Books, 1981), p. 4.

Chapter 14

p. 368: Ellen Goodman, "Speeding Through Modernity," *Roanoke Times and World-News*, September 6, 1994, p. A7; **p. 377:** Charles L. Peifer quote from James E. Loehr, *Stress for Success* (New York: Times Books, 1997), p. 191; **p. 378:** Marsha Sinetar, "Reel Power: Film and Spirit," *New Dimensions*, Summer 1993, p. 17.

Chapter 15

p. 389: Jack Pluckhan quote from Beau Bauman, *The Most Important Thing I've Learned in Life* (New York: Simon & Schuster, 1994), p. 150; **p. 392:** Vernon E. Jordan, Jr.,

"Look Outward, Black America," *Wall Street Journal,* October 27, 1995, p. A14; **p. 403:** Lewis Brown Griggs and Lente-Louise Louw, *Valuing Diversity: New Tools for a New Reality* (New York: McGraw-Hill, Inc., 1995), p. 9.

Chapter 16

p. 420: George Tunick, "Re-educating Chauvinists," *Executive Female,* January/February 1995, p. 82; **p. 425:** Robert Bly, *Iron John* (Reading, Mass.: Addison-Wesley, 1990), p. iv; **p. 427:** *Berkeley Men's Center Manifesto* cited in James Doyle, *The Male Experience* (Dubuque, Iowa: William C. Brown, 1983), p. 288; **p. 430:** Ann Fisher, "Where Women Are Succeeding," *Fortune,* August 3, 1987, p. 86; **p. 442:** Judy Tingley, *Genderflex: Men and Women*

Speaking Each Other's Language at Work (New York: AMACOM, 1994), p. 13.

Chapter 17

p. 453: Amy Saltzman, *Downshifting: Reinventing Success on a Slower Track* (New York: HarperCollins Publishers, 1990), p. 15; **p. 456:** Hugh Prather poem from *Notes to Myself.* Copyright © 1970 by Real People Press. Used by permission of Bantam Books, a division of Bantam Doubleday Dell Publishing Group, Inc.; **p. 463:** Julie Connelly, "How to Choose Your Next Career," *Fortune,* February 6, 1995, p. 45; **p. 467:** Fred Huyghue, "Merging Spirituality with Work," *Business Ethics,* July/August 1994, p. 27; **p. 468:** Susan Smith Jones, "Choose to Be Healthy and Celebrate Life," *New Realities,* September/October 1988, p. 17.

Name Index

Notes begin on page 487. Reference numbers refer to chapter and note number.

Subject Index